# THE KINGFISHER
# GEOGRAPHY
# ENCYCLOPEDIA

**KINGFISHER**
LONDON & NEW YORK

Copyright © Kingfisher 2011
Published in the United States by Kingfisher,
175 Fifth Ave., New York, NY 10010
Kingfisher is an imprint of Macmillan Children's Books, London.

First published 2003 by Kingfisher
This revised and updated edition published 2011 by Kingfisher

Author: Clive Gifford
Consultant: Clive Carpenter

Distributed in the U.S. by Macmillan, 175 Fifth Ave.,
New York, NY 10010
Distributed in Canada by H.B. Fenn and Company Ltd.,
34 Nixon Road, Bolton, Ontario L7E 1W2

ISBN: 978-0-7534-6575-2

Kingfisher books are available for special promotions and premiums.
For details contact: Special Markets Department, Macmillan,
175 Fifth Avenue, New York, NY 10010.

For more information, please visit www.kingfisherbooks.com

Printed in Taiwan
1 2 4 6 8 10 9 7 5 3
1TR/1210/SHENS/(UNTD)/126MA

# THE KINGFISHER
# GEOGRAPHY
# ENCYCLOPEDIA

### KINGFISHER
NEW YORK

# CONTENTS

# Chapter 5

## Southern Europe, The Balkans, The Caucasus, and Asia Minor

# Chapter 6

## Asia

# Chapter 7

## Eastern and Southeast Asia

# INTRODUCTION

Places that were remote to our grandparents are now visited regularly by tourists, while the world is brought into our homes by television. Although our planet is more accessible, it is also more vulnerable. You can explore our fast-changing world through the pages of *The Kingfisher Geography Encyclopedia*. Discover the challenges and environmental threats faced by Earth and its many nations.

This encyclopedia is divided into ten sections. The Physical Earth describes how the planet was formed and then shaped by the forces of nature, by water and ice, by wind and volcanoes. The variety of landscapes, climates, and soils that influence how people live and the rich natural resources that offer opportunities are explored here.

The continents are surveyed, country by country, through eight thematic chapters. Clear maps place each country in its broader setting and show its rivers and mountains, as well as its major towns and cities. Concise fact boxes feature key information about each nation: its area and population, capital, flag, languages and religions, trade, and government system.

The unique story of each country is explained through a summary of its geography and recent history. From the densely populated industrial landscapes of Western Europe and North America to the endangered rain forests of central Africa and the Amazon Basin, learn what makes each country special. The daily lives of people around the globe are pictured—from the harsh desert regions of the Sahara to the icy wastes of Siberia and from the lush, fertile farmland of Southeast Asia to the open savanna grasslands of east Africa.

The last section, Ready Reference, surveys climate, physical features, population, languages, trade, industry, international organizations, and much more in a format that encourages quick and easy access. Ideal for projects and homework, *The Kingfisher Geography Encyclopedia* is also your passport to an enjoyable journey of discovery around the world.

*Clive Carpenter*
Consultant

# THE PHYSICAL EARTH

# FORMATION OF EARTH

**Earth is part of the solar system, where eight planets orbit a star called the Sun. Earth started life approximately 4.54 billion years ago.**

At the center of the solar system is its biggest object, the Sun. It is the strong pull of the Sun's gravity that holds the solar system together and controls the movement of the planets. There are eight major planets in the solar system. Earth is the third closest to the Sun, orbiting at an average distance of 92,960 million mi. (149,600 million km). The solar system is part of the Milky Way, a collection of star systems known as a galaxy.

The Milky Way is just one of what scientists estimate to be between 100 and one trillion galaxies that occupy the universe. The universe is made up of everything in space, and space itself, and is estimated to be between 12 and 14 billion years old. Many theories have been advanced to explain its origins. The most widely accepted is the big bang theory. This states that the universe began when a gigantic explosion of energy started the process of forming matter, time, and space. Huge forces were generated that saw the universe expand with great energy—so much so that the universe is still expanding to this very day.

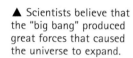

▲ Scientists believe that the "big bang" produced great forces that caused the universe to expand.

► Approximately eight billion years after the start of the universe the Sun formed from a cloud of gas and dust called a nebula. As the nebula condensed it grew intensely hot. Earth was formed from some of the debris blown away from energy produced by the Sun. As matter collided this debris collected together in increasingly large pieces and created Earth.

## BIRTH OF THE SOLAR SYSTEM

Astronomers believe that the Sun formed around 4.57 billion years ago from a huge cloud of gas and dust. As the Sun began to shrink it pulled more and more gas and dust into its center. It became hotter and started to form a central orb surrounded by a spinning disk of gas and dust. Intense heat and energy were generated within the central orb. As the young Sun warmed up it blew a wind of energetic particles through the spinning disk of gas and dust. This drove much of the disk's gases outward, where they cooled and over time formed the solar system's largest planets such as Jupiter and Saturn. The dust and ice left in the disk around the Sun gradually began to form rocky lumps; these collided and joined together. As the objects became bigger the collisions grew more violent. Gradually these bodies formed into planets as dust and gas were drawn to them. The process of building up the planets took around 150 million years.

## EARTH'S DEVELOPMENT

Earth began life as a sphere of dust, rocks, and gases that were drawn together through the force of gravity. As Earth's size and mass increased the pull of gravity gathered in more material and compressed it until it started to melt. Heavier, iron-rich materials moved toward the center to form its dense core, while lighter materials began to form the outer layers. Earth started life as a waterless planet with temperatures too high to let water collect on its hot surface. Water vapor existed in the atmosphere, and as the planet cooled, over 3.8 billion years ago, the vapor began to cool, condense, and fall as rain. Rains that lasted thousands of years are believed to have formed rivers, lakes, early seas, and oceans. Using fossil evidence, scientists estimate that the first life on Earth, single-celled blue-green algae, started around 3.5 billion years ago. Living things with more than one cell are believed to have emerged around 600 million years ago.

▲ Early Earth was a hot, fiery planet with volcanic activity and a surface of liquid rock spewing fumes and gases into the atmosphere. Some gases, mainly nitrogen and carbon dioxide, were prevented from drifting into space by Earth's gravity, forming the early atmosphere.

▲ A mangrove swamp in the Central American country of Belize. Earth is the only known body in space that is able to support and sustain life.

# EARTH'S ROTATION

**As Earth orbits the Sun, it also rotates on its axis like a spinning top. These rotations bring about day and night and cause the seasons.**

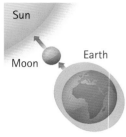

**Spring tide**

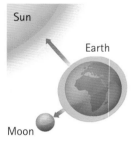

**Neap tide**

▲ As the Moon orbits Earth its gravity pulls water in Earth's oceans toward it. The changes in water level that occur as a result are called tides. The strongest, or spring, tides occur when the Moon and the Sun, which also affect tides, pull in the same direction. Weaker neap tides occur when the Moon pulls at right angles to the Sun.

Earth rotates on its axis at a constant rate as it orbits the Sun. Earth spins eastward on its axis, which is why the Sun appears to rise in the east and set in the west. A complete 360-degree turn is called a planet's rotational period, or day. Earth takes a bit more than 23 hours and 56 minutes to complete a rotational period.

Earth is not quite a perfect sphere. It is slightly squashed, with the diameter at its equator around 24 mi. (38km) greater than its diameter from pole to pole. This is due to its rotation, which forces material out toward the equator. Earth, like the eight other planets in the solar system, travels around the Sun along an elliptical, or oval, path called an orbit. The time taken to complete one orbit is known as a planet's orbital period, or year. Mercury, the planet closest to the Sun, takes 88 days to complete an orbit. In the case of Earth a complete orbit occurs every 365.26 Earth days.

▲When the Northern Hemisphere is tilted toward the Sun, it is summer there. During this time the North Pole is in sunlight for 24 hours each day.

## EARTH'S TILT

Earth's vertical axis is an imaginary line that joins its north and south poles. Earth is tilted toward the Sun along its vertical axis at a constant angle. Earth can be divided along the line of the equator into two halves, the Northern Hemisphere and the Southern Hemisphere. The Earth's tilt creates the seasons. As one hemisphere is tilted more toward the Sun it experiences summer. In the other hemisphere winter occurs. On or close to March 21 and September 23 the daylight hours experienced by the southern and northern hemispheres are equal. These dates are known as equinoxes.

The first day of the winter is usually December 21 in the Northern Hemisphere, which is also the first day of the summer in the Southern Hemisphere.

September 23 is the first day of fall in the Northern Hemisphere and the first day of spring in the Southern Hemisphere. The Sun is directly overhead at the equator.

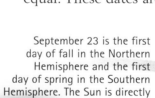

SUN

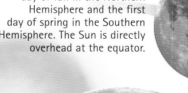

▶ The two hemispheres of Earth experience opposing seasons as Earth orbits the Sun on its tilted axis. From around March 21 to September 23 the Northern Hemisphere is tilted toward the Sun, and the seasons of spring and summer occur there, while the Southern Hemisphere experiences fall and winter.

March 21 is the first day of spring in the Northern Hemisphere and the first day of fall in the Southern Hemisphere.

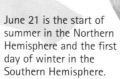

June 21 is the start of summer in the Northern Hemisphere and the first day of winter in the Southern Hemisphere.

# INSIDE EARTH

**Earth is made up of a series of layers that formed early in the planet's history. They include a central core, a mantle, and a surface crust.**

▲ Hot volcanic rocks underneath Earth's surface boil and spurt out water and steam in the form of hot springs called geysers. Old Faithful is just one of more than 3,000 geysers found in Yellowstone National Park in the United States. Each time it erupts between 9,770–11,900 gallons (37,000–45,000 liters) of hot water are expelled.

At Earth's center is its dense core, which is largely made up of iron with a small amount of nickel and other elements. The core is divided into inner and outer regions. The outer core is kept molten, or liquid, by a temperature of more than 7,952°F (4,400°C). The inner core's temperature is higher, in excess of 9,806°F (5,430°C), but is believed to be a solid, or acts like a solid, owing to the intense pressure it experiences. Scientists estimate the pressure on the inner core to be four to five million times the pressure we experience on Earth's surface. Together, the inner and outer core comprise 33.5 percent of Earth's mass. Lying above the outer core is the mantle, the layer that forms 66 percent of Earth's mass. The mantle is largely solid, but with a temperature of over 2,372°F (1,300°C), it can deform and be distorted slowly.

Iron and oxygen are the most common components of Earth. Iron is especially concentrated in Earth's core. Compounds called magnesium silicates, made up of magnesium, silicon, and oxygen, form most of Earth's mantle.

| Iron | Oxygen | Silicon | Magnesium | Nickel | Calcium | Sulfur | Other elements | Aluminum |
|---|---|---|---|---|---|---|---|---|
| 36% | 28.5% | 14% | 13% | 2% | 1.9% | 1.8% | 0.6% | 0.4% |

The final layer, the crust, floats on the mantle and is much thinner than the other layers. There are three types of crust. The continental crust, which forms land, is usually between 20–30 mi. (30–50km) in depth, but in places it can be just 12 mi. (20km) thick or bulge downward beneath mountain ranges to depths of around 40 mi. (65km). The transitional crust averages 9–20 mi. (15–30km) thickness. The oceanic crust found below oceans is thinner, usually between 3–9 mi. (5–15km) thick.

Oceanic crust averages 3–9 mi. (5–15km) thickness

Continental crust averages 20–30 mi. (30–50km) thickness

Molten rock rises to the surface

The mantle forms a 1,796-mi.-(2,890-km-) thick layer

Earth's outer core is 1,400 mi. (2,260km) thick

The inner core is estimated to be 1,515 mi. (2,440km) in diameter

► Earth's different layers float on top of one another. The heaviest layer, the core, is at its center, and the lightest layer, the crust, is on Earth's surface. The crust forms just 0.5 percent of Earth's total mass. The crust is rocky and brittle and can be fractured by earthquakes.

# EARTH'S MAGNETISM

**Earth acts like a large magnet, creating a magnetic field that extends out through the layers of the planet and into space.**

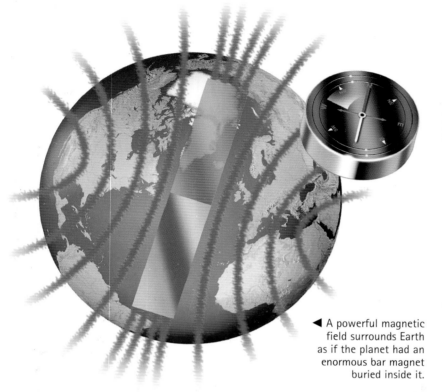

◀ A powerful magnetic field surrounds Earth as if the planet had an enormous bar magnet buried inside it.

An aurora is caused by particles of the solar wind that enter Earth's atmosphere. The particles interact with gases in the atmosphere to create light energy. This aurora borealis, or northern lights, was seen in Alaska.

E arth's magnetic field originates in the molten outer core deep below the crust. There electric currents churning and circulating through the molten material are believed to be behind the creation of Earth's giant magnetic field. The flow of electric currents in the core is continually changing, so the magnetic field produced by those currents also changes. The magnetic north and south poles move and are in different locations from the geographic poles. Currently magnetic north is less than 590 mi. (950km) from the North Pole, and magnetic south is more than 930 mi. (1,500km) from the South Pole. The angle between a geographic pole and a magnetic pole is called magnetic declination. This is vital to know when navigating with a magnetic compass.

## THE MAGNETOSPHERE

Earth's magnetism generates a giant magnetic field that reaches out past Earth's atmosphere and into space. It is called the magnetosphere and is irregularly shaped. The side facing the Sun extends around 43,500 mi. (70,000km) out from Earth, while the side away from the Sun forms a long tail stretching a distance of more than 620,000 mi. (almost one million km). The shape of the magnetosphere is influenced by the solar wind. This is the constant stream of high-energy particles produced by the Sun that moves at a speed of around 250 mi. (400km) per second. The magnetosphere helps protect Earth's atmosphere from the impact of the solar wind. If Earth's magnetism did not exist, the solar wind would strip Earth of its air, and Earth would become incapable of supporting life. Earth's magnetosphere is not unique. Space probes have detected magnetic fields surrounding the planets of Jupiter, Saturn, Uranus, and Neptune.

▼ The shape of Earth's magnetosphere is influenced by the Sun's solar wind. It compresses the magnetosphere on the side facing the Sun and sweeps it out into a long tail away from the Sun.

Magnetosphere

Solar wind particles enter Earth's atmosphere

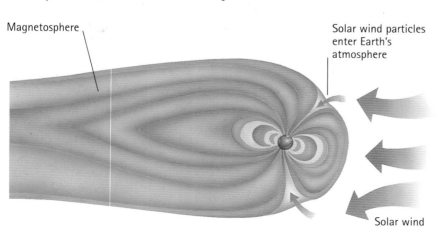

Solar wind

# CONTINENTAL DRIFT

**Earth's outer layer is not a single piece but is made of a number of giant sections, called tectonic plates. The large landmasses at the surface are called continents.**

The continents are constantly moving as the tectonic plates (the crust and the outer part of the mantle) "float" on the semimolten layer below. This process is known as continental drift. The plates are propelled by convection currents in the partly molten mantle. There are seven major plates and eight smaller plates.

### THEORY AND EVIDENCE

Geologists and fossil hunters had puzzled over how identical rock formations and fossils of species could be found in landmasses thousands of miles apart. The theory of continental drift was first put forward by German scientist Alfred Wegener (1880–1930) in 1912. He stated that, more than 100 million years ago, the continents as we know them today emerged from the gradual breakup of one supercontinent, which he called Pangaea. Wegener's ideas were not widely accepted until the 1960s when advances in technology, including laser measurement systems and satellite imaging, supported his theory. Landmasses are currently moving at an average rate of between 0.4–4 in. (1–10cm) per year. Over millions of years continental drift has shaped the continents and many of their features.

**1** From 270 million to 200 million years ago all land was part of one supercontinent, known as Pangaea.

**2** By around 110 million years ago Pangaea had separated into a number of landmasses. Africa and South America were already recognizable.

**3** The continents today. Continental drift is continuing so that in around 50 million years from now North America will separate from South America and will be joined to the continent of Asia.

▶ There are seven major and nine minor plates covering Earth. This map shows the positions of the seven major plates: Eurasian, African, Antarctic, Pacific, North American, South American, and Indo-Australian. The arrows depict the directions in which the plates are currently moving.

The San Andreas Fault in California marks where the Pacific plate and the North American plate meet, slide, and grate past each other.

### PLATE TECTONICS

Plate tectonics is the study and theory of how the plates were created, move, and their effect on the geography of Earth. Over time plates move apart from each other, grind and grate alongside each other, or collide brutally into one another. In all cases they help shape Earth's land features. A boundary between two plates is known as a fault or a fault line. Volcanoes and earthquakes frequently occur at fault lines where the crust is weak or is under extreme stress.

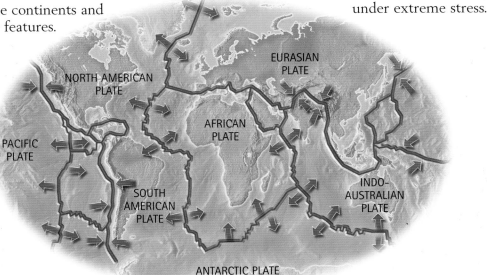

EURASIAN PLATE

NORTH AMERICAN PLATE

AFRICAN PLATE

PACIFIC PLATE

INDO-AUSTRALIAN PLATE

SOUTH AMERICAN PLATE

ANTARCTIC PLATE

# EARTHQUAKES

**Earthquakes are a trembling or shaking of the ground caused by the sudden release of energy stored in the rocks beneath Earth's surface.**

▲ This ancient Chinese earthquake detector dates from around A.D. 130. Earth tremors would cause balanced bronze balls to fall into the frogs' mouths.

▲ A seismograph charts the intensity of Earth's vibrations using a pen held on a balanced pendulum and a roll of graph paper.

E arth's crust is on the move—powerful forces produce large amounts of stress and energy where the crust's plates meet. Plates rub up against each other, collide head on, or one plate can be forced to pass under another. Stresses and strains in the crust build up. When plates suddenly move or slip into a new position, the energy from the stress created can be released as an earthquake. The energy in an earthquake comes in the form of powerful disturbances, called seismic waves, which surge through rocks, moving and distorting them in the process. Earthquakes emit waves in all directions from the point where they start—known as the focus, or hypocenter— less than 43 mi. (70km) below ground. The point on the surface of Earth directly above the focus is called the epicenter. It is usually where the destructive effects of the earthquake are most felt. Some seismic waves travel deep underground through the body of Earth. Other waves travel in a zone close to Earth's surface.

"P" waves travel deep below the ground and stretch and squeeze rock particles as they progress.

"S" waves also travel deep underground but move the rock from side to side.

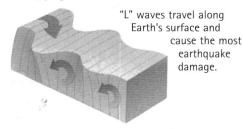

"L" waves travel along Earth's surface and cause the most earthquake damage.

▲ Different types of seismic waves travel by distorting rocks in different ways.

## EARTHQUAKE LOCATIONS

Certain areas of Earth are more prone to earthquakes than others, particularly regions that lie at the boundaries of Earth's plates. The forcing together of the Eurasian, African, and Australian plates, for example, creates a region of earthquake activity that has affected countries as far apart as Portugal, Iran, and India. Earthquakes can also occur away from the boundaries of Earth's plates. Some earthquakes are caused by volcanic activity. As molten rock works its way up it can cause strains on the rocks around it,

▶ In August 1999 an earthquake measuring 7.4 on the Richter scale hit the cities of Izmit and Gölcük in the northwest of Turkey. It killed 17,118 people, injured a further 27,000, and made 200,000 people homeless. A second earthquake struck the region in November 1999. With its epicenter close to the town of Düzce, it killed over 700 people and injured 5,100 others.

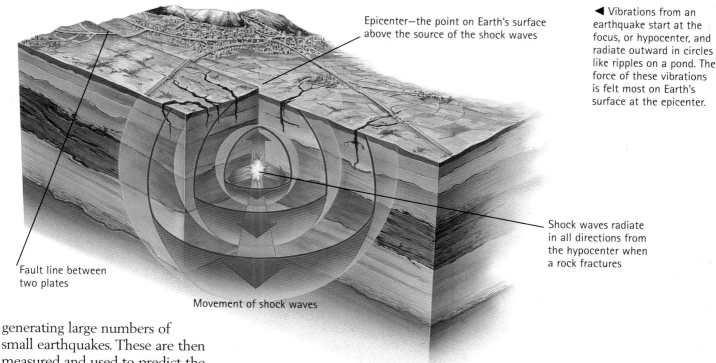

Epicenter—the point on Earth's surface above the source of the shock waves

◀ Vibrations from an earthquake start at the focus, or hypocenter, and radiate outward in circles like ripples on a pond. The force of these vibrations is felt most on Earth's surface at the epicenter.

Shock waves radiate in all directions from the hypocenter when a rock fractures

Fault line between two plates

Movement of shock waves

generating large numbers of small earthquakes. These are then measured and used to predict the likelihood of a major volcanic eruption. Many earthquakes occur in the midocean ridges (see pages 20–21) and account for five percent of all of Earth's seismic activity. These earthquakes are measured by seismologists but rarely affect people since they are so far from inhabited areas. A powerful earthquake sometimes occurs in the center of a plate. The earthquake that struck the Gujarat region of India in 2001 is an example. It caused great devastation, killing more than 30,000 people.

## AFTERSHOCKS AND TSUNAMIS

Further devastation can occur after the waves from a main earthquake have died away. Sometimes an earthquake does not release all of the energy built up in an area. This can cause smaller tremors, or aftershocks, following the main earthquake. These aftershocks can be deadly in an earthquake-hit area, creating even more destruction. Earthquakes can also produce giant ocean waves called tsunamis. These waves, which can also be created by volcanic activity, are believed to start when the ocean floor is tilted or moved during an earthquake. A set of fast-moving waves is created and can travel hundreds of miles across an ocean, reaching speeds of between 450–500 mph (725–800km/h). When the waves reach shallow waters, they grow as

high as 50 ft. (15m), destroying settlements on the coast. Most tsunamis occur in the Pacific Ocean. A tsunami in 2004 killed about 230,000 people around the Indian Ocean. Indonesia was the worst hit.

## MEASURING EARTHQUAKES

Two scales are used to measure earthquakes. The Mercalli scale measures the physical effects of earthquake activity on Earth's surface. The Richter scale measures the energy produced by earthquakes on a scale of 1–10. At 3.5 on the Richter scale the tremors are noticed by most people, at 4.5 some local damage can occur, and at 7.0 or above a major earthquake has occurred.

▼ The blue dots show the sites of past major earthquakes. These are largely distributed along the fault lines marking boundaries between Earth's tectonic plates, shown in green. In these areas Earth's crust tends to be under the greatest pressure, which can also give rise to large amounts of volcanic activity (see pages 10-11).

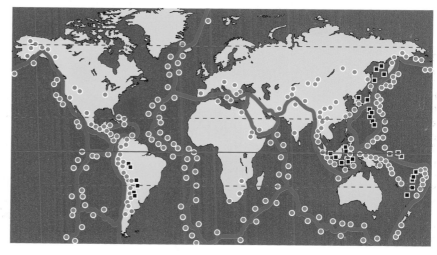

# VOLCANOES

**Volcanoes are openings in Earth's crust that allow gases, ash, and molten rock to rise. This activity is called a volcanic eruption.**

In the upper mantle, where temperatures are high and pressure is low, solid rock becomes molten. This material is called magma. Less dense than the solid rock that surrounds it, magma rises upward and can collect in large reservoirs called magma chambers. As the rising magma gets close to Earth's surface the pressure on the magma decreases. This causes the gases held in the magma to expand. The magma is then forced up and through openings in Earth's surface, creating a volcanic eruption. Once magma has erupted it is called lava. Lava may erupt in explosive bursts or ooze and flow gently down slopes.

Eventually the lava cools, forming rock and new rock formations. Volcanoes are located mainly in places where Earth's crust is weakest, particularly at the boundaries between Earth's plates. Some are found away from these boundaries in areas, such as the Great Rift Valley in Africa, where there is intense crust movement and above places called hot spots. These are locations where a rising plume of especially hot mantle rock is situated and melts Earth's crust, forcing magma up toward the surface.

## VOLCANO TYPES

The types of eruptions and volcanoes vary and depend largely on the properties of the magma, including its composition and consistency. Thin, runny lava, for example, allows gases to escape relatively easily. This tends to make the eruption less violent and allows the lava to flow gently out of the openings. Thin lava is also more likely to flow a long distance after reaching the surface before it cools, hardens, and forms rock. As a result, it tends to form shallow-sloped shield volcanoes. Thick lava flows only a short distance before setting to form steep-sided volcanoes. Thicker molten rock can trap gases, and if the gas content in the magma is high, the chance of a violent eruption is increased. Explosive eruptions can propel ash, red-hot cinders, lava, and pieces of rocks high into the atmosphere. Larger, more dense particles fall back

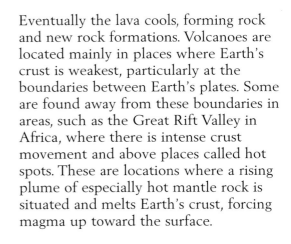

Fissure volcano

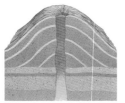
Dome volcano

Ash cinder volcano

Shield volcano

Caldera volcano

Composite volcano

▲ Many different volcano types can form depending on the type of lava and how the volcano erupts.

Volcanic cone

Fumaroles are volcanic openings that leak only gas or steam

Main cone—consists of layers of lava and cinders

◄ This composite volcano has steep slopes formed from layers of cinders and hardened lava that have emerged from previous eruptions. At the center is a vertical opening called a vent. Smaller openings that branch off from the main vent are called side vents. Lying often several miles below is the supply of molten rock in the magma chamber.

Magma chamber

▲ Mount Etna is an active composite volcano on the island of Sicily in the Mediterranean Sea. At more than 10,988 ft. (3,320m) in height, it is the highest volcano in Europe.

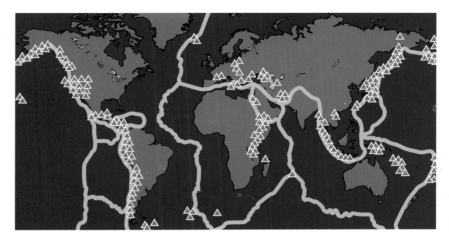

to Earth, but smaller dust particles can travel high into the atmosphere, where they may remain for months or years.

Many volcanoes are found underwater. Some are forced upward by plate activity or erupt enough times to grow in height and rise above sea level to form volcanic islands. Curved chains of volcanic islands, called island arcs, are particularly common in the Pacific Ocean.

Volcanoes are classified as extinct, dormant, or active. There are approximately 850 active volcanoes, although fewer than 30 tend to erupt each year. Dormant volcanoes have been quiet for many years but may erupt in the future. After 600 years of inactivity Mount Pinatubo in the Philippines erupted in 1991, sending ash over 49,200 ft. (15,000km) up into the atmosphere.

## PEOPLE AND VOLCANOES

Some people choose to live and farm the slopes of volcanoes. The ash that settles there is rich in minerals, making fertile growing land. Scientists monitor volcanic activity to predict eruptions and warn people in areas at risk. Seismometers detect Earth tremors caused by an impending eruption, while tiltmeters and Geodimeters™ measure changes in the land shape that may signal volcanic activity.

Bombardment from material thrown into the air from an eruption and the red-hot lava flow are not the only threats to people posed by volcanoes. Volcanic areas can also emit harmful gases in immense quantities. Heat from an eruption poses further threats in the form of large floods, when eruptions melt parts of nearby glaciers, and unstoppable mudflows.

▲ The triangles on this map show the location of active volcanoes around the world. Most volcanoes are found near plate boundaries (shown in yellow) or over hot spots.

▼ The Caribbean island of Montserrat suffered from serious volcanic activity in June 1997. A series of eruptions from both Soufriere Hills and Chance's Peak volcanoes destroyed the town of Plymouth, made thousands of islanders homeless, and killed 19 people.

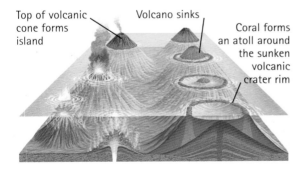

▲ Volcanic islands can form from a volcanic cone that rises above the ocean's surface. Sometimes volcanoes sink, and a new island type, called an atoll, is created from coral, forming a ring where the volcanic crater lay.

Top of volcanic cone forms island

Volcano sinks

Coral forms an atoll around the sunken volcanic crater rim

# ROCKS AND MINERALS

**Rocks are the solid materials that make up Earth's surface. They can be divided into three types— igneous, metamorphic, and sedimentary.**

Rocks consist of chemical compounds called minerals. There are many thousands of different minerals. Some are single elements such as the metals gold and copper. Others are composed of a number of elements such as silicates, which are compounds of silicon, oxygen, and small amounts of other elements.

### IGNEOUS ROCKS

Igneous rocks are formed from hot, molten rock material, called magma, that has cooled and turned solid. The type of igneous rock is determined by the chemical makeup of the magma and the rate at which it cools and solidifies. Many igneous rocks, such as granite, are formed from magma buried deep within the crust of Earth. These rocks cool slowly and, as a result, contain large mineral crystals. Other igneous rocks, such as basalt and obsidian, are created by volcanic activity. They either form from magma that rises and fills cracks close to Earth's surface or erupts onto the surface. In both cases the magma of volcanic igneous rocks tends to cool rapidly, and this creates very small crystals in rocks that give a fine grain or a glasslike appearance.

▲ When basalt lava erupts from volcanic vents and cools, it shrinks and cracks and sometimes forms vertical columns. The Devil's Postpile consists of four- to seven-sided basalt columns and is found in the Sierra Nevada mountain range in California.

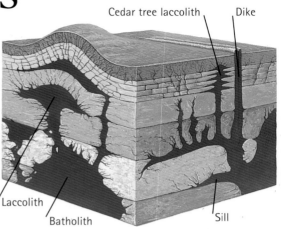

▲ Intrusive igneous rock is pushed up beneath overlying rocks as large masses that have already turned solid. Batholiths are large intrusions of igneous rocks that push away or replace a vast amount of other rock. When an intrusion creates a mushroom shape, it is called a laccolith. A dike is formed when magma fills a fracture in other rock and cools and turns solid. A sill occurs when magma intrudes between layers of sedimentary rock.

### METAMORPHIC ROCKS

Metamorphic rock is rock that has been transformed from other metamorphic, sedimentary, or igneous rocks. These form when extreme temperatures or pressures deep within Earth alter existing rock without melting it or adding new substances to it. There are two main ways in which metamorphism can occur. Hot igneous rocks can force their way, or intrude, into an area. Heat from these igneous rocks bakes and transforms the surrounding rock. For example, through heat limestone can be turned into marble, and sandstone, a sedimentary rock, can be turned into the metamorphic rock quartzite. The second type of metamorphism tends to occur on a larger scale and involves huge pressures

▶ Heat from an igneous intrusion has turned some of the surrounding layers of limestone into marble (right). The pressures generated by mountain layers folding (left) can turn clay materials or shale into slate.

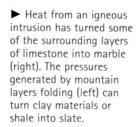

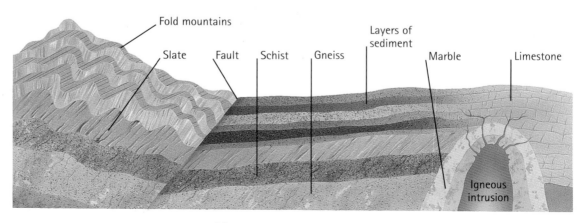

▲ Sedimentary rock can form clearly distinguishable rock layers, or strata. These rocks form part of Death Valley in California.

a rock such as chalk. Chemical sedimentary rocks, such as gypsum, occur when water evaporates, leaving behind minerals as a sediment. Clastic rocks make up 75 percent of all sedimentary rocks. They are formed from other rocks that are worn away by a range of forces when exposed at Earth's surface. These include wind, water, ice, and frost, as well as chemical reactions and the actions of plant roots. The material worn away from these rocks is transported by gravity, wind, water, or ice and eventually is deposited as a layer or bed of sediment. Over time the beds of sediment are slowly compacted by pressure as other material is deposited above them. Eventually the loose pieces of sediment join together to form a solid sedimentary rock such as sandstone.

created by mountains forming and folding. Rocks, such as mudstone and shale, can be transformed under great pressure into metamorphic rocks such as slate, schist, or gneiss.

## SEDIMENTARY ROCKS

Although sedimentary rocks are only a small part of the entire Earth's crust, they make up around three fourths of the planet's surface rock. There are three types of sedimentary rocks: biogenic, chemical, and clastic. Biogenic sedimentary rocks consist of the skeletons and shells of millions of microscopic organisms that have been compressed over time to form

## GEMSTONES AND ORES

Minerals within rocks that are capable of being cut and polished are called gemstones. Certain gemstones, including rubies, opals, and diamonds, are highly prized. Many minerals are concentrated in rocks as impure chemical compounds called ores. For example, aluminum is commonly found in the ore bauxite, while copper is frequently concentrated in an ore called malachite. Ores are mined, and their valuable metal or other minerals are extracted from the rest of the ore using heat and chemical reactions.

▲ An open-air gold mine in Australia. Australia is the third-largest producer of gold behind South Africa and China.

▶ Minerals are often formed underground when heat and pressure transform one rock from another. They can also be formed from evaporation and when hot water and other liquids cool.

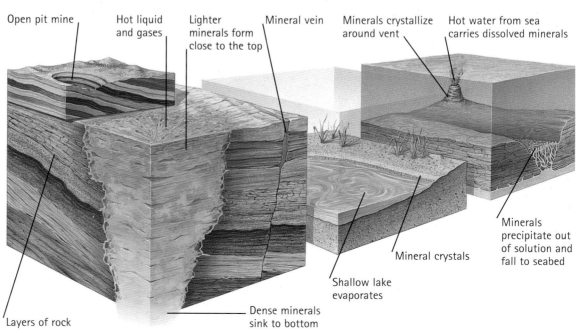

Open pit mine

Hot liquid and gases

Lighter minerals form close to the top

Mineral vein

Minerals crystallize around vent

Hot water from sea carries dissolved minerals

Minerals precipitate out of solution and fall to seabed

Mineral crystals

Shallow lake evaporates

Dense minerals sink to bottom

Layers of rock

# THE ROCK CYCLE

**The rock cycle is a way of charting how rocks change from one type to another. Scientists measure this using geological time.**

Rocks are always changing. The minerals in them are constantly moved and acted upon by the environment. The upper part of Earth—the mantle, crust, and surface—acts as a rock recycling system. The matter that makes up rocks is transported and transformed from one type of rock to another. The rock cycle shows the relationships between igneous, sedimentary, and metamorphic rocks and the ways they are formed and recycled. The basic rock cycle was devised by Scottish geologist and naturalist James Hutton (1726–1797). It starts with the formation of igneous rock when magma cools and solidifies. Particles of igneous rocks, worn away through erosion and weathering, are transported elsewhere and form deposits of sediment. These layers are compacted by the weight of layers above and can become cemented together by minerals to form sedimentary rocks.

▲ Most sediments occur in marine environments, which means that the majority of fossils found are of sea creatures. This fossil is of an ammonite, a group of hard-shelled sea creatures that existed between 400 and 65 million years ago.

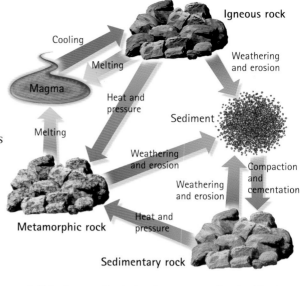

▲ This diagram illustrates the processes involved in the recycling and changing of rocks from one type to another.

Igneous rock

Cooling

Melting

Magma

Weathering and erosion

Heat and pressure

Sediment

Melting

Weathering and erosion

Compaction and cementation

Weathering and erosion

Metamorphic rock

Heat and pressure

Sedimentary rock

Sedimentary rocks are formed at fairly low pressures and temperatures. They are most susceptible to further change when greater pressures and temperatures are applied. Those that become very deeply buried or involved in the processes of mountain building are often changed into metamorphic rocks. Yet more heat can turn solid metamorphic rock into a liquid or molten state, creating magma from which igneous rocks can form. The cycle is not always a simple progress between igneous, sedimentary, metamorphic, and igneous again. For example, metamorphic rock can be worn away to create sedimentary rock. Another exception is that sedimentary rock can be heated to such extreme temperatures that it forms magma, which, when it cools, creates new igneous rock. All three types of rocks can be worn away to generate sediment from which new sedimentary rock is created.

Rocks eroded by ice and frost

Magma (molten rock) underneath Earth's surface

Mountain uplift creates pressures and heat, creating metamorphic rocks

Igneous rock layer forms underneath Earth's surface

River transports rock particles— where they are deposited on the seabed

Sedimentary rock layer buried under other rock layers

Buried rock layer

▲ Deep underground, intense heat and pressure are at work, creating and transforming rocks. New rock is constantly being pushed toward the surface of Earth while existing surface rocks are broken down. These rock fragments are carried and deposited in layers, which may eventually become sedimentary rocks.

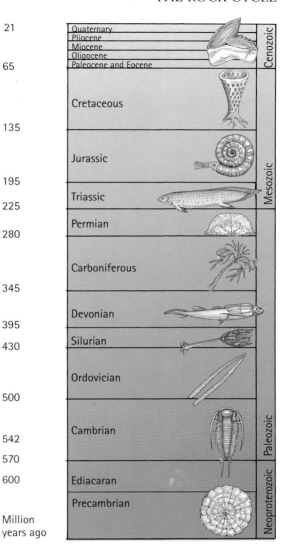

| 21 | Quaternary | | Cenozoic |
| | Pliocene | | |
| | Miocene | | |
| | Oligocene | | |
| 65 | Paleocene and Eocene | | |
| | Cretaceous | | Mesozoic |
| 135 | | | |
| | Jurassic | | |
| 195 | | | |
| | Triassic | | |
| 225 | | | |
| | Permian | | Paleozoic |
| 280 | | | |
| | Carboniferous | | |
| 345 | | | |
| | Devonian | | |
| 395 | | | |
| | Silurian | | |
| 430 | | | |
| | Ordovician | | |
| 500 | | | |
| | Cambrian | | |
| 542 | | | |
| 570 | | | |
| | Ediacaran | | Neoproterozoic |
| 600 | | | |
| | Precambrian | | |
| Million years ago | | | |

▲ Geological time is divided into four eras (right), three of which are then subdivided into periods, each showing a different range of fossilized creatures.

## FOSSILS

Fossils are the remains of dead plants and creatures that have settled in soft sediment that has become sedimentary rock over millions of years. Only the hard parts of living things, such as bones, teeth, and shells, tend to become fossilized. As a result, soft-bodied creatures are rarely discovered. The fossil record has revealed valuable information about life on Earth millions of years ago. It has also provided scientists with an important method of comparing and dating rocks. This is because studies of fossils show that similar life-forms existed at the same time in different parts of the world. The fossil record is one of a number of methods used to date rocks and geological features. Radiometric dating measures the levels of radioactive elements present in rocks. These radioactive elements decay at a constant rate, providing a relatively accurate measure of the age of rocks in millions of years.

▲ At Bryce Canyon in Utah erosion has shaped a range of sedimentary rocks, including limestone and sandstone, into thousands of spires and pinnacles known as hoodoos.

▲ Where rock layers have laid largely undisturbed it is possible to date rocks by their position. Younger rock layers tend to sit above older layers.

## GEOLOGICAL TIME

Modern science estimates that Earth is around 4.54 billion years old. Geological time is a way of presenting this huge span of time. Geological time is divided into a series of four eras stretching back to the formation of the planet over 4.54 billion years ago to the present. The Neoproterozoic era represents over 80 percent of Earth's life, but owing to the constant changes in the rocks, it is the period from which the fewest fossil remains have been discovered. During the early Paleozoic era the first land plants grew, and in time the first forests formed, which would later decompose to create the world's coal reserves. The Mesozoic is the era during which the dinosaurs lived and became extinct.

# MOUNTAIN BUILDING

**Over millions of years mountains have formed, risen, and disappeared, due to the actions of Earth's crust, weathering, and volcanoes.**

▲ The Wilder Kaiser mountain range is part of the Austrian Alps and features mountain summits between 6,230–7,875 ft. (1,900–2,400m). It is a popular skiing and rock-climbing destination.

Mountains are landmasses that are steeply raised above the surrounding area. They are formed mainly through the movement and actions of Earth's crust. The continental crust is made of hard rock, but the immense pressures on the rock can cause softer rocks to bend into folds. The folds can bend over, sink downward, and pile on top of each other like a crumpled blanket. Mountains can be formed from a sequence of folds, piling rock layers one on top of another. Rock layers subjected to severe forces can crack and break, forming fractures and faults. Blocks of land can rise or sink between two faults, forming flat, steep-sided block mountains and long, deep rift valleys.

## CONTINENTAL COLLISION

Continental drift (see page 7) sees the plates of crust move and drive into each other. The crust at the edges of the plates buckles and folds, and faults occur. Land often

▲ Mount Aconcagua, rising to 22,831 ft. (6,960m), is the highest mountain outside of Asia. Part of the South American Andes chain, the mountain is a long-dormant volcano.

rises upward, forming many of the world's mountain chains. The most spectacular example of different plates driving toward each other to form mountains can be found in the Himalayas. There, over 60 million years ago, the Indian subcontinent started to head north, pushing the Tethys Ocean ahead of it. Over a period of around 45 million years the movement continued, with the dense ocean crust pushed under the continental crust beneath Asia. Eventually the Tethys Ocean disappeared, but masses of sediment from its floor

A nappe is a large body of rock that has been moved around 1 mi. (2km) from its original position through faulting or folding

Recumbent folds are where the sides of a fold are pushed over so that it lies close to horizontal

Anticline occurs when folds form an arch

A basin, or trough, formed from folds is called a syncline

Fault

Block mountain, or horst

Rift valley

▲ Parts of Earth's crust are put under great pressure by the movement of plates and other activity. This pressure sees folds and faulting occur that shape the landscape in a number of ways and create a variety of features.

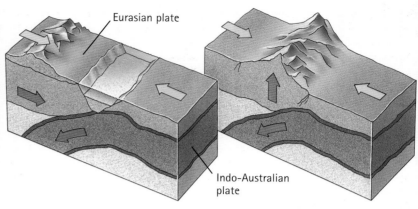

Eurasian plate

Indo-Australian plate

were scooped up and squeezed between the continents, helping form the world's tallest mountain range.

## ERUPTIONS AND EROSION
Some mountains form through other actions rather than directly through plate movements. Volcanic eruptions can form steep-sided, cone-shaped mountains such as Mount Vesuvius in Italy, Mount St. Helens in the United States, and Mount Fuji in Japan. More shallow-sloped volcanoes, called shield volcanoes, can still form mountains such as Mauna Loa and Mauna Kea in Hawaii. Dome mountains are caused by rising magma or igneous rock under Earth's crust that thrust at the rocks above with great force, lifting them into an arch shape. The Black Hills in South Dakota and Wyoming are examples of dome mountains. Erosion can also help form mountains, not by lifting up existing land but by wearing away softer

rock, leaving a core of harder rock standing above the plains around it. Parts of the Ozark Mountains in Arkansas and Missouri were formed in this way. Sometimes a mixture of volcanic activity and erosion forms mountains. Magma that seeps into the crust may be uncovered by erosion to stand above the surrounding area as mountains. Scotland's Cairngorm Mountains, made of granite, are one such example.

## RISE AND FALL
Mountains are far from permanent structures. They continually form, rise, and then are worn down over millions of years. The eroding actions of wind, ice, and water start to reduce mountains' size, with rivers and glaciers transporting debris that they deposit as sediment. Eventually mountains are worn down, while new mountains are formed elsewhere.

▲ Long ago the plate carrying the land we now call India collided with the plate carrying the rest of Asia (left). The sand, mud, and soil on the ocean floor between the plates was slowly squeezed together and pushed up (right) to form the Himalayas.

▼ Fault-block mountains are formed when huge blocks of Earth's crust are tilted on, or pushed up along or close to, a fracture or fault line. These mountains lie near the Moab fault line in Utah.

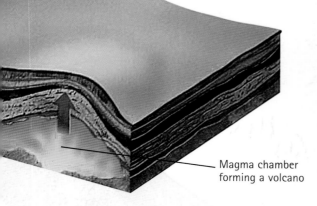

Magma chamber forming a volcano

# RIVERS AND LAKES

Rivers and lakes have a great impact on the world. They shape the land and provide water and habitats for living things.

▲ Rising in Switzerland, where it is fed by meltwaters from glaciers and snow, the Rhine river, here seen in Germany, flows approximately 820 mi. (1,320km) through northern Europe before emptying into the North Sea.

Rivers are large channels of water that carry water from high land toward areas at sea level. Rivers empty into seas, oceans, and lakes. They carry water that comes from rainfall, snow, melting glaciers, lakes, and from water inside Earth called groundwater. Rivers vary greatly in length, with the longest extending more than 3,730 mi. (6,000km). They also vary in the volume of water they carry. The two biggest rivers (in volume), the Amazon in South America and the Congo in Africa, contain roughly 60 percent of the world's river water.

▼ A river starts in high-altitude regions and flows through land down toward sea level. As it makes its journey the speed of its current, or water flow, slows, and its effect on the landscape alters. As the river's flow slows on a floodplain it deposits sediment.

Mountain glacier feeds young river

Fast-moving young river carves out deep V-shaped valley

Oxbow lake

Mature river's course changes in meanders and wide curves

At its mouth the river drops a lot of sediment, which can form a fan-shaped area called a delta

## A RIVER'S LIFE

Rivers tend to start life in higher altitude regions where they are fed by meltwaters from snow, ice, or glaciers or from groundwater. When rain falls on high ground, some of the water disappears into the soil or seeps between cracks in the rocks. In places the ground becomes saturated. The top of this saturated zone is called the water table. When the water table reaches Earth's surface, groundwater can pour out, forming a spring. Water from all sources is drawn by gravity toward sea level and trickles down slopes to form streams that act as tributaries, feeding rivers. The area of land from which a river collects water is called a drainage basin, and the shape of the river and its tributaries is called a drainage pattern. This pattern depends on the type of soil and rock, how steeply the land slopes, and soil movements under the ground. A young river flows fast and relatively

▲ The Amazon river travels 4,006 mi. (6,448km) through South America before emptying into the Atlantic Ocean. More than 20 percent of the freshwater that enters the seas and oceans every year comes from the Amazon.

▶ Oxbow lakes are horseshoe-shaped lakes that were once part of and now lie close to mature rivers.

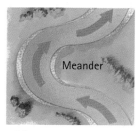

**1** Some meanders will swell into broader loops than others.

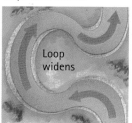

**2** The neck of the loop may narrow as the loop develops.

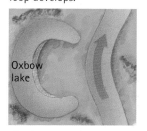

**3** An oxbow lake forms from the old channel.

straight, eroding and cutting through landforms (see page 22). As the river matures it tends to carry more water, flow more slowly, and is more likely to change its course in loops and bends called meanders. Finally, a river empties into a sea, ocean, or large lake at its river mouth.

## LAKES

A lake is a large quantity of standing water surrounded by land. Lakes form wherever water collects, particularly in dips or depressions in the ground, and does not drain away. Lakes can be formed in a variety of ways. Many, including the Great Lakes of North America, are the result of glaciers scooping out bedrock to form large basins. The deepest lakes are the result of movement of Earth's tectonic plates, pushing material aside to create faults and depressions. Crater lakes form in the remains of meteorite craters or in the tops of extinct volcanoes. Artificial lakes can be created by humans deliberately damming rivers or valleys for fishing, irrigation, or for generating electricity. Some lakes are created by the meandering of a mature or old river where a loop in the river is eventually cut off from the main course, forming what is called an oxbow lake. In geological terms lakes are temporary features, forming in many different ways and, in most cases,

disappearing. The water in lakes can evaporate as the climate becomes drier, or they can fill up with sediment, leaving a bog or swamp in their place. Lakes make up a very small percentage of all the freshwater on Earth, but they make excellent habitats for plants and animals. Shallow lakes are often rich in nutrients that foster an abundance of aquatic plants and wildlife.

▼ Lakes can form in valleys that have been blocked by large landslides. An example of this is Moraine Lake in Banff National Park in Alberta, Canada.

# OCEANS AND SEAS

**Water covers more than 71 percent of the planet's surface. Around 97.6 percent of all of Earth's water is contained in the world's seas and oceans.**

▼ Black smokers are vents found on the ocean floor that spout hot, mineral-rich waters. These provide nutrients for deep-sea life-forms such as tubeworms.

All seawater was originally freshwater, but rain falling on land for millions of years has washed minerals, especially salt, from rocks into seas. Typically by weight, seawater is 96.5 percent pure water, 2.9 percent salt, and 0.6 percent other elements, including calcium, fluoride, magnesium, and potassium. The salt content, or salinity, of seawater can vary. Some seas, such as the Baltic Sea, have a much lower salt content owing to the large amounts of freshwater that run into them from rivers. Other seas, such as the Dead Sea, that receive little rainfall and experience a lot of evaporation have a higher salt content. The world's rivers transport around three billion tons of salt into the water every year.

▲ Coral reefs, such as this South Pacific reef, are formed near the ocean's surface by the remains of millions of creatures called polyps.

▼ The Pacific Ocean dominates a large portion of Earth, covering just over one third of the entire planet. It has a surface area of 65,330,000 sq. mi. (169,200,000km²), including neighboring seas. This is more than the total land area of the continents put together.

## MOVING WATER

Waves, tides, and currents move the water within the seas and oceans. Waves stir the ocean's surface and break in shallow waters, eroding, transporting, and depositing debris. Tides caused by the gravitational pull of the Moon result in the oceans and seas rising and falling in a continuous cycle. There are five oceans spanning the planet: the Pacific, Atlantic, Indian, Southern, and Arctic. These five bodies of water are interlinked, and water circulates Earth via ocean currents. Ocean currents are driven particularly by winds, but variations in water density and temperature also cause currents to flow. Ocean currents redistribute water and transfer the heat they absorb from the Sun's rays around the planet, influencing climate.

## THE OCEAN LANDSCAPE

The edges of the continents slope down under the ocean to form continental shelves. These vary in width from a few miles to more than 300 mi. (500km), and some are crossed by large depressions called submarine canyons. The continental shelves end at shallow depths of around 425 ft. (130m). From there continental slopes plunge sharply downward, meeting the ocean floor at the continental rise. Oceanographers estimate the average depth of the ocean floor, or abyss, to be over 13,000 ft. (4,000m). Large parts of the ocean abyss are relatively flat, forming abyssal plains broken by low hills and underwater volcanoes, known as

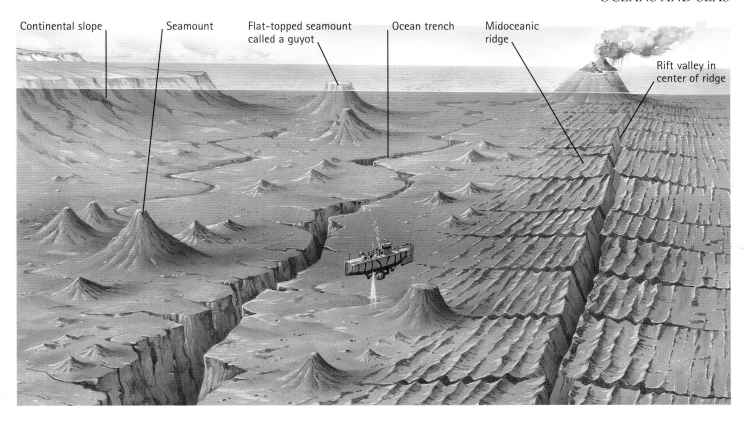

Continental slope · Seamount · Flat-topped seamount called a guyot · Ocean trench · Midoceanic ridge · Rift valley in center of ridge

seamounts, that do not reach sea level. Where the plates of Earth's crust collide deep ocean trenches may form. These are often hundreds of miles wide, thousands of miles long, and are the deepest places on Earth. At 35,994 ft. (10,971m) below sea level, Challenger Deep, part of the Mariana Trench in the Pacific Ocean, is the deepest known place in the world's oceans.

A key feature of most ocean floors is the midoceanic ridge, which features enormous mountain ranges rising almost 5,000 ft. (1,500m) from the ocean floor. These are formed by molten rock rising from Earth's mantle. As it cools and hardens the new ocean crust spreads out from the ridge in both directions. Where the ocean crust meets a continent it tends to sink down, often forming an ocean trench.

## MARINE LIFE

Seas and oceans teem with life. There are around 22,000 species of marine fish and thousands more plants and crustaceans. Most marine life exists in the top 330 ft. (100m) of the oceans, which is called the euphotic zone. Sunlight penetrates this zone and is used by microscopic organisms, called phytoplankton, to convert light energy into food through a process called photosynthesis. Phytoplankton form the first link in marine food chains that support fish, crustaceans, and marine mammals such as seals. Life exists even in the dark ocean depths. In regions below 3,300 ft. (1,000m) plants and creatures have adapted to living where little or no light reaches. Many are scavengers, relying on the sinking of dead plants and animals from upper ocean layers for their food.

▲ The landscape of the ocean floor is varied and contains a range of features. Trenches and ocean ridges are active volcanic and seismic zones.

Wind direction

▲ Currents vary in temperature according to depth. Sometimes cold water rises as an upwelling to replace warmer surface water blown away from the coasts by winds.

◄ Waves begin as up-and-down movements caused by winds that turn in a circular motion as the wave advances. Waves topple over and break as they enter shallow water.

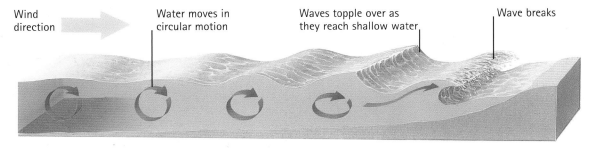

Wind direction · Water moves in circular motion · Waves topple over as they reach shallow water · Wave breaks

# LANDSCAPING BY WATER

Rivers, seas, oceans, and rainwater shape landscapes through erosion and by moving and depositing material to create new landforms.

▲ Wave action has eroded this limestone headland on the Dorset coast in southern England to form a large arch called Durdle Door. When the top of an arch collapses, the tall pillar of rock left behind is called a stack.

▼ The sea erodes landforms with its wave action, compressing air in gaps and cracks in land, forcing rocks apart. Waves frequently undercut a cliff face at its base, causing cliff falls.

Water moving downhill in streams and rivers carries with it any particles that it can move. This material helps erode, or wear away, the land it flows over, creating more loose material—some of which is also carried by the water. Close to its source a river tends to carve out steep, V-shaped valleys. As a river matures it usually erodes the sides of its banks, carving out wider valleys. When a river flows in a bend, its current is faster on the outside of the bend than on the inside. The faster flowing current continues to erode land while sediment is deposited on the inside edge.

When rivers meet harder rock that is more resistant to erosion, rapids and waterfalls can form. Although some waterfalls can form through faults and the action of glaciers (see page 25), most are the result of flowing water undercutting softer rock layers. The amount of eroded material a river can carry depends on the speed it travels. As a river matures it tends to slow in speed and deposit the debris it carries as sediment. When an old-age river floods the lands on either side of its course, it deposits a lot of sediment, forming a floodplain. Over time the buildup of sediment can form fertile growing land such as the Nile floodplain in Egypt.

## LANDSCAPING COASTLINES

Coastlines are constantly being shaped as they are broken down and built up by the action of waves. Waves exert great force on the landscape, and the rocks, pebbles, and sediment they carry and hurl against the land act as powerful eroding tools. Seawater is also slightly acidic and can rot and dissolve limestone and chalk rocks. Many coastlines are formed from a mixture of hard and soft rocks that erode at different rates. Soft rock is worn away into curved bays, with hard rock left behind forming cliffs and headlands. Beaches are formed from some of the loose sediment and stone produced through coastal erosion and from material deposited by rivers as they flow into the sea. Beach material is pulled along sideways by the waves in an action called

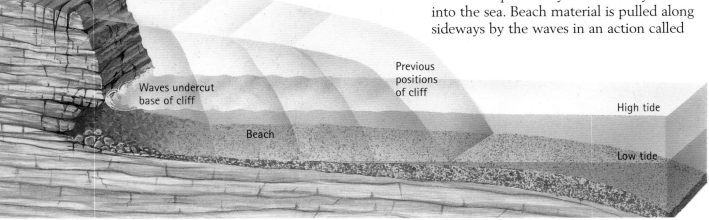

Waves undercut base of cliff

Beach

Previous positions of cliff

High tide

Low tide

▲ The Colorado river has landscaped the surrounding sandstone rock at Canyonlands National Park in Utah to form the spectacular Horseshoe Bend.

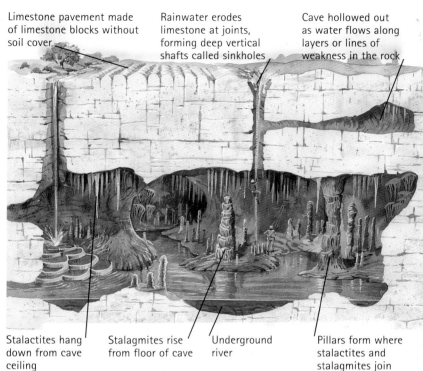

Limestone pavement made of limestone blocks without soil cover.

Rainwater erodes limestone at joints, forming deep vertical shafts called sinkholes

Cave hollowed out as water flows along layers or lines of weakness in the rock

Stalactites hang down from cave ceiling

Stalagmites rise from floor of cave

Underground river

Pillars form where stalactites and stalagmites join

longshore drift. Breaks in the coastline cause these drifts to push beach material out into the sea to form long, thin ridges called spits.

## UNDERGROUND WATER
Water can pass through certain types of rocks. Porous rocks, such as sandstone, have tiny spaces between their grains, allowing water to seep in. Permeable rocks,

such as limestone, have gaps and fractures that water can travel through. Many cave systems are formed through the action of rainwater. As rain falls it dissolves carbon dioxide from the atmosphere and becomes weakly acidic. Some rocks, especially limestone, can be dissolved by rainwater, which gradually widens cracks and joints in the rock. Deep vertical tunnels, called sinkholes, are sometimes created, and large caves are formed by the hollowing out of the underground rock.

▲ Acidic rainwater reacts with limestone, dissolving the rock to landscape features underground. Stalactites and stalagmites are formed from minerals deposited by the water.

▼ Located on the border between Argentina and Brazil, the Iguaçu Falls are a spectacular series of waterfalls stretching over 1.7 mi. (2.7km). Small, rocky, and wooded islands divide the falls into 275 separate waterfalls.

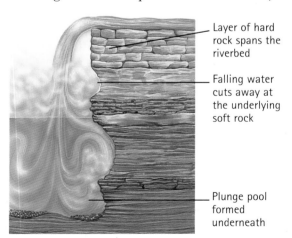

Layer of hard rock spans the riverbed

Falling water cuts away at the underlying soft rock

Plunge pool formed underneath

▲ Waterfalls form when water erodes softer layers of rock downstream, creating a sharp ledge. Over time the the harder rock is eroded as well, creating a gorge.

# LANDSCAPING BY ICE

**Glaciers are giant rivers of ice that have the power to carve out large land features, form lakes, and move soil and rocks hundreds of miles.**

Ice covers a little more than ten percent of Earth's land. During periods in the past this figure was much higher. Long periods of colder, global climates, known as ice ages, have occurred a number of times in Earth's history. Scientists believe that the last Ice Age began around 2.58 million years ago. Glacial periods have occurred between 15 and 22 times in the last two million years. During the last Ice Age ice sheets covered large parts of the Northern Hemisphere. Ice has receded from many of these areas, and its effects on the landscape can be seen clearly. Ice wears down the surrounding rocks as it moves in large masses. The material deposited by ice has formed many lowland areas around the world.

▲ The white area shows the extent of the ice sheets that covered parts of the Northern Hemisphere during the last Ice Age. In places the thickness of the ice reached 9,840 ft. (3,000m).

▼ Lowland areas that emerge from glaciers often contain a number of distinctive features formed through the action of the ice and the moraine it carried and deposited.

### GLACIER FORMATION
Glaciers are large masses of ice that move slowly. There are around 100,000 glaciers found on all of the continents. Over time glaciers form, frequently in mountain valleys that receive heavy, repeated snowfall. Fresh snow is squashed together under pressure from successive layers to form a solid mass called névé. As more snow lands on top of the névé air is

pushed out, driving the snow particles closer together. The grains melt and refreeze, filling all remaining gaps until they form glacier ice. Once the depth of the glacial ice

Meltwater

Terminal moraine

reaches around 100 ft. (30m) gravity forces the ice mass to creep slowly down the valley.

### MOVEMENT AND POWER
Glaciers advance slowly, usually at a rate of between 0.4–3 ft. (1cm–1m) per day. At the base of the glacier, where ice comes into contact with bedrock, the huge pressures generate heat that melts ice to form a layer of meltwater. This helps the glacier slide over the rock. Glaciers move with enormous force and erode the landscape below and to the sides. Water that refreezes in the rock underneath the glacier breaks pieces of rock loose, which freeze into the bottom

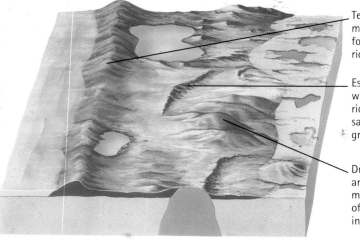

Terminal moraine forms large ridge

Eskers are winding ridges of sand and gravel

Drumlins are smooth mounds that often occur in groups

◀ The Moreno Glacier, found in Argentina's Parque Nacional Los Glaciares, is one of the few major glaciers that is still advancing. The glacier's front face, around 3 mi. (5km) wide and up to 148 ft. (45m) high, moves forward at a rate of around 12 in. (30cm) per day.

▶ Snowfalls feed the top of the glacier. At the lower, front end the glacier melts, forming cold meltwaters. As long as more snow continues to accumulate at the top than melts away at the bottom, the glacier will continue to advance.

Bowl-shaped hollow is called a cirque

Movement of glacier

Crevasses are cracks in the glacier that form when it moves around corners or over bumps

Lateral moraine

The front face of a glacier is commonly known as its snout

of the glacier. These rocks scour and grind the land surface. Rock debris in glaciers is called moraine and can occur in the middle, at the front, or to the sides of the glacier. As the glacier flows down the valley it reaches a location where the temperature rises and is no longer replenished by snowfall.

## AFTER THE ICE

The landscape left behind after a glacier has retreated or disappeared is often altered. In highland areas armchair-shaped hollows, called cirques, jagged pyramidal peaks, and sharp ridges between two glaciers, called arêtes, are often formed by the action of glaciers. Valleys where glaciers have flowed are eroded into a U shape. In many instances the valley

is eroded so deeply that the mouths of smaller, tributary valleys are left high up above the new valley floor. These are called hanging valleys, and water can be seen cascading over them into the main valley as waterfalls. In lowland areas much of the vast amount of moraine carried by glaciers is deposited as glacial drift. This consists of boulders, gravel, sand, and clay and has shaped Earth's surface greatly.

▼ Fjords are glaciated valleys that have been partly flooded by the sea. Geiranger Fjord in Norway is a 9-mi.- (15-km-) long, U-shaped valley created by eroding actions of glaciation.

25

# LANDSCAPING BY WIND

**Wind can have the power to alter landscapes by wearing away rock formations and by transporting sand and other particles.**

The wind's ability to shape the land is particularly powerful in dry, desert regions where there are few plants and very little water to bind particles together. The finer, lighter particles are carried by winds and wear away rock formations to help form a range of landscape features. These include mesas (broad, flat-topped hills with steep sides), buttes (smaller versions of mesas), pedestal rocks, and archways. Winds can blow sands and other loose particles away from an area, leaving exposed a rocky pavement called a hamada. Wind forces sand grains to move via a series of short hops. As the grains land they hit other grains, either bouncing off into the air themselves or forcing other grains to do the same. This process is called saltation. Sand dunes form on lake and sea shores and in deserts. Different types of sand dunes occur based on the wind direction, obstructions, and the sand supply. Where winds blow from one constant direction large, crescent-shaped dunes, called barchans, often form. Star-shaped dunes occur where winds come from all directions.

▲ Wind erosion has bored through soft central rock to create an arch in Delicate Arch, Utah.

▲ These spectacular rock formations in Monument Valley, Utah, are buttes formed by wind erosion.

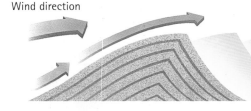

Wind direction

▲ Winds blow over the top, or crest, of the dune, creating a steeper slope on its far side. When winds blow constantly, sand dunes tend to move in the same direction as the wind. A dune may travel as much as 100 ft. (3om) in one year.

▶ The Namib Desert stretches around 1,240 mi. (2,000km) through South Africa, Namibia, and southern Angola. With virtually no rainfall or vegetation, vast seas of moving sand dunes have been formed and shaped by the winds.

# SOIL

**Soil covers much of Earth's land surface and is vital for life. It provides the food and conditions that plants need in order to grow.**

▲ Air and water in the soil are taken in by a plant's roots. Almost half the volume of good agricultural soil, such as this plowed field in Texas, can consist of air and water.

Soil consists of particles of rocks and minerals, gases, water, and humus—dead and decaying plant and animal matter. Soil is formed through many different processes of weathering and erosion that break up underlying bedrock into fragments of rock called regolith and, over time, into smaller particles. These are mixed with the decaying humus and bound together by moisture and the roots of plants that extend down into the soil. Chemical reactions release many of the minerals in the rock particles that enrich the soil with nutrients that are vital for plant growth. These include calcium, potassium, and magnesium. Bacteria, fungi, and other small organisms help decompose, or break down, the dead plant and animal matter on the ground surface or in the soil. This forms the nutrient-rich humus on which much plant growth depends.

Soils vary in type from place to place owing to the climate, vegetation, the local rock types, and other environmental factors. Soil is considered to be a renewable resource, but it can easily be stripped of its nutrients. Most soils tend to be naturally fertile but can be poisoned through pollution or exhausted through extensive farming, which uses the soil's nutrients at a faster rate than can be replaced. Stripping land of its vegetation (see page 40) can result in rich layers of topsoil being washed or blown away, leaving the land infertile.

**Sandy**

**Clay**

**Loamy**

▲ Sandy soils are rough, grainy, hold much air, and allow water to drain rapidly. Clay soils consist of smaller particles that hold less air but retain much water. Loamy soils are a mixture of large and small particles that offer good growing conditions.

Larger soil creatures, such as moles, aid the movement of water and air through the soil as they burrow down, taking humus to deeper levels

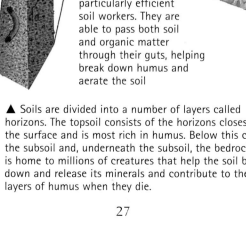

Earthworms are particularly efficient soil workers. They are able to pass both soil and organic matter through their guts, helping break down humus and aerate the soil

A well-developed soil will be full of millions of insects and billions of bacteria and microorganisms

▲ Soils are divided into a number of layers called horizons. The topsoil consists of the horizons closest to the surface and is most rich in humus. Below this comes the subsoil and, underneath the subsoil, the bedrock. Soil is home to millions of creatures that help the soil break down and release its minerals and contribute to the layers of humus when they die.

# THE ATMOSPHERE

**Earth's atmosphere protects its surface from the extremes of space and is the cause of the planet's weather systems.**

Nitrogen 78%

Oxygen 21%

Argon and other gases 1%

▲ Air is a mixture of different gases, including nitrogen (N) at 78%, oxygen (O) at 21%, argon (Ar) at under 1%, and water vapor, which can vary from 0–7%. There are also trace amounts of hydrogen, methane, neon, carbon monoxide, helium, ozone, krypton, and xenon.

▼ Viewed from space, Earth's atmosphere appears as a wispy, fragile arrangement of cloud masses. Yet the atmosphere protects life on Earth from many external hazards, including the solar wind, the intense cold of space, and ultraviolet and other harmful forms of radiation.

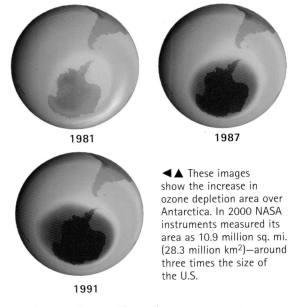

1981

1987

1991

◀▲ These images show the increase in ozone depletion area over Antarctica. In 2000 NASA instruments measured its area as 10.9 million sq. mi. (28.3 million km²)—around three times the size of the U.S.

Earth's atmosphere has evolved over millions of years. Volcanic eruptions helped form the earliest atmosphere, which scientists believe produced much water vapor, nitrogen, and carbon dioxide but little or no oxygen. As the atmosphere cooled much of the water vapor condensed and fell to Earth to form the world's oceans. Oxygen only became an important part of the atmosphere once plant life was established. Plants are capable of capturing and converting light energy into stored energy in a complex process called photosynthesis. Oxygen is released into the atmosphere as a result of photosynthesis. The air contained in the atmosphere today provides creatures with oxygen to breathe and carbon dioxide that helps trap the Sun's energy to warm the planet. The atmosphere also recycles water and protects the planet from harmful radiation.

## LAYERS OF ATMOSPHERE

The atmosphere can be divided into five different layers: the troposphere, stratosphere, mesosphere, thermosphere, and exosphere. These layers merge into one another and vary according to the time of year, so only approximate measurements of their size can be given. The troposphere is the atmospheric layer closest to the ground. It extends between 5–9 mi. (8–15km) up from Earth's surface and is the most dense part of the atmosphere. Air circulates through this layer, and almost all weather is generated within it. Temperatures in the troposphere vary from around 63°F to -67°F (17°C to -55°C). The troposphere's temperature is at its highest close to the ground where the air is heated by Earth's surface. Climbing through this layer, the air

becomes thinner and less capable of holding onto heat. As a result, temperatures decrease on average at a rate of 42°F every 3,280 ft. (or 5.5°C every 1,000m). The stratosphere is drier and less dense than the troposphere and ends around 30 mi. (50km) above Earth's surface. Together, the stratosphere and troposphere contain 99 percent of the atmosphere's air. Extending from a height of around 53 mi. (85km) is the mesosphere, an atmospheric layer that is capable of reflecting radio waves. The thermosphere is also known as the upper atmosphere, and temperatures rise the higher someone climbs through this layer, exceeding 3,092°F (1,700°C). The boundary layer beyond the thermosphere is called the exosphere, and it extends and merges into space. The exosphere contains very little matter, just a small amount of hydrogen and helium.

## OZONE LAYER

Ozone is found in the stratosphere, concentrated in a layer 8–12 mi. (13–20km) above Earth. Ozone performs a vital function, absorbing and scattering much of the ultraviolet radiation that is produced by the Sun. This radiation is harmful to living things, causing skin cancers and damaging plankton, which form the base of the marine life food chain.

A heavily depleted area of the ozone layer over Antarctica was discovered in the late 1970s by the British Antarctic Survey. The main cause is believed to be the release of chlorofluorocarbon (CFC) into the atmosphere. These gases are used as refrigerants, solvents in the electronics industry, and in aerosol cans. When CFCs enter the atmosphere, they react with the ultraviolet radiation, which causes the chlorine in CFCs to destroy ozone molecules, converting them into oxygen. One molecule of chlorine can destroy up to 100,000 ozone molecules. Although international moves to ban the use of CFCs have occurred, any improvements take time since CFCs can last in the atmosphere for 50 to 100 years and take five to ten years to reach the upper atmosphere, where they are broken down.

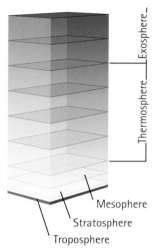

434 mi. (700km)
372 mi. (600km)
310 mi. (500km)
248 mi. (400km)
186 mi. (300km)
124 mi. (200km)
62 mi. (100km)
31 mi. (50km)
6.2 mi. (10km)

Exosphere
Thermosphere
Mesosphere
Stratosphere
Troposphere

▲ The layers of the atmosphere flow into each other in transition zones called pauses. The tropopause, for example, is the zone between the troposphere and the stratosphere.

► The layers of the atmosphere rise upward from Earth's surface, held in place by the force of gravity. Within the different layers a variety of atmospheric features, or phenomena, can be witnessed.

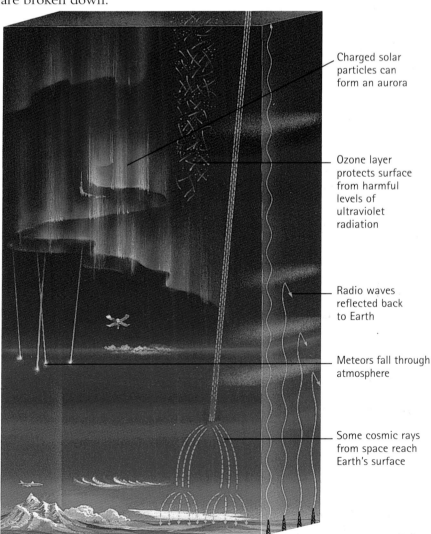

Charged solar particles can form an aurora

Ozone layer protects surface from harmful levels of ultraviolet radiation

Radio waves reflected back to Earth

Meteors fall through atmosphere

Some cosmic rays from space reach Earth's surface

# CLIMATE

The general weather conditions that an environment experiences over a long period of time is called the climate. Climates vary around the world.

Sun's rays

▲ The Sun's rays reach Earth's surface at their most concentrated around the equator. North and south from the equator they strike at a greater angle, and their warming power decreases.

▼ The water cycle is heat-driven by energy from the Sun. Water evaporates from lakes, rivers, and seas into the atmosphere. Plants also let water out into the atmosphere from their leaves. Warm, moist air cools as it rises over high land or meets cooler air. When the cooled air can no longer support all the water it holds as vapor, rain forms and falls to Earth. Water returns to vegetation and to lakes, rivers, and seas, completing the cycle.

The Sun provides Earth with the energy to support life, while its heat drives the planet's weather systems. How the Sun's rays strike Earth's surface help determine the temperature of an area, which, in turn, affects its climate and weather patterns. Earth's curved surface means that different parts of the planet receive differing amounts of the Sun's rays. Around the center of Earth, the equator, temperatures remain high and vary relatively little. This is because the Sun's rays strike almost directly all year long, and Earth's tilt (see page 4) has little effect there. The farther from the equator, the greater the angle with which the Sun's rays strike the surface. This means that they have to travel through more of Earth's heat-absorbing atmosphere and that their energy has to be spread over a wider surface area, lessening their warming effect. This is why the polar regions are also the coldest places on Earth.

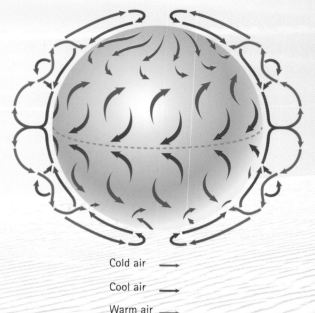

Cold air →

Cool air →

Warm air →

▲ Warm air rises at the equator, where sunlight is strongest, and moves away from the equator toward the poles, drawing cool air behind it. Cold air close to the poles heads in the opposite direction, from cold areas to warmer ones.

## CIRCULATING AIR

Three circles of winds, called circulation cells, blow around each hemisphere of the globe. The cold air in these winds sinks and spreads out until it reaches warmer regions, where the air warms up, rises, and flows back toward the poles. Earth's constant spinning on its axis tends to bend or push winds to one side, a phenomenon known as the Coriolis effect. In the Northern Hemisphere winds are pushed to the right of their intended direction. In the Southern Hemisphere winds are pushed to the left. As air moves it creates differences in air pressure. When warm air rises, it leaves behind an area of lower air pressure. This is because the upward-moving air is not pressing down so hard on Earth's surface. High air pressure areas are formed by air sinking and pressing down with greater force. These areas tend to bring hot, dry weather in the summer and cold, dry weather in the winter. Low pressure areas tend to bring clouds, rain, or snow.

Rain and snow

Water vapor condenses and forms clouds

Transpiration from plants

Water vapor in atmosphere

Rivers flow back to oceans

Evaporation from seas and lakes

Water vapor cools and forms rain

Groundwater runs off

## WATER'S INFLUENCE

Earth's climate is affected by the oceans and their ability to absorb large quantities of the Sun's heat. The top 6.6 ft. of the ocean stores more heat than the entire atmosphere. Ocean currents carry much of this heat around the world and toward the poles, warming landmasses and the lower atmosphere above the ocean. One major ocean current, the Gulf Stream, carries warmth toward northern Europe, helping give that region a mild climate. Areas far inland from oceans tend to have more extreme temperature differences between their winters and summers. The amount of water present on Earth's surface in its oceans, seas, lakes, and rivers and in its atmosphere does not alter. Water, however, does change its state and location in an endless sequence called the water cycle. Water is taken up into the atmosphere through evaporation and the action of plants transpiring. Clouds form when warm air containing water vapor rises, cools, and condenses to form millions of minute water droplets. Rain forms when these droplets collide with each other and form larger droplets that are too heavy for the clouds to support them.

▼ The ground temperature of an area can be affected by how much its surface reflects or absorbs the Sun's energy, known as its albedo. Snow and ice in the Antarctic have a high albedo, meaning that most energy is reflected and little is absorbed.

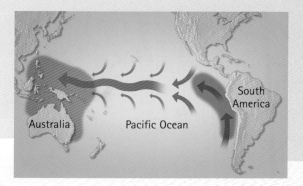

◄ Ocean currents affect the climates of regions, and occasionally major currents can alter, leading to a large impact on climate. In the Pacific Ocean surface ocean currents normally transport warmer water (shown in purple) westward from South America toward Australia.

▶ El Niño is the name given to the occasional reversal in the currents of the Pacific Ocean. During El Niño the warm current flows eastward, causing floods in the Americas and reducing rainfall in Southeast Asia, leading to droughts.

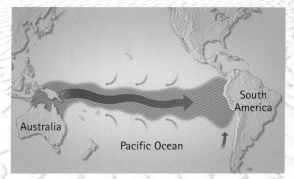

## CLIMATE CHANGE

Although climate is the long-term measure of weather conditions in an area, it is subject to change. Alternating long periods of hot and cold weather have occurred in Earth's distant past many millions of years ago. More recently, in the 1600s, a cooler period occurred known as the Little Ice Age. It is believed to have been linked to a lack of dark patches, called sunspots, on the Sun's surface. Climate change is being closely monitored today as a result of concerns about global warming (see pages 40–41).

▼ Waipoua Forest, found in the Northland region of New Zealand, has a subtropical climate with warm temperatures and relatively high rainfall. These climatic conditions allow lush vegetation to flourish, including giant kauri trees standing between 115–130 ft. (35–40m) tall.

# WORLD CLIMATE ZONES

Climates vary greatly around the world and influence the life that exists in a region. A number of factors influence the climate of a location on Earth, including altitude and distance from seas and oceans. Climate zones are a way of mapping the world's climates.

A major factor in determining climate is a region's distance from the equator. For example, while the regions closest to the equator have a warm and wet tropical climate, the regions farthest from the equator experience an intensely cold and dry polar climate. The temperate climate zone lies approximately halfway between the equator and the poles. This climate zone features mild temperatures and moderate rainfall.

▲ Continental climate zones, such as the central northern U.S., tend to occur inland, long distances away from oceans. Their moderating effects on climate are negligible, so continental climates tend to have large differences between summer and winter temperatures. These climate zones are also dry because the moisture carried by air from the oceans is lost as rainfall earlier in its journey.

▲ The Amazon rain forest is typical of tropical climates that are found close to the equator. Heavy and prolonged rainfall and average temperatures above 77°F (25°C) help produce lush plant growth, which, in turn, provides food and habitats for a large range of creatures.

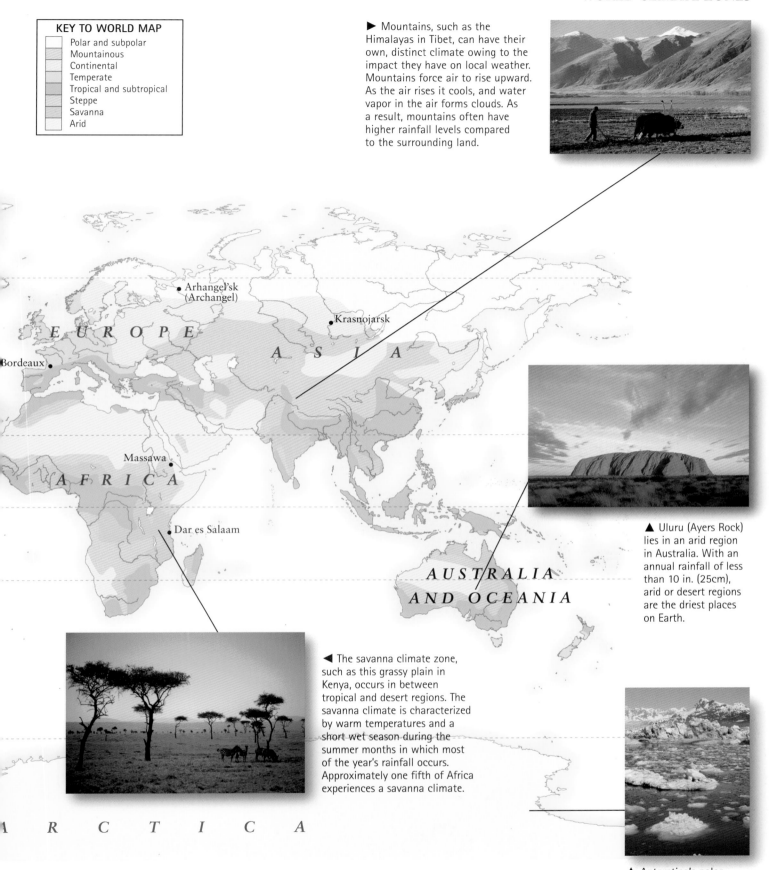

**KEY TO WORLD MAP**
- Polar and subpolar
- Mountainous
- Continental
- Temperate
- Tropical and subtropical
- Steppe
- Savanna
- Arid

► Mountains, such as the Himalayas in Tibet, can have their own, distinct climate owing to the impact they have on local weather. Mountains force air to rise upward. As the air rises it cools, and water vapor in the air forms clouds. As a result, mountains often have higher rainfall levels compared to the surrounding land.

▲ Uluru (Ayers Rock) lies in an arid region in Australia. With an annual rainfall of less than 10 in. (25cm), arid or desert regions are the driest places on Earth.

◄ The savanna climate zone, such as this grassy plain in Kenya, occurs in between tropical and desert regions. The savanna climate is characterized by warm temperatures and a short wet season during the summer months in which most of the year's rainfall occurs. Approximately one fifth of Africa experiences a savanna climate.

▲ Antarctica's polar climate experiences subzero temperatures for most of the year.

33

# WEATHER

**The combination of conditions in Earth's atmosphere and how these frequently change and behave is called the weather.**

▲ Sea mist shrouds San Francisco, California. Mist is a type of cloud close to the surface of Earth and is formed by the cooling of a moist air layer from the land or water below.

Three factors, the amount of water in the air, air temperature, and air movement, are largely responsible for forming the many different types of weather. In some parts of the world weather can vary little over a period of many days or weeks. In other regions weather changes frequently.

## PRECIPITATION AND STORMS

Water that falls to Earth's surface from clouds is called precipitation. Rain is the most common form, but there are others such as snow and sleet. Snowflakes form when water droplets freeze into ice crystals in clouds. If the freezing level is less than 985 ft. (300m) above ground level, the flakes do not have time to melt before reaching the ground and fall as snow. If the freezing level is much higher, the flakes tend to melt and fall as rain. Sleet is a mixture of snow and rain. It occurs when rain encounters a layer of very cold air close to the ground, and some, but not all, the rain freezes. Thunderstorms occur in hot, damp weather where water droplets rise quickly, hit colder air above, and form tall, heaped cumulonimbus clouds. A buildup

▲ Lightning is a massive discharge of electricity from one rain cloud to another or from the cloud to Earth. This lightning storm was photographed in France. Electrically charged water particles occur in storm clouds with positive and negative charges. When they attempt to discharge or move to equalize their charges, they heat up the air to temperatures as high as 54,000°F (30,000°C), which can generate lightning flashes and thunder.

▶ Clouds are classified by their appearance and their height above Earth's surface. Medium-level clouds have their bases between 6,560–23,000 ft. (2,000–7,000m). Below 6,560 ft. (2,000m) are low-level clouds, while high-level cloud formations can extend up to an altitude of 45,900 ft. (14,000m).

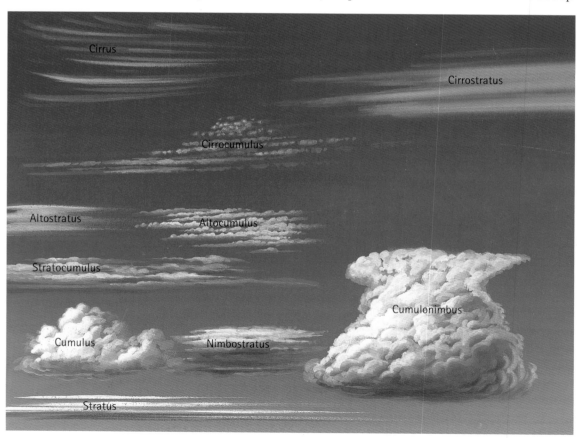

Cirrus

Cirrostratus

Cirrocumulus

Altostratus

Altocumulus

Stratocumulus

Cumulonimbus

Cumulus

Nimbostratus

Stratus

of electrically charged particles in these clouds can generate lightning flashes and thunder. Tornadoes tend to form during violent thunderstorms when hot, fast-moving upward air currents meet a cold, downward air current. The hot and cold currents spiral around each other, forming a tight funnel of clouds in which wind speeds can reach 300 mph (480km/h).

◄ Tornadoes are narrow funnels of fast-moving air usually less than 985 ft. (300m) in width at ground level. They are hard to forecast because they are small, appear quickly, and are usually short-lived.

Powerful storms occur over the seas and oceans of equatorial regions. In the Atlantic and Caribbean they are known as hurricanes, in the Pacific as typhoons, and elsewhere as cyclones. They involve the formation of an intense low pressure core that sucks in warm, moist air moving fast in spirals. As the air rises the water vapor condenses and falls as torrential rain. A large amount of heat is emitted, which makes the air rise even faster and increases the speed of the air moving in and around the storm. Reaching wind speeds of at least 124 mph (199km/h), they move relatively slowly, allowing them to be tracked and warnings given to areas at risk.

## MEASURING WEATHER

Weather details are measured and recorded using many instruments, including barographs, which measure changes in air pressure, and anemometers, which measure wind speed. Satellite imaging is used to track weather systems, radar helps detect cloud patterns and movements, and computers assist in the analysis of weather patterns. Weather maps plot the movement of areas of high and low pressure and chart fronts where cold and warm air meets. Forecasting the weather can be difficult because the weather in one location can later influence weather in another area.

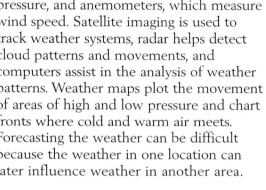

▲ Rainbows form when sunlight strikes water falling through the air at a certain angle, causing the colors of the visible light spectrum to be displayed.

◄ Hurricane Fran photographed by a weather satellite off the coast of the southeastern United States near Florida in 1996. Hurricanes are marked by huge cumulonimbus clouds that rapidly circle the hurricane's center. Warm, moist air rises in a hurricane in a fast-turning spiral. Dry air sinks through the center of the hurricane, known as the eye, where the weather is calm and the sky is clear.

# HUMAN IMPACT

**Human beings have been on Earth only for a small fraction of its 4.57-billion-year history—yet they have transformed large parts of the planet.**

▲ To generate electricity from falling water, hydroelectric power programs often involve large dams built across rivers. The 725-ft.- (221-m-) high, 1,243-ft.- (379-m-) long Hoover Dam on the Colorado river creates an artificial lake measuring 247 sq. mi. (640km²) called Lake Mead.

## CO₂ POLLUTION

Transportation: 70.6%

Other (waste disposal, chemical sprays, etc.): 12.3%

Fuel burning: 10.3%

Industry: 6.8%

▲ Carbon dioxide ($CO_2$) is emitted into Earth's atmosphere by humans in a variety of ways.

▼ One of the largest and most crowded urban areas in the world, Mexico City is also one of the most polluted. Industry and over three-and-a-half million vehicles generate serious air pollution.

The human race started life as hunter-gatherers roaming the land for food. Over time people learned how to raise animals and grow crops. As people started to settle in one place they began to have a great impact on the geography and vegetation of their local area. Human beings are unique among Earth's creatures in being able to alter many aspects of their environment. Early changes were mainly concerned with making land suitable for growing crops, such as clearing plots of trees, rocks, and other obstructions, and diverting water from nearby rivers, streams, and lakes to irrigate crop fields.

### EXPLOITING EARTH'S RESOURCES
As industries developed the need for raw materials and fuels saw the start of people exploiting Earth's resources. These include minerals, ores, and fossil fuels such as coal. Large mines and pits have gouged the surface of Earth as people have sought out building materials, precious metals, and metal ores. Coal mines, oil wells, and natural gas fields have exploited large quantities of Earth's fossil fuel reserves. Most electricity is still generated by burning fossil fuels, such as coal or oil, in power plants. Plastics and many other artificial materials use petroleum products as a raw material. Oil, coal, and metal ores are all known as nonrenewable resources and cannot be replaced at the rate at which humans are using them.

### INCREASING POPULATION
The human population has boomed over the past two centuries, rising from between 700 and 800 million in 1800 to 6.87 billion in 2010. With this massive increase has come major changes in how

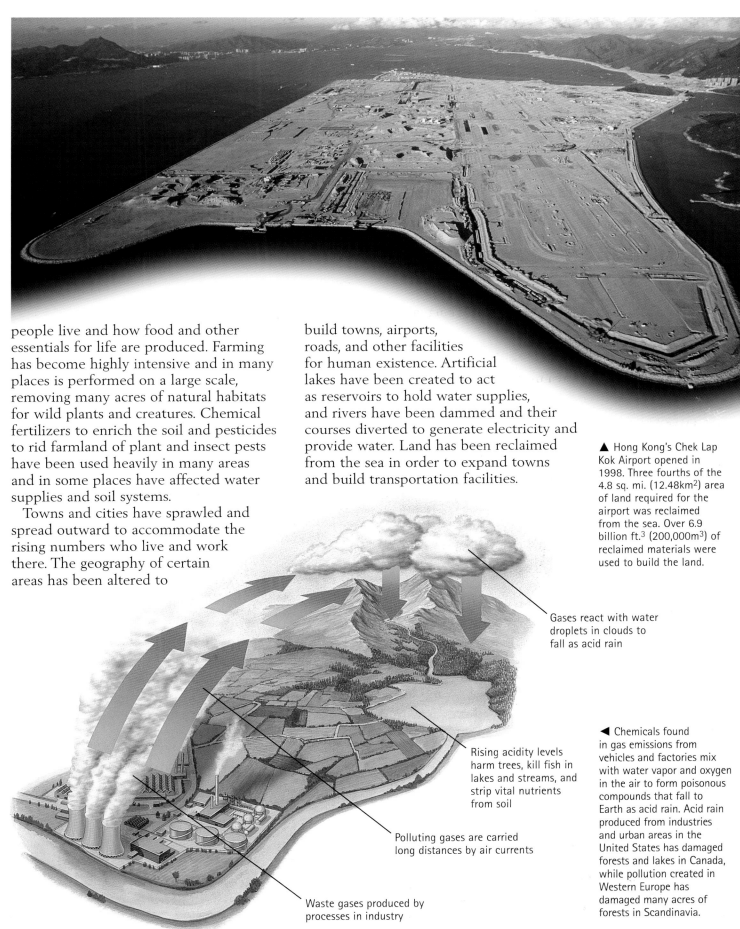

people live and how food and other essentials for life are produced. Farming has become highly intensive and in many places is performed on a large scale, removing many acres of natural habitats for wild plants and creatures. Chemical fertilizers to enrich the soil and pesticides to rid farmland of plant and insect pests have been used heavily in many areas and in some places have affected water supplies and soil systems.

Towns and cities have sprawled and spread outward to accommodate the rising numbers who live and work there. The geography of certain areas has been altered to build towns, airports, roads, and other facilities for human existence. Artificial lakes have been created to act as reservoirs to hold water supplies, and rivers have been dammed and their courses diverted to generate electricity and provide water. Land has been reclaimed from the sea in order to expand towns and build transportation facilities.

▲ Hong Kong's Chek Lap Kok Airport opened in 1998. Three fourths of the 4.8 sq. mi. (12.48km$^2$) area of land required for the airport was reclaimed from the sea. Over 6.9 billion ft.$^3$ (200,000m$^3$) of reclaimed materials were used to build the land.

Gases react with water droplets in clouds to fall as acid rain

Rising acidity levels harm trees, kill fish in lakes and streams, and strip vital nutrients from soil

Polluting gases are carried long distances by air currents

Waste gases produced by processes in industry

◄ Chemicals found in gas emissions from vehicles and factories mix with water vapor and oxygen in the air to form poisonous compounds that fall to Earth as acid rain. Acid rain produced from industries and urban areas in the United States has damaged forests and lakes in Canada, while pollution created in Western Europe has damaged many acres of forests in Scandinavia.

# WORLD POPULATION GROWTH

The total human population of Earth passed six billion in the year 2000. This population is distributed unevenly throughout countries and regions of the world. Countries with similar land areas can contain greatly differing populations.

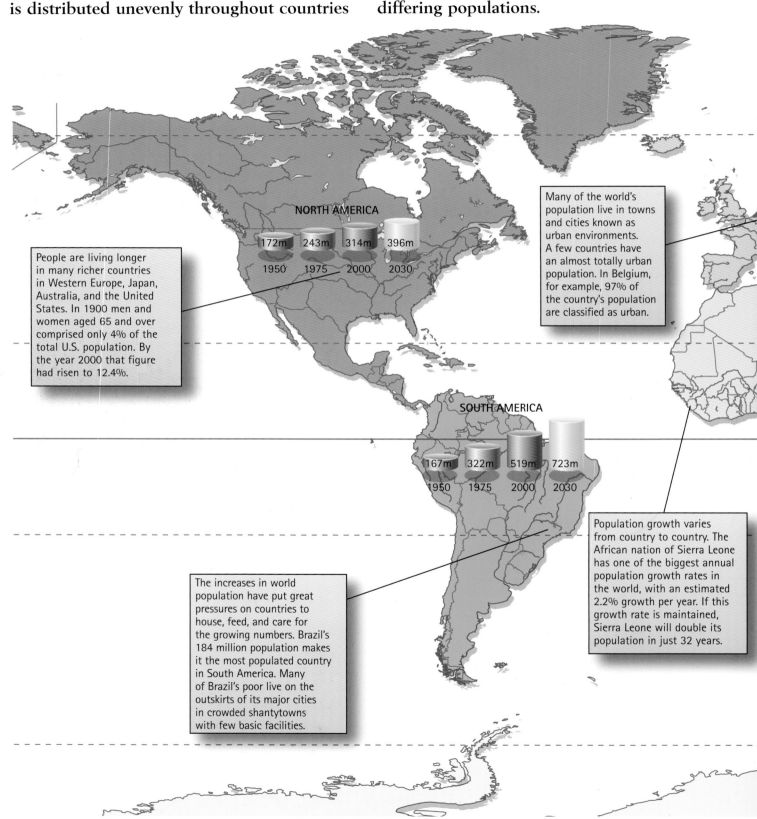

**NORTH AMERICA**

172m — 1950
243m — 1975
314m — 2000
396m — 2030

People are living longer in many richer countries in Western Europe, Japan, Australia, and the United States. In 1900 men and women aged 65 and over comprised only 4% of the total U.S. population. By the year 2000 that figure had risen to 12.4%.

Many of the world's population live in towns and cities known as urban environments. A few countries have an almost totally urban population. In Belgium, for example, 97% of the country's population are classified as urban.

**SOUTH AMERICA**

167m — 1950
322m — 1975
519m — 2000
723m — 2030

The increases in world population have put great pressures on countries to house, feed, and care for the growing numbers. Brazil's 184 million population makes it the most populated country in South America. Many of Brazil's poor live on the outskirts of its major cities in crowded shantytowns with few basic facilities.

Population growth varies from country to country. The African nation of Sierra Leone has one of the biggest annual population growth rates in the world, with an estimated 2.2% growth per year. If this growth rate is maintained, Sierra Leone will double its population in just 32 years.

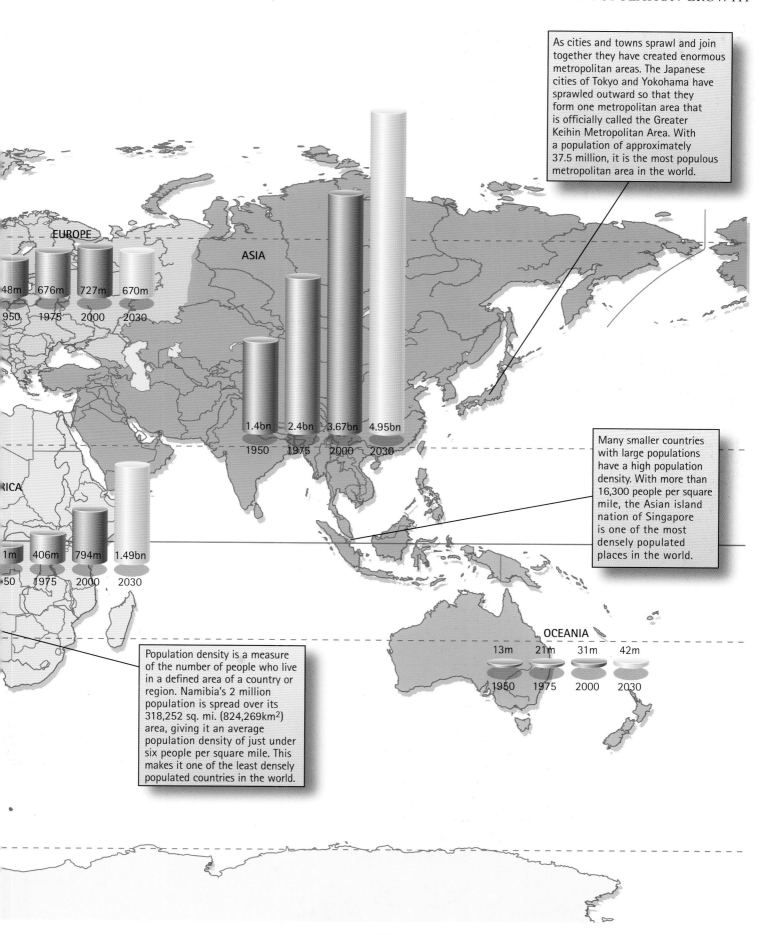

As cities and towns sprawl and join together they have created enormous metropolitan areas. The Japanese cities of Tokyo and Yokohama have sprawled outward so that they form one metropolitan area that is officially called the Greater Keihin Metropolitan Area. With a population of approximately 37.5 million, it is the most populous metropolitan area in the world.

EUROPE

48m  676m  727m  670m

950  1975  2000  2030

ASIA

1.4bn  2.4bn  3.67bn  4.95bn

1950  1975  2000  2030

RICA

1m  406m  794m  1.49bn

50  1975  2000  2030

Many smaller countries with large populations have a high population density. With more than 16,300 people per square mile, the Asian island nation of Singapore is one of the most densely populated places in the world.

Population density is a measure of the number of people who live in a defined area of a country or region. Namibia's 2 million population is spread over its 318,252 sq. mi. (824,269km²) area, giving it an average population density of just under six people per square mile. This makes it one of the least densely populated countries in the world.

OCEANIA

13m  21m  31m  42m

1950  1975  2000  2030

# THE FUTURE

**Earth in the early part of the 21st century continues to evolve and change. In some cases changes are occurring owing to human activity.**

▲ Flood-prone countries, such as Bangladesh, are likely to be even more at risk if global temperatures continue to rise.

▼ When sunlight enters the atmosphere and strikes the surface, some of the Sun's energy is reflected back in the form of infrared radiation. Greenhouse gases tend to absorb this, trapping heat in the atmosphere.

Planet Earth is always changing. Mountains continue to rise, continents are still on the move, while wind, water, and ice erode and shape rock formations. The climate also continues to change. At the current time Earth is warming up faster than in any period in recorded history. Many experts believe that global warming could see an average temperature increase of 35.6°F (2°C) by 2060. Such an increase could result in great changes in weather patterns and local climates, increasing the extent of desertlike areas, harming land and sea ecosystems, and turning some farmlands into wildernesses. A rise in sea levels owing to the melting of parts of the polar ice caps and the thermal expansion of water may see coastal and low-lying areas of land reclaimed by the sea.

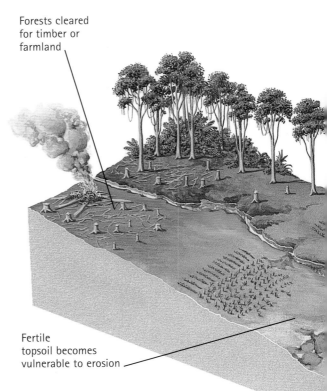

Forests cleared for timber or farmland

Fertile topsoil becomes vulnerable to erosion

▲ Desertification can occur in warm, dry regions removed of their plant cover. Without plant roots to bind the soil, the rainwater runs off the land quickly and soils bake hard and crack and become infertile, desertlike areas.

## ENHANCED GREENHOUSE EFFECT

Scientists believe that part of the change in climate is due to the enhanced greenhouse effect. Greenhouse gases, such as carbon dioxide, methane, and nitrous oxide, are naturally present in Earth's atmosphere. They perform a vital role, helping trap some of the Sun's energy as heat and warming the planet's surface. The enhanced greenhouse effect sees more heat trapped as the result of an increase in the concentrations of greenhouse gases in the atmosphere. These have risen by as much as 25 percent in the past 150 years. Deforestation and the burning of large quantities of fossil fuels, such as oil, in industry and by motor vehicles are believed to be the major causes.

## DEFORESTATION

Forests are often described as the "lungs of the planet" since they take in carbon dioxide from the air and generate much

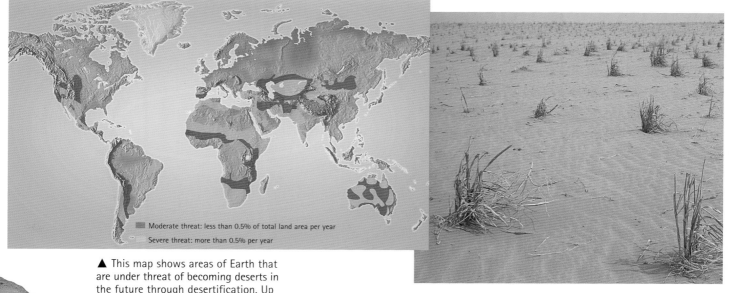

Moderate threat: less than 0.5% of total land area per year

Severe threat: more than 0.5% per year

▲ This map shows areas of Earth that are under threat of becoming deserts in the future through desertification. Up to 23,200 sq. mi. (60,000km²) of new deserts are created every year.

Land becomes dry, cracked, and infertile

## DESERTIFICATION

As the world climate has become hotter and drier desertification, or the expansion of desert environments, has increased. Human activities, such as deforestation and overgrazing livestock, play a major part as well, resulting in ground losing its vegetation cover. The roots of trees and other plants bind soil together, enabling water to be absorbed and further plant life to grow. As land is cleared of its vegetation the topsoil is exposed to the elements and can be washed or blown away, clogging rivers with sediment. When topsoil is blown or washed away, water is no longer retained in the remaining soil, so springs and wells dry up, and fertile land becomes arid and desertlike.

▲ Desertification has seen deserts creep farther into the northern part of the African nation of Sudan, removing farmland that was previously used for growing crops.

▼ Nonpolluting energy-producing methods that use renewable resources, such as these Californian wind turbines, hope to counter further pollution of Earth's atmosphere.

of the oxygen in Earth's atmosphere. Trees and vegetation also recycle water through the process of transpiration, which releases water from the plants' leaves back into the atmosphere. Deforestation occurs when major tracts of forests are destroyed, either cut down for their wood or cleared to create more land for farming, to exploit mineral resources, or to build new settlements. In the past 50 years almost half of the world's forests have disappeared, reducing Earth's ability to convert carbon dioxide into oxygen, leaving more carbon dioxide in the atmosphere. Deforestation also removes vital habitats for living things. For example, the clearing of large areas of forests in Asia has reduced both the territory and prey for tigers. An estimated 100,000 wild tigers were in existence at the start of the 1900s. Today that figure may be fewer than 3,500.

# MAPMAKING

**Maps are graphical representations of Earth that help record and communicate information about the world, as well as help people find their way.**

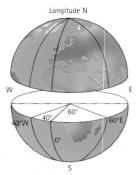

▲ Lines of longitude run from pole to pole over Earth's surface. They are measured in degrees east or west of 0° longitude.

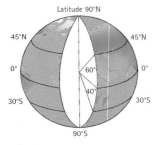

▲ Lines of latitude run around Earth and are measured in degrees north or south from 0° latitude, also known as the equator.

Since ancient times people have been constructing maps. As people traveled greater distances and explored Earth more thoroughly maps have become more accurate and detailed representations of Earth. Maps are drawn to a scale that is often expressed as the ratio between the size of the map and the size of the area it represents. For example, a 1:250,000 scale map would portray one inch on the map as four miles of Earth. Maps of the world may use a larger scale, with one inch equaling 1,600 mi. (1:100,000,000); town plans may use a much smaller scale, with one inch equaling 0.5 mi. (1:31,680).

## LATITUDE AND LONGITUDE

To provide an accurate method of both mapmaking and navigation Earth is crisscrossed with a grid of imaginary lines called latitude and longitude. Lines of latitude run around Earth and lie parallel to the equator. Lines of longitude run from pole to pole and are sometimes called meridians. The lines of latitude are measured in degrees north or

▲ Using a map and a magnetic compass people are able to navigate their way around Earth's surface.

south of the equator. The North Pole has a latitude of 90° north; London, England, is 51.5°north, while Rio de Janeiro, Brazil, is 23° south. The lines of longitude are measured in degrees east or west of an imaginary line that runs from pole to pole and passes through Greenwich in London, known as the prime meridian. The Australian city of Sydney has a longitude of 151° east, while Los Angeles, California, is 118° west. Every place on Earth can be found by combining its longitude and latitude points.

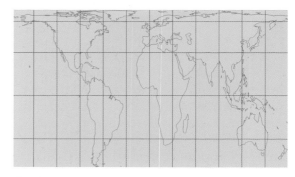

▲ The Peters' projection accurately portrays the extent of land area on maps, but as a result, the shape of landmasses is distorted.

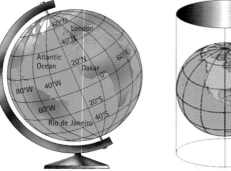

▲ By combining their latitude and longitude locations everywhere on Earth's surface can be pinpointed on a map. For example, the Brazilian city of Rio de Janeiro lies at latitude 22°54'S and longitude 43°11'W.

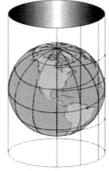

◄▼ Devised by Flemish cartographer Gerardus Mercator (1512–1594), the Mercator projection was one of the first widely used and relatively accurate map projections. However, it distorts the land area closer to the poles, making those regions appear much larger than they actually are.

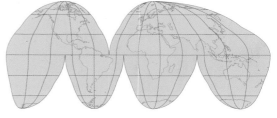

▲ The Homolosine map projects Earth in irregular joined sections. It distorts landmasses less than some other projections and is often used for global thematic maps.

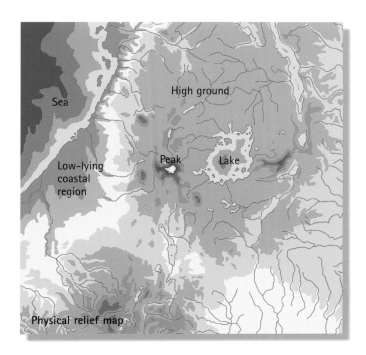

Physical relief map

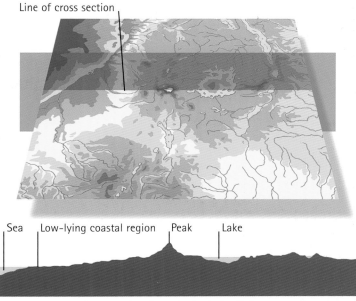

Line of cross section

Sea | Low-lying coastal region | Peak | Lake

Cross section through physical relief map

## MAP PROJECTIONS

Earth is a three-dimensional sphere, while a map is usually a two-dimensional flat piece of paper. Map projections are ways in which cartographers convert Earth's curved surface into a flat image. There are many different projections, but all involve shrinking or stretching parts of the globe. Some projections, such as Peters', represent the relative land areas accurately but distort the land shape. Others, such as the Mercator, distort the land area greatly. Some modern projections, such as Goode's Homolosine projection, have used mathematics to divide Earth into sections in order to convey land area and shape more accurately.

## MAP TYPES

Different types of maps are constructed for a range of purposes. A political map shows the boundaries of the countries of the world. A physical map shows the natural features of the land using different colors or contour lines to show the varying elevations of land areas. A number of different maps and charts are produced to aid navigation, from hiking or cycling maps to maps depicting the main sea lanes for shipping. Maps can also be used to display types of data that varies throughout the world or by region. Thematic maps can show population density or land use, for example.

## MAPPING DEVELOPMENTS

Mapping Earth is a task performed to this day. Modern cartographers use the many advances in technology that have occurred since World War II (1939–1945) to produce highly detailed and accurate maps. Aerial photography, satellite imaging systems, and other methods of remote sensing generate highly detailed data that can be analyzed by Geographic Information Systems (GIS). Running on powerful computers, GIS programs are able to produce maps layered with different information. These can be altered, updated, and printed.

▲ A physical relief map shows the varying heights, or elevations, of the terrain in an area, as well as physical features such as rivers and mountains. This map uses colors to represent different elevations, from purple (the highest points) through brown and yellow to green (the lowest points) on land. The lighter blues are used for more shallow waters and the darker blues for deeper.

▼ Maps are only flat diagrams of Earth's surface. They do not show all of its physical and human-made features. Modern high-resolution photographs taken from the air or from space show further detail and are often used to make advanced and accurate maps for civilian and military use.

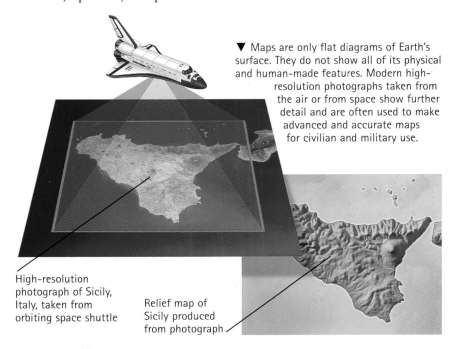

High-resolution photograph of Sicily, Italy, taken from orbiting space shuttle

Relief map of Sicily produced from photograph

# THE PHYSICAL EARTH

**A physical map of the world represents Earth's evolving landscape, mountain ranges, plains, and deserts and its rivers, lakes, and seas.**

Earth's major physical features are found on both land and deep underwater. The longest mountain range on Earth is actually underwater. The Mid-Ocean Ridge consists of a series of ridges on the bottom of the world's oceans and extends around 40,400 mi. (65,000km) in total length. Mountains form major physical features on all of the continents. The Alps are Europe's largest mountain range, while the Rockies extend over 3,000 mi. (4,800km) through North America. While the world's highest mountain range is the Himalayas in Asia, the longest mountain range is the Andes, found on the western side of South America. With a length of 4,470 mi. (7,200km), the Andes has an average elevation of 12,000 ft. (3,660m).

## ISLANDS

Thousands of islands dot Earth's surface, including over 13,700 islands that form Indonesia and comprise the largest archipelago, or island chain, in the world. Islands vary in size from tiny rocky outcrops and coral atolls to giant landmasses such as Madagascar and Borneo. Although Australia is surrounded by water, it is often classified as the world's smallest contintent. The largest island in the world is Greenland, with an area of 840,000 sq. mi. (2,175,600km²).

## WATER FEATURES

Water has had a major influence in shaping the land. Water has eroded soft rock to form wide valleys or has—over millions of years—carved out deep gorges. The spectacular Grand Canyon in the U.S. is the world's largest gorge, measuring 277 mi. (446km) in length and averaging 10 mi. (16km) in width. Moving water has also deposited fertile sediment on riverbanks and floodplains to create farmland. The ribbon of land on both sides of the world's longest river, the Nile, is where the large majority of Egypt's population live.

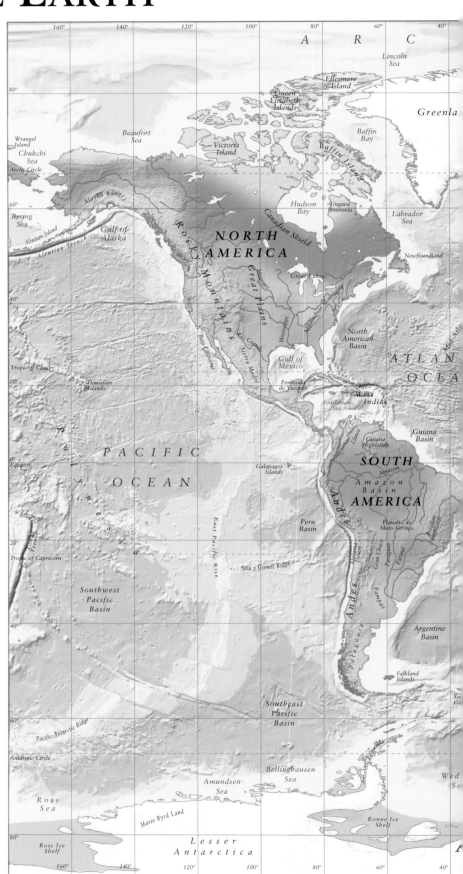

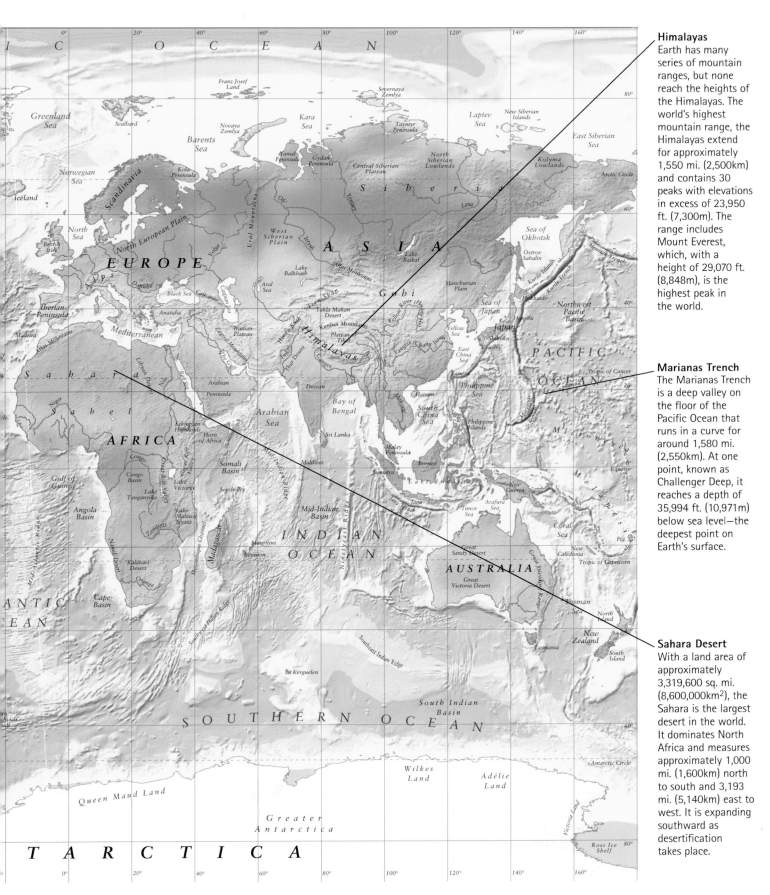

**Himalayas**
Earth has many series of mountain ranges, but none reach the heights of the Himalayas. The world's highest mountain range, the Himalayas extend for approximately 1,550 mi. (2,500km) and contains 30 peaks with elevations in excess of 23,950 ft. (7,300m). The range includes Mount Everest, which, with a height of 29,070 ft. (8,848m), is the highest peak in the world.

**Marianas Trench**
The Marianas Trench is a deep valley on the floor of the Pacific Ocean that runs in a curve for around 1,580 mi. (2,550km). At one point, known as Challenger Deep, it reaches a depth of 35,994 ft. (10,971m) below sea level—the deepest point on Earth's surface.

**Sahara Desert**
With a land area of approximately 3,319,600 sq. mi. (8,600,000km²), the Sahara is the largest desert in the world. It dominates North Africa and measures approximately 1,000 mi. (1,600km) north to south and 3,193 mi. (5,140km) east to west. It is expanding southward as desertification takes place.

# COUNTRIES OF THE WORLD

Every part of Earth's land surface belongs to or is claimed by one of its 197 independent countries. The oldest country with defined borders is San Marino, thought to have been established in A.D. 301. Kosovo became the newest independent nation in 2008.

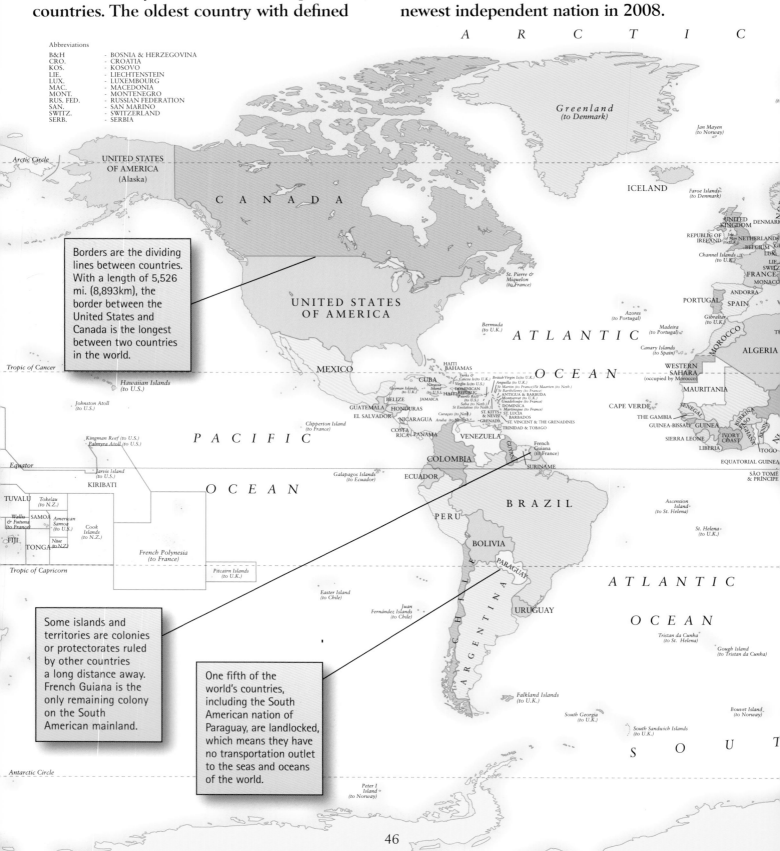

Abbreviations
| | |
|---|---|
| B&H | - BOSNIA & HERZEGOVINA |
| CRO. | - CROATIA |
| KOS. | - KOSOVO |
| LIE. | - LIECHTENSTEIN |
| LUX. | - LUXEMBOURG |
| MAC. | - MACEDONIA |
| MONT. | - MONTENEGRO |
| RUS. FED. | - RUSSIAN FEDERATION |
| SAN. | - SAN MARINO |
| SWITZ. | - SWITZERLAND |
| SERB. | - SERBIA |

Borders are the dividing lines between countries. With a length of 5,526 mi. (8,893km), the border between the United States and Canada is the longest between two countries in the world.

Some islands and territories are colonies or protectorates ruled by other countries a long distance away. French Guiana is the only remaining colony on the South American mainland.

One fifth of the world's countries, including the South American nation of Paraguay, are landlocked, which means they have no transportation outlet to the seas and oceans of the world.

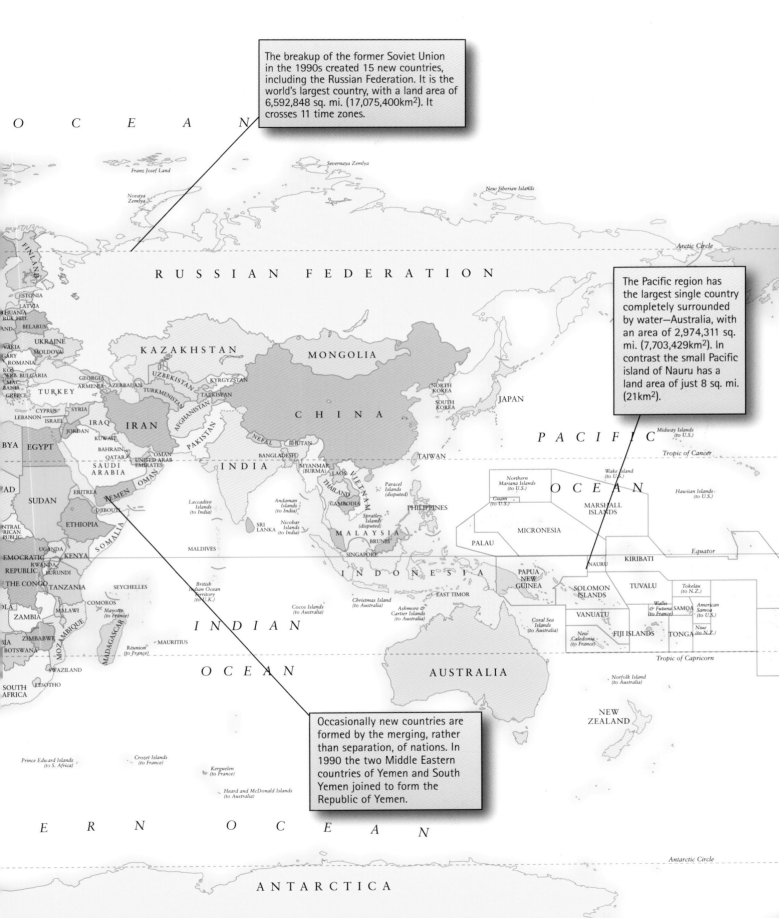

The breakup of the former Soviet Union in the 1990s created 15 new countries, including the Russian Federation. It is the world's largest country, with a land area of 6,592,848 sq. mi. (17,075,400km²). It crosses 11 time zones.

The Pacific region has the largest single country completely surrounded by water—Australia, with an area of 2,974,311 sq. mi. (7,703,429km²). In contrast the small Pacific island of Nauru has a land area of just 8 sq. mi. (21km²).

Occasionally new countries are formed by the merging, rather than separation, of nations. In 1990 the two Middle Eastern countries of Yemen and South Yemen joined to form the Republic of Yemen.

# EARTH STATISTICS

## PLANETARY DATA

| | | | |
|---|---|---|---|
| Estimated age | 4.54 billion years | Orbital period (year) | 365.24 days |
| Diameter at the equator | 7,926 mi. | Rotational period (day) | 23 hours and 56.1 minutes |
| Diameter at the poles | 7,900 mi. | Average temperature | 57°F |
| Circumference at the equator | 24,901 mi. | Surface area | 196,937,600 sq. mi. |
| Circumference at the poles | 24,850 mi. | Land area | 57,392,900 sq. mi. (29.1%) |
| Average distance from the Sun | 92.96 million mi. | Total water area | 139,544,700 sq. mi. (70.9%) |
| Distance between Moon and Earth | 238,855 mi. | Ocean area | 129,443,850 sq. mi. |

### THE WORLD'S OCEANS BY AREA

| | |
|---|---|
| Pacific | 65,328,500 sq. mi. |
| Atlantic | 29,638,000 sq. mi. |
| Indian | 26,469,500 sq. mi. |
| Southern | 7,848,300 sq. mi. |
| Arctic | 5,427,000 sq. mi. |

### THE WORLD'S MAJOR SEAS BY AREA

| | |
|---|---|
| South China Sea | 1,148,500 sq. mi. |
| Caribbean Sea | 1,062,900 sq. mi. |
| Mediterranean Sea | 966,400 sq. mi. |
| Bering Sea | 875,800 sq. mi. |
| Gulf of Mexico | 595,800 sq. mi. |
| Sea of Okhotsk | 589,800 sq. mi. |
| East China Sea | 482,300 sq. mi. |
| Hudson Bay | 475,800 sq. mi. |
| Sea of Japan | 389,000 sq. mi. |
| Andaman Sea | 308,000 sq. mi. |
| North Sea | 222,100 sq. mi. |

### DEEPEST POINTS OF OCEANS AND SEAS

| | |
|---|---|
| Pacific Ocean | 35,994 ft. |
| Atlantic Ocean | 27,493 ft. |
| Caribbean Sea | 25,217 ft. |
| Indian Ocean | 24,442 ft. |
| Southern Ocean | 23,737 ft. |
| Arctic Ocean | 18,051 ft. |
| Gulf of Mexico | 17,070 ft. |
| South China Sea | 16,453 ft. |
| Mediterranean Sea | 16,345 ft. |
| Bering Sea | 13,442 ft. |
| Sea of Japan | 12,277 ft. |

### MAJOR RIVERS BY LENGTH

| | |
|---|---|
| Nile, Africa | 4,145 mi. |
| Amazon, South America | 4,006 mi. |
| Chang Jiang (Yangtze), Asia | 3,914 mi. |
| Mississippi-Missouri, North America | 3,741 mi. |
| Yenisey-Angara, Asia | 3,442 mi. |
| Huang He (Yellow), Asia | 3,395 mi. |
| Ob-Irtysh, Asia | 3,361 mi. |
| Paraná-Río de la Plata, South America | 3,032 mi. |
| Congo, Africa | 2,920 mi. |
| Lena, Asia | 2,734 mi. |

### WORLD'S HIGHEST MULTIPLE WATERFALLS

| | |
|---|---|
| Angel, Venezuela | 3,212 ft. |
| Tugela, South Africa | 3,107 ft. |
| Utigordfoss, Norway | 2,625 ft. |
| Mongefoss, Norway | 2,539 ft. |
| Mutarazi, Zimbabwe | 2,500 ft. |
| Yosemite, U.S. | 2,425 ft. |
| Espelandsfoss, Norway | 2,306 ft. |
| Ostre Mardolafoss, Norway | 2,152 ft. |
| Tyssestregene, Norway | 2,119 ft. |
| Cuquenán, Venezuela | 1,902 ft. |

### MAJOR LAKES BY AREA

| | |
|---|---|
| Caspian Sea, Asia-Europe | 143,550 sq. mi. |
| Superior, North America | 31,800 sq. mi. |
| Victoria, Africa | 26,800 sq. mi. |
| Huron, North America | 23,000 sq. mi. |
| Michigan, North America | 22,300 sq. mi. |
| Tanganyika, Africa | 12,700 sq. mi. |
| Great Bear, North America | 12,300 sq. mi. |
| Baikal, Asia | 12,000 sq. mi. |
| Malawi/Nyasa, Africa | 11,400 sq. mi. |
| Great Slave, North America | 11,000 sq. mi. |

### LARGEST ISLANDS BY AREA

| | |
|---|---|
| Greenland | 839,772 sq. mi. |
| New Guinea | 317,000 sq. mi. |
| Borneo | 287,400 sq. mi. |
| Madagascar | 226,658 sq. mi. |
| Baffin | 183,810 sq. mi. |
| Sumatra | 182,860 sq. mi. |
| Honshu | 88,976 sq. mi. |
| Great Britain | 84,816 sq. mi. |
| Ellesmere | 82,119 sq. mi. |
| Victoria | 81,930 sq. mi. |

### HIGHEST MOUNTAINS BY CONTINENT

| | |
|---|---|
| Asia, Mount Everest | 29,070 ft. |
| S. America, Aconcagua | 22,831 ft. |
| N. America, Mount McKinley | 20,320 ft. |
| Africa, Mount Kilimanjaro | 19,335 ft. |
| Europe, Elbrus | 18,506 ft. |
| Antarctica, Vinson Massif | 16,062 ft. |
| Oceania, Puncak Jaya | 16,503 ft. |

### WORLD'S 10 HIGHEST MOUNTAINS

| | |
|---|---|
| Everest, Himalayas | 29,035 ft. |
| K2, Karakoram | 28,244 ft. |
| Kanchenjunga, Himalayas | 28,146 ft. |
| Lhotse, Himalayas | 27,862 ft. |
| Makalu, Himalayas | 27,763 ft. |
| Cho Oyu, Himalayas | 26,847 ft. |
| Dhaulagiri, Himalayas | 26,735 ft. |
| Manaslu, Himalayas | 26,699 ft. |
| Nanga Parbat, Himalayas | 26,699 ft. |
| Annapurna, Himalayas | 26,487 ft. |

### 10 LARGEST COUNTRIES BY AREA

| | |
|---|---|
| Russian Federation | 6,592,848 sq. mi. |
| Canada | 3,849,674 sq. mi. |
| United States | 3,717,813 sq. mi. |
| China | 3,691,442 sq. mi. |
| Brazil | 3,300,171 sq. mi. |
| Australia | 2,974,311 sq. mi. |
| India | 1,269,219 sq. mi. |
| Argentina | 1,068,300 sq. mi. |
| Kazakhstan | 1,049,155 sq. mi. |
| Sudan | 967,500 sq. mi. |

### 10 COUNTRIES WITH HIGHEST HUMAN POPULATION

| | |
|---|---|
| China | 1,328,886,000 |
| India | 1,148,000,000 |
| United States | 304,060,000 |
| Indonesia | 234,181,000 |
| Brazil | 183,889,000 |
| Pakistan | 162,508,000 |
| Bangladesh | 142,460,000 |
| Russian Federation | 141,904,000 |
| Nigeria | 140,003,000 |
| Japan | 127,918,000 |
| | |
| World Population | 6,870,000,000 |

### POPULATION OF WORLD'S LARGEST CITIES (URBAN AREAS)

| | |
|---|---|
| Tokyo, Japan | 37,520,000 |
| Seoul, South Korea | 21,300,000 |
| Mexico City, Mexico | 19,232,000 |
| São Paulo, Brazil | 19,226,000 |
| New York City, U.S. | 19,007,000 |
| Mumbai (Bombay), India | 18,196,000 |
| Osaka, Japan | 17,640,000 |
| Delhi, India | 15,048,000 |
| Kolkata (Calcutta), India | 14,277,000 |
| Shanghai, China | 14,231,000 |
| Jakarta, Indonesia | 13,660,000 |
| Buenos Aires, Argentina | 13,361,000 |
| Los Angeles, U.S. | 12,873,000 |
| Dhaka, Bangladesh | 12,797,000 |
| Istanbul, Turkey | 12,574,000 |
| Moscow, Russian Federation | 12,410,000 |
| Cairo, Egypt | 12,200,000 |

## HIGHS AND LOWS

**DRIEST RECORDED PLACE ON EARTH**
Calama in Chile's Atacama Desert has zero average annual rainfall.

**WETTEST RECORDED PLACE ON EARTH**
Tutunendo, Colombia, with 463 in. average annual rainfall.

**COLDEST RECORDED TEMPERATURE**
Vostok station, Antarctica (-128°F)

**HOTTEST RECORDED TEMPERATURE**
Al Aziziyah, Libya (136°F)

# THE ARCTIC,
# NORTH AMERICA,
# AND CENTRAL
# AMERICA

# THE ARCTIC

The Arctic is the area circling the North Pole and extending south to include the Arctic Ocean and the northernmost parts of three continents: Asia, Europe, and North America. Surrounding the North Pole and extending outward is a gigantic ice sheet, bigger than all of Europe. Much of this polar ice cap floats on the Arctic Ocean. The ice cap recedes in the summer, with large chunks breaking off to form icebergs. In the winter, when the temperatures can fall as low as -76°F (-60°C), it increases in size again. Despite the hostile climate and living conditions, the Arctic is home to a number of large mammals, including polar bears, walrus, and seals. It has also been inhabited for thousands of years by peoples such as the North American Inuits and the European Lapps (Samis).

▼ Part of Greenland covered in glacial ice meets the sea near the settlement of Cape York, 124 mi. (200km) south of Qaanaaq.

# GREENLAND

**Greenland is the world's biggest island. It is a dependency of Denmark but is 50 times bigger. Much of the land is covered by a large ice cap.**

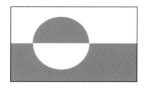

**Area:** 840,000 sq. mi. (2,175,600km²)
**Population:** 56,000
**Capital:** Nuuk (15,000)
**Main languages spoken:** Inuktitut, Danish
**Main religion:** Lutheran
**Currency:** Danish krone
**Main exports:** fish and fish products, minerals, (gold, mobium, uranium, iron, diamonds)
**Government:** self-governing dependency of Denmark

▼ The small village of Savissivik lies on the west coast of Greenland. It was originally founded by Inuit people who made iron tools using the iron contained in meteorites discovered in the area.

Greenland lies mainly within the Arctic Circle, and its landscape is dominated by a giant ice sheet that covers 84 percent of the island. The action of glaciers has created a complex coastal landscape with many fjords and offshore islands. Almost all of Greenland's small population live on the coast, particularly on the southwestern side, where the climate is not as bitterly cold as in the interior. Only one percent of the island's total area can be farmed; hardy vegetables, such as beets and turnips, are grown, and small herds of sheep, goats, and reindeer are raised for their meat. The Arctic waters around the coast provide good catches of salmon, cod, and shrimp, and fish processing is Greenland's major industry. The island has no railroads and only 93 mi. (150km) of roads. The main forms of transportation are air, boat, and snowmobile. The people of Greenland are a mixture of descendants of Inuit, Danish, and Norwegian settlers. Although Denmark is around 1,300 mi. (2,000km) away, all Greenlanders are Danish citizens. After a long campaign the island was

allowed to rule itself from 1979 onward, although Denmark remains in control of foreign affairs. A 31-member parliament, called the Landsting, is elected every four years. Following a referendum in 1982 Greenland withdrew from the European Union, which it had joined in 1972.

# NORTH AMERICA

The third-largest continent, North America lies completely in the Northern Hemisphere. Its 9.3 million sq. mi. (24.2 million km²) of land stretches deep into the Arctic Circle and extends southward through Central America to join South America. The continent consists of three large countries—Canada, the United States, and Mexico—as well as a cluster of smaller countries in Central America. Young, folded mountains run almost the entire length of the continent's western side and contain a number of volcanoes. A large proportion of this western area has been shaped by the movement of the plates of Earth's crust. Much of North America is uninhabited, especially the land in the far north, while many of the region's 535 million population live in large towns and cities. Fertile land exists throughout the continent, and many of the countries have large reserves of minerals and fossil fuels. Economically the continent is dominated by the U.S., the world's richest and most powerful nation. The Central American nations tend to be poorer and reliant on trade and aid from the U.S. and, to a lesser extent, Canada and Mexico.

▲ The Chrysler Building was built between 1928 and 1930 and is just one of New York City's many skyscrapers.

▼ A bison grazes on a plain in Wyoming close to the Rocky Mountains. This 2,000-mi.- (3,200-km-) long mountain chain runs from the southwestern U.S. to Canada's British Columbia.

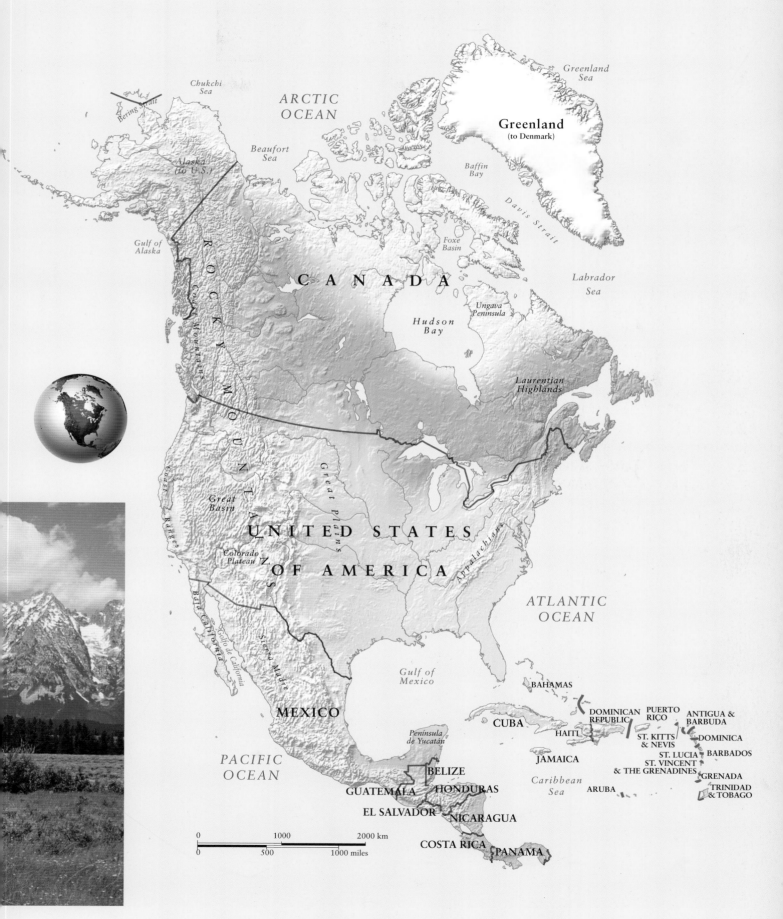

ARCTIC
OCEAN

*Chukchi
Sea*

*Bering Strait*

*Greenland
Sea*

**Greenland**
(to Denmark)

*Beaufort
Sea*

*Baffin
Bay*

Alaska
*(to U.S.)*

*Davis Strait*

*Gulf of
Alaska*

C A N A D A

*Foxe
Basin*

*Labrador
Sea*

*Ungava
Peninsula*

*Hudson
Bay*

*Laurentian
Highlands*

*Great
Basin*

*Great Plains*

U N I T E D   S T A T E S

*Colorado
Plateau*

O F   A M E R I C A

*Appalachians*

ATLANTIC
OCEAN

*Baja California*

*Golfo de California*

*Sierra Madre*

*Gulf of
Mexico*

BAHAMAS

**MEXICO**

DOMINICAN
REPUBLIC

PUERTO
RICO

ANTIGUA &
BARBUDA

*Península
de Yucatán*

**CUBA**

HAITI

ST. KITTS
& NEVIS

DOMINICA

PACIFIC
OCEAN

**BELIZE**

JAMAICA

BARBADOS

ST. LUCIA
ST. VINCENT
& THE GRENADINES

**GUATEMALA**

**HONDURAS**

*Caribbean
Sea*

ARUBA

GRENADA

**EL SALVADOR**

**NICARAGUA**

TRINIDAD
& TOBAGO

**COSTA RICA**

**PANAMA**

| 0 | | 1000 | | 2000 km |
|---|---|---|---|---|

| 0 | 500 | 1000 miles |
|---|---|---|

# CANADA

**With the longest coastline of any nation, Canada is a huge country that occupies the northernmost part of North America and extends deep into the Arctic Circle.**

**Area:** 3,849,674 sq. mi. (9,970,610km²)
**Population:** 33,740,000
**Capital:** Ottawa (1,220,000)
**Main languages spoken:** English, French
**Main religions:** Roman Catholic, United Church, Anglican
**Currency:** Canadian dollar
**Main exports:** motor vehicles, other machinery and transportation equipment, mineral fuels, lumber, newsprint and wood pulp, foodstuffs (particularly cereals)
**Government:** confederation with parliamentary democracy

▼ The St. Lawrence river runs from the most easterly of the Great Lakes, Lake Ontario, through the Canadian cities of Montreal and Quebec (pictured) before emptying into the Gulf of St. Lawrence. The river provides a vital shipping link between the industrial centers of the Great Lakes and the Atlantic Ocean.

Canada is the second-largest country in the world—only Russia is bigger. It has long coasts with the Arctic, Atlantic, and Pacific oceans and shares two separate land borders with the U.S. To the east it borders Alaska, while its main border is to the south and extends almost 4,000 mi. (6,400km). Canada has a varied landscape that includes rugged mountain ranges, ice-covered wastelands, fertile prairies, and temperate lowlands and plains. Islands account for almost one sixth of its total land area, with Baffin Island being the fifth-largest island in the world.

## A LAND OF LAKES AND TREES

Canada contains more lakes and inland waters than any other country in the world. Within its borders lie over 30 lakes with an area bigger than 507 sq. mi. (1,313km²). Canada's longest river is the Mackenzie-Peace river, which runs for 2,635 mi. (4,241km), but the St. Lawrence is the most important for trade and shipping. This river helps form more than 2,480 mi. (4,000km) of linked waterways connecting the Great Lakes to the Atlantic Ocean. It is estimated that as much as 25 percent of the world's entire freshwater sources are found in Canada. Forests cover more than 35 percent of the entire country. Trees, such as spruce, pine, cedar, and maple, are common.

## PEOPLE AND RESOURCES

Canada is one of the world's least densely populated countries with an average of nine people per square mile. Huge areas, especially in the cold north, are unpopulated. Most people live in a fairly narrow belt in the southern part of the country where the climate is milder than the icy, harsh north. Although Ottawa is its capital, Canada's two largest cities are Toronto, with a population of 5.62 million, and Montreal, with a population of 3.81 million. Canada was settled by English- and French-speaking peoples. Today people of European origin form more than two thirds of its population. The country has rich mineral resources and large areas of fertile farmland.

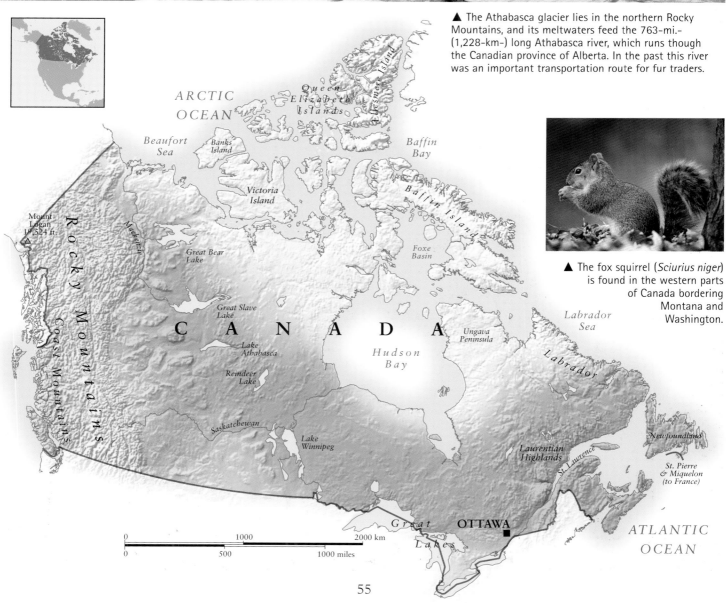

▲ The Athabasca glacier lies in the northern Rocky Mountains, and its meltwaters feed the 763-mi.-(1,228-km-) long Athabasca river, which runs though the Canadian province of Alberta. In the past this river was an important transportation route for fur traders.

ARCTIC
OCEAN

*Queen
Elizabeth
Islands*

*Ellesmere Island*

*Beaufort
Sea*

*Banks
Island*

*Baffin
Bay*

*Victoria
Island*

*Baffin Island*

Mount
Logan
19,524 ft.

R o c k y   M o u n t a i n s

*Mackenzie*

*Great Bear
Lake*

*Foxe
Basin*

*Great Slave
Lake*

C A N A D A

*Labrador
Sea*

C o a s t   M o u n t a i n s

*Lake
Athabasca*

*Hudson
Bay*

*Ungava
Peninsula*

*Labrador*

*Reindeer
Lake*

*Saskatchewan*

*Lake
Winnipeg*

*Laurentian
Highlands*

*Newfoundland*

*St. Lawrence*

*St. Pierre
& Miquelon
(to France)*

*G r e a t*   **OTTAWA** ■
*L a k e s*

ATLANTIC
OCEAN

▲ The fox squirrel (*Sciurius niger*) is found in the western parts of Canada bordering Montana and Washington.

| 0 | 1000 | 2000 km |
| 0 | 500 | 1000 miles |

# EASTERN CANADA

**Eastern Canada includes the industrial and farming heartlands of Quebec and Ontario, Canada's biggest city—Toronto—and its seat of government in Ottawa.**

Canada is divided into ten provinces and three northern territories. Six of these provinces form eastern Canada: Ontario, Quebec, New Brunswick, Prince Edward Island, Newfoundland and Labrador, and Nova Scotia.

### SHAPED BY GLACIERS

Canada was shaped mainly by glaciation. The glaciers that remain in the northern part of the country are remnants of a giant ice sheet that once covered the country. Glaciation is responsible for many of eastern Canada's distinctive geographical landmarks—from the low, rolling hills found on Prince Edward Island and Nova Scotia to the magnificent Niagara Falls, which lies between Lake Erie and Lake Ontario. Eastern Canada is made up of three different geographical regions: the Canadian Shield, the Appalachian Mountains to the east, and, in between, a rich area of agricultural land called the Great Lakes–St. Lawrence lowlands.

The Canadian Shield takes its name from the hard bedrock of gneiss and granite that lies underneath the surface. This rock is estimated to be more than three billion years old. The shield occupies half of all of Canada. It extends southward from the large inland sea called Hudson Bay down through the provinces of Ontario and Quebec to reach the northern shore of Lake Superior. Scraped by the advance and retreat of glaciers, the region contains many rivers and lakes and tends to have a thin soil that supports boreal forests containing evergreen trees.

### THE ATLANTIC PROVINCES

The four Atlantic provinces are: New Brunswick, Prince Edward Island, Newfoundland and Labrador, and Nova Scotia. They are the smallest provinces of Canada and were also the first to be settled by Europeans. Large parts of these provinces are covered by the Appalachian Mountains—an ancient mountain range that has been worn down by glaciers in the past to create low, rolling hills that are often heavily forested. Valleys full of fertile soil often lie between these hills, so farming is a key industry in all four provinces. The smallest of all the provinces is Prince Edward Island, which lies in the Gulf of St. Lawrence and has an area of just 2,185 sq. mi. (5,659km²). Half of the island is covered in dense forests of both deciduous trees, such as

▲ Canada's parliament buildings are found in the eastern Canadian city of Ottawa. First opened in 1866, the buildings show a British influence, with the tower bearing a striking resemblance to the Houses of Parliament buildings in London, England.

▼ Built in 1976, the 1,815-ft.- (553-m-) high CN Tower is the most notable landmark in the busy Ontario city of Toronto. The tower receives around two million visitors every year.

▲ Seal Cove is a fishing village in the Atlantic province of New Brunswick. It is situated on Grand Manan Island in the Bay of Fundy.

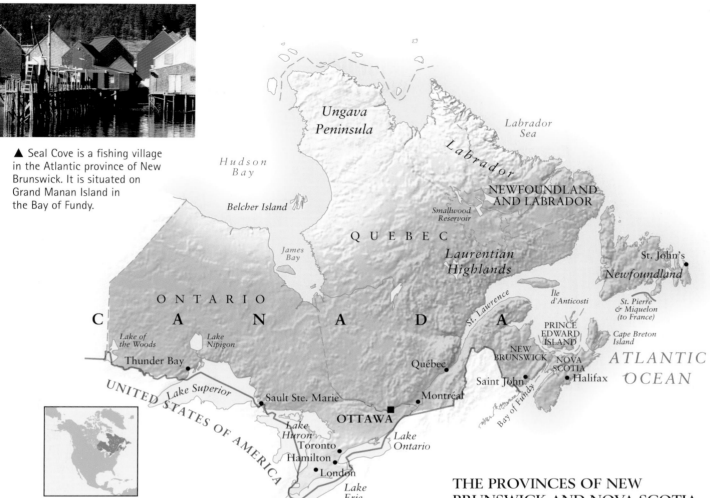

maple and birch, and coniferous trees such as the white pine. Farming and fishing are the most important industries for the island's 141,000-strong population. Around one fourth of the land is farmed, with the most valuable products including dairy products, fruit crops such as raspberries and blueberries, and vegetables such as peas, beans, and potatoes. Newfoundland and Labrador is the newest Canadian province. It joined Canada in 1949 and consists of a mainland area, Labrador, and the large island of Newfoundland. Newfoundland has always been the traditional center of Canada's fishing industry. The Grand Banks area off the eastern coast of the island is a continental shelf that extends around 250 mi. (400km). The arrival of a series of ocean currents there has helped create one of the world's richest fishing grounds. Overfishing has caused fish stocks to drop, and there are now quotas in place that have dimished the local industry.

## THE PROVINCES OF NEW BRUNSWICK AND NOVA SCOTIA

Lying between Quebec and Maine, New Brunswick is almost rectangular in shape with an area of 28,355 sq. mi. (73,439km²). Large fishing grounds in the Bay of Fundy and the Gulf of St. Lawrence, as well as mines and some manufacturing factories, sustain many of the province's 749,000 people. With most of its land covered in forests, logging and timber products, such as pulp and paper, are a vital part of the province's economy. Forests also cover a large part of New Brunswick's eastern neighbor, the province of Nova Scotia. Bordering the Atlantic Ocean, Nova Scotia was home to the first permanent European settlement in Canada, which was founded by French settlers in 1605. The province has a long history of ship- and boatbuilding, which continues to this day, supplemented by mining for coal and other minerals, as well as fishing. Nova Scotia's largest settlement, Halifax, is a major shipping port all year round.

on the climate, making it milder and increasing the number of frost-free days. This allows a range of fruit to be grown, including peaches and pears. In the southeastern corner of Ontario, on the banks of Lake Ontario, lies Toronto, Canada's largest city. Toronto is a cosmopolitan city with a booming population of over five million people.

### CENTRAL GOVERNMENT
Ontario is also the home of Canada's national government in the country's capital city, Ottawa. The British North America Act of 1867 united much of Canada, but independence was only recognized in 1931. Canada is a federal union, which means that power is divided between the provinces and the central

▲ This hat store in Québec City displays its signs in both English and French. Canadian law gives its citizens the right to choose whether to receive many official services in English or French.

▼ Completed in 1959, the St. Lawrence Seaway opened up a major shipping route from the Great Lakes to the Atlantic Ocean. In 2007, more than 2,000 vessels passed between Montreal and Lake Ontario, carrying around 55 million tons (50 million metric tonnes) of cargo and thousands of passengers.

### THE POWERHOUSE PROVINCES
Ontario and the southern part of the province of Québec are the agricultural and industrial powerhouses of Canada. Fifty percent of all Canadians live in this region, where approximately 70 percent of all of Canada's manufactured goods are made. The second-largest province in terms of area, Ontario's population of 13,069,000 is growing quickly in size as more and more people flock to the industrial, commercial, and governmental center of the country. Curving around the shore of Lake Ontario is Canada's industrial heartland, known as the Golden Horseshoe. Large steel factories, car manufacturers, meat-processing plants, and ship- and aircraft-building factories exist in this region. They make use of the transportation links provided by the lake and its connection to the Atlantic Ocean by the St. Lawrence Seaway. Southern Ontario also has large stretches of prime agricultural land. Sixty percent of revenue from farming is derived from livestock, and much of the crop output of the region is used as food for farm animals. The two closest Great Lakes, Lake Ontario and Lake Erie, have a modifying effect

government. The Canadian parliament consists of two houses: the Senate, whose members are appointed and serve until the age of 75, and the House of Commons, whose members are elected once every five years or whenever parliament is dissolved and a general election called.

## FRENCH-SPEAKING CANADA

Canada has two official languages: English and French. This reflects the patterns of settlement that saw British and French arrivals from the 1600s on. Conflicts over territories and land rights saw a number of wars fought, with the British gaining overall control but the French settlers remaining. Although French-speaking Canadians live in the Atlantic provinces and throughout Canada, they are concentrated in the province of Quebec, the area that French fur traders and farmers first settled. Around 90 percent of Canadians whose first language is French live in Quebec. Lying to the east of Ontario, Quebec is blessed with many resources and good farmland. The province has rich mineral reserves and generates more electricity through hydroelectric power than any other province. On many occasions Quebec has only narrowly resisted breaking away from the rest of Canada. Although the capital of the province is the city of Quebec, its largest settlement is Montreal. A busy port and financial center, Montreal stands on an island where two rivers meet and contains nearly four million people, most of whom speak French as their first language.

▼ The spectacular Horseshoe Falls in Canada are part of Niagara Falls, which extend into both Canada and the U.S. Believed to have been formed around 12,000 years ago when glaciers retreated, around 1.3 million gallons (5 million liters) of water pass over Niagara Falls every second. They attract around 15 million visitors every year.

# WESTERN CANADA

**Rich in natural resources, western Canada features mountainous British Columbia and the three "prairie provinces" of Manitoba, Saskatchewan, and Alberta.**

▲ Grizzly bears are found in western Canada, especially in more mountainous regions. They are one of the largest meat-eating land creatures, but they are also an endangered species.

▼ Vancouver is Canada's third-largest city and is situated on the Canadian mainland opposite Vancouver Island. It has a large natural harbor, which has helped make it the center of British Columbia's sea trade.

Three of western Canada's four provinces are dominated by the Great Plains, which run through large parts of Alberta, Saskatchewan, and Manitoba. The plains feature fertile soils and large deposits of fossil fuels. Manitoba, the flattest of the three provinces, is known as "the land of 100,000 lakes," with many lakes being created through glaciation. There are many rivers and lakes in the northern half of Saskatchewan, while the Rocky Mountains and their foothills extend into the southwestern corner of Alberta. The northern regions of all three provinces tend to be heavily forested, and timber industries are a major contributor to the local economies. British Columbia is the only Canadian province with a Pacific coastline and is more mountainous, with two enormous mountain ranges running along much of its length.

## BRITISH COLUMBIA

British Columbia is separated from Alberta by the Rocky Mountains, which run throughout its length and continue north into the Yukon Territory. West of the Rockies lie heavily forested lands, natural grasslands, and large numbers of lakes. Another mountain range, the Coast Mountains, define much of the province's coastal area, with glaciation having carved out many islands and fjords. The Queen Charlotte Islands to the north and the 285-mi.- (460-km-) long Vancouver Island are the largest islands. The province's landscape is naturally beautiful and sustains much wildlife, including grizzly and black bears, elks, and waterfowl. The animals' habitat is preserved in the form of 675 parks, or protected areas, which attract around 24 million visitors every year. A feature of the province is its large forests, which contain a big percentage of Canada's commercially sold wood—trees that can be used for timber, pulp, paper, and other industries. Wood processing, mining, tourism, and service industries are the biggest employers of the province's 4.46 million people. Most of the population live in the southwest, with 60 percent living in just two cities: Victoria and Vancouver, Canada's third-largest city.

▲ The Maligne river flows from the Canadian Rocky Mountains through Jasper National Park in the province of Alberta.

Victoria is the province's capital and is located on Vancouver Island. It is built on the site of the first permanent European colony, which was established in 1843. Facing the Pacific Ocean and the Far East, British Columbia is increasingly trading and building commercial ties with Japan, China, and other Asian nations. Although half of the people of the province are of British origin, there are also Native Americans and people originally from Continental Europe. The province is also home to North America's largest Chinese community outside of San Francisco, California.

## WARM SUMMERS—COLD WINTERS

Some distance from both the Pacific and Atlantic oceans, the three "prairie provinces" have a continental climate. This means large differences between warm summer and cold winter temperatures. For example, Manitoba's largest city, Winnipeg, records an average January temperature of -4°F (-20°C), and average temperatures in July are 68°F (20°C) higher. In southwestern parts of Alberta, the closest of the three provinces to the Pacific Ocean, mild winds from the Pacific—called the chinook—tend to raise the cold winter temperatures a little.

▲ After Russia, Canada is the world's largest producer of barley, an important cereal crop. More than 90 percent of the country's total production of 12 million tons (10.7 million metric tonnes) is grown in western Canada. It is grown on Canada's Great Plains and is harvested with automated machinery.

▼ Lying on the eastern slopes of the Rockies and famous for its spectacular mountain scenery, Banff National Park is also Canada's oldest national park, first opened in 1883.

## FARMING AND FUELS

The warm summer conditions, along with the large expanses of flat, fertile plains, have made the three "prairie provinces" highly productive farming areas. Alberta, for example, has more than six million cattle and calves. It is by far the largest beef-producing province in Canada. Only a small part of the beef is used within the state. The rest is shipped to other parts of Canada and also to the U.S. Saskatchewan produces more than half of the wheat grown in Canada and also has large farmlands devoted to growing rye, flaxseed, and other crops. Manitoba's central location in Canada has made it an important trading, transportation, and distribution center for farming and food products. Around 60 percent of its population live in and around the capital city of Winnipeg. Food production and packaging are major industries in all three provinces, while fossil fuels are exploited, particularly in Alberta, which supplies 80 percent of Canada's natural gas, and Saskatchewan. More than 18,000 active oil wells in Saskatchewan produce around one fifth of Canada's total oil output.

All three provinces receive low rainfall averaging between 15–18 in. (38–46cm) per year but enjoy a large number of sunny days in both the summer and the winter. The town of Estevan in Saskatchewan is considered the sunshine capital of Canada, with an average of more than 2,500 sunshine hours per year. The most eastern parts of the fourth province, British Columbia, also feature a continental climate, but much of this province is affected greatly by its closeness to the Pacific Ocean. Warm, moist air from the Pacific not only helps create milder winters but also brings heavy rainfall, between 52–152 in. (132–386cm) per year.

# NORTHERN CANADA

Northern Canada consists of three sparsely populated territories: Yukon, the Northwest Territories, and Nunavut. Four fifths of these territories are wilderness areas.

▲ Northern Canada is the main home of the polar bear. Since 1973 hunting restrictions have helped it survive.

▼ Cutting a hole in the ice, this Inuit fisherwoman fishes for arctic char.

The three territories of northern Canada are among the most sparsely populated regions in the world. In the Northwest Territories and Nunavut there is one person for every 18 sq. mi. (46km²), while in Yukon there is one person per 5.5 sq. mi. (14km²). Yukon occupies 186,661 sq. mi. (483,452km²), yet over half of its entire population lives in a single town, Whitehorse. Icy tundra occupies large parts of these territories to the north, and permafrost is widespread. Many of northern Canada's peoples are either Native American Indians or traditional Arctic people such as the Inuit. Hunting, fishing, trapping, mining, and forestry are the main sources of work.

## NUNAVUT

The boundaries defining Canada's two territories were redrawn in 1999, creating the newly formed Nunavut territory. Nunavut is the most northerly region in Canada and includes the thousands of islands in the Arctic Ocean that form the Arctic archipelago. Nunavut is a self-governing homeland for the Inuit people, who form 85 percent of the territory's total population of around 32,000. Nunavut means "Our Land" in the Inuit language. More than one third of Nunavut's population is under 15 years of age.

# UNITED STATES OF AMERICA

**The U.S. is the third-largest and the most powerful country in the world. A world leader in manufacturing industries, it has an abundance of natural resources.**

**Area:** 3,717,813 sq. mi. (9,629,091km²)
**Population:** 304,060,000
**Capital:** Washington, D.C. (5,281,000)
**Main languages spoken:** English, Spanish
**Main religions:** Roman Catholic, Baptist, Methodist
**Currency:** U.S. dollar
**Main exports:** machinery and transportation equipment (particularly road vehicles), chemicals, food, scientific and related equipment
**Type of government:** federal republic with strong democratic tradition

▼ Independence Day in the U.S. commemorates the adoption of the Declaration of Independence in 1776. Held every 4th of July, it is celebrated with large fireworks displays such as this one over Florida's largest city, Miami.

The United States of America gets its name from its administrative divisions. Each of its 50 states has its own courts and government, which wield much local power. Mainland U.S. consists of 48 states that share borders and occupy the width of North America, stretching from the Pacific Ocean to the Atlantic Ocean. Alaska, which borders western Canada, and the Pacific islands of Hawaii are the remaining two states.

Two large mountain ranges dominate the country's landscape. To the west the Rocky Mountains form a high altitude spine, with some peaks rising to more than 13,000 ft. (4,000m). To the east the Appalachian mountain system runs almost parallel to the Atlantic Ocean for approximately 1,500 mi. (2,400km). The Appalachians are older, lower in height, with large parts covered with forests. In between much of the land consists of giant plains crossed by many rivers. The U.S.'s longest river is the Mississippi. Its main tributary is the Missouri, and together they form the fourth-longest river in the world. To the north the U.S. shares a border with Canada. The countries share ownership of the Great Lakes, the series of lakes that run along their border.

The United States is rich in natural resource—from metals, such as lead and iron, to oil and timber. More than one fifth of the world's known reserves of coal lies within its borders. Large parts of the plains running through the center of the country have fertile soils that are used to grow corn and other cereal crops on a huge scale and as grazing land for the U.S.'s 97 million cattle.

◀ The bald eagle is the national bird of the U.S.

### AMERICA'S PEOPLE
Populated by Native Americans for many thousands of years, the first Europeans arrived and settled particularly along the U.S.'s eastern coast in the 1600s and 1700s. The Revolutionary War (1775–1781) finally resulted in the nation freeing itself from British rule. The new country encouraged settlers and immigrants for many decades, and the U.S. today is a "melting pot" of different peoples and cultures. Around 69.8 percent of the people are of European origin, 13.2 percent Hispanic, 12.8 percent African, three percent Asian, and 1.2 percent Native American.

▲ The U.S.'s landscape varies greatly and includes flat, temperate grasslands, rugged mountains, and arid wilderness regions such as this area of New Mexico.

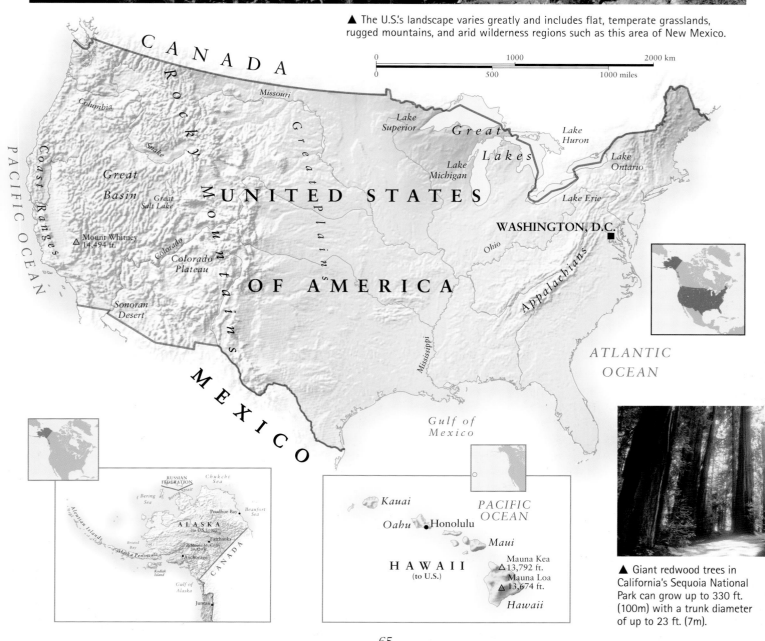

▲ Giant redwood trees in California's Sequoia National Park can grow up to 330 ft. (100m) with a trunk diameter of up to 23 ft. (7m).

# EASTERN U.S.

The site of the first European arrivals to the United States, the eastern U.S. is as rich in land resources as it is in history.

▲ The East Coast of the U.S. has many excellent natural harbors around which ports and fishing settlements have developed such as Rockport on Cape Ann peninsula in Massachusetts.

▲ This marble statue of former U.S. president Abraham Lincoln is the centerpiece of the Lincoln Memorial, a building located in Potomac Park in the capital city of Washington, D.C.

▼ The White House in Washington, D.C. was designed by Irish-American architect James Hoban and was originally called the Executive Mansion.

The eastern U.S. borders the Atlantic Ocean with a long, irregular coastline, which, in places, is indented with many bays and inlets. Two eastern U.S. states, Pennsylvania and New York, have shorelines with the two most easterly Great Lakes, Erie and Ontario. The geography of the region changes as you travel both south and inland. The Atlantic coastal plain broadens as the land runs southward, while the Appalachian mountain system lies inland. Running almost parallel to the Atlantic coast, the Appalachians extend more than 1,400 mi. (2,250km) from the Canadian province of Quebec southward through the eastern U.S., where they reach as far south as Alabama. They form many mountain ranges, including the Green Mountains of Vermont, the Catskill Mountains found in New York state, and the Blue Ridge Mountains, which run through Georgia, North Carolina, West Virginia, and Virginia. The Appalachians are some of the oldest mountains anywhere in the world. Their heavily eroded formations are rich in mineral deposits, including coal, iron

ore, and zinc. The region includes the collection of six northeastern states known as New England, as well as the mid-Atlantic states of New Jersey, Delaware, Maryland, Pennsylvania, and Virginia. West Virginia sits inland and is the only one of the eastern states that does not have a shoreline with either a Great Lake or the Atlantic Ocean. Some forest areas of these states have been cleared for farmland and for the many large towns and cities that house the region's 71.3 million people. However, 75 percent of West Virginia, for example, is still covered in trees, while 60 percent of Virginia, 55 percent of Pennsylvania, and 43 percent of Maryland remain forested. Although there are extensive farmlands in many eastern states, manufacturing industries and services are extremely important to state economies. In New Jersey, for example, agriculture accounts for only one percent of the state's total revenue.

## SETTLEMENT

The Appalachian Mountains played an important role in early European settlement of the U.S. Their heavily forested heights formed an obstacle to further inland travel, which prompted many people to settle to their east, forming the first major colonies. The first successful English colony was established in Jamestown, now in the state of Virginia, in 1607. In 1620 English Puritans escaping religious persecution landed in what is now Massachusetts and founded Plymouth Colony. Most of the major events of the U.S.'s colonial period, including the Revolutionary War, took place in the eastern United States. The first major protest at British rule, the Boston Tea Party (1773), took place in Boston harbor in the state of Massachusetts; the important Battle of Saratoga (1777) was fought in what is now New York state; and the U.S. Constitution was framed in the city of Philadelphia, Pennsylvania, in 1787. This document lays down the structure and powers of government in the U.S., and although there have been 27 amendments to its contents, much remains in place to this day.

▼ The fall season in the states of New England sees the leaves of the deciduous trees there turn beautiful shades of orange, yellow, and red. This autumnal scene is from Vermont.

## GOVERNMENT

The U.S. system of government splits powers between the 50 states and a national government called the federal government. Both state and national governments have powers to collect taxes, borrow money, build roads, and provide welfare services. In addition, the national government has powers to make foreign policies and treaties with other nations, provide military forces, and print money. The offices of the federal government are also split between the lawmakers (the legislature), the law administrators (the executive branch, including the president), and the law interpreters and enforcers (the law courts). All three arms of the federal government have their headquarters in Washington, District of Columbia (usually shortened to D.C.). It was chosen in 1790 as the seat of national government. On the eastern banks of the Potomac river, Washington, D.C. was originally a territory created by land donated from the two neighboring states of Maryland and Virginia. Washington has developed into a major city, with one third of its permanent workers employed by the federal government. The Capitol building in Washington, D.C. is the home of Congress, the law-making body of the United States, and is split into two branches, the House of Representatives and the Senate. The members of both branches are chosen by

▲ A nighttime view over part of Manhattan in New York City shows how skyscrapers, including the Empire State Building (center), shape the view of its skyline.

public elections, and both meet separately. Close by is the Supreme Court, which makes the ultimate decisions on disputes in law. Pennsylvania Avenue links the Capitol building with the White House, the home of the president of the U.S.

## NEW ENGLAND STATES

Six northeastern states—Maine, New Hampshire, Rhode Island, Vermont, Connecticut, and Massachusetts—are collectively known as the New England states. It was in this region that most of the earliest arrivals to the U.S. came ashore and settled in pioneer towns and villages. Some of the country's most highly regarded places of learning have their homes in New

▲ The impressive 307-ft.-(94-m-) high Statue of Liberty sits on a small island in the harbor of New York City. The statue was given by France to the U.S. in 1876 to celebrate 100 years of U.S. independence.

▼ Located at the meeting point of a number of rivers, including the 980-mi.-(1,580-km-) long Ohio river, Pittsburgh, Pennsylvania, is one of the busiest inland river ports in the entire U.S.

## NEW YORK CITY

Lying in the southeastern corner of New York state is the giant metropolis of New York City, which started life as a fur-trading post at the mouth of the Hudson river. It is now one of the world's largest, busiest, and richest cities and a world center for finance and business. New York City sits on both the mainland and a collection of 50 islands, the largest being Manhattan. For the past 200 years it has been the main gateway into the U.S., and huge waves of immigrants have settled there, giving it a mixed racial background. The 2000 census estimated the New York City population to be 68 percent white, 16 percent black, 6 percent Asian and Pacific islander, and 10 percent other races.

▲ The world's largest market for the trading of securities, the New York Stock Exchange has traded from Wall Street in Manhattan since 1817.

England. These include Massachusetts Institute of Technology (MIT) and Harvard University in Massachusetts and Yale University in Connecticut. The New England states draw large numbers of tourists who are attracted to both the region's history and its rich landscapes of hills, mountains, and picturesque forests of mainly deciduous trees. Rhode Island, with an area of 1,212 sq. mi. (4,000km²), is the smallest state in the U.S. The most northerly New England state, Maine, has over 85 percent of its 33,265 sq. mi. (86,156km²) of land covered in thick forests. It is also famed for its rugged, irregular coastline, created mainly by glaciation in the last Ice Age. The highest peak in New England, Mount Washington (6,288 ft./1,917m), is found in northern New Hampshire close to the border with Maine.

▲ Baseball is one of the most popular sports in the U.S. Here at Oriole Park at Camden Yards stadium in Baltimore, Maryland, the Baltimore Orioles play against the Boston Red Sox. Both teams are from the eastern United States.

# MIDWEST AND THE GREAT LAKES

**A major location for manufacturing and trade and home to the world's largest cereal-farming operations, this region plays a major part in the U.S. economy.**

▲ Cities like Detroit, Michigan, and Chicago, Illinois, have been synonymous with manufacturing industries such as the production of motor vehicles. This Chicago-based Ford assembly plant manufactures around 250,000 vehicles per year.

▼ Almost one fifth of all wheat grown in the U.S. comes from the state of Kansas. Approximately half of the wheat grown in Kansas is exported overseas.

Most of the land that makes up the interior of the U.S. is part of a giant plateau that runs from the Rocky Mountains in the west across the interior of the country. Within this plateau there are a number of hill and mountain ranges, including the Smoky Hills of Kansas and the Black Hills of South Dakota and Wyoming. South and North Dakota and northwestern Nebraska are also home to a region of rugged, strangely shaped rock masses and hills called badlands. Unable to support more than sparse vegetation, they were formed by erosion, assisted by short periods of heavy rains followed by long periods of droughts. A large part of the interior consists of the Great Plains, while a region called the Corn Belt, stretching from western Ohio to the central part of Nebraska, is one of the largest crop-growing regions in the world.

## THE GREAT PLAINS

The Great Plains occupy a large area of southern Canada and extend south to cover the land east of the Rocky Mountains and west of the Mississippi

▲ Built on the southwestern shores of Lake Michigan, Chicago is the U.S.'s third-most-populous city behind New York City and Los Angeles. Its location makes it a vital junction for air, water, and land transportation.

river. The Great Plains include parts of North Dakota, South Dakota, Montana, Wyoming, Colorado, Nebraska, and Kansas, as well as parts of the southern states of Oklahoma, New Mexico, and Texas. Much of the Great Plains region was once covered by a vast inland sea, and sedimentary deposits make up the rock strata, which tend to lie horizontally underneath the land surface. The Great Plains was once one of the largest areas of grasslands in the world, supporting giant herds of bison estimated to total more than 50 million. Much of the grassland featured a rich, fertile topsoil and was heavily exploited by farmers from the 1800s on. Years of overfarming led to dust bowls— prolonged droughts and dust storms—due to the erosion of topsoil. However, modern farming and irrigation techniques have seen North America's grasslands return to intensive farming, both in raising large herds of livestock and in growing cereal crops, including rye, barley, alfalfa, and wheat. A little more than 75 percent of the world's wheat exports are produced in this region.

▶ The bison is the largest land mammal in North America. Around 50 million bison roamed the central U.S. before the arrival of European settlers with guns in the 1800s.

## THE MISSOURI AND MISSISSIPPI

The Missouri river flows across the central U.S. It is second in length only to the Mississippi, which it flows into just north of the city of St. Louis. Together, the Missouri and the Mississippi travel almost the length of the country and drain much of the central interior. The Mississippi remains an important transportation link, with large barges and ships carrying bulk cargo such as petroleum products, coal, sand, gravel, and iron ore. The Missouri is harnessed by the Missouri River Basin Project, which irrigates large areas of farmland and provides energy via hydroelectric power plants.

## THE GREAT LAKES

The Great Lakes were formed during the last Ice Age when glaciation helped to scour and hollow out increasingly broad and deep depressions from stream valleys. The resulting five large lakes hold an estimated 20 percent of the world's freshwater and 90 percent of the freshwater of the U.S. Lake Michigan is the only one of the five Great Lakes that lies completely within the borders of the U.S. The other four lakes— Erie, Ontario, Huron, and Superior—span the border between the U.S. and Canada. They are all joined to form a giant drainage system, which sees water flow from Lake Superior through the other lakes before finally entering the sea in the Gulf of St. Lawrence. The lakes are large enough to have an effect on the climate of the land around them. They make the winters warmer and the summers cooler. Together, the lakes drain a region approximately 300,000 sq. mi. (777,000km$^2$) in size known as the Great Lakes Basin. Around one fifth of the United States' total population lives within the area of the Great Lakes Basin.

▼ A shopping mall found in the city of Columbus, Ohio—the state capital since 1816.

▲ The 630-ft.- (192-m-) high Gateway Arch in St. Louis, Missouri, commemorates the city's historic status as the gateway to the west.

▲ Mount Rushmore in South Dakota features 59-ft.- (18-m-) high faces of four U.S. presidents carved into the rock.

## THE GREAT LAKE STATES

The Great Lake states are considered to be Ohio, Michigan, Indiana, Illinois, Wisconsin, and, sometimes, Minnesota. These states form the traditional industrial heartland of the U.S., where the majority of heavy engineering goods, such as motor vehicles and industrial machinery, are produced. The engineering and manufacturing industries developed in the region in the 1800s and 1900s. Raw material resources, such as iron ore and coal, were readily available, and the lakes allowed transportation by boats over long distances. Large settlements sprang up on many shores of the Great Lakes, acting as industrial centers, ports, and trading communities. These have developed into some of the U.S.'s largest cities, including Cleveland on Lake Erie and Milwaukee and Chicago on Lake Michigan. Detroit, which sits on the Detroit river between Lake Erie and Lake Huron, became the world's most famous motor-vehicle city. Large numbers of people—particularly new immigrants from overseas, especially Europe, and black people from the southern states—came to work in the industrial north. The mixture of cultures spawned new art and music forms, including electric blues music originating in Chicago and soul music centered around Detroit. Economic problems in many heavy industries and cheaper competition from overseas have more recently forced the Great Lake states to turn to other industries, including finance, electronics, and tourism. This is also an important farming region. More than 75 percent of Illinois, for example, is devoted to farming, with the state being the U.S.'s largest producer of soybeans. Wisconsin is known as a major dairy-farming state, producing over ten percent of the U.S.'s milk and large quantities of cheese.

▼ Millions of years of water and wind erosion created the strange and spectacular rock formations found in Badlands National Park in South Dakota.

## NATIVE AMERICANS

Native American peoples had lived throughout much of North America for thousands of years before the arrival of European explorers and settlers. Although early contact tended to be peaceful, if wary, and linked to trade, gradually tensions built up, and conflicts occurred as the settlers wanted more land to farm and to exploit mineral resources. By the 1800s a crisis point had been reached. The buffalo, or bison, herds on which many Native American tribes depended had been killed in their millions, and thousands of settlers, mainly from Europe, were pushing farther west, seeking to claim lands belonging to tribes. Wars erupted as the many different Native American tribes attempted to keep control of all or part of their tribal lands. Many of these conflicts occurred in the Midwest and in the states surrounding the Great Lakes. For example, the forced resettlement of the Sauk and Fox tribes resulted in the Blackhawk War of 1832, fought in Wisconsin and Illinois. Perhaps the most famous of all conflicts was the Battle of Little Big Horn (1876) between U.S. cavalry, led by General George Custer, and the combined forces of Sioux and Cheyenne Native Americans, led by Crazy Horse and Sitting Bull. This battle took place in Montana and saw Native American tribes overpowered by the settlers' forces. The 1890 massacre of Sioux men, women, and children at Wounded Knee in South Dakota signaled the end of the conflict. Today Native Americans account for one percent of the country's total population. They are found in small numbers in all states, but the greatest numbers are in the four adjoining southern states of Oklahoma, New Mexico, Arizona, and California. Each of the states has populations of more than 200,000 Native Americans.

▲ Yellowstone National Park was founded in 1872 and is the oldest national park in the U.S. It is world famous for its hot springs, geysers, waterfalls, and abundant wildlife. The park stretches across parts of Montana, Wyoming, and eastern Idaho and is home to more than 200 species of birds.

▲ Colorado's heavy snowfall on its mountains attracts thousands of skiers to resorts such as Powderhorn and Aspen.

# THE SOUTH

**The southern United States has a distinctive character created by its landscape, economy, and the character of its people.**

▲ New Orleans, Louisiana, is known for its rich mixture of cultural influences, which reflect varying periods when it has been a French and Spanish colony. For example, jazz first developed in the city. In August 2005, New Orleans was devastated by a violent hurricane named Katrina.

▼ The Mesa Montosa lies in New Mexico. The river, the Río Chuviscar, originates in this landform and eventually flows into the larger Río Conchos across the border in Mexico.

The southern states of the U.S. have a varied geography and climate. Some have a warm, temperate climate, while others, such as Louisiana and Florida, have a subtropical climate with hot, humid summers and, in most places, mild winters. Most of the two most southerly states, Florida and Texas, remain warm all year-round. In the states that surround the Gulf of Mexico moderate-to-heavy rainfall is often increased by thunderstorms. On average, between five and eight tropical storms or hurricanes hit some part of the coast surrounding the Gulf every year.

## THE LANDSCAPE

The Appalachian mountain chain extends into the southern U.S., reaching the states of North Carolina, Georgia, and Alabama. Other major mountain ranges include the Cumberland Mountains, which cross eastern Tennessee, north Georgia, and northeastern Alabama. The Ouachita Mountains are found to the west, spanning much of Arkansas and southeastern Oklahoma. Of the southern states,

▲ White Sands National Park is located in southwestern New Mexico. These white gypsum sand dunes are shifted by winds to create ever-changing landscapes.

only New Mexico, Arkansas, Tennessee, and Oklahoma do not have a coastline with either the Atlantic Ocean or the Gulf of Mexico. Florida has both, with the eastern side of its peninsula facing the Atlantic and its western side facing the warmer waters of the Gulf. Four more states border the Gulf. Louisiana and Texas have long coastlines, while Alabama and Mississippi have only small Gulf shores. West of Texas lies New Mexico, where the Great Plains extend into the eastern one third of the country, while much of the remainder consists of mountains and desert valleys.

## THE MISSISSIPPI PLAINS AND DELTA

The Mississippi is the region's largest river and also the longest in the U.S., at 2,350 mi. (3,780km) long (the Mississippi-Missouri combined is 3,740 mi./6,020km long. It flows south, where it forms much of the border between Tennessee and Arkansas, as well as the state of Mississippi's two western borders with Arkansas and Louisiana. The river meanders through the central southern states before its final journey through southern Louisiana, before emptying into the Gulf of Mexico close to New Orleans at an average rate of five million gallons (19 million liters) per second. The Mississippi's course has changed many times in the past few thousands years and has created a giant river delta measuring around 4,630 sq. mi. (12,000km²). This is still expanding as more sediment is deposited by the river emptying into the Gulf.

The power of the Mississippi to deposit sediment is not just seen at its delta. Large alluvial plains extend on both sides of the river as it flows through the southern states. These have been created over long periods of time and measure between 37–74 mi. (60–119km) in width. Because the plains are low-lying, the severe risk of flooding is battled in a number of ways, including storage reservoirs in the northern part of the river, dams, and large embankments, or levees, which now run for an estimated 1,600 mi. (2,600km) along its length.

▼ An inhabitant of the Appalachian Mountains of North Carolina plays his banjo. Folk songs from the Appalachian Mountains originated from Celtic folk music introduced by 18th- and 19th-century settlers from the British Isles.

▼ The Rio Grande runs for more than 1,860 mi. (3,000km²), flowing through New Mexico and forming the border between Texas and Mexico. Here it flows through Big Bend National Park in Texas.

## THE COTTON BELT

Cotton is the world's largest nonfood crop and is used to make around half of all the world's textiles. In 2001 the U.S. was the world's second-largest producer of raw cotton, most of it grown in the Cotton Belt that sweeps across the southern states. This region provides ideal climatic conditions for cotton, which has been grown there since the time of the earliest European settlers. Today much production has moved west to California and Arizona, but Mississippi, Arkansas, Louisiana, and Texas are still leading producers.

▼ The American alligator lives in the swamplands of the South in Alabama, Florida, and Georgia. Adults can grow up to 11.8 ft. (3.6m) in length.

## SLAVERY

Cotton, tobacco, rice, and sugarcane were major crops for the early European settlers in the southern states. As farms and plantations grew in size farmers turned to slavery to create the large workforce required. Millions of black Africans were imported by slave traders into the South. By 1790 black people made up one third of the South's population. Controversy grew around the morality of slavery, and the issue split the U.S., with the North opposing it. In 1860–1861, 11 southern states withdrew from the rest of the U.S. to form the Confederate States of America. This was the start of the Civil War (1861–1865). The southern states lost the war, and as a result, their economy was devastated. Although slavery was abolished, conditions barely improved for many decades, and many African-Americans migrated to the industrial North.

## CHANGING ECONOMIES

Although traditional crops, such as cotton, are still grown in the region, the southeastern states have moved into other areas to strengthen their economies. Modern cash crops, such as soybeans and peanuts, have grown in importance, while Alabama, North Carolina, Arkansas, and Georgia are the leading U.S. producers of poultry. Oil from the Gulf of Mexico, as well Louisiana and Mississippi, helps supply raw materials to chemical and manufacturing industries. Engineering and electronics have grown in importance in the South, prompted in part by the U.S. military and NASA, the national space agency. Tourism has become a major source of revenue, with the cities of New Orleans, Miami, and most of Florida proving to be top destinations for foreign tourists. Florida's wetlands, which cover almost one fifth of its land and include Everglades National Park, are a major attraction, as are as its beach resorts on both the Atlantic and Gulf coasts. Florida is a leading citrus fruit producer, and its warm climate is attractive to older, retired citizens.

## TEXAS

Texas is the second-biggest state in the U.S. and is also the third most populous. Much of its western area lies within or near the Great Plains region. The state is one of the most important agricultural producers in the country and is a leading grower of a large range of crops— from watermelons to spinach. Cattle farming is a major industry, and the state has many huge cattle ranches. Texas has developed independently of its neighbors, due in part to its huge reserves of fossil fuels. Wealth from extracting these fuels—from processing oil and from the manufacturing industry— has financed the creation of large, modern cities, including Dallas, Houston, and Austin, the capital.

▲ A NASA space shuttle blasts off from its launch site at Cape Canaveral on the east coast of Florida.

▼ These ranch hands herd cattle into a feedlot. A head count in 2000 revealed that Texas contained 15 million cattle.

# WESTERN U.S.

**From the high volcanic mountains of the north to the Grand Canyon and the flat, dry deserts in the south, the western U.S. has a dramatic range of scenery.**

▲ Organ Pipe Cactus National Monument in Arizona is one of several national parks that preserve portions of the Sonoran Desert. The park covers more than 330,630 acres.

▲ Convict Lake is found in the eastern Sierra Nevada Mountains. The 0.81-mi.- (1.3-m-) long lake is named after a gunfight in 1871 involving escaped prisoners on its shores.

The western U.S. is a land of contrasts. It contains major centers of population, including San Francisco and Los Angeles in California, as well as some of the least inhabited parts of the country. It is home to some of the most high-tech regions and centers in North America, while other parts of its land are owned by native peoples who have lived there for thousands of years. Geographically the region contains a number of the United States' highest and lowest, as well as wettest and driest, places. This part of the United States is made up of a several distinct and different geographical regions. Inland the giant Rocky Mountains separate a lot of the western U.S. from states farther east. They run through a large part of the state of Idaho before progressing deep into Canadian territory. To the south there are large areas of mostly flat desert, which stretch across the border and into northern Mexico. The large state of California has a complex geography partly created by a major fault line in Earth's tectonic plates called the San Andreas Fault. The fault runs through approximately 650 mi. (1,050km) of the state. California has an enormous central valley flanked by the Sierra Nevada Mountains to the east and ranges of coastal mountains to the west. Lower-lying areas of California are found in the central valley and along much of the Pacific coast west of the coastal mountains, as well as to the southeast, in flat, desert areas that include the Mojave Desert. North of central California is the region known as the Pacific Northwest, which runs from northern California through Oregon and Washington state. It features coastal ranges of mountains and the Cascade Range, which is farther inland. East of California and the Pacific Northwest much of the landscape consists of what geographers call intermontane (between mountain) basins and plateaus, including the Great Basin (see page 81), bounded to the east by the Rockies.

◄ One of the western U.S.'s most notable landmarks is the Golden Gate Bridge, found in San Francisco, California. Completed in 1937, the bridge's main span measures 4,200 ft. (1,280m) in length and is suspended from two cables hung from towers 745 ft. (227m) high.

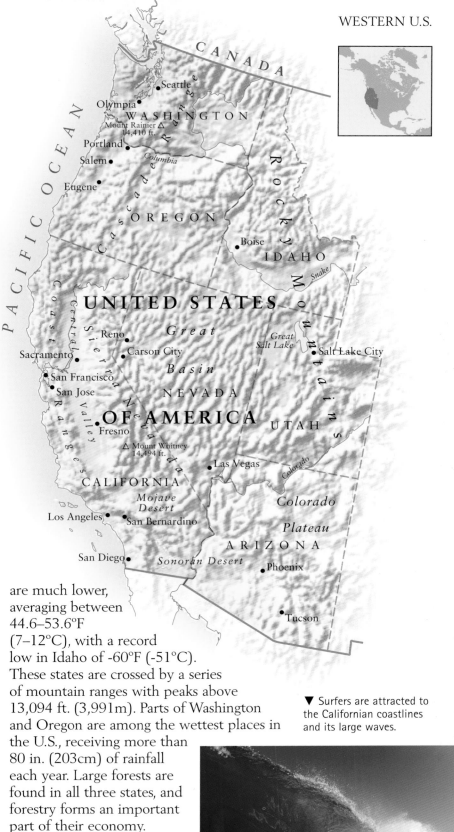

## HOT AND COLD, DRY AND WET

To the north and south of the western U.S. lie vastly different landscapes. Much of Arizona and parts of Nevada and southern California are covered in hot, arid deserts. The largest desert in the region is also the largest in all of North America. Called the Sonoran Desert, it covers an area of around 119,700 sq. mi. (310,000km²) and extends from northwestern Mexico and includes southwestern Arizona and southeastern California. Death Valley is an extremely dry desert area in California and Nevada that receives just 2 in. (5cm) average rainfall each year. There the highest temperature ever in the U.S. was recorded: 134.1°F (56.7°C). In contrast temperatures in the northern states of Idaho, Oregon, and Washington are much lower, averaging between 44.6–53.6°F (7–12°C), with a record low in Idaho of -60°F (-51°C). These states are crossed by a series of mountain ranges with peaks above 13,094 ft. (3,991m). Parts of Washington and Oregon are among the wettest places in the U.S., receiving more than 80 in. (203cm) of rainfall each year. Large forests are found in all three states, and forestry forms an important part of their economy.

◀ In less than one century Los Angeles has grown from a town of 50,000 people to a metropolitan area with around 12,873,000 residents. It is famous as the home of Hollywood—the heart of the U.S. movie industry.

▼ Surfers are attracted to the Californian coastlines and its large waves.

79

## CALIFORNIA'S INDUSTRIES

California is the state with the biggest population. It is home to 36.6 million people, a figure that has increased by 13.6 million in only 30 years. Many people are drawn to this western state for the glamour of its major movie, music, and entertainment industries, as well as its business opportunities. California is the home of one of the largest and most profitable high-tech and computing regions in the world. Nicknamed "Silicon Valley," this industrial region stretches a distance of more than 425 mi. (684km) along two valleys. Many leading computer manufacturers have their headquarters and research centers there, and Silicon Valley employs many thousands of people and generates hundreds of millions of dollars. Traditional industries in California, such as aerospace and shipbuilding, still exist. However, light industries, such as electronics and service industries including entertainment, tourism, and banking, are extremely important in the state's major cities of San Francisco and Los Angeles.

Around 4.2 million people live in the metropolitan area of San Francisco, while the metropolitan area of Los Angeles is the largest urban area in the the western U.S. with a population of more than 12.8 million people. Built on a large coastal plain, this cosmopolitan urban region is linked by an enormous network of freeways, which has created serious air-pollution problems in the area. To the south of Los Angeles lies its port, Los Angeles-Long Beach. It is the biggest cargo-handling port on the U.S. Pacific coast.

▲ A field of mustard seed in California's Napa Valley. California is also famous for its grapes, which are used in its wine industry.

▲ Death Valley in California, a depression 282 ft. (86m) below sea level, is the lowest point in the entire U.S.

▼ Rows of slot machines and gambling tables abound in the many casinos found in the city of Las Vegas, Nevada.

▲ Lying in Arizona, the Grand Canyon is one of the most famous geological features in the world. Carved out of the surrounding rock by the Colorado river, the canyon is over 272 mi. (438km) long and, in places, more than 1 mi. (1.6km) deep.

## U.S.'S LEADING FOOD PRODUCER

If it were a nation, California would have a place in the world's top-ten food producers. Half of the U.S.'s fruit and vegetables and 15 percent of its milk are produced within its borders. California is also home to the largest single wine producer, Ernest Gallo, which produces around two million bottles each day. There are many reasons to explain California's success as a farming area beyond rich, fertile soil. Much of the state has a warm, subtropical climate that encourages long growing seasons. There are many variations in local climates depending on distance to the Pacific Ocean and height above sea level. Different crops make use of these varying subclimates so that California grows more than 200 different foods. A lot of research and investment has led to heavy use of the latest technology and farming techniques, as well as extensive irrigation schemes (especially throughout the Central Valley), which has enabled this dry region to produce half of the state's farm output.

▲ The golden eagle
is found throughout the
Pacific coast of the U.S.
and in Mexico, where
it is the national bird.
Its wingspan can reach
up to 7.5 ft. (2.3m).

## THE GREAT BASIN

The Great Basin covers an area of more
than 310,000 sq. mi. (802,900km²). It
occupies most of the state of Nevada, the
western half of Utah, as well as smaller parts
of Oregon, Idaho, and California. Widest in
the north, the Great Basin narrows and
decreases in height as it extends south. The
basin consists of broad valleys and rugged
mountain blocks. The Sierra Nevada
mountain range to the west prevents winds
carrying moist air from the Pacific Ocean
from reaching the basin. Most of the
moisture falls as rain before reaching the
basin. As a result, most of the Great Basin
has a desert climate, with total rainfall
between 6–12 in. (15–30cm) per year.
Natural plant and animal life is limited
except in areas where artificial irrigation
programs water. The Great Basin is a region
that features interior drainage. This means
water from rivers and streams empties into
desert flats and seeps underground rather
than emptying into a sea or ocean. The
region's largest lake is the Great Salt Lake in
northern Utah. It is fed mainly by melting
snow from mountains and from a number
of small rivers. This shallow lake has an
average area of around 2,728 sq. mi.
(7,066km²) but varies greatly in size owing

to evaporation and the amount of water it
receives.

It is one of the saltiest freshwater lakes
in the world. Industrial plants that extract
and process the lake's salt are situated on its
shores.

## LIFE IN THE GREAT BASIN

Compared to many parts of the U.S., the
Great Basin is a hostile environment. Large
parts of the Great Basin lie uninhabited,
but major towns and cities do exist. Much
of the agriculture is concerned with raising
cattle and sheep and only contributes a
small amount to the area's economy. The
region's greatest resource is its wealth of
minerals. Mining for deposits of silver, gold,
and other metals helped develop
settlements such as Carson City, the capital
of Nevada. Today Nevada remains the
leading state producer of gold and mercury,
while Utah is among the leading producers
of silver, copper, and iron ore. Salt Lake City
is a major manufacturing center. It is also
home to the Church of Jesus Christ of
Latter-day Saints—the Mormon religion
whose pioneers established the city in the
late 1840s. Much of Nevada's growth in
cities and population is linked with the
legalization of gambling in 1931. Las Vegas
opened its first casino in 1941, and today a
population of more than 1.8 million people
are reliant on its status as one of the world's
leading gaming and gambling centers.

▼ Part of the Cascade
Range, which lies in the
center of Washington
state, Mount Rainier is
a dormant volcano that
is made up of five major
glaciers. With a peak
14,410 ft. (4,392m) above
sea level, it is the third-
highest peak on the
mainland U.S.

# ALASKA

**The largest and most northern part of the U.S, the vast, icy wilderness of Alaska was bought from Russia in 1867.**

▲ Built in the 1970s, the Trans-Alaska Pipeline runs for 798 mi. (1,284km), carrying crude oil from Alaska's northern coast to the city of Valdez in the south.

▼ At 20,320 ft. (6,194m) above sea level, Mount McKinley is the highest point in all of North America. The mountain is known to Native Americans as Denali, which means "the high one."

Lying at the northwestern tip of the North American continent, Alaska is separated from the Russian Federation by the seas that course through the Bering Strait. The 591,004 sq. mi. (1,530,693km²) state includes frozen tundra to the north, large taiga forests, hundreds of small lakes, and a southern peninsula that stretches out westward. Beyond it lies the Aleutian Islands, a long island chain. Alaska has a rugged geography with large mountain ranges bordering the Pacific and running inland. In total, the state has 39 mountain ranges that hold 17 of the 20 highest peaks in the entire United States.

## PEOPLE AND ECONOMY

It was across the Bering Strait at least 30,000 years ago that the first people were thought to have entered North America. Descendants of these first arrivals include the Inuit and Aleut peoples, who today make up around one tenth of Alaska's total population of 683,000. Oil and petroleum exploitation dominate the Alaskan economy, producing almost one third of its income.

Forestry and fishing are the state's other key resources, while tourism is also on the rise. Visitors are attracted to Alaska's harsh landscapes and its national parks, which contain a rich range of wildlife, including black bears, brown bears, and polar bears, moose, and large herds of caribou.

► Alaska is home to the world's largest population of gray wolves.

# HAWAII

**Hawaii is the name given to a group of 132 atolls and islands, along with the largest island in the group. In 1959 these Pacific islands became the 50th state of the U.S.**

The islands of Hawaii form a 1,488-mi.- (2,395-m-) long arc through the Pacific Ocean. Some smaller islands are coral atolls, but most of the islands are the topmost parts of giant volcanoes that extend more than 29 ft. (9m) up from the Pacific Ocean floor and break the water's surface. Only the volcanoes found on the island of Hawaii, known as the "Big Island," are thought to be still active, although the region experiences earthquake activity. The landscape of the Hawaiian islands is a dramatic mixture of volcanic peaks, steep cliffs, sandy beaches, and deep valleys covered in forests. The climate is tropical, with the northeast trade winds bringing rain. Large parts of the islands are covered in lush, tropical vegetation. Apart from Hawaii, there are seven other large islands. One of these, Oahu, is home to over two thirds of the islands' 1,283,000 population, as well as the islands' largest and capital city, Honolulu. The people of Hawaii are ethnically diverse, with those of European (31 percent), Japanese (20 percent), Filipino (14 percent), and Polynesian (13 percent) descent the largest groups. Fishing is important to the economy in Hawaii; however, tourism is the islands' single biggest industry and is worth more than $10 billion every year.

▼ The beautiful weather, sandy beaches, and excellent surfing in the waters of the Pacific attract many tourists from all over the world to the islands of Hawaii.

# BERMUDA

**The most northerly coral islands in the world, Bermuda lies in the Atlantic Ocean around 560 mi. (900km) off the coast of the U.S. It remains a British dependency.**

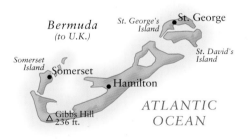

**Area:** 21 sq. mi. (54km²)
**Population:** 62,000
**Capital:** Hamilton (11,500)
**Main language spoken:** English
**Main religions:** Anglican, Methodist
**Currency:** Bermudian dollar
**Main exports:** re-exported pharmaceuticals
**Type of government:** self-governing dependency of U.K.

Bermuda consists of more than 150 islands that have a base of volcanic rock with coral formations lying above. The population relies on collecting and storing rainfall for their water supply. The island chain has a mild, humid climate aided by the warm Gulf Stream ocean current. The islands are covered in rich vegetation, including mangrove hedges and many flowering plants. Yet there is very little agricultural land, and flowering lilies are Bermuda's only agricultural export. Tourists, although falling in numbers throughout the 1990s, are still a major contributor to the economy, with more than 80 percent of visitors coming from the U.S. The remainder of Bermuda's economy is reliant on service industries such as insurance. Discovered in 1503 by Spaniard Juan Bermudez, the chain of islands came under British rule in 1684. Although still a dependency of the U.K., Bermuda became self-governing in 1968. The population, who are mainly descendants of former black slaves or Portuguese or British settlers, enjoy a high standard of living and in 1995 rejected a move for full independence.

# CENTRAL AMERICA

Bounded by the Pacific Ocean to the west and the Caribbean Sea to the east, Central America is a land bridge, known as an isthmus, that links the rest of North America with the South American continent. It is dominated by the country of Mexico, south of which lies a further seven countries: Belize, Guatemala, Nicaragua, El Salvador, Honduras, Costa Rica, and Panama. Around 40 percent of the land area of these countries is covered in rain forests that harbor a rich variety of wildlife. Much of Central America, from southern Mexico southward, is mountainous, and the region is one of the most active volcanic areas in the world. Water falling from high land is harnessed to generate almost half of the region's electricity via hydroelectric power. Farming is the main activity of the majority of Central Americans, with many crops, such as corn and beans, grown on small family farms. Approximately half of all farm products are exported out of the region. The five most important export products are: coffee, cotton, sugar, beef, and bananas. Central America has been inhabited by a series of ancient civilizations, including the Aztec, Maya, Olmec, and Toltec. The region has seen many wars and conflicts since the arrival of Spanish explorers in the 1500s.

▼ Mexico City, the capital of Mexico, struggles to accommodate around 19.2 million inhabitants. Many people live in slums without sanitation. The lack of environmental controls contributes to one of the world's worst air problems.

▲ The Mayan pyramid of Altun Ha in Belize is one of many ancient sites found in Central America. It attracts millions of tourists every year, providing the relatively poor region with much-needed income and employment.

MERICA

Río Grande

Sierra Madre Oriental

C   O

MEXICO CITY

Gulf of Mexico

Península de Yucatán

BELMOPAN

**BELIZE**

**GUATEMALA**

**HONDURAS**

GUATEMALA CITY

SAN SALVADOR

**EL SALVADOR**

TEGUCIGALPA

**NICARAGUA**

MANAGUA

Caribbean Sea

Lago de Nicaragua

SAN JOSÉ

PANAMA CITY

**COSTA RICA**

**PANAMA**

COLOMBIA

◄ The blue morpho butterfly with its spectacular metallic-blue wings is found in Costa Rica's forests and feeds mainly on fallen fruit.

0                    1000 km
0              500 miles

# MEXICO

**About one fifth of the size of the U.S., with which it shares a major land border, Mexico is the most populous Spanish-speaking nation in the world.**

**Area:** 756,066 sq. mi. (1,958,201km²)
**Population:** 103,264,000
**Capital:** Mexico City (19,232,000)
**Main language spoken:** Spanish
**Main religion:** Roman Catholic
**Currency:** Mexican peso
**Main exports:** manufactured goods (including machinery and transportation equipment), crude petroleum, agricultural goods (particularly sugar, fruit, and meat)
**Type of government:** federal republic

▼ The center of Mexico City is the Zócalo, or Plaza of the Constitution. It contains the huge Metropolitan Cathedral, which was built in the 1600s and added to in the 1800s.

Mexico is at its broadest to the north where it borders the U.S. The country narrows as it runs in a curve southward and eastward. It ends in land borders with Guatemala and Belize and in a square-shaped peninsula jutting into the Gulf of Mexico called the Yucatán peninsula. The Yucatán is formed mainly of limestone rocks and is low-lying, with an average height above sea level of only 100 ft. (30m). Mexico has a second peninsula that is very different in shape and landscape, Baja California. It extends around 760 mi. (1,225km) south from California, creating the Gulf of California and bordering the Pacific Ocean on its western side. Much of Baja California consists of high mountain ranges of more than 9,840 ft. (3,000m).

### THE CENTRAL PLATEAU
The center of Mexico is a huge, high plateau that is open to the north but bounded by two large mountain chains: the Sierra Madre Oriental to the east and the Sierra Madre Occidental to the west. This plateau

▲ Cancún is a major vacation resort found just off the east coast of the Yucatán peninsula. Growing from a small island village in the 1970s, it now has more than 30,000 hotel rooms and attracts tourists from around the world.

forms around half the total area of Mexico and slopes downward from the west to the east. To the south the plateau rises to form a region that is crossed by many mountains and volcanoes. Lying an equal distance between the cities of Veracruz and Puebla is Citlaltépetl, a volcano that is the country's highest point. On the far side of the mountain ranges from the central plateau the land forms huge, low-lying coastal plains. The plains facing the Gulf of Mexico are fringed with swamps, lagoons, and sandbars. Mexico has relatively few

▲ A busy market day for local Mexicans in the south of the country. Mexican markets, known as *mercados*, exist all over the country and are a major way in which goods are traded between local people.

▼ Ancient Mayan people lived throughout large parts of Mexico and left behind many impressive structures and sites. This ancient Mayan pyramid is called the Temple of the Inscriptions. It is found in Palenque, 70 mi. (110km) southeast of the city of Villahermosa.

major rivers and lakes. Its largest lake is Lake Chapala, which covers around 420 sq. mi. (1,080km²) and is found near Guadalajara, Mexico's second-largest city. The country's longest river, the Río Grande (also known as the Río Bravo del Norte), forms more than 1,240 mi. (2,000km) of border between Texas and Mexico before emptying into the Gulf of Mexico.

## HOT AND COLD LAND

From mountain peaks permanently covered in snow to hot, dry deserts and lush, wet rain forests, Mexico has a varied range of landscapes and climates. Climate tends to change with both the height of the land above sea level and its latitude. Land below 2,990 ft. (910m) is known as *tierra caliente* (hot land), between 2,990–5,900 ft. (910–1,800m), *tierra templada* (temperate land), and above 5,900 ft. (1,800m), *tierra fria* (cold land). Mexico City, for example, lies in the *tierra templada* and has a cool, dry climate with only a small variation in temperature (averaging between 54–63°F/12–17°C) throughout the year. In the north of Mexico temperature extremes are much greater, and maximum temperatures can rise to more than 113°F (45°C). This intense heat, along with low rainfall, often below 10 in. (25cm) per year, results in vast desert and semidesert areas. Much of central and southern Mexico is relatively dry as well,

and it is only in the tropical regions in the far south and southeast of the country that rainfall is heavy. The wettest regions of Mexico are to the south and in the Yucatán; these areas can receive more than 120 in. (300cm) of rainfall per year.

▲ Mexico City has an estimated three million cars that are responsible for much of its air pollution.

▼ Fibers from the leaves of the sisal plant are used to make strong ropes that do not deteriorate quickly in saltwater. Here sisal leaves are harvested for a rope-making factory in the Yucatán peninsula's largest city, Mérida.

## PLANTS AND ANIMALS

Mexico's wide range of landscapes and climates create habitats for a great variety of living things. Even in the hottest and driest desert areas in the north, plants such as yuccas and many species of cacti flourish, while insects, lizards, coyotes, and armadillos also live in arid regions. Mexico has approximately 212,360 sq. mi. (550,000km$^2$) of forests that cover more than 20 percent of its land. In the hot and humid far south of the country rain forests exist that provide habitats for monkeys, jaguars, anteaters, and many species of birds and lizards. On the slopes of the Sierra Madre ranges and other mountains large forests of pines and other coniferous trees grow below an altitude of around 13,120 ft. (4,000m). Creatures that live in these mountainous forests include bears, wild pigs, and ocelots. Owing to continuing deforestation, many creatures in Mexico's forests have become endangered as their habitat is destroyed.

## RESOURCES AND INDUSTRY

Agriculture, forestry, and fishing make up four percent of Mexico's economy. Much farming is conducted on a small scale, but irrigation remains a problem. Coffee and sugar are Mexico's two most important food exports. The country has large reserves of many minerals and is the world's leading producer of silver and one of the largest producers of zinc and lead. Mexico has large reserves of oil, much of which is located offshore. Processing oil and natural gas and manufacturing a wide range of products generate more revenue than any other sector. Manufacturing industries include food-processing plants, paper mills, and clothing factories. The country is also the world's tenth-largest assembler of motor vehicles. A feature of Mexican industry, especially around Mexico City and near the U.S. border, are Maquiladora industries. These occur when well-known, brand-name products from one country are made under license in another country where workforce costs are lower. In northern Mexico there are more than 2,000 Maquiladoras producing clothes, computers, shoes, and other goods.

▼ A train runs over a viaduct in the Copper Canyon in the Sierra Madre Occidental Mountains.

▲ Iguanas are common throughout southern Mexico, and in the southeast of the country they are sometimes smoked over an open fire and eaten as a delicacy.

Native American origin, who form around 60 percent of the population. The mixture of European and native groups contribute to Mexico's rich culture, reflected in its music, art, textiles, and its range of native foods and dishes, many of which use over 200 different species of chili as flavorings.

## UNITED STATES OF MEXICO

Mexico's full, official name is the United States of Mexico. The country is divided into 32 administrative regions—31 states and a federal district located in its capital, Mexico City. This giant urban area has grown in size and population to extend beyond the federal district. Smaller settlements, once outside of the city, have been swallowed up as the metropolitan area has sprawled outward. Around 19.2 million people are estimated to live in and around Mexico City, making it one of the world's largest urban areas. Over half of Mexico's industry is located in or near the city, which is surrounded by mountains on all sides. These mountains trap the air around the city and increase the levels of air pollution caused by motor vehicles and industry. Air pollution is a serious health problem in Mexico City.

## MEXICO'S PEOPLE

Mexico has been home to a number of ancient civilizations, including the Olmec, Maya, and Aztec. The Aztecs settled in Mexico around A.D. 1200 and built their capital city, Tenochtitlán, on the site of present-day Mexico City. Most of the Aztec civilization was destroyed by Spanish explorers in the early 1500s. Called New Spain, Mexico was under Spanish rule until it became independent in 1821. Native Americans make up approximately 30 percent of Mexico's total population of 103.3 million. The largest group are mestizos, people of mixed Spanish and

▼ The highest point in Mexico—and the third highest in North and Central America—Citlaltépetl is a dormant volcano standing 18,365 ft. (5,598m) above sea level.

# GUATEMALA

**Guatemala is a mountainous country that experiences both earthquakes and volcanic activity. It contains the largest continuous area of rain forest in Central America.**

**Area:** 42,042 sq. mi. (108,889km2)
**Population:** 14,362,000
**Capital:** Guatemala City (3,104,000)
**Main languages spoken:** Spanish, Mayan languages
**Main religion:** Roman Catholic
**Currency:** quetzal
**Main exports:** coffee, sugar, bananas, petroleum, clothing
**Type of government:** republic; limited democracy

▼ Lying between Mazatenango and Guatemala City, Lake Atilán fills part of a large sunken crater, or caldera, created by an enormous volcanic explosion.

Almost two thirds of Guatemala are covered in mountains. There are two main mountain ranges that cross the country. To the north is a series of older mountains that have been heavily eroded yet still stand almost 9,850 ft. (3,000m) in height in some places. To the south the mountains are younger and contain more than 30 volcanoes, five of which are still active. Soil mixed with volcanic ash has washed down from the Sierra Madre Mountains to create a narrow plain of excellent growing land along Guatemala's Pacific coast. Although it lies in the tropics, the cooler seas it borders and its range of high- and low-lying land create a number of different climates. On the Pacific coast temperatures tend to average more than 86°F (30°C), while in the highlands above 5,900 ft. (1,800m) temperatures between 50–60°F (10–16°C) are more common. The dry season is when most of the country's 1.5 million tourists visit. Most tourists are from the U.S. and Mexico.

## EL PETÉN

Approximately one third of Guatemala is made up of low-lying land in the northern region called El Petén. This area consists of plains and small, knobby hills made largely of limestone rocks. Dense rain forests cover most of the region, providing habitats for a great variety of creatures, including the jaguar. This big cat is the largest predator in Central America. Few rivers run through El Petén since most of the rainfall it receives drains underground. Transportation links are sparse, although a major road and airport connect the region's main town, Flores, with the rest of the country.

## THE PEOPLE OF GUATEMALA

Guatemala was the center of the ancient Maya civilization, which flourished between A.D. 300 and A.D. 900. Almost half of all Guatemalans are descendants of the ancient Maya and other native Indian peoples, while just over half are mestizos—people of mixed Indian and European origins. Farming dominates the lives of 50 percent of the workforce. Cereals and fruit are grown for local use, and coffee is the most important export crop. The country is also one of the world's largest producers of cardamom seeds, a popular spice. After many decades of dictators ruling without elections, as well as violent civil wars, Guatemala is currently peaceful but faces problems in health care and education. For example, 36 percent of adult women cannot read or write.

◄ Approximately 1.7 percent of Guatemala's rain forests, home to a large range of wildlife, is removed every year for its timber and to clear new land for farming.

# BELIZE

Bordering the Caribbean Sea, the small country of Belize contains a varied mixture of landscapes and peoples. It became independent in 1981.

**Area:** 8,867 sq. mi. (22,965km²)
**Population:** 333,000
**Capital:** Belmopan (20,000)
**Main languages spoken:** English, Spanish, Mayan, Garifuna (Carib)
**Main religions:** Roman Catholic, Protestant
**Currency:** Belize dollar
**Main exports:** sugar, orange and grapefruit juice, bananas, fish, clothes
**Type of government:** parliamentary democracy

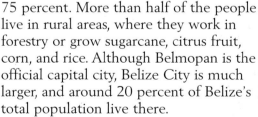

Known as British Honduras until 1973, Belize is a country of two distinct geographical sections. The northern half, which borders Mexico, is mainly low-lying and contains many swamps close to the coast. The southern half begins with grassy savannas and rises to mountain ranges. Over 40 percent of Belize is covered in forests that flourish in the country's subtropical climate. The forests provide hardwoods such as mahogany, rosewood, and chicle, the gum of which is used to make chewing gum. Off Belize's coastline is a chain of coral reefs and small sandy islands called cays.

Running for approximately 180 mi. (290km), this chain is the largest coral reef in the Western Hemisphere. Several hundred thousand tourists visit Belize every year, mainly for its beaches and the reef but also for its historic sites. Belize was once a part of the Mayan empire, and many ancient sites remain. Its

► Keen-billed toucan

people are a mixture of many cultures, with mestizos and creoles accounting for 75 percent. More than half of the people live in rural areas, where they work in forestry or grow sugarcane, citrus fruit, corn, and rice. Although Belmopan is the official capital city, Belize City is much larger, and around 20 percent of Belize's total population live there.

▼ El Castillo is part of an ancient Mayan site found in the mountainous west of the country.

# HONDURAS

The third-largest country in Central America, Honduras is dominated by mountain ranges. It borders Nicaragua, Guatemala, and El Salvador.

**Area:** 43,277 sq. mi. (112,088km²)
**Population:** 7,320,000
**Capital:** Tegucigalpa (1,416,000)
**Main language spoken:** Spanish
**Main religion:** Roman Catholic
**Currency:** lempira
**Main exports:** coffee, bananas, shrimp and lobsters, clothing, gold
**Type of government:** republic; limited democracy

Honduras has a long coastline with the Caribbean Sea and a short coast alongside the Pacific Ocean. The Caribbean coast features several important ports, including Le Ceiba and, offshore, the Bay Islands (Islas de la Bahia), which are popular tourist destinations. The country's lowland areas are found near the coasts and in large river valleys that crisscross the highlands of Honduras. Much of the country is mountainous. The highest mountains are found in the western and central areas and were created by volcanic activity. In the hot, humid lowland areas rain forests cover large stretches of land. On the mountains forests of oak and pine trees dominate.

### A DEVELOPING NATION

Honduras is less industrialized than its neighbors, and its people are among the poorest in the Western world. Foreign aid and investment have helped set up food-processing plants, as well as industries producing rum, cooking oil, cement, and paper. The country's mountains contain vast deposits of metal ores, particularly, silver, zinc, lead, and gold. Underground mines have been excavated to extract these metals for industry. Most people farm land or work for owners of large plantations on which bananas, coffee, and exotic fruit and flowers are grown for sale overseas. Honduras was once the world's leading exporter of bananas, and this crop still accounts for almost 14 percent of the country's income. Much of the highland areas are unsuitable for farming, but the terrain allows 80 percent of the country's electricity to be generated by hydroelectric plants, harnessing the power of falling water.

▲ Discovered by Christopher Columbus in 1512, the Bay Islands lie in the Caribbean Sea off the north coast of Honduras and attract many tourists and divers.

▶ Many Hondurans work on plantations owned by foreign companies growing coffee and bananas. These women, employed by the U.S.-owned Chiquita company, are washing bananas.

# EL SALVADOR

The smallest nation in Central America, El Salvador's landscape is a mixture of lowlands and high volcanic mountains.

**Area:** 8,124 sq. mi. (21,041km²)
**Population:** 6,095,000
**Capital:** San Salvador (1,731,,000)
**Main language spoken:** Spanish
**Main religion:** Roman Catholic
**Currency:** U.S. dollar
**Main exports:** coffee, clothing, pharmaceuticals, sugar, consumer goods
**Type of government:** republic

El Salvador is bordered to the east and north by Honduras and to the west by Guatemala. Behind its 200-mi.- (320-km-) long coast with the Pacific Ocean the land forms a narrow coastal plain before rising to a large central plateau dominated by several chains of mountains, around 20 volcanoes, and deep valleys. More than 280 rivers and large streams flow across the country, mostly carrying water to the Pacific Ocean. Of all the Central America nations south of Mexico, El Salvador has the least amount of forests. In the past much of the land would have been covered in trees, but many years of clearing the land for agriculture now mean that only around six percent of the land remains forested.

## NATURAL RESOURCES

El Salvador's mountainous backbone has been settled by native Indian people for many thousands of years. The slopes of the volcanic mountains were covered in nutrient-rich soils that have attracted farmers since the earliest times. El Salvador has little in the way of mineral resources such as gold, iron, or oil. The mountains and hills, however, do help generate much of the country's electricity. Fast-falling

▲ San Salvador is El Salvador's capital and largest city. The World Bank estimates that around one third of the country's entire population live in extreme poverty. Many of these people live in slums in San Salvador and other cities.

water turns turbines in hydroelectric power plants to generate around two thirds of El Salvador's electricity. A further ten percent is created by a large geothermal power plant. This taps into the heat below Earth's surface.

## RICH AND POOR

El Salvador is the most densely populated country in Central America, with an approximate average of 780 people per square mile. The vast majority are mestizos—people of mixed native Indian and European descent. For many years just 14 families owned 75 percent of the country's land, but reforms are now changing that, and small plots of land are being handed over to many more people. After a devastating 13-year civil war that ended in 1991 the gap between the rich and poor remains large, with wealth still concentrated in the hands of a few people. The U.S. is El Salvador's main trading partner and is responsible for 35 percent of its imports and 48 percent of its exports, which include clothing, machinery, and cash crops such as fruits, coffee, and sugarcane.

▼ Pineapples are one of a number of fruit, including avocados, mangoes, and papaya, grown in the rich soils of El Salvador.

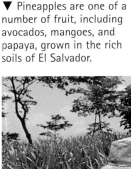

# NICARAGUA

**Nicaragua is considered one of the most beautiful countries in Central America, but earthquakes and human conflict have left their mark.**

**Area:** 50,450 sq. mi. (130,670km²)
**Population:** 5,142,000
**Capital:** Managua (1,260,000)
**Main language spoken:** Spanish
**Main religion:** Roman Catholic
**Currency:** gold cordoba
**Main exports:** coffee, meat, sugar, shrimp, lobster
**Type of government:** republic; limited democracy

▼ Nicaragua's capital city, Managua, lies on the southern shore of Lake Managua. The city was badly damaged by earthquakes in 1931 and 1972. Parts of its center have never been rebuilt.

Nicaragua has a varied landscape with dramatic variations in terrain throughout the country. The eastern region of Nicaragua, bordering the Caribbean Sea, is known as the Mosquito Coast (Costa de Mosquitos). Partially covered in rain forests and featuring many lagoons and river deltas, this area is a coastal plain that extends more than 45 mi. (70km) inland from the sea. The western side of Nicaragua has a drier climate and is mainly savanna grasslands and some forests. In between are two long chains of mountains that contain more than 40 volcanoes. These volcanoes are partly responsible for the great amount of earthquake activity that Nicaragua experiences. In 1992, for example, a large earthquake made 16,000 people homeless. Nicaragua has a tropical climate with a wet season between May and October. Parts of Nicaragua receive more than 122 in. (310cm) of rainfall each year. The eastern side of Nicaragua has been hit by hurricanes on many occasions. In 1998, for example, Hurricane Mitch (which also devastated El Salvador and caused a lot of damage in Honduras) took the lives of over 1,800 Nicaraguans and also destroyed much of the country's banana, sugar, and coffee crops.

## LIVING NEAR THE LAKES

The southern part of Nicaragua is dominated by a giant basin in which lie Lake Managua and Lake Nicaragua, the largest lake in Central America. Lake Nicaragua is 110 mi. (177km) long and is 36 mi. (58km) wide at its widest point. The lake contains more than 400 islands, and their picturesque location makes them popular visitor destinations. It is the only freshwater lake in the world to contain a number of sea fish, including swordfish and sharks. Research shows that these fish came from the Caribbean Sea and made their way to the lake via the San Juan river, one of four main rivers that flow from the lake. Most of Nicaragua's population live and work in the lowlands between the Pacific Ocean and the shores of Lake Nicaragua and Lake Managua. The soil in this region is rich in nutrients, and crops, including cotton, corn, rice, bananas, and beans, are grown for local markets and for export.

## TROUBLES

Nicaragua has suffered from many natural disasters such as hurricanes and earthquakes. It also experienced years of civil war in the 1980s. The Somoza family, who ruled for more than 40 years, was overthrown in 1979, and the left-wing Sandinista government that replaced them was removed from power in 1990. The years of unrest have left Nicaragua's public services in a poor condition. To revive the economy, new industries are being developed, but many Nicaraguans have emigrated to work, sending home money to their families in Nicaragua.

# COSTA RICA

**Costa Rica is one of the most peaceful and prosperous of the Central American nations. Growing coffee is the mainstay of rural life in this country.**

**Area:** 19,730 sq. mi. (51,100km²)
**Population:** 4,439,000
**Capital:** San José (1,500,000)
**Main language spoken:** Spanish
**Main religion:** Roman Catholic
**Currency:** Costa Rican colon
**Main exports:** bananas, coffee, fish, flowers, electronic components
**Type of government:** republic

Costa Rica spans the width of the narrow Central America isthmus. The land on both coasts tends to be low-lying. The eastern side receives more rain than the western, but both coastal areas have a number of mangrove swamps and white, sandy beaches. The land rises from the coasts in the center and south, with high, rugged mountains created by volcanic activity. Between the main mountain ranges lies a large plateau on which the majority of Costa Ricans live. The country has a tropical climate with relatively heavy rainfall. Its rain forests cover around one third of its land and help provide homes for an abundance of plant and animal life.

## PEOPLE AND PROSPERITY

Costa Rica's population is unusual in the region in that they are mainly of European descent. Indigenous Amerindians account for less than one percent of the total population, while around three percent of people are black. Agriculture occupies 14 percent of its workforce, with sales of bananas and coffee earning the country almost 40 percent of its income. Costa Rica generates the majority of its electricity using hydroelectric power. The mining of metal ores, particularly bauxite, is becoming more important, as is tourism. Since its 1948 civil war Costa Rica has largely been a nation at peace. It has the most extensive welfare

▲ The macaw is just one of 725 different species of birds found in Costa Rica.

▶ Here is a local fruit market in Costa Rica. Bananas are one of the country's major export earners.

▲ Costa Rica was the first country in the region to grow and export coffee. Coffee growing on plantations supports around half of the population and has been the country's leading export for more than 100 years.

state in Central America. Compulsory education is free up until the age of 15, and Costa Rica is home to 14 universities. The country has a well-developed health care system to which it devotes almost 25 percent of its total expenditure. As a result, Costa Ricans have a life expectancy of 78 years, the best in Central America. However, the country does have economic problems. Reduced U.S. aid, the rising price of imported oil, and falling prices for coffee and bananas, which it exports, have caused large debts to build up.

# PANAMA

The small country of Panama links the continents of North and South America. Its 48-mi.- (77-km-) long canal also links the Pacific and Atlantic oceans.

**Area:** 29,340 sq. mi. (75,990km²)
**Population:** 3,228,000
**Capital:** Panama City (892,000)
**Main languages spoken:** Spanish, English
**Main religions:** Roman Catholic, Protestant
**Currency:** balboa (U.S. currency is also legal tender)
**Main exports:** bananas, shrimp, coffee, clothing, fish
**Type of government:** constitutional republic

Panama occupies a relatively narrow strip of land, known as an isthmus, bordered by the Caribbean Sea to the east and the Pacific Ocean to the west. Two sets of mountains run the length of Panama, and between these ranges are many low-lying hills, lakes, and more than 400 rivers and streams. Panama has a tropical climate with particularly heavy rainfall on its eastern side. There lush rain forests grow, and Panama is home to more than 2,000 species of tropical plants. On its western, Pacific side the land tends to receive less rainfall, and scrub forests are common. The scrub forests of Darien National Park in the south of Panama are virtually uninhabited and untouched by humans. Panama's coastline is indented by many bays and lagoons.

### THE PANAMA CANAL
One of the biggest engineering feats in the world, the Panama Canal was finally opened in 1914. The canal and its dredged entrances stretch 50 mi. (81km) through Panama, linking the Atlantic and Pacific oceans. To sail between these oceans without using the canal involves a 7,460-mi.- (12,000-km-) long trip around the southernmost tip of South America. More than 14,000 individual journeys through the canal are made by ships every year, and the tolls that are paid are a major source of income for Panama. Traffic can travel in both directions, and three sets of giant locks raise and lower the water level, altering it by 85 ft. (26m) during the course of the journey. The canal was built by the U.S., which assisted Panama in obtaining independence from Colombia in 1903. At the end of 1999, following a 20-year handover period, full control of the canal was passed to Panama.

### AN INTERNATIONAL GATEWAY
The Panama Canal has made the country an international gateway for shipping, trade, and finance. Panama has a free-trade

zone around the canal, and tax-free banking attracts customers from all over the world. Panama also has one of the largest fleets of merchant ships in the world. Most of these ships are registered in Panama but are owned by foreign companies.

The warm climate and fertile soil allow the rural population of Panama to grow enough food for the country to be largely self-sufficient. Rice, corn, and beans are the main staple crops, with bananas, coffee, and sugar grown for export abroad. Shrimp is also an important export product.

▲ Due to its shipping and banking interests and also because of the revenue collected from running the Panama Canal, Panama City, the country's capital, is one of the wealthiest cities in Central America. In 2007 the government began a major enlargement of the Panama Canal, to be completed by 2014.

▲ The Miraflores Locks on the Panama Canal raise or drop 55.1 ft. (16.8m)—the difference between the elevation of the waters of Miraflores Lake and the Pacific Ocean.

# THE CARIBBEAN AND SOUTH AMERICA

# THE CARIBBEAN

The Caribbean islands form a broken bridge of land 1,990 mi. (3,200km) long between the South American country of Venezuela and the southeastern U.S. state of Florida. The islands form a boundary separating the Atlantic Ocean from the Caribbean Sea. The region's climate is largely tropical, with most islands experiencing a wet season between June and November. The Caribbean is also one of the regions most at risk from the threat of hurricanes. The Carribean is comprised of three groups of islands. The Bahamas are the most northerly; the Lesser Antilles, which include the islands of Antigua & Barbuda, Grenada, and Trinidad & Tobago are the most easterly; while the Greater Antilles contain the largest islands such as Cuba, Jamaica, and the large island of Hispaniola shared by the states of Haiti and the Dominican Republic. The region is named after some of the earliest known inhabitants of the area, the Carib people. In 1492 Christopher Columbus and his crew became the first European visitors when they landed in the Bahamas. He mistakenly thought he had reached Asia, which led to the region being called the West Indies. In the centuries since Columbus's discovery most of the Caribbean has seen colonial rule by the Spanish, French, British, Danish, and Dutch.

► These Cuban workers are harvesting tobacco, a major crop in Cuba and several other Caribbean islands. Cuba, with a land area of 42,804 sq. mi. (110,861km²), comprises almost half the total land area of the Caribbean region.

◄ The landscape and climate of the U.S. Virgin Islands make it a popular tourist destination. Sandy beaches often fringed with palm trees are found throughout the Caribbean.

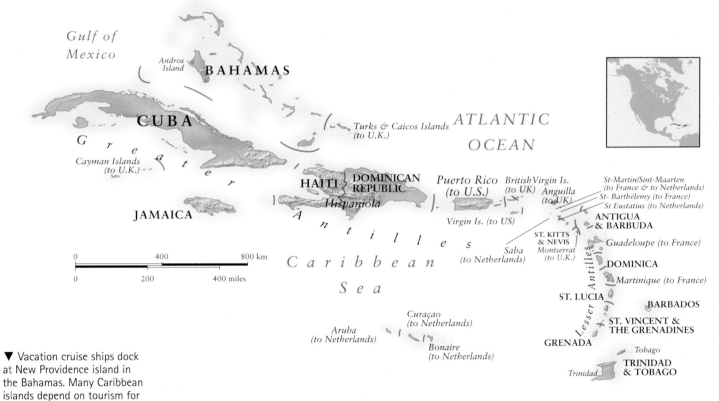

*Gulf of Mexico*

*Andros Island*

**BAHAMAS**

**CUBA**

*G r e a t e r*

*Cayman Islands (to U.K.)*

**JAMAICA**

**HAITI**

**DOMINICAN REPUBLIC**

*Hispaniola*

*A n t i l l e s*

*Turks & Caicos Islands (to U.K.)*

*ATLANTIC OCEAN*

*Puerto Rico (to U.S.)*

*British Virgin Is. (to UK)*

*Anguilla (to UK)*

*Virgin Is. (to US)*

*St-Martin/Sint-Maarten (to France & to Netherlands)*

*St- Barthélemy (to France)*

*St Eustatius (to Netherlands)*

**ANTIGUA & BARBUDA**

**ST. KITTS & NEVIS**

*Saba (to Netherlands)*

*Montserrat (to U.K.)*

*Guadeloupe (to France)*

**DOMINICA**

*Martinique (to France)*

**ST. LUCIA**

**BARBADOS**

**ST. VINCENT & THE GRENADINES**

**GRENADA**

*L e s s e r   A n t i l l e s*

*Caribbean Sea*

*Curaçao (to Netherlands)*

*Aruba (to Netherlands)*

*Bonaire (to Netherlands)*

*Tobago*

**TRINIDAD & TOBAGO**

*Trinidad*

```
0        400        800 km
0   200       400 miles
```

▼ Vacation cruise ships dock at New Providence island in the Bahamas. Many Caribbean islands depend on tourism for a large part of their revenue.

# CUBA

**Cuba is the largest, most varied, and one of the most beautiful of all Caribbean islands. Long but narrow, it lies just 89 mi. (144km) south of the state of Florida.**

**Area:** 42,804 sq. mi. (110,861km²)
**Population:** 11,239,000
**Capital:** Havana (2,175,000)
**Main language spoken:** Spanish
**Main religion:** Roman Catholic
**Currency:** Cuban peso
**Main exports:** minerals (nickel and chromite), fish products, tobacco, sugar
**Type of government:** communist state

▼ This old steam train is carrying harvested sugarcane to a refinery. Sugar was once the main export for Cuba, but the industry has shrunk, and in 2009 only 1.4 million tons (1.3 million metric tonnes) were produced.

Cuba extends approximately 780 mi. (1,260km) roughly east to west, and its widest point measures 119 mi. (191km). It is separated from mainland United States by the Straits of Florida and from the island of Hispaniola by the Windward Passage. Its closest neighbor is Jamaica, 86 mi. (139km) away. Hundreds of natural bays, reefs, and peninsulas give Cuba a shoreline of 2,320 mi. (3,735km). Its territory includes one major island, the Isla de la Juventud (Island of Youth), and many tiny islets.

Cuba is less mountainous than its neighbors in the Greater Antilles, with around one fourth of its land covered in high elevations. The main mountain system of the Caribbean crosses southeastern Cuba, where it is called the Sierra Maestra. Most of the remainder of Cuba is lowlands. Cuba is part of a limestone platform related to the limestone areas of the Yucatán peninsula in Mexico, in Florida, and in the Bahamas. The country's longest river, the Cuoto, runs west to east and passes 12 mi. (20km) north of Bayamo. However, only small boats are able to navigate it.

▲ Tobacco grown in Cuba is used to make the country's world-famous cigars. In 2004 Cuba exported 230 million cigars. Today only the most expensive are hand rolled.

## FARMING IN CUBA

Around 80 percent of Cuba's soil has been created by rain falling on red limestone, producing deep, fertile soil. Around 20 percent of the land is covered with forests of pine and mahogany. Much of the remainder is pastureland for the country's 4.6 million cattle or cropland. Cuba has a mostly hot climate, with heavy seasonal rainfall, and many crops flourish, including rice, coffee, citrus fruit, and tobacco, which is used to make its world-famous cigars. Cuba's chief crop was sugar, and the island used to be one of the world's leading producers. The loss of a guaranteed customer, the Soviet Union, brought the industry to crisis, and sugar is no longer the main export.

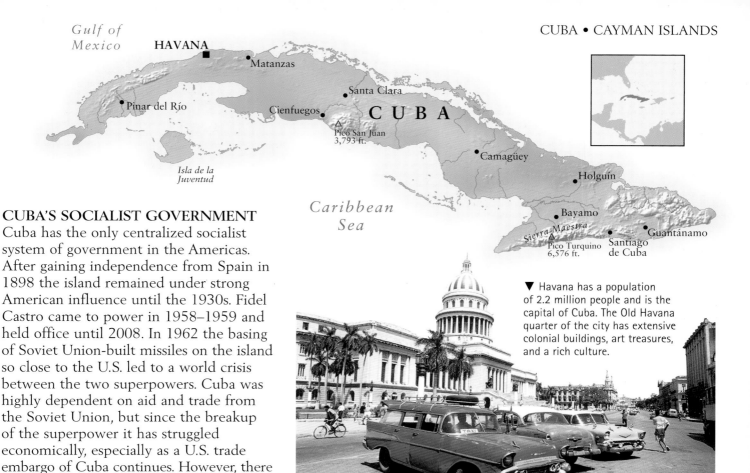

Gulf of Mexico

HAVANA
Matanzas
Pinar del Río
Santa Clara
Cienfuegos
CUBA
Pico San Juan
3,793 ft.
Isla de la Juventud
Caribbean Sea
Camagüey
Holguín
Bayamo
Sierra Maestra
Pico Turquino
6,576 ft.
Guantánamo
Santiago de Cuba

## CUBA'S SOCIALIST GOVERNMENT

Cuba has the only centralized socialist system of government in the Americas. After gaining independence from Spain in 1898 the island remained under strong American influence until the 1930s. Fidel Castro came to power in 1958–1959 and held office until 2008. In 1962 the basing of Soviet Union-built missiles on the island so close to the U.S. led to a world crisis between the two superpowers. Cuba was highly dependent on aid and trade from the Soviet Union, but since the breakup of the superpower it has struggled economically, especially as a U.S. trade embargo of Cuba continues. However, there has been greater exploitation of nickel, as well as increasing tourist numbers.

▼ Havana has a population of 2.2 million people and is the capital of Cuba. The Old Havana quarter of the city has extensive colonial buildings, art treasures, and a rich culture.

# CAYMAN ISLANDS

**World-renowned for their beautiful beaches, the three islands that comprise the Caymans lie around 180 mi. (290km) northwest of Jamaica.**

Cayman Islands (to U.K.)
Little Cayman
Cayman Brac
Grand Cayman
George Town
Bodden Town
Caribbean Sea

**Area:** 100 sq. mi. (259km²)
**Population:** 39,000
**Capital:** George Town (25,000)
**Main language spoken:** English
**Main religions:** Anglican, Roman Catholic
**Currency:** Cayman Islands dollar
**Main exports:** manufactured consumer goods, turtle products
**Type of government:** dependency of U.K.

The Cayman Islands consist of Cayman Brac, Little Cayman, and Grand Cayman, the largest of the group. All three islands are low-lying, feature excellent beaches, and are fringed by spectacular coral reefs that are home to a rich range of marine life. Mangrove swamps cover a little under one third of the land, although there are no natural streams on any of the islands. Among the vegetation found on the islands are coconut palms and banana, mango, and breadfruit trees. Turtles raised on a government turtle farm provide food, shell, and leather, which is sometimes fashioned into souvenirs for the Cayman's large number of tourist visitors. Cayman Brac is approximately 12 mi. (19km) long and 1 mi. (1.6km) wide. Its land is riddled with

caves and dozens of shipwrecks, which are popular sites for divers. Little Cayman is only around 5 mi. (8km) long, and much of its area is given over to a wildlife sanctuary for iguanas and wild birds. More than half of the Cayman Islands' population is located in its capital, George Town, where more than 500 bank offices from many countries take advantage of the Cayman Islands' low levels of taxation. The Caymans were administered by Jamaica from 1863. When Jamaica became independent in 1962, they remained a British dependency. The governor of the islands, who represents Great Britain, works with a legislative assembly that consists of 18 members, 15 of whom are elected.

# JAMAICA

**Jamaica is a mixture of mountainous and lowland regions that are densely populated. It lies around 90 mi. (145km) south of Cuba.**

**Area:** 4,244 sq. mi. (10,991km²)
**Population:** 2,692,000
**Capital:** Kingston (895,000)
**Main language spoken:** English
**Main religions:** Protestant, Church of God
**Currency:** Jamaican dollar
**Main exports:** bauxite, agricultural products, food, beverages, clothing
**Type of government:** parliamentary democracy

▼ Kingston's bustling Coronation Market is where many Jamaicans sell a wide range of farm produce, including peppers, bananas, tobacco, yams, and mangoes. Jamaica grows almost the entire world supply of allspice.

Jamaica has beaches like many other Caribbean islands, but much of its land is mountainous. In the northwest limestone rock forms a series of steep ridges and flat basins that have many sinkholes. To the northeast the land rises to form the island's main mountain range. Called the Blue Mountains, the highest of its summits, Blue Mountain Peak, is also the highest point in the Caribbean. The lowlands are largely covered in farms, with sugar, bananas, coffee, and vegetables being the main crops, although sugar production has greatly declined. Agriculture employs around one fifth of the Jamaican workforce, and the island has over 440,000 goats and a similar number of cattle. Mining is one of Jamaica's most important industries. Bauxite—an ore from which aluminum is extracted—has been mined on the island since the 1950s, and aluminum ore and products account for more than 50 percent of the country's exports. Tourism is vital, with more than 3.2 million visitors to the island in 2008.

### KINGSTON

Kingston is the capital of Jamaica and is the largest English-speaking city in the entire Caribbean. It is the center of government of the island, which is divided into 14 parishes. The city was founded in 1692 after an earthquake destroyed much of the capital at that time, Port Royal. Kingston is situated on one of the largest natural harbors in the world and is overlooked by a highland area. The city is a busy port, a manufacturing center for clothing and food processing, and a tourist destination for cruise ships. The city's architecture is a mixture of traditional colonial buildings, modern tower blocks, rich mansions, and poor slum areas. Reggae music developed particularly in the deprived areas of Kingston and made reggae musician Bob Marley a world-famous Jamaican.

# THE BAHAMAS

One of the most prosperous states in the region, the Bahamas are a collection of 700 islands, plus 2,000 rocky islets, located in the northwestern Caribbean.

**Area:** 5,382 sq. mi. (13,939km²)
**Population:** 347,000
**Capital:** Nassau (211,000)
**Main language spoken:** English
**Main religions:** Baptist, Roman Catholic, Anglican
**Currency:** Bahamian dollar
**Main exports:** petroleum, crayfish, machinery and transportation equipment, salt
**Type of government:** independent commonwealth

An island archipelago, the Bahamas are spread over 89,960 sq. mi. (233,000km²) of ocean, with the closest neighboring landmasses being the state of Florida and, to the south, Cuba. Most of the islands are low-lying with mangrove swamps and reefs around their edges. The islands have no rivers but contain many tropical plants including orchids and jasmine, as well as a rich bird life. Thousands of tourists are attracted to the Bahamas for the scenery, beaches, and warm climate. Average daily temperatures rarely slip below 64°F (18°C), even in the winter. Only around 40 of the 700 islands are inhabited. Andros is the largest island, while Grand Bahama has much of the Bahamas' industry, especially in Freeport. Over half of the Bahamas' population lives in Nassau, its capital. The islands have become a center for financial services.

◄ Beautiful palm-fringed beaches, clear seas, and a year-round warm climate attract visitors to the Bahamas.

# TURKS & CAICOS ISLANDS

The Turks & Caicos are two island groups whose cays and islands rise more than 6,560 ft. (2,000m) from the sea floor. They are a British crown colony.

**Area:** 165 sq. mi. (430km²)
**Population:** 33,000
**Capital:** Cockburn Town (5,000)
**Main language spoken:** English
**Main religions:** Anglican, Methodist
**Currency:** U.S. dollar
**Main exports:** salt, lobster, fish
**Type of government:** dependency of U.K.

The Turks & Caicos Islands are an extension of the Bahamas chain and consist of eight major islands and over 30 largely uninhabited cays. The two island groups are separated by a 22-mi.- (35-km-) wide trench called the Turks Island Passage, which is over 7,220 ft. (2,200m) deep. Much of the land is sandy and rocky and covered in scrubs and cacti. The climate is warm and constant, averaging between 75–90°F (24–32°C) throughout the year. Rainfall averages between 21–28 in. (54–72cm) per year, and drinking water is relatively scarce. Irrigation and careful management of the available water allow crops, including beans, corn, and citrus fruit, to be grown. In 1678 salt traders

from Bermuda started to clear much of the island to create salinas—salt-drying pans—in which salt was dried and then taken on ships and traded. Salt remained a key industry until the 1960s, but today tourism, fishing, and financial services are the main sources of revenue. In 2009 the U.K. suspended the islands' constitution and imposed direct rule after evidence of corruption.

# HAITI

**Occupying the western third of the tropical island of Hispaniola, Haiti has few natural resources, and agriculture forms the basis of its economy.**

**Area:** 10,710 sq. mi. (27,750km²)
**Population:** 9,923,000
**Capital:** Port-au-Prince (2,296,000)
**Main languages spoken:** Haitian Creole, French
**Main religions:** Roman Catholic, Protestant, voodoo
**Currency:** gourde
**Main exports:** textiles and clothing, handicrafts, coffee
**Government:** republic; limited democracy

Haiti is mountainous, with five distinct mountain ranges separated by deep valleys and plains. The lowland areas are densely populated, with around 80 percent of the country's population living in rural areas. Around one third of Haiti's land can be farmed, and most farms are small plots on which families grow only enough to feed themselves. The most common subsistence crops are corn, bananas, and cassava. Larger estates and plantations exist where crops, including coffee, sisal, and sugar, are grown for export. Much of Haiti's farmland suffers from soil erosion, and large tracts of its forest areas have been removed to create new farmlands and to produce charcoal. Ninety-five percent of its people are descendants of black slaves employed to grow sugarcane by the Spanish and the French colonial powers. In 1804 a slave revolt enabled Haiti to gain independence from France. In 2010 Haiti suffered a major earthquake that killed about 230,000 people and wrecked Port-au-Prince.

▶ Haitians are the poorest people in the entire Caribbean region, and many of them live in slums. Poverty is one reason for the country's long history of political instability.

# DOMINICAN REPUBLIC

**Occupying the western two thirds of Hispaniola, the Dominican Republic is the second-largest and second-most-populous country in the Caribbean.**

**Area:** 18,700 sq. mi. (48,433km²)
**Population:** 9,884,000
**Capital:** Santo Domingo (3,310,000)
**Main language spoken:** Spanish
**Main religion:** Roman Catholic
**Currency:** Dominican peso
**Main exports:** nickel, raw sugar, coffee, gold
**Government:** republic; democracy

The Dominican Republic is a mountainous country, with large areas of fertile lands in valleys between the peaks and in the lower-lying lands near the coast. A wide range of crops is grown on these lands, including tobacco, sugar, and cocoa. In 2000, 1.29 million tons of fruit and berries were harvested. The Dominican Republic has the largest and fastest-growing economy in the Caribbean. Large reserves of ores containing nickel and gold are mined, while construction and telecommunications industries have expanded at a rapid rate. Tourism has also increased in importance, with many vacation cruise ships stopping in its natural harbors. The country has established a number of free-trade zones within its borders. Overseas companies employ more than 200,000 people, making clothes, footwear, and electronic goods. The land was twice visited by Christopher Columbus, and the city of Santo Domingo was established in 1496 by his brother, Bartholomew. It is the oldest European settlement in the entire Americas. Today Santo Domingo is the capital of the Dominican Republic.

# PUERTO RICO

**The most easterly of the Greater Antilles Islands, Puerto Rico is a mountainous island with a tropical climate and rich plant life.**

**Area:** 3,425 sq. mi. (8,870km²)
**Population:** 3,954,000
**Capital:** San Juan (2,601,000)
**Main languages spoken:** Spanish, English
**Main religion:** Roman Catholic
**Currency:** U.S. dollar
**Main exports:** chemicals and chemical products, food, electronics, clothing
**Government:** dependency of U.S.

Puerto Rico is separated from the Dominican Republic by a stretch of the Caribbean called the Mona Passage. Part of a key shipping lane to and from the Panama Canal, the island has benefited from shipping and trade industries, especially since its capital city, San Juan, is located on the site of one of the largest natural harbors in the Caribbean. Around three fifths of the country is mountainous, with coastal lowlands in which dairy farming and coffee growing are the most important farming activities. The island was claimed by the explorer Christopher Columbus in 1493 and was a

▶ These Puerto Ricans are working in a rum distillery on the island. Rum uses sugar as its principal ingredient, and the alcoholic drink is exported to many countries.

Spanish colony until 1898, when the U.S. gained control. Many U.S. businesses have invested in the island, and the economy is increasingly reliant on manufacturing and service industries. Almost 90 percent of the island's exports go to the U.S.

---

# VIRGIN ISLANDS

**Lying east of Puerto Rico, these islands form the economically strong dependency of the U.S. and the smaller, less prosperous British Virgin Islands dependency.**

**Virgin Islands (U.S.)**

**Area:** 136 sq. mi. (352km²)
**Population:** 110,000
**Capital:** Charlotte Amalie (28,000)
**Main language spoken:** English
**Main religions:** Baptist, Roman Catholic
**Currency:** U.S. dollar
**Main exports:** refined petroleum, rum, watches, fragrances
**Type of government:** dependency of U.S.

**British Virgin Islands**

**Area:** 59 sq. mi. (153km²)
**Population:** 21,272
**Capital:** Road Town (8,500)
**Main language spoken:** English
**Main religions:** Anglican, Roman Catholic
**Currency:** U.S. dollar
**Main exports:** fish, gravel, fruit
**Type of government:** self-governing dependency of U.K.

The capital of the British Virgin Islands, Road Town, is on its largest island, Tortola. Most of the islands are of volcanic origin, with the exception of the second-largest, Anegada, which is a coral and limestone atoll. The islanders engage in rum making, raising livestock, and fishing, but tourism accounts for three fourths of revenue. The economy of the U.S. Virgin Islands is also largely based on tourism, with more than one million visitors per year. Bought from Denmark by the U.S. in 1917, the U.S. Virgin Islands consist of many small, hilly, volcanic islands. A giant oil refinery located on St. Croix accounts for almost all of the islands' exports.

# ST. KITTS & NEVIS

The first British colonies in the Caribbean since the 1620s, St. Kitts & Nevis is a federation formed by a pair of islands separated by a 2-mi.- (3-km-) wide channel.

**Area:** 104 sq. mi. (269km²)
**Population:** 46,000
**Capital:** Basseterre (17,000)
**Main languages spoken:** English, English Creole
**Main religion:** Protestant
**Currency:** East Caribbean dollar
**Main exports:** electronic goods, foodstuffs, electronics
**Type of government:** constitutional monarchy

Both the islands of St. Kitts & Nevis were formed by volcanic activity, and both feature a high volcanic peak at their center. The islands bask in a tropical climate with high rainfall, but both have been hit by a number of hurricanes that have caused widespread damage. Although much land has been cleared for farming, there are large areas of rain forests, wetlands, and grasslands in which a great variety of plants and creatures live. St. Kitts & Nevis has little mineral or energy resources. Almost all fuel for energy has to be imported, mainly in the form of oil from Mexico and Venezuela. St. Kitts, the larger of the two islands, is also the home

of the federation's capital, Basseterre, which is an important port and receives much trade from cruise ships. The city of Basseterre is a financial and industrial center for the eastern Caribbean. Charlestown is the largest town on Nevis. Once inhabited by Carib and Arawak Indians, the population of St. Kitts & Nevis is now almost entirely of African or mixed African-European descent. The islands gained independence from Great Britain in 1983, and in 1998 a vote for Nevis to withdraw from the federation just failed to gain the necessary two-thirds majority.

---

# ANGUILLA & MONTSERRAT

Anguilla is a flat limestone coral island, while Montserrat is more mountainous and features seven active volcanoes. Both are British dependencies.

**Anguilla**

**Area:** 37 sq. mi. (96km²)
**Population:** 11,600
**Capital:** The Valley (1,200)
**Main languages spoken:** English, Creole
**Main religions:** Anglican, Roman Catholic
**Currency:** East Caribbean dollar
**Main exports:** lobsters, fish, livestock, salt
**Type of government:** dependency of U.K.

**Montserrat**

**Area:** 38 sq. mi. (98km²)
**Population:** 9,300
**Temporary capital:** Brades (200)
**Main language spoken:** English
**Main religions:** Anglican, Methodist
**Currency:** East Caribbean dollar
**Main exports:** electronic components, food, cattle
**Type of government:** dependency of U.K.

First occupied by British settlers in 1650, the present-day population of Anguilla is mainly descendants of African and European peoples. Anguilla's income is derived from lobster fishing, salt mining, and tourism. It has a dry, sunny climate.

Montserrat's economy has been more varied than Anguilla's, with vegetable farming, cotton growing, and

manufacturing industries. The island is dominated by a series of active volcanoes. In 1997 eruptions of the Soufrière Hills volcano east of the capital, Plymouth, destroyed the town. Brades is now the temporary capital. Refugees from the eruption have now largely returned to Montserrat.

# ANTIGUA & BARBUDA

**Colonized by Great Britain from the 1600s before becoming independent in 1981, Antigua & Barbuda is a nation almost totally dependent on tourism for its income.**

Codrington • Barbuda

**ANTIGUA & BARBUDA**   *ATLANTIC OCEAN*

**ST. JOHN'S**

*Caribbean Sea*   All Saints • Antigua

**Area:** 171 sq. mi. (442km2)
**Population:** 77,000
**Capital:** St. John's (45,000)
**Main languages spoken:** English, English Creole
**Main religion:** Anglican
**Currency:** East Caribbean dollar
**Main exports:** re-exported petroleum products, fruit
**Type of government:** constitutional monarchy

Antigua & Barbuda consist of three islands. Antigua is by far the most important, being the largest and where an estimated 98 percent of the population live. The remainder inhabit Barbuda, a low-lying coral island, while a tiny third island lies uninhabited. Unlike most of the other members of the Leeward Islands group, Antigua has no forests, few trees, and no rivers. With only a few springs, droughts occur, even though approximately 40 in. (100cm) of rain falls every year. Few native animals exist, but the islands are home to over 100 species of birds. After the closure of the sugar farming industry in the 1970s the islands have come to depend on their beaches to lure tourists, as well as developing a finance and banking industry. Two military bases on Antigua have been leased to the U.S. Ninety percent of Antigua & Barbuda's population are the descendants of black slaves brought to the islands. Light industry, assembling goods for export, has been encouraged by the government.

# GUADELOUPE

**Two contrasting islands, one a high-peaked volcanic island, the other a lower-lying coral island, form the majority of the land of Guadeloupe.**

*Guadeloupe (to France)*   *ATLANTIC OCEAN*

Grande-Terre   La Désirade

Sainte-Rose •   Les Abymes
Pointe-à-Pitre •
*Basse-Terre*   Le Gosier
Basse-Terre •   Soufrière △ 4,812 ft.   *Marie-Galante*
*Caribbean Sea*   • Grand-Bourg
Les Saintes

**Area:** 629 sq. mi. (1,628km2)
**Population:** 401,000
**Capital:** Basse-Terre (46,000)
**Main language spoken:** French
**Main religion:** Roman Catholic
**Currency:** euro
**Main exports:** bananas, sugar, rum
**Type of government:** dependency of France

Guadeloupe is an archipelago made up of two major islands, Basse-Terre and Grande-Terre, and many smaller islands. On Basse-Terre the summit of the active volcano, Soufrière, is one of the wettest landmarks in the Caribbean and can receive more than 315 in. (800cm) of rain in a year. In contrast the coastal areas of the islands receive around 51 in. (130cm). While Basse-Terre is home to the capital, Grande-Terre is more heavily populated, with Pointe-à-Pitre the main port and commercial center. Guadeloupe depends heavily on tourism and aid from France.

The Guadeloupe archipelago is part of the Lesser Antilles island group. The islands of St.-Martin and St.-Barthélemy, 137 mi. (220km) to the north, were ruled from Guadeloupe but they became separate French dependencies in 2007.

# DOMINICA

A mountainous, volcanic island with many hot springs, Dominica has a great variety of wildlife and a large number of protected parks and reserves.

**Area:** 285 sq. mi. (739km²)
**Population:** 71,000
**Capital:** Roseau (20,000)
**Main languages spoken:** English, French patois
**Main religions:** Roman Catholic, Protestant
**Currency:** East Caribbean dollar
**Main exports:** bananas, soap, fresh vegetables, limes, coconuts
**Type of government:** parliamentary democracy

A high ridge forms the backbone of Dominica, which slopes down toward the sea and contains more than 300 rivers and streams. The mountains are covered in dense woodlands, thickets, and rain forests, much of which is protected in a series of national parks and reserves. Dominica has a varied plant and animal life, with more than 130 species of birds. Many creatures, including opossums, iguanas, crabs, and freshwater shrimp, are collected as food.

Much of the island's electricity is generated from a hydroelectric plant found in the center of the island. Dominica was one of the few Caribbean islands whose native Indian inhabitants managed to stop becoming a colony of a European nation until the late 1700s. Around 3,000 descendants of the Carib Indians still live on the island.

# MARTINIQUE

Martinique is one of the most beautiful and rugged islands in the Caribbean, with volcanic peaks, dense rain forests in the mountains, and narrow, fertile valleys.

**Area:** 436 sq. mi. (1,128km²)
**Population:** 398,000
**Capital:** Fort-de-France (133,000)
**Main language spoken:** French
**Main religion:** Roman Catholic
**Currency:** euro
**Main exports:** bananas, refined petroleum, rum
**Type of government:** dependency of France

The island of Martinique has an average elevation of more than 2,950 ft. (900m) above sea level. Narrow plains around the coast and a plain in the center of the island are the only flat areas. Its highest point, the volcano Montagne Pelée, destroyed the town of St. Pierre, killing more than 28,000 people in 1902. Around one third of the island remains covered in forests, with large amounts of tropical hardwoods. Colonized by the French in 1635, the island remains a dependency of France. France maintains an oil refinery on the island in which crude oil from Venezuela and Trinidad & Tobago is processed and shipped elsewhere. The majority of its population are of either African or mixed African-European descent. Agriculture and service industries, particularly tourism, are the main sources of income.

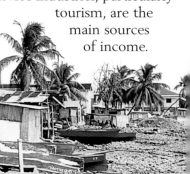

# ST. LUCIA

**Explored by Spain and then France, the volcanic island of St. Lucia became a British territory in 1814 and became independent in 1979.**

**Area:** 238 sq. mi. (617km²)
**Population:** 158,000
**Capital:** Castries (61,000)
**Main languages spoken:** English, French patois
**Main religion:** Roman Catholic, Protestant
**Currency:** East Caribbean dollar
**Main exports:** bananas, other foodstuffs, live animals, clothing
**Type of government:** parliamentary democracy

St. Lucia's mountains are heavily wooded and contain many fast-moving streams and rivers. The legacy of its volcanic origins can be found at many points around the island. A volcanic crater and bubbling mud pools releasing sulfur gases are found in Soufrière, a town that is overlooked by twin volcanic peaks. To the south of the island lies an area that contains a chain of 18 volcanic domes and a number of craters. The island has many fine beaches, some of which are covered in black volcanic sand in the southwest. St. Lucia is one of the larger banana producers in the Caribbean. The seas around the island are fished heavily—in 2005, almost 1,650 tons (1,500 metric tonnes) of fish, such as tuna, dolphin, and kingfish, were caught.

▼ Overlooking Jalousie Plantation harbor on the western side of St. Lucia are the Pitons. These two volcanic domes have elevations of 2,618 ft. (798m) and 2,460 ft. (750m).

# ST. VINCENT & THE GRENADINES

**St. Vincent & the Grenadines consist of one main island, St. Vincent, and the northern part of the chain of 600 islands and islets called the Grenadines.**

**Area:** 150 sq. mi. (389km²)
**Population:** 103,000
**Capital:** Kingstown (26,000)
**Main languages spoken:** English, French patois
**Main religions:** Anglican, Methodist, Roman Catholic
**Currency:** East Caribbean dollar
**Main exports:** bananas, flour
**Type of government:** constitutional monarchy

The island of St. Vincent makes up 89 percent of the area and 95 percent of the population of the nation. The island is rugged with little flat land, and its northern one third is dominated by an active volcano called Soufrière, which erupted a number of times during the 1900s. The central and southern sections of the island fall sharply from mountainous heights to the sea, with rocky cliffs and black sand beaches on the eastern side. Most of the islands of the Grenadines are less rugged and tend to be surrounded by coral reefs. Several of the Grenadines, including Mustique and Bequia, have become exclusive resort islands for

◄ On Dominica fishermen use seine nets to catch schools of fish that swim near beaches.

wealthy foreign visitors. Bananas are the most important farm crop, and there are also small food-processing, cement, clothing, and rum-making industries. St. Vincent & the Grenadines is less wealthy than many of its neighbors, and high unemployment has led to emigration, which continues.

# BARBADOS

**The most easterly of all Caribbean islands, Barbados is around 21 mi. (34km) long, with an economy based on agriculture, tourism, and other service industries.**

**Area:** 166 sq. mi. (430km²)
**Population:** 272,000
**Capital:** Bridgetown (92,000)
**Main languages spoken:** English, Bajan (English Creole)
**Main religions:** Roman Catholic, Protestant
**Currency:** Barbados dollar
**Main exports:** sugar, chemicals, food and beverages, manufactures
**Type of government:** parliamentary democracy

Barbados is formed from coral limestone and is largely flat with a few rolling hills in the north. The west coast has a number of white-sand beaches, while the east coast has a rocky shoreline. Sugarcane production now accounts for less than half of the cultivated land. Oil found on the island provides around one third of the country's energy needs. Founded in 1628, Bridgetown is the island's capital and commercial port. Ninety percent of the population are of African descent, and roughly one third of Barbados' people, known as Bajans, live in or around Bridgetown. The original inhabitants of Barbados were Arawak Indians, who are believed to have been driven off the island by the warlike Carib Indians around 1200. The island lay deserted until a colony was established in 1627 by British settlers. Barbados has been independent from the U.K. since 1966, and tourism now employs one third of the workforce. Remnants of traditional British customs and buildings have earned it the nickname "Little England" by its Caribbean neighbors.

► Cars head through an arch in Bridgetown, the capital of Barbados and the island's largest port.

# GRENADA

**Grenada consists of one major island and several of the southern Grenadine islands, including Carriacou. It is famous for its spices and agricultural produce.**

**Area:** 133 sq. mi. (344km²)
**Population:** 103,000
**Capital:** St. George's (37,000)
**Main languages spoken:** English, French patois
**Main religions:** Roman Catholic, Protestant
**Currency:** East Caribbean dollar
**Main exports:** fish, cocoa, nutmeg, bananas, clothing
**Type of government:** parliamentary democracy

Grenada's geography is quite varied, with a hilly interior covered in lush vegetation, deep valleys through which fast-flowing streams run, several mountain lakes, and 45 beaches around its coastline. Its tropical climate features 60 in. (150cm) of rainfall per year on its coasts and more than double that amount on the mountain slopes. Created by volcanic activity, the island has a rich, black soil in which many crops flourish. Grenada is known in the Caribbean as the "Isle of Spice" and is the world's largest producer of nutmeg and mace. It also produces large amounts of cinnamon, cloves, pepper, and ginger. Limes, cocoa, and bananas are also grown. Grenada was a French colony from 1650 until it was captured by British forces in 1762. Gaining independence in 1974, two military coups, one in 1979, the second in 1983, were followed by U.S. forces invading the island and establishing a new government. Tourism has since become important after an international airport was built in Point Salines near the capital, St. George's.

▲ A plantation worker separates strands of the spice mace from cloves.

# TRINIDAD & TOBAGO

One of the few Caribbean nations with oil reserves, the two islands of Trinidad & Tobago are the most southerly islands in the Caribbean.

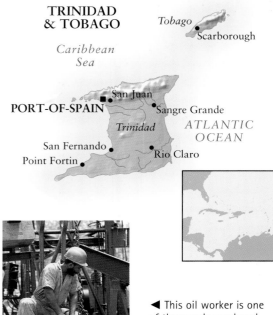

**Area:** 1,980 sq. mi. (5,128km²)
**Population:** 1,262,000
**Capital:** Port-of-Spain (303,000)
**Main languages spoken:** English, English Creole
**Main religions:** Roman Catholic, Protestant, Hindu
**Currency:** Trinidad & Tobago dollar
**Main exports:** petroleum, ammonia, iron, steel
**Type of government:** parliamentary democracy

L ying close to the coast of Venezuela, where the Orinoco river empties into the Atlantic Ocean, Trinidad is a geological extension of South America. Trinidad's major resources are fossil fuels. Large reserves of oil and natural gas have been exploited both on the island and just offshore. In the southwest of the island lies one of the world's largest sources of natural asphalt, used for road building. Unlike most Caribbean nations, Trinidad & Tobago's population come from a great range of backgrounds. Those of African and East Asian descent each form around 40 percent. There are also many people of European, Chinese, and South American origin.

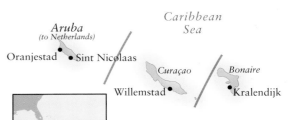

◀ This oil worker is one of thousands employed in Trinidad's 30 oil fields. In 2007 these fields produced a combined output of 59.6 million barrels.

# ARUBA, CURAÇAO, & SINT-MAARTEN

Aruba, Curaçao, and Sint-Maarten are countries making up part of the Netherlands. All have limited natural resources but flourishing tourist industries.

### Aruba

**Area:** 75 sq. mi. (193km²)
**Population:** 106,000
**Capital:** Oranjestad (26,000)
**Main languages spoken:** Papiamento, Dutch
**Main religion:** Roman Catholic
**Currency:** Aruban florin
**Main exports:** live animals, art objects, electrical equipment
**Type of government:** self-governing dependency of the Netherlands

### Curaçao

**Area:** 171 sq. mi. (444km²)
**Population:** 142,000
**Capital:** Willemstad (119,000)
**Main languages spoken:** Papiamento, Dutch
**Main religion:** Roman Catholic
**Currency:** Curaçao florin
**Main exports:** petroleum products, consumer goods
**Type of government:** self-governing dependency of the Netherlands

### Sint-Maarten

**Area:** 13 sq. mi. (34 km²)
**Population:** 41,000
**Capital:** Philipsburg (29,000)
**Main languages spoken:** English, Dutch
**Main religion:** Protestant Church in the Netherlands
**Currency:** Sint-Maarten florin
**Main exports:** re-exported goods, mainly consumer goods
**Type of government:** self-governing dependency of the Netherlands

T hese three countries, found in the Lesser Antilles, have all recently become self-governing dependencies of the Netherlands. Aruba and Curaçao are islands, while Sint-Maarten is the southern half of the island of St. Martin (the northern half is a French dependency).

Other Dutch islands in the Caribbean include Curaçao's neighboring island, Bonaire, and Saba and St. Eustatius (see map on page 99).

▶ Willemstad, with its Dutch-style buildings, is the main town on Curaçao.

# SOUTH AMERICA

South America is the fourth-largest continent, with a total surface area of 6,878,024 sq. mi. (17,814,000km²). It extends from the Caribbean Sea southward, a distance of 4,600 mi. (7,400km), to Cape Horn, and its maximum width is 3,200 mi. (5,160km). The Brazilian Shield and the smaller Guyana Shield to the north, as well as the Patagonian Shield to the southwest, are the oldest geological parts of the continent. Running along the entire western edge of the continent is the much younger Andes mountain range, with many peaks more than 19,685 ft. (6,000m). A large part of the interior is a series of basins in which three large rivers—the Amazon, the Orinoco, and the Paraguay-Paraná—drain much of the continent's water into the Atlantic Ocean. The largest lowland region of South America is the enormous Amazon basin, the world's largest river basin, covering an area of more around 2.7 million sq. mi. (seven million km²). Much of its extent is covered in lush, tropical rain forests. South America has been inhabited for many thousands of years with advanced native cultures, including the Chavin, Moche, Chimu, and Inca civilizations. South America's population more than doubled between 1960 and 2000, and in 2009 the continent's population was 394.4 million.

▲ These small houses are made of adobe mud bricks and lie on the shore of Lake Titicaca, which straddles the border between Bolivia and Peru.

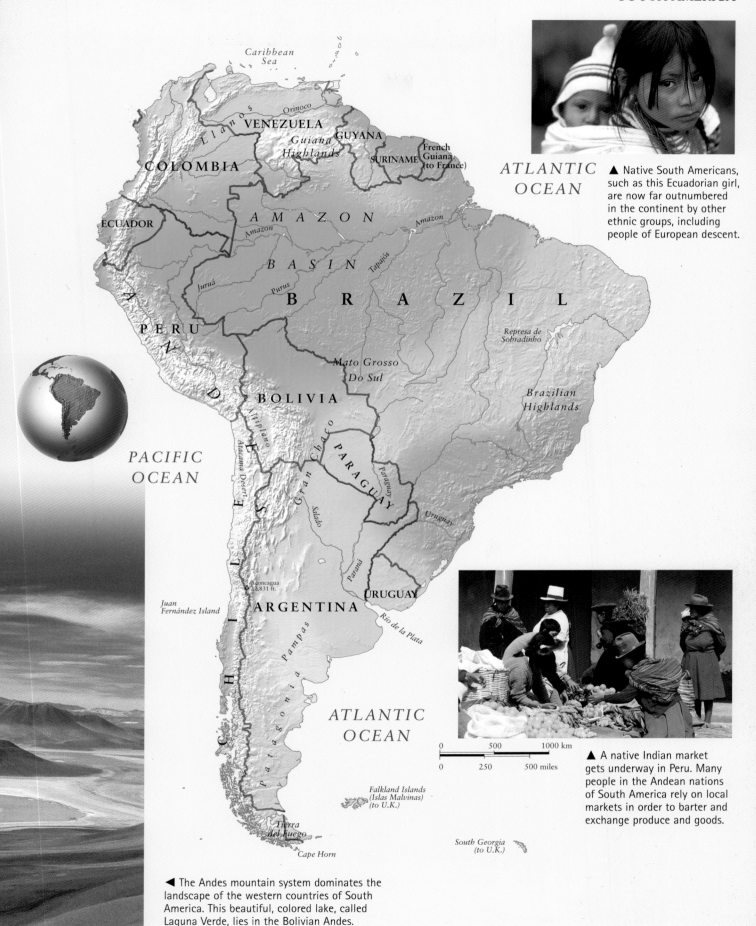

Caribbean
Sea

*Orinoco*

*Llanos*

VENEZUELA   GUYANA

*Guiana
Highlands*   SURINAME   French
Guiana
(to France)

COLOMBIA

ECUADOR

A M A Z O N

*Amazon*   *Amazon*

B A S I N

*Juruá*   *Purus*   *Tapajós*

B R A Z I L

P E R U

*Represa de
Sobradinho*

*Mato Grosso
Do Sul*

*Brazilian
Highlands*

BOLIVIA

*Altiplano*

*Atacama Desert*

A   N   D   E   S

*Gran Chaco*

PARAGUAY

*Paraguay*

*Salado*

*Uruguay*

*Paraná*

ATLANTIC
OCEAN

▲ Native South Americans,
such as this Ecuadorian girl,
are now far outnumbered
in the continent by other
ethnic groups, including
people of European descent.

PACIFIC
OCEAN

△ Aconcagua
22,831 ft.

*Juan
Fernández Island*

ARGENTINA

URUGUAY

*Río de la Plata*

*Patagonia*   *Pampas*

C   H   I   L   E

ATLANTIC
OCEAN

0        500       1000 km
0    250      500 miles

▲ A native Indian market
gets underway in Peru. Many
people in the Andean nations
of South America rely on local
markets in order to barter and
exchange produce and goods.

*Falkland Islands
(Islas Malvinas)
(to U.K.)*

*Tierra
del Fuego*

Cape Horn

*South Georgia
(to U.K.)*

◄ The Andes mountain system dominates the
landscape of the western countries of South
America. This beautiful, colored lake, called
Laguna Verde, lies in the Bolivian Andes.

113

# NORTHERN SOUTH AMERICA

Northern South America is the widest part of the continent and includes the world's highest navigable lake, Lake Titicaca, which forms part of the border between Peru and Bolivia. It also includes the world's highest waterfalls in Venezuela and the mighty Amazon river. Second only to the Nile as the world's longest river, the Amazon drains a region of 2,722,020 sq. mi. (7,050000km²). The rain forests that cover the lands surrounding the river and its tributaries are some of the last major wild regions in the world and contain the richest range of species of living things found anywhere on Earth. Brazil is the dominant country in terms of land area, population, and economic importance. It shares a border with every country in the region, with the exception of Ecuador and Chile. The lands bordering the Atlantic Ocean were the first to be explored and claimed as colonies of European nations. Although all of continental South America is now independent, with the exception of French Guiana, its colonial heritage is evident. English, Dutch, French, and Portuguese are the official languages of Guyana, Suriname, French Guiana, and Brazil respectively, while Spanish is the official language of the other nations.

▲ Around half of Ecuador's entire population are native Indians. The majority of native Indian peoples in northern South America can be found in the Andean countries of Peru, Bolivia, Colombia, and Ecuador.

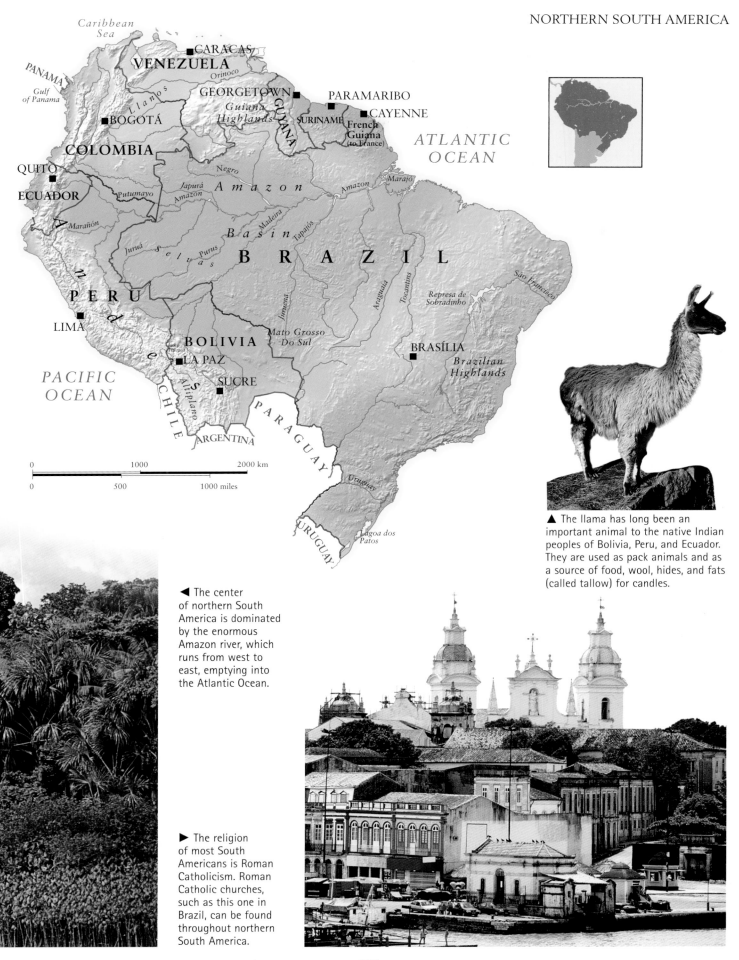

*Caribbean Sea*

**VENEZUELA**

CARACAS

*Orinoco*

PANAMA

*Gulf of Panama*

BOGOTÁ

*Llanos*

GEORGETOWN

*Guiana Highlands*

GUYANA

PARAMARIBO

SURINAME

CAYENNE

French Guiana (to France)

**COLOMBIA**

QUITO

**ECUADOR**

*ATLANTIC OCEAN*

*Marañón*

*Negro*

*Amazon*

*Japurá*

*Amazón*

*Putumayo*

*Amazon*

*Marajó*

A

n

d

e

s

**P E R U**

*B a s i n*

*Juruá*

*Selvas*

*Purus*

*Madeira*

*Tapajós*

**B R A Z I L**

*Xingu*

*Araguaia*

*Tocantins*

*São Francisco*

*Represa de Sobradinho*

LIMA

*Titicaca*

**BOLIVIA**

LA PAZ

SUCRE

*Altiplano*

*Mato Grosso Do Sul*

BRASÍLIA

*Brazilian Highlands*

*PACIFIC OCEAN*

CHILE

A

n

d

e

s

PARAGUAY

ARGENTINA

*Uruguay*

URUGUAY

*Lagoa dos Patos*

| 0 | 1000 | 2000 km |
|---|---|---|

| 0 | 500 | 1000 miles |
|---|---|---|

▲ The llama has long been an important animal to the native Indian peoples of Bolivia, Peru, and Ecuador. They are used as pack animals and as a source of food, wool, hides, and fats (called tallow) for candles.

◄ The center of northern South America is dominated by the enormous Amazon river, which runs from west to east, emptying into the Atlantic Ocean.

► The religion of most South Americans is Roman Catholicism. Roman Catholic churches, such as this one in Brazil, can be found throughout northern South America.

# VENEZUELA

**During the 1900s Venezuela underwent a transformation from one of the poorest South American countries to one of the wealthiest.**

**Area:** 352,145 sq. mi. (912,050km²)
**Population:** 28,384,000
**Capital:** Caracas (3,875,000)
**Main language spoken:** Spanish
**Main religion:** Roman Catholic
**Currency:** bolivar
**Main exports:** petroleum and petroleum products, basic manufactured goods, bauxite, aluminum, chemicals
**Type of government:** federal republic; limited democracy

▼ The flat, grassed plains of the Llanos in central Venezuela provide good grazing ground for large livestock herds. The cattle ranchers, or cowboys, are called *llaneros*.

Venezuela shares borders with Brazil to the south, Colombia to the west, and Guyana to the east. Its coastline meets the Caribbean Sea in the northern part of the country and the Atlantic Ocean to the east, in which around 70 islands belonging to Venezuela lie. Mainland Venezuela has a number of geographical regions. In the center are low-lying plains covered in grassland vegetation called the Llanos. The rugged granite Guiana Highlands are situated in the south and southeast and are only sparsely inhabited. Much of the northern portion of Venezuela is made up of a series of narrow coastal plains and large mountains, including two branches of the Andes. These define part of the Venezuela-Colombia border and include the country's highest peak, Pico Bolivar (16,427 ft./ 5,007m). In between these two mountain ranges lie the swampy lowlands surrounding Lake Maracaibo. Most of the Llanos and Guiana Highlands are drained by the 1,700-mi.- (2,740-km-) long Orinoco river.

▼ An oil terminal on the edge of Lake Maracaibo. Although Venezuela has many other mineral resources, crude and refined oil account for almost four fifths of the revenue made through exports.

## OIL AND LAKE MARACAIBO

Lake Maracaibo is actually a large inlet of the Caribbean Sea lying in northwestern Venezuela. It extends southward from the Gulf of Venezuela for approximately 130 mi. (210km). Many rivers flow into this stretch of water, some of which are also important transportation routes for ships. The waters in the northern part of Lake Maracaibo are salty and stagnant since the tides mix seawater with freshwater. In the southern portion of the lake the water is fresh. A 5-mi. (8-km) bridge spans the

▼ Angel Falls is the waterfall with the highest drop in the world. The falls, which are located in the Guiana Highlands, drop a long 3,212 ft. (979m).

outlet of the lake. The discovery of oil reserves in and around the lake has transformed the Venezuelan economy. The first productive oil well was drilled in 1914, and many foreign-owned companies helped develop the oil fields until the oil industry was nationalized in 1975. The oil reserves are immense and are one of the largest supplies outside of the Middle East. Venezuela produces 2.6 million barrels of oil per day, and oil refining, processing, and shipping industries have developed around the area. Two large cities, Cabimas—on the shoreline of Lake Maracaibo—and the port of Maracaibo, have flourished as a result.

117

▲ The Orinoco river flows from the Guiana Highlands through the Llanos before emptying into the Atlantic Ocean.

▼ Caracas is a modern-day city with towering office blocks, yet large shantytowns housing the poor can be found on the nearby hills.

## HISTORY AND PEOPLE

Venezuela was inhabited by native Indian peoples for many centuries before the arrival of European explorers and settlers. Until the early 1800s Venezuela was controlled by Spain, which imported Asian and African slaves to work the lands. An independence movement grew in the late 1600s and early 1700s. Led by the Venezuelan general Simón Bolivar, victory was finally achieved over Spanish forces in 1821. Venezuela, along with Ecuador and Colombia, became the republic of Great Colombia. In 1830 Venezuela withdrew from Great Colombia and became an independent nation. The population of Venezuela reflects its colonial past, with people of mixed Native American and European descent (mestizos) making up two thirds of the population. Unmixed Native Americans comprise only two percent of the population. A small number of Native Americans still maintain their traditional way of life deep in Venezuela's forests. The most notable group is the Yanomami, who live in the remote forests of the Orinoco river basin in southern Venezuela and across the border in northern Brazil. There are between 10,000 and 17,000 Yanomami in existence; around one third of the population died in skirmishes with gold prospectors and miners in the 1970s or from diseases introduced by these outsiders. In 1991 Brazil set up a 36,000-sq.-mi. (93,000-km²) homeland for the Yanomami, but many remain inside Venezuela's borders.

## CITY DWELLERS

Venezuela is a country of huge tracts of uncultivated land. Grasslands occupy half of the country, and different types of forests cover around two fifths. Less than five percent of the land is cultivated, although this farmland produces large amounts of staple crops, including bananas, corn, and rice. Around 15 million cattle, 4.5 million pigs, and 4 million goats are also raised. The majority of Venezuela's people live in cities and towns—around 93 percent of the population live in urban areas. The largest city is the capital, Caracas, which has existed for more than four centuries.

# GUYANA

**Guyana means "land of many waters" in local native Indian language, reflecting the many rivers that cross its area. It gained independence from the U.K. in 1966.**

**Area:** 83,044 sq. mi. (215,083km²)
**Population:** 751,000
**Capital:** Georgetown (138,000)
**Main languages spoken:** English, Amerindian dialects
**Main religions:** Christian, Hinduism, Islam
**Currency:** Guyanan dollar
**Main exports:** sugar, gold, rice, bauxite, timber
**Type of government:** republic

Guyana is a country of dense interior rain forests, many parts of which have been barely touched by humans. Ninety percent of its people live on a relatively narrow coastal plain bordering the Atlantic Ocean. Parts of this plain have been formed by land reclaimed from the sea, creating over 120 mi. (200km) of dikes and canals. Rice, sugar, coconuts, corn, and coffee are grown on the coastal plain, which is never more than 40 mi. (64km) wide. Guyana's longest river is the Essequibo, which measures 628 mi. (1,010km) and is partly navigable by small boats along stretches of its length. Diamond-digging industries occur on parts of many of Guyana's rivers, while mining for bauxite is Guyana's chief mineral resource. The Dutch were the first colonial power to reach Guyana, where they established settlements along the Essequibo river in 1615. They grew a range of crops, including sugarcane and cocoa, and imported slaves from Africa. During the early 1800s Great Britain took over the Dutch colonies of Berbice, Demerara, and Essequibo, which became British Guiana in 1831. Slavery was outlawed in 1834, and the great need for plantation workers led to a large influx of immigrants, mainly from the Indian subcontinent. Today around half of the population is of East Indian descent, and around 43 percent are of African descent.

▲ A Guyanan forestry worker in the process of felling a tree. Forests cover around four fifths of the country's land.

► Situated in central Guyana, Kaieteur Falls is between 295–344 ft. (90–105m) at its top and falls 741 ft. (226m). Over time the falls have eroded a gorge around 5 mi. (8km) long.

# SURINAME

**Previously called Dutch Guiana, the independent republic of Suriname has a small population that is one of the most varied in South America.**

**Area:** 63,040 sq. mi. (163,270km²)
**Population:** 493,000
**Capital:** Paramaribo (243,000)
**Main languages spoken:** Dutch, Sranang English, Hindustani
**Main religions:** Protestant, Roman Catholic, Islam
**Currency:** Surinamese guilder
**Main exports:** bauxite, shrimp and fish, rice, aluminum, petroleum
**Type of government:** republic

▼ Suriname's largest industry, the mining, processing, and exporting of the aluminum ore bauxite, forms the basis of its economy. Here barges carrying bauxite arrive at Suralco refinery.

Suriname consists of three distinct geographical areas: a coastal plain that is narrow and marshy in places, a small plateau area that is covered in savanna grasslands and forests, and a large tract of dense rain forests. The rain forest makes up around 90 percent of the country, and few roads penetrate it. Unlike its immediate neighbors, French Guiana to the east and Guyana to the west, Suriname has a number of huge lakes, including one of the largest artificial lakes in South America just south of Brokopondo, created by damming a river for hydroelectric power. Only a small portion of Suriname's land is used for agriculture, with rice being the major crop. The English established plantations on the banks of the Suriname river in 1651 and founded the settlement on which Suriname's capital city, Paramaribo, now lies. In 1667 England and the Netherlands exchanged lands in the Americas. The English swapped their territories in Suriname. In exchange they received the territory of New Amsterdam, which is now known as New York City. The Dutch imported many slaves to work on plantations, not just from Africa but from many parts of Asia, and this has given the country its varied cultural background. Around 37 percent of the population are Asian Indians, while 31 percent are Creoles, and 15 percent are of Indonesian origin. There are also populations of Chinese and the descendants of Africans and native people. The Netherlands granted Suriname independence in 1975 but remains a major aid donor, providing 80 percent of Suriname's tourists. Many Surinamese have emigrated to the Netherlands. Before 1991 the country suffered from a lack of political stability, with the military often intervening in affairs.

# FRENCH GUIANA

**An overseas dependency of France, French Guiana consists of a narrow belt of flat land at the coast that rises to higher ground blanketed in lush rain forests.**

**Area:** 33,400 sq. mi. (86,504km²)
**Population:** 213,000
**Capital:** Cayenne (77,000)
**Main language spoken:** French
**Main religion:** Roman Catholic
**Currency:** euro
**Main exports:** timber and wood products, bauxite
**Type of government:** dependency of France

French Guiana is situated on the northeast coast of South America and is bordered by Brazil to the south and the east and by Suriname to the west. An area bounded by the Maroni river is under dispute between Suriname and French Guiana. Most of the country is covered in rain forests that rise from low elevations near the coast to mountains that lie on the frontier with Brazil. The rain-forest region is largely uninhabited by humans but has a rich variety of wildlife, including many species of monkeys, tapirs, anteaters, ocelots, and caimans, a relative of the crocodile family. French Guiana has a tropical climate with high humidity and heavy rainfall, especially in its interior. The heaviest rain falls from January to June, and the average rainfall in the country's capital, Cayenne, on the coast, is approximately 150 in. (380cm). Cayenne is the country's largest town and its chief port. French Guiana exports bananas, sugar, aluminum ores, and timber. With only one percent of the country's land devoted to agriculture, many foods have to be imported.

The French first established a colony in Cayenne in 1637, and French Guiana remains the last remaining colony on mainland South America. From 1852 until the 1950s it was notorious as the place where France sent its most hardened convicts. Penal colonies were established in Cayenne and on a nearby small islet in the Atlantic Ocean known as Devil's Island. Most of French Guiana's population live near the coast and are people of mixed white, Native American, and black African origin called creoles. Small numbers of Native Americans live in the rain forests and highlands of the country's interior, which is largely untouched by modern life.

▲ Almost nine tenths of French Guiana are covered in rain forests that provide timber, oils, fibers, and foods for many of the dependency's population.

▲ An *Ariane 4* rocket blasts off from Kourou satellite launch base in French Guiana in May 2002. Kourou is the launch site for European Space Agency projects, and the town nearby has grown to become the third largest in French Guiana.

121

# COLOMBIA

**Colombia is troubled politically, but it is a country blessed with rich wildlife, fertile land, and large mineral resources.**

**Area:** 440,762 sq. mi. (1,141,568km²)
**Population:** 44,978,000
**Capital:** Bogotá (8,494,000)
**Main language spoken:** Spanish
**Main religion:** Roman Catholic
**Currency:** Colombian peso
**Main exports:** petroleum products, coffee, chemicals, clothing, cut flowers. (The illegal export of cocaine and marijuana produces much revenue.)
**Type of government:** republic; limited democracy

Colombia's short border with the southernmost part of Panama marks the northern end of the South American continent. The western part of the country is mostly mountainous with three large ranges from the Andes mountain system: the Cordillera Occidental, Central, and Oriental. Between the three ranges are several large valleys. The Magdalena river flows north through the eastern part of these valleys. In addition to the three chains of Andes Mountains, the landscape of the western part of Colombia is also marked by an isolated mountain range to the north of the region. Containing Colombia's highest peak, Pico Cristóbal Colón (18,942 ft./ 5,775m), it is the highest coastal mountain range in the world. More than half of Colombia consists of lowland areas. The more northerly lowlands are the Llanos, which are the low-lying plains that run east into and throughout much of Venezuela. South of the Llanos are further lowlands that form part of the Amazon river basin and tend to be covered in thick rain forests. Many of the region's rivers provide a key—and sometimes only—transportation link to isolated areas in the lowlands.

## COLOMBIA'S CLIMATE

Colombia's climate is mainly tropical with not much change throughout the year since the country lies close to the equator. However, there is a lot of variation in temperature and rainfall based on altitude and also based on location near the mountain ranges, some of which cast a rain shadow over nearby lowlands. Above around 9,840 ft. (3,000m) the climate is cold, with temperatures ranging from 0–55°F (-18– 13°C). Mountain peaks in the Andes that extend above 14,760 ft. (4,500m) are permanently capped in snow and ice. Generally Colombia receives moderate to heavy rainfall with no completely dry season.

◀ Colombia's capital city, Bogotá, sprawls over a sloping plain at the base of two mountains. The city features two of the oldest universities in South America: the University of Santo Tomás (founded in 1580) and the Xavier Pontifical University (founded in 1622).

▼ A large coffee plantation near the city of Manizales in western Colombia. Founded in 1848, Manizales is a major trading and transportation center for coffee, cocoa, and gold.

▲ This stone statue, one of several hundred created by an unknown civilization, is located in San Augustin Archaeological Park near the source of the Magdalena river.

### RICH PLANT AND ANIMAL LIFE

Colombia is home to a huge range of plant and animal life and is considered one of the most biodiverse countries in the world. More than 130,000 species of plants have been identified within its borders, and it has as many different animal species as Brazil, which is ten times its size. Larger creatures include the jaguar, spectacled bear, ocelot, tapir, and many species of monkeys. Colombia also has more than 1,500 bird species, thought to be the most of any nation. Deforestation for cattle ranching, for farmlands and for Colombia's timber industry has caused environmental problems, including the risk of landslides.

### COLOMBIA'S RESOURCES

Colombia has large mineral resources, including copper, lead, and mercury—91,940 lb. (41,500kg) of gold were recovered in 2008, mainly from many small mines, while emerald gemstones are mined in an area northeast of Bogotá. The country has large reserves of fossil fuels; it has the biggest reserves of coal in South America, while its oil fields produce an average of 670,000 barrels per day. Most of its oil fields are found in the Magdalena Valley and near the border with Venezuela. Despite the abundance of fossil fuels, 70 percent of Colombia's electricity, used to fuel its many industries, come from hydroelectric power plants, which make use of the many rivers flowing quickly down the mountains.

### COLOMBIA'S AGRICULTURE

Agriculture employs about 18 percent of the Colombian workforce, with coffee being the most important cash crop. Other important crops are bananas, cotton, corn, rice, and potatoes. Unfortunately the crops believed to generate the most revenue are coca (used to make cocaine) and cannabis. Colombia is one of the world's largest producers of these drugs, which are illegal in most countries. The power of the producers of illegal drugs has added to the already significant problems with maintaining law and order in the country. Colombia has been in a state of near civil war for decades.

# ECUADOR

**Ecuador is the smallest Andean country but has a varied landscape. It also governs the world-famous Galapagos Islands in the Pacific Ocean.**

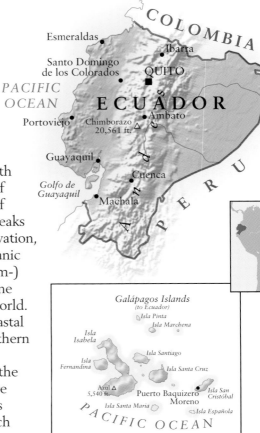

**Area:** 103,930 sq. mi. (269,178km²)
**Population:** 14,203,000
**Capital:** Quito (1,686,000)
**Main languages spoken:** Spanish, Quechua
**Main religion:** Roman Catholic
**Currency:** U.S. dollar
**Main exports:** petroleum, bananas, shrimp, coffee, cocoa, cut flowers
**Type of government:** republic; limited democracy

▼ Quito is located on the slopes of a volcano in a valley among the Andes. The oldest of all South American capital cities, Quito has many well-preserved Spanish colonial buildings, including 86 churches.

E cuador has three distinct geographical areas: two sets of lowlands split by a highland region that runs through the country from north to south. The highland region consists of two chains of mountains that are part of the Andes. The mountains contain 22 peaks that are over 13,800 ft. (4,200m) in elevation, as well as around 30 mountains of volcanic origin, including the 19,342-ft.-(5,897-m-) high cone volcano Mount Cotopaxi—one of the highest active volcanoes in the world. To the west of the highlands are the coastal lowlands bordering the Pacific. The northern coastal lowlands are largely covered in tropical rain forests, while to the south the land is more arid, and vegetation is more sparse. East of the Andes Mountains lies Ecuador's Amazon basin lowlands, which are covered in dense rain forests.

## ECUADOR'S ECONOMY

Ecuador's economy is based mainly on agriculture, fishing, and oil. More than 440,000 tons (400,000 metric tonnes) of fish are caught every year, although overfishing now threatens certain marine life. Ecuador's oil industry produces over 486,000 barrels per day, making oil the single largest export earner. Ecuador's rugged countryside allows it to produce over 70 percent of its electricity from hydroelectric power plants. Several metals are mined, while the government of Ecuador controls a large salt-mining industry. Guayaquil, in the south of the country, is Ecuador's main industrial center and its biggest port. Quito, in the north, remains the governmental and cultural capital.

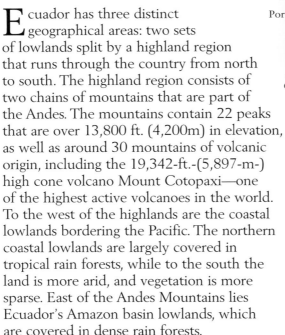

## ECUADOR'S PEOPLE

Like all of the Andean nations, Ecuador was colonized by the Spanish and only obtained independence in the 1800s. Wars with Peru between 1904 and 1942 saw the country lose a lot of territory. Unlike most South American countries, the Amerindian population is large; pure-blooded Quechua Amerindians make up 25 percent of the population. Most speak the Quechua language used in the times of the Inca civilization. People of mixed European and Amerindian descent make up a further 65 percent of the population. Ecuador is the most densely populated South American country, with an average of approximately 133 people per square mile.

## GALAPAGOS ISLANDS

Ecuador's major island territories lie around 620 mi. (1,000km) from its coastline in the Pacific Ocean. The Galapagos Islands comprise 19 islands and many islets and rocks, most of which are formed from lava piles. Lava rock forms the islands' shorelines, with higher ground containing

▲ Found on the Galapagos Islands, the giant tortoise can grow to lengths of just over 3 ft. (1m), weigh over 550 lbs. (250kg), and live for over 100 years.

▼ Ecuadorians herd some of the country's 2.1 million sheep down from the slopes of the inactive volcano Chimborazo, the country's highest point. Permanently snow-capped from around 15,090 ft. (4,600m) upward, the volcano gets its name from the Quechua Amerindian for "mountain of snow."

▲ Around 66 percent of Ecuadorians live in towns and cities. The country's most populous city, Guayaquil, contains over two-and-a-half million people.

most of the islands' plant life. Although some remains of Inca pottery have been found in places, the Galapagos are believed to have been uninhabited for most of their existence. Isolated from other landmasses, the islands are home to a large number of unusual species of plants and creatures not found elsewhere. Most of the Galapagos Islands' animals are thought to have originated long ago in South and Central America, but they have adapted and evolved into separate species. For example, the marine iguana is the only iguana that swims and feeds on seaweed. Other unusual creatures include flightless cormorants and giant tortoises, which can weigh over 550 lbs. (250kg) and are believed to be the longest-living land creatures. Ecuador has had to control visitor numbers to the islands in order to conserve their future welfare. Laws ban further settlements and development.

# PERU

**Peru is the third-largest country in South America and has a long Pacific Ocean coastline. The interior features the Andes Mountains and rain forests.**

**Area:** 496,225 sq. mi. (1,285,216km²)
**Population:** 28,221,000
**Capital:** Lima (8,473,000)
**Main languages spoken:** Spanish, Quechua, Aymará
**Main religion:** Roman Catholic
**Currency:** new sol
**Main exports:** copper, fish and fish products, zinc, coffee, petroleum, gold
**Type of government:** republic

Peru can be divided into three geographical regions: the coast, a jungle interior, and, between them, the highlands, or sierra. Peru's narrow coastal region runs the entire length of the country for 1,500 mi. (2,410km). Facing the Pacific Ocean, this region is mostly dry, although many of the valleys near the coast are farmed using modern irrigation techniques. In contrast the jungle interior receives heavy rainfall—as much as 150 in. (380cm) in places. This region covers more than half of Peru's land and is divided into highland and lowland regions. The highland area is found on the eastern flanks of the Andes at altitudes between 1,600–9,185 ft. (490–2,800m). Covered in thick rain forests, the lowland area is part of the Amazon river basin and includes Peru's longest rivers, the Ucayali and the Marañón. These rivers join 50 mi. (80km) south of Iquitos to form the Amazon river.

## PERUVIAN HIGHLANDS

The Peruvian highlands cover approximately 30 percent of Peru and consist of large numbers of mountain peaks, over 170 of which rise above 15,910 ft. (4,850m).

Temperatures vary with altitude and can range from 19–70°F (-7–21°C). This region has a mixture of arid areas and some fertile growing land, usually found in deep valleys. Most people who live there either work in mining or practice subsistence farming. The area is also home to Lake Titicaca, a large lake of over 3,200 sq. mi. (8,300km²) that, at an altitude of over 12,470 ft. (3,800m), is the highest navigable lake in the world.

▼ Local Aymará Native Americans fish the waters of Lake Titicaca. The Aymarás use boats built out of reeds and rushes in the same way as their ancient ancestors did.

## PEOPLE OF THE INCA EMPIRE

Peru has been the home of a number of ancient native cultures, including the Nazca, Chimú, and Chavín civilizations. The country was also at the center of the great Inca empire, which had its capital in Cusco in southern Peru. Despite great destruction by the Spanish, many remains of the Incas' former glory lie throughout Peru and are one of the biggest attractions for the two million tourists who visit the country each year. While around 37 percent of Peru's population are people of mixed European and Amerindian descent, the largest population group is Amerindian, who comprise 45 percent of Peruvians. Spanish was the sole official language until 1975, when Quechua, an Amerindian language, was also made an official language. Aymará, another important Amerindian language, was added in 1980.

## PERU'S POLITICS AND ECONOMY

Exploiting oil and natural gas and mining metal ores are major industries in Peru. The country ranks as one of the world's leading producers of silver, lead, and copper. Agricultural land is relatively limited, but the use of terraces cut into the mountain and hillsides, as well as irrigation in dry coastal areas, allows a range of crops to be grown, especially corn, sugarcane, rice, and potatoes. Fishing is a major industry but, along with farming, has been hit by the change in weather patterns known as El Niño (see page 31). This has reduced fish stocks off the coast of Peru and caused large floods and landslides to damage harvests. Further hardships have hit Peru's population, 45 percent of whom the UN estimates to live below the poverty line. Historically, Peru has had long periods of military rule and, in the 1980s and 1990s, suffered Maoist guerrilla insurgency. In the 21st century Peru has achieved stability and economic growth.

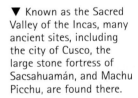

▲ A Peruvian market draws traditionally dressed local native Indian people to sell and trade produce and goods.

▼ Known as the Sacred Valley of the Incas, many ancient sites, including the city of Cusco, the large stone fortress of Sacsahuamán, and Machu Picchu, are found there.

# BOLIVIA

Most of the population of Bolivia, one of the poorest South American countries, live on a high plateau, called the Altiplano, between Andes mountain ranges.

**Area:** 424,165 sq. mi. (1,098,581km²)
**Population:** 10,028,000
**Capitals:** La Paz (1,726,000) and Sucre (265,000)
**Main languages spoken:** Spanish, Quechua, Aymará
**Main religion:** Roman Catholic
**Currency:** boliviano
**Main exports:** natural gas, zinc, soybeans, petroleum, gold, tin
**Type of government:** republic; limited democracy

Bolivia is a landlocked country, so it has no sea or ocean coastline. It borders five South American countries: Peru and Chile to the west, Brazil to the north and east, and Paraguay and Argentina to the south. The largest expanse of water is formed by Lake Titicaca, which sits on the country's border with Peru. The country's most notable highland areas consist of two mountain ranges that run almost south to north through the western side of the country. The more westerly of these two mountain ranges includes a number of active volcanoes on its steep slopes, so this area is the least inhabited part of Bolivia. The more easterly range, in which Bolivia's twin capital cities of La Paz and Sucre are situated, is more densely populated. Its eastern slopes are densely covered by forests. This region is the wettest part of the Bolivian Andes and receives around 53 in. (135cm) of rain per year, mostly falling in just three months of the year. To the north and the east the land descends into part of a huge lowland area called the Oriente. This is made up of low alluvial plains, large swamp areas, and tropical forests.

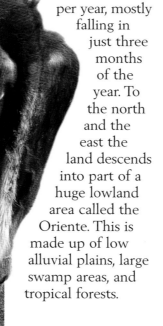

◄ Life in rural areas is often very harsh. Around 40 percent of the Bolivian workforce grow crops or raise livestock for a living.

## THE ALTIPLANO

Lying between the two Andean mountain ranges is a large high-altitude plateau called the Altiplano. The Altiplano is a series of basins lying at around 12,000 ft. (3,650m) above sea level. Approximately 500 mi. (800km) long, the plateau is almost 200 mi. (320km) wide at its broadest point. Lakes Titicaca and Poopó occupy two of the basins, while salt flats inhabit several others. The northern half of the region receives moderate rainfall, while the southern region is dry. Most rain comes during summer thunderstorms in January and February. Cold winds sweep through the entire plateau, keeping average temperatures under 54°F (12°C), with subzero temperatures during the winter. The land has thin soil, and grasses, scrub bushes, and small trees are the main vegetation.

This harsh landscape actually provides homes for the majority of Bolivians. Many live in towns, work in the mining region based around Oruro, or farm the land and raise herds of alpacas and llamas. Successive Bolivian governments have urged people to move from the Altiplano to the Oriente, where the discovery of fossil fuels and the possibility of large-scale forestry and growing tropical crops have provided a boost to the country's economy. The Oriente is now the engine of Bolivia's development. The population has increased especially in and around the Oriente's main town, Santa Cruz, which is now the fastest growing city in Bolivia.

▲ Most crops grown in Bolivia are traded in markets and consumed within the country. These include corn, potatoes, wheat, and soybeans.

▼ The imposing San Francisco Church is found in La Paz. At an elevation of between 10,660–13,450 ft. (3,250–4,100m), La Paz is the highest capital city in the world. More than two thirds of all of Bolivia's manufacturing industry are based in La Paz.

## MINING AND NATURAL GAS

The Spanish explorers who came to Bolivia in the 1500s discovered reserves of silver, with the mine established at Potosi becoming famous as the world's largest. The boom in silver production soon ended, and now Bolivia, independent from Spanish rule since the middle of the 1800s, relies on other mining industries to prosper. The country has reserves of a number of minerals but has not invested in exploiting them all. Large-scale tin production, which first started in 1895, replaced silver as the main metal mined. For the first half of the 1900s Bolivia was the world's largest tin producer and still ranks as one of the top-ten countries. Other metals are also mined, including zinc, tungsten, uranium, copper, and lead. Almost half of Bolivia's electricity is generated by hydroelectric power programs, but the country also has reserves of oil and natural gas. Natural gas is Bolivia's biggest export, although food products, zinc, petroleum, and silver are also important to the country's economy.

## LIVING IN BOLIVIA

Many Bolivians are poor and struggle to make a living. The country once had a Pacific coastline but lost the land during the war with Chile in 1879–1885. It then lost further important territory in the Chaco War (1932–1935). Its isolated position in South America, poor transportation links owing to the rugged geography of the land, and frequent changes of government have not aided development. While there is wealth in the larger towns and cities, life in rural areas tends to be harsh. Doctors and health-care services are hard to find outside of the towns and cities, and many children are not immunized against diseases. Many Bolivian farmers have turned to cultivating coca—even though it is used to make the illegal drug cocaine.

# BRAZIL

**The largest country in South America, Brazil has a rapidly industrializing economy, a growing population, and incredibly rich wildlife and mineral resources.**

**Area:** 3,300,171 sq. mi. (8,547,404km²)
**Population:** 183,889,000
**Capital:** Brasília (3,508,000)
**Main languages spoken:** Portuguese, Spanish, English, French
**Main religion:** Roman Catholic
**Currency:** real
**Main exports:** iron and steel products, nonelectrical machinery, iron ore, road vehicles, soy beans, coffee
**Type of government:** republic; democracy

▼ Brazil has outlawed a lot of the deforestation that occurs in the Amazon basin. However, laws are hard to police in such a huge area, and illegal forestry to recover valuable tropical hardwoods accounts for most of the deforestation occurring in the Amazon.

Brazil shares a border with every country in South America, with the exception of Chile and Ecuador. The country is a federal republic divided into 26 separate states, with a federal district based in the city of Brasília. The country has a great variety of landscapes over its huge area, but there are a small number of major geographical regions. To the north and east, where Brazil borders four other South American countries, lie the Guiana Highlands, which run into Suriname and Guyana. This region of mountains and valleys includes Pico da Neblina. With an elevation of 9,823 ft. (2,994m), this mountain is the country's highest peak and was only discovered in the 1950s. Most of northern and western Brazil is home to a large part of the Amazon basin, containing the Amazon and its hundreds of tributary rivers, as well as the largest rain-forest region in the world. In the center and south of the country are the Brazilian Highlands. This area is a large plateau of ancient rocks that

▲ The ornate opera house in Manaus was built in 1896. Situated on the Negro river, Manaus is the capital of the Amazonas state and is home to half the state's population.

is divided by low mountain formations and has been weathered over thousands of years to create deep river valleys. Much of the Brazilian Highlands are covered in scrubland or forests.

### THE AMAZON BASIN
Although the giant basin and rain forest through which the Amazon runs lie in a number of South American countries, the river's greatest extent is located in Brazil.

ATLANTIC OCEAN

Mount Roraima 9,217 ft.

*Guiana Highlands*

COLOMBIA
VENEZUELA
SURINAME
French Guiana (to France)
GUYANA

*Negro*
*Japurá*
*Amazon*
*Amazon*
Macapá
*Marajó*
Belém
São Luís
Fortaleza

*A m a z o n*
Manaus
*Amazon*

*B a s i n*
*Madeira*
*Iriri*
*Tapajós*
*Xingu*
Natal

*S e l v a s*
*Juruá*
*Purus*
**B R A Z I L**
Recife

PERU
Porto Velho
*Teles Pires*
*Araguaia*
*Tocantins*
*São Francisco*
*Represa de Sobradinho*

Rio Branco
BOLIVIA
*Guaporé*
*Jamena*

Salvador

*Mato Grosso Do Sul*
Cuiabá
Goiânia
■ BRASÍLIA
*Brazilian Highlands*

PARAGUAY
*Paraguay*
Campo Grande
*Paraná*
Belo Horizonte
Vitória

Campinas
Nova Iguaçu
São Paulo
Rio de Janeiro
Santos

Curitiba

ARGENTINA
*Uruguay*
Porto Alegre

URUGUAY
*Lagoa dos Patos*
*Lagoa Mirim*

▲ Found in many parts of central and southern America but most common in Brazil, the jaguar is the largest wild cat species in either North or South America.

The Amazon basin covers over one third of Brazil, and large parts of the rain-forest-covered region remain unsurveyed or have only been recently explored. The Amazon forest contains the largest single reserve of biological organisms in the world. No one knows how many species of living things exist in the Amazon, but scientists estimate the number could be as high as five million, which could equal almost one third of the entire world's living organisms. What is not in doubt is that the Amazon basin is extraordinarily rich in wildlife. At one time around five million Native Americans lived in the Amazonian rain forests, but this number

is closer to 200,000 today. The major tribes still inhabiting the Amazon include the Tikuna, the Yanomami, which are also found in Venezuela, the Xavante, and the Guajajara.

## DEFORESTATION IN THE AMAZON

The rain forest is shrinking, occasionally owing to forest fires but mainly owing to human impact. Deforestation to clear lands for mining, farming, or for timber and other products has seen more than 15 percent of the entire rain forest destroyed since the early 1970s. As much as 13,510 sq. mi. (35,000km$^2$) have been lost in individual years. Deforestation of the Amazon has become an international issue, with aid programs and initiatives designed to slow or halt the cutting down of trees. Yet governmental plans to construct a huge dam and road network to help develop industry may threaten even greater areas of the rain forest.

▲ Rio de Janeiro's carnival is a giant festival billed as the largest party in the world and features parades, music, and dancing.

▼ Standing on Corcovado peak, 2,582 ft. (787m) above sea level, the statue of Christ the Redeemer looks over the city of Rio de Janeiro.

## A COFFEE AND MINING GIANT

No country produces more coffee than Brazil. The world leader, Brazil produces around 2.9 million tons (2.6 million metric tonnes) of this lucrative crop, most of which is exported. Sugarcane, soy beans, cocoa, corn, and oranges are also major export crops, and many more crops, including potatoes, cotton, tobacco, and rice, are grown. Brazil has some of the richest mineral deposits in the world, although their full extent is not known since the entire country has not been surveyed. Brazil has iron ore reserves estimated at a minimum of 53 billion tons (48 billion metric tonnes) and large reserves of other metal ores, including bauxite, lead, nickel, and manganese. Ninety percent of the country's electricity is generated by hydroelectric power plants. Brazil's resources are used by the country's giant manufacturing industry to produce large quantities of products, including motor vehicles, chemicals, clothing, and textiles.

## BRAZIL'S CLIMATE

Brazil has a generally warm and humid climate, but there is great variation in local areas. Cities on plateaus, such as Brasília, have mild climates with average daily temperatures of around 66°F. Cities on the coast, such as Rio de Janeiro, have warmer climates. The hottest part of Brazil is the northeast, where in the dry season between May and November temperatures above 100°F are often recorded. Most of Brazil receives moderate rainfall; the wettest areas lie in the Amazon basin.

## BRAZIL'S PEOPLE

More than half of Brazil's population is under 30 years of age, and the population has more than tripled in the last 60 years.

Brazilians are a mix of different origins, with the Native Americans who first settled the country now comprising less than one percent of the population. Most of the early European settlers were Portuguese, and from the 1500s to the 1800s they brought back between three and four million black Africans to Brazil as slaves. People of mixed descent from European, African, and Native American backgrounds comprise the majority of Brazil's population. Brazil also has the largest population of Japanese outside of Japan. Arriving mainly as poor farmers in the 1920s, over two million people of Japanese origin now live in Brazil. Monumental migration from rural to urban areas has occurred. Some Brazilians are very wealthy, but income is distributed with huge inequalities—and millions are desperately poor. Large shantytowns surrounding major cities see people living in squalor with little water or sanitation.

## BRAZILIAN CITIES

Unlike many South American countries, Brazil has many major cities: São Paulo is the country's biggest, most populous city, while Rio de Janeiro is its most famous city internationally and its cultural center. Neither is the official capital of the country, a role given to the purpose-built city of Brasília. In the 1950s, as part of initiatives to encourage people to move into the Brazilian interior, this new capital city was constructed. Brasília now houses the national seat of government and many foreign embassies. The largest Brazilian city, however, is also one of the country's oldest colonial settlements—São Paulo. Founded in 1554 on a plateau 2,490 ft. (760m) above sea level, São Paulo has boomed in the last 120 years as, first, coffee growing and exports and, later, industry brought wealth and employment to the region. Today it is at the center of an urban area that houses approximately 19,226,000 people. This makes it the most populous urban area in South America and the third largest in the world. Lying around 47 mi. (75km) inland from the Atlantic Ocean, São Paulo is home to more than 20,000 industrial plants and factories and is also the financial center of Brazil. Rio de Janeiro is a major tourist and business destination. It was the capital until 1960 and remains a major metropolis and the entry point for most of the country's five million or so tourists who arrive every year.

▲ Poverty and housing shortages mean that many millions of Brazilians live with little water, sanitation, or other basic facilities in shantytowns, known as *favelas*, that surround the country's major cities.

▼ Located in the modern capital city of Brasília, the National Congress building forms part of the official parliamentary buildings of Brazil.

# SOUTHERN SOUTH AMERICA

The four nations that make up southern South America contrast in size, shape, and geography. The geography varies from the seemingly endless flat plains of the Pampas to the spectacular and rugged Andes mountain system. The region's climate varies just as greatly—from the rainless hot deserts of northern Chile to the icy wastelands of extreme southern Argentina. Running along the western coast is Chile, 2,670 mi. (4,300km) long but rarely more than several hundred miles wide. Smaller and more compact are the landlocked nation of Paraguay and the smallest country in southern South America—Uruguay. Argentina is the largest country in the region and the second largest in the continent. Together the four countries have an area of approximately 1,585,335 sq. mi. (4,106,000km²). However, vast areas of land are sparsely inhabited or uninhabited. In contrast to the Andean nations, Native American peoples in all of these countries (except for Paraguay) make up very small proportions of the population. Most of these peoples can trace their descent back to European settlers in the past 400 years. Traditionally important, farming remains the backbone of the economy of the region, although, with the exception of Paraguay, the nations of southern South America are increasingly dependent on industry and services for revenue.

▲ The Torres del Paine National Park lies in the extreme south of Chile, more than 1,550 mi. (2,500km) south of the country's capital city, Santiago. It is renowned for its unspoiled mountain and river scenery.

PERU

BOLIVIA
PARAGUAY
BRAZIL

PACIFIC
OCEAN

Atacama Desert

Gran Chaco

Pilcomayo

Paraguay

ASUNCIÓN

Salado

A n d e s

Aconcagua
22,831 ft.

SANTIAGO

C H I L E

ARGENTINA

Paraná

URUGUAY

BUENOS AIRES

MONTEVIDEO

Río de la Plata

Pampas

Colorado

Río Negro

Isla Grande
de Chiloé

P a t a g o n i a

ATLANTIC
OCEAN

0        500        1000 km

0        250        500 miles

Strait of Magellan

Tierra
del Fuego

Cape Horn

▼ Cattle and livestock raising is important in all four
southern South American countries. The Pampas region
is an area of flat plains found in Argentina, large parts of
which are used to raise the country's huge herds of cattle
and sheep. Argentina has about 52 million cattle and
about 15 million sheep.

# PARAGUAY

A relatively unknown and isolated country, Paraguay is divided into two geographical regions. The eastern half is the more populous.

**Area:** 157,048 sq. mi. (406,752km²)
**Population:** 6,230,000
**Capital:** Asunción (1,660,000)
**Main languages spoken:** Spanish, Guaraní
**Main religion:** Roman Catholic
**Currency:** guaraní
**Main exports:** soy, flour, cotton, oilseed and vegetable oil, electricity
**Type of government:** republic; limited democracy

▼ Oxen are used as beasts of burden throughout rural Paraguay. Fifty percent of the country's roads are unpaved, and few people own vehicles.

Paraguay's borders are largely created by rivers such as the Paraná, Paraguay, and Pilcomayo, which form much of the border with Argentina. The Paraguay river also divides the country into two very different geographical regions. To the east is the Paraneña region, which increases in elevation to form a series of low-lying mountains near the border with Brazil. To the west lies the Chaco region. This is a huge plain averaging around 410 ft. (125m) in altitude above sea level. It covers more than 60 percent of the country, and in the summer rainy season large parts are flooded and become temporary swamplands. Paraguay's people are mainly descendants of native Amerindians. Agriculture is the key occupation of most of Paraguay's workforce. Half of the country's population live in rural areas, growing a wide range of crops, including cotton, sugarcane, wheat, bananas, and sweet potatoes. Livestock raising, especially cattle, is very important. There are 10.5 million cattle raised on the grasslands,

as well as sheep and horses. Paraguay is much less industrialized than its neighbors. However, electricity from the Itaípu dam powers growing industries. Asunción is Paraguay's capital and its largest city. It is built on low-lying hills overlooking the Paraguay river at the point where it joins the Pilcomayo river. Asunción and Ciudad del Este are the two chief manufacturing and trading cities in Paraguay.

# URUGUAY

**The smallest country in southern South America, Uruguay is a land of rolling plains and low-lying hills. Most of the land is used to raise livestock.**

**Area:** 68,037 sq. mi. (176,215km²)
**Population:** 3,445,000
**Capital:** Montevideo (1,750,000)
**Main language spoken:** Spanish
**Main religion:** Roman Catholic
**Currency:** Uruguayan peso
**Main exports:** meat and other animal products, live animals, textiles and clothing, vegetables
**Type of government:** republic

Uruguay is one of the few countries in South America that does not have a tropical or subtropical climate. Its location some distance from the equator and its position facing the Atlantic Ocean give the country a warm temperate climate with relatively high rainfall (around 37 in./95cm per year) and average temperatures of 50°F (10°C) in the winter and 72°F (22°C) in the summer. Cold wind storms, called *pamperos*, can occur during the winter, but few parts of Uruguay ever experience frost. The natural vegetation is tall prairie grasslands with relatively few forest areas. Almost 90 percent of the country is suitable for agriculture, but only one tenth of this land is used for growing crops such as corn, wheat, and rice. Much of the remaining land supports the giant herds of livestock, particularly cattle and sheep, that roam Uruguay's plains. For such a relatively small country Uruguay is a major sheep-farming nation and an important exporter of wool.

Uruguay's people bear few traces of the original native Amerindian inhabitants. Less than one percent of the population are either solely or part native Amerindian. The large majority of people are immigrants from Europe or from Brazil and Argentina. Uruguay's capital city, Montevideo, sprawls along the northern banks of the Río de la Plata and is the center of Uruguayan business and food- and wool-processing industries. Large-scale migration from the

▲ A market stall in the Barrio Reus district of Montevideo, Uruguay's capital city. Montevideo is Uruguay's main port and is the site of its state university.

country to the city means that around half of the entire country's population live in or close to the city. Uruguay was the first South American country to establish a state welfare system and has a high level of literacy (98 percent) and good health care.

▼ A shepherd tends his flock in eastern Uruguay. The country has around 16 million sheep.

# CHILE

Chile is a nation of natural extremes in its landscapes and especially its climate. Volcanoes, icy wastelands, and temperate plains are all part of this highly developed country.

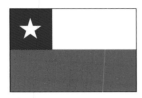

**Area:** 292,135 sq. mi. (756,626km²)
**Population:** 17,094,000
**Capitals:** Santiago (6,886,000). Valparaiso (804,000) is the legislative capital
**Main language spoken:** Spanish
**Main religions:** Roman Catholic, Protestant
**Currency:** Chilean peso
**Main exports:** copper, iron ore, fruit, food products, paper and paper products
**Type of government:** republic; democracy

▼ Founded in 1849, Punta Arenas lies on the stretch of water known as the Straits of Magellan, which links the Atlantic and Pacific Oceans. The city's 116,000 inhabitants work in industries processing and transporting oil, mutton, wool, and timber.

Chile shares borders with Argentina, Peru, and Bolivia and has the longest Pacific coastline of any South American country. Around 2,300 mi. (3,700km) west of its coast in the southern Pacific Ocean lies Easter Island, which is owned by Chile. Several other small islands in the Pacific are also under Chilean control. Chile owns the western part of the island group of Tierra del Fuego in the extreme south of the continent.

## A CHANGING LANDSCAPE

Around 2,670 mi. (4,300km) long but averaging only 110 mi. (175km) in width, Chile's landscape is dominated by the Andes Mountains, which run along the entire length of the country. Northern Chile includes one of the driest places in the world, the Atacama desert. Parts of this arid area have never received any recorded rainfall. South of this area lies a large temperate region where most of Chile's towns and cities and agricultural land are found. The southern central region of Chile is renowned for its natural beauty and contains many lakes and large areas of forests. If you move farther south, the mild climate changes to a cold, windswept region. Rainfall is high here, reaching as much as 161 in. (410cm) per year. Cape Horn is the most southerly point of both Chile and the South American continent and is just 400 mi. (650km) away from Antarctica.

▲ Magellanic penguins breed on the southern Chilean coast and islands, including Tierra del Fuego.

▲ The Atacama desert is one of the driest places on Earth. It features salt mines and copper reserves that are exploited by the largest open-pit mine in the world.

▶ Located 34 mi. (55km) northeast of Puerto Montt, Mount Osorno is 8,700 ft. 2,652m) high and is just one of hundreds of volcanoes found within the Andes Mountains that run through Chile. A cone volcano with its topmost part covered in glaciers, Osorno is a young volcano that last erupted in the 1830s.

## CHILEAN PEOPLE AND ECONOMY

The large majority of Chile's people are mestizos. Native Amerindians make up around one twentieth of the total population, and most live in the Andes in northern Chile and along the southern coast. Almost 90 percent of all Chileans live in central Chile, with more than one third living in and around the capital city of Santiago. Parliament meets in Valparaiso, the country's main port. The exploitation of minerals, including salt and metals, is a major industries in the country, with Chile remaining the world's largest producer of copper. Agriculture in the center of the country produces fruit crops for export and provides grapes for a flourishing and world-famous wine industry. The fast-flowing rivers found in the Andes have been harnessed for hydroelectric power to generate just over half of Chile's electricity.

# ARGENTINA

**The second-largest country in South America, Argentina's territory includes large areas of rich pastureland where some of the largest cattle herds in the world graze.**

**Area:** 1,068,300 sq. mi. (2,766,890km²)
**Population:** 39,356,000
**Capital:** Buenos Aires (12,047,000)
**Main languages spoken:** Spanish, English, Italian
**Main religion:** Roman Catholic
**Currency:** Argentine peso
**Main exports:** meat, wool, cereals, manufactured goods, machinery and transportation equipment
**Type of government:** republic; democracy

▼ Ushuaia is the capital of the Argentinian province of Tierra del Fuego, Antarctica, and South Atlantic islands. Founded in 1884 and with around 63,000 inhabitants, Ushuaia lies at a latitude of 54.8°S, making it the southernmost large settlement in the world.

Forming the southeastern part of South America, Argentina is a large plain that rises in elevation from the Atlantic Ocean westward to the country's border with Chile. There some of the highest peaks of the Andes are found, including Aconcagua, with an elevation of 22,831 ft. (6,960m). The Andean region of Argentina is sparsely inhabited by miners and sheep herders. To the north, where Argentina borders Bolivia and Paraguay, lies the Gran Chaco region, which contains large forested areas and swamplands. South of this are the large rolling plains of the Pampas region, where Argentina's largest city, Buenos Aires, is located. Farther south lies Patagonia, a vast, inhospitable region.

## ARGENTINA'S CLIMATE

Because Argentina is a long country—approximately 2,070 mi. (3,330km) from north to south—its climate varies greatly. In the northeast there is a small tropical region, while the Gran Chaco has subtropical temperatures. Most of Argentina has a temperate climate that gets colder farther south. Rainfall varies greatly, with Argentina's capital city, Buenos Aires, averaging around 37 in.

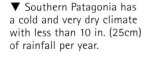

▲ Argentina is one of the foremost polo-playing nations. Many of the world's best polo ponies are thoroughbred horses from either Argentina or the southwestern U.S.

▼ Southern Patagonia has a cold and very dry climate with less than 10 in. (25cm) of rainfall per year.

(95cm) per year. To the south and the west much less rain falls, and the semiarid climate restricts the types of plants that can grow there. In the Argentinian Andes hot, dry winds, called *zondas*, travel across the mountains, absorbing moisture but not forming clouds and rain.

## PATAGONIA
The southernmost region of Argentina, Patagonia is a vast, frequently windswept plain with an area of approximately 300,000 sq. mi. (777,000km²). Much of the region experiences a dry climate, but the northern portion of the region is warm enough to be able to support large farms growing alfalfa grass, vegetables, and some fruit, as well as raising huge flocks of sheep. Argentina has approximately 15 million sheep, many millions of which are found in Patagonia. Tourism has become important in the region. Argentina has more than 20 national parks, a number of which are located in Patagonia, along with wildlife reserves and other protected areas. However, Patagonia's biggest impact on the country's economy is increasingly due to its reserves of oil, natural gas, and coal, as well as metal ores such as iron, tungsten, lead, and gold.

▲ Buenos Aires is Argentina's largest city and effectively became its capital in 1816. The city is a major transportation terminus in South America, and it has the largest railroad center and is the continent's largest port.

## THE PAMPAS
The Pampas get their name from a Quechua Indian word meaning "flat surface" and are a vast series of largely treeless plains that cover most of central Argentina. The region is split in half based on climate. The Humid Pampas runs from the coast inland and receives moderate to heavy rainfall. The soils are deep, heavy, and rich. Farther inland the Dry Pampas is a larger area but supports fewer people and has less crop-growing land. Originally covered in grassland vegetation, most of the Pampas region has been turned into farmland, with huge pastureland and ranches for the country's large herds of cattle, which number around 52 million.

▲ Argentinian ranchers, known as gauchos, herd cattle across the plains of the Pampas. A national symbol of Argentina, the gauchos were originally nomadic cowboys who traded herds of cattle and horses. Many gauchos now work as cattle hands on individual ranches.

## ARGENTINA'S HISTORY AND PEOPLE

Argentina received its name, meaning "land of silver," from Spanish explorers who reached the region in the 1500s. In 1580 Spaniards established a colony on the site of what would become the major city of Buenos Aires. After repelling an attempted British invasion in 1806–1807 the country declared independence from Spain in 1816, beginning a long internal conflict for power. A series of fierce battles with the country's Native American population occurred in the 1870s and resulted in a major decline in their number. Today there are an estimated 700,000 Native Americans living in Argentina. Waves of immigrants from Europe (particularly Italy, Spain, and the United Kingdom) and the Middle East (particularly Syria and Lebanon) arrived in the late 1800s and early 1900s. These immigrants transformed the country's agriculture and its infrastructure such as railroads and ports. As a result, Argentina has a different mix of peoples compared to most South American countries, with particularly strong Italian-Argentine, British-Argentine, and Jewish communities. Until the economic crisis of 2002 a relatively large number of Argentinians enjoyed a high standard of living compared to the rest of South America. The crisis forced many into poverty; the United Nations estimates that 14 percent of Argentinians live below the poverty. The economy recovered, but Argentina's economic status has diminished.

▼ Considered one of the natural wonders of South America, Iguaçu Falls lies in the northeast of the country. It is four times the width of North America's Niagara Falls and falls a distance of 236 ft. (72m).

# SOUTH ATLANTIC ISLANDS

**Lying in the icy waters of the south Atlantic Ocean are a number of largely barren, ice-covered islands that include South Georgia and the South Sandwich Islands.**

▲ The third-largest penguin species, the gentoo penguin is found on the South Sandwich Islands, where it nests on rocky shorelines.

South Georgia is the largest of the south Atlantic islands and lies around 810 mi. (1,300km) southeast of the Falkland Islands. Largely covered in ice, it is mountainous and has a rugged coastline. The small population consists mainly of military personnel and scientists, who reside in a small settlement formerly used by whalers. The South Sandwich Islands are a group of six glacier-covered volcanic islets 470 mi. (760km) southeast of South Georgia. British ownership of these islands and South Georgia is disputed by Argentina.

# ST. HELENA, ASCENSION, & TRISTAN DA CUNHA

**A small, isolated collection of islands make up the British dependency of St. Helena and include the islands of St. Helena, Ascension, and Tristan da Cunha.**

**Area:** 159 sq. mi. (441km²)
**Population:** 5,600
**Capital:** Jamestown (2,400)
**Main language spoken:** English
**Main religions:** Anglican, Baptist
**Currency:** local issue of U.K. pound
**Main exports:** canned and frozen fish, handicrafts
**Government:** dependency of U.K.

▶ The slopes of Green Mountain on Ascension are one of the few places where fruit and vegetables are grown on the island.

A rugged, mountainous island created by volcanic activity, St. Helena sits in the south Atlantic Ocean around 1,190 mi. (1,920km) from the west coast of Africa. Large cliffs face the ocean on its north, east, and west sides, while deep valleys are carved into its mountainous interior. Over half the island's population lives in Jamestown, a natural harbor and port for shipping. Potatoes, corn, and flax are grown, but most of the economy is subsidized by the United Kingdom, with additional

▲ St. Helena was the last place of exile for the French leader Napoleon Bonaparte.

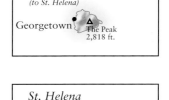

*Ascension Island*
*(to St. Helena)*
Georgetown • △ The Peak 2,818 ft.

*St. Helena*
*(to U.K.)*
Jamestown • △ Diana's Peak 2,699 ft.

*Tristan da Cunha*
*(to St. Helena)*
Edinburgh △ Queen Mary's Peak 6,760 ft.
*Inaccessible Island*
*Nightingale Island*

revenue generated through the port. Ascension lies over 700 mi. (1,130km) northwest of St. Helena and is used as a military base. Its rugged, volcanic landscape provides habitats for thousands of sea turtles and sooty terns. The small population of the volcanic islands of Tristan da Cunha grows potatoes and catches crayfish. The main island is dominated by a volcano that last erupted in 1961, causing the island to be evacuated.

# FALKLAND ISLANDS

**Located in the southern Atlantic Ocean, the Falkland Islands are a dependency of the U.K. Their ownership is disputed by Argentina, which calls them Islas Malvinas.**

Falkland Islands (Islas Malvinas) (to U.K.)

ATLANTIC OCEAN

West Falkland
Port Howard
East Falkland
Mount Usborne △ 2,312 ft.
Stanley
Goose Green
Darwin
Bluff Cove
Weddell Island
Port Stephens

**Area:** 4,699 sq. mi. (12,170km²)
**Population:** 2,500
**Capital:** Stanley (2,100)
**Main language spoken:** English
**Main religion:** Anglican
**Currency:** U.K. pound
**Main exports:** sheep products, fish, squid
**Type of government:** dependency of U.K.

▼ With a permanent population of around 20 people, Port Howard is the second-largest settlement on West Falkland island. The Falklands have around 500,000 sheep.

The Falklands consist of two main islands, East and West Falkland, and approximately 200 smaller islets. The two major islands are hilly, and their coastlines are heavily indented with many drowned river valleys that form natural harbors. The climate is cool, very windy, and wet. The average winter temperature is 35°F (2°C), while the average summer temperature is approximately 50°F (10°C). Rain falls around 250 days of the year, with almost constant winds averaging 19 mph (31km/h). The islands' vegetation reflects the harsh conditions, with few trees and mainly grasses and low-lying scrub bushes. The grasslands act as pastureland for the main farming activity on the island—sheep raising. East Falkland is the site of the islands' biggest settlement, Stanley. Eighty-five percent of all Falkland Islanders live in this town, which contains the islands' only hospital. Many of the older buildings in Stanley were constructed from locally quarried stone and timber salvaged from shipwrecks. Timber today is just one of many items that has to be imported.

Situated on the site of a large natural harbor, Stanley is the main terminal for imports of food, coal, oil, and clothing, as well as exports of wool and sheepskins. A dependency of the United Kingdom, disputes over the ownership of the islands with Argentina have continued for many decades. Negotiations came to crisis point in April 1982 with the invasion of the islands by Argentina. A bloody ten-week war ended with British military forces reoccupying the islands. Today the islands are self-supporting through the sale of fishing and oil-prospecting licenses to foreign companies.

# EUROPE

# EUROPE

Europe is considered an individual continent, but it is actually part of the Eurasian landmass that extends eastward through Asia. Its landscape varies from icy, rugged mountain ranges, such as the Alps, to temperate forests and warm regions, particularly around the Mediterranean Sea. Europe is the second-smallest continent, and its land area is not that much greater than the country of Australia. However, its population of around 730 million makes it the second-most-populous continent and the most densely populated of all. The birthplace of modern industry and exploration, a number of European countries, particularly Spain, France, Great Britain, Portugal, and the Netherlands, claimed lands all over the world as colonies from the 1400s onward. Rich in history that extends back thousands of years, Europe has many divisions of language and nationality and over 60 native languages. The continent has seen a lot of conflict and changing boundaries. The most recent redrawing of borders came in the 1990s with the reunification of East and West Germany into one nation, the splitting of Czechoslovakia into Slovakia and the Czech Republic, and the breakup of the former country of Yugoslavia into seven republics. Europe's largest nation is also its most easterly. The Russian Federation emerged from the breakup of the Soviet Union in the early 1990s.

▲ The capital of the Russian empire for over two centuries, St. Petersburg is the Russian Federation's second-largest city. It is located on the delta of the Neva river and contains many elaborate buildings, including this church, the Church of Our Savior.

◄ Many countries in southern Europe border the Mediterranean Sea, which provides thousands of tons of fish every year. They are sold at markets such as this one in Marseille in the south of France.

Norwegian
Sea

North Cape

Novaya Zemlya

Barents
Sea

Vesterålen
Lofoten

Kola
Peninsula

White
Sea

Ural Mountains

▲ The red deer
is found mainly
in forest areas in
northern Europe.

NORWAY

SWEDEN

FINLAND

Gulf of Bothnia

RUSSIAN

FEDERATION

North
Sea

DENMARK

Gulf of Finland

Saaremaa

ESTONIA

Gotland

LATVIA

Öland

Baltic
Sea

Bornholm

LITHUANIA

Kaliningrad
(to RUSS FED.)

THERLANDS

GERMANY

-LUXEMBOURG

POLAND

BELARUS

CZECH
REPUBLIC

SLOVAKIA

UKRAINE

SWITZ.

LIECH.

AUSTRIA

Carpathians

MOLDOVA

L P S

SLOVENIA

HUNGARY

ROMANIA

Sea of
Azov

Caspian Sea

CROATIA

CRIMEA

NACO

SAN
MARINO

BOSNIA-
HERZEGOVINA

SERBIA

Caucasus

Apennines

Adriatic Sea

MONT.

KOSOVO

BULGARIA

Black Sea

VATICAN CITY

urian
ea

Corsica
(to France)

ITALY

MACEDONIA

ALBANIA

Sardinia
(to Italy)

Tyrrhenian
Sea

GREECE

Aegean
Sea

Ionian
Sea

Peloponnese

Sicily

MALTA

Crete

Rhodes

▶ Europe is one of the most industrialized continents, and
this steelmaking plant is located in the Ruhr Valley in western
Germany's central and southern territory, one of the largest
industrialized regions in the world.

# NORTHERN EUROPE

Northern Europe includes a varied collection of countries, from the large economic powerhouses of Germany, France, and the United Kingdom to the tiny nation of Luxembourg. Much of the region's landscape has been shaped by glaciation, which has left behind land features such as Norway's complex coastline made up of over 100,000 islands and fjords. The three largest islands in the region are Iceland and the two islands that comprise the United Kingdom and Ireland. All three islands are located in the north Atlantic. Much of northern Europe was once covered in forests, but a growing population and the demands of industry have cleared much of the land. The largest forests remain in Norway, Sweden, Finland, and Germany. Although large parts of northern Europe are farmed, the economies of most of the region's countries are dominated by manufacturing industries and services such as banking. These have helped give the majority of the region's people a high standard of living. Most of the countries receive large numbers of tourists. France is the world's leading destination, with over 79.3 million visitors each year. Most of the countries in the region are members of the European Union, which has its major centers in France, Belgium, and Luxembourg.

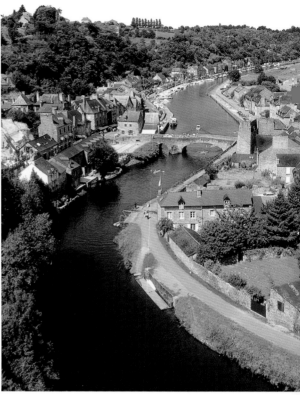

▼ Northern Sweden is home to some of the last large wilderness areas in northern Europe. The region contains over 390 sq. mi. (1,000km²) of virgin fir and pine forests.

▲ Northern Europe is crisscrossed by rivers, and many of the region's towns developed along a riverbank. This is the market town of Dinan in northwestern France.

REYKJAVIK
ICELAND

North Cape

Norwegian
Sea

Vesterålen
Lofoten

ATLANTIC

OCEAN

Faroe Islands
(to Denmark)

Shetland Islands
(to U.K.)

Outer Hebrides

Orkney Islands

N
O
R
W
A
Y

S
W
E
D
E
N

FINLAND

Gulf of Bothnia

RUSSIAN FEDERATION

OSLO

HELSINKI

STOCKHOLM

Gulf of Finland

Vänern

Vättern

UNITED
KINGDOM

North
Sea

DENMARK
COPENHAGEN

Gotland

Öland

Baltic
Sea

Bornholm

REP. OF
IRELAND
DUBLIN

Celtic
Sea

Isle of Man
(to UK)

LONDON

English Channel
Channel Islands
(to U.K.)

NETHS.
THE HAGUE
AMSTERDAM

BELGIUM
BRUSSELS

PARIS

LUX.
LUXEMBOURG

Elbe

Rhine

BERLIN

GERMANY

POLAND

CZECH
REPUBLIC

Seine
Loire

FRANCE

Bay of
Biscay

Garonne

Rhône

SWITZ.

A
L
P
S

Mont Blanc
15,777 ft △

Massif
Central

LIECH.

AUSTRIA

ITALY

SPAIN

Pyrenees

ANDORRA

MONACO

Ligurian
Sea

Mediterranean
Sea

Corsica
(to France)

0        250        500 km
0    125        250 miles

▶ A windmill in the Netherlands. In contrast to Scandinavia,
northern Belgium and the Netherlands are flat and barely rise
above sea level.

# NORWAY

**A mountainous and rugged country, Norway is the most northerly and westerly of the mainland Scandinavian nations and one of the most sparsely populated in Europe.**

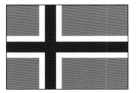

**Area:** 125,050 sq. mi. (323,878km²)
**Population:** 4,799,000
**Capital:** Oslo (876,000)
**Main language spoken:** Norwegian
**Main religion:** Evangelical Lutheran (Church of Norway)
**Currency:** Norwegian krone
**Main exports:** petroleum and natural gas and their products, machinery and transportation equipment, metals and metal products
**Type of government:** hereditary constitutional monarchy

▼ The first major discovery of oil was made at the Ekofisk field in the North Sea in 1969. Large oil terminals, such as this Statoil terminal, assist in processing and export.

Norway is a long, narrow country that runs northeast to southwest along the Scandinavian Peninsula and broadens out to the south where it borders the North Sea. An extended portion of the North Sea, called the Skagerrak, separates Norway from Denmark, and it shares a long land border with Sweden and much shorter, northerly borders with Finland and the Russian Federation. Norway has Arctic dependencies: the uninhabited island of Jan Mayen and the Svalbard archipelago. The Norwegian mainland consists of a large number of high plateaus called *vidder*. These are often very mountainous and are still covered in glaciers in the far north.

The Norwegian people live mostly in settlements along the coast, including the important cities of Bergen, Trondheim, and Stavanger, or in the southeast of the country where the capital city of Oslo is located.

## A COUNTRY OF WATER

Norway's western coastline is so indented that in a country that measures 1,650 mi. (2,650km) in length the coastline measures 13,264 mi. (21,347km). Along most of the coastline's length lie hundreds of islands collectively known as the *skerryguard*. These islands provide some shelter from the open sea, allowing Norwegian people to use the fjords and bays as excellent natural harbors. Most of this coastline is kept free of ice, despite lying in northern latitudes, due to the warm Gulf Stream current. Much of the country's landscape has been shaped by the various periods of glaciation. Norway has hundreds of rivers and streams that crisscross the country, as well as thousands of lakes. The largest lake is Lake Mjøsa (Mjoesa), which covers an area of 140 sq. mi. (362km²)and is situated in the southeast of the country, around 43 mi. (70km) north of Oslo. The lake often freezes during the winter months.

## FARMING, FORESTRY, AND FISHING

Approximately three percent of Norway's land can be farmed, and most of this land lies in the southeastern part of the country. Fodder crops, grown to feed livestock, such as hay, some cereals (including rye, oats, and barley), and root vegetables, are the most common crops. Pigs, sheep, and cattle are all raised. Over one fourth of its land remains covered in forests, and wood pulp and paper industries are as important as farming. No part of Norway is too far from the sea, and Norwegians have long relied on the sea for fishing, transportation, port trade, and boat- and shipbuilding industries. Norway has one of the largest fleets of merchant ships in the world, and its fishing industry, despite depletion of many fishing grounds, still catches around 2.4 million tons (2.2 million metric tonnes) of fish each year.

## AN OIL-RICH NATION

Norway's traditional industries have declined in favor of light industries, including furniture making, electronics, and oil and chemical processing. The discovery of large reserves of oil and natural gas off the Norwegian coast in the 1960s made a large difference to the country's economy. Today Norway is western Europe's largest oil producer, producing around 2.5 million barrels per day. Because Norway generates 99 percent of its own electricity from hydroelectric power, it is able to export a large proportion of its oil. This has helped give its population one of the highest standards of living in the world, with low unemployment and extensive social services.

▲ The spectacular Holmenkollen ski jump, near Oslo, is the world's oldest and is the site of Norway's annual ski festival held in March.

▼ The fishing village of Nusfjord on the island of Flakstadøya, one of the Lofoten islands, is located at the site of a picturesque natural harbor created by the process of glaciation.

# SWEDEN

**Sweden has a highly developed welfare state and advanced industries that help give its population a very high standard of living.**

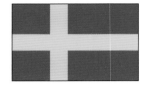

**Area:** 173,732 sq. mi. (449,964km²)
**Population:** 9,256,000
**Capital:** Stockholm (1,981,000)
**Main language spoken:** Swedish
**Main religion:** Evangelical Lutheran (Church of Sweden)
**Currency:** Swedish krona
**Main exports:** machinery and transportation equipment (mainly motor vehicles and electrical machinery), paper products, chemicals, iron and steel products
**Type of government:** constitutional monarchy

▼ The northern area of Sweden is part of a region called Lapland (Samiland), which extends into Norway, Finland, and Russia. Samiland has an Arctic climate, and dogsleds are still used in areas for transportation.

The kingdom of Sweden is the largest of the three Scandinavian countries and is also the most populous. Its eastern coast faces the Gulf of Bothnia and the Baltic Sea, while its much shorter western coast is an outlet to the North Sea. Sweden's main land border is with Norway, and to the west Sweden is mountainous just like its neighbor. To the northwest the Kölen Mountains contain Sweden's highest points. In central, eastern, and southern regions the landscape is less rugged and consists mostly of plateaus and gently rolling lowlands. Periods of glaciation have left behind many lakes. Sweden has more than 4,000 lakes over 0.39 sq. mi. (1km²) in size, while its largest, Lake Vänern, occupies 2,180 sq. mi. (5,650km²). Sweden also has many rivers, most of which flow eastward, emptying into the Gulf of Bothnia and the Baltic Sea.

### USING THE LAND
Around half of Sweden is covered in forests, most of which are situated to the north. Sweden exploits this huge resource and has become a leading producer of paper and timber products, with many timber-processing factories along its eastern coast. Less than seven percent of the country is suitable for farming, but intensive techniques mean that Sweden is able to be self-sufficient in a number

◄ The long waterfront street of Strandvagen in central Stockholm links the Old Town (Gamla Stan) with Diplomat Town, so-called because it contains many foreign embassies.

of crops, including wheat, barley, and potatoes, as well as raising large herds of pigs and cattle. Sweden generates 40 percent of its electricity from hydroelectric power. Much of this energy is used to power the country's industries, some of which use locally extracted minerals. Sweden has large reserves of iron ore and other metals but lacks coal or oil reserves and has to import these from Norway, Russia, and elsewhere.

## SWEDEN'S CITIES

Sweden's largest city, Stockholm, has been the capital for over 600 years. Built on a series of islands linked to the neighboring mainland by a mixture of ancient and modern bridges, it is one of the most elegant and picturesque capital cities in the world. It is also Sweden's second-biggest port and is the country's largest industrial area, with machine making, advanced telephone, and computer technologies and printing, chemical, and metalworking industries.

Stockholm is home to the country's national lawmaking body, the Riksdag. Just outside Stockholm is the official residence of the country's monarchy. Sweden's largest port is the city of Göteborg, found on its western coast. Located on the southernmost tip of Sweden, Malmö is a major port and trading center, likely to increase in importance since a 10-mi.- (15.5-km-) long transportation link, called the Øresund Fixed Link, was completed in 2000. This major engineering feat comprises 2 mi. (3.5km) of tunnels, 5 mi. (7.8km) of bridges, and 2.5 mi. (4km) of human-made islands linking Malmö to the capital city of Denmark, Copenhagen. It provides Sweden with a direct rail and road link with mainland Europe, building on its attempts to integrate more fully into Europe since joining the European Union in 1995.

▲ A member of the Sami people, formerly known as Lapps, in traditional dress. There are around 80,000 Sami found in Sweden, Finland, Norway, and Russia.

▼ The city of Göteborg lies on Sweden's western coast and is the largest port in Scandinavia, handling 43.5 million tons (39.5 million metric tonnes) of cargo per year.

# FINLAND

Finland is a low-lying country of lakes and forests. Physically isolated and remote from much of Europe, Finland joined the European Union in 1995.

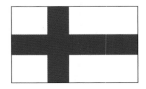

**Area:** 130,558 sq. mi. (338,145km²)
**Population:** 5,300,000
**Capital:** Helsinki (1,082,000)
**Main languages spoken:** Finnish, Swedish
**Main religion:** Evangelical Lutheran (Church of Sweden)
**Currency:** euro
**Main exports:** metal products and machinery, paper and paper products, electrical equipment, wood
**Type of government:** constitutional republic

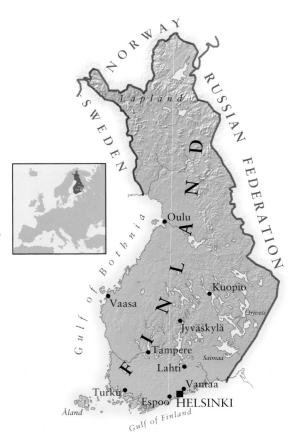

Lying between Russia to the east and Sweden to the west, Finland also shares a land border with Norway to the north. The western coast of Finland faces Sweden, separated by the Gulf of Bothnia. The Gulf of Finland, to the south, flows into the Baltic Sea and separates Finland from the small Baltic nation of Estonia. Most of Finland is relatively level, with an average elevation of between 393–622 ft. (120–190m). The coast of Finland, although not quite as indented with fjords as Norway, is still marked by thousands of mostly small islands. Many of these are found in the southwest, where an island chain called the Turun, or Turku, archipelago extends westward to the autonomous Åland Islands. The Åland Islands are made up of over 6,500 rocky reefs and granite islands, of which only 35 are inhabited. The landscape of Finland was greatly altered by glaciation in the past. Experts estimate that glaciers, several miles thick, forced Earth's crust downward by many feet. Since the glaciers and their weight have disappeared much of Finland is rising up from the sea at rates of as much as 0.4 in. (1cm) per year.

### THE LAND OF THE MIDNIGHT SUN

The northern part of Finland, a little over one fourth of its territory, lies within the Arctic Circle. It is the hilliest region of the country and rises into mountains to the northwest close to the border with Norway. In its most northerly region the sun does not set for 73 days in the summer and shines for 24 hours each day. This gives the region its nickname of "The Land of the Midnight Sun." In the same area during the dark winter period, called *Kaamos* in the Finnish language, the sun does not rise above the horizon for 51 days.

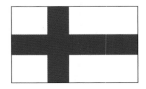

▲ A member of the Lapp (Sami) people fishes in the Arctic by cutting a hole in the ice through which he can extend his fishing line.

### LAKES AND FORESTS

Finland's scenery is dominated by large tracts of forests, which are found over three fourths of its land. More than 1,100 species of trees and plants are found in Finland. While some deciduous trees, such as aspen and elm, are found in the south, the large majority of its trees are coniferous and include pine and spruce. The forests provide habitats for a range of wildlife, including wild geese and swans and mammals such the Arctic fox, lynx, and wolf. Finland's forests are definitely its most important natural resource. Many exports come from its forests, including timber, young trees, wood chippings, and paper. Lacking large reserves of coal and oil, wood is one of only two naturally occurring fuels. The other is peat, which is mostly found in large peat bogs in the northern one third of the country. Finland has around 87,000 lakes that make

◄ Reindeer differ from other species of deer in that both males and females have antlers. Reindeer are herded by the Lapp (Sami) people found in Finland and elsewhere in Scandinavia. Their skins are used to produce clothing, boots, and tents, while their meat and milk are a source of food. Reindeer are also used as pack animals in some isolated regions.

▲ Part of the harbor area found in Finland's capital city of Helsinki.

up around ten percent of its land area. The largest of its inland waterways is Saimaa in southeastern Finland, which measures approximately 1,700 sq. mi. (4,400km²). Part of a complicated network of natural waterways, which includes 120 other lakes containing a total of 14,000 islands, the waters of the Saimaa flow to Lake Ladoga in Russia, the largest lake in Europe.

## HISTORY AND INDUSTRY

Positioned between Sweden and Russia, Finland has been governed by both of these nations for long periods of its history. From 1323 to 1809 it was under Swedish rule before becoming a territory of Russia until 1917, when it declared its independence. Finland's capital city was founded in 1550. It was moved to its present position on a small peninsula extending out into the Gulf of Finland in 1640. Helsinki has traditionally relied on its position as an important port, although all except one shipping channel is icebound from January to April or May every year. In the 1900s Finland developed an advanced industrial economy. Metal extraction and metalworking industries, along with engineering and electronics, account for just over half of all the money made through exports. Finland is particuary known for making cell phones and for modern design. Helsinki is its industrial and commercial center and also the home of the parliament, the Eduskunta. Its area includes almost 20 percent of the country's population.

▼ Koli National Park is located on the western shore of Lake Pielinen approximately 60 mi. (95km) east of Kuopin. The Koli hills are remnants of a mountain chain that formed almost two billion years ago. Over 120,000 visitors a year come to admire the views and hike through the trails that line the park.

# DENMARK

**The smallest and most densely populated of the Scandinavian countries, Denmark consists of a peninsula and 406 islands.**

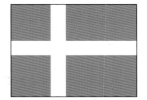

**Area:** 16,638 sq. mi.
(43,094km²)
**Population:** 5,511,000
**Capital:** Copenhagen
(1,168,000)
**Main language spoken:**
Danish
**Main religion:** Evangelical
Lutheran (Church of
Sweden)
**Currency:** Danish krone
**Main exports:** machinery,
pig meat, pharmaceuticals,
furniture, textiles and
clothing, dairy products
**Type of government:**
consitutional monarchy

Mainland Denmark occupies the Jutland Peninsula, which extends north from Germany almost 210 mi. (340km) into the North Sea. The portion of the North Sea that lies between Sweden and Denmark's eastern coast is called the Kattegat, and the arm of the North Sea that separates Norway from northwest Denmark is called the Skagerrak. In the south of Jutland Denmark has a 42-mi.-(68-km-) long border with Germany. The Jutland Peninsula makes up around 70 percent of Denmark's land area. The remainder is made up of a large series of islands mostly found to the east of Jutland. The country is responsible for two self-governing territories: the Faroe Islands and the world's biggest individual island, Greenland.

### A LOWLAND, TEMPERATE COUNTRY

Denmark is one of the lowest and flattest countries in the world. Almost the entire country is low-lying, with an average elevation of only 100 ft. (30m) above sea level. The 227 sq. mi. (588km²) island of Bornholm, lying east of Denmark in the Baltic Sea, is an exception since it is covered with rocky hills. The western coast of Jutland is indented with lagoons, spits, and sandbars. Fjords

cut into parts of the eastern coast. The largest fjord, Limfjorden, slices right through the northern part of the Jutland Peninsula and broadens into a complex series of inland waterways. Denmark's climate is temperate with mild summers, when temperatures can reach 77°F (25°C), and cold, rainy winters, when the average daily temperatures hover around freezing point. Winter temperatures are up to 50°F (10°C) warmer than average for this latitude. The warming effect of the Gulf Stream, which sweeps northward along the west coast of the country, is the reason for Denmark's milder-than-typical climate.

▲ The Tivoli Gardens is a large area in the center of Copenhagen that was opened in 1843. It includes concert halls, cafés, flower gardens, and an amusement park.

► Nyhavn Canal in Copenhagen is lined with picturesque buildings—many dating back to the 1500s. Most immigrants to Denmark and one fifth of the entire Danish population live in or around Copenhagen. The city is situated on the island of Sjaelland.

## A FARMING NATION

Denmark's manufacturing and service industries are very important to the economy, although the country has few mineral resources. However, Denmark has natural gas reserves and extensively harnesses wind power. Almost two thirds of its land is used for farming. Centuries of cultivation have improved the land's ability to grow crops, particularly cereals, of which wheat, followed by barley and rye, are the most important. Much of Denmark's farmland is used to support livestock, particularly pigs and cattle. In 2008, Denmark had 13.5 million pigs, two million cattle, and produced nearly four million tons of barley. It also has a large fishing fleet of around 2,500 vessels, which catch over one million tons of fish every year.

## THE DANES

Denmark has been occupied for thousands of years but took its name from the Danes—a people from Sweden who colonized the region around A.D. 500. Denmark's oldest town, Ribe, near Esbjerg, was an international trading center as far back as A.D. 850. Scandinavian peoples make up 96 percent of its population. People of German origin are found close to Denmark's border with Germany, and there are small numbers of Turks, Iranians, Pakistanis, and some refugees from countries such as the former Yugoslavia and Somalia. Denmark's people enjoy one of the highest standards of living in the world.

▲ The south Denmark island of Fyn has large expanses of fertile land on which cereal crops and fruit are grown.

# FAROE ISLANDS

**Lying in the North Atlantic Ocean halfway between Norway, Iceland, and Scotland, the Faroes are a group of islands that are a self-governing territory of Denmark.**

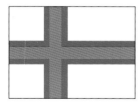

**Area:** 540 sq. mi. (1,399km²)
**Population:** 48,800
**Capital:** Tórshavn (17,000)
**Main languages spoken:** Faroese, Danish
**Main religions:** Evangelical Lutheran (Church of Sweden), Plymouth Brethren
**Currency:** Faroese krone
**Main exports:** fish and fish products
**Type of government:** self-governing dependency of Denmark

The Faroe Islands are clustered closely together and are separated by deep fjords. The islands were shaped by volcanic action and subsequent erosion, which has created sharp cliffs and towering stacks on a number of the islands and has deposited a relatively thin layer of soil in many places. Almost constant high winds mean that the islands have few naturally occurring trees, although some have been planted in artificially sheltered areas. Large flocks of seabirds are found on the islands' coasts, while a thick grass layer in many areas provides food for sheep. However, the majority of Faroe Islanders are engaged in fishing industries. The seas around the islands are rich in fish, including cod and haddock, and the prospects of offshore oil

exploration have increased following an agreement signed in 1999 between Denmark and the United Kingdom.

# ICELAND

**Lying in the north Atlantic Ocean, Iceland is a young, volcanic island. Its population relies largely on the fishing industry for trade.**

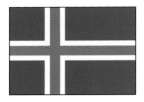

**Area:** 39,699 sq. mi. (102,819km²)
**Population:** 319,000
**Capital:** Reykjavík (201,000)
**Main language spoken:** Icelandic
**Main religion:** Evangelical Lutheran (Church of Sweden)
**Currency:** Icelandic krona
**Main exports:** frozen fish, shrimp and lobsters, salted fish, fresh fish, aluminum
**Type of government:** constitutional republic

▲ Thermal springs are found in various parts of Iceland and are harnessed to heat many buildings. Erupting hot springs, called geysers, got their name from an example found on Iceland called Geysir.

► Around two thirds of Iceland's population live in Reykjavík, its capital city. The center of Iceland's fishing and fish-processing industries, Reykjavík is also home to Iceland's only university and the world's oldest ongoing law-making body, the Althing (established in A.D. 930).

Iceland is just 178 mi. (287km) east of Greenland and 496 mi. (798km) northwest of Scotland. Most of its landscape consists of a rocky plateau dotted with mountains. Its entire area is elevated between 1,970–3,120 ft. (600–950m) above sea level. Around 15 percent of the land is covered in ice or snowfields. The coastline is indented with deep bays, steep cliffs, and fjords on the east and northwest, while the south coasts tend to be more low-lying. Geologically, Iceland is a very young country and still in the process of formation. Iceland sits on a major geological fault—the mid-Atlantic rift—which makes it one of the most volcanically active countries in the world.

### THE ICELANDIC PEOPLE
Celtic people from Ireland and Norse people from Scandinavia were Iceland's first settlers, and almost all of the country's population are their descendants. Iceland was first ruled by Norway and then Denmark, before independence in 1918.

Greenland Sea

Ísafjördhur
Saudhárkrókur
Akureyri
Breidhafjördehur

**ICELAND**

Faxaflói
Akranes
REYKJAVÍK
Vatnajökull
Keflavík
Selfoss
△Hvannadalshnúkur 6,950 ft.

Vestmann Islands • Vestmannaeyjar

**ATLANTIC OCEAN**

▲ Sea fishing contributes more than 70 percent of all export income to the Icelandic economy. The biggest customers are the United Kingdom and Germany.

Almost all electricity and much heating is generated by abundant hydroelectric and geothermal power, which is used to smelt aluminum. In 2009 Iceland's economy faltered when its major banks collapsed.

# BRITISH ISLES

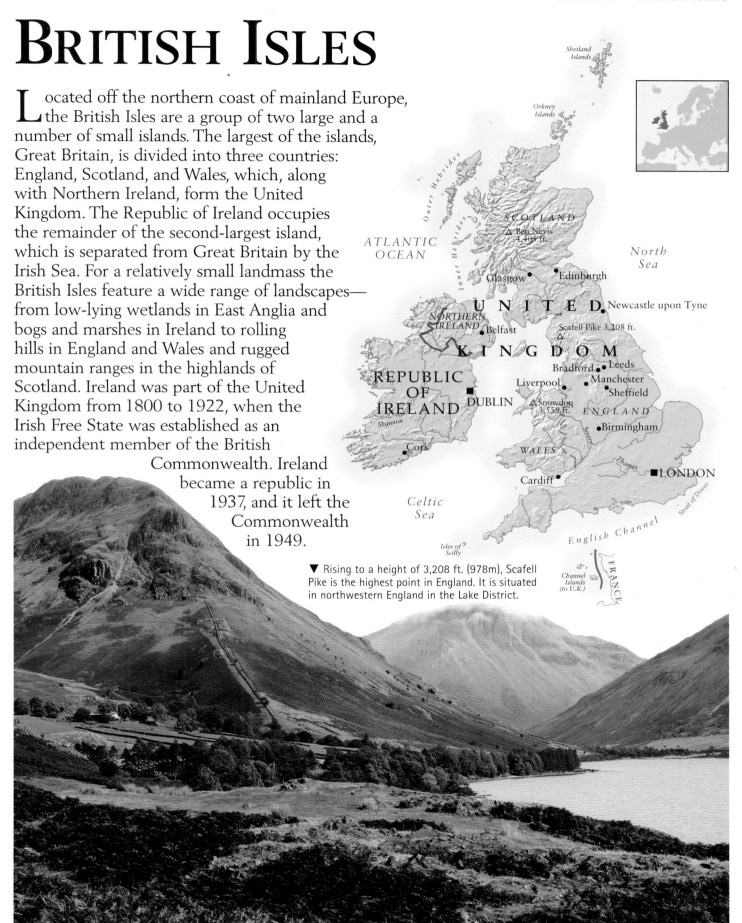

Located off the northern coast of mainland Europe, the British Isles are a group of two large and a number of small islands. The largest of the islands, Great Britain, is divided into three countries: England, Scotland, and Wales, which, along with Northern Ireland, form the United Kingdom. The Republic of Ireland occupies the remainder of the second-largest island, which is separated from Great Britain by the Irish Sea. For a relatively small landmass the British Isles feature a wide range of landscapes— from low-lying wetlands in East Anglia and bogs and marshes in Ireland to rolling hills in England and Wales and rugged mountain ranges in the highlands of Scotland. Ireland was part of the United Kingdom from 1800 to 1922, when the Irish Free State was established as an independent member of the British Commonwealth. Ireland became a republic in 1937, and it left the Commonwealth in 1949.

Shetland Islands

Orkney Islands

Outer Hebrides

ATLANTIC OCEAN

Inner Hebrides

SCOTLAND

△ Ben Nevis 4,405 ft.

North Sea

Glasgow • Edinburgh

UNITED

NORTHERN IRELAND

• Belfast

Newcastle upon Tyne

Scafell Pike 3,208 ft. △

KINGDOM

REPUBLIC OF IRELAND

Shannon

DUBLIN

Bradford •• Leeds

Liverpool • • Manchester
• Sheffield

△ Snowdon 3,559 ft.

ENGLAND

Severn

• Birmingham

Cork

WALES

Thames

Cardiff

■ LONDON

Celtic Sea

English Channel

Strait of Dover

Isles of Scilly

Channel Islands (to U.K.)

FRANCE

▼ Rising to a height of 3,208 ft. (978m), Scafell Pike is the highest point in England. It is situated in northwestern England in the Lake District.

# IRELAND

One of the most westerly European nations, the Republic of Ireland occupies much of the island of Ireland and consists of farmland, lakes, and mountains.

**Area:** 27,137 sq. mi. (70,285km²)
**Population:** 4,240,000
**Capital:** Dublin (1,046,000)
**Main languages spoken:** English, Irish (Gaelic)
**Main religion:** Roman Catholic
**Currency:** euro
**Main exports:** machinery and transportation equipment, chemical products, food products (particularly dairy products and meat), manufactured goods
**Type of government:** parliamentary republic

The Republic of Ireland is located on the most westerly part of the Eurasian landmass and, like Great Britain, was once part of the European mainland. Great Britain and Ireland became separated only around 11,000 years ago owing to melting glaciers and rising sea levels. Ireland's landscape consists of a large central plain almost completely surrounded by highlands near the coast. The plain is relatively low, averaging around 300 ft. (90m) in height and broken in many places by low hills, lakes, and rivers. The country's main river is the Shannon, which rises in the north of the country and forms a long estuary south of Limerick. A broad, slow-moving river, at 231 mi. (372km) in length, the Shannon is the longest river in the British Isles.

### THE EMERALD ISLE

Ireland's climate is moderated by the warm waters of the North Atlantic Drift, which help make the winters milder than other places in a similar latitude. The average daily temperature in the winter is between 40–45°F (4–7°C)—as much as 57°F (14°C) warmer than comparable places of a similar latitude. The opposite effect occurs in the summer, when average temperatures are

The map shows:
ATLANTIC OCEAN

Malin Head, Letterkenny, NORTHERN IRELAND (to U.K.), Donegal Bay, Sligo, Ballina, Castlebar, Longford, Drogheda, REPUBLIC OF IRELAND, Galway, Athlone, DUBLIN, Galway Bay, Dún Laoghaire, Bray, Ennis, Portlaoise, Wicklow Mountains, Carlow, Limerick, Kilkenny, Shannon, Clonmel, Tralee, Waterford, Wexford, Carrauntoohil △ 3,414 ft., Killarney, Cork, Mizen Head, Dundalk

▲ Found in the center of Dublin, St. Patrick's Cathedral was founded in 1191, although a church had been on its site since the A.D. 400s. At 300 ft. (91m) in length, St. Patrick's is one of the largest cathedrals in Ireland.

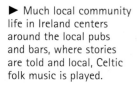

▶ Much local community life in Ireland centers around the local pubs and bars, where stories are told and local, Celtic folk music is played.

▲ A sheep market in the town of Ballinrobe, 16 mi. south of Castlebar in County Mayo. In 2009 there were over five million sheep in the Republic of Ireland.

## A CHANGING ECONOMY

For a long period Ireland's economy relied on traditional methods of agriculture, with crops such as sugar beets, potatoes, and cereals grown. Many pigs were kept, sheep grazed on mountain slopes, and cattle were raised in the center and south of the country. Agriculture remains important, but Ireland's economy is changing dramatically. Farming has been modernized with financial assistance from the European Union. Around six percent of its workforce is now employed in agriculture. Many more people work in new manufacturing industries, such as electronics and computing, and in the food, drink, and clothing industries. However, in 2008–2009 a banking and building industry crisis damaged development. Ireland's beautiful landscape, history, and culture have been heavily promoted to foreign visitors, and in 2009 6.9 million tourists visited the country.

▲ An Irish peat cutter removes chunks of peat, which has been used for many centuries as a fuel. Peat is the remains of dead, rotted plants that have been squeezed together. When it is burned, peat generates heat. Several power plants in Ireland are powered by peat.

kept to a relatively cool 59–63°F (15–17°C). With the warming ocean currents and Atlantic winds come plenty of rain. It tends to rain on two out of three days throughout the year, and average rainfall can be as high as 100 in. (250cm) in the mountains of the southwest. This heavy rainfall helps promote the thick grass, moss, and wild plants and flowers that cover much of the country and give Ireland the nickname "the Emerald Isle." Peat bogs, which occupy around ten percent of the land, are homes for rare wild plants but are threatened owing to peat's continued use as a fuel to generate power and also as a fertilizer. Many small mammals, including stoats, hare, and foxes, along with over 120 species of native birds, inhabit the country.

## TRADITIONAL LIFE

All of Ireland has a long tradition of settlement stretching back at least 9,000 years. Around 2,400 years ago Celts arrived from mainland Europe. Since that time Ireland was often isolated from the rest of Europe—for example, it was never part of the Roman Empire—which led to its people developing a rich and different culture and language called Gaelic. English has taken over from Gaelic as the most widely spoken language and, although still taught in schools, is only the first language of a dwindling number of people in rural areas. Other elements of Irish culture still flourish in Celtic art, literature, and various forms of music.

▶ Found on the western coast of Ireland, the Cliffs of Moher are a series of shale and sandstone cliffs that reach heights in excess of 655 ft. (200m).

# UNITED KINGDOM

A union of four countries—England, Scotland, Wales, and Northern Ireland—the densely populated United Kingdom lies off the coast of northwest Europe.

**Area:** 94,243 sq. mi. (244,088km²)
**Population:** 61,383,0020
**Capital:** London (8,278,000)
**Main languages spoken:** English, Welsh, Scottish, Gaelic
**Main religions:** Christian churches (Anglican, Roman Catholic, Methodist), Islam
**Currency:** pound sterling
**Main exports:** electrical equipment, chemicals, road vehicles, petroleum and petroleum products
**Type of government:** kingdom; democracy

▲ The London Eye towers 443 ft. (135m) over the Thames river. More than 15,000 passengers can travel in its pods each day.

▲ London was the first city to have a subway. The London Underground opened in 1863 and now serves more than 260 stations.

▶ The prehistoric stone circle of Stonehenge in southern England was built between 3200 and 1000 B.C. It is one of the most important prehistoric monuments in Europe.

The United Kingdom's territory consists of the island of Great Britain, a northeastern portion of Ireland, and a large number of smaller islands off its coast. Due to the warming effect of the Gulf Stream, the country has a temperate climate with relatively high rainfall and milder winters than usual for its latitude. Its location, at a point where many seas and air currents meet, means that its weather is extremely changeable. In general the south of the country tends to be warmer, and the west of the country tends to receive more rainfall.

## A VARIED LANDSCAPE

For such a small area the landscape of the U.K. has great variation, from lowland areas barely above sea level to rugged mountain ranges in Scotland, Wales, and the north of England. Around half of Scotland consists of the Highlands and a large number of islands off its coast, while Wales' landscape is dominated by the Cambrian Mountains, which run through much of the principality from north to south. Northern Ireland is a region of rolling plains with some low mountains. Northern England features hills and low mountain ranges, while most of the rest of the country is relatively flat with occasional areas of gentle hills.

The U.K. has a large number of rivers crisscrossing its land—most of the major cities are sited on rivers; for example, London is located on the Thames, and Newcastle is on the Tyne. The longest river is the Severn (220 mi./354km), which flows from central Wales to southwest England. Scotland's heavily indented coastline, and its

many lakes—known as lochs—reveal the past action of glaciers that have greatly shaped the country's landscape.

Glaciation also scoured out river valleys to form the lakes in the scenic Lake District of northwest England.

▼ At a height of 800 ft. (244m), Number One, Canada Square—known as the Canary Wharf building—is the tallest in the United Kingdom. It is a landmark in the Docklands area of London, which has been redeveloped since the 1980s from old, disused docks and warehouses to become a major financial, media, and business center.

The Lake District is also the home to England's highest point, Scafell Pike. Mount Snowdon is the highest point in Wales, and Ben Nevis is the highest point in Scotland and all of the British Isles. The U.K.'s largest lake is Northern Ireland's Lough Neagh, which is located just 12 mi. (20km) west of Belfast.

### FLORA, FAUNA, AND FARMING

Most of the U.K. was once covered in forests, but thousands of years of human settlement and activity have reduced these areas dramatically. Although replanting programs have been in place since the early 1900s, the U.K. has one of the lowest levels of tree cover in Europe. Coniferous trees, such as pine, are found in Scotland, while the most common trees elsewhere are beech, ash, oak, and chestnut. The largest animal found in the wild is the red deer, found in Scotland and on Exmoor in southwestern England, while smaller mammals found in the wild include foxes, voles, shrews, mice, and squirrels. The hedgerows, moors, and coasts of the U.K. provide habitats for many species of birds, but all fauna and much of the U.K.'s rich collection of wildflowers have suffered from habitat destruction and air and water pollution. Around seven percent of the U.K. is under a degree of protection as national parks. These include Snowdonia in North Wales, the Lake District, and areas of the North York Moors, 9 mi. (15km) south of Middlesbrough. Much of the U.K. is farmed, with belts of cropland and large areas of pastures on which livestock herds are grazed. Although only one percent of the workforce is employed in agriculture, the U.K. is self-sufficient in 60 percent of all types of food and animal feed.

▲ Canals, such as the Trent and Mersey in the Midlands of England (opened in 1777), were built to transport materials and goods during the Industrial Revolution. Today the majority of canals are used for leisure cruising.

## THE FIRST INDUSTRIALIZED NATION

The United Kingdom was the first country in the world to undergo an industrial revolution. Based on industries, including coal, iron, steel, and textiles, the U.K. became wealthy through inventing and pioneering the machines and factory processes used in industry. However, coal mining, steelworking, shipbuilding, and other heavy industry have been in decline for many years.

In their place have come fast-growing service industries and high-tech companies, medicine and chemical manufacturers, industrial researchers, and engineering firms. Aided by large offshore oil and natural gas reserves, the U.K. is the sixth-biggest economy in the world today and is a major international trading power.

## CROWDED ISLANDS

The United Kingdom is Europe's fourth-most-populous nation after Russia, Germany, and France (although the U.K. is less than half the size of France). The population density is around 640 people per square mile, with 90 percent living in or around major towns and cities. In the past century the urban areas of the U.K. have sprawled outward, creating both new towns, such as Milton Keynes, halfway between London and Birmingham, and large urban areas called conurbations such

as the many towns around Birmingham. The majority of the population of each of the three countries of Great Britain are situated in the south. The south coast of Wales includes the cities of Swansea, Cardiff, and Newport, while Scotland's two largest cities of Glasgow and Edinburgh are both south of the Highlands. The southeast is the most densely populated portion of England and is dominated by London. Founded by the Romans in A.D. 43, London is one of the world's foremost cities. Its prosperity is founded mostly on services, such as insurance, finance, and trading, while its many historic buildings and parks attract millions of tourists every year.

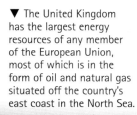

▲ Sitting on a giant volcanic rock that towers over Scotland's capital city, Edinburgh Castle has been the main Scottish royal fortress for many centuries.

▼ The United Kingdom has the largest energy resources of any member of the European Union, most of which is in the form of oil and natural gas situated off the country's east coast in the North Sea.

◀ The Millennium Stadium is the national stadium of Wales and hosts concerts and sports events. It has a sliding roof and seats over 72,000 spectators.

The Northern Ireland Assembly, held in the city of Belfast, has been troubled by problems between the Protestant majority and the Catholic minority. The U.K. head of state is officially the monarch, but power is held by the prime minister, usually the leader of the majority political party in the House of Commons in Westminster, London.

▲ Over 11 million cattle, including this Highland Breed, are raised in the U.K. The outbreak of foot-and-mouth disease in 2001 caused more than one million cattle to die.

## A COLONIAL POWER
From the 1600s to the 1900s the U.K. was one of the world's major colonial powers, with the British empire laying claim to territory on every continent and exploiting its colonies' resources and peoples in order to grow wealthy and powerful. Most of its former colonies are now independent but are part of a loose alliance of states known as the Commonwealth. The U.K. still controls a number of dependencies as far away as the Falkland Islands in the south Atlantic and Turks & Caicos in the Caribbean. Closer to home are the Isle of Man, lying between Ireland and Great Britain, and Jersey and Guernsey, lying off the northern coast of France. All of these dependencies have their own legal systems, but the U.K. government is responsible for their external affairs. The U.K. continues to exert international influence through its close relationship with the U.S. and as a member of the European Union.

▲ The symbol of the Celtic cross is found at standing signs and statues, especially in Scotland and Northern Ireland.

▼ Giant's Causeway on the north coast of Northern Ireland was formed over 50 million years ago from volcanic lava that cooled to form over 40,000 basaltic pillars.

## THE U.K.'S PEOPLE
In the past the U.K.'s position as an island nation lying close to mainland Europe saw it undergo periods of both isolation and invasion. Migration by Celtic people, occupation by the Romans, and waves of invasion and settlement by Danes, Saxons, Vikings, and the Normans have all left their mark. Most of the U.K. population descended from these invaders and settlers. Sizable communities of other ethnic groups do exist, including people from former British colonies in Africa, the Caribbean, and south Asia, as well as Chinese, Jewish, and European peoples. Although Celtic languages still exist, especially in Wales, the dominant language is English, which is primarily a blend of Anglo-Saxon and Norman French.

## FOUR COUNTRIES IN ONE
The U.K. has a complex political history. England and Wales were united by the 1500s, and the 1707 Act of Union formed the Kingdom of Great Britain, including Scotland. For a period from 1801 to the 1920s Great Britain and all of Ireland were ruled as one nation. Wales, Scotland, and Northern Ireland have their own national identity, different elements of culture, and a degree of government devolved away from the U.K. national government based in London. In 1999 the Scottish Parliament and the National Assembly for Wales were opened, giving these two countries more control over their own affairs.

# BELGIUM

One of the Benelux countries (along with Luxembourg and the Netherlands), Belgium is an industrialized nation in which 97 percent of its people live in urban areas.

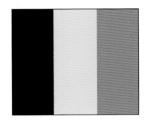

**Area:** 11,787 sq. mi. (30,528km²)
**Population:** 10,667,000
**Capital:** Brussels (1,049,000)
**Main languages spoken:** Flemish (Dutch), French, German
**Main religions:** Roman Catholic, Protestant
**Currency:** euro
**Main exports:** machinery and transportation equipment, chemicals (particularly plastics), food, diamonds, metal products, textiles
**Type of government:** parliamentary democracy

The north of Belgium has a similar landscape to the Netherlands. It is a flat coastal plain, barely rising more than a few feet above sea level and is laced with river deltas and canals. Most of the coastline is marked by a belt of giant sand dunes that are among the largest in Europe. South of the coastal plain is a central plateau region that contains the country's best farming land. The southeastern area of the country is part of the Ardennes region, a rocky, heavily forested region with an average elevation of 1,510 ft. (460m). Belgium's main river, the Meuse, is linked with other rivers and canals, giving the country almost 1,000 mi. (1,600km) of inland waterways, most of which can be traveled by large boats.

## A TRADING NATION

Belgium's location between a number of European countries, plus its access to the oceans via the Scheldt estuary, on which the port of Antwerp lies, has made it a major trading nation. Belgium's manufacturing industries include metalworking, steel, cloth, and carpet making, and heavy engineering. Much of the electricity required by these industries is supplied by nuclear power, which generates almost two thirds of Belgium's electricity. Lacking large reserves of raw materials, Belgium imports many of them raw and exports finished or semifinished goods. Millions of tons of imports and exports pass through the port of Antwerp. Situated around 50 mi. (80km) inland from the North Sea, Antwerp is one of the largest ports in Europe.

▲ Work building the City Hall in Belgium's capital city of Brussels started in 1402. The imposing tower is 315 ft. (96m) high.

▶ The Atomium stands in Heysel Exhibition Park in Brussels and has become a symbol of the city. Designed for the 1958 World's Fair, the 394-ft.- (120-m-) high structure is an aluminum model of a carbon molecule magnified 165 billion times.

## LANGUAGE DIVISIONS

Belgium is divided into three federal districts that reflect, in part, its centuries-old language divisions between its Flemish or Dutch-speaking people, known as Flemings, and its French-speaking people, called the Walloons. Flanders, its northern district, is principally home to the Flemings, while the southern district, Wallonia, is populated mainly by French speakers. Bilingual signs in Flemish and French are common throughout the country, while a small German-speaking minority lives in the extreme east of the country. The third district, the land in and around Brussels, its capital city, has a mixed population. Brussels is home to one tenth of Belgium's population and is an international business center. The city is also the administrative center of the European Union and home to the major headquarters of the North Atlantic Treaty Organization (NATO).

▲ The picturesque city of Ghent, located in western Belgium, lies at the joining point of two rivers. These rivers, along with many canals, crisscross the city, dividing it into many small islands linked by more than 200 bridges.

# LUXEMBOURG

**A small nation bordering Germany, the Netherlands, and France, Luxembourg is a center for finance and for the European Court of Justice.**

**Area:** 998 sq. mi. (2,586km²)
**Population:** 494,000
**Capital:** Luxembourg (130,000)
**Main languages spoken:** Luxembourgian, English, German, French
**Main religion:** Roman Catholic
**Currency:** euro
**Main exports:** machinery and transportation equipment, plastics and rubber, textiles, processed food
**Type of government:** constitutional monarchy

Luxembourg's landscape can be divided into two areas. The northern one third consists of densely forested hills and many narrow valleys with fast-flowing streams. The southern two thirds have a more gentle landscape of meadows, vineyards, and forests. The southwest is heavily industrialized with large iron and steelworks and some chemical and food-processing plants.

The people of Luxembourg enjoy the highest standard of living in Europe. Almost one third of Luxembourg's workers are foreigners, many of them employed by more than 200 banks, including the European Investment Bank, which are based in the country. Luxembourg is also home to the European Court of Justice. Most of the country's population speak two or three languages.

French is the main language used in the courts, while German is the language used in newspapers and literature. For centuries Luxembourg was ruled by other countries, and it finally regained complete independence in 1839.

# THE NETHERLANDS

**Lying between Germany and Belgium with a long North Sea coastline, the Netherlands is one of the lowest-lying countries in the world.**

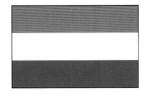

**Area:** 16,033 sq. mi. (41,526km²)
**Population:** 16,486,000
**Capitals:** Amsterdam (1,497,000); The Hague—seat of government (1,008,000)
**Main language spoken:** Dutch
**Main religions:** Roman Catholic, Protestant Church of the Netherlands
**Currency:** euro
**Main exports:** machinery and transportation equipment (particularly motor vehicles), food (mainly meat and dairy products), chemicals and chemical products, petroleum
**Type of government:** parliamentary democracy under a constitutional monarch

Geographically, the Netherlands can be divided into two regions, the Low Netherlands to the north and west and a smaller region of gently rolling land, called the High Netherlands, to the southeast. The average elevation of the High Netherlands is below 164 ft. (50m). Because the Netherlands has no high hill ranges or mountains, the climate varies little from area to area, with only a slight difference in temperatures and rainfall between the coast and inland areas. The Netherlands has a temperate maritime climate shared by much of northwestern Europe. The winters are mild, while the summers are kept cool by westerly winds. Rainfall averages around 30 in. (73cm) per year.

## BELOW SEA LEVEL

The country derives its name from the Dutch word for low-lying land, and around one fourth of its land lies below sea level. Much of the country has been reclaimed from the sea or fortified to stop rivers from submerging the surrounding area.

From the 1200s onward barriers were built to stop water from getting in, and windmills were used to pump out excess water. By the 1800s the Netherlands had over 9,000 windmills. Polders are areas of drained land surrounded and protected by embankments called dikes. Today there are over 5,000 polders in the Netherlands, the largest of which was the result of the Zuyder Zee works, during which time the inland sea, the Zuyder Zee, became a lake and 637 sq. mi. (1,650km²) of land were created.

▶ Opened in 1996, the Erasmus Bridge provides a link over the river at the major European port of Rotterdam. Rising to a height of 455 ft. (139m) and spanning a width of 2,625 ft. (800m), the bridge took seven years to construct. Its steel deck contains lanes for vehicles, a tram track, two footpaths, and two cycle paths.

▲ Around 27,000 acres of fruit, vegetables, and flowers are grown under glass in the Netherlands. More than one tenth of this is devoted to growing peppers, which are shown here being harvested for export.

Without dikes and dams the most densely populated part of the Netherlands—around half of the country's land area—would be submerged by the North Sea and the country's rivers.

## EUROPE'S LARGEST PORT

Located at the center of the most industrialized and populated area in the world is the port of Rotterdam. Originally a fishing village, Rotterdam was seriously damaged in the two world wars but has since developed into the world's largest port and is a major oil refining and trading center. It has a prime location 20 mi. (30km) inland from the North Sea and lies at the mouths of two important European rivers, the Rhine and the Meuse. Tens of thousands of cargo barges, loaded and unloaded at Rotterdam, travel the Rhine, taking raw materials and goods into France, Germany, and the heart of Europe. Every year, nearly 660 million tons (600 million metric tonnes) of goods enter Dutch ports, particularly Rotterdam. Shipping is not the only way goods are transported. Giant pipelines carry oil and petroleum products to other parts of the Netherlands, to Belgium, and to Germany.

▶ The picturesque city of Amsterdam, with its well-preserved buildings, 160 canals, and hundreds of bridges, is a popular tourist destination for foreign visitors.

## THE DUTCH PEOPLE

The Netherlands is one of the world's most densely populated nations, more than 1,000 people per square mile. A proportion of the country's population are immigrants from Turkey, Morocco, and former Dutch colonies, including parts of Indonesia, Suriname, and the Netherlands Antilles. Half of the country is farmed, and Dutch farming is among the most advanced and intensive in the world. The Netherlands has one of the 20 largest and most powerful economies based on its transportation and trade services, including tourism and the engineering, chemical, and electronics industries.

# GERMANY

**The fourth-largest economy in the world, Germany lies at the heart of Europe and is a vital part of the European Union.**

**Area:** 137,847 sq. mi. (357,021km²)
**Population:** 82,002,000
**Capital:** Berlin (4,298,000)
**Main language spoken:** German
**Main religions:** Protestant, Roman Catholic
**Currency:** euro
**Main exports:** road transportation equipment, chemicals and chemical products, other machinery, electrical equipment, foodstuffs
**Type of government:** federal republic

Germany extends from the Alps in the south to a northern coastline that borders both the North Sea and Baltic Sea, a maximum distance of 544 mi. (876km). The country's territory extends into islands in both seas, most notably the islands of Rügen, Hiddensee, and Fehmarn in the Baltic Sea and the East and North Frisian Islands in the North Sea. The country shares 2,250 mi. (3,621km) of borders with nine countries: France, Luxembourg, the Netherlands, and Belgium to the west; Switzerland and Austria to the south; Denmark to the north; and Poland and the Czech Republic to the east.

▼ Heavy industry, such as this chemical factory near the Elbe river, remains an important part of the German economy, although services and light industries, such as electronics, contribute more to the economy.

**LOWLANDS AND UPLANDS**
Germany's landscape is varied, including heavily forested hills and mountains, plains and lakes, and many winding rivers.

The country can be split into three main geographical regions. A large lowland belt lies to the north and stretches from the Netherlands to Poland. It contains dry, sandy plains with moors (bogs) and heaths. The second major geographical area is the Central Uplands, which divides northern Germany from the south. It consists of a number of hill and mountain ranges, river valleys, and plateau areas. Its highest point reaches 3,747 ft. (1,142m) above sea level. The southern part of Germany consists mainly of hills and mountains, the lower slopes of which are heavily forested. Part of southern Germany lies in the Alps mountain system and is known as the Bavarian Alps.

## GERMANY'S FORESTS

Germany is a heavily populated industrial country, but it is large enough to also include huge areas of relatively untouched forests. Around 30 percent of Germany is forested, and around one third of this area is covered with deciduous trees, such as beech, oak, and birch, while the remainder consists of firs, pines, and other coniferous trees. Half of all Germany's forested areas are owned by the state or by the local community, while farmers and forestry companies manage and harvest fast-growing coniferous trees for timber, paper, and other wood-based products. The Bavarian Forest in southeast Germany is the largest mountain forest in Western Europe. Germany's most famous forest, the Black Forest, is in the southwest of the country and covers an area of over 1,970 sq. mi. (5,100km²) and attracts thousands of tourists from Germany and elsewhere to view its scenery and picturesque lakes.

▲ A horseshoe bend in the Saar river. This river starts its life in the northern Vosges Mountains of France and meanders in a northwesterly direction through Germany before becoming a tributary of the Mosel river.

▼ A major financial and commercial center that hosts many international trade fairs every year, Frankfurt is also the home of the European Central Bank. The city's airport is also among the busiest in Europe.

## A GOOD FARMING CLIMATE

Germany is situated in the moderately cool zone between the Atlantic Ocean and the continental climate of Eastern Europe. Almost all of the country features a temperate climate, with rainfall occurring throughout the year and long periods of overcast skies even when rain does not fall. The country has an average annual temperature of 48°F (9°C), and sharp changes in temperature are rare, although there is a great difference between the seasons. In the winter the average temperature is between 35°F (2°C) in the lowland areas and 21°F (-6°C) in the mountains. In the warmest month of the year, July, temperatures are between 64°F (18°C) in low-lying regions and 68°F (20°C) in the sheltered valleys of the south. In parts of the southern region of Germany called Bavaria occasional warm winds, called Föhns, pass over the northern Alps and can cause abrupt melting snow. With a long growing season free of frost, over 28 in. (70cm) of rain fall each year, and few extremes of temperature, Germany's climate is suitable for many forms of farming. The country is home to 27 million pigs, 13 million cattle, and 110 million chickens and

is one of the world's top-ten producers of cereal crops such as barley. Despite less than three percent of the country's population employed in growing crops, Germany is a major producer of potatoes and other root vegetables, as well as hops used to make beer. Food- and drink-processing is one of the largest employers in Germany, with the country being the second-largest beer brewer after the U.S. and one of the top-ten wine producers in the world.

## THE RHINE AND OTHER RIVERS

Germany's biggest river is the Rhine, which flows from the Alps in Switzerland through or along the boundaries of Austria, Liechtenstein, France, Germany, and the Netherlands before emptying into the North Sea. A broad river, the Rhine acted as a natural boundary in historic times and is now a vital transportation link. Giant barges carrying millions of tons of cargo travel its length. In 1992 the 106-mi.- (171-km-) long Main-Donau-Kanal was opened. This links the Danube, which flows through Eastern Europe, with the Rhine, allowing heavy cargo to be carried through the center of Europe. Apart from the Rhine and Main, a further ten major rivers flow through Germany. These include the Elbe, Ems, and Main. All are navigable along most of their length and provide important transportation links for the industries that are found along their banks.

▲ The New Town Hall with its ornate tower lies in the Marienplatz in the heart of the city of Munich. In the Middle Ages this square was the site of markets, festivals, and tournaments.

▼ The distinctive buildings of the Markplatz (marketplace) in the medieval town of Rothenberg, around 40 mi. (65km) south of Nuremberg.

East Germans help to break down the Berlin Wall in 1989. A landmark in the history of Germany, the Berlin Wall had divided Germany into two nations for over 35 years. Most of the wall is now dismantled, but some parts have been preserved—most notable of which is the East Side Gallery. This 4,318-ft.- (1,316-m-) long stretch features 106 paintings.

Consequently, Germany is the world's second-largest exporter. Over one fourth of the German workforce is employed by the manufacturing industry, ranging from heavy factory machinery to household electrical goods. It was the fourth-largest producer of motor vehicles in the first decade of the 21st century. Germany has greatly suffered from pollution and environmental damage, with almost 50 percent of the trees of the Black Forest affected by acid rain. The country was one of the first industrialized nations to take environmental problems seriously, and the Green Party now holds a large number of seats in the Bundestag— the German Parliament. Pressure from the Green Party and environmental groups has resulted in Germany tightening its pollution controls and starting to phase out its nuclear power plants.

## INDUSTRY AND ENVIRONMENT

Germany's modern wealth and power is founded on its manufacturing and processing industries, many of which are located in the Ruhr in the west of the country—a European center of heavy industry.

▲ Designed by architect Carl Gotthard Langhans and completed in 1791, the Brandenberg Gate in Berlin lay close to the border, separating the former East Germany and West Germany. Since reunification in 1990 the 62-ft.- (19-m-) high gateway has become a symbol of united Germany.

▼ A shipyard building located in Stralsund in northeast Germany. Located on an inlet of the Baltic Sea, Stralsund was founded in the 1200s and passed through Swedish control before becoming part of Prussia in 1815.

▲ A giant beer hall in Munich is in full swing as the city's Oktoberfest celebrates Germany's food, drink, and entertainment.

▼ The church of Ramsau is situated in the mountainous area of southeast Germany. It lies close to a mountain lake.

## TRANSPORTATION AND CITIES

Germany has excellent land, sea, and air transportation links. More goods and people travel by road than any other mode, with 400,410 mi. (644,400km) of roads, including 7,830 mi. (12,600km) of highways. Many of the country's major cities are linked by high-speed rail links along which InterCity Express (ICE) trains travel at 174 mph (280km/h). Regular flights between the major cities don't take much more than one hour. Germany has a large fleet of oceangoing merchant ships that sails from ports such as Bremen and Hamburg, the country's biggest port and third-largest urban area.

## CONFLICT AND DIVISION

Germany has spent many more years as separate states than it has as one nation. Around 3,000 years ago a number of tribes settled in the Rhine and Danube river valleys. The Romans named the area Germania after one of these tribes, the Germani. Until the 1800s the region was home to many different states but was unified into one nation in 1871. Germany suffered greatly after its defeat at the end of World War I in 1918. Under Adolf Hitler the country was again defeated at the end of World War II in 1945. Germany was then divided into four zones occupied by the U.K., France, the U.S., and the Soviet Union. By 1949 the occupation zones had become two separate nations. The Soviet occupation zone became the German Democratic Republic, or East Germany. The Federal Republic of Germany, or West Germany, comprised the three remaining zones. Both nations joined the security organizations of their previous occupying powers—West Germany was a part of NATO, while East Germany belonged to the Warsaw Pact. Germany was reunited in 1990 after the breakup of the Soviet Union. West Germany's 11 *Länder*, or states, were joined by five new additions from East Germany: Brandenburg, Mecklenburg-West Pomerania, Saxony, Saxony-Anhalt, and Thuringia. Since then Germany has had to deal with the economic and social issues that come with reuniting two sets of people who have spent more than 40 years living apart.

# FRANCE

**The largest country in Western Europe, France has a long history of political, economic, and cultural influence that continues to this day.**

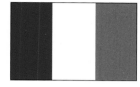

**Area:** 211,210 sq. mi. (547,030km²)
**Population:** 61,796,000
**Capital:** Paris (10,170,000)
**Main language spoken:** French
**Main religion:** Roman Catholic
**Currency:** euro
**Main exports:** machinery and transportation equipment, agricultural products (particularly food and wine), chemical products, plastics
**Type of government:** republic

▼ The TGV high-speed train travels at speeds of up to 186 mph (300km/h), linking Paris with major cities throughout France.

Sixty percent of France lies below 820 ft. (250m) in elevation. Much of this land consists of gently rolling plains with occasional rocky outcrops and hills and large river valleys. To the northwest of the country the regions of Brittany and Normandy are more hilly and have heavily indented coastlines. France contains a number of distinct highland areas. To the northeast the Vosges are a series of gently rounded summits over 200 million years old. South of the Vosges are the Jura Mountains, which extend into Switzerland and reach 5,610 ft. (1,710m) at their highest point. The Jura and Vosges are dwarfed by the French Alps found in the east of France. Peaks include Mont Blanc, the highest in western Europe. The south-central highland plateau, called the Massif Central, was formed around 300 million years ago. Covering around 15 percent of the country, it was disturbed by the formation of the Alps 65 million years ago. Volcanic activity ceased in the region around 10,000 years ago, leaving behind many extinct cones, outcrops, and pointed hills called *puys*. A number of France's major rivers begin their life in the Massif Central, including the Loire. This and other rivers, including the Seine and the Rhône, have carved out large valleys and have helped create fertile lands.

▲ A major landmark in Paris and symbol of France, the Eiffel Tower was built between 1887 and 1889 out of 8,050 tons (7,300 metric tonnes) of wrought iron. Breathtaking views of Paris greet those who ascend the 985-ft.-(300-m-) high tower.

▼ The spectacular Mont-Saint-Michel is a rocky islet in the Gulf of St. Malo cut off from the mainland of northwestern France at high tide. The islet has been the site of a monastery since A.D. 966, and the church on the summit was first built in the 1000s.

## FRANCE'S BORDERS AND TERRITORY

France's other significant mountain range, the Pyrenees, acts as a natural border to the southwest, separating France from Spain. To the southeast, near the French city of Nice, France surrounds the tiny principality of Monaco. The remainder of France's land borders are to the east with Belgium, Luxembourg, Germany, Switzerland, and Italy. France is divided into 96 "départements" and four overseas "départements": Réunion in the Indian Ocean, Martinique and Guadeloupe, both in the Caribbean Sea, and French Guiana in South America. In addition, there are overseas territories that include French Polynesia, New Caledonia, Wallis and Futuna Islands, St. Pierre and Miquelon, Mayotte, and Saint Martin. France also lays claim to a portion of the continent of Antarctica. Corsica, the fourth-largest island in the Mediterranean, is part of France. Two thirds of Corsica consist of granite-based mountains, with over 20 peaks rising more than 6,560 ft. (2,000m) in elevation. The island has a population of approximately 299,000 people.

## THE FRENCH COASTLINE

France is situated on the western side of continental Europe with long north and west-facing coastlines, as well as a coastline with the Mediterranean. This location has enabled France, in the past, to grow strong as a trading and colonial power. To the north France borders the North Sea and the English Channel. Northern ports, such as Le Havre, handle large amounts of shipping, particularly passenger ferries. At its narrowest point, in the Straits of Dover, France and the U.K. are no more than 19 mi. (30km) apart. The year 1994 saw the opening of the Channel Tunnel (Eurotunnel), which runs underneath the English Channel, providing a rail link between the two countries. Almost all of France's Atlantic coastline lies to the west within the large Bay of Biscay close to towns, such as Bordeaux, that have developed as ports. The Mediterranean coastline is a major tourist destination and includes resort towns such as Cannes, 10 mi. (16km) from the city of Nice.

## FRANCE'S CLIMATE

The climate of France is temperate but with some regional variations. In the north and west of the country winds from the Atlantic bring large amounts of moisture in the air, changeable weather, and help produce cool summers and mild winters. The region around Paris, known as the Paris Basin (Île-de-France), has a more continental climate. The area receives heavy rainfall in the spring and fall and thunderstorms in the summer. In eastern France and in the Massif Central region the temperature range is greater between the winter and the summer. In the south of the country, particularly in the southeastern region of Provence, a warmer, Mediterranean climate prevails. Average daily temperatures there range between 63–84°F (17–29°C) in the summer, while only very rarely falling below 32°F (0°C) in the winter. Southern France can feel the effects of the Mistral—a strong, cold, dry wind that can blow for several days at a time, reach speeds of over 80 mph (130km/h), and cause damage to crops. The amount of precipitation varies greatly throughout France, with some northern lowlands receiving less than 12 in. (30cm) and some mountain areas receiving over 51 in. (130cm) per year.

## FARMING AND FOOD

France is one of the biggest agricultural producers and exporters in the world. A great variety of crops are grown, from cereals and root vegetables to asparagus, silk, flax, and tobacco. Almost 20 million cattle and close to 300 million poultry are also raised. Fruit growing is widespread, and much of the output of grapes, apples, and other fruit is used to make drinks and sauces. France is a renowned producer of wines and spirits, usually named after their region or area of production such as Burgundy or Bordeaux. The French have developed a rich and diverse cuisine that varies from region to region. Along the eastern coast fish-based dishes are common, while every region has its own variety of pastries and rich breads, meat dishes, desserts, and cheeses. France is the second-largest producer of cheese in the world.

▲ A field of lavender in the southern region of Provence. Lavender grows to between 24-35 in. (60–90cm) in height and is cultivated in many places in France for its sweet-smelling oil used in perfumes and potpourri.

▲ A cellar worker attends racks of champagne at the Veuve Clicquot vineyards. This luxury sparkling wine gets its name from the Champagne region close to the city of Reims.

▲ The European Parliament building in Strasbourg, in northeast France, opened in 1999. Members of the European Parliament are elected by voters of countries in the European Union.

▼ Outdoor eating and drinking at sidewalk cafés is a feature of life in France. This café is located on the Champs Elysées, a famous broad avenue in Paris that runs from the Arc de Triomphe—a distance of 1.17 mi. (1.88km).

## INDUSTRY AND THE ENVIRONMENT

Although it was slow to industrialize, France has become a major industrial power since World War II. It has been aided by large reserves of minerals, including some of the richest deposits of iron ore in Europe. Coal, particularly from the north and the east, was once plentiful but is dwindling. France is one of the countries most committed to using nuclear power to supply its electricity needs. Around 78 percent of its electricity is generated from nuclear power plants. The country is also a key engineering center of Europe, with many companies devoted to producing machinery, cars, and defense products. The water and air pollution caused by these industries have had a detrimental effect on the country's environment. France's 37 million acres of forests and woodlands have suffered some acid rain damage but not as much as some of its eastern neighbors.

## THE CULTURAL CAPITAL

As the world's most popular visitor destination, with more than 79 million arrivals in 2008, tourism is a vitally important part of the French economy. People travel all over the world to visit its many attractions—from the pilgrimage center of Lourdes at the foot of the Pyrenees and its winter ski resorts in the Alps to the unspoiled countryside of its river valleys and the warmth and glamour of coastal towns such as Nice. Paris is the number-one destination. More than just France's capital, the city exerts a dominant influence in government, business, and culture over the rest of the country. Paris dwarfs all other French cities. Its metropolitan area is the home of one sixth of the country's people and is around seven times the size of France's next largest city, Marseille. The Île de la Cité is a small island on the Seine river first populated by a Celtic tribe over 2,200 years ago. Paris has since developed around this point, with the river winding its way through the city.

The city has had a long and turbulent history. It was occupied during both world wars and became the focal point of the French Revolution (1789–1799), which overthrew the succession of kings who had ruled France for over 1,300 years. The legacy of France's long history can be found throughout Paris in such famous sites as Notre Dame cathedral, the Sorbonne university, and the Louvre museum.

## FRANCE'S PEOPLE

Over 90 percent of French people were born in the country, are white, and speak French. In the distant past France was a trading crossroad and was settled by waves of different people, including Celts, Visigoths from Italy, and Vikings. The ancient Greeks started a trading colony in what is now the major city and port of Marseille over 2,600 years ago, while much of France later came under the control of the Roman Empire. A colonial power in the 1700s to 1900s, much of North Africa, parts of West Africa, the Caribbean, Southeast Asia, and many islands in the Pacific all came under France's colonial rule. Although almost all of its colonies are now independent, large numbers of people from former French colonies, especially from North Africa, are now resident in France along with sizable communities of Portuguese, Italian, Spanish, and Turkish people.

▲ French cakes and sweets are frequently enjoyed by the French and visitors alike. This food stall is part of a market in the city of Nice in southeast France.

# MONACO

**Bordering the Mediterranean Sea and completely surrounded by France, Monaco has a largely rugged landscape and a mild climate.**

**Area:** 0.77 sq. mi. (2km²)
**Population:** 31,100
**Capital:** Monaco (31,100)
**Main languages spoken:** French, Monegasque, English, Italian
**Main religion:** Roman Catholic
**Currency:** euro
**Main exports:** chemicals, plastics, electronic goods
**Type of government:** constitutional monarchy

Although land reclaimed from the sea has increased its area by 20 percent since 1964, Monaco remains the second-smallest nation in the world. Less than one fourth of Monaco's population was born in the country. Its population has grown, due to a large number of celebrities, businesspeople, and athletes attracted by low taxes settling there. Light industries, including cosmetics and clothing, are dwarfed in economic importance by the nation's banks and insurance industries. Monaco has been ruled by one family, the Grimaldis, for over seven centuries. The National Council of 18 elected members helps run the country, along with the current head of the Grimaldi family, Prince Albert II.

▶ Attracted by Monaco's mild climate and its status as a tax haven, millionaires have made their homes among the luxury apartments that overlook the Mediterranean Sea.

179

# CENTRAL EUROPE

The region of central Europe consists of a number of small- to medium-size nations, as well as the larger country of Poland and the tiny state of Liechtenstein. Much of the region lies on the north European plain and has a relatively low elevation, but to the south of the region the Alps, central Europe's principal mountain range, is found. Stretching in an arc measuring almost 745 mi. (1,200km), the highest and most densely populated mountain range in all of Europe is found through much of Switzerland and Austria, as well as extending into France, Italy, Slovenia, and the extreme south of Germany. The most important river in the region is the Danube, which starts its life in Germany's Black Forest and flows through Austria, Hungary, and Slovakia before continuing through Eastern Europe and emptying into the Black Sea. Politically, the region has seen great change in both ancient and more modern times. Only Switzerland, which has remained neutral since 1815, has stayed out of the many wars, conflicts, and border changes that have occurred in the region. Today the nations of central Europe all have mixed economies where agriculture and food processing remain important but have been overtaken by industry and services, especially tourism.

▲ Central Europe's major river, the Danube, is pictured here (top) flowing through the Hungarian capital city of Budapest. Under Soviet influence until 1991, Hungary now has a growing tourist industry.

▼ Approximately 80 million tourists visit central Europe every year, with Switzerland and its spectacular mountain scenery one of the region's leading destinations.

Baltic
Sea

Kaliningrad LITHUANIA
(Russia)

BELARUS

GERMANY

P O L A N D

WARSAW

Oder

Vistula

UKRAINE

PRAGUE

CZECH
REPUBLIC

SLOVAKIA

Danube

VIENNA

BRATISLAVA

BUDAPEST

GERMANY

AUSTRIA

HUNGARY

ROMANIA

FRANCE

VADUZ

LIECH.

Rhine

BERN

SWITZERLAND

A

L

P

S

ITALY

SLOVENIA

CROATIA

Danube

SERBIA

Matterhorn △
14,685 ft.

△ Dufourspitze
15,199 ft.

| 0 | | 150 | | 300 km |
|---|---|---|---|---|

| 0 | 750 | | 150 miles |
|---|---|---|---|

# SWITZERLAND

**The most mountainous country in all of Europe, Switzerland's people speak a number of languages and enjoy a prosperous life.**

**Area:** 15,940 sq. mi. (41,285km²)
**Population:** 7,593,000
**Capital:** Bern (346,000)
**Main languages spoken:** German, French, Italian, Romansh
**Main religions:** Roman Catholic, Protestant
**Currency:** Swiss franc
**Main exports:** machinery, electronics, chemical products, precision instruments, watches, jewelry
**Type of government:** federal republic

Switzerland borders France to the west, Lichtenstein and Austria to the east, Germany to the north, and Italy to the south. It has a landscape of high mountain peaks and lush green valleys and plateaus, with around 20 percent of its land covered in forests. The country's main rivers, which include the Rhine and the Rhône, flow in different directions and finally empty into three different seas, the North Sea, the Mediterranean Sea, and the Black Sea. To the west winds from the Atlantic Ocean carry much moisture and cause rainfall. In the east the climate is drier and has sharper differences in temperature. Generally the lower-lying areas of plains and valleys enjoy a temperate climate, while the low-lying region south of the Alps receives warmer weather.

### THE MOUNTAINS OF SWITZERLAND

Over two thirds of its area are covered in two sets of mountain ranges. To the west, the Jura Mountains form a natural border between Switzerland and France. Between the Alps and the Jura Mountains lies the Swiss Plateau, a region with an average elevation of 1,296 ft. (395m) and dotted with many low hills. The country is home to one fifth of the entire Alps mountain system, which runs roughly east to west across much of the south and central regions. The Alps are most spectacular along Switzerland's southwestern border with Italy. Famous peaks over 13,120 ft. (4,000m) include the Matterhorn and Dufourspitze.

### FARMING, TRADE, AND TRANSPORTATION

Swiss farming and industry have had to adapt to the country's landscape and location in order to prosper. The terrain makes farming difficult, yet the Swiss people are self-sufficient in certain farm products, including beef, dairy products, and wheat. Swiss dairy products, including cheeses and chocolate, are exported around the world. Apart from fast-flowing rivers to

▼ The Reuss river in the Swiss city of Luzern is crossed by seven bridges. The town is a German-speaking center.

generate hydroelectric power, Switzerland has few natural resources for industry. The country depends on importing raw materials, processing them, and using them for manufacturing goods, particularly small items of high value, including watches, medicines, electronics, scientific instruments, and handicraft products. Transporting raw materials in and finished goods out of the country relies on rivers and good road and rail links. Switzerland has worked with other nations to build a number of road and rail tunnels through its mountainous borders. Although Switzerland is landlocked, it has a national fleet of over 170 vessels that operate from foreign ports or from Basel, a city located on the Rhine.

## MANY LANGUAGES

Switzerland's people speak a variety of languages. German is spoken as a first language by 65 percent of the population, French by 18 percent, and Italian by ten percent. Swiss-German is very different from regular German, but because it is not a written language, regular German is used for newspapers and other print media. French is most often spoken and used in and around Geneva and in the west. Romansh is the fourth official language, although it is only spoken by less than one percent of the population.

## A NATION APART AND AT PEACE

Switzerland has remained neutral in wars and conflicts for almost two centuries. Internally the country has remained stable and grown wealthy as a financial and banking center. These and other service industries employ over half of the workforce. The country has become the home of a number of major world organizations, including the Red Cross and the World Health Organization, both of which have their headquarters in the city of Geneva. The European headquarters of the United Nations is also sited in Switzerland, although the country only voted to join the UN in 2002. In 2001 over three fourths of voters rejected the proposal to join the European Union.

▲ Switzerland's famous Emmenthal cheese is pressed for around 20 hours, and the holes found in the cheese occur owing to gases trapped inside.

▼ The town of Lauterbrunnen is located 62 mi. (100km) east of Lausanne in a steep river valley that contains famous waterfalls, including the Trümmelbach and the Staubbach falls.

# AUSTRIA

**Famous for its mountain scenery and its historic and cultural sites, Austria is a landlocked country dominated by the foothills and mountains of the Alps.**

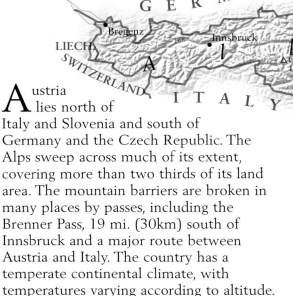

**Area:** 32,378 sq. mi. (83,858km²)
**Population:** 8,355,000
**Capital:** Vienna (1,984,000)
**Main language spoken:** German
**Main religions:** Roman Catholic, Protestant
**Currency:** euro
**Main exports:** machinery and transportation equipment, chemicals, paper and paper products, iron and steel
**Type of government:** parliamentary democracy

▼ Traditional dancing at a winter ball in Vienna. The winter ball season is a major part of Viennese social life and lasts for around seven weeks, from New Year's Eve onward.

Austria lies north of Italy and Slovenia and south of Germany and the Czech Republic. The Alps sweep across much of its extent, covering more than two thirds of its land area. The mountain barriers are broken in many places by passes, including the Brenner Pass, 19 mi. (30km) south of Innsbruck and a major route between Austria and Italy. The country has a temperate continental climate, with temperatures varying according to altitude. The summers tend to be relatively short and mild, while the winters are cold and last three months or more in the valleys.

Austria is crossed by a number of rivers, including the Danube and its tributaries such as the Inn. Broad green valleys covered in lush meadows and pastureland frequently separate the mountains, while dense forests cover large portions of the mountains' lower slopes. Almost all of the croplands in Austria are situated in the northeast, while dairy farming is common in the mountain valleys.

## ELECTRICITY AND INDUSTRY

The fast-flowing rivers and mountainous landscapes help Austria generate vast amounts of hydroelectric power, enabling it to sell excess energy to neighboring countries. More than 70 percent of Austria's electricity is generated this way, much of which is used by industry to produce iron, steel, and aluminum. Such raw materials are used in manufacturing industries to build ships, machine tools, and motor vehicles. A feature of Austrian industry is the large number of factories and companies making and selling craft goods, including porcelain, fine glassware, jewelry, and traditional clothing. Much of Austria's industry

is centered around Vienna, the capital of the country. More than one fifth of the country's population live in Vienna, which is counted as one of the nation's nine *Bundesländer*, or provinces.

## HISTORY AND GOVERNMENT

People have lived in Austria since prehistoric times, but the country rose to prominence from the 1200s onward under the rule of one family, the Hapsburgs. The country became the center of a vast empire, which, at its peak, included Hungary and many other nations such as Spain and the Netherlands. The cities of Vienna and Salzburg became major European centers of culture and the arts. Two world wars devastated the country and left it occupied by Soviet, U.S., British, and French forces. Austria regained its independence in 1955 and, in 1995, joined the European Union.

▲ The Tirol province of Austria is highly mountainous, with over 300 peaks above 9,840 ft. (3,000m) in elevation. Between the peaks are lakes, dense forests, and lush meadows that attract many walkers in the summer and winter sports enthusiasts in the winter. The largest city in the Tirol is Innsbruck, with a population of 192,000.

# LIECHTENSTEIN

The world's sixth-smallest nation, Liechtenstein is perched between the Rhine river and the Alps. Its neighbor, Switzerland, provides many of its services.

**Area:** 62 sq. mi. (160km²)
**Population:** 35,400
**Capital:** Vaduz (5,100)
**Main language spoken:** German
**Main religions:** Roman Catholic, Protestant
**Currency:** Swiss franc
**Main exports:** machinery and transportation equipment, metal products, dental products, hardware
**Type of government:** hereditary constitutional monarchy

Liechtenstein is not as mountainous as its neighbors, Austria and Switzerland. During the winter it may experience heavy snowfall and temperatures below 32°F (0°C), but its summer is warm, with maximum temperatures as high as 82°F (28°C), allowing grapes and corn to be cultivated. On the plain near the Rhine river livestock is raised. First formed in 1719, the tiny principality has managed to stay independent and has flourished, giving its inhabitants one of the highest standards of living in the world. Low tax rates have attracted foreign businesses and banking, while sales of postage stamps generate almost one tenth of the country's income. Liechtenstein has no airport; the closest is found in the Swiss city of Zurich. Like its neighbor, Switzerland, Liechtenstein is not a member of the European Union.

# HUNGARY

A landlocked country in central Europe, Hungary has a mixed economy and one of the most beautiful capital cities in Europe.

**Area:** 35,919 sq. mi. (93,030km²)
**Population:** 10,031,000
**Capital:** Budapest (1,915,000)
**Main language spoken:** Hungarian
**Main religions:** Roman Catholic, Calvinist, Lutheran
**Currency:** forint
**Main exports:** industrial goods, consumer goods, machinery, food (cereals, meat, and dairy products)
**Type of government:** parliamentary democracy

The Danube river divides Hungary into two regions. To the east lies the Great Plain, or Great Alföld, which covers more than half of Hungary. Although mountains lie along its northern border, the Great Plain is a mainly low-lying region crossed by Hungary's second major river, the Tisza. West of the Danube is a hilly region called Transdanubia. It contains the Bakony Mountains, which are close to Lake Balaton, the largest freshwater lake in central Europe. Hungary has a continental climate with cold, cloudy winters, late summers, and heavy rainfall in the spring and summer.

## FROM AGRICULTURE TO INDUSTRY
The black-colored soils of the Great Plain are extremely rich in nutrients. Coupled with its mild, dry climate in which rainfall is heaviest during the growing season, Hungary's farms have flourished. Fruit growing, wine making, and cereal and vegetable planting are the biggest users of cropland. Hungary was a mainly agricultural country until World War II, when its industries started to grow, in part aided by financing from the Soviet bloc of communist nations to which Hungary belonged from 1949 until 1989. Steelmaking and aluminum and cement production were among the largest industries, with leather goods, cars, factory machinery, and fertilizers also important. Unchecked industrial development in some of the regions generated a great deal of air and water pollution. Lake Balaton and stretches of the Danube are heavily polluted, while deciduous forests, which consist mainly of beech and oak trees, have also suffered.

▼ The Elizabeth Bridge is one of many bridges that cross the Danube river, linking both sides of the city of Budapest. It was first completed in 1903 and then rebuilt between 1961 and 1964.

## THE MAGYARS

In the past Hungary was a larger country with large minorities of Germans, Croats, and Romanians, but its land area shrunk after World War I when it lost its border provinces. Today over 95 percent of Hungarians are Magyars, descendants of a mixture of tribes that settled in Hungary over 1,100 years ago. The ancient Magyars had a strong culture, much of which is still kept alive today, especially in the towns and villages of the Great Plains. There aspects of traditional life—from weaving and embroidery to traditional dress, folk stories, and music—can still be found.

## BUDAPEST—QUEEN OF THE DANUBE

Hungary's capital and largest city, Budapest, is, in fact, an amalgam of three individual cities with long histories—Obuda became the first center of Hungary in the 900s; Buda, on the western bank of the Danube, was the former royal capital of the Hungarian empire; Pest, on the eastern bank, developed as a center of trade and industry and for long periods was under the control of German rulers. In 1849 the first bridge across the Danube connecting Buda and Pest was opened, uniting the cities. Budapest is nine times larger than the second-largest Hungarian city, Debrecen, which lies in a farming region in eastern Hungary. Budapest is home to universities and colleges that teach more than one half of all Hungarian students. Known as the "Queen of the Danube," the city attracts many of the country's ten million tourists. In 2004, Hungary became a member of the European Union.

▶ Built between 1880 and 1902, the tall, domed parliament building in Budapest is 879 ft. (268m) long and 403 ft. (123m) wide.

▲ A father and son play Romany folk music on their violins on the banks of Lake Balaton. Situated approximately 56 mi. (90km) southwest of Budapest, Lake Balaton measures 229 sq. mi. (592km²) and is central Europe's largest freshwater lake.

# CZECH REPUBLIC

A small, hilly country in the center of
Europe, the people and settlements of the
young Czech Republic have a long history.

**Area:** 30,450 sq. mi.
(78,864km²)
**Population:** 10,468,000
**Capital:** Prague (1,427,000)
**Main languages spoken:**
Czech, Slovak
**Main religions:** Roman
Catholic, atheist,
Protestant, Orthodox
**Currency:** Czech koruna
**Main exports:**
manufactured goods
(including textiles),
industrial machinery, motor
vehicles, chemicals, fuel
**Type of government:**
republic

▼ Prague Castle has a
long history but today is
the home of the president
of the Czech Republic.

On January 1, 1993 the
former federal republic
of Czechoslovakia was dissolved,
and two new nations were created:
the Czech Republic and Slovakia.
The Czech Republic is the larger,
more populous, and more industrialized
of the two nations. It is actually the most
industrialized of the former communist
nations of central Europe. The country is
landlocked and lies 200 mi. (322km) from
the Adriatic Sea and 203 mi. (326km)
from the Baltic Sea. It shares borders with
four nations: Germany to the west and
north, Poland to the north and east,
Austria to the south, and Slovakia to the
southeast. Mountain ranges form a large
part of its borders, including the
Carpathians, which separate the country
from Slovakia, and the Sudety Mountains,
which run west of the city of Ostrava and
form most of the border with Poland.
Most of the country inside this ring of low
mountains consists of a large basin called
the Bohemian Massif. The country is
split into two regions—to the east lies
Moravia, and to the west
lies Bohemia.

## COLD WINTERS AND WARM SUMMERS

The Czech Republic has a
humid, continental climate
and does not experience the
effects of ocean air masses.
As a result, the winters tend to be colder and the
summers warmer than in other European nations
at similar latitudes. Easterly winds from Siberia
force the temperatures down to below freezing
during the winter, and snowfalls are often heavy
on the high ground. A little under two thirds of
the country are covered in forests, particularly of
spruce, pine, and beech trees—almost 42 million
ft.³ (12 million m³) of timber were produced in
2008. Farming has been modernized, and cereal
crops and root vegetables are the most widely
grown. In 1999 there were 11,580 sq. mi.
(30,000km²) of cultivated land.

## MODERNIZING OLD INDUSTRIES

For over one century the Czechs have relied on heavy industry based around their large deposits of coal, reserves of copper, lead, and zinc, and their central trading location in Europe. With economic independence in 1993 came the realization that many of their industries were neither modern nor efficient enough to compete in the world market. Successive Czech governments have spent large amounts of revenue, as well as securing loans, to modernize many of their industries. Foreign companies have been eager to invest in the country, with its skilled workforce and stable government. The Czech Republic's single largest industry is engineering, followed by food production, electronics, chemicals, rubber, asbestos, and iron and steel. The country's biggest trading partner is Germany, which accounted for 28 percent of its exports and 29 percent of its imports in 2008.

▲ The Budweiser brewery in the southern Czech Republic town of Ceské Budejovice. Situated close to the Vltava river, the town has been a center of the beer-brewing industry for 700 years.

## THE CZECH REPUBLIC'S HERITAGE

The Czech Republic has only been in existence for little more than a decade, and Czechoslovakia, the country of which it was once part, was only established in 1918. However, the Czech people have a long history of settlement in the area dating back 1,500 years. The modern-day capital of the country, Prague, was a major European city by the 1300s and flourished as a center of culture, the arts, and learning for over 500 years. Much of Prague's older buildings and town layout have survived many conflicts, including the two world wars and Soviet occupation. It is one of the most beautiful capitals in Europe and is a major tourist destination. The Czech Republic has developed its tourism industry, and in 2004, it became a member of the European Union.

▼ Located in the south of the Czech Republic, around 25 mi. (40km) south of the city of Brno, the Palava Hills form a biosphere reserve in which the country's forests and other wild plant and animal life are officially protected.

# POLAND

A large nation in northern central Europe, Poland's present borders were fixed in 1945 after the end of World War II.

**Area:** 120,728 sq. mi. (312,685km2)
**Population:** 38,153,000
**Capital:** Warsaw (2,220,000)
**Main language spoken:** Polish
**Main religion:** Roman Catholic
**Currency:** zloty
**Main exports:** manufactured goods, machinery and transportation equipment, consumer goods, food (particularly poultry, eggs, pork, fruit, and vegetables)
**Type of government:** republic

The Republic of Poland borders seven other nations. Its land consists mainly of plains with low hills to the north, with the southern third of the country mainly occupied by highland areas. Along the country's southern border are the Carpathian Mountains. The Tatras, a mountain range within the Carpathians, is a protected national park and contains peaks over 7,860 ft. (2,400m) in elevation. It is one of 23 national parks within Poland's borders.

## A CHANGEABLE CLIMATE

Essentially Poland has a warm summer and a cold winter, but its location means that its climate is influenced by many different air fronts, which lead to variable, changeable weather. Cold polar air from Russia and Scandinavia meets warmer air currents from south of the country, as well as air currents from the west. Poland is sometimes described as having six seasons, with its spring and fall periods both split into two different sets of climatic conditions.

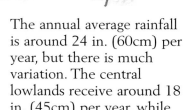

The annual average rainfall is around 24 in. (60cm) per year, but there is much variation. The central lowlands receive around 18 in. (45cm) per year, while in the mountain regions rainfall can be as high as 57 in. (145cm) per year. In the winter snow covers most of the mountainous areas of Poland and half of the plains.

▼ Wawel Castle lies in the city of Kraków, one of the most ancient settlements in Poland. The castle overlooks the Vistula river and for centuries was the site where Polish kings were crowned.

The largest city in northern Poland, Gdansk is a major shipbuilding and boat and ship repair center on the Baltic Sea coast.

## CHANGING BOUNDARIES

The name Polska, or Poland, has applied to part of northern central Europe that has changed its area and boundaries many times. It originally came from a people known as the Polaine who settled on the lowlands between the Oder and Vistula rivers in the 900s and 1000s. At its peak in the 1400s Poland's extended borders made it the largest country in Europe. Three centuries later, in the period 1772–1795, it ceased to exist as its territory was divided by the major powers of Austria, Prussia, and Russia. Poland received its independence from Russia in 1918 but was again overrun in 1939, prompting the onset of World War II. Part of the communist Soviet bloc in the mid- to late 1900s, the country was the first in central and Eastern Europe to break from communist rule in 1989. The following year the opposition leader, Lech Walesa, became president. Closer ties with the West led Poland to join the European Union in 2004.

▲ Found in the Old Town Square in Warsaw, the statue of the fighting mermaid with raised sword and shield is called Syrenka. A national symbol, images of Syrenka are found on city buildings throughout Warsaw.

## POLAND'S RIVER SYSTEMS

Poland has more than 2,480 mi. (3,990km) of navigable rivers and lakes, which have been historically important as trade and transportation routes. The Oder river starts in the Czech Republic but flows through the west of Poland, forming part of its border with Germany. About 530 mi. (854km) long, it is joined by a canal to the Vistula, or Wisla—Poland's longest river. The Vistula is navigable for almost all of its 650 mi. (1,047km) length, from the Carpathian Mountains to the Gulf of Danzig. Many of Poland's important cities, including Kraków and the capital, Warsaw, lie on its banks.

## PEOPLE AND WORK

Poland has substantial mineral and agricultural resources. It has the world's ninth-largest reserves of coal, in addition to deposits of copper, sulfur, zinc, lead, and silver. Its industrial region around Katowice is one of Europe's largest. The main agricultural crops are cereals, such as barley and wheat, and potatoes, sugar beets, and hay. The country contains approximately 5.7 million beef and dairy cattle and 19 million pigs. Around 30 percent of Poland is covered in forests, but the thriving forestry industry has been damaged by high levels of air and water pollution from heavy industries.

▼ Lying 9 mi. (14km) southeast of Kraków are the Wieliczka salt mines. Comprising a vast network of 2,148 chambers and passages totaling 200 mi. (320km) in length, many of the older chambers are decorated with sculptures carved out of rock salt. Worked since the 1200s, these are the oldest operational salt mines in Europe.

# SLOVAKIA

A small, landlocked country in central Europe, Slovakia was formed from the separation of the two halves of Czechoslovakia in 1993.

**Area:** 18,933 sq. mi. (49,036km²)
**Population:** 5,412,000
**Capital:** Bratislava (449,000)
**Main languages spoken:** Slovak, Hungarian
**Main religions:** Roman Catholic, Protestant
**Currency:** euro
**Main exports:** semimanufactured products, machinery and transportation equipment, chemicals, manufactured goods, food
**Type of government:** republic

Slovakia is bordered by five nations: Poland, Austria, the Ukraine, Hungary, and the Czech Republic. Much of the country is mountainous to the north and west, while the southern region consists of fertile lowlands on which crops, such as corn, wheat, and potatoes, are grown. Slovakia has a continental climate with warm summers and cold winters. Eighty-six percent of the country's people are Slovaks—a distinct ethnic group that has lived in the region for more than 1,000 years. People of Hungarian origin make up a further ten percent of the population, reflected in the fact that Slovakia's capital, Bratislava, was the capital of the kingdom of Hungary from the 1500s until the 1700s.

## INDUSTRY AND ENVIRONMENT

Slovakia has reserves of copper, lead, iron, and lignite (brown coal) but has to import most of its oil and natural gas. Hydroelectric power from plants located on the Váh and other rivers provides an important source of energy, while Slovakia is also building nuclear power plants. A large-scale hydroelectric project in Gabcíkovo, 25 mi. (40km) southeast of Bratislava, which involved damming the Danube river, has caused environmental concerns. Slovakia has high levels of industrial pollution, which have affected its forests and inland waterways. Around 39 percent of all Slovakian workers are employed in industries such as iron- and steelmaking and motor vehicle manufacturing. Many thousands more work in food-processing factories producing products such as beer and sheep's cheese. Most of the country's industry is centered around the capital, Bratislava, or Kosice. In 2004, Slovakia became a member of the European Union.

► The Tatra, or Tatry, mountain range is the highest range of the Carpathian Mountains, which lie along the Poland–Slovakia border. The range consists of more than 300 peaks, and its lower slopes are heavily forested with pine and spruce trees that provide habitats for animals, including bears and eagles. A popular year-round vacation destination, visitors come to hike its mountain trails and to view its many picturesque mountain lakes.

# SOUTHERN EUROPE, THE BALKANS, THE CAUCASUS, AND ASIA MINOR

# SOUTHERN EUROPE

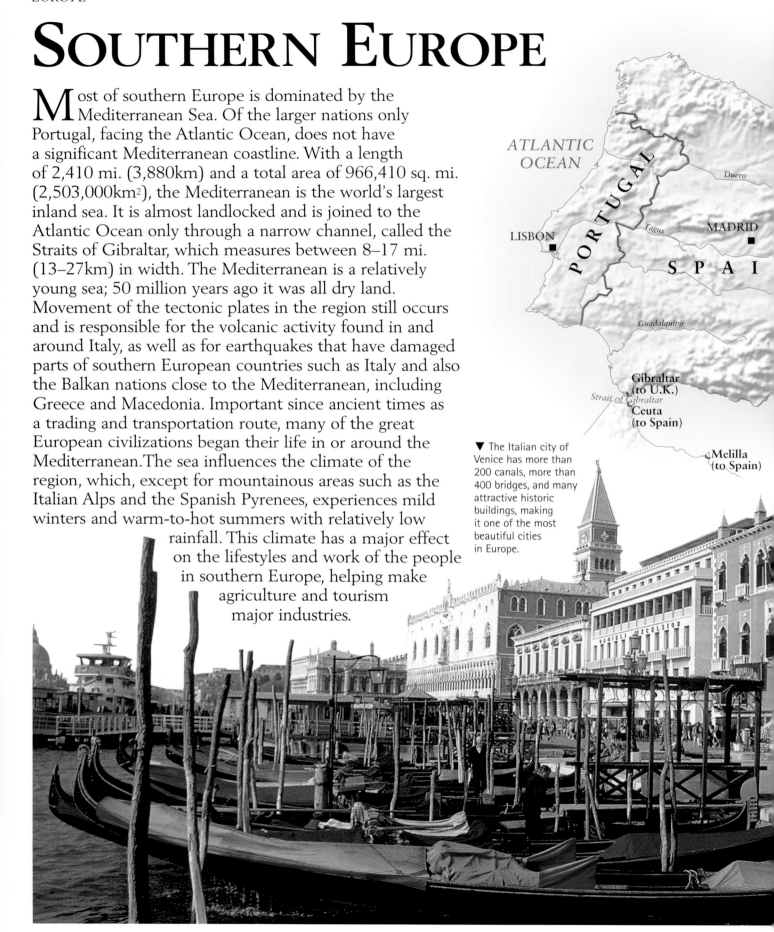

Most of southern Europe is dominated by the Mediterranean Sea. Of the larger nations only Portugal, facing the Atlantic Ocean, does not have a significant Mediterranean coastline. With a length of 2,410 mi. (3,880km) and a total area of 966,410 sq. mi. (2,503,000km²), the Mediterranean is the world's largest inland sea. It is almost landlocked and is joined to the Atlantic Ocean only through a narrow channel, called the Straits of Gibraltar, which measures between 8–17 mi. (13–27km) in width. The Mediterranean is a relatively young sea; 50 million years ago it was all dry land. Movement of the tectonic plates in the region still occurs and is responsible for the volcanic activity found in and around Italy, as well as for earthquakes that have damaged parts of southern European countries such as Italy and also the Balkan nations close to the Mediterranean, including Greece and Macedonia. Important since ancient times as a trading and transportation route, many of the great European civilizations began their life in or around the Mediterranean. The sea influences the climate of the region, which, except for mountainous areas such as the Italian Alps and the Spanish Pyrenees, experiences mild winters and warm-to-hot summers with relatively low rainfall. This climate has a major effect on the lifestyles and work of the people in southern Europe, helping make agriculture and tourism major industries.

ATLANTIC OCEAN

PORTUGAL

Duero

Tagus

LISBON ■

MADRID ■

S P A I

Guadalquivir

Gibraltar (to U.K.)

Strait of Gibraltar

Ceuta (to Spain)

Melilla (to Spain)

▼ The Italian city of Venice has more than 200 canals, more than 400 bridges, and many attractive historic buildings, making it one of the most beautiful cities in Europe.

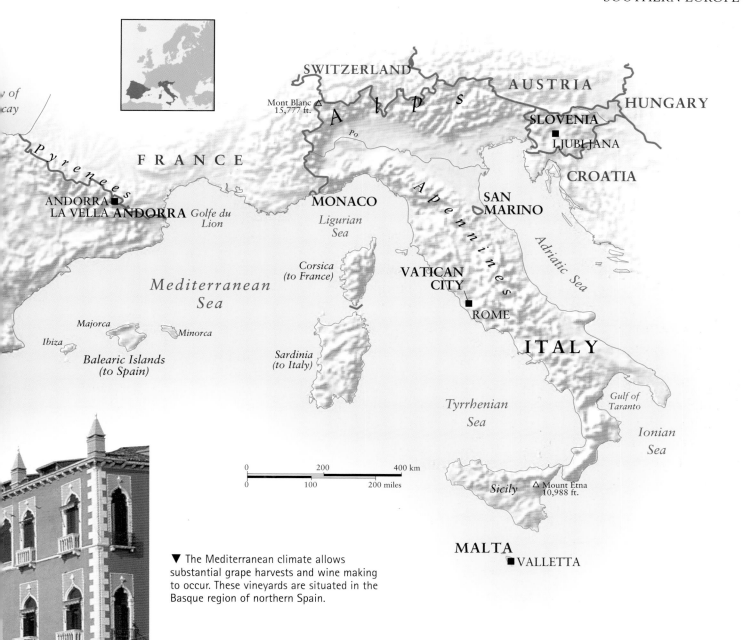

SWITZERLAND

Mont Blanc
15,777 ft.

A l p s

AUSTRIA

HUNGARY

SLOVENIA

LJUBLJANA

CROATIA

Po

FRANCE

A
p
e
n
n
i
n
e
s

SAN
MARINO

MONACO

Ligurian
Sea

ANDORRA

LA VELLA **ANDORRA** *Golfe du
Lion*

Adriatic
Sea

*Pyrenees*

VATICAN
CITY

ROME

*Mediterranean
Sea*

Corsica
(to France)

**ITALY**

*Majorca*

*Minorca*

*Ibiza*

*Balearic Islands
(to Spain)*

Sardinia
(to Italy)

Gulf of
Taranto

*Tyrrhenian
Sea*

*Ionian
Sea*

| 0 | 200 | 400 km |
| 0 | 100 | 200 miles |

△ Mount Etna
10,988 ft.

*Sicily*

y of
cay

**MALTA**

VALLETTA

▼ The Mediterranean climate allows
substantial grape harvests and wine making
to occur. These vineyards are situated in the
Basque region of northern Spain.

195

# SPAIN

The fourth-largest nation in Europe, Spain was once the center of a giant colonial empire and possesses a rich culture, history, and fine architecture.

**Area:** 194,897 sq. mi. (504,782km²)
**Population:** 46,158,000
**Capital:** Madrid (6,123,000)
**Main languages spoken:** Castilian (Spanish), Catalan, Galician, Basque
**Main religion:** Roman Catholic
**Currency:** euro
**Main exports:** transportation equipment, agricultural products, machinery
**Type of government:** constitutional monarchy

Spain is the sixth-most-populous nation in Europe. It shares land borders with Portugal, Gibraltar, and two nations in the Pyrenees Mountains: France and Andorra. Spanish territory includes the Balearic and Canary islands and three smaller island groups off the coast of Africa. Spain has a long Atlantic coastline to the north and northwest of the country, and on its eastern side it borders the Mediterranean Sea.

### CLOSE TO AFRICA

Spain occupies four fifths of the Iberian Peninsula, the European landmass closest to Africa. It is separated from North Africa by the Straits of Gibraltar—the Mediterranean's narrow outlet to the Atlantic Ocean. Spain administers two small areas in the north African country of Morocco called Ceuta and Melilla. Close to the straits on the Spanish mainland is the British dependency of Gibraltar. This 2.5-sq.-mi. (6.5-km²) territory is home to almost 28,000 people, most of whom are engaged in tourism and shipping. Spain and the U.K. have been contesting the dependency's sovereignty for many years. A referendum in 2002 saw Gibraltarians vote in favor of staying part of the U.K., and in 2006, Spain and the U.K. resolved many outstanding problems.

### THE MOUNTAINS AND THE MESETA

Spain has a number of large mountain ranges that cross different parts of the country, as well as a huge central plain, called the Meseta, which occupies almost half of the Spanish mainland. To the north lie the Pyrenees and, westward, the Cordillera Cantabrica Mountains, which run close to Spain's northern

▲ Flamenco originated in southern Spain in the 1700s and is an exciting mixture of dance, guitars, and percussion instruments.

coastline with the Atlantic before veering southward toward northern Portugal. To the east mountains run southeast from the Cordillera Cantabrica toward the Mediterranean Sea, while south of the central plain lies the Sistemas Béticos. The Meseta covers an area of around 8,100 sq. mi. (210,000km²) and has an average elevation of 2,296 ft. (700m). It contains the oldest geological features of the Iberian Peninsula. Much of the plain is treeless, and water is drained by two major rivers, the Duero and the Tagus, and their tributaries. A series of block mountains, called Sistema Central, occurs in the middle of the Meseta. There is a marked difference in soil quality between the east and west parts of the Meseta. The underlying limestone rocks of the eastern plains have been weathered to form richer soils and provide good agricultural areas.

## CLIMATE AND FARMING

Most of Spain has an essentially warm Mediterranean climate that varies with altitude and location. While temperatures in parts of northern Spain fall below 32°F (0°C) in the winter, Málaga, on the south coast, has an average daily winter temperature of 57°F (14°C). Most of the country receives less than 24 in. (60cm) of rainfall each

year, and droughts frequently occur in the Meseta. Farmers in many regions rely on irrigation systems to transport water to their fields, and the problem of desertification is growing. Spain is traditionally an agricultural nation that grows a wide range of crops, from sugar beets and cereals to citrus fruit and grapes. The country has industrialized rapidly in the past four decades, but farming and food processing remain very important. Spain is also one of the world's leading wine makers.

▲ The Guggenheim museum was opened in the industrial city of Bilbao in 1997 and within a year had received 1.3 million visitors. Covered in titanium sheets, it is a supreme example of modern architecture.

▼ These Spaniards are harvesting grapes near the southern city of Málaga. In 2000 Spain produced 6.6 million tons (6 million metric tonnes) of grapes.

▲ The layout of the city of Toledo is dominated by the Alcázar, a fortress palace built in the 1300s and since renovated on several occasions. Toledo lies in central Spain on the Tagus river, not far from Madrid.

▼ The giant cone of the volcano El Teide lies at the center of Tenerife, the largest of the Canary Islands. El Teide reaches an elevation of 12,195 ft. (3,718m) and is the highest point in the islands and Spain.

## A VARIETY OF CULTURES

Until the 1400s many waves of settlers had helped make Spain a patchwork of different states with varying cultures. Following the Roman conquest of the native Iberian people settlers and invaders from northern Europe arrived, as well as Muslim people from North Africa. Between the 800s and 1300s the land was a flourishing center of Islamic arts, culture, and science that influenced the architecture and society for centuries afterward. Spain has been very influential in European art, architecture, literature, and music, and traditional art forms and entertainment have survived to this day. Several regions in Spain have maintained their own distinct culture and identity, including the Basques in northern Spain and the Catalans in the east and

northeast of the country. After the Spanish Civil War (1936–1939) Spain was ruled by a dictator, General Francisco Franco, until 1975. During his leadership minority languages and customs were banned. Separatist movements in the Basque region and Catalonia, which had existed before Franco's rise to power, strengthened in their demands for independence from Spain. Democratic elections and a new constitution were established in the late 1970s. The 19 regions now have varying degrees of self-rule, some with considerable autonomy.

## CITY LIVING

With a move to more manufacturing and service industries has come a migration of Spaniards from the countryside to towns and cities. Around 78 percent of Spaniards now live in towns and cities—of which Madrid is the biggest, as well as being the capital and seat of government. Unusually for a European capital city, Madrid, which sits in the center of the Meseta, is neither located on one of the country's major rivers nor on the coast, like Barcelona, Spain's second-largest city. Barcelona is a major Mediterranean port and the center of a large and densely populated industrial region.

## A MAJOR COLONIAL POWER

In the late 1400s Spain became united as one nation under the rule of Queen Isabel and King Ferdinand. At around the same time some of the first major explorations of other continents by Spanish sailors were underway. These resulted in Spain building up a large colonial empire. By 1600 Spain controlled parts of North and South America, much of Central America, and a number of Caribbean islands. The Spanish empire also included Portugal, the Netherlands, Austria, and parts of France, Germany, and Italy. Conflicts from the mid-1600s onward caused Spain to lose its European territories by 1714 and, by 1850, almost all of its South American colonies.

## A TOURISM GIANT

Spain is one of the world's top-three tourist destinations, but in 2009–2010 the number of visitors declined by around ten percent. More than half of all visitors come from Germany and the U.K., lured by the warm climate, the beaches of the Mediterranean, particularly those of the Costa del Sol, Costa Blanca, and Costa Brava, and major cities of culture and history such as Barcelona, Madrid, and Valencia. The country's two main island groups—the Balearics in the Mediterranean and the Canary Islands in the Atlantic—have also become major tourist destinations. The Canaries are the remains of steep-sided volcanic cones, and their land is rugged with relatively sparse vegetation. Year-round sunshine and mild winters not only attract many tourists but

also enable bananas and tomatoes to be grown for export. The Balearics include the islands of Majorca, Minorca, and Ibiza, which have become popular vacation destinations. Development on a huge scale has transformed large parts of both groups of islands and has led to environmental concerns.

▲ Café customers sit and enjoy the views found in the Plaza Mayor in the center of Spain's capital, Madrid. The plaza was built in the early 1600s and was originally used by royalty to watch plays, bullfights, and royal pageants.

# ANDORRA

**A small, mountainous principality in the Pyrenees, Andorra has existed as a separate state since 1278 and relies on tourism and its status as a tax haven.**

**Area:** 181 sq. mi. (468km²)
**Population:** 84,500
**Capital:** Andorra la Vella (38,000)
**Main languages spoken:** Catalan, French, Castilian
**Main religion:** Roman Catholic
**Currency:** euro
**Main exports:** tobacco and cigarettes, furniture
**Type of government:** parliamentary coprincipality

Andorra lies in the eastern Pyrenees, bordering both France and Spain. Its land consists of sharp mountain peaks, mountain slopes, and a series of valleys. Andorra has a large number of natural sources of hot water known as thermal rock springs. The summers are dry and relatively warm, but in the winter snowfall and cold temperatures mean that its mountain slopes are covered with snow for many months. Only four percent of its land can be cultivated; much of the remainder is forested. Andorra relies on its snowfall to lure winter visitors in their millions. Visitors at other times are attracted by its charm and tranquillity. Andorra's heads of state are the coprinces—French

and Spanish authorities who in modern times have been the Spanish Bishop of Urgel and the French president. In 1993 Andorra introduced a new constitution that gave its inhabitants free elections and the right to join trade unions. In the same year Andorra joined the United Nations, although France and Spain still remain responsible for its defense. Native-born Andorrans make up only around 30 percent of the population. Most of the remainder are immigrants from France and Spain. Andorra la Vella is the highest capital in Europe.

# PORTUGAL

**Lying on the far west of southern Europe, Portugal is a long, rectangular-shaped country. It is one of the most rural countries in Western Europe.**

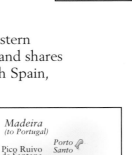

**Area:** 35,672 sq. mi. (92,391km²)
**Population:** 10,627,000
**Capital:** Lisbon (2,672,000)
**Main language spoken:** Portuguese
**Main religion:** Roman Catholic
**Currency:** euro
**Main exports:** textiles and clothing, machinery and transportation equipment, footwear, food, chemicals
**Type of government:** republic

▼ Built on seven hills around the estuary of the Tagus river, Lisbon is a major European city and important deep-water port.

Portugal occupies the southwestern part of the Iberian Peninsula and shares borders in the north and east with Spain, while facing the Atlantic Ocean to the south and west. Northern Portugal is mountainous. The highest part is a highland region that in the winter is snow-covered and popular for skiing. Much of the forests that cover around 35 percent of the country are also found in the north. Portugal's major river, the Tagus, rises in western Spain and divides Portugal into its northern and southern regions. The Douro and the Guadiana rivers, both of which also flow into Spain, are the other major rivers. South of the Tagus the land is much flatter and more low-lying. Much of it consists of vast plains that are divided from the south coast by a mountain range. The south coast region, known as the Algarve, is popular as a tourist destination.

## TRADITIONAL FARMING

Around ten percent of Portugal's population are engaged in farming, while more than 30 percent live in rural areas. The dry soil and climate of the southern part of the country have allowed olives, grapes, and fruit to flourish, and Portugal is renowned worldwide for the production of table wine and two fortified wines, madeira and port, named after the city of Oporto. Cereal grains are grown, and livestock

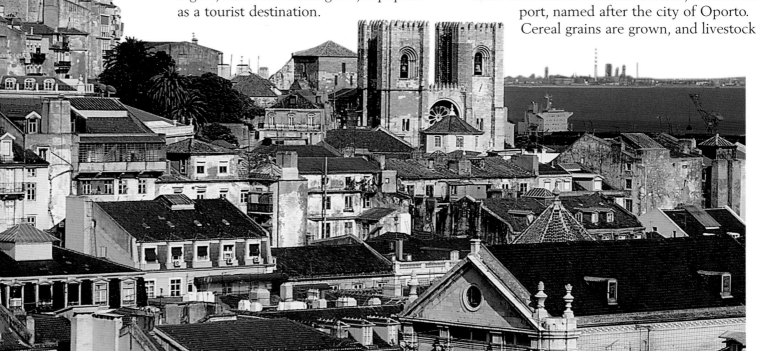

◄ Almost 15 million tourists visit Portugal every year, and a large proportion of them come to the Algarve region in the south of the country. It is renowned for its wide, sandy beaches and warm climate.

▲ This distinctively styled pottery is from Sintra, a small collection of towns and villages on the slopes of the Sintra mountains around 15 mi. (24km) from Lisbon.

are raised on the flatter uplands, as well as on the plains near the coast. Traditional agricultural methods are still practiced in large parts of Portugal. As a result, wild birds and animals have been able to flourish without losing their natural habitats. In the last 20 years Portugal has undergone major economic changes. In particular it has increased its levels of light manufacturing industries, including clothing, footwear, and paper and food processing.

## A SEAFARING NATION

Portugal's long coastline with the Atlantic has meant that—for hundreds of years—many of its people have relied on fishing and trade to make a living. This is still partly the case today, with major ports, such as Lisbon and Oporto, and large fishing fleets. Trawlers fish the Atlantic for cod, hake, mackerel, halibut, and anchovies, while sardines account for one third of all fish catches. In more shallow waters near the coast oysters and other shellfish are harvested. From the 1400s onward Portuguese explorers traveled the world, and the country became a colonial power, with colonies in Africa, South America, and Asia. In 1999 Portugal relinquished control over the last European colony in the Far East when it handed Macau back to China. Today most of Portugal's trade is conducted with other members of the European Union.

► Portugal is the world's leading producer of cork, the thick bark of a particular evergreen oak tree that grows in abundance in the country.

## ISLANDS AND ADMINISTRATION

Portugal first won its independence from Moorish Spain in 1143 and was ruled by a monarch until 1910, when it became a republic. Portugal is divided into 25 regions and communities, which include the Atlantic island groups of Madeira and the Azores. Madeira consists of three small islands and one main island on which its capital, Funchal, is located. Covered in subtropical and tropical plants, Madeira, a popular vacation destination, is around 620 mi. (1,00km) southwest of Portugal. The Azores are a group of nine volcanic-formed islands and smaller islets. They lie just over 745 mi. (1,200km) west of Lisbon.

# ITALY

Unified as one country in 1860–1871,
Italy is now a major European industrial
country with a large agricultural base.

**Area:** 116,324 sq. mi.
(301,277km²)
**Population:** 59,619,000
**Capital:** Rome (3,402,000)
**Main language spoken:**
Italian
**Main religion:**
Roman Catholic
**Currency:** euro
**Main exports:** machinery
and transportation
equipment, electrical
machinery, precision
machinery, chemicals,
textiles, clothing and
shoes, processed metals
**Type of government:**
republic

▼ The city of Naples
was founded around 2,600
years ago by the ancient
Greeks. Today it is one of
Italy's largest ports and
is the center of industry
in southern Italy.

Much of Italy extends
into the Mediterranean
Sea as a long peninsula. It is
bordered by five different nations
to the north: France, Switzerland,
Monaco, Austria, and Slovenia,
while two tiny independent states
are within its territory, San
Marino and Vatican City. In
the northeast of the country
is Italy's largest plain, the
Plain of Lombardy, which
is drained by Italy's longest
river, the 405-mi.- (652-
km-) long Po river. Running
along the western coast of Italy
from Genoa in the north to Naples in
the south are a series of lowlands separated
by mountains, plains, and peaks. This region,
along with the Plain of Lombardy, has
Italy's most fertile soil and is the most
densely populated part of the country.

## HILLS, MOUNTAINS,
## AND VOLCANOES

Much of Italy is covered by hills and
mountains. To the north and part of the
Alps, lie the Dolomites, so named because
many of their peaks are topped
with formations of

dolomite rock. On the southern side of the
Alps is a series of large lakes, including Lago
di Como, Lago di Garda, and Lago Maggiore.
Fast-flowing rivers and streams are harnessed
to provide northern Italy with around half of
its electricity needs. Along the eastern part of
Italy, running from north to south over almost

the entire length of the country, are the Apennine Mountains. These mountains form the backbone of the country and rise to a height of almost 9,840 ft. (3,000m) in the Gran Sasso range, east of the capital city of Rome. A fault line running through the western coast to Sicily features several active volcanoes, including Mount Etna in Sicily and Mount Vesuvius, close to Naples.

## SICILY

Italy's territory includes Sicily, the largest island in the Mediterranean, which is separated from the southwestern tip of the mainland by the Straits of Messina. Most of

Sicily is a plateau of between 656–1,640 ft. (200–500m) in elevation, with higher mountains to the north and several isolated volcanic peaks. The most famous of these is Mount Etna, which rises to 10,998 ft. (3,350m) and is Europe's highest active volcano. Sicily's warm, dry climate allows large crops of citrus fruit, grapes, and olives to be grown, despite the island often suffering drought conditions. Fishing is extremely important to the island economy, with around one fourth of all Italian fishing vessels based in Sicily. The island is also one of the world's leading producers of sulfur, while other mineral deposits include iron and coal.

▲ The Marmolada Massif is part of the Dolomites mountain range in northern Italy. The highest peak in the Dolomites, the Marmolada Massif, is also home to the biggest glacier in the eastern Alps.

▼ Tomato pickers hard at work harvesting their crop. Italy is the second-largest grower of tomatoes in the world and processes much of its crop into sauces and pastes used in Italian cuisine.

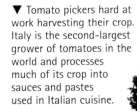

heartland of the country, producing, among other things, chemicals, iron and steel, electrical consumer goods, textiles, and over one million motor vehicles per year. Major industrial cities in the north, including Milan and Turin, are home to giant Italian companies such as Fiat and Olivetti. Northern Italy is one of the most prosperous regions in all of Europe, which is in marked contrast to the south of the country, which is poor and suffers from high unemployment. There, among its terrain of rugged hills and dry soils, traditional methods of agriculture and small-scale industries remain the dominant way of life. Poverty has forced many southern Italians to migrate to the north, and around two thirds of the country's population live in cities and towns.

## ITALY'S ATTRACTIONS

Italy is one of the world's top-five tourist destinations, with its warm Mediterranean climate, scenic lakes and mountains, remains of ancient Rome, and ski resorts in the winter. In 2008, nearly 43 million tourists flocked to Italy to experience its amazingly rich history, culture, and cuisine. Italy's cuisine is varied and extensive, with hundreds of regional dishes and more than 50 different cheeses. The country is also the second-largest wine producer in the world. More than 100,000 historical sites are found throughout Italy, a legacy of the country's past historic wealth and power as the center of the Roman Empire and, from the 1300s onward, the birthplace of new thinking in science, philosophy, and the arts—called the Renaissance. As the home of opera, as well as dozens of influential artists, architects, writers, and composers, Italy's culture is world renowned.

▲ One of the most famous architectural features of Rome is the Scalinata della Trinità dei Monti, or Spanish Steps. Constructed in the early 1700s, the steps are a magnet for tourists and outdoor artists and lead to the 16th-century church of Trinità dei Monti at the top.

## SARDINIA

North of Sicily, the island of Sardinia is also mountainous, with its best farmland in the southwest of the island, where a large plain is situated. Cereals, olives, tobacco, and grain are the chief crops, while the mining industry extracts lead, copper, zinc, and salt from the island. Sardinia's population of more than 1.6 million lives in a number of towns, mostly situated around the island's coast. The island's capital is Cagliari, which is also the principal port of Sardinia.

## NORTH-SOUTH DIVIDE

Italy is divided into 20 administrative regions, but geographers and economists have defined two Italys: the north and the south. Particularly since World War II the north has become the industrial

▶ Italy is one of the foremost manufacturers of motor vehicles in Europe, including the distinctive red Ferrari, Europe's most famous make of luxury sports car. Ferrari was formed in 1939 by Enzo Ferrari and has run a successful Formula One race car team since the 1940s.

# SAN MARINO

The third-smallest nation in Europe, San Marino was established in the A.D. 300s and is completely surrounded by Italy. It relies on tourism for much of its income.

**Area:** 24 sq. mi. (61km²)
**Population:** 31,000
**Capital:** San Marino (4,400)
**Main language spoken:** Italian
**Main religion:** Roman Catholic
**Currency:** euro
**Main exports:** building stone, wine, wheat, ceramics
**Type of government:** republic

Located in central Italy in the Apennine mountain range, San Marino is a tiny country with a maximum length of around 9 mi. (14km). Its landscape is dominated by Monte Titano, which has three individual peaks. Each of these peaks is topped by a medieval fortress: la Rocca, la Cresta, and Montale. The land to the northeast of the mountain slopes gently toward the Romagna Plain, while to the southwest there are a number of hills. Several large streams run through San Marino, including the Ausa and Marano. The country is crowded, with an average population density of over 1,283 people per square mile. Hewn out of the steep slopes of Monte Titano is the nation's capital, also called San Marino.

Agriculture and stone quarrying were important in the past, but today San Marino relies on tourism for around three fifths of its income. The spectacular location of San Marino's settlements and their history, along with the mild climate, lure three million tourists within its borders every year. Three fourths of these are Italians, and many tourists arrive via the Italian city of Rimini, the closest airport to San Marino.

# VATICAN CITY

The world's smallest independent state, Vatican City, or Holy See, is encircled by the city of Rome. It is home to the head of the Roman Catholic Church, the pope.

**Area:** 0.17 sq. mi. (0.44km²)
**Population:** 560
**Capital:** Vatican City
**Main languages spoken:** Italian, Latin
**Main Religion:** The Vatican is the headquarters of the Roman Catholic church.
**Currency:** euro
**Main Exports:** none
**Type of government:** theocracy

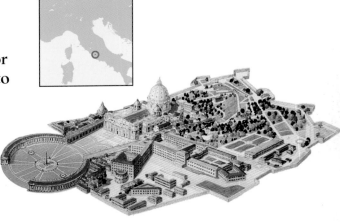

Vatican City lies near the Tiber river and is cut off from Rome by its medieval walls. All food, goods, and energy supplies have to be imported. Vatican City's economy is unlike any other nation in the world. Money comes from investments and from the churches and followers of Roman Catholicism around the world. In addition, admission charges and sales of literature and souvenirs to the hundreds of thousands of tourists who visit provide a large proportion of the state's income. The Vatican's form of government is a theocracy. The person elected pope for life by the Roman Catholic Church has supreme control over the country's laws and government. Security is the task of the 100-strong Vatican army called the Swiss Guard.

▶ Built in the 1500s, St. Peter's Basilica in Vatican City is one of the world's largest religious buildings.

205

# SLOVENIA

**Formerly part of Yugoslavia, Slovenia is a small, scenic, and mountainous country that gained its independence in 1991.**

**Area:** 7,827 sq. mi. (20,273km²)
**Population:** 2,010,000
**Capital:** Ljubljana (248,000)
**Main languages spoken:** Slovenian, Serbo-Croatian
**Main religion:** Roman Catholic
**Currency:** euro
**Main exports:** machinery and transportation equipment, chemicals, foodstuffs
**Type of government:** republic

▼ A market in progress in the Slovenian capital city of Ljubljana. Located on the banks of two rivers, the city has been a major transportation center for many centuries. Today it is an industrialized city with large heavy engineering and paper, soap, and chemical factories.

Slovenia borders Italy to the west, Hungary to the east, Austria to the north, and Croatia to the south. The country has a small 28.9-mi.-(46.6-km-) long coastline with the Adriatic Sea. Much of the northern and western parts of Slovenia are occupied by mountains, which are heavily forested on their lower slopes. Almost half of Slovenia is covered in forests, which still provide habitats for small numbers of bears, wolves, and lynx. The eastern portion of the country lies on a barren limestone plateau. Over millions of years the erosive actions of rainwater in this region have formed some of the most impressive cave systems in Europe, including the 12-mi.- (19.5-km-) long Postojna caves.

Slovenia has a continental climate with cold winters and warm summers. Forty-five percent of the country's population live in small farming communities, where cattle and sheep raising are the most important activities. In the northeast of Slovenia, where the climate is warmer, wine making is an important industry. Brown coal, lead, zinc, and uranium are among the minerals found within its borders, and Slovenia has a small but flourishing manufacturing industry. Despite being ruled by other nations for long periods of their history, the Slovenian people, over 85 percent of whom are descendants of Slavs, have retained much of their rich culture and craft skills. Slovenia's people enjoy relatively high standards of living. Since gaining independence in 1961, the country has built up close ties with the West, and in 2004, it joined the European Union.

# MALTA

**Strategically located in the Mediterranean Sea between Europe and North Africa, Malta has been an important trading center for more than 2,000 years.**

MALTA

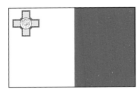

**Area:** 122 sq. mi. (316km²)
**Population:** 414,000
**Capital:** Valletta (204,000)
**Main languages spoken:** Maltese, English
**Main religion:** Roman Catholic
**Currency:** Maltese lira
**Main exports:** machinery and transportation equipment, manufactures (mainly textiles, clothing and footwear), chemicals
**Type of government:** parliamentary democracy

The Maltese archipelago consists of three inhabited islands—Malta, Gozo, and Comino—and two uninhabited islands. They lie in the middle of the Mediterranean Sea around 56 mi. (90km) south of the Italian island of Sicily and more than 155 mi. (250km) from the coast of North Africa. Malta is the largest of the islands. Measuring 17 by 9 mi. (27 x 14.5km) at its greatest extent, the island's 85-mi.- (137-km-) long coastline is rocky and contains many low cliffs, bays, and natural harbors. There are also a number of sandy beaches, which, along with the country's warm, dry climate and long history, attract over one million vacationers every year. Away from the coast Malta's landscape is one of mainly low hills, with small farming fields cut into the hill slopes as terraces. Crops are grown on the terraces, including feed for livestock, flowers, and citrus fruit. Malta has no rivers and little surface water. It relies on desalination plants, which produce freshwater from seawater, for its water supply. Lying northwest of Malta and linked by a regular ferry service, the island of Gozo is less populated but has more fertile soils in which grapes, other fruit, and vegetables are grown. The Maltese islands' strategic location has seen them occupied by the ancient Phoenicians, Greeks, Romans, Normans, Arabs, and Turks. The last colonial power to control Malta was Great Britain, from which Malta became independent in 1964. Malta has few natural resources, and shipping and trade remain vitally important to its economy. In 2004, Malta became a member of the European Union.

▼ Lying on the southeastern coast of Malta, the harbor and town of Marsaxlokk has been a site of the Maltese fishing industry for many centuries.

# THE BALKANS

The Balkans region of Europe gets its name from the Balkan Peninsula, which juts into the Mediterranean Sea. The peninsula's coastline faces Italy across the Adriatic Sea on its western side and terminates to the south with the fragmented coastline of Greece and its many island groups. The Mediterranean Sea reaches its greatest depth off the coast of Greece, where a maximum depth of 16,345 ft. (4,982m) has been recorded. "Balkan" comes from the Turkish word for mountains, and mountains and rugged hills are a major feature of the region's landscape. Much of the region was part of the Turkish empire for many centuries. As it declined in the late 1800s and early 1900s rivalries between different ethnic groups in the territory north of Greece led to new states being formed. After World War I a large portion of the Balkans was combined into a new nation, which became known as Yugoslavia. The tensions between the ethnic groups in Yugoslavia turned into direct conflict, with fierce fighting and thousands of deaths after the breakup of that country in 1991. Today the region contains a number of new and young nations involved in an uneasy peace that are seeking to rebuild after war and to create stable societies.

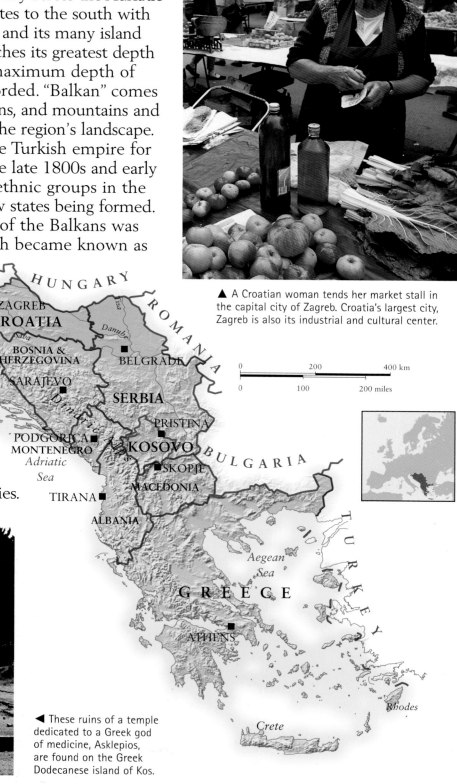

▲ A Croatian woman tends her market stall in the capital city of Zagreb. Croatia's largest city, Zagreb is also its industrial and cultural center.

◀ These ruins of a temple dedicated to a Greek god of medicine, Asklepios, are found on the Greek Dodecanese island of Kos.

208

# CROATIA

Founded in A.D. 800 and part of Yugoslavia during the 1900s, Croatia lies on the crossroad between central Europe and the Mediterranean countries.

**Area:** 21,831 sq. mi. (56,542km²)
**Population:** 4,435,000
**Capital:** Zagreb (786,000)
**Main language spoken:** Croatian
**Main religions:** Catholic, Orthodox
**Currency:** kuna
**Main exports:** basic manufactures, machinery, chemicals, fuels, food
**Type of government:** parliamentary democracy

▼ The ancient historic town and port of Dubrovnik is one of the most scenic settlements in all of Croatia. Originally founded in the A.D. 600s, it is overlooked by Mount Srjd and features heavily fortified stone city walls.

Croatia borders Slovenia and Hungary to the north, while its eastern border with Serbia is partly defined by the Danube river. Croatia wraps around the northern and western sides of Bosnia & Herzegovina and extends along the Adriatic Sea with one 12-mi. (20-km) break, giving Bosnia & Herzegovina a short Adriatic coastline. The remaining Croatian territory, which includes the city of Dubrovnik, is cut off from the rest of Croatia and has a short border with Montenegro. The western part of Croatia is known as Dalmatia and is a rocky and relatively barren land. Changes in sea level have drowned mountain valleys, creating many steep islands and small, rocky peninsulas. This western part of Croatia experiences a Mediterranean climate, while the remainder of the country's climate is continental with colder winters. Croatia's large river, the Sava, flows into the Danube. Around one fifth of the country is devoted to agriculture, with the most fertile region in the east. Pigs, chickens, and dairy cattle are raised, while cereal crops cover almost two thirds of the land. Other important produce includes sunflower seeds, soybeans, and sugar beets. The country has rich mineral resources, including oil and coal, and today, following the damaging conflicts of the 1990s, much aid and investment is being introduced into rebuilding its former industries. The Croatian tourist industry has revived and is again an important sector of the economy.

# BOSNIA & HERZEGOVINA

**Bosnia & Herzegovina became independent of Yugoslavia in 1992 and is now rebuilding following a devastating civil war.**

**Area:** 19,741 sq. mi. (51,129km²)
**Population:** 3,840,000
**Capital:** Sarajevo (393,000)
**Main language spoken:** Serbo-Croatian
**Main religions:** Islam, Catholic
**Currency:** convertible mark
**Main exports:** food, timber, basic manufactures
**Type of government:** republic; limited democracy

▼ The city of Mostar is surrounded by high, barren mountains. Formerly home to Roman Catholic Croats, Bosnian Muslims, and Serbs, the city was heavily damaged during the civil war, and today Serbs no longer live there.

Bosnia & Herzegovina lies in the Balkans bordering Serbia, Montenegro, and Croatia. The country's rugged landscape is very mountainous in the north, while to the south there are flatter, more fertile regions. Cereal crops and flax are grown in the north, while tobacco, fruit, and cotton are important in the south. Large parts of the country lie on a barren limestone plateau. Underground rivers flow through this area, and there are many mineral springs. Almost half of the country is covered in forests of oak, beech, and pine trees. Since the time of the Roman Empire many different religious and cultural groups have settled here. The country's main ethnic groups today are Croats, Serbs, and the largest group, ethnic Bosniaks, most of whom are Muslims. Following the savage civil war many people emigrated, and the population dropped by one fourth.

The country is now made up of two self-governing states, the Muslim-Croat Federation and the Serbian Republika Srpska. Bosnia & Herzegovina is now trying to revive its industries.

# SERBIA

**Formerly part of Yugoslavia and then of a loose union
called Serbia & Montenegro, landlocked Serbia became
a separate nation in 2006.**

**Area:** 29,913 sq. mi.
(77,474km²)
**Population:** 7,350,000
**Capital:** Belgrade
(1,597,000)
**Main languages spoken:**
Serbian
**Main religion:** Serbian
Orthodox
**Currency:** dinar
**Main exports:** iron and
steel, clothing, wheat, fruit
**Type of government:**
republic; democracy

Serbia occupies a strategic location in
the Balkans, sharing borders with eight
countries. In the north, which has a
continental climate, there are large plains
and low hills. To the east lie areas of
limestone hills and basins; in the south,
mountains form barriers. When Yugoslavia,
of which Serbia was the largest constituent
republic, dissolved in the early 1990s,
Serbia embanked on a "Greater Serbia"
policy, aiming to unite all Serbs in one
state. This led to a series of wars with
other former-Yugoslav republics, a
NATO bombing campaign, international
trade sanctions against Serbia, and a
bitter civil war in the Kosovo region,
which has a majority of ethnic
Albanians. A UN administration
removed Kosovo from
Serbian control in
1999, and in 2008
Kosovo
declared

independence. Serbia adopted a democratic
system in 2000 and has attempted to
rebuild its economy. The country has
reserves of bauxite, copper, lead, and other
minerals and its industries include
metallurgy, food processing, textiles, motor
vehicles, and growing cereals, vegetables,
and fodder crops.

▼ Serbian
refugees from
Kosovo work on
a farm in central
Serbia.

# MACEDONIA

A landlocked nation with great scenic beauty, the former Yugoslav republic of Macedonia was once part of the ancient Greek Empire.

**Area:** 9,928 sq. mi. (25,713km²)
**Population:** 2,049,000
**Capital:** Skopje (527,000)
**Main languages spoken:** Macedonian, Albanian
**Main religions:** Macedonian Orthodox, Roman Catholic
**Currency:** dinar
**Principal exports:** basic manufactures, machinery and transportation equipment, food products, chemicals
**Type of government:** republic; limited democracy

Macedonia has steep-sided hills and mountains, deep valleys, and large forests. The capital, Skopje, was severely damaged by an earthquake in 1961. It has been rebuilt and is a major market center and industrial region. Part of the former Yugoslavia, Macedonia became independent in 1991, although Greece has disputed its name and its flag. Most people are Macedonian Slavs, but Albanian-speaking people make up 21 percent of the population. Tensions led to an uprising by ethnic Albanians in 2001, but peace was restored and the Albanians were granted autonomy.

# MONTENEGRO

A small, mountainous country, Montenegro maintained its independence from the 1400s until 1918. It declared independence again in 2006.

**Area:** 5,333 sq. mi. (13,812km²)
**Population:** 626,000
**Capital:** Podgorica (143,000)
**Main language spoken:** Serbian
**Main religions:** Serbian and Montenegrin Orthodox
**Currency:** euro
**Main exports:** metal products (particularly aluminum), manufactures, electricity
**Type of government:** republic; democracy

In 1918 Montenegro was absorbed by Yugoslavia. After 1945, when Yugoslavia became a communist federation, Montenegro became a constituent republic. When Yugoslavia dissolved in the early 1990s, Montenegro remained in federation with Serbia. However, the country increasingly grew to resent Serbian dominance, and in 2006 Montenegro declared independence. Montenegro's Adriatic coast attracts foreign tourists. Coal and hydroelectric facilities provide enough electricity to meet the country's needs, and mining and metallurgy, particularly aluminum smelting, are important industries. There is little arable land, and farmers raise livestock in the hills and grow cereals, fruits, vegetables and olives in the limited lowlands.

▼ Supporters of Montenegro's independence celebrate in Podgorica in May 2006, after winning the vote for separation from Serbia.

# ALBANIA

**One of the poorest and least developed nations in Europe, Albania remained isolated from the outside world for much of the 1900s.**

**Area:** 11,100 sq. mi. (28,748km²)
**Population:** 3,170,000
**Capital:** Tirana (484,000)
**Main languages spoken:** Albanian, Greek
**Main religions:** Islam, Albanian Orthodox, Roman Catholic
**Currency:** lek
**Main exports:** manufactured goods, chromium and copper, food and tobacco, textiles
**Type of government:** republic; limited democracy

▼ Founded in the 1600s and lying on the Ishm river, Tirana is Albania's capital and largest city.

Albania is found on the western part of the Balkan Peninsula facing the Adriatic Sea, with Montenegro to the north, Serbia, Kosovo, and Macedonia to the east, and Greece to the south. The country can be divided into two geographical regions. To the west is an area of coastal lowlands. Although some of this land is marshy, much of it contains fertile soils and is heavily farmed, as well as being the most densely populated part of the country. Much of the rest of Albania consists of highlands and mountains. Albania's major rivers begin their life in the mountains and flow in a western direction, emptying into the Adriatic Sea.

Over 50 percent of the country's workforce is employed in agriculture, with wheat, corn, potatoes, and sugar beets being the major crops, while there are some 1.9 million sheep. Albania's population is one of the least mixed in Europe—97 percent of its people are ethnic Albanians. Most of the 1900s was spend in isolation from the rest of the world under a communist dictatorship. As a result, the country is less developed, and despite its reserves of metals, gas, and oil, its industry and economy lags behind the rest of Europe. Albania's people are among the poorest in Europe, and many young Albanians emigrate to seek work. There are more ethnic Albanians overseas than in Albania itself.

# KOSOVO

**Kosovo, formerly part of Serbia, unilaterally declared independence in 2008.**

**Area:** 4,203 sq. mi. (10,887 km²)
**Population:** 2,153,000
**Capital:** Pristina (197,000)
**Main language spoken:** Albanian
**Main religion:** Sunni Islam
**Currency:** euro
**Principal exports:** metal products, leather, raw materials
**Type of government:** republic; limited democracy

Kosovo is culturally and linguistically Albanian. The region was the heart of the medieval Serbian empire but Serb migration from the 1600s reduced the Serb population to a minority. Today, Kosovo is largely agricultural and is one of the least developed parts of the Balkans.

Nationalism among the Kosovars (ethnic Albanians) increased in the late 1980s, when Kosovo was still part of Serbia and Yugoslavia, and in 1989 Serbia revoked Kosovo's autonomy. From 1998 Serbian forces conducted a campaign against Kosovo, killing many Kosovars and forcing about 800,000 into exile. NATO ousted Serbian forces, and in 1999 the UN placed Kosovo under a transitional administration. Attempts to achieve a solution failed. Kosovo declared independence, which has been recognized by most Western countries, but not by Serbia.

# GREECE

Greece is one of the oldest civilizations in Europe, although it only gained independence from Turkey in 1832.

**Area:** 50,949 sq. mi. (131,957km²)
**Population:** 11,214,000
**Capital:** Athens (3,188,000)
**Main language spoken:** Greek
**Main religion:** Greek Orthodox
**Currency:** euro
**Main exports:** textiles, food, beverages, tobacco, petroleum products, minerals, cotton
**Type of government:** parliamentary republic

Greece is a highly fragmented landmass, with a heavily indented coastline that measures over 2,485 mi. (4,000m). The country occupies the southernmost part of the Balkan Peninsula and curves around the northern and eastern edge of the Aegean Sea. The country's land borders are to the north with Albania, Macedonia, Bulgaria, and Turkey. Two large gulfs almost split the southern portion of the mainland, the Peloponnese Peninsula, from the rest of mainland Greece. Much of the country consists of highland areas. The Pindus Mountains are Greece's largest mountain range. Greece's mountains are young and are still being built, resulting in many earthquakes. Most of Greece has a Mediterranean climate with mild, rainy winters, with average daily temperatures rarely below 50°F (10°C), and subtropical, dry and warm summers. Temperatures are cooled slightly by a system of seasonal breezes popularly known locally as the Meltemia. Greece's northern forests are home to wildcats, roe deer, and small numbers of brown bears, lynx, and wild boar. Jackals and wild goats are found in the south. Much of Greece, especially its western wetlands, is visited in the winter by flocks of migratory birds.

▼ Lying on the Saronic Gulf, the city of Piraeus first served as a port for the city of Athens, around 5 mi. (8km) inland, almost 2,500 years ago. Developed in the 1900s, Piraeus is now Greece's largest port.

## FAMILY FARMING

Only 22 percent of Greece's territory consists of arable land. The rest is rocky scrubland, both mountains and forests. Greek agriculture employs almost one fifth of the country's workforce, despite poor soils and soil erosion in places. It has received much assistance from the national government and the European Union, which Greece joined in 1981. Most farms are small and family-owned, on which warm weather crops, including olives, grapes, and citrus fruit, are grown. The leading export crop is tobacco, with cotton, olive oil, and Greek cheeses also important. Sheep and goats are raised, while fishing is strictly controlled to protect the Mediterranean Sea from overfishing.

## THE GREEK ECONOMY

Greece relies on tourism and agriculture for a major part of its economy. The country has few mineral reserves, with some exceptions such as bauxite. Its industries include textiles, cement, telecommunications, and processed foods. The Greek merchant fleet is the largest home-owned fleet of vessels in the world, and shipbuilding and trading services are a major part of the economy. European Union assistance has reduced poverty in Greece, but the country suffered a major financial crisis in 2010, requiring EU aid.

## THE ISLANDS OF GREECE

One fifth of Greece's land area consists of more than 2,000 islands, of which only 154 are inhabited. These are divided into many groups, including the Ionian Islands to the west and the Cyclades to the southeast. A number of Greece's islands lie just off the coast of Turkey, the country with which Greece has had territorial disputes. With an area of 3,219 sq. mi. (8,336km²), Crete is the largest of the Greek islands and the fifth largest in the Mediterranean. Three mountain ranges run across the island, forming a spine and creating the deep and scenic gorges for which Crete is famous. Home to the Minoan civilization from 3500 B.C., Crete was also one of the major birthplaces of the ancient Greek civilization, which became centered around the modern day capital of Athens. The Olympic Games, which started in ancient Greece more than 2,500 years ago, returned to Athens in August 2004.

▲ A crowded pedestrian crossing in the bustling city of Athens. As a result of thousands of people migrating from the countryside to the capital city of Greece, Athens has a high population density and suffers badly from heavy air pollution.

▼ The remains of hundreds of ancient Greek buildings can be found throughout Greece. This theater in Epidaurus once held around 2,000 spectators.

# EASTERN EUROPE

Eastern Europe stretches westward from the eastern part of the Russian Federation, bordered by the Ural Mountains, to the Baltic states of Latvia, Lithuania, and Estonia in the north of Europe and the countries of Belarus, Ukraine, Moldova, Romania, and Bulgaria to the south. Two seas provide vital trading links for the region: the Baltic Sea to the west and the Black Sea to the south. While mountain chains exist in parts, much of Eastern Europe is part of the Great European Plain, which extends deep into western Russia. Although the soil is poor in some parts of the plain, in other regions it is fertile enough to support extensive cereal crop farming, especially in Ukraine and western Russia. All of the countries of this region were, until the late 1980s, either part of the former Soviet Union or a member of the communist power bloc of countries controlled by that nation. Most of the countries of Eastern Europe are seeking to modernize their industry to compete with the countries of Western Europe, and closer ties between both halves of the continent are being forged. The Baltic states of Latvia, Lithuania, and Estonia joined the European Union in 2004, while Bulgaria and Romania joined in 2007.

▼ St. Basil's Cathedral stands in Red Square in the center of Moscow, the capital of the Russian Federation. Completed in 1679, the church was built to commemorate the military conquests of the Russian czar known as Ivan the Terrible.

▼ Transylvania, in Romania, consists of a high plateau surrounded by mountains. The region is extensively farmed and contains reserves of minerals such as coal, silver, and gold.

*Novaya Zemlya*

*Barents Sea*

*Kola Peninsula*

FINLAND

*White Sea*

Ural Mountains

*Pechora*

*Northern Dvina*

*Lake Onega*

*Lake Ladoga*

RUSSIAN

FEDERATION

*Gulf of Finland*

■ TALLINN

ESTONIA

*Volga*

*Kama*

■ MOSCOW

■ LATVIA

RIGA ■

LITHUANIA

*Kaliningrad (RUSSIA)*

■ VILNIUS

■ MINSK

BELARUS

*Volga*

*Ural*

POLAND

*Don*

KAZAKHSTAN

KIEV ■

UKRAINE

*Dniester*

SLOVAKIA

Carpathians

HUNGARY

MOLDOVA

■ CHISINÂU

*Dnieper*

*Sea of Azov*

*Caspian Sea*

ROMANIA

CRIMEA

*Elbrus △18,506 ft.*

Caucasus

■ BUCHAREST

*Danube*

*Black Sea*

SERBIA

BULGARIA

KOSOVO

■ SOFIA

MACEDONIA

| 0 | 400 | 800 km |

| 0 | 200 | 400 miles |

GREECE    TURKEY

# ESTONIA

**Dense forests, low hills, and a lengthy coastline are key features of the smallest and most northern of the three Baltic states.**

**Area:** 17,462 sq. mi. (45,227km²)
**Population:** 1,340,000
**Capital:** Tallinn (432,000)
**Main languages spoken:** Estonian, Russian
**Main religions:** Evangelical Lutheran, Russian Orthodox
**Currency:** kroon
**Main exports:** chemicals, machinery, food products, textiles and clothing, wood and paper
**Type of government:** republic

Estonia borders its Baltic state neighbor of Latvia to the south and the Russian Federation to the east. It faces the Baltic Sea to the west and an arm of the Baltic, called the Gulf of Finland, to the north. Estonia is a low-lying country, with two thirds of its land below 164 ft. (50m) in elevation. Its land is crossed by around 7,000 streams and rivers, as well as more than 1,000 lakes, which together make up around five percent of the country's area. Lake Peipus is Estonia's largest lake. It forms much of the Estonian border with Russia and is Europe's fifth-largest freshwater lake. A further ten percent of Estonian territory comes in the form of islands lying a short distance off its Baltic coastline. The two largest islands are Saaremaa, where livestock raising is the main activity, and Hiiumaa, on which most of its workforce, many of whom are of Swedish origin, fish for a living. Trees cover around 45 percent of the country and provide habitats for many creatures, as well as the raw materials for Estonia's large timber, furniture making, and paper industries. Metalworking, engineering, and the mining and processing of oil shale into fuels and chemicals are the country's chief industries.

Estonia's small population gives the country one of the lowest densities in Europe, with just 78 people per square mile. The country derives its name from a people called the Ests who settled in the region around 2,000 years ago. Around two thirds of the population are native Estonians whose language and descent are closely related to the Finns. Russians form the largest minority group, comprising 26 percent of the population. Seven out of ten Estonians live in major towns and cities such as the capital, Tallinn, the industrial city of Narva, and Pärnu, a popular summer vacation resort with a warmer climate than much of the country.

▲ Tallinn dates back to the 1200s when crusading knights built a castle on the site. The city has developed and retained many charming historic buildings, which have survived fires and wars. Tallinn is visited by several hundred thousand foreign tourists every year.

► A sailing boat in the choppy waters of the Bay of Tallinn. The waterfront of Estonia's capital city is in the background.

**Map labels:** Gulf of Finland, TALLINN, Maardu, Kohtla-Järve, Rakvere, Narva, Sillamäe, RUSSIAN FEDERATION, Hiiumaa, Haapsalu, Paide, ESTONIA, Lake Peipus, Saaremaa, Pärnu, Viljandi, Tartu, Baltic Sea, Gulf of Riga, Voru, LATVIA

# LATVIA

**Latvia is the most industrialized of the Baltic states. A flat, wooded, and marshy country, it uses its coastline for trade and fishing.**

**Area:** 24,946 sq. mi. (64,610km²)
**Population:** 2,261,000
**Capital:** Riga (787,000)
**Main languages spoken:** Lettish, Lithuanian, Russian
**Main religions:** Lutheran, Roman Catholic, Russian Orthodox
**Currency:** lat
**Main exports:** timber and paper products, textiles, food and agricultural products, machinery
**Type of government:** republic

▼ Lying on the southern shore of the Gulf of Riga, the capital city of Riga is Latvia's major port and is home to around one third of the entire country's population.

Latvia is a low-lying country, with 98 percent of its territory below 656 ft. (200m) in elevation. It borders Belarus and the Russian Federation to the east, and a large part of its coast curves around to form much of the Gulf of Riga. Sheltered from the Baltic by the large Estonian island of Saaremaa, the Gulf of Riga provides warm water harbors, including Liepaja, Ventspils, and the country's largest port and capital city, Riga. Latvia has thousands of small rivers and streams, only 17 of which are longer than 56 mi. (90km). The longest is the Daugavapils, which begins its life in northwestern Russia and flows through Latvia, emptying into the Gulf of Riga. Frozen from December to April and with a series of rapids and shallows, the river is not navigable by large shipping. It is, however, used to provide hydroelectricity and to float timber to transport it from

Latvia's wooded interior to the ports on its coast. Over half of Latvia's forests consist of pine trees, while forests of oak are also common. Trees cover around 40 percent of the country's land and contribute to a sizable timber industry. Apart from peat from the bogs that cover almost one tenth of the country and limestone and dolomite rocks for building, Latvia has few natural resources. It is reliant on the Russian Federation for imports of oil and other fuels, although oil has recently been discovered in the east of the country. Dairy and livestock farming occupy many Latvians in rural areas, while two thirds of its people live in towns and cities. Around 60 percent of the population are Latvians, with Russians forming a large minority of about 28 percent. Smaller minorities of Ukrainians, Belarusians, and Poles exist.

**INDEPENDENCE AND GOVERNMENT**
Latvia has been ruled by foreign powers, including Sweden and, later, Poland, for most of its history. In the 1700s the country was absorbed into the large Russian empire of Peter the Great. It seized independence in 1919 and remained independent until the Soviet Union took control after World War II. Since independence in 1991 the country has restored the 1922 constitution, and the government is headed by a president elected by the Saeima, a 100-member parliament elected by free vote for terms of four years. Latvia joined the European Union in 2004.

# LITHUANIA

**The most southerly of the Baltic states, Lithuania has a short west-facing coastline. Most of its people work in heavy industry or farming.**

**Area:** 24,946 sq. mi. (64,610km²)
**Population:** 3,350,000
**Capital:** Vilnius (570,000)
**Main languages spoken:** Lithuanian, Polish, Russian
**Main religion:** Roman Catholic
**Currency:** litas
**Main exports:** textiles, chemicals, mineral products, machinery
**Type of government:** republic

▼ Lithuanians pray in front of the altar of a church containing an icon of the Virgin Mary. Around 79 percent of Lithuanians are Roman Catholic.

Lithuania borders Latvia to the north, Belarus to the south and east, and Poland to the southwest. Its land is mainly a series of plains and low hills dotted with many lakes and crossed by over 20 rivers. The largest river, the Neman, is around 582 mi. (937km) long and drains much of the country. Lithuania's short coastline with the Baltic Sea is the location of much of the world's amber, the fossilized resin from prehistoric trees used to make jewelry. It is also the site of the Courland Spit, a 59-mi.- (95-km-) long bank of sand dunes stretching south from the port of Klaipéda and enclosing the Courland Lagoon. Over one fourth of the country is forested, and it has five national parks and four national wildlife reserves. Lithuania was a powerful independent state 700 years ago, but from the 1500s

onward it became part of Poland and, later, Russia. It declared independence in 1918, only to become occupied by the Soviet Union from 1944 until 1991, when it again achieved independence. Native Lithuanians comprise around 85 percent of the population, and Poles and Russians make up the largest minorities.

# BELARUS

A flat, low-lying nation with many lakes in the north and large marshlands in the south, Belarus became independent from the former Soviet Union in 1991.

**Area:** 80,134 sq. mi. (207,546km²)
**Population:** 9,672,000
**Capital:** Minsk (1,829,000)
**Main languages spoken:** Byelorussian, Russian
**Main religion:** Eastern Orthodox
**Currency:** Belarussian ruble
**Main exports:** trucks and tires, diesel fuel, synthetic fibers, refrigerators, fertilizer, milk and dairy products
**Type of government:** republic

The hill range that runs diagonally through Belarus forms a ridge that divides the country into two areas of lowlands. The northern area has a number of gentle hills and many of the country's 11,000 small lakes. South of the ridge lies a large marshy plain drained by the Pripet river and its tributaries. This region comprises the largest area of unreclaimed marshland in Europe. To the west where Belarus borders Poland lies the Belovezhskaya Forest. Much of this forest is protected to create Europe's largest nature reserve, the home of the otherwise rare wisent, or European bison.

## DEVASTATED TWICE

Over two million Belarussian people lost their lives during World War II, which devastated many of its towns and cities. In 1986 the Chernobyl nuclear power station in neighboring Ukraine exploded, and 70 percent of the radioactive fallout landed on Belarus territory. Close to three million people were seriously affected, and soil, streams, and rivers were contaminated. Around 15 percent of the country's forests and 20 percent of its farmland remain too radioactive for their products to be used. The cost of cleaning up the region, rehousing people, and dealing with the long-term effects of the world's biggest nuclear accident has put severe strain on the country's health service and economy, despite aid from other nations and charities.

▼ A monument overlooks part of the Belarussian city of Minsk. The nation's largest settlement, almost all of Minsk was reconstructed from 1944 onward. The city has barely changed since independence.

## A DECLINING ECONOMY

Around 14 percent of the country's workforce is engaged in agriculture, but industry contributes more to the economy. When it was part of the former Soviet Union, many heavy industrial factories and processing plants were built in Belarus to process the raw materials extracted from other parts of the Soviet Union, especially Ukraine. As an independent nation and one with relatively few mineral resources, Belarus has struggled since independence. It has largely kept its old Soviet-style economy and has privatized or modernized very little of its industry to make it more competitive in the world market. As a result, production has declined, and the country faces huge economic problems. Its main industrial center is in and around the capital city, Minsk. In Minsk many products, including farm machinery, motor vehicles, machine tools, and electrical goods, are manufactured and assembled. The country retains close ties with Russia, which it relies on for around three fifths of its imports and 32 percent of its exports. Belarus remains heavily dependent upon Russia for oil and gas. The country is a dictatorship in which opposition is restricted.

# UKRAINE

**Bordering the Black Sea to the south, Ukraine is one of the most economically powerful of the former Soviet states.**

**Area:** 233,090 sq. mi. (603,700km$^2$)
**Population:** 46,144,000
**Capital:** Kiev (2,923,000)
**Main languages spoken:** Ukrainian, Russian
**Main religions:** Ukrainian Orthodox, Ukrainian Catholic
**Currency:** hryvna
**Main exports:** ferrous metals, machinery, minerals, chemicals
**Type of government:** republic; democracy

▼ A combine gathers and processes a cereal crop in Ukraine. The country is one of the world's leading producers of cereals, such as wheat, and is the largest producer of sugar beets.

Ukraine is the third largest of the former states of the Soviet Union, after the Russian Federation and Kazakhstan. Most of Ukraine consists of fertile plains, known as steppes, and plateaus. Much of the northern part of the country is covered in dense forests largely consisting of pine, oak, and spruce trees. Mountains are found only to the west of the country and in the Crimean Peninsula, which juts out into the Black Sea. Ukraine has a long shoreline with the Black Sea and also borders the Sea of Azov, which measures approximately 14,500 sq. mi. (37,555km$^2$). Shallow and with low salt levels owing to the large number of rivers that deposit freshwater, the Sea of Azov is almost entirely landlocked. It has just one marine opening to the south connecting it with the Black Sea. Ukraine generally has a continental climate with warm summers and cold winters, especially in the east of the country. The Crimean coastline, however, has a

Mediterranean climate with hotter summers. The levels of rainfall vary greatly depending on the region, with more rain in the north and west of the country and heavy snowfalls in the country's mountainous areas.

## RICH IN MINERALS

An estimated five percent of the entire world's mineral reserves are found within Ukraine. The country has the world's largest reserves of manganese and titanium and the third-largest iron ore reserves. In 2007 Ukraine produced more than 62.5 million tons (56.7 million metric tonnes) of iron ore. Despite declining dramatically since independence, the metal industry remains Ukraine's single most important industrial area. It contributes approximately one fifth of its GDP and one fourth of all of its exports. The country has giant coal reserves, the largest of which are situated to the east around the city of Donets'k. However, it has only small oil and gas reserves and has to import more than four fifths of these fuels for its energy needs.

## EASTERN EUROPE'S CEREAL GIANT

Ukraine has extremely rich soil, and its millions of acres of flat land allow a range of cereal crops to be grown in bulk. Formerly known as "the breadbasket of the Soviet Union," Ukraine has traditionally produced a huge surplus of agricultural and food products, which it exported to other parts of the former Soviet Union or to countries in Eastern Europe. In the late 1980s Ukraine contributed more than one fourth of the entire Soviet Union's agricultural output. However, since independence farm production has

plummeted to under half of 1991 levels. Some of Ukraine's farmland was contaminated by the radioactive fallout from the 1986 nuclear disaster at Chernobyl. Industries linked to agriculture, such as producing factory machinery and processing foods, tend to be outdated and struggle to keep up with demand. As a result, there are often shortages of certain basic foods. A number of foreign companies have started operations within Ukraine, looking to modernize parts of its industry and utilize its trained and educated workforce. Since independence in 1991 the population, 78 percent of which are of Ukrainian descent, with 17 percent comprising Russians, have seen the gap between the rich and poor increase greatly.

▲ Ukrainian coal miners work at the pit face. Ukraine has large coal reserves, enough to sustain production at the current rate for at least 300 years.

# MOLDOVA

**Moldova is the smallest and most densely populated of the former Soviet republics. The country is landlocked and is one of the poorest nations in Europe.**

**Area:** 13,078 sq. mi. (33,873km²)
**Population:** 3,958,000
**Capital:** Chisinau (755,000)
**Main languages spoken:** Moldovan, Russian
**Main religion:** Eastern Orthodox
**Currency:** Moldovan leu
**Main exports:** food and agricultural goods, machinery, textiles, metals
**Type of government:** republic; limited democracy

Moldova is surrounded on three sides by Ukraine, while it shares a border with Romania to the west. The country is low-lying with an average elevation of only 460 ft. (140m), but much of its land is hilly. Hundreds of short streams and rivers cross the land, the longest being the Dniester, which flows through the east of Moldova and empties into the Black Sea in Ukraine.

## A FARMING NATION

More than seven tenths of Moldova's land is covered in a rich black soil that can be farmed. Wheat, tobacco, corn, and sunflower seeds are among the main crops, while grapes tend to be grown in the south of the country. Moldova's wine-making industry is one of the few industries that has flourished since the country gained independence in 1991. Agriculture is the leading employer of Moldova, providing work for 41 percent of the country's workforce and generating

many of its exports. Food processing accounts for 42 percent of the country's industrial output. With only limited mineral resources and poor transportation links, the country's economy has struggled, and Moldavians are among the poorest people in Europe. Moldova was once part of Romania, and almost two thirds of its people are of either Moldavian or Romanian descent. Two large minorities—Ukrainians and Russians—make up a further one fourth of the population. Many Russians and Ukrainians live east of the Dniester river, in a breakaway region called the Dniester Republic, or Transnistria.

▲ A church wedding takes place in the country's capital city of Chisinau. Many Moldavians are followers of the Romanian Orthodox Church.

▶ Moldavians harvest potatoes in a small field. Most agriculture in Moldova is farmed by cooperatives of people working together.

# ROMANIA

**Achieving independence in 1878, Romania is a country with a Black Sea coastline. Its land is a mixture of mountains and lowlands.**

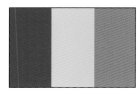

**Area:** 91,699 sq. mi. (237,500km²)
**Population:** 21,623,000
**Capital:** Bucharest (2,100,000)
**Main languages spoken:** Romanian, Hungarian, German
**Main religions:** Romanian Orthodox, Roman Catholic, Protestant
**Currency:** Romanian leu
**Main exports:** textiles, mineral products, footwear, chemicals, machinery
**Type of government:** republic

▼ A large portion of Bucharest was demolished in the 1980s to build the huge Palace of the People (now Parliament Palace). Even though parts of the building remain incomplete, it is the second-largest administrative building in the world behind the United States' Pentagon.

Romania borders Hungary to the northwest, Ukraine to the north, Moldova to the east, Bulgaria to the south, and Serbia to the west. It also has a strategically important coastline on the Black Sea. The Danube river flows along most of the border with Bulgaria, providing an important transportation route for inland shipping. The Danube forms a large delta as it empties into the Black Sea.

## MOUNTAINS, FORESTS, AND FARMING

Much of north and central Romania is covered by two large mountain ranges. Running east to west are the Transylvanian Alps, which include the country's highest point, the 8,344-ft.- (2,544-m-) high Varful Moldoveanu. North of these mountains is a large, hilly plateau that is bordered to the north and east by the Carpathian Mountains. Forests cover more than one fourth of the country and provide homes for a wide range of wild animals, including wolves, deer, bear, wild boars, and lynx. Forty five percent of Romania's land is suitable for agriculture.

## NATURAL RESOURCES

Most of the raw materials used in Romania's industries are imported, and its once important oil and natural gas reserves are fast dwindling. Romania's major natural resources are its fertile soils and its fast-moving rivers, which are harnessed for hydroelectricity generation. The country also has deposits of lead, zinc, and sulfur. Much of Romania's industrial and agricultural exports are transported out of the country's biggest port, Constanta. Romania became a member of the European Union in 2007 and benefits from exports to EU markets. The country is replacing obsolete industrial facilities.

# BULGARIA

**A mountainous country bordering the Black Sea in southeastern Europe, Bulgaria has had a long and colorful history.**

**Area:** 42,855 sq. mi. (110,993km²)
**Population:** 7,607,000
**Capital:** Sofia (1,247,000)
**Main language spoken:** Bulgarian
**Main religions:** Bulgarian Orthodox, Islam
**Currency:** lev
**Main exports:** food, textiles, clothing, footwear, machinery, iron and steel
**Type of government:** republic

Bulgaria is a country with varied scenery. Plateaus, plains, hills, and mountains are all found in its territory. The two largest mountain ranges are the Balkans, which run west to east through the center of the country, and the Rhodope Mountains to the southwest. Bulgaria's climate is temperate with marked differences between the four seasons. To the south and around the Black Sea the temperatures are milder in the winter and warmer than average in the summer, reaching a daily average of 84°F (29°C) in July and August.

### A COUNTRY IN TRANSITION

Bulgaria was ruled by the Turkish Ottoman Empire from the late 1300s until 1878, before becoming fully independent in 1908. A communist ally of the former Soviet Union until 1990, the country has since become a multiparty democracy. Its economy is recovering after major crises in 1995, 1997, and 1999, but Bulgaria is still readjusting to economic independence, which has meant that cheap supplies of high-quality coal, oil, and iron from the Soviet Union are no longer available. In 2007 Bulgaria joined the European Union, but its economy faces problems, including corruption. Foreign investment and economic reforms are transforming the country.

Bulgars make up 84 percent of the population, while Turks account for nine percent. Around 70 percent of the people live in cities and towns.

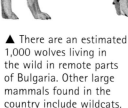

▲ There are an estimated 1,000 wolves living in the wild in remote parts of Bulgaria. Other large mammals found in the country include wildcats, elks, and bears.

▶ Bulgaria's National Assembly building lies in the center of its capital city of Sofia. It was built in three stages between 1884 and 1928 from plans by the Austrian architect Yovanovich.

# RUSSIA

The world's largest nation, the Russian Federation crosses two continents and nine time zones. Its people are undergoing great changes to their way of life.

**Area:** 6,592,848 sq. mi. (17,075,400km²)
**Population:** 141,904,000
**Capital:** Moscow (12,410,000)
**Main languages spoken:** Russian, Tatar, Ukrainian, Chuvash, Bashkir, Chechen, Mordovinian
**Main religions:** Russian Orthodox, Islam
**Currency:** Russian ruble
**Main exports:** fuels and lubricants, ferrous and nonferrous metals, machinery and transportation equipment, chemicals, precious metals, timber and forestry products
**Type of government:** republic; democracy

Russia is a gigantic nation extending almost 6,200 mi. (10,000km) west to east and more than 2,480 mi. (4,000km) north to south at its greatest extent. Vast plains cover much of Russia's territory, while mountain ranges are found mainly in the eastern and southern regions. The Ural Mountains, running north to south, divide western, European Russia from eastern, Asian Russia. Much of Russia experiences a continental climate, although there is great variation both in climate and vegetation in such a large country, with large temperate regions, giant forests, and vast tracts of icy wastelands to the north. The country has large areas of fertile farmlands and a great wealth of mineral resources. It is one of the world's leading producers of fossil fuels and a wide range of metals. The largest and most powerful republic of the former Soviet Union, Russia has had to deal with a number of political and economic problems since its independence in 1991.

▲ With an area of 800,000 sq. ft. (73,000m²), the giant Red Square is the focal point of the city of Moscow. On its west side lies the tomb of the communist leader Lenin, in front of which a changing-of-the-guard ceremony is occurring.

# WESTERN RUSSIA

**The most economically powerful part of the Russian Federation, western Russia is the home of the country's largest cities and most of its productive farmland.**

Western Russia borders Kazakhstan, Georgia, and Azerbaijan to the south and has coastlines with both the Caspian and Black seas. To the west the country borders Ukraine, Belarus, Latvia, Lithuania, and Finland and, to the far north, Norway. Its territory includes the enclave of Kaliningrad, which is separated from the rest of Russia by Lithuania and Latvia. Western Russia is mostly part of the Great European Plain, which increases in width eastward.

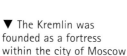

▲ The ornate marble halls of a Moscow underground railroad station. The Moscow Metro was built in the 1930s and now contains more than 186 mi. (299km) of tracks.

▼ The Kremlin was founded as a fortress within the city of Moscow in 1156. Rebuilt on several occasions, it is now used as the central seat of the Russian government.

## THE KOLA PENINSULA AND BARENTS SEA

The highest elevations of western Russia are found in the Caucasus in the southwest and in the Kola Peninsula, which faces the Barents Sea to the east. The Barents Sea is a shallow arm of the Arctic Ocean and is subject to freezing during the winter. However, warm waters from the Gulf Stream keep a coastal shipping lane open throughout the year. Western Russia's two largest islands, which form the archipelago called Novaya Zemlya, are found in the Barents Sea. Perched on the Kola Peninsula is the strategically important port of Murmansk. A major Russian naval base, the city also has fishing, shipbuilding, and marine research facilities.

## THE URAL MOUNTAINS

The Great European Plain extends east until it reaches the Ural Mountains. Formed by continental drift that forced Siberia and Europe together, the Urals are around 250 million years old. Erosion has worn these mountains down so that they now have an average elevation of 1,968 ft. (600m). The Urals are, however, rich in important minerals, including coal, iron ore, platinum, lead, chromium, and copper. West of the southern Urals several industrial cities, including Perm and Ufa, have sprung up owing to the extraction and processing of these minerals and the development of manufacturing industries.

## THE FERTILE TRIANGLE

The large majority of Russia's farmland lies in western Russia in what is called the "fertile triangle." The fertile triangle extends from the Black Sea to the Baltic Sea along Russia's western borders and stretches from the area of the city of St. Petersburg southeast to the southern Ural Mountains. In the fertile triangle large

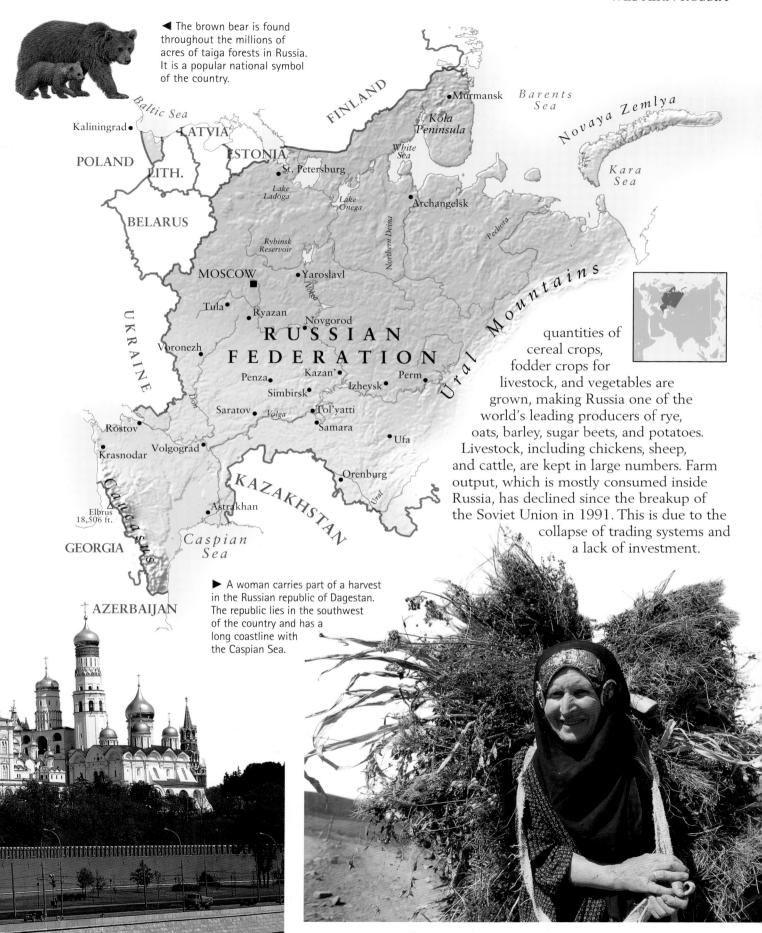

◄ The brown bear is found throughout the millions of acres of taiga forests in Russia. It is a popular national symbol of the country.

Baltic Sea

FINLAND

*Barents Sea*

*Novaya Zemlya*

Murmansk

*Kola Peninsula*

*White Sea*

*Kara Sea*

Kaliningrad•

LATVIA

POLAND

ESTONIA

LITH.

St. Petersburg

*Lake Ladoga*

*Lake Onega*

Archangelsk

*Pechora*

BELARUS

*Rybinsk Reservoir*

*Northern Dvina*

MOSCOW ■

Yaroslavl•

UKRAINE

Tula•

Ryazan•

Novgorod•

R U S S I A N
F E D E R A T I O N

*Volga*

Voronezh•

*Ural Mountains*

Penza•

Kazan'•

Perm•

Simbirsk•

Izhevsk•

Saratov•

*Volga*

Tol'yatti•

Samara•

Ufa•

*Don*

Rostov•

Volgograd•

Orenburg•

Krasnodar•

KAZAKHSTAN

*Ural*

*Caucasus*

Elbrus
18,506 ft.

Astrakhan•

GEORGIA

*Caspian Sea*

AZERBAIJAN

quantities of cereal crops, fodder crops for livestock, and vegetables are grown, making Russia one of the world's leading producers of rye, oats, barley, sugar beets, and potatoes. Livestock, including chickens, sheep, and cattle, are kept in large numbers. Farm output, which is mostly consumed inside Russia, has declined since the breakup of the Soviet Union in 1991. This is due to the collapse of trading systems and a lack of investment.

► A woman carries part of a harvest in the Russian republic of Dagestan. The republic lies in the southwest of the country and has a long coastline with the Caspian Sea.

▲ A large area of apartment buildings offers accommodation for some of Moscow's 12.4 million inhabitants. Apart from being Russia's largest and most politically dominant city, Moscow is also the spiritual center of the Russian Orthodox Church.

## TWIN CITIES OF POWER

Russia has a long history of settlement and has been a powerful force in Europe and Asia for hundreds of years. Two cities have been its capital and center during its history—Moscow and St. Petersburg. The first Russian leader to use the title of emperor was Peter the Great, who founded the city of St. Petersburg in the early 1700s. The city became the home of the czars—the Russian royal family—from 1713 onward. Its position connected to the Baltic Sea by the Gulf of Finland enabled St. Petersburg to rise as a trading power and to become a major cultural center of eastern Europe. Today St. Petersburg is Russia's second-largest city and the home of many large industries, especially engineering, chemicals, and shipbuilding, as well as being its largest seaport. A system of rivers and artificial inland waterways links St. Petersburg in the south to the Caspian Sea and also to the White Sea and Volga river.

Moscow was founded as a city in 1138 and was the capital of Russia prior to the establishment of St. Petersburg. It became the capital again in 1918 after communist forces toppled the czar and came to power. For 70 years Moscow was the capital city of the former Soviet Union. During this period its industry boomed—it produced around one sixth of the entire Soviet Union's industrial output. Moscow has sprawled into a giant city and is the home of both the leader of the country, the president, and the highest legislative body, the Federal Assembly.

Around 78 percent of Russia's people live in towns and cities, but the nation's population is sharply declining and some villages have become deserted.

▼ Novgorod is a major transportation terminus and industrial center, producing cars, airplanes, and electrical goods. It lies on the Volga river. The Volga is navigable along almost all of its 2,194-mi. (3,531-km) length and is the longest river in Europe.

# EASTERN RUSSIA

**Russia east of the Ural Mountains is a sparsely populated land of mountains, rivers, and icy wastelands where huge resources remain largely untapped.**

▲ A train on the Trans-Siberian railroad passes by Lake Baikal. The lake holds 85 percent of all of Russia's lake water and around one fifth of the entire world's lake water. The Trans-Siberian railroad runs a long distance of 5,777 mi. (9,297km) from Moscow to Vladivostok on eastern Russia's Pacific coast. In the late 1990s the entire trip took six days.

East of the Ural Mountains, Russia stretches more than 3,100 mi. (5,000km) eastward to form a long coastline with the Pacific Ocean. Eastern Russia borders three nations to the south: Kazakhstan, Mongolia, and China. Most of the Russian territory near Mongolia and China is part of a series of mountain ranges, including the Yablonovy and Stavonoy ranges.

Geographically, eastern Russia is often divided into four broad regions: the southern mountain ranges mentioned above, the West Siberian Plain, the Central Siberian Plateau, and the Russian Far East. Each of these regions is vast, has large tracts of barely inhabited territory, and has much variation in rock formations, landscape, and vegetation.

## THE SIBERIAN PLAIN

To the east of the Urals is the gigantic West Siberian Plain. This area stretches around 1,180 mi. (1,900km) from west to east and around 1,490 mi. (2,400km) from north to south. It covers an area of more than 965,255 sq. mi. (2.5 million km²). Over half of the plain lies at elevations below 328 ft. (100m), and only in the south does the land rise above 820 ft. (250m). Much of the plain is poorly drained and consists of some of the world's largest swamps and floodplains. Important cities include Omsk and Chelyabinsk, which is located near the Urals in a rich coal-mining region. The long Yenisey river flows broadly south to north, a distance of 2,200 mi. (3,540km), where it completes its journey, discharging more than 5 million gallons (19 million liters) of water per second. Together with its tributary, the Angara, the two rivers flow 3,440 mi. (5,540km). The valley it has formed acts as a rough dividing line between the West Siberian Plain and the Central Siberian Plateau.

▲ Eastern Russia has large untapped oil reserves, but oil exploitation of much of the region is beset with problems, including transportation and the hostile climate.

▼ A camp of Koryak nomads is pitched amidst the icy tundra of northeast Russia. The Koryak continue traditional ways of living, mainly herding reindeer and hunting for furs. Koryak people who live on the coast fish, especially for crabs.

## THE CENTRAL SIBERIAN PLATEAU AND FAR EASTERN RUSSIA

The Central Siberian Plateau is, in fact, several plateaus lying between 984–2,296 ft. (300–700m) in elevation. Mountains border the plateaus to the south and much of the east. The region is rich in mainly untapped mineral resources.

Far Eastern Russia has a complex geography consisting of many mountain ranges formed in different ways. A major feature of the region is the Kamchatka Peninsula, which juts southward into the Sea of Okhotsk, itself an arm of the Pacific Ocean. The peninsula has many volcanic peaks, some of which are still active. The highest is the 15,580-ft.- (4,750-m-) high Kliuchevskoi volcano, the highest point in the

Russian Far East. Along with the Caucasus in the southwest of Russia, Kamchatka is one of Russia's main areas of earthquake activity. The volcanic chain continues from the southern tip of Kamchatka through the Kuril Islands. This island chain extends for approximately 745 mi. (1,200km), ending close to Hokkaido—the northern island of Japan. The islands contain 100 volcanoes, of which around one third are either dormant or active. Some of the southernmost Kuril Islands have their ownership disputed by Japan. Located on the far south of the Far Eastern Russian mainland, the city of Vladivostok is the largest in the region. Founded as a military naval outpost in 1860, Vladivostok now has a population of 579,000. It is an important port and is a base for fishing and whaling fleets.

## TUNDRA AND TAIGA

Eastern Russia's main zones of vegetation vary with latitude and run from north to south. To the south are steppes, plains of grassland that form eastern Russia's best farmland. The northernmost reaches of Russia, stretching the entire width of the country, consist of tundra. These are largely icy and treeless plains with very cold winters and limited plant life. South of the tundra are large belts of forests called taiga. These are the world's largest forest regions and consist of coniferous trees such as Siberian cedar, fir, pine, and larch.

## RIVERS AND LAKES

Russia is crossed by more than 100,000 rivers; most of the longest are found in the east. The Ob-Irtysh river system, for example, flows a distance of 3,361 mi. (5,409km) from western China north through Siberia before emptying into the Arctic Ocean. Around 84 percent of Russia's surface water is located east of the Urals in its rivers and lakes. The largest lake, Lake Baikal, is found in central south Siberia. Measuring 395 mi. (636km) and varying between 9–50 mi. (15–80km) in width, the lake reaches a depth of 5,315 ft. (1,620m), making it the world's deepest freshwater lake.

## RUSSIA'S PEOPLE

Russia's population is a striking multicultural mix in both the eastern and western portions of the country. When it was the dominant part of the Soviet Union throughout much of the 1900s, ethnic Russians made up around 83 percent of its population. Many republics of the Soviet Union containing other ethnic groups started to press for independence during the 1980s. Reforms, such as *glasnost* (openness) and *perestroika* (restructuring), were introduced by the Soviet Union's leader, Mikhail Gorbachev. They were attempts to modernize the way the country was run and to give some of these republics more control. However, by December 1991 the Soviet Union split into 15 independent republics, of which the Russian Federation is the largest. Ethnic Russians now make up 83 percent of the population, but there are large minority groups, including more than five million Tatars—Islamic peopls who descended from the Mongols who invaded Russia over 750 years ago. In total, over 120 different nationalities and ethnic groups are found within the country's borders. Russia's people have faced many changes in the past. They are currently witnessing further, enormous, and often difficult changes in the way their country and businesses are run. Health and other social services are in crisis, and crime is rising. Most Russians are having to deal with a drop in their standard of living.

▲ A woman watches a helicopter run by the state airline, Aeroflot, depart from a landing site near her isolated village in the far east of Russia. In many isolated parts of eastern Russia air transportation is the only way to travel outside the local area.

# THE CAUCASUS AND ASIA MINOR

A land bridge between Europe and Asia since prehistoric times, the region that includes the Caucasus and Asia Minor has a long and complex history. Wave after wave of armies, traders, and settlers have passed through the region, which is bounded by three different seas: the Mediterranean Sea, the Black Sea, and the Caspian Sea. As a result, there is a large number of different ethnic groups, languages, and cultures found in the region. The area's largest and most populous nation is Turkey, which straddles the traditional boundaries that separate Asia from Europe. East of Turkey lie three countries—Georgia, Armenia, and Azerbaijan—which sit between the Black Sea and the Caspian Sea. These three nations, all part of the former Soviet Union, are sometimes collectively known as the pair of mountain ranges that dominate their territory, the Caucasus. The land of the Caucasus nations is rugged yet fertile in places. Many of the mountain slopes are covered in coniferous trees, while a large number of rivers cross the land and empty into the Black Sea, the Caspian Sea, or the Sea of Asov to the north. Large mineral deposits, including oil, natural gas, and various metal ores, are found throughout the region.

▲ The enormous extinct volcano of Mount Ararat straddles the border between Turkey and Armenia and has a diameter of approximately 25 mi. (40km) at its base. The mountain has two peaks, the higher of which lies in Turkey and reaches an elevation of 16,850 ft. (5,137m)

# GEORGIA

**A mountainous country bordering the Black Sea, Georgia was a part of the former Soviet Union until 1991.**

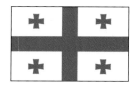

**Area:** 26,831 sq. mi. (69,492km²)
**Population:** 4,632,000
**Capital:** Tbilisi (1,107,000)
**Main languages spoken:** Georgian, Russian
**Main religions:** Georgian Orthodox, Islam, Russian Orthodox
**Currency:** lari
**Main exports:** food products, ferrous metals, wine, scrap metal
**Type of government:** republic; limited democracy

Georgia borders Turkey, Armenia, and Azerbaijan to the south and the Russian Federation to the north. The Caucasus Mountains define the country's northern border and are home to its highest point, Mount Shkhara. The southern part of Georgia is crossed by the Lesser Caucasus Mountains. Sandwiched between the two mountain ranges are lower-lying lands, including the valley of the country's major river, the Kura. Lower-lying areas also exist in the east and the west of the country. To the west the region close to the Black Sea was formerly swamps and wetlands, but much land has been reclaimed. This region now forms the most productive farmlands of Georgia. The warm, humid climate in that area allows citrus fruit, tea, grapes, and tobacco to be grown. Farther inland less rain falls, and the climate is continental with cold winters. Glaciers and snow cover the upper reaches of most of the Caucasus Mountains. Large forests of birch, beech, and oak grow over the lower mountain slopes. Almost two fifths of the country is forested.

▼ A man stands close to one of the medieval towers found in Georgia. Most of the around 200 surviving towers date back to the 1100s, but a few are more than 1,000 years older.

## A CROSSROAD

Despite its rugged terrain, trade routes through Georgia have been established for thousands of years. The country's status as a crossroad resulted in its highly diverse population. Ethnic Georgians make up around 71 percent of the population, but there are also around 100 different ethnic groups. Tensions between groups, especially in the Abkhazia region in the northwest of the country, led to conflict in the 1990s and in 2008. As a result, Abkhazia and South Ossetia have declared independence and are virtually under Russian control. Most Georgian people live in poverty, although improving transportation links, tourism promotion, and exploiting the country's largely untapped oil reserves bring hope of a better quality of life.

# ARMENIA

Once the smallest republic of the former Soviet Union, Armenia is a landlocked, mountainous country with an average elevation of around 5,900 ft. (1,800m).

**Area:** 11,484 sq. mi. (29,743km²)
**Population:** 3,238,000
**Capital:** Yerevan (1,111,000)
**Main language spoken:** Armenian
**Main religion:** Armenian Orthodox
**Currency:** dram
**Principal exports:** various machinery and equipment, minerals, diamonds, metals
**Type of government:** republic; limited democracy

▼ Armenian peasants dig in potato fields in northern Armenia. Potatoes, along with wheat, tobacco, and other vegetables, are the main crops grown in the country.

Armenia is one of the most rugged countries in all of Eurasia, with large mountains and steep-sided valleys. Many smaller rivers and streams cross the land and provide the country with hydroelectric power. There are also many waterfalls, river rapids, and mountain lakes. Armenia's largest lake, Lake Sevan, lies in the Caucasus Mountains and measures approximately 363 sq. mi. (940km²). It holds more than 85 percent of all of the standing water found in Armenia. Parts of the country are susceptible to earthquakes; in 1988 one devastated the country's second-largest city of Gyumri. Armenia was one of the most industrialized and wealthiest states in the former Soviet Union, with a variety of industries, including machine building, chemicals, canned goods, and leather products. Since independence in 1991 Armenia has been in conflict with Azerbaijan over Nagorno Karabakh, an area of Azerbaijan with a largely Armenian population. The cost of war included fuel shortages that damaged many of the country's industries. Armenia's transportation and communications links are old and in need of repair and modernization in many places. Its capital city, Yerevan, is one of the oldest cities still in existence, with archaeological evidence of settlement for more than 5,000 years. Ethnic Armenians make up more than 93 percent of the country's population. There are more people of Armenian descent living overseas.

# AZERBAIJAN

**A mountainous and oil-rich country, Azerbaijan has been beset by economic difficulties and territorial disputes.**

**Area:** 33,436 sq. mi. (86,600km²)
**Population:** 8,922,000
**Capital:** Baku (1,889,000)
**Main languages spoken:** Azeri, Russian, Armenian
**Main religions:** Islam, Orthodox
**Currency:** manat
**Principal exports:** petroleum and petroleum products, cotton, machinery, food products
**Type of government:** republic; limited democracy

Azerbaijan is ringed by mountains on almost all sides, except to the east where it borders the Caspian Sea. To the north lie the Russian Federation and Georgia, Iran lies to the south, and Armenia lies to the west. Azerbaijan and Armenia's border is complex, with enclaves of both nations surrounded by the lands of the other and some territory disputed. The largest disputed area, Nagorno Karabakh, was the subject of violent conflict during the 1990s. The Greater and Lesser Caucasus mountain ranges run through Azerbaijan, and the fast-flowing rivers that flow down the mountain slopes are not only harnessed to generate electricity, but they are also diverted and used for water reservoirs and irrigation systems. Parts of Azerbaijan, particularly the peaks of the Caucasus Mountains and the extreme southeast of the country, receive heavy rainfall, but much of the remainder of the country is warm and dry, receiving less than 12 in. (30cm) of rain per year. Irrigation enables the farmers to grow cereal crops, tobacco, grapes, and cotton. Agriculture still employs 39 percent of the workforce. Unlike its Caucasus

neighbors, the people of Azerbaijan are mostly Muslims. They are descended from people who conquered the territory more than 900 years ago. The country not only has large natural gas reserves but also big deposits of oil.

▲ Azeri fishermen bring in their catch from the Caspian Sea. In 2001 9,356 tons (8,488 metric tonnes) of fish were caught in the Caspian.

▼ One century ago Azerbaijan was the world's leading producer of oil, but the industry declined as oil was discovered in many other places in the world.

# TURKEY

**A large country with extensive mountains and long coastlines, Turkey straddles the point where southern Europe and Asia meet and has a long history.**

**Area:** 300,948 sq. mi. (779,452km²)
**Population:** 70,586,000
**Capital:** Ankara (3,764,000)
**Main languages spoken:** Turkish, Kurdish, Arabic
**Main religion:** Islam
**Currency:** Turkish lira
**Main exports:** textiles and clothing, iron and steel, electrical and electronic machinery, fruit
**Type of government:** republic; limited democracy

Geographically, Turkey's territory is found in both Asia and Europe. Although 97 percent of its land lies in Asia and is known as Anatolia, or Asia Minor, the country is generally accepted as part of Europe, takes part in many European organizations, and has applied to join the European Union. Turkey is a country of rugged highland areas with a large central plateau. Four fifths of the country lie more than 1,640 ft. (500m) in elevation, and the key lowland areas are found on the coasts. Most of Turkey is part of the great Alpine-Himalayan mountain belt, and several large ranges run east to west through the country. A highland area runs along the Black Sea coastline, and the Taurus Mountains are found in the south of the country. Mostly composed of limestone, these mountains contain many caves, potholes, and underground streams. The far east of Turkey is home to both the country's highest point, Mount Ararat, and its largest lake, Lake Van, with an area of 1,434 sq. mi. (3,713km²). Turkey lies on a major fault line and often experiences severe earthquakes.

## SURROUNDED BY SEAS

Almost all of Turkey's northern border is a 991-mi.- (1,595-km-) long coastline with the Black Sea. To the south and the west of Turkey are the Mediterranean and Aegean seas. Its Aegean coastline is heavily indented and contains many of the country's 159 islands. To the northwest of the country lies the Sea of Marmara, which is connected to both the Black Sea and the Aegean Sea through two narrow straits. The Sea of Marmara separates the European part of Turkey from the Asian part. The sea has an area of 4,301 sq. mi. (11,140km²).

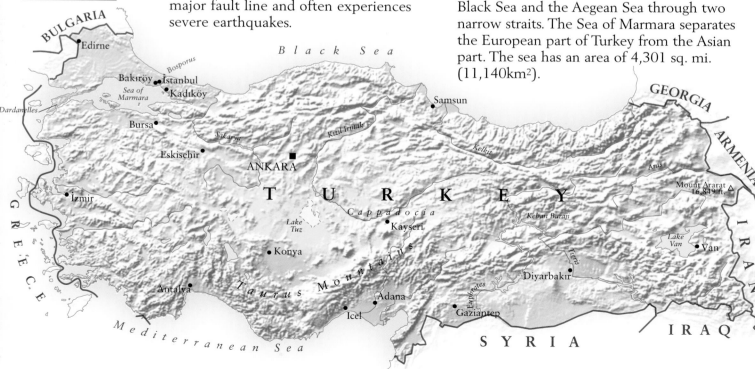

◄ Hagia Sophia lies in Turkey's most populous city, Istanbul. Completed in the A.D. 500s, the church is one of the finest artefacts from the Byzantine civilization. Once known as Constantinople, Istanbul served as the capital of both the Byzantine and Ottoman empires in the past.

fruit, and nuts. Around 29 percent of the workforce are engaged in farming, and Turkey is self-sufficient in many basic foods. Turkey is also relatively rich in mineral deposits, including coal, oil, and a number of metals. More than one third of the country's electricity is generated by hydroelectric power, particularly from fast-flowing rivers such as the Tigris.

## WHERE WEST MEETS EAST

Turkey's strategic location, at the point where the three continents of Africa, Asia, and Europe are closest, has meant that the region has been traveled and settled since ancient times. Its land has seen the birth of many civilizations, including the ancient Hittites, Persians, Romans, and Arabs. Turks today are descended from these and other peoples and make up the majority of the population, with the largest minority being Kurdish peoples.

▲ Turkish men enjoy their tea drinking in the Youth Park in the city of Ankara. The country's second-largest city, Ankara became its capital when Turkey was formed in 1923.

▼ The stepped terraces of Pammukale in southwest Turkey attract many visitors who bathe in their hot waters. The limestone terraces have been formed over thousands of years from calcium-rich springs.

## CLIMATE AND COUNTRY

Turkey has a range of climates based largely on altitude and closeness to the sea. The land bordering the Black Sea has hot summers and mild winters with high humidity and relatively heavy rainfall. In the Mediterranean and Aegean regions the climate is equally warm but drier, with most rainfall in the winter. Farther inland the country experiences a dry, continental climate. The range of climates allows a variety of crops to be grown, including cereals, cotton, tobacco,

# CYPRUS

The third-largest island in the Mediterranean, Cyprus is situated 50 mi. (80km) south of the Turkish coast. The country is currently divided into Greek and Turkish zones.

**Area:** 3,572 sq. mi. (9,251km²), of which 1,295 sq. mi. (3,355km²)are in the Turkish-controlled zone
**Population:** 1,041,000 including Turkish settlers in the north
**Capital:** Nicosia (284,000)
**Main languages spoken:** Greek, Turkish, English
**Main religions:** Greek Orthodox, Islam
**Currency:** euro
**Main exports:** clothing, potatoes, citrus fruit, pharmaceuticals, cement
**Type of government:** republic

▼ This orchard is located in the Troodos Mountains in the southwest of Cyprus. The island's warm climate allows a large range of fruit to be grown.

Cyprus consists of a central plain with mountains to the south and north of the island. The largest mountain chain, the Troodos Mountains, covers much of the southwest of the island. Much of Cyprus's forests have been cleared, and scrub grass and bushes are the most common vegetation. The island has no permanent rivers. Pasturelands used to graze sheep, goats, and pigs cover one tenth of the land area. The main crops grown include wheat, potatoes, tobacco, and grapes, which are used in Cyprus's wine-making industry. The island enjoys a warm Mediterranean climate with an average annual temperature of 69°F (21°C). Average annual rainfall is less than 20 in. (50cm), although parts of the Troodos Mountains can receive 41 in. (105cm).

## A DIVIDED ISLAND

Cyprus has been a colony of a number of nations, including Greece, Egypt, and the Ottoman Empire. Greek Cypriots make up around 78 percent of the population, with almost all of the

remainder of Turkish descent. Cyprus became independent from the United Kingdom in 1960, but in 1974 Turkey invaded the island and gained control of its northern one third. It later established the Turkish Republic of Northern Cyprus, but this has not been recognized by the rest of the world. Cyprus remains divided, with a United Nations peacekeeping force based there. In 2002 the European Union invited Cyprus to join it. In April 2004 Turkish Cypriots voted to reunite Cyprus, but the Greek Cypriots voted against it. As a result, only the south was admitted to membership of the EU, in May 2004.

# ASIA

# ASIA

Covering an area of 17.4 million sq. mi. (44.6 million km), Asia is the world's largest continent. It is geologically active, with many of the world's most active volcanoes within its territory, particularly to the east, where the continent faces the Pacific Ocean. Asia is also home to many of the planet's physical extremes, including the lowest point, the Dead Sea in Jordan, and the highest point, Mount Everest in the Himalayas. Central Asia is considerably more mountainous than other continents, with the Himalayas just one of many ranges. To the south the most notable features are several major peninsulas: the Arabian Peninsula to the west, the Indian subcontinent and the Indochina Peninsula, which extends into the South China Sea, and the large island archipelagos found in Southeast Asia. Every form of climate and vegetation zone is present in this continent, from icy tundra and large arid deserts to tropical rain forests and highly fertile plains and river valleys. Around 16 percent of Asia is covered in forests, with the largest found in Siberia, China, and Southeast Asia. Although parts of Tibet, Siberia, and a region of Saudi Arabia are virtually unpopulated, the continent is also home to the world's two most populous countries—China and India. Approximately one third of the entire world population is found within their borders. Although the people in Asia's most developed nations, such as Japan, enjoy a high standard of living, many are desperately poor.

▲ Bicycles and beasts of burden constitute most of the traffic in this busy street in the northern Indian city of Jaipur.

▼ Nomadic people herd horses in the isolated countryside of Mongolia. Nomadic people traveling with herds of livestock comprise around 25 percent of Mongolia's population.

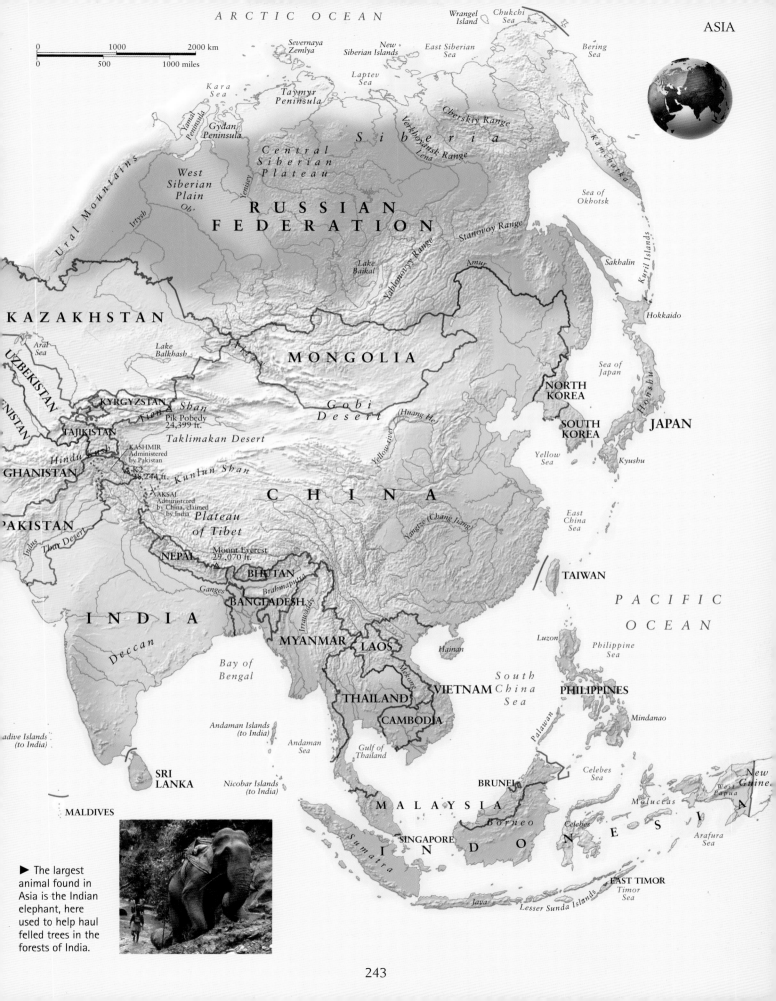

ARCTIC OCEAN

0    1000    2000 km
0   500   1000 miles

*Wrangel Island*    *Chukchi Sea*

*Severnaya Zemlya*    *New Siberian Islands*    *East Siberian Sea*    *Bering Sea*

*Kara Sea*    *Taymyr Peninsula*    *Laptev Sea*    *Cherskiy Range*

*Yamal Peninsula*    S    i    b    e    r    i    a    *Verkhoyansk Range*    *Kamchatka*

*Gydan Peninsula*    *Central Siberian Plateau*    *Lena*

*West Siberian Plain*    *Yenisey*    *Sea of Okhotsk*

*Ob*    *Irtysh*    RUSSIAN FEDERATION

*Ural Mountains*    *Sakhalin*    *Kuril Islands*

*Stanovoy Range*    *Amur*    *Hokkaido*

KAZAKHSTAN    *Lake Baikal*    *Yablonovyy Range*

*Aral Sea*    *Lake Balkhash*    MONGOLIA    *Sea of Japan*

UZBEKISTAN    *Altai*    *Gobi Desert*    NORTH KOREA    *Honshu*

KYRGYZSTAN    *Tien Shan*    *Huang He*    JAPAN

*Pik Pobedy 24,399 ft.*    SOUTH KOREA

TAJIKISTAN    *Taklimakan Desert*    *Yellow river*    *Yellow Sea*    *Kyushu*

*Hindu Kush*    KASHMIR Administered by Pakistan

GHANISTAN    K2 28,244 ft.    *Kunlun Shan*    CHINA    *East China Sea*

AKSAI Administered by China, claimed by India

PAKISTAN    *Plateau of Tibet*    *Yangtze (Chang Jiang)*

*Indus*    *Thar Desert*    NEPAL    *Mount Everest 29,070 ft.*    TAIWAN

BHUTAN    *Brahmaputra*    PACIFIC OCEAN

*Ganges*    BANGLADESH

INDIA    *Deccan*    MYANMAR    LAOS    *Hainan*    *Luzon*    *Philippine Sea*

*Bay of Bengal*    *Irrawaddy*    *Mekong*    VIETNAM    *South China Sea*    PHILIPPINES    *Mindanao*

*Andaman Islands (to India)*    THAILAND    CAMBODIA    *Palawan*

*Andaman Sea*    *Gulf of Thailand*    *Celebes Sea*

*adive Islands (to India)*    SRI LANKA    *Nicobar Islands (to India)*    BRUNEI    *Celebes*    *Moluccas*    *West Papua*    *New Guine*

MALDIVES    MALAYSIA    *Borneo*    *Celebes*    *Arafura Sea*

SINGAPORE    I    N    D    O    N    E    S    I    A

*Sumatra*    EAST TIMOR    *Timor Sea*

*Java*    *Lesser Sunda Islands*

▶ The largest animal found in Asia is the Indian elephant, here used to help haul felled trees in the forests of India.

# MIDDLE EAST

The Middle East has been the birthplace of many important civilizations and major world religions such as Christianity, Judaism, and Islam. Much of the region's terrain is hostile, with large sandy or rocky deserts and rugged mountain regions. Smaller areas of fertile lands exist around coastlines and in river valleys and basins. Much of the region was underdeveloped until the discovery of huge reserves of oil in the early 1900s. The Middle East now produces over one third of the world's daily oil output, and many countries have been transformed by oil revenue. Although the region has an ancient history, many of the national boundaries are relatively new, drawn up by particular Western colonial powers in the early and mid-1900s. Partly as a result, the region has had a turbulent recent history with disputes over land and resources, as well as conflicts between different religious groups. The latest conflict in 2003 saw international forces invade Iraq.

In 1948 Israel was founded in Palestine as a Jewish homeland. The Palestinians rejected a United Nations (UN) proposal to divide Palestine between them and Israel. In the ensuing war, Israel ejected hundreds of thousands of Palestinians from their land. This led to five wars and countless terrorist attacks by Palestinians upon Israel. In 1967 Israel occupied Gaza and the West Bank, where Israelis have since founded settlements. The UN regards the occupation and settlements as illegal. In 1993 the Palestinians recognized Israel, and Israel gave them limited self-rule in the West Bank and Gaza. However, the peace process has stalled, despite the withdrawal of Israel from Gaza in 2005. Palestinian missile attacks on Israel led it to invade southern Lebanon in 2006. The international community recognizes the right of Palestinians to have their own independent state in Gaza and the West Bank, but Israel continues an economic blockade of Gaza.

◀ The Red Sea, shown here at the port of Aqaba in Jordan, is one of the world's busiest waterways. It is linked via the Suez Canal to the Mediterranean Sea, thus providing a shipping route between Europe, the Middle East, and Asia.

ARMENIA
AZERBAIJAN
AZ.
TURKMENISTAN
AFGHANISTAN
PAKISTAN

TURKEY

Caspian Sea

Lake Urmia

Qolleh-ye Damavand 18,381 ft.
Elburz △ Mountains

SYRIA

TEHRAN

Buhayrat ath Tharthar

LEBANON
BEIRUT ■
Mediterranean Sea
■ DAMASCUS

IRAQ
■ BAGHDAD

Dasht-e Kavir

I R A N

Iranian
Plateau

Dasht-e Lut

West Bank
a Strip
■ AMMAN
ISRAEL
JERUSALEM
JORDAN

Syrian Desert

Euphrates

Tigris

Zagros Mountains

Karun

KUWAIT

KUWAIT

The Gulf

Strait of Hormuz

An Nafud

Arabian

BAHRAIN
MANAMA ■
■ QATAR
DOHA
ABU DHABI ■
UNITED ARAB EMIRATES

OMAN

Gulf of Oman

MUSCAT ■

Al Hijaz

■ RIYADH

SAUDI ARABIA

Red Sea

Peninsula

Ar Rub' al Khali
(Empty Quarter)

OMAN

Arabian Sea

Asir

Al Mahrah

INDIAN OCEAN

SANA ■ YEMEN

Hadramawt

Gulf of Aden

Socotra
(to Yemen)

0        350        700 km
0    185        370 miles

◀ Part of one of Saudi Arabia's many major oil fields. Oil and natural gas exploration, extraction, and processing are the Middle East's biggest export earners.

▶ Known as "ships of the desert," camels have provided transportation across the large desert regions of the Middle East for many centuries.

# SYRIA

A large Arab nation, Syria borders Turkey, Iraq, Lebanon, Jordan, and Israel. Israel has occupied Syrian territory in the Golan Heights since 1967.

**Area:** 71,498 sq. mi. (185,180km2), including areas of the Golan Heights occupied by Israel
**Population:** 20,367,000
**Capital:** Damascus (2,100,000)
**Main languages spoken:** Arabic, Kurdish, Armenian
**Main religions:** Sunni Islam, other Islam, Christian
**Currency:** Syrian pound
**Main exports:** crude petroleum and petroleum products, vegetables and fruit, cotton, textiles and fabrics
**Type of government:** republic (under military regime)

▲ A textile printer at work in a souk in the city of Aleppo. With a population of 2,330,000, Aleppo is Syria's second-largest city.

Syria consists of three main geographical regions. The most westerly is a coastal plain that contains the country's best farmland and is home to the majority of its population. Syria's Mediterranean coastline extends around 112 mi. (180km) between the borders of Turkey and Lebanon and is the location of the two major ports of Tartus and Al Ladhiqiyah (Latakia). Dividing much of the coastal plain from the interior are mountain ranges and several fertile basins in which large cities have developed. East of the mountains lie plateaus and a great expanse of rock and gravel desert. The Syrian Desert makes up over half of the country and extends into northern Saudi Arabia, Jordan, and western Iraq. The desert is bounded to the north by a region of fertile land through which the Euphrates river flows. A dam built on the river generates almost 35 percent of the country's electricity.

## AGRICULTURE
Syria was a predominantly agricultural nation until the early 1960s, when large-scale state industries were developed. Agriculture still employs 17 percent of the workforce, with around 18,590 sq. mi. (48,150km2) of cropland in which barley,

wheat, olives, tobacco, fruit, and vegetables are grown. The most important cash crop is cotton. Almost all crop farming depends on irrigation systems since, even in the wettest regions, most rain falls in the winter. Large parts of the country north of the Syrian Desert are not cultivated but are used as pastures for Syria's 14.5 million sheep and 1.1 million goats.

## POWER AND INDUSTRY
The areas in and around the Syrian cities of Damascus, Aleppo, and Homs have become the chief industrial centers. In these regions oil and tobacco are processed, chemicals are produced, cotton-based textiles are woven,

▼ Huge olive groves span low hills in Syria. Syria is the world's fifth-largest producer of olive oil.

and a wide range of handicrafts, including silk, leather, and glass goods, are made. The development of Syria's oil industry has made it the country's largest export earner, but reserves are dwindling and Syria will be a net oil importer by 2015. Oil pipelines cross Syria to link it to Iraq, Jordan, and the Mediterranean coast.

## ARAB PEOPLE

Syria has been settled continuously for many thousands of years by different civilizations, including the Egyptians, Hittites, Babylonians, and Persians. Although Syria was part of the Ottoman Empire from the 1500s until 1918, its modern population is largely descended from Arab people who conquered the country in the 600s and ruled for 800 years. Over 90 percent of the population are of Arab descent, with the largest minorities being Kurds, who are found near the Turkish border, and Armenians. Syria's capital, Damascus, is one of the world's oldest surviving cities and claims to be the oldest continuously inhabited capital city in the world. Situated in the southwestern corner of the country, Damascus is located at the border of a fertile plain and at the foot of mountains that divide Syria from Lebanon.

▲ Lively markets, known as souks, are a feature of towns in Syria and other Arab nations. The large, bustling Souk al-Hamidiye is found in Damascus.

# ISRAEL

Established as a homeland for Jewish people in 1948, Israel stands apart from the rest of the Middle East, with which it has been in conflict since its formation.

**Area:** 7,876 sq. mi. (20,400km²), excluding areas annexed by Israel (East Jerusalem and the Golan Heights)
**Population:** 7,338,000, including Golan Heights and East Jerusalem
**Capital:** Jerusalem (757,000); Jerusalem is not recognized as the capital of Israel by the international community
**Main languages spoken:** Hebrew, Arabic, English
**Main religions:** Judaism, Islam
**Currency:** new shekel
**Main exports:** machinery and transportation equipment, cut diamonds, chemicals, clothing, food, software
**Type of government:** republic

Israel is located at the eastern end of the Mediterranean Sea and is bordered by Egypt, Lebanon, Syria, Jordan, and the occupied territories of Gaza and the West Bank. Its most southerly point is a short Red Sea coastline, which has been developed as a tourist center. The country has a variety of landscapes, including hills that run from the north into its center and a large depression, part of the Great Rift Valley, along its most eastern lands. Israel's coastal plain runs parallel to the Mediterranean Sea and is bordered by stretches of fertile farmland extending up to 25 mi. (40km) inland. This plain contains over half of Israel's population, most of its industry, and much of its agriculture. To the south lies the dry and rugged Negev Desert.

## ISRAEL'S ECONOMY AND PEOPLE
Although agriculture has been developed using advanced techniques and irrigation, the country's economy is dominated by service, defense, and manufacturing industries. Israel is a major world center for the cutting and polishing of gems and has large computing, machine-making, and chemical industries. Tourism, although declining since the late 1990s, has been important, with visitors attracted by the warm climate and the religious history of a land that holds importance for three of the world's major religions: Islam, Christianity, and Judaism. In the 1990s Israel's economy expanded, partly owing to the mass immigration of large numbers of highly skilled Jews from the former Soviet Union. They joined

▼ A gardener plants a tree at a kibbutz. Some farms in Israel are organized as *kibbutzim*, settlements and communities in which people share their income and property.

▼ Jerusalem is Israel's second largest city. In 1950 Israel proclaimed Jerusalem as its capital although the United Nations does not recognize this and almost all countries maintain their embassies in the coastal city of Tel Aviv.

248

a highly mixed population consisting of approximately 81 percent Jewish and 18 percent Arab peoples. An open immigration policy to Jewish people around the world has resulted in Jews from over 100 countries settling in Israel.

## AID, TRADE, AND CONFLICT

The U.S. maintains a strong relationship with Israel. It is its largest trading partner, and it donates more aid to Israel than any other nation. Israel trades heavily with a number of European countries but very little with its immediate Arab neighbors. The country has been in political and sometimes military conflict with these neighbors over its territory and ultimate existence. A series of wars since Israel's formation saw Israel occupy parts of the neighboring countries. The Gaza Strip on the Mediterranean coast was once part of Egypt. The West Bank and East Jerusalem were once part of Jordan, while Golan Heights was previously Syrian territory. Israel's strained relationship with its Arab neighbors and the violence between Jews and Palestinians mean that over one fourth of the national budget is spent on defense. The major issue remains the fate of the Palestinians. Despite Israel's 2005 withdrawal from the Gaza Strip, which raised hopes of a Palestinian state, conflict in the region continues.

# GAZA & THE WEST BANK

**Gaza and the West Bank are two poor, crowded, disputed territories inhabited by Palestinians who wish to form their own state.**

**Area:** 2,416 sq. mi. (6,257km²) (Gaza 146 sq. mi./378km²; West Bank 2,270 sq. mi./5,879 km²)
**Population:** 3,767,000 (Gaza 1,417,000; West Bank 2,351,000)
**Acting capital:** Ramallah (27,000)
**Main language spoken:** Arabic
**Main religion:** Sunni Islam
**Currency:** Israeli new sheqel
**Main exports:** olives, fruit, vegetables
**Type of government:** partly self-governing territory with areas under Israeli occupation

When Israel was created in Palestine in 1949, the majority of Palestinians were exiled. The remaining Palestinian territories, Gaza and the West Bank, were annexed by Egypt and Jordan, respectively. In 1967 Israel occupied both Gaza and West Bank. In 1993 Israel and the PLO (Palestine Liberation Organization, which had been founded to drive Israel from Palestine) concluded a provisional peace accord and, the following year, some Palestinian areas gained autonomy. Israel transferred additional areas to the PLO in 1996, 1998, and 2000 but, at the same time, constructed Israeli settlements (illegal under international law) on occupied territory on the West Bank. By 2000 the peace process had ground to a halt. In 2007 the militant Hamas movement seized control of Gaza, which was subject to massive Israeli attacks in 2008–2009.

# LEBANON

**Occupying a narrow strip of land along the eastern coast of the Mediterranean Sea, Lebanon is a nation that is rebuilding after a prolonged civil war.**

**Area:** 3,939 sq. mi. (10,201km²)
**Population:** 3,754,000
**Capital:** Beirut (1,171,000)
**Main languages spoken:** Arabic, Armenian, French, English
**Main religions:** Islam, Christian
**Currency:** Lebanese pound
**Main exports:** re-exports, food, jewelry, metals, machinery and transportation equipment
**Type of government:** republic

Lebanon is a small country bordered to the south by Israel and on its north and eastern sides by Syria. The country consists of a coastal plain that rises to a pair of mountain ranges in the east. Between these mountain ranges lies a large, fertile valley, the Bekaa. Lebanon has two main climatic zones. Its coast with the Mediterranean experiences warm, dry summers and rainy, yet mild, winters. Inland, in the Bekaa valley, the summer months are hot and dry. The Litani river runs through the valley and is harnessed to provide hydroelectricity, as well as irrigation for both the southern part of the valley and, via a mountain tunnel, water for part of the coastal plain. Compared to many countries in the region, Lebanon receives relatively high rainfall. Farming is a key occupation both in the coastal plain and in the Bekaa, with crops including cereals, vegetables, and a large range of fruit.

## CIVIL WAR AND RECONSTRUCTION

The site of ancient Phoenician cities built over 3,000 years ago, Lebanon was a prosperous nation and a commercial and trading center. Beirut, its capital city, attracted many tourists. The country's complex ethnic background features many different Christian and Muslim groups. Tensions between religious groups were responsible for a civil war that started in 1975 and devastated most of the country. After a stable period in the 1990s, Israel invaded Lebanon in 2006 in order to attack terrorist groups in the south, which were causing a lot of damage.

▲ The majestic cedars of Lebanon, some of which are 1,500 years old, are a national symbol. Much of Lebanon was once covered in huge forests, but these now occupy less than eight percent of its land.

▶ New hotels and apartment buildings, viewed from a beach café, show how Beiruit is redeveloping and attracting large numbers of tourists after many years of devastating conflicts.

# JORDAN

Lying between Saudi Arabia, Israel, Syria, and Iraq, the almost landlocked, small Arab kingdom of Jordan became fully independent in 1946.

**Area:** 34,495 sq. mi. (89,342km²)
**Population:** 5,850,000
**Capital:** Amman (1,700,000)
**Main languages spoken:** Arabic, English
**Main religions:** Sunni Islam, Christian
**Currency:** Jordanian dinar
**Main exports:** chemicals and chemical products, reexported petroleum, phosphate fertilizers, potash, fruit, vegetables, and nuts
**Type of government:** kingdom; limited democracy

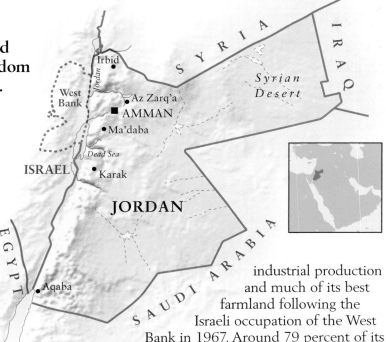

Jordan has three distinct geographical regions: the Jordan valley to the west, an eastern desert region, and, between them, an area of highlands and plateaus. Western Jordan has a Mediterranean climate with hot, dry summers, cool, wet winters, and two short transitional seasons. The remaining three fourths of the country have a largely desert climate with less than 10 in. (25cm) of rainfall per year. Water shortages are a major problem in Jordan, which also lacks large oil and other major mineral reserves—with the exception of phosphates, which, along with with fertilizer and potash, are the country's major exports. Less than five percent of its land is capable of supporting crops, which include tomatoes, fruit, wheat, and olives. Sheep are the country's most important livestock, with an estimated 1.5 million in 2008. Jordan lost around one fifth of its industrial production and much of its best farmland following the Israeli occupation of the West Bank in 1967. Around 79 percent of its people, many of them displaced Palestinians, live in cities, including Amman, the capital.

### THE JORDAN VALLEY

Part of the Great Rift Valley of Africa, the Jordan valley extends down the entire western flank of the country. The valley contains the Jordan river, which is heavily exploited to irrigate the surrounding land and provide water for the local population. This river flows into the Dead Sea, which, at 1,338 ft. (408m) below sea level, is the lowest point on the surface of Earth.

▲ Tourism is a major source of revenue for Jordan, and many visitors flock to see the ruins of the ancient city of Petra. Petra's stunning buildings, including this tomb known as the Treasury of the Pharaohs, are carved out of red sandstone cliffs.

▶ Lying on the Gulf of Aqaba, an arm of the Red Sea, the city of Aqaba is Jordan's only port. It is also used as a base for divers who visit the rich coral reef farther south in the gulf.

# IRAQ

Iraq is a nation of mountains, deserts, and fertile plains. It was invaded by a U.S.-led coalition in 2003 but regained sovereignty in 2004.

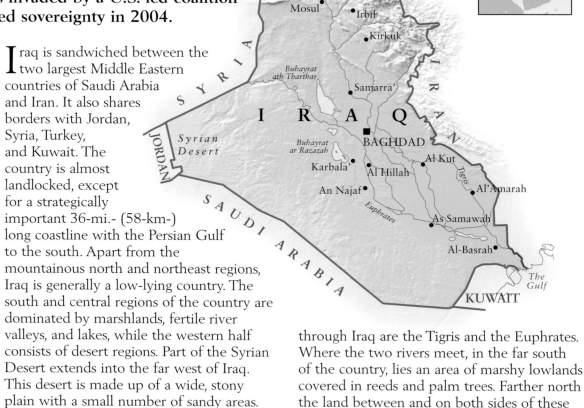

**Area:** 169,235 sq mi. (438,317km²)
**Population:** 29,682,000
**Capital:** Baghdad (6,200,000)
**Main languages spoken:** Arabic, Kurdish
**Main religions:** Shi'a Islam, Sunni Islam
**Currency:** Iraqi dinar
**Main exports:** crude petroleum and petroleum products
**Type of government:** republic; virtual dictatorship

▲ An image of Saddam Hussein, Iraq's leader from 1979 until the U.S.-led invasion of Iraq in 2003, adorns a Baghdad street.

▶ Situated in a suburb of Iraq's capital, Baghdad, the Kadhimain mosque was built in 1515 and is decorated with gold minarets and ornate designs.

Iraq is sandwiched between the two largest Middle Eastern countries of Saudi Arabia and Iran. It also shares borders with Jordan, Syria, Turkey, and Kuwait. The country is almost landlocked, except for a strategically important 36-mi.- (58-km-) long coastline with the Persian Gulf to the south. Apart from the mountainous north and northeast regions, Iraq is generally a low-lying country. The south and central regions of the country are dominated by marshlands, fertile river valleys, and lakes, while the western half consists of desert regions. Part of the Syrian Desert extends into the far west of Iraq. This desert is made up of a wide, stony plain with a small number of sandy areas. Wadis, watercourses that are dry for most of the year, carry waters from heavy rains in the winter. Summer temperatures in the plains and deserts are very hot, and winter temperatures are generally mild. These regions receive little rainfall. The northeast is cooler and wetter, especially in the mountains.

## LAND BETWEEN THE RIVERS

Iraq covers a region known in ancient times as Mesopotamia, a Greek word meaning "land between the rivers." The two major rivers that flow through Iraq are the Tigris and the Euphrates. Where the two rivers meet, in the far south of the country, lies an area of marshy lowlands covered in reeds and palm trees. Farther north the land between and on both sides of these two large rivers consists of fertile plains crisscrossed by many natural and artificial waterways and lakes. For over 6,000 years this region has been cultivated and settled by a number of ancient civilizations, including the Sumerians, Babylonians, and

252

Assyrians. Today this region is where most Iraqis live. Many are engaged in agriculture, either raising livestock or growing cereal crops and a large range of fruits. Before the 1991 Gulf War Iraq produced 80 percent of the world's dates.

## OIL AND WAR

Oil was first discovered in Iraq in 1927, and since that time the country has become one of the world's leading oil producers. Before 1990 the country rose to become the world's third-leading oil producer. Iraq also has one of the world's largest reserves of sulfur, an element widely used in industry. Much of the oil revenue was channeled into building a large military force. Iraq invaded Iran in 1980, and by the time a ceasefire was struck in 1988 over 300,000 Iraqis had lost their lives. Two years later the country occupied the small, oil-rich state of Kuwait. In 1991 a coalition of nations led by the U.S. pushed Iraq's forces out of Kuwait. Following United Nations sanctions after the Gulf War Iraq was only able to use its enormous oil reserves for domestic use until 1996, when limited and supervised exports were allowed. As a result, the country's gross national product (GNP) was cut in half. Damage inflicted on the country during the Gulf War and the subsequent embargoes on trade have disrupted both agriculture and industry. As a result,

▼ Poor treatment of the Kurdish minority by the Iraqi government has generated thousands of refugees. Here a Kurd from Iraq sits in a refugee camp inside the Turkish border.

there was widespread poverty and hardship, especially among the poorer sections of Iraqi society. Iraq, under the strict leadership of Saddam Hussein, remained isolated. In March 2003 an international coalition force led by the U.S. invaded Iraq. It overthrew Saddam Hussein and his regime. The international forces sought to rebuild the country and to set up democratic institutions. Elections were held in 2005 and 2009, but conflict continued, with attacks on the international forces as well as violence between communities.

▼ A group of Iraqi Arab women walk in front of a bomb-damaged building in the capital city of Baghdad. Iraqis are predominantly Arab people, with Kurds the one large minority.

# IRAN

The most populous and second-largest nation in the Middle East, the Islamic Republic of Iran is a rugged country with huge fossil fuel deposits.

**Area:** 633,948 sq. mi. (1,641,918km²)
**Population:** 70,496,000
**Capital:** Tehran (11,850,000)
**Main languages spoken:** Farsi (Persian), Turkic, Kurdish, Luri
**Main religions:** Shi'a Islam, Sunni Islam
**Currency:** rial
**Main exports:** petroleum and natural gas, carpets, pistachios, iron and steel
**Type of government:** Islamic republic

Iran is bordered by seven nations and has coastlines with three large seas: the Gulf of Oman, the Persian Gulf, and the Caspian Sea. The country's main geographical features are several large mountain ranges and a giant plateau. Lying in the center of the country, the Iranian Plateau extends eastward into central Asia. Around 4,000 ft. (1,220m) in elevation, the plateau is hot, dry, and contains two large deserts in the northeast and east—the Dasht-e Kavir (69,500 sq. mi./180,000km²) and the Dasht-e Lut (over 64,000 sq. mi./166,000km²)—which occupy most of the northeast and east of the central plain. There are a large number of climatic regions throughout Iran. Yet, although the northern mountains bordering the Caspian Sea receive heavy rainfall, Iran is a country in which precipitation is relatively scarce and is dependent on the seasons.

▲ One of hundreds of carpet workshops found in the central Iranian city of Esfahan. The city is a center of textile mills that process cotton, silk, and woolen cloth for manufacturing clothing and carpets.

## IRANIAN MOUNTAINS

Iran's longest mountain range—the Zagros—stretches from the northwest of the country close to the border with Armenia southward and southeastward along the Persian Gulf, where it ends near the Strait of Hormuz, which link the Persian Gulf and the Gulf of Oman. Its terrain includes

many peaks over 9,840 ft. (3,000m), while many of its deep valleys are fertile and are farmed. The Elburz mountain range runs along the southern shore of the Caspian Sea. The highest of its volcanic peaks is Qolleh-ye Damavand (18,381 ft./5,604m), Iran's highest point. The northern slopes of the Elburz Mountains are densely covered with deciduous trees, forming the largest area of vegetation in Iran. Many of Iran's seasonal rivers start in these mountains and flow north into the Caspian Sea. The country's capital city, Tehran, is located on the southern slopes of the Elburz Mountains at a height of around 3,510 ft. (1,070m).

## AN OIL ECONOMY

Iran's economy is closely tied to its natural resources; 85 percent of its export revenues are derived from oil and gas. Iran contains around 11 percent of the known global oil reserves and one sixth of the world's total reserves of natural gas. Under modernizing programs introduced by Shah Mohammad Reza Pahlavi—the country's monarch from 1953 to 1979—Iran developed oil-processing and transportation industries at a number of large ports on its Persian Gulf coast, including Bandar-e' Abbas and Abadan. Industries, such as chemicals, textiles, machinery, and cement production, were also developed.

## REVOLUTION AND WAR

The Iranian people are deeply religious, and all aspects of life are heavily influenced by the Islamic faith. In 1979 the shah was overthrown in a revolution, and Iran was declared an Islamic republic. Iran outlawed many Western influences and strictly enforced a code of Islamic law. In the 1980s Iran fought an eight-year-long border war with Iraq, and more than 400,000 Iranians died. The country's support for strong Islamic rule elsewhere has brought it into conflict with neighbors and Western nations, and its ambition to become a nuclear power may lead to the imposition of international sanctions.

▲ A petroleum refinery found in the city of Abadan. Located at the northernmost end of the Persian Gulf, Abadan is a major center of oil processing and transportation.

▼ Iranian farmworkers prepare to gather harvested crops. Agriculture contributes 11 percent of the GDP, with important crops including wheat, barley, rice, sugar beets, tobacco, and wool.

# SAUDI ARABIA

**The desert kingdom of Saudi Arabia covers much of the Arabian Peninsula and is the largest and wealthiest oil-producing nation in the Middle East.**

**Area:** 830,000 sq. mi. (2,149,690km²)
**Population:** 23,980,000
**Capital:** Riyadh (4,550,000)
**Main language spoken:** Arabic
**Main religion:** Sunni Islam
**Currency:** riyal
**Main exports:** petroleum, petrochemicals, natural gas
**Type of government:** monarchy with council of ministers

Saudi Arabia borders seven countries and is connected to an eighth, Bahrain, by a highway. The country is about one fourth of the size of the U.S. and has 1,640 mi. (2,640km) of coastline, approximately 1,090 mi. (1,760km) with the Red Sea to the west and the remainder with the Persian Gulf. A narrow coastal plain between 9–40 mi. (15–64km) in width extends along the Red Sea coast, and a range of mountains runs farther inland and parallel to this plain. These mountains increase in height as they extend southward, reaching the country's highest point on the slopes of Jabal Sawda (10,276 ft./3,133m). A large plateau stretches out to the northeast of Saudi Arabia, reaching a maximum height of 5,904 ft. (1,800m) and dropping in altitude as it slopes down toward the Gulf in the east. To the south and southeast Saudi Arabia contains the world's largest continuous sand desert, the Ar Rub' al Khali, or Empty Quarter. In parts of this hostile environment rain has not fallen for years.

▲ Excess gas is burned off at an oil well in Saudi Arabia. Oil and natural gas are transported around the country to refineries and ports via over 10,540 mi. (16,960km) of pipelines.

## WATER AND AGRICULTURE

Saudi Arabia's climate is generally hot and dry. Temperatures can reach 122°F (50°C) on summer days, although nights are cool, and frosts occur in the winter. Rainfall is generally low; the capital city, Riyadh, receives an average of 33 in. (85cm) per year, although the Asir Mountains tend to receive three to four times as much. Saudi Arabia's generally dry climate means that the country has no permanent rivers or large lakes. Agriculture has traditionally been restricted to livestock herded by nomadic Bedouin Arabs, with crops only grown in the mountainous Asir region in the southwest of

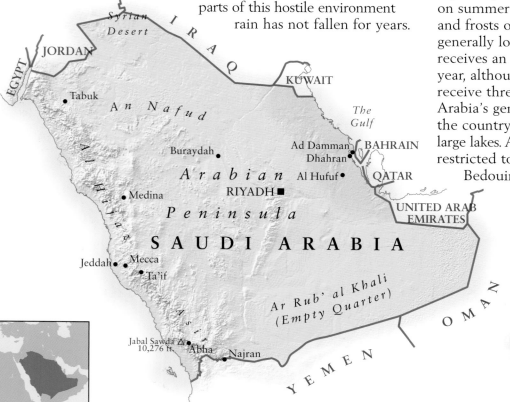

256

the country and in the oases that dot the desert landscape north of the Empty Quarter. Huge desalination projects, where the seawater is processed, the salt removed, and freshwater created, have helped generate millions of gallons of water. Desalination, along with recent irrigation projects, has helped reclaim many square miles of desert and turn it into fertile land. As a result, Saudi Arabia's farming sector is growing. The country's leading crops are wheat, barley, dates, dairy products, and a range of fruit. Sheep, goats, and camels are the most commonly raised livestock.

## WORLD'S BIGGEST OIL PRODUCER

Oil was first discovered in Saudi Arabia in 1936, and in 2008, 9.2 million barrels per day were produced. The country has the world's largest oil and natural gas reserves—almost 22 percent of the entire world's oil deposits. As a result, oil revenues not only dominate the country's economy, making up over 90 percent of exports, but they also give the country great importance in the global economy. Its oil region lies primarily in the east along the Gulf. The enormous revenue from oil has been used to build modern cities, develop infrastructure, ports, hospitals, and schools, and bring electricity to towns. It has also been used to develop other industries such as chemicals, metalworking, and medicines.

## INDEPENDENCE AND GOVERNMENT

Although the region has a long history and has been settled for thousands of years, the actual kingdom of Saudi Arabia is a fairly young nation. It emerged in the early 1900s as Abd al-Aziz ibn Saud

(1882–1953) conquered successive territories in the Arabian Peninsula, beginning with Riyadh in 1901 and ending largely in 1920 with the incorporation of the region of Asir. The year 1932 saw the formation of the kingdom of Saudi Arabia by Abd al-Aziz ibn Saud. Descendants of the Saud family continue to run the country, with absolute power invested in the monarch. In 1993 the reigning monarch, King Fahd ibn Abdul Aziz, introduced political reforms, creating a Consultative Council of 60 members who advise the king. A bill of rights was also established, and power was given to the local governments of the 13 provinces into which Saudi Arabia is divided. However, Saudi Arabia still remains a nation dominated by one family who makes all key political appointments. There are no political parties, and strong media censorship is imposed. Satellite television, for example, was banned in 1994, while there are strict rules regarding the Internet and religion.

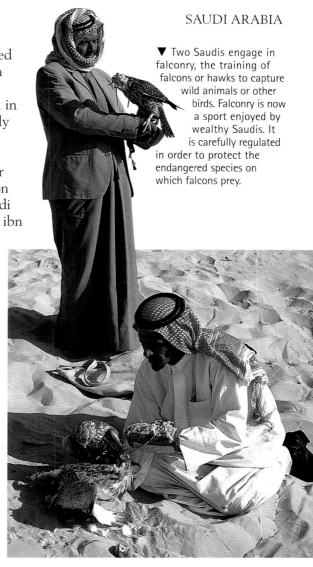

▼ Two Saudis engage in falconry, the training of falcons or hawks to capture wild animals or other birds. Falconry is now a sport enjoyed by wealthy Saudis. It is carefully regulated in order to protect the endangered species on which falcons prey.

▼ A Bedouin camel train winds its way across the Saudi Arabian desert. Many Bedouins are no longer nomadic and now work in the oil industry or have settled in cities.

▲ Saudi stock traders monitor prices of companies' shares in their business suite in the city of Riyadh. The Tadawul, the Saudi stock market, is now the largest in the Arab world.

▼ Pilgrims at the Great Mosque in Mecca surround the Kaaba, the holiest place on Earth to Muslims.

## A REGIONAL SUPERPOWER

As the wealthiest of the Middle East nations Saudi Arabia has strong ties and great influence with both its Arab neighbors and the Western world. This power has increased as the country has grown richer and has made more contributions to military and economic operations in the Middle East. It has also funded a number of aid and investment projects in the Gulf and Middle East region and frequently contracts U.S., Japanese, French, and British companies for defense and civil-engineering projects. Many Saudis are sent overseas to Europe and North America to complete their higher education.

## THE BIRTHPLACE OF ISLAM

The world's second-largest religion has its origins within Saudi Arabia. The founder of Islam, the Prophet Muhammad (c. A.D. 570–632), was born in the city of Mecca, around 40 mi. (70km) inland from the Red Sea port of Jeddah. The Islamic calendar began in A.D. 622, the year of the hegira, or Muhammad's flight from Mecca. He returned to capture the city in A.D. 630, and it is now the holiest city in the Islamic world. Every Muslim strives to make the religious pilgrimage, known as a hajj, to Mecca once in their lifetime, and millions of Muslims visit Mecca every year. There they attend the Great Mosque, or Al-Haram, a religious place of worship large enough to hold 300,000 people. In the center of the Great Mosque's courtyard lies the Kaaba, a small building in which the Black Stone of Mecca is housed. It is the holiest shrine in the entire Islamic world. Medina, 211 mi. (341km) north of Mecca, is also a holy city and houses Muhammad's tomb. Saudi Arabia is run as a strict Muslim state in which Islamic law, *sharia*, is paramount. Women have no role in public life, are prevented from taking jobs in many fields, apart from teaching and health care, and cannot obtain driving licenses. Strict Islamic punishments for certain crimes are enforced, generating criticism from international human rights groups.

# KUWAIT

**Dwarfed by its neighbors, Saudi Arabia, Iraq, and Iran, Kuwait is an intensely oil-rich nation that is still recovering from the effects of the 1990 Iraqi invasion.**

**Area:** 6,880 sq. mi. (17,818km²)
**Population:** 2,496,000
**Capital:** Kuwait City (1,290,000)
**Major language spoken:** Arabic
**Major religion:** Islam
**Currency:** dinar
**Main exports:** petroleum and petroleum products (account for more than 95 percent of exports)
**Type of government:** emirate; limited democracy

Kuwait is located on the northernmost end of the Gulf. Its territory includes a number of islands in the Gulf, most of which are uninhabited. The country's landscape is flat and almost featureless. It consists largely of a rolling sandy plateau that rises in the west to an elevation of 948 ft. (289m) near the country's borders with Saudi Arabia and Iraq. Average annual rainfall is around 5 in (13cm), there is little surface water, and the country relies on advanced desalination projects for most water. Fertile soil is minimal. The one major exception is the oasis at Al Jahrah, 30 mi. (50km) west of Kuwait City. The remaining few areas of natural vegetation occur in salt marshes in the northeast and along parts of the coast. Green areas in Kuwait's large towns and cities have been created using imported soil. Fishing is the country's only major food-related industry, with shrimp the most profitable catch.

## OIL, INVASION, AND REBUILDING

Beneath Kuwait's barren, featureless land lie enormous oil and smaller, but still significant, natural gas deposits. Kuwait has an estimated eight percent of the world's proven reserves of crude oil and, in 2009, produced around 2.3 million barrels every day. This is a recovery from a major slump that followed the invasion of the country by Iraq in 1990. The Iraqi invasion and subsequent war, in which an international coalition forced Iraqi troops to withdraw, proved to be both an economic and ecological disaster. In 2003 Kuwait became a base for large numbers of international coalition forces that invaded Iraq.

▼ An oil worker in Kuwait works on one of the country's many modern oil rigs. Kuwait's oil industry employs thousands of foreign workers, mainly from southern Asia and other Arab nations.

# BAHRAIN

**Lying in the Persian Gulf between Qatar and Saudi Arabia, the small kingdom of Bahrain consists of one large and a number of smaller islands.**

**Area:** 276 sq. mi. (716km²)
**Population:** 1,107,000
**Capital:** Manamah (290,000)
**Main languages spoken:** Arabic, English, Farsi, Urdu
**Main religions:** Shi'a Islam, Sunni Islam
**Currency:** Bahraini dinar
**Main exports:** petroleum and petroleum products, basic manufactures
**Type of government:** kingdom; virtual dictatorship

Bahrain Island, the nation's main land area, has a rocky center and is linked to the Saudi Arabian mainland by a large highway. The island's climate is hot and extremely dry, with no more than 4 in. (10cm) of rainfall annually. Imported soil, irrigation, and drainage programs have helped Bahrain grow some fruit and vegetables. Bahrain was the first Gulf state to start producing oil in commercial quantities, but the nation's reserves are heavily depleted and may run out in the next 10 to 20 years. Investment in other industries, including aluminum production, chemicals, and plastics, has occurred, while many educated Bahrainis work in flourishing service industries such as insurance and banking. The country, run by the powerful al-Khalifa family, owns one fourth of the region's Gulf Air airline. Bahrain came under the protection of the United Kingdom in the 1800s and declared independence in 1971. English is still widely spoken by both the Arab population and the large communities of foreign workers.

▶ Part of the large business district in Bahrain's capital city, Manamah. The city is connected to the nearby island of Al Muharraq, on which the country's airport is located.

# QATAR

**The emirate of Qatar occupies a peninsula jutting out into the Persian Gulf. It is a flat, dry desert land with particularly high reserves of natural gas.**

**Area:** 4,412 sq. mi. (11,427km²)
**Population:** 838,000
**Capital:** Doha (723,000)
**Main languages spoken:** Arabic, English
**Main religion:** Sunni Islam
**Currency:** Qatari riyal
**Main exports:** petroleum and natural gas, chemicals
**Type of government:** traditional monarchy

Qatar shares land borders with the United Arab Emirates and Saudi Arabia. Much of Qatar consists of rolling deserts, with some low hills to the west facing the coast. Rainfall is very low, less than 4 in. (10cm) per year, and tends to fall only in heavy storms during the winter. Some freshwater is tapped from underground sources, but Qatar relies on desalination plants, which process seawater into freshwater. Not much land is suitable for farming, but irrigation programs do allow melons, tomatoes, and eggplants to be cultivated. Fishing off the peninsular coast is important, with around 5,500 tons (5,000 metric tonnes) of fish caught per year. Qatar has one of the smaller reserves of oil in the Middle East but has the world's third-largest natural gas deposits.

**A NATIVE MINORITY**
Only one in five of the country's population was born in Qatar. Since oil production began large numbers of foreign workers have been employed in Qatar, especially people from Iran, Pakistan, and India. The native people are descendants of nomadic Bedouin Arabs. Now over 95 percent of native Qataris live in cities, and many small villages and settlements lie abandoned. Ruled by the ath-Thani family, Qatar has grown very wealthy from its oil and natural gas reserves. The country's population has a high standard of living, with no income tax and free health and education services.

# UNITED ARAB EMIRATES

A federation of seven states, or emirates, the United Arab Emirates lies on the Gulf and is a dry desert land that is prosperous from gas and oil revenues.

**Area:** 32,280 sq. mi. (83,600km²)
**Population:** 4,765,000
**Capital:** Abu Dhabi (578,000)
**Main languages:** Arabic, Persian, English, Hindi, Urdu
**Main religions:** Islam, Christian, Hinduism
**Currency:** dirham
**Main exports:** crude and refined petroleum, natural gas, manufactures, dates
**Type of government:** constitutional monarchy

The United Arab Emirates is a land of mainly low-lying deserts and salt flats with an average elevation of under 492 ft. (150m). To the east the land rises sharply to a height of 5,009 ft. (1,527m) along the border with Oman. The country has a long coastline with the Persian Gulf and a short coast facing the Gulf of Oman. The waters in the Gulf of Oman are much deeper and richer in nutrients and support a vibrant fishing industry. In 2009, 99,000 tons (90,000 metric tonnes) of fish were caught. The country is extremely dry, with as little as 2 in. (5cm) of rainfall per year, rising to 6 in. (15cm) per year in the mountainous areas. Agriculture is only possible via irrigation.

In 1971 the United Arab Emirates formed as a federation comprising the seven emirates of Abu Dhabi, Dubai, Sharjah, Ajman, Umm al-Qaiwain, Ras al-Khaimah, and Fujairah. Formerly known as the Trucial States, the federation was formed after British forces left the region. Abu Dhabi was the largest of the states in land area and is home to the country's political capital city of the same name. Along with the sizable city of Dubai, these are the two main

industrial centers of the country. Oil extraction and processing dominates the country's economy. The United Arab Emirates has approximately eight percent of the world's proven reserves of oil and produces over three million barrels per day. The world's largest artificial port, 19 mi. (30km) south of the city of Dubai, has become a major transportation terminus for the Gulf nations. The United Arab Emirates has used some of its oil revenue to develop other industries, including finance, metal production, and tourism, as well as providing high-quality transportation links and other services for its people. The citizens of the U.A.E. have the highest income per capita in the entire Arab world and pay no income tax.

▲ The United Arab Emirates is largely self-sufficient in many fruit, including dates, here being harvested from palm trees.

▶ The New Souk market building (right) sits in front of a Muslim mosque in the city of Sharjah. The city's population has increased 25 times over since 1968 as foreign workers, predominantly male, have arrived to work in the oil and other industries. Today over two thirds of the entire country's population are male.

# OMAN

**Located strategically at the entrance to the Persian Gulf, Oman has large oil reserves but is one of the least developed of the Gulf states.**

**Area:** 119,500 sq. mi. (309,500km2)
**Population:** 2,867,000
**Capital:** Muscat (829,000)
**Main language spoken:** Arabic
**Main religion:** Ibadhi Islam
**Currency:** Omani rial
**Main exports:** petroleum, re-exports
**Type of government:** absolute monarchy

▼ This rugged mountain landscape is found in the Musandam Peninsula, an exclave of Oman separated from the rest of the country by territory belonging to the United Arab Emirates.

The terrain of Oman is dominated by a vast desert plain that covers over three fourths of the country. In the north lie mountains that rise to heights of over 9,840 ft. (3,000m). The narrow coastal plain, which is fertile in places, is separated from the desert interior by a range of hills that runs southwest parallel to the Arabian Sea. The country has a 1,300-mi.- (2-092-km-) long coastline with both the Gulf of Oman and the Arabian Sea. The coastline has a variety of terrain, including deepwater inlets, long, sandy beaches, mangrove lagoons, coral reefs, and rocky islets. There are no major rivers or lakes in Oman, and with a warm, dry climate with less than 4 in. (11cm) of rainfall per year, there is little agriculture. Oman is reliant on irrigation and concentrates on export crops such as limes and dates. Fishing is important, especially to Omani people living in small coastal settlements. Oman is ruled by a sultan who appoints a cabinet and council of regional representatives. The country has no political parties or law-making assembly. Oil dominates the economy and was first discovered in Oman in 1964. The country started large-scale oil production in 1967. From 1970 onward Oman has undergone a rapid transformation. Previously there were few schools, few communications links, and only 6 mi. (10km) of paved roads. Using oil revenues, Oman, under the leadership of Sultan Qaboos, has developed a modern infrastructure and public services. This process is still continuing. For example, many new schools have been built since 1996, and the country's literacy rate has risen rapidly to over 81 percent.

# YEMEN

A union of two former nations, Yemen is the newest country in the Middle East. It occupies the rugged and arid southwestern corner of the Arabian Peninsula.

**Area:** 203,850 sq. mi. (527,970km²)
**Population:** 20,901,000
**Capital:** Sana (1,708,000)
**Main language spoken:** Arabic
**Main religion:** Islam
**Currency:** Yemeni rial
**Main exports:** petroleum, food and live animals, crude minerals
**Type of government:** republic; dictatorship

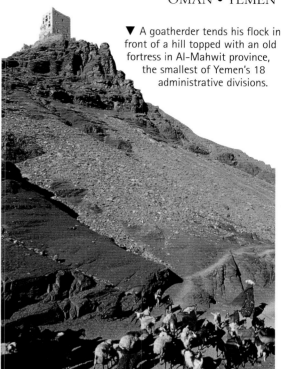

▼ A goatherder tends his flock in front of a hill topped with an old fortress in Al-Mahwit province, the smallest of Yemen's 18 administrative divisions.

Yemen shares land borders with Oman to the east and Saudi Arabia to the north, both of which were finally agreed in 1992–2000 following disputes. Yemen's territory also includes a small number of islands, the largest of which is Socotra, with an area of 1,382 sq. mi. (3,579km²). The country has coastlines with both the Red Sea and the Gulf of Aden, which flows out into the Indian Ocean. Yemen's location has been strategically important since ancient times, with Aden a major port for over 2,000 years. The country's landscape is varied and consists of a semidesert plain facing the Red Sea that then rises to form mountains and plateaus that are cut by deep valleys. East of the central region the landscape is rugged deserts and mountains. Rainfall varies depending on location, with the southern coast receiving less than 4 in. (10cm) per year, while up to 30 in. (75cm) falls in the western mountain region. The wettest area of Yemen is also the most highly populated, with Sana, the largest city and capital, and other major towns such as Ibb and Ta'izz.

The vast majority of Yemenis are Muslim Arabs, and the population is one of the most rural of all Arab nations. More than half of the workforce are engaged in agriculture, often farming small plots of land. Ancient terraces cut into the mountainsides provide extra farmland. Wheat, millet, and other cereal crops are vital staple foods, along with citrus fruit, tomatoes, and some vegetables. The main cash crops for export are coffee and cotton. Mocha coffee has been exported from Yemen for 1,200 years. Today oil is the dominant export, accounting for the majority of the country's export revenue. Yemen was formed in 1990 when the Yemen Arab Republic (North Yemen) and the People's Democratic Republic of Yemen (South Yemen) unified. The newly formed nation supported Iraq during the 1991 Gulf War, and reprisals followed, with Saudi Arabia and Kuwait expelling many Yemeni migrant workers. This has had a severe effect on the economy, with a high unemployment rate. There was a brief civil war in 2004, and since 2010 Shia rebels have controlled part of the north.

▲ A Yemeni market worker trades and sells qat. The leaves of this evergreen shrub have a mild stimulating effect when chewed, a popular practice in Yemen.

# CENTRAL ASIA

A region of extremes in terrain, Central Asia lies south of the Russian Federation and borders the Middle East to the west and Pakistan and China to the east. People, particularly nomadic livestock herders and traders, have lived in the area for many thousands of years. Part of the region lay on the Silk Road, an overland route used since 100 B.C. to carry goods, especially silk, between China and Europe. Yet today most of Central Asia is hampered by a lack of transportation facilities owing to its mountainous and desert terrain, as well as its general lack of ocean ports. Kazakhstan and Turkmenistan have coastlines with the inland Caspian Sea, but the other nations of the region are landlocked. The entire region is faraway from the world's oceans and experiences a continental climate with great extremes in temperature. Generally Central Asia is dry, and water is at a premium. Irrigation is vital to most crop growing but is placing great strains on freshwater lakes and rivers. Further environmental problems of desertification and pollution caused by industry and nuclear facilities have attracted much concern. Five of the six countries in Central Asia—Kazakhstan, Turkmenistan, Uzbekistan, Kyrgyzstan, and Tajikistan—were all former republics of the Soviet Union but became independent in 1991. The Russian Federation continues to exert influence on the region as a major trading partner, and Russians make up large minorities in a number of the countries.

▲ Traveling through a mountain pass, these Afghani traders are carrying opium. The United Nations estimates that Afghanistan grows more than 60 percent of the world's illegal supplies of opium.

▼ This fisherman plies his trade on the Aral Sea, which straddles the border between Uzbekistan and Kazakhstan. Falling water levels have caused the extinction of most of the fish species and have devastated the fishing economy of the area.

R U S S I A N  F E D E R A T I O N

*Ural*

*Caspian
Depression*

**K A Z A K H S T A N**

*Mugozbary*

*Kazakh*

ASTANA

*Irtysh*

*Altai*

*Lake
Zaysan*

*Uplands*

*Lake
Balkhash*

*Lake
Alakol*

*Aral
Sea*

*Ustyurt
Plateau*

*Caspian Sea*

*Zaliv
Kara-Bogaz
Gol*

*Kizilkum*

*Syr Darya*

BISHKEK

*Kirghiz Range*

*Lake
Issyk Kul'*

Pik Pobedy
24,399 ft.
△

**KYRGYZSTAN**

*Tien Shan*

C H I N A

TASHKENT

**UZBEKISTAN**

*Altai Range*

*Karakum*

**TURKMENISTAN**

*Amu Darya*

DUSHANBE

**TAJIKISTAN**

Qullai Ismoili Somoni
△24,583 ft.

*Pamirs*

ASHGABAT

**I R A N**

*Hindu Kush*

KABUL

300    600 km

150    300 miles

**AFGHANISTAN**

P A K I S T A N

*Dasht-
i-Margo*

*Helmand*

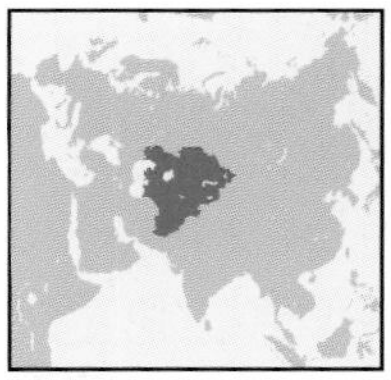

▼ Workers attach new lengths
of pipe to an oil rig operating in
a southern Kazakhstan oil field.
Kazakhstan produces more than
1.5 million barrels of oil per day.

# KAZAKHSTAN

The biggest of the central Asian states and the ninth-largest country in the world, Kazakhstan is a land of deserts and plains with vast mineral reserves.

**Area:** 1,049,155 sq. mi. (2,717,300km²)
**Population:** 15,776,000
**Capital:** Astana (639,000)
**Main languages spoken:** Kazakh, Russian
**Main religions:** Islam, Russian Orthodox
**Currency:** tenge
**Main exports:** oil and natural gas, rolled ferrous metals, refined copper, cereals, coal
**Type of government:** republic

▲ A *Soyuz-Fregat* rocket launch occurring at the Baikonur Cosmodrome. The site of the former Soviet Union's space program, it lies approximately 124 mi. (200km) northwest of the city of Qyzylorda.

Much of Kazakhstan's vast area consists of grassy plains, known as steppes, that cover the north and some of the central regions of the country. The south and south-central regions of the country are covered by deserts, while to the extreme east and south the land rises to form several high mountain ranges. This area features the country's highest point, Mount Khan Tangiri (22,943 ft./6,995m). In contrast, the western part of the country, which borders the Caspian Sea, has a low point of 92 ft. (28m) below sea level. Kazakhstan has a continental climate with great extremes of temperature and rainfall. The mountains to the east, for example, can receive an annual average rainfall of 60 in. (150cm). Most of the country receives between 8–16 in. (20–40cm) per year, while parts of the central desert region receive no more than 4 in. (10cm). Much farming relies on irrigation from the country's rivers and lakes. The largest lake entirely in Kazakhstan is Lake Balkhash, which has an area of 6,720 sq. mi. (17,400km²). Russians form 30 percent of the nation's population, and there are large minorities of Ukranians, Tatars, and Uzbeks. The Kazahks

▲ Founded in 1824 as a fortress settlement, Kazakhstan's capital city of Astana has been known as Akmolinsk, Tselinograd, and Aqmola in the past. Its status is a duty-free tax zone to encourage foreign investment.

are the biggest ethnic group in the country, making up 53 percent of the population. Historically most Kazahks lived a nomadic life, but during the 1900s many were forced to settle in one place. Mining is the largest industry, while agriculture remains important. Kazakhstan has enormous reserves of many minerals, including lead, zinc, chromium, and tungsten, as well as coal, iron ore, and nickel. Large oil and natural gas deposits are found in the Caspian Sea, and the country has formed partnerships with foreign companies in order to exploit these reserves.

# UZBEKISTAN

Uzbekistan is the most populous country in central Asia. It has huge mineral resources, but its infrastructure is limited, and many of its people are poor.

**Area:** 172,740 sq. mi. (447,400km²)
**Population:** 27,767,000
**Capital:** Tashkent (2,210,000)
**Main languages spoken:** Uzbek, Russian
**Main religions:** Islam, Eastern Orthodox
**Currency:** som
**Main exports:** light industrial products, petroleum, cotton, gold, food
**Type of government:** republic

Uzebekistan is one of only two countries in the world that are doubly landlocked— surrounded by other landlocked countries (Liechtenstein is the other). Approximately one third of the country's territory consists of mountains and foothills to the east and southeast, where they merge with the mountain ranges of neighboring Kyrgyzstan and Tajikistan. Most of the remainder consists of dry desert plains. Uzbekistan's continental climate is characterized by low rainfall levels of between 8–16 in. (20–40cm) per year across the country. Farming tends to rely on irrigation and occurs mainly to the east and in the fertile river valley of the Amu Darya, which feeds the Aral Sea. Overuse of river and lake water for irrigation has caused severe ecological problems. Cotton is the most important crop, followed by tobacco, fruit, and vegetables, but the country produces only one third of the cereals it requires and has to import the rest. Uzbek people comprise around 80 percent of the population, Tajiks five percent, Kazakhs four percent, and

▲ Uzbekistan is one of the world's leading producers of cotton.

Russians and Tatars make up around two percent each. The country's population is concentrated in the south and east of the country. Many live in towns and cities that date back many centuries. Samarqand is one of the oldest cities in central Asia. Tashkent is the country's capital and is the center of Uzbekistan's manufacturing and heavy industry, which includes car and aircraft production, farm machinery, and jewelry, using gold from several large mines in the Kizilkum Desert.

▼ Since 1960 the Aral Sea has shrunk in area 80 percent, due to overuse of the rivers that have fed it for thousands of years. In addition to the stranded boats, the salt and sand left behind have made the surrounding land unsuitable for agriculture.

# TURKMENISTAN

The least populous central Asian country, Turkmenistan is an isolated, largely desert nation with large natural gas reserves.

**Area:** 188,460 sq. mi. (488,100km²)
**Population:** 6,550,000
**Capital:** Ashgabat (828,000)
**Main languages spoken:** Turkmen, Russian, Uzbek
**Main religions:** Islam, Eastern Orthodox
**Currency:** manat
**Main exports:** natural gas and oil products (almost 70 percent of exports), cotton, textiles
**Type of government:** republic

Four fifths of the land of Turkmenistan consist of the large, flat Karakum Desert, famous for its black sands, which experiences maximum temperatures in excess of 122°F (50°C). Turkmenistan has a very dry climate with extremes of temperature; in the winter temperatures can fall below -22°F (-30°C). The country's principal river, the Amu Darya, flows through the eastern part of the country. Near the country's border with Afghanistan some of its waters are diverted along a 680-mi.-(1,100-km-) long irrigation canal westward to Ashgabat. The Karakum Canal is the world's largest irrigation canal and brings water to farmlands along its route, enabling cotton, wheat, silk, and fruit, among other crops, to be grown. Many people in the country suffer from health problems, owing to the scarcity of clean water. Turkmenistan's largest city, Ashgabat, was rebuilt after an earthquake in 1948. It is well known as the center of the country's cotton and textiles industries. However, these are second as export earners to oil and natural gas. From 1991 to 2006, Turkmenistan was kept isolated by dictator Saparmurat Niyazov.

# TAJIKISTAN

**The smallest and poorest central Asian nation, Tajikistan is also the most mountainous. Over half of the country lies above 9,840 ft. (3,000m).**

**Area:** 55,250 sq. mi. (143,100km²)
**Population:** 7,374,000
**Capital:** Dushanbe (695,000)
**Main languages spoken:** Tajik, Uzbek, Russian
**Main religions:** Sunni Islam, Shi'a Islam
**Currency:** Tajik rouble
**Main exports:** aluminum (over half of exports), electricity, cotton fibers, fruit, vegetable oil
**Type of government:** republic

Mountains cover more than 90 percent of Tajikistan, with the highest peaks found in the Pamirs in the southeast of the country. Mountain glaciers feed many streams, which allows the country to generate surplus electricity in order to support both its own aluminum industry and to export to neighboring nations. Only six percent of the country is farmed. Irrigation allows parts of the country's lowlands to be used to grow a range of crops, including cotton, fruit, and mulberry trees. Tajikistan has substantial reserves of a number of minerals, including mercury, silver, gold, and over one tenth of the world's proven reserves of uranium. However, the mountainous terrain makes mining and transportation extremely difficult. The country is named after the Tajik people, who are descended from Iranians and comprise around 80 percent of the country's population. The Uzbeks are the largest minority group, comprising 15 percent. Most of the country's people are followers of the Islamic religion. A civil war following independence in 1991 and the emigration of highly skilled Russian workers are key causes of a decline in the country's industries. Around 60 percent of the population live in poverty, with poor health-care facilities.

# KYRGYZSTAN

**A mountainous republic, Kyrgyzstan is the most rural central Asian nation. The country's economy relies on mining its extensive mineral deposits.**

**Area:** 76,640 sq. mi. (198,500km²)
**Population:** 5,363,000
**Capital:** Bishkek (835,000)
**Main languages spoken:** Kyrgyz, Russian
**Main religions:** Islam, Russian Orthodox
**Currency:** som
**Main exports:** food products, metals, machinery, cotton, wool
**Type of government:** republic

◄ A yurt formed from a frame of wooden poles covered in cloth acts as a portable summer home for nomadic livestock herders in Kyrgyzstan.

Kyrgyzstan's landscape is dominated by mountains that extend through much of the country and into neighboring China. The highest peaks in these snow- and ice-covered mountains rise to over 22,960 ft. (7,000m) in elevation. Overlooked by the Tien Shan Mountains in the east of the country lies Ozero Issyk-Kul', one of the world's largest mountain lakes and the fourth deepest in the world. The country experiences a continental climate, with average daily temperatures in the valleys reaching 81°F (27°C) in July and 25°F (-4°C) in January. Reserves of many minerals, including gold, coal, iron, zinc, mercury, and natural gas, are found within its mountains. Despite less than seven percent of the land being suitable for farming, agriculture employs larger numbers of people than any other sector. The raising of sheep and the herding of cattle, goats, and horses, all for their meat and milk, are widespread. The country is politically unstable and experienced revolutions in 2005 and 2010.

# AFGHANISTAN

A mountainous nation, Afghanistan has been torn apart by conflict over the past 30 years. Most of its people live in poverty.

**Area:** 249,347 sq. mi. (645,807km²)
**Population:** 24,970,000
**Capital:** Kabul (2,536,000)
**Main languages spoken:** Pashtu, Dari (Persian), Turkic
**Main religions:** Sunni Islam, Shi'a Islam
**Currency:** afghani
**Main exports:** dried fruit and nuts, carpets and rugs, wool and hides, cotton
**Type of government:** republic; virtual dictatorship

▼ Afghanistan's forbidding mountainous landscape has hampered transportation and trade and leaves many small settlements isolated.

Almost three fourths of Afghanistan are covered in mountains and highland areas. Principal among its mountains is the Hindu Kush range, which extends around 500 mi. (800km) through central Afghanistan and into Pakistan and Tajikistan. The highest peaks there rise to over 22,960 ft. (7,000m), and the average altitude of the region is approximately 14,104 ft. (4,300m). The Hindu Kush forms a natural and imposing barrier between the country's northern plains, its major farmlands, and the rest of the country. South and southwest of the Hindu Kush lies a flat plateau with an average height of approximately 3,280 ft. (1,000m). Most of this plateau is covered in deserts. The soil there supports little life, except for the immediate lands around the rivers that run through the region. Chief among these is the Helmand river, Afghanistan's longest, which begins its

life approximately 50 mi. (80km) south of Kabul and flows through the Dasht-i-Margo Desert into Iran. Afghanistan's climate varies with elevation, but generally the country experiences cold winters and hot summers, in which temperatures in the southern deserts can exceed 113°F (45°C). All of the country receives low levels of rainfall; the average annual precipitation is around 12 in. (30cm). Droughts sometimes cause serious problems for the country's farmers.

## AFGHAN PEOPLE

Afghanistan has a long history going back over 5,000 years, and its people come from a range of origins—the main groups are: Pashtuns, Tajiks, Hazaras, and Uzbeks. Over 30 languages are spoken, and many Afghans speak their own local language, as well as one of the two official languages. Ninety-nine percent of the population are Muslims. Most Afghans are rural people who depend on farming to live. The flat northern plains and foothills are where the majority of crops, including corn, rice, wheat, cotton, and nuts, are grown. Many Afghans raise sheep and goats that provide milk, as well as wool for making rugs—one of the key crafts of the country. Several million Afghans still live nomadic lives tending small herds of livestock.

## A SUCCESSION OF WARS

Afghanistan's strategic position between central Asia and the Indian subcontinent has seen it invaded and fought over a number of times in its past. In 1979 the Soviet Union invaded the country to support an unpopular government, and a lengthy war was fought between Soviet and government forces and the mujahideen—rural tribesmen supported by the United States and Pakistan—that continued for ten years. Further conflicts between different Afghan groups occurred before a strict Islamic group, the Taliban, came to power in 1996. The Taliban was deposed by the United States and its allies in 2001. These conflicts caused devastation, but some progress was made in 2004 and 2005 when democratic institutions were established that provided education for women and helped rebuild the country's infrastructure. However, fighting continued, especially in the south, where the Taliban has a lot of support. The south is also a major producer of opium. International coalition forces, trying to stamp out the opium trade, have met much opposition. By 2010, the Afghan authorities controlled little beyond Kabul.

▲ A school for female students in Kandahar, which opened in January 2002. Afghan women have a literacy level of 14 percent—the lowest level in the world.

# SOUTH ASIA

South Asia is one of the oldest centers of permanent human settlement and is the birthplace of several of the world's major religions. Extremes of terrain and climate are found in south Asia—from the permanently snow-capped peaks of the towering Himalayas to the giant, very low-lying floodplains that are found in India and comprise most of Bangladesh. Large parts of the region are subject to monsoon winds that bring heavy rainfalls in the summer but that also cause floods and storms. However, huge crop failures are caused if the rain fails. Over one fifth of the world's population lives in south Asia, many in abject poverty as fast-growing populations outpace countries' abilities to provide for their people. The region is dominated by the large and populous nation of India. Two of its neighbors, Pakistan and Bangladesh, were formerly parts of India when it was under British rule. These two nations are predominantly populated by Muslims, while Hindus are the majority in India and Nepal, and Buddhists live in Sri Lanka and Bhutan.

▲ Completed in 1978 after 20 years of work, the Karakoram Highway runs for 500 mi. (800km) through some of the most hostile terrain in Asia to link China with the Pakistani city of Islamabad.

▼ Hindu Indians bathe in the Ganges, the holy river for south Asia's large Hindu population.

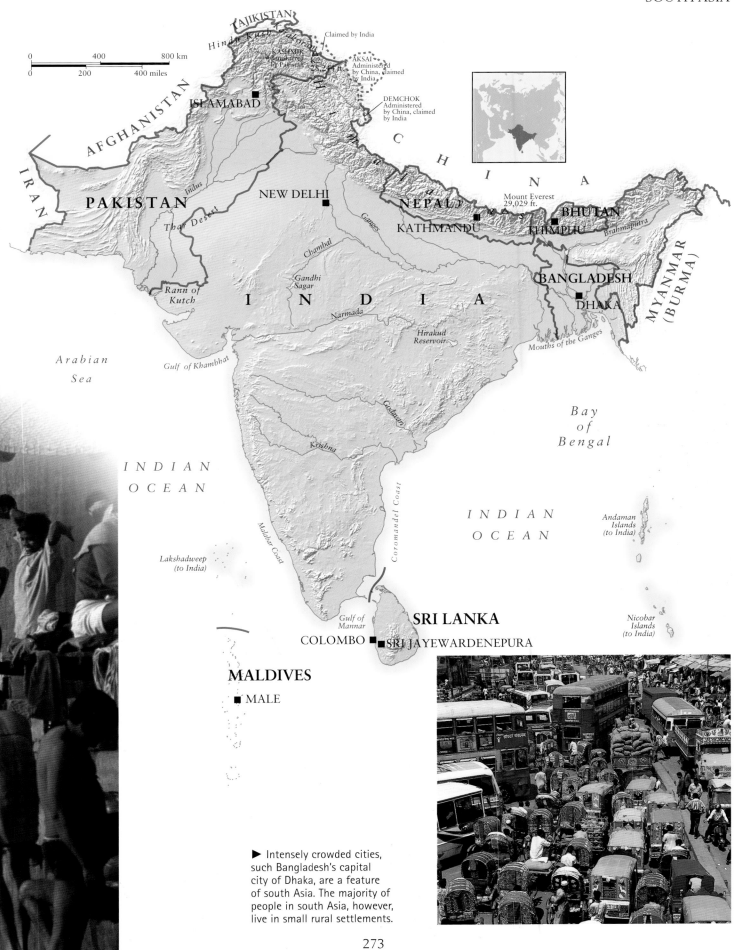

TAJIKISTAN

Hindu Kush *Karakoram*

Claimed by India

KASHMIR
Administered
by Pakistan

AKSAI
Administered
by China, claimed
by India

DEMCHOK
Administered
by China, claimed
by India

0   400   800 km
0   200   400 miles

**AFGHANISTAN**

IRAN

ISLAMABAD

**PAKISTAN**

*Indus*

NEW DELHI

*Thar Desert*

*Rann of
Kutch*

**I N D I A**

*Chambal*

*Gandhi
Sagar*

*Narmada*

*Gulf of Khambhat*

*A r a b i a n
S e a*

*Ganges*

C H I N A

Mount Everest
29,029 ft.

**NEPAL**

KATHMANDU

**BHUTAN**

THIMPHU

*Brahmaputra*

**BANGLADESH**

DHAKA

*Mouths of the Ganges*

**MYANMAR
(BURMA)**

*Hirakud
Reservoir*

*Godavari*

*Krishna*

*B a y
o f
B e n g a l*

*I N D I A N
O C E A N*

*I N D I A N
O C E A N*

*Malabar Coast*

*Lakshadweep
(to India)*

*Coromandel Coast*

*Andaman
Islands
(to India)*

*Gulf of
Mannar*

**SRI LANKA**

*Nicobar
Islands
(to India)*

COLOMBO   SRI JAYEWARDENEPURA

**MALDIVES**

MALE

▶ Intensely crowded cities,
such Bangladesh's capital
city of Dhaka, are a feature
of south Asia. The majority of
people in south Asia, however,
live in small rural settlements.

# PAKISTAN

**The Islamic Republic of Pakistan borders Afghanistan, Iran, and India. It is a country of dramatic and contrasting scenery, people, and cultures.**

**Area:** 307,374 sq. mi. (796,095km²) excluding 33,649 sq. mi. (87,150km²) of the Pakistani-held areas of Kashmir and the disputed Northern Areas (Gilgit, Baltistan, and Diamir)
**Population:** 162,508,000
**Capital:** Islamabad (1,600,000)
**Main languages spoken:** Urdu, English, Punjabi, Sindhi, Pashtu
**Main religions:** Sunni Islam, Shi'a Islam
**Currency:** Pakistani rupee
**Main exports:** textiles, clothing, rice, leather goods, cotton, manufactures
**Type of government:** republic

The landscape of Pakistan is partly divided by the Indus river system, which enters the country in the northeast and flows southward before emptying into the Arabian Sea. The Indus Plain, found mostly along the eastern side of the river, varies in width between 50–205 mi. (80–330km) and is the most densely populated and farmed region of Pakistan. A series of mountain ranges, including the Toba Kakar Range, dominate the northern regions of the country, and Pakistan is crossed by part of the Thar Desert in the southeast. The country's climate varies greatly according to elevation and region, but most of Pakistan suffers from scarce rainfall, with droughts common.

▲ A bustling street in the city of Faisalabad in northeast Pakistan. Faisalabad is a major transportation terminus and industrial center with engineering works, cotton, sugar, and flour mills, and large textile factories.

## FARMING AND INDUSTRY

Around 43 percent of the working population are involved in agriculture. Pakistan produces many crops, is self-sufficient in cereals, and is one of the world's leading producers of cotton, which provides the raw material for a giant textiles industry. However, farming faces a number of environmental challenges, including saltwater logging of the soil, droughts, and floods. Although around 60 percent of Pakistanis live in rural areas, the country has a number of large cities. Lahore is a major distribution and trading center for the surrounding heavily industrialized areas. Hyderabad is a center of heavy industry, while Karachi, lying on the coast, is Pakistan's chief port and the most populous city of all. Manufacturing, services, and mining a range of minerals are all major employers in the country.

## INDEPENDENCE AND POLITICS

The lands that now comprise Pakistan have been invaded and controlled by many different peoples, including Persians, Huns, Turks, and Arabs. European traders started to visit the area in the 1500s, and by the mid-1700s the region, including the territory of both India and Pakistan, was under British rule. Demands for independence grew until 1947, when the region was partitioned into India, containing mainly Hindus, and

a separate Muslim nation of East and West Pakistan. Separated by 992 mi. (1,600km) of land, cultural and political differences grew between the two regions, leading to war in 1971, with East Pakistan becoming independent as Bangladesh. Pakistan has experienced much instability, with military coups, assassinations, and rule by the army for many years. Strict Islamists control some border regions, and there is increasing political and religious violence in Pakistan. A serious dispute over the region of Kashmir on the border between India and Pakistan has existed since 1947.

## PAKISTAN'S PEOPLE

The people of Pakistan are a racial mixture of various groups who have moved to and settled in the region over thousands of years. The five largest ethnic groups are: Punjabis, Pashtuns, Sindhis, Balochis, and Muhajirs. Punjabis comprise 45 percent of the country's population, and their language is the most commonly spoken. Pashtuns and Sindhis together make up 30 percent of the population. When Pakistan was separated from the Hindu state of India in 1947, millions of Muslims left India to settle in Pakistan. These people and their descendants are the Muhajirs, who tend to speak Urdu. Ninety-six percent of Pakistanis are Muslim. While a wealthy elite, mainly Punjabis, live in considerable luxury, a large proportion of Pakistan's population barely survives. The country has one of the lowest access rates to doctors, hospitals, and essential medicines in the world. Malaria, tuberculosis, and other diseases are common, and food and water shortages are widespread.

▲ Sugarcane being harvested in the province of Sind in southeast Pakistan. Pakistan produces around 70 million tons (64 million metric tonnes) of sugarcane every year.

▼ Distinctive trucks wait for the road ahead to clear on the mountainous Karakoram Highway. This road took the efforts of over 24,000 workers to complete.

# INDIA

**Home to over one billion people, India is a vast and diverse country with much variety and richness in culture. India is also the world's largest democracy.**

**Area:** 1,269,219 sq. mi.
(3,287,263km²)
**Population:** 1,148,000,000
**Capital:** New Delhi
(15,048,000)
**Main languages spoken:**
Hindi, English, 14 regional
official languages
**Main religions:** Hinduism,
Islam
**Currency:** Indian rupee
**Main exports:**
agricultural products,
diamonds and jewelry,
clothing, machinery and
transportation equipment,
metals with iron and
steel, cotton, petroleum
**Type of government:**
federal republic

India is the seventh-biggest country in the world and the second most populous. It shares borders with six countries, mostly to the north and including Myanmar, Nepal, and Bhutan. India surrounds the country of Bangladesh on three sides and is involved in long-running disputes over territory with its two other neighbors, Pakistan to the northwest and China to the north. Its landscape is incredibly varied, with dry desert regions, lush, wet highlands, vast plains, and plateaus. The country is also home to a large part of the world's youngest and highest mountains—the Himalayas. The Himalayas and their foothills form a massive geological barrier across almost all of northern India, extending a distance of over 1,430 mi. (2,300km). They were formed and continue to rise owing to the immense forces that are pushing the Indian subcontinent northward toward China. Extending south from the highlands region, much of India consists of a giant peninsula jutting out into the Indian Ocean. The Arabian Sea lies to the west of India and to the east lies the Bay of Bengal.

## THE NORTHERN PLAINS

Lying south of the Himalayas is a huge belt of flat land known as the Northern Plains. Much of this land surface has been formed by rivers, including the Ganges and Brahmaputra, depositing sediment on great floodplains and deltas and creating extremely rich and fertile soils. Many of India's rivers start their life in the Himalayas, among them the Ganges.

▼ Situated in Kashmir in northwest India, Lake Dal is known for its beautiful location, lotus flowers, and its striking lake dwellers, who live in wooden houseboats and tend floating gardens.

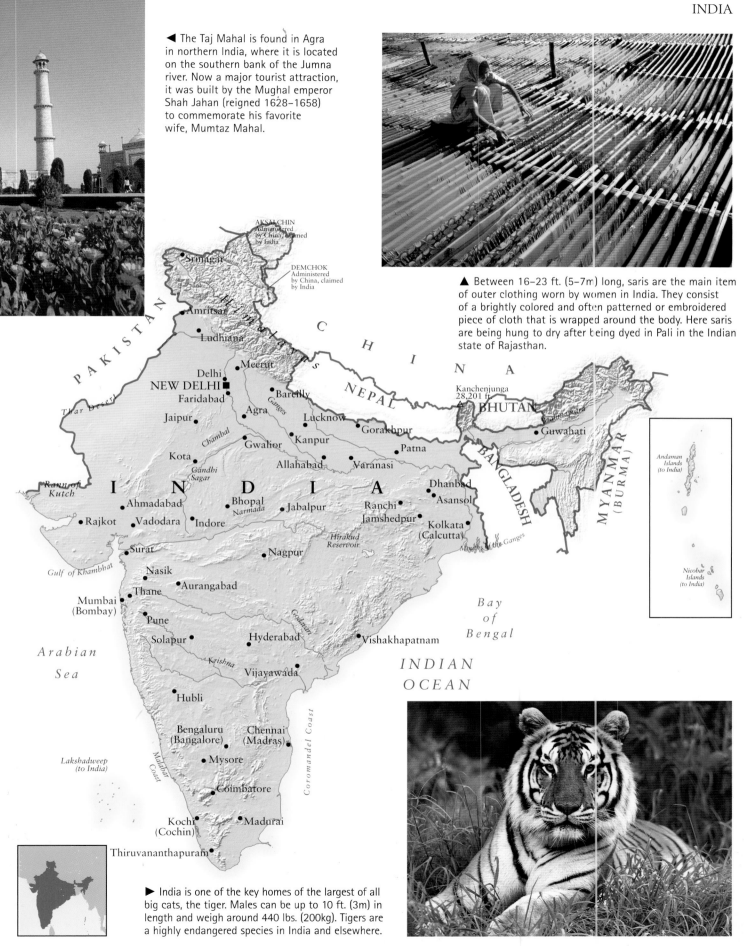

◄ The Taj Mahal is found in Agra in northern India, where it is located on the southern bank of the Jumna river. Now a major tourist attraction, it was built by the Mughal emperor Shah Jahan (reigned 1628–1658) to commemorate his favorite wife, Mumtaz Mahal.

▲ Between 16–23 ft. (5–7m) long, saris are the main item of outer clothing worn by women in India. They consist of a brightly colored and often patterned or embroidered piece of cloth that is wrapped around the body. Here saris are being hung to dry after being dyed in Pali in the Indian state of Rajasthan.

► India is one of the key homes of the largest of all big cats, the tiger. Males can be up to 10 ft. (3m) in length and weigh around 440 lbs. (200kg). Tigers are a highly endangered species in India and elsewhere.

277

The wide, slow-moving Ganges river is just over 1,550 mi. (2,500km) long and drains almost one fourth of the country. The Ganges has created the wide, flat Gangetic Plain, which lies in both India and Bangladesh. This region is heavily populated and farmed by millions of Indians who rely on water from the river. A largely low-lying region, it is subject to flooding and typhoon storms. In marked contrast to the plains, the arid Thar Desert lies to the northwest and crosses the Indian-Pakistan border. South of the plains is the Deccan Plateau, an area of around 1,970 ft. (600m) average elevation that covers much of central and southern India. On both sides of the plateau are coastal mountains. India has highly varied plant and animal life, from arctic plants in the high mountains to tropical flowers, rhinoceroses, tigers, and many other big cats. The country provides habitats for more than 1,100 species of birds.

▲ An Indian guide to the city palace of Jodhpur. Located in northwest India, the city is a major trading center for the surrounding farmlands and is famous for its handicraft products, including ivory, glass, cloth, and leather goods.

## FARMING AND FISHING
Agriculture is the backbone of India's economy. It employs 52 percent of the workforce directly, as well as providing raw materials for some of the country's

▲ Indians with camels cross part of the Thar Desert. Over one million camels are used as the main beasts of burden in the dry desert regions of India.

other key industries, particularly the textiles, jute, and sugar industries. Although most farming is largely conducted in ways unchanged for centuries, advances in technology, fertilizers, and irrigation have seen more and more land come under cultivation. Almost 232,000 sq. mi. (600,000km$^2$) of land are now irrigated by canal or well systems, and over half of India's land is cultivated. Huge farms and plantations do exist, growing cash crops such as coffee, tea, cotton, and jute. Yet thousands of farms are tiny—less than one tenth of a square mile in size—and many rural families struggle to grow enough to feed themselves. Fishing is carried out along all of India's coastline and also in its major rivers. Sea fishing accounts for more than two thirds of all catches. Most fishing is conducted in simple unmotorized vessels, although the Indian government is investing in ocean-going trawlers.

▼ A reminder of British rule in India, Mumbai's Victoria Station was completed in 1887 and was built on the site of the first train route in Asia, which opened in 1853.

part of India's agriculture, with many of the country's 282 million cattle and 94 million water buffalo used as beasts of burden and sources of milk.

## MINING AND INDUSTRY
India has large reserves of many minerals—from oil and coal to zinc, copper, silver, and gold. It has developed a number of sizable industries based on its natural resources, including large-scale steel production and engineering industries. Millions of Indians are employed in the textiles industry, mostly in small-scale businesses. Helped by foreign investment in the 1990s, India built up large computer software, telecommunications, and other modern industries. Based in and around the city of Mumbai (Bombay), India's movie industry, nicknamed "Bollywood," produces more movies per year than anywhere else in the world.

▼ Hindus bathe in the Ganges river in the northern city of Varanasi. Formerly known as Benares, Varanasi is home to more than 1,500 religious buildings. Hindus believe that bathing in the Ganges cleanses them of sin.

## RICE AND SPICES
India has more land devoted to growing rice than any other country in the world and became self-sufficient in rice production in the late 1970s. India consumes most of the rice it grows. It is also one of the world's largest producers of a number of other crops, including sugarcane, tea, cotton, corn, pulses, and wheat. A major grower of many of the world's spices and flavorings, India is renowned for its rich cuisine and the enormous variety of regional dishes. In contrast, most Indians have a simple diet. Livestock raising is an important

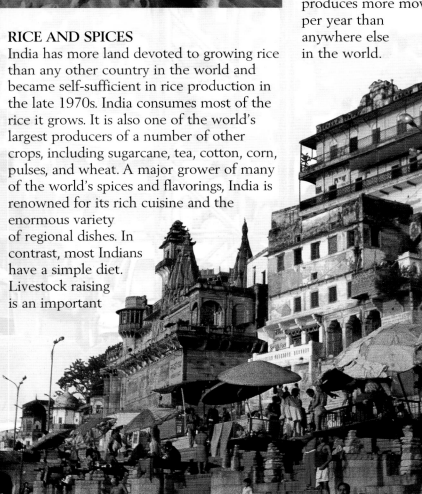

## AN ENORMOUS POPULATION

With around two percent of the world's land area, India supports more than 15 percent of the world's population. Although it is still a predominantly rural country, India has an urban population of more than 340 million and three of the top-ten largest metropolitan areas in the world: Mumbai (Bombay) with 18.2 million people; Delhi with almost 15.1 million; and Kolkata (Calcutta) with 14.3 million people. Extremes of wealth and poverty coexist in India. The country's wealthy middle classes number more than 150 million, yet under four percent of Indian households have an annual income of more than $2,500. The United Nations estimates that 25 percent of the population live below the poverty line, many in city slums or without homes.

▲ Pilgrims flock to the Har Mandir Sahib, or Golden Temple, in Amritsar, the most sacred shrine to followers of the Sikh religion. Originally built in 1604 and rebuilt in the 1800s, the Golden Temple sits on a small island surrounded by the Pool of the Nectar of Immortality, called Amrita Sar, from which the city gets its name.

## LANGUAGE, RELIGION, AND CASTE

The country has been settled since prehistoric times, and waves of different invaders and settlers have been absorbed, giving the country a rich culture. This is reflected in the two official, 14 recognized, and several hundred more languages spoken in the country, of which Hindi is the most widely used. Although 81 percent of the people are Hindu, India is also home to one of the world's largest Muslim populations, numbering more than 154 million. The varied religions found in India include more than 60 million Christians, around 20 million Sikhs, as well as Buddhists, Parsis, and Jains. A complex caste system exists in India in which people are placed in one of around 3,000 social class positions that limit where they can work, who they can interact with, and who they can marry. Despite government reforms, the caste system remains an important factor in Indian life.

## THE WORLD'S LARGEST DEMOCRACY

India gained independence from British rule in 1947 and established its present constitution in 1949. The country is a multiparty democracy with an electorate

◄ Farmers plow rice paddy fields in the southeastern Indian state of Tamil Nadu. Indian farmers rely on the monsoon season, from June to November, for water to irrigate their crops.

## JAMMU AND KASHMIR

Jammu and Kashmir is a region on the northern borders of India and Pakistan. Famous for its natural beauty, the region is home to K2 (or Mount Godwin Austen), at 28,244 ft. (8,611m) the world's second-highest mountain, and 12.4 million people. Both India and Pakistan claim the region as a part of their own territory. After several armed conflicts the area was separated, with the eastern region, including the valley of Kashmir, Jammu, and Ladakh, administered by India. The potential for conflict to flare up into full-scale war remains, with both countries having tested nuclear devices in the 1990s. Partly as a result of the ongoing problems over Jammu and Kashmir, defense spending is high. India keeps one of the world's largest military forces, made up of around one million personnel.

▲ A crowded train operates on part of India's enormous railroad system. Approximately 39,700 mi. (64,050km) of tracks link the country and carry millions of passengers and millions of tons of cargo.

▼ Shimla lies on the southern slopes of the Himalayas and was the summer capital of British India between 1865 and 1939. In 1971 a meeting of Indian and Pakistani leaders formed the Simla Agreement, dividing Jammu and Kashmir.

so large that it is the largest democracy in the world. India has a federal form of government with 28 states, each with a large amount of control over their own affairs, and seven union territories with less control. Each state is headed by a governor who is appointed for a five-year term by the country's head of state, the president. The prime minister is the holder of most political power in India. He and his Council of Ministers are responsible to the parliament, which is based in New Delhi. India's parliament consists of two chambers, the Rajya Sabha (Council of States) and the Lok Sabha (House of the People).

# BANGLADESH

Lying on the Bay of Bengal and bordered by India and Myanmar, Bangladesh was formerly West Pakistan before it gained its independence in 1971.

**Area:** 56,980sq. mi. (147,570km²)
**Population:** 142,460,000
**Capital:** Dhaka (12,797,000)
**Main languages spoken:** Bengali, Bihari
**Main religions:** Islam, Hinduism
**Currency:** taka
**Main exports:** clothing, jute manufactures, fish and shrimp, hides and leather
**Type of government:** parliamentary democracy

Much of the land of Bangladesh is a low-lying floodplain formed by two large rivers, the Ganges and the Brahmaputra. These and other rivers carry meltwaters from the Himalaya mountains southward to empty into the Bay of Bengal. Few places in the world are more susceptible to floods than Bangladesh. Some parts of the country can receive over 2,000 in. (5,080cm) of rainfall annually, and approximately two thirds of the land are flooded for part of the year. The floods often result in great loss of life and crops and property damage. The coastal regions of Bangladesh are also prone to cyclones. These intense storms can generate 23-ft.- (7-m-) high waves and wind speeds of over 150 mph (240km/h). The rich soils created by sediment left by rivers in the delta region and a long growing season create fertile farming conditions.

Bangladesh is the world's leading producer of jute, a natural fiber particularly used in making rope, string, baskets, and rough forms of paper. Sugarcane and tea are other important crops grown for export. However, most of the agriculture in the country is on a small scale, and many Bangladeshi farmers struggle to grow enough food to feed their families. Rice is the most important crop, along with pulses, such as lentils, and a range of vegetables. Around 1.5 million tons (1.4 million metric tonnes) of fish, mainly freshwater varieties, are caught each year. The water that damages Bangladesh's land and threatens its people is also harnessed to irrigate farmlands in the dry season and to generate electricity. In the past Bangladesh's mineral reserves were untapped. However, recent discoveries of large natural gas reserves are now being exploited, with pipelines carrying the gas to the major industrial center of Dhaka and the major port of Chittagong.

▼ A traffic jam of pedestrians and bicycle rickshaws occupies a crowded street in Dhaka, the capital of Bangladesh. However, around 73 percent of Bangladeshis live in small rural villages.

# NEPAL

**Home to Mount Everest and many other Himalayan peaks, Nepal has developed a financially important tourist industry.**

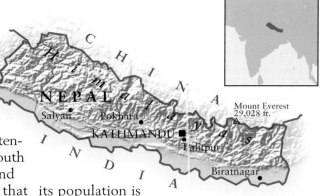

**Area:** 56,826 sq. mi. (147,181km²)
**Population:** 27,677,000
**Capital:** Kathmandu (1,150,000)
**Main languages spoken:** Nepali, many dialects
**Main religions:** Hinduism, Buddhism
**Currency:** Nepalese rupee
**Main exports:** basic manufactures, textiles and clothing, food
**Type of government:** republic; limited democracy

▶ Offerings are left at the Swayambunath temple, a Buddhist temple near the capital city of Kathmandu. Only 11 percent of the Nepalese population are Buddhists. Eighty-one percent are Hindus.

Four fifths of Nepal are covered in mountains, with eight of the world's ten-highest peaks within its borders. To the south of the country the land is lower-lying and forms an area of plains and marshlands that runs across the border with India. This region contains both hardwood and bamboo forests, which provide homes for tigers, leopards, and some elephants. Most of Nepal's population live in these southern plains or in the large central valley, in which the country's largest city, Kathmandu, is found. Farming dominates the economy, with most Nepalese engaged in growing crops and raising livestock such as goats and buffalo. Nepal's hard to develop and mountainous location has made large-scale industry hard to develop. Carpets and textiles are the main manufacturing industries. Nepal once attracted 500,000 tourists each year to its mountains and historic and religious sites, but numbers fell owing to instability. Nepal is a poor country in which over one third of its population is undernourished. Maoist insurgency destabilized Nepal, and after the massacre of most of the royal family in 2001 and the imposition of a royal dictatorship in 2002–2004 and 2005–2006, Nepal became a republic in 2008.

# BHUTAN

**A mountainous, landlocked kingdom surrounded by China and India, Bhutan remains one of the most isolated and unknown of all nations.**

**Area:** 17,950 sq. mi. (46,500km²)
**Population:** 696,000
**Capital:** Thimphu (79,000)
**Main languages spoken:** Dzongkha (Bhutanese), Nepalese
**Main religions:** Lamaistic Buddhism, Hinduism
**Currency:** ngultrum
**Main exports:** electricity, cement, timber, fruit, vegetables
**Type of government:** limited democracy

The northern part of Bhutan is located in the Great Himalayas, with mountain peaks rising to elevations of over 23,950 ft. (7,300m). In the center of the country are the lower-lying Lesser Himalayas. Between many of these mountain peaks are wide, fertile valleys. The only portion of Bhutan that is not mountainous is the Duars Plain, which is a narrow strip along the southern border covered largely in dense forests. The people of Bhutan are among the most rural in the world. Only 36 percent are estimated to live in towns, and around 63 percent are dependent on farming. Sheep and cattle are raised, while yaks, used for transportation, meat, and wool, are herded on colder mountain slopes. Only 47 percent of the country's adults are able to read and write, and the country's industries and infrastructure remain underdeveloped. India is Bhutan's key trading partner, accounting for around 63 percent of imports and 86 percent of exports. Bhutan is a strongly traditional Buddhist society. Until 1999 TV was banned, and tourism still remains restricted.

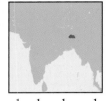

# SRI LANKA

A British colony until 1948, Sri Lanka is a pear-shaped island lying off the coast of India. However, from 1983 to 2009, its people experienced a violent civil war.

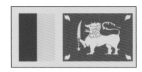

**Area:** 25,330 sq. mi. (65,610km²)
**Population:** 20,450,000
**Capitals:** Colombo, the administrative capital, and Sri Jayewardenpura, the legislative capital (combined population 2,477,000)
**Main languages spoken:** Sinhala, Tamil, English
**Main religions:** Buddhism, Hinduism, Christian, Islam
**Currency:** Sri Lankan rupee
**Main exports:** textiles, clothing, tea, diamonds, coconut products
**Type of government:** republic

▼ Much of Sri Lanka's tea is grown on large plantations in the central highlands, where cooler temperatures allow the tea plants to grow slowly and with more flavor. In 2008, 351,000 tons (318,500 metric tonnes) of tea were grown.

Sri Lanka's main geographic feature is an extensive area of rugged highlands in the central and southern parts of the island. These include peaks rising up over 4,920 ft. (1,500m), steep river gorges, and large plateaus. North of the highlands the land consists of more gently rolling plains crisscrossed by a number of rivers. Lying close to the equator, the island has an essentially tropical climate, while the central highlands are cooler and temperate. Sri Lanka has an average of 47 in. (120cm) of rainfall per year, but parts of the southwest of the country can receive between two and three times more. This wet zone is also the most densely populated part of the country. Sri Lanka has no fossil fuel reserves, relying instead on hydroelectricity to supply around one half of its electricity needs. It does have reserves of iron ore and graphite and is a major source of a number of semiprecious and precious gemstones. Around 32 percent of the population work in agriculture. The most common crop is rice, which is grown primarily as a local food source. Almost 3 million tons (2.7 million metric tonnes) of rice were produced in 2007, yet the country has to import more rice and many other foodstuffs. Only 12 percent of Sri

Lanka's farmland is used to grow tea, but the country is the world's largest tea exporter.

## SINHALESE AND TAMIL PEOPLES

Sri Lanka's population consists largely of two peoples: the Sinhalese, who are mainly Buddhist and comprise around 74 percent of the population, and the Tamils, most of whom are Hindus, who make up around 9 percent. Both peoples have inhabited Sri Lanka for over 1,400 years. Tensions between them spilled over into violent civil war from 1983 onward. Many Tamils, especially in the north and east of Sri Lanka, want an independent state. Conflict between government forces and the Tamil rebel group, called the Liberation Tigers of Tamil Eelam (Tamil Tigers), has brought over 70,000 deaths. From 2002, international mediators tried to achieve peace in Sri Lanka, but Sri Lankan forces intensified their efforts against the rebels in 2006 and, in 2009, finally defeated the remnants of the LTTE.

# INDIAN OCEAN ISLANDS

The third-largest of the oceans, the Indian Ocean extends from the eastern coast of Africa east to the Australian coast. A number of islands are contained in its waters; most are considered geographically to be part of the continent of Africa, although they have been settled by people of both African and Asian descent. The exception is the Maldives island group, which is considered part of Asia. Apart from Madagascar, which has an area larger than the European country of France, the remaining islands tend to be relatively small. Lush vegetation is found on many islands, yet the terrain often allows only small areas of land to be farmed. Tourism, encouraged by the palm-fringed beaches of the islands, is the biggest-growing industry.

# MALDIVES

**A chain of over 1,200 coral islands, of which around 200 are inhabited, the Maldives lies southwest of India. Tourism dominates the economy of these isles.**

**Area:** 115 sq. mi. (298km²)
**Population:** 299,000
**Capital:** Male (104,000)
**Main language spoken:** Dihevi
**Main religion:** Sunni Islam
**Currency:** rufiya
**Main exports:** fish, clothing, textiles
**Government:** republic; limited democracy

The Maldives consists of a 472-mi.- (760-km-) long series of island groups in the Indian Ocean. All of the islands are low-lying, with none over 6.5 ft. (2m) in height, and many are under threat from rising sea levels owing to global warming. Many have sandy beaches fringed with lush palm trees and other vegetation. The islands lie in the tropical zone and have a hot climate, with an average temperature of 80.0°F (26.7°C). Moist, seasonal winds, known as monsoons, blow across the islands, bringing an annual average of 60 in. (152cm) of rain, mainly between May and August. The two major food resources on the islands are coconut palms and breadfruit trees. However, the islands' most important resource is fish, with more than 204,000 tons (185,000 metric tonnes) of fish, especially tuna, landed each year. Fish account for the greater part of the islands' exports, but beach tourism dominates the economy, with 655,000 visitors in 2009.

MALE

M A L D I V E S

▼ A typical small, low-lying island in the Maldives.

# MADAGASCAR

The fourth-largest island in the world, Madagascar lies in the Indian Ocean. It is a poor country and is best known for its many unique plant and animal species.

**Area:** 226,658 sq. mi. (587,041km²)
**Population:** 17,594,000
**Capital:** Antananarivo (1,432,000)
**Main languages spoken:** Malagasy, French
**Main religions:** indigenous beliefs, Christian, Islam
**Currency:** Malagasy franc
**Main exports:** coffee, vanilla, shrimp, cotton, cloves
**Type of government:** republic

Madagascar was once part of the African continent, from which it split approximately 50 million years ago. Its current position is around 250 mi. (400km) east of Africa, separated by the Mozambique Channel. Highlands run north to south through the island and drop sharply to the east. To the west they descend more gently to a coastal plain. Almost all of Madagascar was once covered in forests, but much of the land has now been cleared. Areas of the island are covered in a rich, red soil that is suitable for farming. Isolated from mainland Africa, over three fourths of the island's species of plants and animals are not found anywhere else in the world. Large amounts of foreign aid have been targeted to protect many of these species and their habitats, which are under threat from deforestation and soil erosion.

### MADAGASCAR'S PEOPLE

The island's people are of a range of origins, with the largest groups descendants of Indonesian peoples believed to have settled on the island

over 1,000 years ago. Today most Madagascans are engaged either in agriculture or in industries that process livestock and crops into products, including foods, sisal rope, sugar, and textiles. The main staple food is rice, while cassava, beans, taro, and bananas are widely grown. Over ten million cattle exist on the island, many of which are a type of humped cattle called zebu. Madagascar is one of the poorest countries in the world. It struggles to import enough food to help feed its population, which is growing at a rate of three percent every year. Health and education services are also underdeveloped, but the country's development is hampered by political instability.

► Lemurs are a member of the primate family that includes monkeys, apes, and humans. They are only found naturally in the wild on Madagascar. Forty distinct species of lemurs have been cataloged.

286

# COMOROS & MAYOTTE

An island archipelago between Africa and Madagascar, Comoros and Mayotte consists of the nation of Comoros and the French dependency of Mayotte.

**Comoros**
**Area:** 719 sq. mi. (1,862km²)
**Population:** 669,000
**Capital:** Moroni (40,000)
**Main languages spoken:** Arabic, Comorian, French
**Main religions:** Sunni Islam, Roman Catholic
**Currency:** Comorian franc
**Main exports:** vanilla, ylang-ylang, cloves
**Type of government:** republic; limited democracy

Volcanic action created the three major islands and the number of islets that comprise Comoros. Njazidja is the largest and the youngest. Its highest point, Le Kartala, is an active volcano. Most Comorians fish or farm small areas of land, growing cassava, rice, and sweet potatoes for food, and coffee, vanilla, and other crops for export. Despite half of the workforce being engaged in farming or fishing, over half of all food is imported. Mayotte, a neighboring island to the east, remained a dependency of France after the Comoros became independent in 1974.

**Mayotte**
**Area:** 234 sq. mi. (376km²)
**Population:** 186,000
**Capital:** Mamoudzou (53,000)
**Major languages spoken:** Mahorian, French
**Main religion:** Sunni Islam
**Currency:** euro
**Main exports:** ylang-ylang, vanilla
**Type of government:** dependency of France

---

# SEYCHELLES

Consisting of 105 islands lying 992 mi. (1,600km) from the east coast of Africa, the Seychelles was formerly a British colony before achieving independence in 1976.

**Area:** 176 sq. mi. (455 km²)
**Population:** 83,000
**Capital:** Victoria (25,000)
**Main languages spoken:** English, French, Creole
**Main religions:** Roman Catholic, Anglican
**Currency:** Seychelles rupee
**Main exports:** canned tuna, re-exported petroleum products, frozen fish
**Type of government:** republic

▼ Tourists attracted to unspoiled scenery and beaches in the Seychelles help fuel the tourism industry, which employs over 30 percent of the islands' workforce.

The Seychelles consists of the Mahé group, which are mainly granite islands, and other islands largely formed from coral. The granite islands rise to over 1,970 ft. (600m), and many contain small streams. In contrast, the coral-based islands rarely rise above 30 ft. (9m) and tend to have no freshwater. Forty-six of the islands are inhabited, but 98 percent of the population live on the four main islands: Mahé, Praslin, Silhouette, and Felicité. Mahé is the largest and most populous of the Seychelles. The islands have a tropical climate, and many are covered in thick, lush vegetation. In places where land has been cleared for farming crops, such as tea, cinnamon, tobacco, bananas, and sweet potatoes, are cultivated. Many tropical fruit also grow on the islands. The Seychelles greatest natural resources are the fish-rich seas and the white, sandy beaches. The beaches and warm climate have enabled the Seychelles to attract more than 300,000 tourists every year.

# RÉUNION

A French overseas dependency, Réunion is an island in the Indian Ocean. Its inhabitants rely on growing sugarcane, tourism, and financial aid from France.

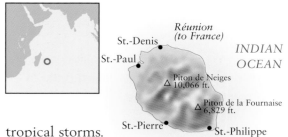

**Area:** 970 sq. mi. (2,510km²)
**Population:** 794,000
**Capital:** St.-Denis (172,000)
**Main languages spoken:** French, Creole
**Main religion:** Roman Catholic
**Currency:** euro
**Main exports:** sugar, machinery, lobsters
**Type of government:** dependency of France

Réunion is the largest of the Mascarene Islands, which lie in the western Indian Ocean. The island is located around 110 mi. (180km) southwest of Mauritius and around 420 mi. (680km) east of Madagascar. Volcanic in origin, most of Réunion's landscape consists of mountains that rise to their highest point of 10,066 ft. (3,068m) at Piton de Neiges in the center of the island. The climate is tropical, although cooler at higher altitudes, and there is much variation in rainfall. On the south and eastern sides rainfall is extremely heavy and can exceed 160 in. (406cm) per year, while on the north and western sides rainfall can be lower than 40 in. (102cm) per year. The island sometimes suffers from powerful tropical storms. The island was uninhabited when it was discovered by Portuguese explorers in the 1500s. In 1643 it was claimed by France, who named it Bourbon and imported slaves from Africa to work on sugar plantations. Renamed Réunion in 1793, the island became an overseas dependency of France in 1946. Réunion's economy has relied on agriculture for many years, particularly sugarcane, which has been the island's major crop for over one century. Other export products include rum, vanilla, and essences used in perfumes. The island's inhabitants are of mainly mixed African, Asian, and French descent.

# MAURITIUS

Mauritius is an island republic in the Indian Ocean. Once a colony of the Netherlands, France, and then Great Britain, it achieved independence in 1968.

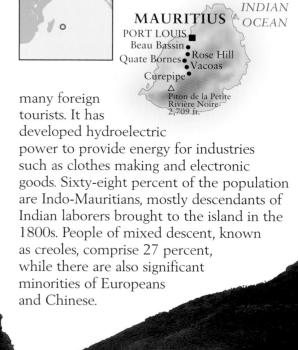

**Area:** 790 sq. mi. (2,040km²)
**Population:** 1,269,000
**Capital:** Port Louis (175,000)
**Main languages spoken:** Indo-Mauritian, Creole
**Main religions:** Hinduism, Christian, Islam
**Currency:** Mauritian rupee
**Main exports:** clothing, sugar, flowers, fish
**Type of government:** republic

Mauritius lies approximately 500 mi. (800km) east of the large island of Madagascar and consists of one large, dominant island with the name Mauritius and a number of smaller islands. Formed by volcanic activity, Mauritius has a mountainous southern region, a central plateau, and a lower-lying plain in the north. Traditionally reliant on sugarcane growing and processing, Mauritius has broadened its range of industries. Its white-sand beaches and coral reefs, together with its tropical climate, have attracted many foreign tourists. It has developed hydroelectric power to provide energy for industries such as clothes making and electronic goods. Sixty-eight percent of the population are Indo-Mauritians, mostly descendants of Indian laborers brought to the island in the 1800s. People of mixed descent, known as creoles, comprise 27 percent, while there are also significant minorities of Europeans and Chinese.

► Sugarcane plantations cover half the cultivated land and make up 15 percent of the country's export earnings.

# EASTERN AND SOUTHEAST ASIA

# EASTERN ASIA

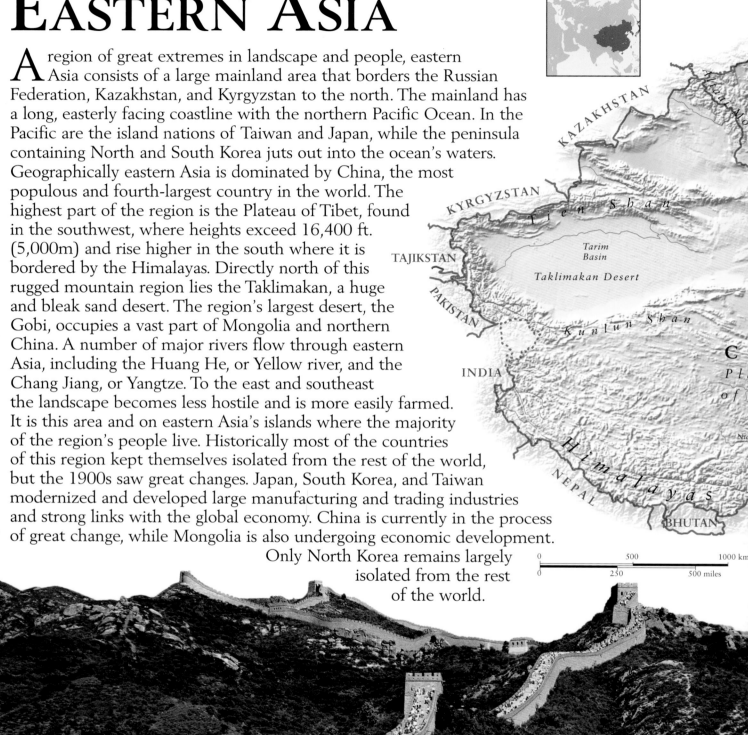

A region of great extremes in landscape and people, eastern Asia consists of a large mainland area that borders the Russian Federation, Kazakhstan, and Kyrgyzstan to the north. The mainland has a long, easterly facing coastline with the northern Pacific Ocean. In the Pacific are the island nations of Taiwan and Japan, while the peninsula containing North and South Korea juts out into the ocean's waters. Geographically eastern Asia is dominated by China, the most populous and fourth-largest country in the world. The highest part of the region is the Plateau of Tibet, found in the southwest, where heights exceed 16,400 ft. (5,000m) and rise higher in the south where it is bordered by the Himalayas. Directly north of this rugged mountain region lies the Taklimakan, a huge and bleak sand desert. The region's largest desert, the Gobi, occupies a vast part of Mongolia and northern China. A number of major rivers flow through eastern Asia, including the Huang He, or Yellow river, and the Chang Jiang, or Yangtze. To the east and southeast the landscape becomes less hostile and is more easily farmed. It is this area and on eastern Asia's islands where the majority of the region's people live. Historically most of the countries of this region kept themselves isolated from the rest of the world, but the 1900s saw great changes. Japan, South Korea, and Taiwan modernized and developed large manufacturing and trading industries and strong links with the global economy. China is currently in the process of great change, while Mongolia is also undergoing economic development. Only North Korea remains largely isolated from the rest of the world.

KAZAKHSTAN

Altai Mo

KYRGYZSTAN

Tien Shan

TAJIKSTAN

PAKISTAN

Tarim Basin

Taklimakan Desert

Kunlun Shan

C

Pla of

INDIA

Himalayas

NEPAL

BHUTAN

| 0 | 500 | 1000 km |
| 0 | 250 | 500 miles |

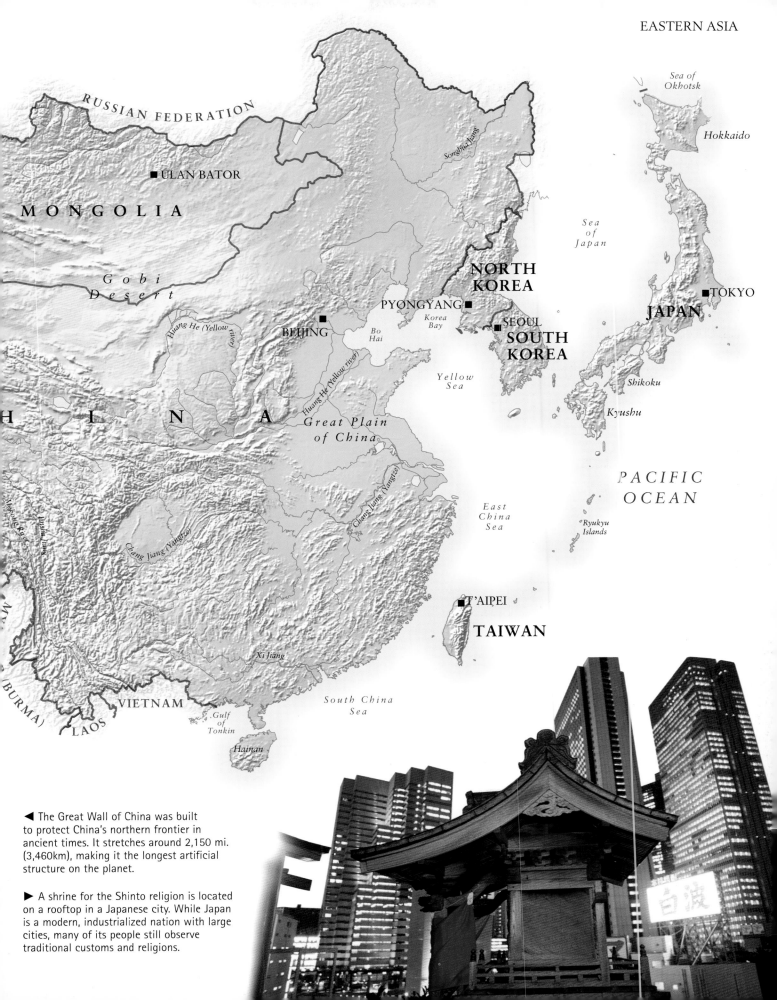

RUSSIAN FEDERATION

■ ULAN BATOR

M O N G O L I A

*G o b i
D e s e r t*

*Huang He (Yellow river)*

■ BEIJING

*Songhua Jiang*

*Sea
of
Japan*

Hokkaido

NORTH
KOREA

PYONGYANG ■

*Korea
Bay*

*Bo
Hai*

SEOUL ■
SOUTH
KOREA

JAPAN

TOKYO ■

H           I           N           A

*Huang He (Yellow river)*

*Great Plain
of China*

*Yellow
Sea*

Shikoku

*Kyushu*

*Chang Jiang (Yangtze)*

*East
China
Sea*

*PACIFIC
OCEAN*

*Ryukyu
Islands*

*Mekong Kiang*

*Dasha Jiang*

*Chang Jiang (Yangtze)*

■ T'AIPEI

TAIWAN

*Xi Jiang*

*South China
Sea*

(BURMA)

VIETNAM

LAOS

*Gulf
of
Tonkin*

*Hainan*

◄ The Great Wall of China was built
to protect China's northern frontier in
ancient times. It stretches around 2,150 mi.
(3,460km), making it the longest artificial
structure on the planet.

► A shrine for the Shinto religion is located
on a rooftop in a Japanese city. While Japan
is a modern, industrialized nation with large
cities, many of its people still observe
traditional customs and religions.

# CHINA

The home of advanced civilizations stretching back over 5,000 years, the People's Republic of China is the world's most populous and fourth-largest country.

**Area:** 3,691,442 sq. mi. (9,560,790km²)
**Population:** 1,328,886,000
**Capital:** Beijing (10,301,000)
**Main languages spoken:** Mandarin, Yue, Wu, Hakka, Xiang, Gan, Minbei, Minnan, Cantonese
**Main religions:** officially atheist; Buddhism, Taoism, Islam, Christian
**Currencies:** renminbi (yuan), Hong Kong dollar (legal only in Hong Kong), and pataca (legal only in Macau)
**Main exports:** machinery and equipment, textiles and clothing, footwear, toys and sports goods, minerals and metal products, electrical goods and office equipment
**Type of government:** Communist-Party-led state

▼ The high-rise waterfront of Hong Kong reflects this former British colony's status as one of the world's leading trade, banking, and finance centers. In 1997 control of Hong Kong was handed back to China.

China has an 8,990-mi.- (14,500-km-) long Pacific coastline and land borders of around 13,670 mi. (22,000km) with a total of 14 other nations. With enormous variation in climate and landscape, China can be broadly divided into three key regions: the southwest, the east and the north, and the northwest. The southwest is a cold, mountainous area containing the world's highest plateau, the Plateau of Tibet. Much of this region consists of frozen wastelands, marshlands, and salt lakes and is sparsely inhabited. The eastern region of China is where the majority of the country's huge population reside. Much of eastern China is at elevations below 1,312 ft. (400m), although highland regions do exist. Many rivers crisscross its land, which, over time, has created large floodplains and deltas that are fertile farming areas. The largest of China's rivers—and the longest in Asia—is the Chang Jiang, or Yangtze; 700 tributaries flow into the Chang Jiang as it completes its 3,920-mi.- (6,300-km-) long journey, flowing essentially eastward from the Kunlun Shan Mountains through central China before emptying into the Pacific just north of Shanghai. The

northwestern regions of China are largely highlands marked by large desert basins and some mountains. East of these areas the giant Gobi Desert extends through northern central China. Desert areas cover around 27 percent of China and are increasing annually owing to deforestation and overuse of dry soil on farms near deserts. Winds from the north generate giant sandstorms that envelop towns and cities, hamper transportation, and damage farmland. A 70-year project called the Great Green Wall seeks to plant millions of trees along the southern borders of the Gobi to help bar the further spread of deserts.

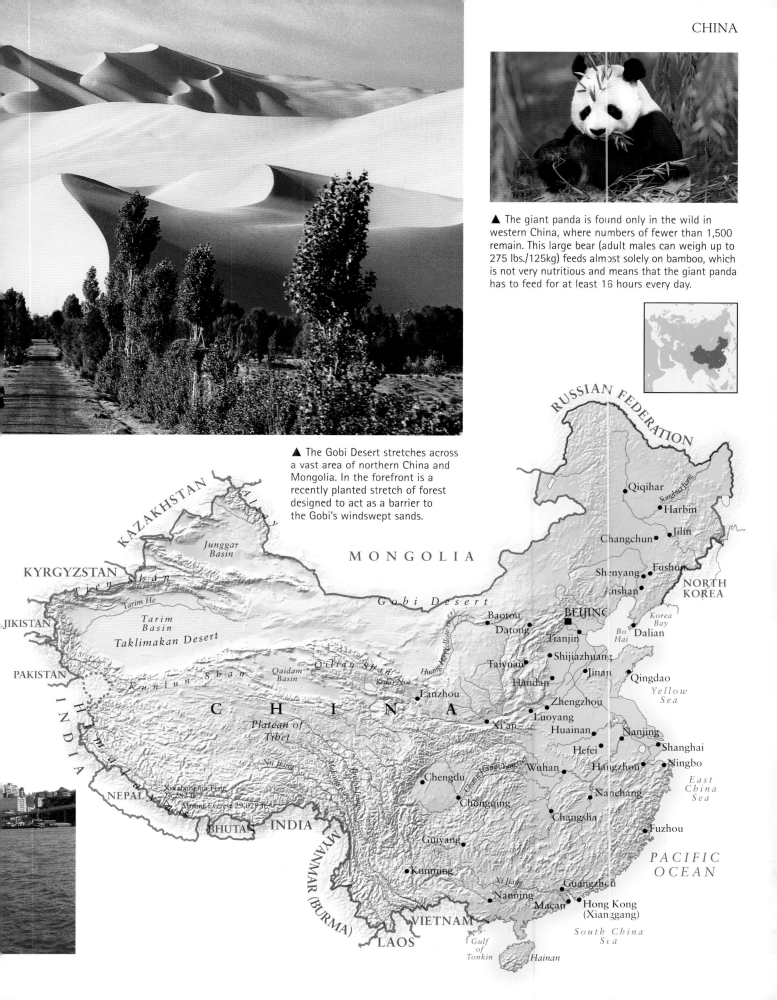

▲ The giant panda is found only in the wild in western China, where numbers of fewer than 1,500 remain. This large bear (adult males can weigh up to 275 lbs./125kg) feeds almost solely on bamboo, which is not very nutritious and means that the giant panda has to feed for at least 16 hours every day.

▲ The Gobi Desert stretches across a vast area of northern China and Mongolia. In the forefront is a recently planted stretch of forest designed to act as a barrier to the Gobi's windswept sands.

RUSSIAN FEDERATION

KAZAKHSTAN

*Altay*

*Junggar Basin*

MONGOLIA

KYRGYZSTAN

*Tien Shan*

*Tarim He*

*Tarim Basin*

Taklimakan Desert

TAJIKISTAN

PAKISTAN

*Kunlun Shan*

*Qaidam Basin*

*Qilian Shan*

*Koko Nor*

*Gobi Desert*

*Huang He (Yellow River)*

Baotou

Datong

BEIJING

Tianjin

Qiqihar

Harbin

Jilin

Changchun

Shenyang

Fushun

Anshan

NORTH KOREA

*Korea Bay*

Dalian

*Bo Hai*

CHINA

*Plateau of Tibet*

Lanzhou

Taiyuan

Handan

Shijiazhuang

Jinan

Zhengzhou

Luoyang

Xi'an

Qingdao

*Yellow Sea*

INDIA

*Himalaya*

NEPAL

Xixabangma Feng 26,282 ft.

Mount Everest 29,029 ft.

BHUTAN

INDIA

*Nu Jiang*

*Mekong River*

*Salween River*

Chengdu

Chongqing

*Chang Jiang (Yangtze)*

Wuhan

Huainan

Hefei

Nanchang

Changsha

Nanjing

Hangzhou

Shanghai

Ningbo

*East China Sea*

Fuzhou

MYANMAR (BURMA)

VIETNAM

LAOS

Guiyang

Kunming

Nanning

*Xi Jiang*

Guangzhou

Macau

Hong Kong (Xianggang)

PACIFIC OCEAN

*Gulf of Tonkin*

Hainan

*South China Sea*

## CHINA'S CLIMATE

China's climate varies greatly over its large area. Temperatures increase from north to south, and rainfall increases from northwest to southeast. Northeast China has a continental climate with warm and humid summers, long, cold winters, and rainfall under 30 in. (75cm) per year. The central lowlands contain the hottest areas of China and have an annual rainfall of 30–43 in. (76–110cm). The south is wetter, while the extreme subtropical south experiences monsoons. The northwest is arid, continental, and has cold winters. Western China experiences an extreme climate owing to its altitude and long distance from the sea. Rainfall is low in Tibet, where there are ten months of frost.

▼ Located 230 mi. (370km) northwest of Guangzhou, the spectacular scenery around the settlement of Guilin has been formed by erosion of the limestone rocks. Many tall pinnacles covered in vegetation exist, along with extensive and beautiful cave systems.

## A FARMING GIANT

Around 43 percent of the workforce are engaged in agriculture. One third of all cultivated land is sown with rice, which dominates farming in southern China and is the country's key staple food. Other cereal crops, particularly wheat, corn, millet, and barley, are also vital, along with oilseeds, soybeans, root vegetables, sugarcane, and sugar beets. China is also one of the world's leading growers of a number of crops, including peanuts, cotton, and tea. China's livestock numbers are

◄ Water buffalo are popular beasts of burden in China, especially in the wetter, rice-growing regions. In 2003 there were an estimated 23 million water buffalo in the country.

enormous, with 500 million pigs, 610 million ducks, and 3.6 billion chickens. Fish is also a vital part of the Chinese diet. Unusually, more than one half of China's annual catch consists of freshwater fish from rivers, lakes, and fish farms.

## MINING AND INDUSTRY

China has enormous mineral resources within its borders and is the world's leading producer of coal, graphite, and a number of commercially valuable metals, including titanium and tungsten. Mining also extracts large amounts of other metals, particularly iron ore, tin, copper, and bauxite, the ore from which aluminum is made. Much of the country's iron ore is concentrated in the northeast, which remains the center of the heavy metals industry. Oil production in 2008 was around 3.8 million barrels per day, although older oil fields in the east of the country have dwindling reserves. Energy

supplies are heavily reliant on burning coal, which has led to high levels of pollution in the cities. Since coming to power the communist government has made huge attempts to build up China's industries in order to compete in the world's markets. Steelmaking and metalworking industries, processing oil into chemicals, artificial fibers, and plastics, and the manufacture of fertilizers, heavy machinery, farm machinery, and railroad and motor vehicles are all major industries. China's textiles industry is the world's largest. Since the late 1980s, China has opened its borders to foreign investment and joint ventures with other countries. As a result, the economy has expanded rapidly. By 2008, China had the world's third-largest economy after the U.S. and Japan. However, most of the economic growth and prosperity have occurred in "special economic zones" in the east and in coastal areas. In other parts of China, especially the west, people contend with poor transportation, undeveloped industries, and a lower standard of living.

▲ Located in China's capital city of Beijing, the Temple of Heaven was traditionally where Chinese emperors used to pray to the gods for good harvests. Built in the 1400s, this beautiful temple was constructed from wood without using nails.

▼ A center of trade in Asia before the communists came to power, the bustling city of Shanghai is again attracting foreign visitors and trade.

▲ More than seven million people live in the small but heavily built-up Special Autonomous Region of Hong Kong. It is one of the world's most densely populated areas.

▼ Since it was built in the 1600s the breathtaking Potala Palace has been the traditional home of Tibet's spiritual leader, the Dalai Lama, who now lives in exile.

## COMMUNIST CHINA

While China makes large reforms to advance its economy in line with the world market, changes in the strict way the country is run have been minimal. The Chinese Communist Party (CCP) was formed in 1921 and came to power in 1949 after a bitter struggle with nationalist forces over a period of two decades. This struggle culminated in a four-year-long civil war (1945–1949) in which an estimated 12 million people died. The CCP, under its leader, Mao Zedong, embarked upon a huge series of reforms to transform much of China's economy and society. Some have been successful such as improving education and health care and developing new infrastructure and industries. Women's role in society has been improved, and China has grown as an economic power. Other policies, such as the Great Leap Forward in the late 1950s, proved to be disastrous. An attempt to reorganize China's rural people into farming and industrial communes saw harvests fall and an estimated 20 million people die of starvation. Communist China has also practiced much censorship of the media and has abused human rights to quell criticism. The Cultural Revolution (1966–1976) saw chaos and thousands of people executed. In more recent times student uprisings have also been violently suppressed.

## ONE FIFTH OF ALL PEOPLE

In 1949 there were an estimated 500 million people in China. By 2009, China's population had more than doubled, to

◀ Construction work on the Three Gorges Dam across the Chang Jiang river lasted from 1994 to 2009. This enormous 1.2-mi.- (2-km-) wide dam is a part of the world's biggest hydroelectric power program, scheduled to open in 2011. It is being built to generate enormous quantities of electricity and to allow large ships sail into China's interior. Environmentalists are concerned at the vast area of the river valley, which has been flooded, displacing over 1.5 million people.

▼ Chinese women work on an assembly line building electronics equipment. Electronics and electrical goods manufacturing are fast-growing industries in China. Around 90 million TV sets were produced in China in 2009.

more than 1.33 billion. Managing and feeding about one fifth of the world's population is a huge task, and China has sometimes embarked upon methods that are criticized by the outside world. For example, to curb the high birth rate China introduced very strict one-child-per-family policies in the 1970s. Greater family planning has resulted in a low birth rate, but still over 11 million Chinese babies are born every year. The continued rise in China's population is due mainly to the dramatic increase in life expectancy. Since 1950 better health care and the eradication of certain diseases have resulted in life expectancy more than doubling to just over 70 years. Despite industrialization and the growth of large cities, approximately 57 percent of China's population is rural. During its rule the communist government has attempted many policies to prevent the migration of rural peoples to its towns and cities, but city sizes are still increasing. China has more large cities than any other nation, with more than 60 having a population of over one million.

▲ Bordering Myanmar, Vietnam, and Laos to the south and Tibet to the west, the Chinese province of Yunnan is a region of plateaus and mountains.

▼ Discovered in 1974, the Terracotta Army is a collection of more than 6,000 full-size statues of soldiers and animals made from terracotta clay. An astonishingly large and beautiful collection of sculptures, the figures were designed to guard the tomb of the emperor Shi Huangdi, who ruled in the 200s B.C.

## PEOPLE, RELIGION, AND HISTORY

China contains over 55 different ethnic groups, but an estimated 91.5 percent are of Han Chinese origin. The largest minority, the Zhuang, are related to the Thai people and number more than 17 million. There are also sizable minorities of Manchu, Hui, Miao, and Uyghur peoples. Many of the largest populations of ethnic minorities are found in the border areas of China. Just over half of the Chinese people consider themselves nonreligious, while one fifth practice one of many forms of traditional folk religions. In addition, there are millions of Chinese who follow Buddhism, Islam, Taoism, and various forms of Christianity. Over 3,000 years ago the Zhou Dynasty arose, during which time the teachings of the philosopher Confucius (551–479 B.C.) became important, and his theories influence Chinese society to this day. The short-lived Qin Dynasty (221–206 B.C.) saw the unification of much of China and the building of the Great Wall along the country's northern frontier. The Han (202 B.C.–A.D. 220), Tang (618–907), and Song (960–1279) dynasties were times of great advances in science and the arts. The Mongols completed the first foreign conquest of the Chinese empire in the 1200s and were followed by the Ming Dynasty and then China's last dynasty, the Qing, which ended in 1912 when the country became a republic.

## AUTONOMOUS REGIONS

China has a number of autonomous regions in which a degree of local rule has been granted. Inner Mongolia to the north, Guangxi Zhuang to the south, and Xinjang Uyghur to the northwest are three of the largest of these regions, but in each dissent against Chinese rule has often been suppressed by force.

The best-known autonomous region of China is Tibet in the southwest. Cut off from neighboring areas by giant mountain chains on three sides, ethnic Tibetans make up over 90 percent of the total population of 2.8 million. Tibetans developed their own form of Buddhism led by the Dalai Lama as their national and spiritual leader. By turns independent or under Chinese rule for much of its existence, China invaded Tibet in 1950–1951. Since that time there has been much religious persecution of the Tibetan people, with many Buddhist monasteries, books, and artwork destroyed.

On China's south coast is the former British colony of Hong Kong, which was returned to China in 1997. Like Macau, a former Portuguese colony, it is an important trading center and has been made a Special Autonomous Region with some local self-rule.

# TAIWAN

**Officially known as the Republic of China, this large island lies 100 mi. (165km) off the coast of mainland China. Taiwan is in dispute with China over its independence.**

**Area:** 13,969 sq. mi. (36,179km²), including Quemoy and Matsu islands
**Population:** 23,120,000
**Capital:** Taipei (6,776,000)
**Main languages spoken:** Mandarin, Taiwanese
**Main religions:** Buddhism, Taoism, Confucianism, Christian
**Currency:** new Taiwan dollar
**Main exports:** nonelectrical machinery, electrical machinery, plastic articles, textiles, synthetic fibers, chemicals
**Type of government:** democracy

▼ A food stall in a night market in Taiwan's largest city, the capital, T'aipei. Since World World II Taiwan has undergone rapid urbanization.

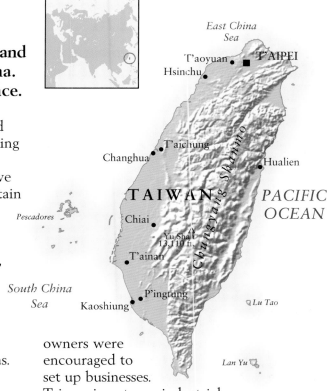

Taiwan consists of Taiwan Island and a number of smaller islands, including Pescadores. More than 60 percent is mountainous, with over 150 peaks above 9,840 ft. (3,000m). Many of the mountain slopes are covered in forests. Most Taiwanese live along the broad and fertile coastal plains to the west and south. Taiwan has heavy annual rainfall, with a tropical climate in the south and a subtropical climate in the higher elevations in the north. Agriculture contributes to less than two percent of Taiwan's income, with the major crops being rice, corn, pineapples, and bananas. The Taiwanese fishing industry is important and exports mainly to Japan.

## ECONOMIC SUCCESS
Taiwan has relatively few mineral resources and is not an oil producer but has become an economic success. Land reforms in the 1950s gave many farm workers control of land, while former land owners were encouraged to set up businesses.

Taiwan is a strong industrial nation, with four fifths of its industry devoted to manufacturing a wide range of products, particularly electrical and electronic goods, textiles, plastics, and motor vehicles. Since the early 1990s Taiwan has been one of the world's top-five producers of computer hardware. The Taiwanese people have one of the highest standards of living in Asia.

## TAIWAN AND CHINA
Formerly called Formosa, Taiwan became part of the Chinese empire in 1624 and for half a century (1895–1945) was ruled by the Japanese. In the late 1940s the communist takeover of China saw almost two million people flee to Taiwan. The former leader of China, Chiang Kai-shek, refused to recognize the Communist Party government and established his own administration on the island. Mainland China still considers Taiwan to be one of its provinces, and in 1971 Taiwan lost its seat in the UN. Today only a small number of countries recognize Taiwan as an independent nation, and the country's relationship with China dominates politics. With one of the world's top-ten largest armies, a large proportion of the government's expenditure goes to defense.

# MONGOLIA

A large, remote country of mountains, plains, and deserts, Mongolia was once the center of a powerful empire. Today this isolated nation is one of the poorest in Asia.

**Area:** 603,900 sq. mi. (1,564,100km²)
**Population:** 2,684,000
**Capital:** Ulan Bator (1,072,000)
**Main language spoken:** Khalkha Mongol
**Main religion:** Tibetan Buddhism
**Currency:** tugrik
**Main exports:** mineral products (particularly copper), live animals, textiles (cashmere and wool), animal products (including hides)
**Type of government:** republic

Mongolia is surrounded by the Russian Federation to the north and China to the south. Much of its land consists of a plateau lying between 2,952–4,920 ft. (900–1,500m) in elevation. This plateau is broken up by mountain ranges, especially to the west, where the Altai Mountains rise to heights of above 13,120 ft. (4,000m). Large, grass-covered prairies exist in the northeast and northwest of the country, supporting flocks of sheep and herds of goats, cattle, and horses. Central and southeastern Mongolia are covered by the hostile Gobi Desert. This giant desert measures over 990 mi. (1,600km) west to east and over 590 mi. (950km) north to south. Its surface consists largely of rock and gravel. To the southeast the Gobi is extremely arid and supports minimal life. Elsewhere in the Gobi tough grass, scrubs, and thornbushes provide meager vegetation for the herds and groups of Mongolia's nomadic desert dwellers. Water comes from the occasional shallow lake and watering holes.

## CLIMATE, RESOURCES, AND PEOPLE

Mongolia's climate is harsh, with great extremes in which the temperature can vary as much as 86°F (30°C) in a single day. The summers tend to be short, cool to mild with low rainfall, and have many clear days. The winters are long and bitterly cold with temperatures ranging between 5 and -22°F (-15 and -30°C).

► This Mongolian farmer cuts and harvests hay using Bactrian camels to pull his simple plow. Over 250,000 camels are raised in the country, mainly as beasts of burden.

◄ A young child fetches water from a frozen river near the Mongolian capital city of Ulan Bator.

Especially severe winters, called Zud, can devastate the livestock on which many Mongolians depend. This happened in 2009–2010. Agriculture and the processing of agricultural products into foods, cloth, and leather goods are a vital part of the Mongolian economy. Mongolia is also rich in a number of minerals, including iron ore, coal, copper, lead, and tungsten. The country's harsh climate and isolated location have so far prevented much of its mineral resources from being exploited.

From 1206 onward Mongolia was the center of the great Mongol empire, which extended throughout much of Asia and was feared for its fierce horse-riding warriors. Today the people live in one of the most undeveloped nations in Asia. Transportation links are sparse. The country has just 1,755 mi. (2,824km) of paved roads and limited water and rail links. Many Mongolians have given up their rural way of life and have moved to towns. An estimated 36 percent live below the poverty line.

▼ Nomadic Mongolian herders eat a meal inside their large, portable, tentlike home—a yurt.

# NORTH KOREA

**North Korea is run by a communist government that has kept this mountainous country isolated since the Korean Peninsula was partitioned in 1948.**

**Area:** 47,399 sq. mi. (122,762km²)
**Population:** 24,052,000
**Capital:** Pyongyang (2,581,000)
**Main language spoken:** Korean
**Main religions:** nonreligious majority; Buddhism, Confucianism, Chondogyo
**Currency:** won
**Main exports:** minerals, metallurgical products, armaments, agricultural products, textiles
**Type of government:** communist state

▼ A political festival in progress in a stadium in North Korea's capital city of Pyongyang. Only people who are loyal to the strict communist regime are allowed to live in the city.

The Democratic People's Republic of Korea occupies the northern half of the Korean Peninsula. Four fifths of its land are mountainous, with many slopes covered with forests of coniferous trees. The mountains rise in elevation to the north, where Paektu-San (9,000 ft./2,744m), the country's highest peak, is located. Most of the east coast of the country is steep and rugged with few islands. To the west the slopes are more gentle and end in plains and a network of river estuaries. The country's lowlands, comprising one fifth of the land, are found mainly in the west and are where most of its people live. Farming is also concentrated there, and the country's major crops are rice, corn and other cereals, potatoes, and other vegetables. North Korea has a continental climate with hot summers and cold winters. The climate is influenced by both the cold winds from Siberia and the monsoon winds from east Asia. During the summer months the monsoons bring much of the country's rainfall.

## AN ISOLATED COMMUNIST NATION

Since its formation North Korea has been run by a strict communist government, with the military exerting a powerful influence. The state owns almost all farms and industries and distributes the wealth among its people. In practice loyal members of the Korean Workers Party (KWP), the only political party allowed by law, benefit more than others. The country's media is state-controlled, and opponents of the government are often dealt with harshly.

◄ Opened in 1984, the Mansudae Assembly Hall in Pyongyang is one of the major governmental buildings of North Korea. It is used to hold sessions of the Supreme People's Assembly.

While other communist nations have changed greatly, North Korea has remained apart and largely isolated. Trade and communications with the rest of the world are limited. This closed nation has recently opened its borders to aid and limited foreign investment as its economy has declined. Important industries in North Korea include the mining of coal, iron ore, tungsten, zinc, and other metals and heavy and engineering industries producing refined metals, machinery, and chemicals. The country produces almost two thirds of its electricity from hydroelectric power, but shortages are common. From 1995 to 1999 successive droughts and floods damaged vast tracts of farmland and brought a famine to North Korea in which as many as two million people died. Chronic food shortages remain.

## NORTH AND SOUTH RELATIONS

The Korean Peninsula had a long history of settlement and civilization before coming under, first, Chinese and, by 1910, Japanese control. In 1948 the peninsula was partitioned into two separate nations. Two years later North Korea launched an invasion of South Korea in an attempt to unify Korea under a single communist government. The Korean War (1950–1953) was a bitter conflict in which North Korea was supported by China, and South Korea was supported by a coalition of forces, mainly from the U.S. By the end of the war over one million Koreans and many thousands of foreign troops had died. Relations between the two nations have remained difficult, with many incidents since this time. Despite a summit meeting between the two countries' leaders in 2000, the first time they had ever met directly, there remains considerable tension between North and South. In 2006 and 2009 North Korea tested nuclear devices, and the country's emergence as a nuclear power raised international concern.

▼ A class for North Korean schoolchildren is held outside. North Korean education starts with preschool. Education emphasizes science and technology, and English is compulsory as a second language for students above the age of 14.

# SOUTH KOREA

Occupying the southern half of the Korean Peninsula, South Korea industrialized rapidly and is now one of Asia's most powerful nations.

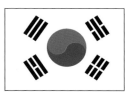

**Area:** 38,402 sq. mi. (99,461km²)
**Population:** 50,034,000
**Capital:** Seoul (21,300,000)
**Main language spoken:** Korean
**Main religions:** Christian, Buddhism
**Currency:** won
**Main exports:** electronic products, machinery and transportation equipment (including motor vehicles), steel, ships, textiles, clothing and footwear
**Type of government:** republic, with power centralized in a strong executive

Over two thirds of South Korea are mountainous, with the largest lowland areas to the west and the south. South Korea's western coastline is indented, and most of the country's 3,000 islands lie off this coast in the Yellow Sea. The largest of Korea's islands is Cheju, south of the mainland. With a subtropical climate, many fruit are grown there, and the island attracts tourists to its spectacular scenery. Ullung, the largest island off the eastern coast, serves as a major fishery base. In 2006 a total of 3.3 million tons (3 million metric tonnes) of fish were caught by South Korean vessels. The country's only land border is with North Korea to the north. It features the demilitarized zone, or DMZ, a 2.5-mi.- (4-km-) wide strip of land that runs from the west coast to the east coast of the peninsula. Thousands of troops from the forces of the two countries are stationed on both sides of the DMZ. Tensions remain high between the two nations.

▼ Sungnyemun, or the South Gate, was originally a grand entrance to the capital city of Seoul and is the oldest wooden structure in the city. Seoul was also the capital of Korea from the late 1300s until 1948.

## THE KOREAN PEOPLE

The population of the Korean Peninsula is unique in Southeast Asia in that it is made up almost entirely of one single ethnic group that has lived in the region for over 2,000 years. Between 1950–1990 the country's population more than doubled. Large numbers of people, particularly the young, moved to South Korea's cities, and now 81 percent of the population are urban. Farming is still important in rural areas, with rice, potatoes, and cereals the biggest crops. The country's high population density has created environmental pressures, with serious air pollution in some cities.

## AN ECONOMIC MIRACLE

South Korea had a largely agricultural and underdeveloped economy before the 1960s. From 1962 onward a series of five-year plans sought to build up the country's manufacturing industries, assisted by investment from foreign companies and aid, particularly from Japan and the U.S. South Korea's economy boomed as a result, growing by around nine percent every year between 1970 and the early 1990s. The country has become a giant in manufacturing areas such as shipbuilding, motor vehicle manufacturing, high-tech electronics, and computers. Much of the industry is run by enormous enterprises—known as *chaebol*, or conglomerates—such as Samsung or Hyundai. Most of its major industrial centers are located on or near the coastline, allowing ships to import many fuels and raw materials and to transport manufactured goods all over the world. The country's biggest port is Pusan, which is also South Korea's second-largest city after Seoul. South Korea has relatively few mineral resources, apart from raw materials used in the cement, glass, and ceramics industries. It is not an oil producer but refines crude oil imported from other nations. Around 40 percent of its electricity is generated using nuclear power.

▲ Cranes in Hyundai Heavy Industries' giant shipbuilding yard in the city of Ulsan. The world's largest shipbuilders, Hyundai Heavy Industry accounts for around 15 percent of the global shipbuilding market. South Korea is the world's 15th-largest economy.

▼ South Korean border guards in the heart of the demilitarized zone (DMZ), a heavily armed border zone separating North and South Korea.

# JAPAN

The island nation of Japan lies on the western edge of the Pacific Ocean. A land of ancient and rich culture, the country has become a world economic superpower.

**Area:** 145,877 sq. mi. (377,819km²)
**Population:** 127,918,000
**Capital:** Tokyo (37,520,000)
**Main language spoken:** Japanese
**Main religions:** Buddhism, Shintoism
**Currency:** yen
**Main exports:** motor vehicles, electrical and electronic equipment (particularly semiconductors and computers), office machinery, chemicals, scientific and optical equipment, iron and steel products
**Type of government:** parliamentary democracy

Japan is an island archipelago that extends over 1,800 mi. (2,900km) in a roughly north-south direction. It is separated from mainland Asia to the west by the Sea of Japan. The country's territory includes more than 1,000 smaller islands and four main islands, which are from north to south: Hokkaido, the most rural, Honshu, the largest, Shikoku, and Kyushu. South of Kyushu the Ryuku island chain, including Okinawa Island, arcs in a southerly direction toward Taiwan. Japan's four main islands are located close enough for them all to be linked by tunnels, bridges, or highways. Together they comprise almost 98 percent of Japan's landmass and are where the large majority of Japanese live.

Japan's climate is varied in part owing to the fact that its land covers around 17 degrees of latitude. Winds from Siberia and cold ocean waters influence the climate of Hokkaido and northern Honshu, where the summers are short and the winters are long and severe, with plenty of snowfall.

Hokkaido's largest city, Sapporo, is a renowned winter sports center. Southern Honshu, Shikoku, and Kyushu enjoy longer, warmer, and more humid summers and milder winters partly created by warmer Pacific winds and the warm, fast-moving Kuroshio ocean current, which travels northeast from the Philippines. Typhoons can strike between June and October. The heavy rains and fierce winds can damage houses and crops. The Ryuku islands experience a subtropical climate. Precipitation also varies greatly, with Hokkaido the driest region, averaging just over 40 in. (100cm) per year. In contrast, central Honshu's mountains can receive 150 in. (380cm) per year.

## JAPANESE FLORA AND FAUNA

Japan has rich plant life, with over 17,000 species. Forests cover over 60 percent of the land, particularly coniferous forests, although large parts of Honshu are covered in deciduous trees. Larger land animals include bears, wild boars, deer, and one species of monkey, the Japanese macaque. Over 400 species of birds exist.

## VOLCANOES AND EARTHQUAKES

Japan is located on the meeting point of three of Earth's tectonic plates, and its landscape has been shaped by plate movement for millions of years. Japan's terrain is largely mountainous, with coastal plains on which almost all of the country's cities are located. More than 200 volcanoes exist, of which 77 are considered active. Examples of the volatility of Earth's crust below can be seen both in the numerous hot springs and occasional tsunamis, which tend to strike the country's eastern coast. An estimated 800–1,000 earthquakes strike Japan every year.

▲ A bullet train on the Shinkansen high-speed railroad line passes by a rice paddy—a typical Japanese scene of the traditional alongside the modern. The Shinkansen trains offer some of the most rapid land transportation in the world, reaching speeds in excess of 160 mph (260km/h).

◄ A national symbol of Japan, the spectacular volcanic cone of Mount Fuji (Fuji san) lies approximately 60 mi. (100km) west of Tokyo. With a height of 12,385 ft. (3,776m), it is Japan's highest point. Although it has not erupted since 1707, Mount Fuji is not considered extinct and could erupt again in the future.

▼ Hikone Castle, one of the best preserved in Japan, lies on the eastern shore of Lake Biwa, around 33 mi. (53km) northeast of Kyoto. Construction of the castle began in 1603, and the city of the same name developed around it.

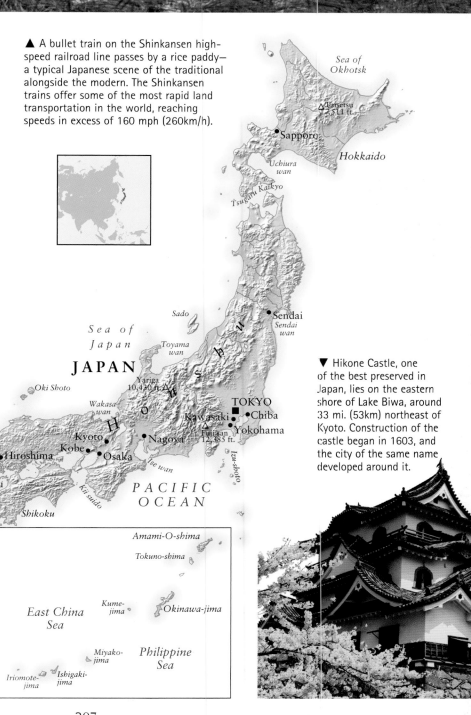

### Map labels

Sea of Okhotsk
Taisetsu 7,511 ft.
Sapporo
Hokkaido
Uchiura wan
Tsugaru Kaikyo
Sado
Sea of Japan
JAPAN
Toyama wan
Sendai
Sendai wan
Oki Shoto
Yariga 10,430 ft.
Wakasa wan
TOKYO
Tsushima
Kawasaki
Chiba
Yokohama
Kyoto
Nagoya
Fuji san 12,385 ft.
Kobe
Izu-shoto
Osaka
Ise wan
Yamaguchi
Hiroshima
Fukuoka
Kitakyushu
Kii suido
PACIFIC OCEAN
Shikoku
Nagasaki
Kumamoto
Amami-O-shima
Kagoshima
Tokuno-shima
Kyushu
Tanega-shima
Yaku-shima
Kume-jima
Okinawa-jima
East China Sea
Tokara Retto
Miyako-jima
Philippine Sea
Amami Oshima
Iriomote-jima
Ishigaki-jima

▲ A Japanese rocket is assembled at a Mitsubishi Heavy Industries factory. Japan is one of the small and exclusive group of nations that has launched space vehicles. Its first satellite was launched in 1970, and the Nozomi space probe reached Mars in 2003.

## AGRICULTURE AND FISHING

Although only around 13 percent of the country is suitable for cultivation, advanced, intensive farming and irrigation methods and government support have enabled Japan to be self-sufficient in its key staple foodstuff, rice. More than 40 percent of the cultivated land is devoted to rice production, but other crops are grown, including potatoes, sugar beets, onions, cucumbers, and mandarin oranges. Fish and seafood are a major part of the Japanese diet, and the country's fishing fleet is one of the biggest in the world. Japan has also developed aquaculture, or fish-farming techniques.

## PEOPLE AND CITIES

Japan's rugged landscape means that little more than one fifth of its area is habitable, yet the country is the tenth-most populous in the world. People tend to live in densely populated towns and cities, especially on Honshu, which accounts for four fifths of the population. The capital, Tokyo, in which 37.5 million people live, is the world's largest metropolitan area. Ninety-nine percent of Japanese share the same ethnic and cultural background. Small minorities of Koreans, a native people of northern Japan called the Ainu, and small handfuls of foreign workers also exist. Japan has a rapidly aging population. By 2009, 22 percent of its people were aged over 65.

## A RICH AND UNIQUE CULTURE

Most Japanese practice Buddhism as a religion but also follow some traditions of the Shinto religion. For long periods of history Japan has remained

▼ A busy street scene at the heart of the world's largest metropolis, Tokyo. The city was known by the name of Edo until 1869, when it became the capital of Japan.

isolated from the rest of the world, absorbing influences from afar. This, along with its cramped living conditions, has given rise to a complex series of manners and behavior. Respect for elders, superiors, and companies is strong, and many ceremonies and traditions exist that are unique to the country. Japan's art, literature, music, and drama are world renowned, and the Japanese are among the world's most avid readers—68.5 million newspapers are sold every day, and around 1.5 billion books are sold every year.

## A DYNAMIC ECONOMY

Japan first industrialized in the late 1800s, retaining its own culture but borrowing industrial ideas from the West. At around the same time it started to expand its empire, fighting wars with China and Russia and capturing much territory in east Asia. In World War II Japan was aligned with Germany and suffered a devastating defeat, surrendering after atomic bombs were dropped on Hiroshima and Nagasaki. Japan rebuilt its economy, embracing new technology. Forced to disband its costly military forces and helped by foreign aid, the Japanese economy boomed until the 1990s. By that time it had become the second-wealthiest and technologically most advanced economy in the world. Japan owns more than half of the world's industrial robots and has heavily invested

in higher education and research. It is one of the world's leading producers of many goods, as well as chemicals, textiles, and steel. Japan's government works closely with industry, many workers are employed for life, and many Japanese companies trade with each other in relationships called *keiretsu*, which makes it difficult for foreign companies to sell into Japan. In the past Japan was ruled by clans, emperors, and rival feudal lords called shoguns. Japan still has an emperor, but his position is ceremonial, and power lies with the prime minister and the largest party in the Diet, or parliament.

▲ Ritsurin Park is one of the largest and most beautiful of Japan's many traditional gardens. It was built during the Edo Period (1603–1868) and covers an area of 8,395,850 sq. ft. (780,000m²).

▼ The traditional Japanese thatched roofed housing, known as *Gassho-zukuri*, has made Shirakawa village a UNESCO World Heritage site and a popular destination for tourists from Japan and overseas.

# SOUTHEAST ASIA

Lying east of India and south of China, Southeast Asia consists of a mainland region and over 15,000 islands stretching through the Indian and Pacific oceans. Over 13,700 of these islands form the nation of Indonesia and the biggest island in the region, Borneo, which is the third largest in the world. Lying on the meeting points of three of Earth's major tectonic plates—the Eurasian, Indian-Australian, and Pacific—much of the mainland is mountainous, while the majority of the islands have been formed through volcanic action. The region remains one of the most volcanically active on Earth. Southeast Asia has been settled for thousands of years, and there is a great diversity of languages and cultures. Buddhism is the most popular religion among the people of the mainland nations, while Islam is practiced by around two fifths of Southeast Asians, in part owing to the large Muslim population in Indonesia. Sizable Christian and Hindu communities also exist in the region. From the 1500s and 1600s into the 1900s almost all of Southeast Asia was under rule by the colonial powers of Great Britain, France, Portugal, and the Netherlands. While war and conflict have devastated some of the nations of this region, most have developed modern, industrial, and service economies, which has brought prosperity and has led to the growth of large, modern cities.

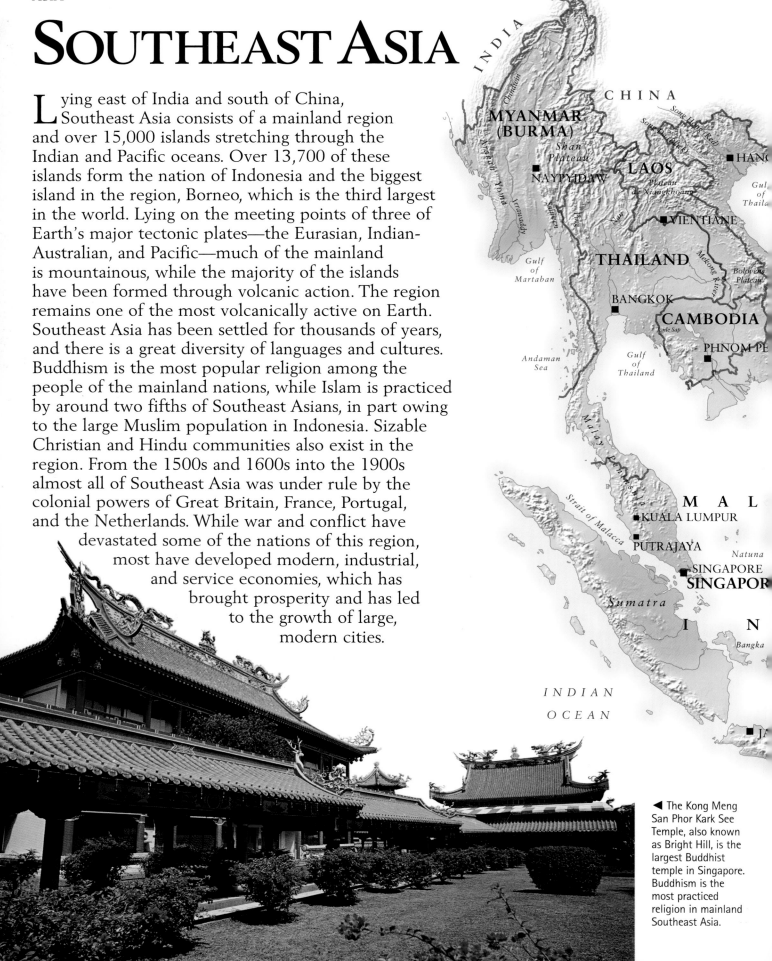

◀ The Kong Meng San Phor Kark See Temple, also known as Bright Hill, is the largest Buddhist temple in Singapore. Buddhism is the most practiced religion in mainland Southeast Asia.

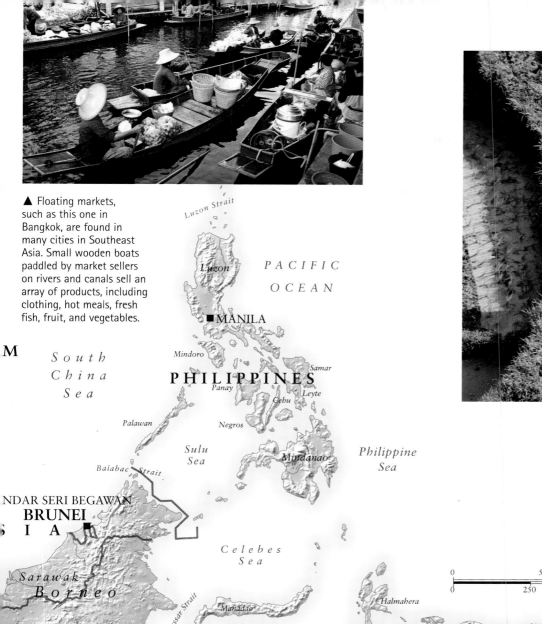

▲ Floating markets, such as this one in Bangkok, are found in many cities in Southeast Asia. Small wooden boats paddled by market sellers on rivers and canals sell an array of products, including clothing, hot meals, fresh fish, fruit, and vegetables.

▲ A worker tends a rice field on the Indonesian island of Bali. Rice is the single most important crop in Southeast Asia, and in many places two crops are grown each year. The region experiences a tropical climate with heavy rainfall in most areas.

▶ Many Southeast Asian cities, such as Malaysia's largest, Kuala Lumpur, have developed and grown at a rapid rate in the past 50 years.

Luzon Strait

PACIFIC
OCEAN

Luzon

■ MANILA

M

South
China
Sea

Mindoro

Samar

PHILIPPINES

Panay

Cebu
Leyte

Palawan

Negros

Sulu
Sea

Mindanao

Philippine
Sea

Balabac Strait

NDAR SERI BEGAWAN

BRUNEI

S I A

Celebes
Sea

O N E S I A

Sarawak

Borneo

Makassar Strait

Manadao

Molucca
Sea

Halmahera

Celebes

Seram

West
Papua

New Guinea

Moluccas

PAPUA
NEW
GUINEA

ava
Sea

Banda
Sea

Kepulauan
Kai

Kepulauan
Aru

Flores
Sea

Kepulauan
Tanimbar

Arafura
Sea

Bali Lombok Sumbawa Flores

DILI ■

EAST
TIMOR

Lesser Sunda Islands

Timor

Sumba

500 km

1000 km

250

500 miles

# THAILAND

**Thailand is a rapidly industrializing country with a large tourist industry. In 2006 the prime minister was removed from power during a military coup.**

**Area:** 198,115 sq. mi. (513,115km²)
**Population:** 67,041,000
**Capital:** Bangkok (11,971,000)
**Main languages spoken:** Thai, Chinese
**Main religion:** Buddhism
**Currency:** baht
**Main exports:** electrical machinery (particularly computers and transistors), nonelectrical machinery, seafood and live fish, clothing, rice, plastics
**Type of government:** kingdom; limited democracy

▼ Wat Phra Si Sanphet is a beautiful Buddhist monastery found in Ayutthaya, the ancient capital of Thailand.

A series of mountain ranges cross Thailand and are at their highest and most extensive in the north. The Khorat Plateau, to the northeast, comprises over one fourth of the country's land area. This flat, relatively barren land is the poorest region of the country. The fertile central plains are the most densely populated part of Thailand. This region includes the Bangkok metropolitan area and is known as "Thailand's Rice Bowl." The country produced more than 33 million tons (30 million metric tonnes) of rice in 2008 and is one of the world's top-three exporters of rice. South of the central plains is the part of Thailand that occupies the Malay Peninsula and includes a number of beautiful islands and beaches. Tin mining, rubber cultivation, and fishing are also practiced in this region. Thailand's annual fish and

shellfish catch in 2007 was 3 million tons (2.7 million metric tonnes). The country experiences a warm and wet tropical climate, with the peninsula in the south receiving almost twice the amount of the rainfall of central and northern areas. Thailand is rich in natural resources. Among the known mineral deposits are tin, coal, gold, lead, zinc, and precious gemstones. Oil production is minimal, but Thailand exploits its natural gas reserves. Around 28 percent of the country is forested with large, valuable hardwood forests, especially in the north and coastal areas. Many species of animals, including elephants, tigers, leopards, crocodiles, gibbons, and 50 species of snakes, inhabit the jungles and forests.

## INDUSTRIALIZATION AND MIGRATION

Thailand has industrialized greatly since the 1970s and 1980s, with electronics and textiles the key industries, while the service sector is dominated by tourism, with over 14 million tourists in 2007. The gap in the standard of living between people in urban and rural areas has widened dramatically, leading to a large migration of the

◀ Thailand's capital city, Bangkok, has exploded in population numbers and size in the past 40 years. The MBK shopping and entertainments center in the heart of Bangkok is just one of many modern developments in the city.

population into Thailand's towns and cities. Bangkok, in particular, is straining under the huge increase in population, with some of the worst traffic congestion and pollution anywhere in the world. The first stage of Bangkok's mass transit system was opened in 1999, and there are initiatives to relocate industries away from Bangkok.

## THE KING AND HIS PEOPLE

Around 80 percent of the people of Thailand are Thai, a people believed to have originated in southwest China and moved to Southeast Asia around 2,000 years ago. The Chinese are the largest minority group, making up around 11 percent of the population, and there are smaller numbers of Malay Muslims, Cambodians, and Vietnamese. The hills of the far north and northeast are home to approximately 650,000 tribespeople with their own culture and language. Eighty-five percent of Thais practice Buddhism, but many Muslims live in the southern regions that border Malaysia. In 1932 a new constitution moved much political power from the monarch to the people. However, the country's King Bhumibol Adulyadej has remained as monarch since 1946 and wields great influence, but the country has been politically unstable in the 21st century.

▼ A floating restaurant on the banks of the Mae Nam Khwae Noi river, known in English as the Kwai river. The river rises on the border with Myanmar west of Nakhon Sawan. It is known outside of the country for the bridge built across it by Allied prisoners of war during World War II.

# MYANMAR (BURMA)

**Beset by political troubles, Myanmar is an agricultural nation with large tracts of hardwood forests. It is one of the least known of all Southeast Asian countries.**

**Area:** 261,228 sq. mi. (676,577km²)
**Population:** 52,171,000
**Capital:** Naypyidaw (418,000)
**Main languages spoken:** Burmese, Shan, Karen, Rakhine
**Main religion:** Buddhism
**Currency:** kyat
**Main exports:** clothing, food, live animals, wood and wood products, precious stones, natural gas
**Type of government:** military

Myanmar is bordered by Bangladesh, India, China, and Thailand. It is a highly mountainous country with giant and largely impassable mountain ranges running in a horseshoe shape along its western, northern, and eastern sides. Lower mountains are also found in more central areas. The mountains reach their highest in the northern range, where the peak of Hkakado Razi reaches 19,289 ft. (5,881m), making it the highest point in Southeast Asia. Enclosed within the horseshoe of mountain ranges are the country's lowland areas, comprised mainly of valleys and deltas of the Chindwin and Irrawaddy rivers. The rich, fertile soils and the monsoon climate in this region make it the center of the country's agriculture, employing the majority of Myanmar's people, principally growing rice, pulses, corn, and sugarcane. Myanmar extends south, occupying a narrow western strip of the Malay Peninsula. Its coastline tends to be rocky with some good natural harbors. The Irrawaddy is the country's principal river. It originates in the Chinese region of Tibet and flows north to south through almost the entire length of Myanmar. Navigable for over 870 mi. (1,400km), it is an important transportation route, especially for the movement of timber.

◄ Myanmar laborers cut and transport bamboo for a government project. Bamboo is used as an important building material for houses, especially in the countryside.

▼ One of over 2,000 Buddhist pagodas found in the city of Pagan. A historic center of Myanmar in the past, Pagan was founded in 849 on the banks of the Irrawaddy river and lies around 300 mi. (500km) north of Rangoon.

## OVEREXPLOITATION OF RESOURCES

Almost half of Myanmar is forested, and the supplies of teak and other hardwoods are among the country's most valuable resources, though at severe risk from overexploitation. Along the coasts there are tidal mangrove forests and, in the mountainous north, pine forests. The country has varied wildlife, including rare creatures such as red pandas, rhinoceroses, and tigers—the latter two species are sometimes killed to make medicinal products. A number of minerals are mined, including copper, lead, and silver, and also sapphire and ruby gemstones. Industry is limited, under state control, and mainly confined to processing farming and timber products.

## A BUDDHIST STRONGHOLD

Buddhism is the religion of around 70 percent of the population. Buddhism has a great influence on the everyday life of most of Myanmar's population, with Buddhist temples the center of most villages and small towns. Small minorities of Christians, Muslims, and Hindus also live in the country.

## INEQUALITIES AND CONFLICTS

Burmans comprise around 56 percent of the population, with smaller numbers of many ethnic groups, including Shan, Karen, Kachin, Mon, and Chin peoples. Largely ruled by the military since independence from the British in 1948, the country has seen internal conflict between the majority Burmans and these minority groups become widespread and violent. Opposition is not tolerated, and human rights abuses are frequent. The military brutally suppressed pro-democracy protests in 2007, and the authorities used forced labor to construct public works.

▼ Over 100 different species of trees are commercially exploited in Myanmar's forests such as this one 30 mi. (50km) west of the city of Tanggyi. Teakwood is the single most important commodity.

# VIETNAM

**Vietnam is a country of great river deltas, mountain chains, and coastal plains. Its people endured long periods of war and oppression during the 1900s.**

**Area:** 127,149 sq. mi. (329,315km²)
**Population:** 85,790,000
**Capital:** Hanoi (2,632,000)
**Main languages spoken:** Vietnamese, French, Chinese, English
**Main religions:** Buddhism, Roman Catholic, Taosim, indigenous beliefs
**Currency:** dong
**Main exports:** crude petroleum, fish and fish products, coffee, rice, rubber, clothing
**Type of government:** communist

▼ Vietnamese fishermen use small, simple boats to navigate West Lake near the capital city of Hanoi. In 2005 approximately 2.8 million tons (2.5 million metric tonnes) of fish, crab, and shrimp were caught, mainly from the South China Sea but also from inland rivers and streams. However, many freshwater and marine fishing grounds are now in danger of being overfished.

The Socialist Republic of Vietnam is a long, S-shaped country that borders China to the north and has a 1,990-mi.-(3,200-km-) long coastline. The northwest of the country is mountainous, with the country's highest point, the peak of Fan Si Pan, reaching an elevation of 10,309 ft. (3,142m). Almost two thirds of the country are dominated by highlands, with the crest of this mountain range forming most of Vietnam's long westerly border with Laos and, farther south, Cambodia. Much of the mountain slopes are forested or have been cleared to create plantations growing tea, rubber, and coffee. Vietnam is one of the world's five-largest exporters of coffee. To the east of the highlands the land forms a long coastal plain bordering the Gulf of Tonkin and the South China Sea. Fishing is important to many Vietnamese living on this plain.

Vietnam has a mainly tropical climate with warm-to-hot temperatures and heavy rainfall. Seasonal monsoon winds bring rains and occasional typhoons during the summer and fall. In the mountainous north the climate is subtropical with cooler temperatures.

## TWO RIVER DELTAS

The narrow strip of land that links the north of the country to the south is vulnerable to typhoons, and a series of sea dikes protects many villages from the worst weather. Vietnam's large and fertile river deltas (the Red, or Song Hong, river in the north and the Mekong in the south) are where rice production and a large proportion of the country's population are concentrated. Agriculture is the mainstay of Vietnam's economy, and rice is the dominant crop. Despite a large migration to cities, the Vietnamese population is still one of the most rural in Southeast Asia, with fewer than 30 percent living in urban areas.

## 20TH-CENTURY WARS

Vietnam was home to a number of ancient civilizations before being dominated by China for many centuries. The country came under French rule in the 1800s, but this ended in the French Indochina War (1946–1954). Vietnam was then partitioned into northern and southern halves as a temporary measure. Tension between the communist north and the largely anticommunist south mounted, and in 1964 a full-scale war erupted. The conflict involved hundreds of thousands of troops from the U.S. and other nations. The 1973 ceasefire saw the U.S. withdraw its troops, and in 1975 the South Vietnamese capital of Saigon fell to northern forces. Vietnam has since been run by a staunchly communist government.

## REPAIR AND RENOVATION

Repairing the extensive damage done to much of the country during the Vietnam War has been a major undertaking. Almost 8 million tons (7 million metric tonnes) of bombs were dropped during the conflict, towns and cities were devastated, and unexploded land mines are still a threat. Five percent of Vietnam's forests were destroyed, and almost 50 percent were damaged by chemical weapons, which stripped trees of their leaves. Since 1986 the country has pursued an economic policy called *doi moi*, meaning "renovation." Investment from foreign companies was sought, trade links with other nations have been engaged, private enterprise has been encouraged, and in 2000 the country's first stock exchange opened. Industry is largely concentrated in the north, while Vietnam produces 305,000 barrels of oil per day. In the 1990s Vietnam started to encourage tourists from noncommunist nations, and in 2008 around 3.9 million tourists visited the country, attracted by its history, culture, and areas of natural beauty.

▲ A busy market in Ho Chi Minh City. The city was once the capital of South Vietnam. Known as Saigon before reunification, it is Vietnam's largest city, with a population of over four million, and is also a major shipping port.

# CAMBODIA

**Cambodia is a land of great history and natural beauty that has been beset by conflicts throughout the second half of the 1900s.**

**Area:** 69,900 sq. mi. (181,035km2)
**Population:** 13,389,000
**Capital:** Phnom Penh (1,326,000)
**Main languages spoken:** Khmer, French
**Main religion:** Theravada Buddhism
**Currency:** riel
**Main exports:** clothing, logs and timber, rubber, rice, fish
**Type of government:** constitutional monarchy

The center of Cambodia is a large, low-lying basin, the Tonle Sap, surrounded by a broad plain that is drained by the country's biggest river, the Mekong. To the southeast of the basin lies the Mekong delta, which extends into Vietnam before reaching the South China Sea. To the north and the southwest of the basin lie several mountain ranges, while highlands are in the northeast of Cambodia. These merge into the highlands in the center of the country that extend into Vietnam. In the center of the basin lies Southeast Asia's largest lake, also called Tonle Sap. This shallow lake varies enormously in size. At its smallest it measures around 1,040 sq. mi. (2,700km2), with depths of between 3–10 ft. (1–3m). During the wet monsoon season, between June and November, the high waters of the Mekong feed into the lake, greatly increasing its size to around 4,020 sq. mi. (10,300km2) and its depth to between 30–46 ft. (9–14m).

## USING ITS NATURAL RESOURCES

Cambodia is poorly endowed with mineral reserves, but, in contrast, the country has relatively rich resources from the natural world. These include plentiful fish from its rivers and lakes, which are often fermented or salted to preserve them. The well-watered lowlands of Cambodia allow rice farming to dominate the country's agriculture. Almost 80 percent of all cultivated land is used for rice, with other crops including mangoes, bananas, and pineapples. Rubber, grown in the east of the country, is an important cash crop, along with corn, peppers, sesame, and cassava. A large proportion of the country is covered in forests, much of it tropical hardwoods such as teak and mahogany. However, deforestation is one of the most serious problems facing the country, with as much as half of its tree cover having disappeared in the past 50 years.

## FROM KINGDOM TO KHMER ROUGE

Cambodia came under French rule in the 1800s. Regaining independence in 1954, the country underwent a period of stability before exploding into conflict from the late 1960s onward. Following the Vietnam War that enveloped the region a violent communist regime, called the Khmer Rouge, swept to power. Between

1975–1979 as many as 1.5 million people were murdered, including most of the country's professional class of workers. The Khmer Rouge was ousted, and Cambodia is now a kingdom again. However, ongoing conflicts and changes of government have continued, with the result that Cambodia is one of Southeast Asia's poorest countries.

▲ Houses on stilts stand in the waters of Tonle Sap lake, where many Cambodians engage in carp raising and fishing. Fish is a major part of many Cambodians' diets.

▼ Constructed during the reign of King Suryavarman II, the 12th-century ruler of the Khmer kingdom, Angkor Wat is a gigantic Hindu temple built of stone and measuring 3,280 ft. (1,000m) in length.

# LAOS

**The most sparsely populated nation in Southeast Asia, Laos is an isolated, poor, and mountainous nation ruled by a communist government.**

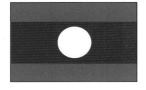

**Area:** 91,430 sq. mi. (236,800km²)
**Population:** 5,622,000
**Capital:** Vientiane (698,000)
**Main languages spoken:** Lao Loum, Lao Theung, Lao Soung
**Main religions:** Buddhism, traditional beliefs
**Currency:** kip
**Main exports:** wood products, clothing, electricity, coffee, tin
**Type of government:** communist

▼ Laotian farmers tend vegetables grown in the rich soil of the banks of the Mekong river. Over half of the country's population live in the lowland areas of Laos, especially along the banks of the Mekong.

The Lao People's Democratic Republic shares borders with five nations: Vietnam, Thailand, Cambodia, Myanmar, and China. Around 70 percent of its land features mountains that run northwest to southeast and reach their highest elevation in the worth of the country at Mount Bia, with an elevation of 9,246 ft. (2,819m). Approximately 55 percent of Laos is covered with forests of different types. In the north these are mostly tropical rain forests, while to the south tropical vegetation mixes with deciduous hardwood trees such as teak and rosewood. Large tracts of bamboo jungle can also be found in the south. Despite timber from these forests being one of Laos' principal exports, the forests help support a wide and varied range of wildlife, including tigers, leopards, panthers, and wild oxen called gaurs. Laos has a tropical monsoon climate with two distinct—wet and dry—seasons. The wet season runs from May to October, with rainfall almost every day and high humidity levels. During this period between 51–90 in. (130–230cm) of rain falls in the central regions of the country. In the south rainfall can reach over 120 in. (300cm).

## THE MEKONG RIVER

Much of Laos' westerly border with Thailand and Myanmar is formed by the winding Mekong river, which extends over 1,120 mi. (1,800km) through Laos. Most of the country's major towns and cities are located on the Mekong, which can be navigated by boat south of the city of Louangphrabang. The people of Laos belong to over 65 different ethnic groups, with very diverse customs and lifestyles. The large majority of Laotians work the land, mainly growing rice, as well as sweet potatoes and corn. Raising livestock, including water buffalo and pigs, is important, as is the illegal growing and selling of opium poppies. The lands adjacent to the Mekong make up the

most extensive lowland area in Laos and are the site of much of the country's farming.

## LANDLOCKED AND ISOLATED

Laos is the only landlocked country in Southeast Asia. Its rugged terrain of mountains and forests along most of its borders has hampered the country's industrial, transportation, and trading development with neighboring nations. Laos has no railroads, and roads are few in number and generally of poor quality. Most of the country's freight is transported by river, especially along the Mekong. Prior to 1994 foreign visitors to Laos arrived largely by air since there was no major road link to other countries. The Australian-funded Friendship Bridge was opened in 1994. It spans the Mekong river at Vientiane, the country's capital city, and links Laos to Thailand by road. Until 1986 the country was as isolated politically as it is

geographically. After more than two decades of internal power struggles Laos became a one-party communist state in 1975 and restricted its foreign relations to a few communist nations, especially Vietnam. From 1986 the country started slowly to reintegrate with the world community, and its largest single trading partner today is Thailand. Laos is reliant on foreign aid and investment, while its industry remains undeveloped and its mineral resources unexploited. Around eight percent of babies die before reaching adulthood, and Laotians have a low average life expectancy of 57 years.

▲ Buddhist monks collect food in the morning from the local people for their one meal per day. Buddhism is the religion of 58 percent of Laotians.

▼ A Khmu tribe family sits around the fire in their two-room house before dinner. The Khmu mainly live in small villages on mountain slopes near the Thailand-Laos border. They survive on subsistence agriculture, supplemented by fishing, hunting, and trading.

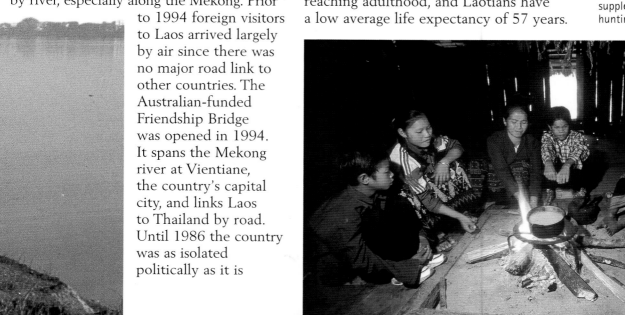

# BRUNEI

**Brunei is located on the northwest coast of the island of Borneo. Gaining independence in 1984, the country is rich in fossil fuel reserves.**

**Area:** 2,226 sq. mi.
(5,765km²)
**Population:** 409,000
**Capital:** Bandar Seri
Begawan (283,000)
**Main languages spoken:**
Malay, English, Chinese
**Main religion:** Islam,
Buddhism, Christian
**Currency:** Brunei dollar
**Main exports:** crude
petroleum, natural gas,
petroleum products
**Type of government:**
independent sultanate

▼ Oil exploitation
in Brunei is mainly
concentrated offshore.
Brunei's oil fields produce
approximately 175,000
barrels of oil per day.

Brunei faces the South China Sea to the north and shares a border with Malaysia, dividing Brunei in half. The country consists of a narrow coastal plain lined largely with mangrove swamps, while the interior rises to form hill ranges covered mainly in rain forests. The country's highest point, Pagon (5,930 ft./ 1,850m), lies in the southeast of the country. Within Brunei's border are 33 islands that make up 1.4 percent of the country's total land area. Most of these islands are uninhabited and are important breeding grounds for certain endangered species of birds, flying foxes, and monkeys. Brunei has a tropical climate with rainfall averaging over 80 in. (200cm) per year and a narrow temperature range averaging between 75–88°F (24–31°C). Most streams and rivers flow north to the coast. This includes the Belait river, the longest in the country, which runs close to the country's western border. A large proportion of Brunei, almost 80 percent, is covered in rain forests. This lush tree cover is filled with animal life, including Asian elephants, leopards, many species of monkeys, and numerous reptiles and birds.

## OIL AND BRUNEI'S PEOPLE

By the 1500s Brunei was an independent sultanate, or kingdom, controlling almost the entire island of Borneo. Following a decline in influence it became a British protectorate in 1888. The indigenous people of Brunei now comprise just three percent of the population. People of Malay descent make up two thirds of Brunei's population, and there are large minorities of Chinese and Indians. Most of Brunei's nonindigenous and non-Malay population arrived when oil was found in 1929. The exploitation of the country's large oil and natural gas reserves completely dominates the economy of this small nation. Oil revenues have made the country's leader, Sultan Sir Muda Hassanal Bolkiah, one of the wealthiest people in the world. The people he rules have also benefited from the oil revenues with a generally high standard of living. There is no income tax, and there are high levels of medical care and education, as well as subsidized food and housing. However, political parties were banned in 1988, and all government workers are banned from political activity. Although Brunei's mixed population follows a number of religions, the country is more inclined to its state religion of Islam.

# SINGAPORE

An island city-state, Singapore is one of the most prosperous and modernized Asian countries, with a standard of living equal to Western Europe.

**Area:** 272 sq. mi. (704km²)
**Population:** 4,839,000
**Capital:** Singapore (4,839,000)
**Main languages spoken:** Chinese, Malay, Tamil, English
**Main religions:** Buddhism, Taoism, Islam, Christian, Hinduism
**Currency:** Singaporean dollar
**Main exports:** machinery and transportation equipment, consumer goods, chemicals, petroleum products
**Type of government:** republic

Singapore lies just off the southernmost tip of the Malay Peninsula, separated from Malaysia by a narrow body of water. The two countries are linked by a highway carrying road and rail links and a road bridge. The country consists of one major island, Singapore Island, and a collection of 60 smaller islands. Singapore's land is mostly flat and low-lying with several small hills. Singapore remains reliant on neighboring Malaysia for some of its freshwater supplies. Lying close to the equator, the country has a tropical climate with an average annual temperature of 80.9°F (27.2°C) and heavy rainfall, averaging over 95 in. (242cm) per year, especially between November and March. Singapore was once covered completely in rain forests, but much of the land has been cleared and swamps and marshlands drained and reclaimed. Now only five percent of the land remains forested, much of this lying in protected reserves.

Singapore was barely settled before a British colonial administrator, Sir Stamford Raffles, founded Singapore City in 1819 as a trading post. Singapore grew as a port and naval base following the opening of the Suez Canal in 1869. The country is now one of the most densely populated nations in the world, with Chinese immigrants making up approximately 77 percent of the population and Malays (14 percent) and Indians (seven percent) the largest minorities. Although Singapore has to import all fuel and raw materials, the country has vibrant manufacturing industries, particularly electrical and electronic goods. The country also has large oil refining and chemicals industries.

▲ Singapore is the world's largest container port and third-largest port.

► Singapore's high-rise financial district is the financial capital of the region. Over one fourth of the country's income is derived from financial and business services.

# MALAYSIA

**A multiethnic nation with rich natural resources, Malaysia has had one of Southeast Asia's fastest-growing economies in the past 30 years.**

**Area:** 127,355 sq. mi. (329,847km²)
**Population:** 28,307,000
**Capitals:** Kuala Lumpur—legislative and diplomatic capital (4,815,000); Putrajaya—administrative capital (12,000)
**Main languages spoken:** Malay, English, Chinese dialects
**Main religions:** Islam, Hinduism, Buddhism, Christian
**Currency:** ringgit
**Main exports:** electronics, machinery, transportation equipment, petroleum and petroleum products, wood and wood products, rubber, textiles, chemicals
**Type of government:** federal parliamentary democracy with a constitutional monarchy

Malaysia is divided into two geographical areas separated by the South China Sea and lying around 400 mi. (650km) apart. Peninsula Malaysia occupies the southern portion of the Malay Peninsula, bordering Thailand to the north and close to the islands of Singapore to the south. It accounts for around 40 percent of the country's landmass and is divided by several central mountain chains, with poorly drained lowlands to the south, a narrow, forested belt to the east, and broader, fertile plains to the west. The western plains are the most densely populated and developed part of Malaysia. In contrast the two states of Sabah and Sarawak, which make up East Malaysia over 370 mi. (600km) away, are barely developed. Home to around 20 percent of the country's population, the land of East Malaysia consists of a coastal plain with many swamps, rising to densely forested hills and valleys before rising further to mountains. At 13,451 ft. (4,101m), Mount Kinabalu in Sabah is the country's highest peak.

### TROPICAL CLIMATE AND WILDLIFE

Malaysia has a tropical climate with warm-to-hot temperatures and high humidity. The west coast of Peninsula Malaysia experiences a rainy season from September until to December, while the east coast, as well as East Malaysia, has its rainy season from October to February. The country has an extremely biodiverse environment in which around 8,000 different flowering plants exist.

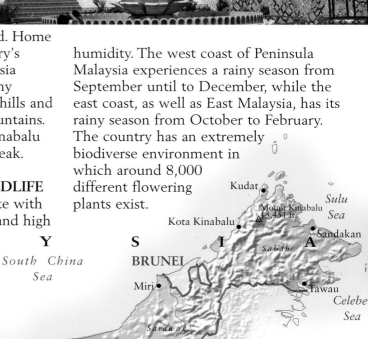

► Kek Lok Si Buddhist temple is situated at Ayer Itam on the island of Penang. The temple features gardens, shrines, a turtle pond, and the 98-ft.- (30-m-) high pagoda of Ten Thousand Buddhas.

◀ A short distance from the coast of Sabah, the island of Pulau Sipadan is a coral seamount covered in dense jungles and surrounded by seas containing rich marine life.

▼ The 1,483-ft. (452-m) Petronas Twin Towers in Kuala Lumpur were the world's tallest buildings from 1998 to 2004. Completed in 1996, the towers are the headquarters of the national oil company of Malaysia.

East Malaysia has one of the largest and most varied bird populations in the world, and elephants, rhinoceroses, leopards, tigers, orangutans, and gibbons are among its larger animal species. Attracted by its wildlife, highland and rain-forest scenery, climate, and beaches along the peninsula coast, more than 17 million tourists visited Malaysia in 2007.

## ABUNDANT NATURAL RESOURCES

Much of Malaysia's economic success is due to its rich natural resources. Oil deposits, particularly offshore of Sabah and Sarawak, are large, allowing Malaysia to produce over 725,000 barrels of oil per day. Sizable deposits of natural gas also exist, and metal ores, including tin, bauxite, copper, and gold, are mined. Much of Peninsula Malaysia's forests have been cleared for plantations, farmland, and settlements. The East Malaysia state of Sarawak still contains some of the largest and oldest original tropical forests on Earth. However, deforestation is the country's biggest environmental issue, with logging one of Malaysia's prime industries. The country is the world's largest exporter of tropical hardwood, logs, and timber, mostly from Sarawak. The World Bank estimates that trees are being felled at three times the rate they can be replaced.

## SUBSISTENCE AND PLANTATION FARMING

Agriculture is a declining sector of the Malaysian economy, but it still employs approximately 13 percent of the workforce. A large number of agricultural workers farm their own small plots of land. Rice is the most common staple food, but the country is not self-sufficient and must import it. Vast plantations growing tea, tropical fruit, sugarcane, and especially cocoa and rubber dominate farming for export. Malaysia is one of the world's top-ten cocoa producers and was once the world's largest rubber producer. The country still ranks as one of the top-five largest producers of natural rubber. This is despite production declining owing to labor shortages, with workers increasingly becoming employed in the country's growing manufacturing industries. Many plantation owners are switching to other crops—palm oil in particular—that are possible to grow and harvest using machinery.

## THIRTEEN STATES, MANY PEOPLE

Malaysia has been inhabited for over 30,000 years and is now a "melting pot" of different ethnic groups and cultures.

▲ These unusual, knifelike limestone pinnacles rise above the densely forested slopes of Gunung Mulu, Sarawak's largest national park.

▼ Malaysia is the world's largest producer of palm oil, used in the manufacture of soaps, ointments, margarine, and cooking oils. This plantation worker is loading palm fruit bunches into a container for transportation to a refinery.

▶ Logging is a huge industry in Malaysia, despite concerns about deforestation. To counter this there have been moves away from selling raw timber to manufacturing furniture. This now accounts for one fourth of all of Malaysia's exports from wood and wood products.

The Orang Asli are the original native people of Peninsula Malaysia, who now number just over 60,000. Larger numbers of indigenous people exist in East Malaysia. These include the Iban, Bidayuh, and Kadazan, the most numerous of some 30 different people, who together comprise approximately eight percent of Malaysia's total population. Approximately 50 percent of Malaysians are Malays, while 24 percent are of Chinese and eight percent of Indian origin. In addition, there are more than one million immigrants, mostly from the Philippines and Indonesia, working mainly in low-paid industries. Islam is the national religion of Malaysia, although religious freedom and toleration mean that almost all of the world's major religions are practiced in the country. Tensions between the traditionally wealthier Chinese and the Malay peoples have seen, since 1970, affirmative action in education, jobs, and business in favor of Malays.

## A DEVELOPING SUCCESS STORY

In the early 1970s, 70 percent of Malaysia's exports consisted of rubber and tin. In just 25 years the economic situation completely changed. In the early 21st century, more than 75 percent of exports were manufactured goods. The rapid growth of industry in Malaysia since the 1960s was, in part, due to the New Economic Policy (NEP), introduced in 1970 following large, violent riots in the country. It aimed at

production of electrical and electronic equipment, motor vehicles, and chemicals. Today Malaysia is one of the world's leading exporters of high-tech components such as computer chips and disk drives. George Town and towns and cities around Kuala Lumpur are the key centers for the country's booming computer industry. Peninsula Malaysia is home to the large majority of the country's industry and has seen living standards rise for much of its population.

### ADVANCED DEVELOPMENT BY 2020

Although Malaysia is developing rapidly and is much wealthier than in the past, it still suffers economic and social problems. A major economic crisis in 1998 slowed growth dramatically, and there are shortages of skilled workers in some industries. Away from the cities and especially in East Malaysia many people's standard of living has not risen greatly, and a large number remain below the poverty line. Major government policies to complete Malaysia's transformation into an advanced nation by 2020 include greater technical education, improved health care, and the use of advanced technology. A new city has been developed, Putrajaya, to be the new administrative capital, 22 mi. (35km) south of Kuala Lumpur.

▲ Malaysia has become a major oil and natural gas producer, with its fields off the coast of Sarawak and Sabah yielding around 727,000 barrels per day.

changing the country's economic structure, where businesses had traditionally been owned by the Chinese population, and developing a range of new industries. Around 36 percent of Malaysia's labor force are now employed in manufacturing, especially the processing of export commodities, such as rubber, tin, oil, wood, and metals, and the

▼ The Cameron Highlands in Perak state, on the western coast of Peninsula Malaysia, are the center of the country's tea plantations such as the Sungai Palas Estate.

# INDONESIA

**A gigantic island archipelago, Indonesia is a sprawling land of great natural and human diversity and is the fourth-most-populous nation in the world.**

**Area:** 735,298 sq. mi. (1,904,413km²)
**Population:** 234,181,000
**Capital:** Jakarta (13,660,000)
**Main languages spoken:** Bahasa Indonesian, English, Dutch, Javanese
**Main religions:** Islam, Protestant
**Currency:** Indonesian rupiah
**Main exports:** crude petroleum and natural gas, electrical goods, plywood, processed rubber, clothing
**Type of government:** republic; democracy

Indonesia consists of around 13,700 islands that extend around one eighth of Earth's circumference. Sumatra is the most westerly of the larger islands and is separated from western Malaysia and Singapore by the Strait of Malacca. Papua, occupying the western part of the island of New Guinea, is Indonesia's most easterly territory. The large majority of the population live on five islands: Java, Sumatra, Papua, Celebes, and Kalimantan— the Indonesian part of the island of Borneo. The country experiences a tropical climate with a small temperature range between the seasons owing to the islands' location close to the equator. Temperatures differ mainly with height, with only some highland areas of Papua receiving snowfall. Rainfall varies more, with the highest amount of rainfall occurring in the mountainous regions of Kalimantan, Sumatra, Celebes, and Papua, which receive in excess of 120 in. (300cm) per year. Most lowland areas receive between 63–87 in (160–220cm).

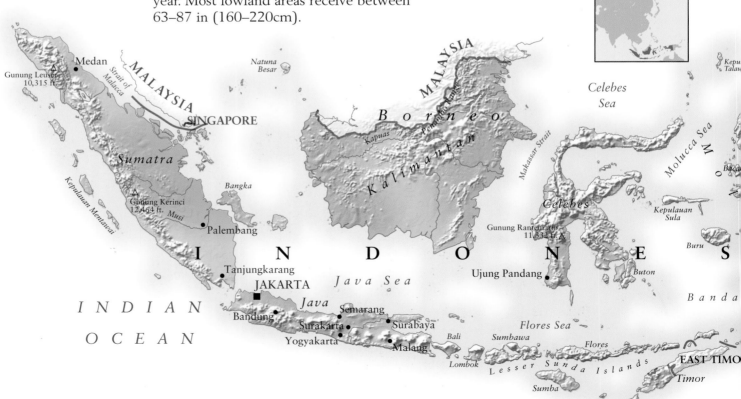

▲ At 7,846 ft. (2,392m), Mount Bromo, on the eastern end of the island of Java, is one of the highest active volcanic peaks on the island.

## INDONESIA'S VOLCANOES

Much of Indonesia's land has been shaped by volcanic activity, with most islands featuring a mountainous interior. The ashes, lava, and mud flows from successive eruptions have helped create fertile soils in many places. Indonesia's territory contains over 128 active volcanoes, with Java containing 22. Of Indonesia's volcanoes, none is more famous than Krakatoa. Located between Java and Sumatra, Krakatoa generated the largest explosion in recorded history when it erupted in 1883. The gigantic explosion destroyed three fourths of the island and was heard 2,500 mi. (4,000km) away in Brisbane. Earthquakes also cause devastation. In 2004 an earthquake off northwest Indonesia triggered a tsunami that killed about 200,000 people, more than 100,000 of them in Indonesia.

▼ Located on the northwest coast of Java, the city of Jakarta is the country's commercial and financial center. A sprawling urban area, much of which lies on a low, flat plain that is subject to swamping, Jakarta is Southeast Asia's most populous urban area.

*Jazirah Doberai*

*Papua*

*Mamberamo*

*Puncak Jaya 16,498 ft.*

*Kesunumgan Maoke*

A

*New Guinea*

*Kepulauan Aru*

**PAPUA NEW GUINEA**

*Arafura Sea*

82 percent of the country was covered in forests. Cutting down forests to clear land and for logging gradually increased throughout the 1900s as Indonesia developed large and economically important paper, timber, and wood pulp industries. Deforestation throughout the late 1990s was at an estimated rate of 7,700 sq. mi. per year (20,000km²), placing hundreds of species, such as the orangutan, under threat of extinction. More than half of all timber produced is estimated to come from illegal logging.

## ASIAN AND AUSTRALASIAN ANIMALS

Indonesia spans the dividing line between two of the world's major animal communities, the Asian and the Australasian. As a result, Australasian creatures, such as the echidna, cockatoo, and bandicoot, can be found on the most easterly islands, while the more northerly and westerly landmasses contain Asian species, including tigers, Asian elephants, and tapirs. The isolated location of many of Indonesia's islands has resulted in many species that are unique not only to Indonesia but also to individual islands. These include the world's largest lizard, the 13-ft.- (4-m-) long Komodo dragon, which is only found on two small islands—Rinca and Komodo—off the west coast of Flores.

▲ This worker is tapping the trunk of a rubber tree to release liquid latex. Producing about 2.9 million tons (2.6 million metric tonnes) of rubber in 2007, Indonesia is one of the world's three dominant natural rubber producers.

▼ A series of terraces cut into a hillside in Bali is occupied by rice paddies. Rice is the staple diet of most Indonesians, and in 2009, 67 million tons (61 million metric tonnes) were produced.

## ASIA'S LARGEST TROPICAL RAIN FORESTS

The tropical climate, high rainfall, and fertile soil are largely responsible for the vast array of natural life found throughout Indonesia. There are thousands of plant and animal species, although many are now under threat. Indonesia has the largest tracts of untouched rain forests in the world outside of the Amazon in South America. At the start of the 1900s over

▲ The Krakatoa volcano is found between the islands of Java and Sumatra and was the site of a gigantic eruption in the 1800s. Giant tsunamis (tidal waves) as high as 130 ft. (40m) were a major cause of the death toll, which reached over 36,000. Minor eruptions continue to this day.

## LIVING OFF THE LAND AND SEA

Since ancient times the people of Indonesia have made great use of their rich and diverse natural environment. For example, many thousands of different plant species are used in traditional herbal medicine known as Jamu. Over 2,000 years ago Indonesian people in the coastal areas were already using irrigation systems to grow rice, while people in the interior tended to practice slash-and-burn agriculture, where forest areas are cleared and crops planted. Although less than 20 percent of Indonesia is cultivated, the country produces large amounts of many different crops. Rice is the key staple food, but after periods of self-sufficiency Indonesia now has to import a great deal of rice to feed its growing population. Other vital crops include cassava, corn, soybeans, peanuts, and sweet potatoes. For such a populous nation livestock herds are relatively small, with around 15 million goats, 12 million cattle, and 10 million pigs. Chickens, however, are raised in large numbers; there were over one billion in Indonesia in 2006. Many Indonesians who have small farms near rivers, lakes, or the coast also fish part-time. Large-scale sea fishing has increased with Japanese assistance.

▼ The striking Buddhist monument of Borobudur is found on Java. It was built between A.D. 778–850 and was hidden by volcano ash and vegetation from around the 900s until it was discovered in the 1800s.

▲ A small river settlement in West Sumatra.

gas (LNG) and has relied on oil reserves to generate much of its export income. In 2008 Indonesia produced 1.1 million barrels per day, but oil production is declining. Concerns that Indonesia will soon become an importer of fuels have led to fossil fuel exploration of remote areas and the possibility of more stations being built.

## RAPID INDUSTRIALIZATION

Although agriculture and the exporting of raw materials have dominated the economy, Indonesia has industrialized rapidly in the past 40 years. Larger industries, mainly controlled by the state, process metals, oil, wood, and wood products and produce chemicals, cement, glass, rubber goods, machinery, and fertilizers. Indonesia has also become involved in high-technology fields such as electronics and aerospace. The country has a large textile industry, including batik, a technique for handprinting cloth. Despite the country's huge resources and growing industries, the Indonesian economy is fragile, with political instability, high unemployment, and large foreign debts. Progress has not occurred evenly, with Java and its neighboring islands the most economically developed but with great poverty elsewhere.

## INDONESIA'S RESOURCES

Much of Indonesia's farmland is devoted to growing cash crops on large plantations. Indonesia is one of the world's top-three rubber producers, the third-largest grower of coffee, and a leading producer of coconuts, tobacco, cacao, and a number of spices. Apart from the resources provided by the living world, Indonesia has large mineral reserves. The country has rich deposits of tin, copper, gold, bauxite, and nickel. In addition, Indonesia is the world's largest exporter of liquefied natural

▼ Indonesian tea pickers at work. In 2008 Indonesia produced 166 million tons (151 million metric tonnes) of tea; this represented four percent of the world total.

## PEOPLE AND HISTORY

Indonesia had been settled for thousands of years before it came under Dutch control at the end of the 1600s. In 1945 Indonesia declared itself independent, an act recognized by the Netherlands in 1949 after a violent conflict. Indonesia is the most populous nation in Southeast Asia, and its population has grown dramatically throughout the 1900s. Despite family-planning campaigns, the country's population is growing by 2.8 people every year. Overcrowding on the most populous islands resulted in transmigration, whereby over 3.5 million people were relocated to less populated parts of the country. This created some new jobs but also damaged the traditional cultures. Indonesia's people come from around 300 different ethnic groups speaking over 250 distinct languages. The Javanese, the largest ethnic group in Indonesia, represent 41 percent of the population. Traders from India brought Hinduism and Buddhism to Indonesia almost 2,000 years ago, while Islam reached Sumatra in the 1200s. This religion spread throughout much of Indonesia, and there are now over 207 million Muslims—making it the world's largest Islamic country. Conflicts between different ethnic and religious groups have marred Indonesia since independence. Governments have tried to suppress the traditional cultures of many local ethnic groups, which has increased conflict. East Timor became independent of Indonesia in 2002, while Aceh province in Sumatra achieved local self-government in 2005. But nationalist movements are still active in other areas. The number of tourists attracted to Indonesia rose rapidly in the 1980s and 1990s, but political instability since then has badly damaged the tourist trade. In 2002, terrorist bombs on Bali caused almost 200 deaths.

▲ Two of Kelimutu's three beautiful colored lakes. Kelimutu is a volcano located on the island of Flores, east of Java, and is in the middle of one of Indonesia's national parks.

▼ Members of the Organisasi Papua Merdeka (OPM) in their traditional dress on Papua. A collection of different tribal groups, the OPM has been fighting for Papua's independence from Indonesia since the 1960s.

# EAST TIMOR

Sometimes known by its Portuguese name, Timor-Leste, East Timor was recognized as an independent country in May 2002 after a long struggle.

**Area:** 5,743 sq. mi. (14,874km²)
**Population:** 1,081,000
**Capital:** Dili (212,000)
**Main languages spoken:** Portuguese, Tetum
**Main religion:** Roman Catholic
**Currency:** U.S. dollar
**Main exports:** timber (sandalwood), coffee, marble
**Type of government:** republic

▼ Two East Timorese farmworkers gather in a harvest. The people of East Timor are a diverse mixture of more than 15 ethnic groups, including some Indonesians and Chinese. Many are Roman Catholic, reflecting its long period as a Portuguese colony.

The island of Timor lies in the Malay Archipelago. East Timor occupies the eastern half of the island, the island of Pulau Kambing, and the enclave of Ambeno (also known as Oecusse). This lies on the northern coast of the remainder of Timor, which is part of Indonesia.

East Timor has a mostly mountainous landscape, with elevations rising inland to 9,721 ft. (2,963m). In the north the mountains rise almost immediately from the sea, while in the south there is a wide coastal plain that is broken up by river deltas and swampland. The country has a tropical climate with temperatures remaining high throughout the year but with great variations in rainfall. The southern side of the island tends to receive more rainfall, and the foothills are covered in bushes and trees, including eucalyptus. The northern side is more arid, and droughts can occur in the long dry season between May and November.

## SUBSISTENCE AND CASH-CROP FARMING

The people of East Timor rely largely on farming, with corn the most important staple food, followed by rice, cassava, millet, and sweet potatoes. Buffalo, cattle, goats, and poultry are raised and traded. Outside the main settlements most trade occurs through barter. Cash crops include coffee, coconuts, cloves, and sandalwood trees, from which sandal oil, used in perfumes, is extracted. In 2005 Australia and East Timor agreed to share valuable oil and natural gas deposits under the seas that lie between them.

## BLOODSHED AND INDEPENDENCE

Portugal colonized the island in the 1500s, and East Timor remained a colony until 1975 when the Portuguese withdrew. Within ten days Indonesian forces invaded and declared East Timor part of Indonesia. Horrible human rights abuses occurred, and over 100,000 East Timorese died resisting the Indonesian occupation. In a referendum on East Timor's future in 1999 almost four fifths of the vote supported independence. East Timor was administered by the UN for almost three years after armed groups, supported by the Indonesian military, killed hundreds and destroyed much of the country's largest city, Dili. Much aid and investment has since poured into East Timor.

# THE PHILIPPINES

**The sprawling island nation of the Philippines occupies the northernmost part of the Malay Archipelago and lies in the western Pacific Ocean.**

**Area:** 115,860 sq. mi. (300,076km²)
**Population:** 88,575,000
**Capital:** Manila (11,553,000)
**Main languages spoken:** Pilipino, English
**Main religions:** Roman Catholic, Protestant, Islam
**Currency:** Filipino peso
**Main exports:** electronic equipment (particularly computer components), machinery and transportation equipment, clothing, coconut oil, wiring
**Type of government:** republic; limited democracy

▼ The capital city of Manila is at the heart of a sprawling metropolis that contains five individual cities and houses more than 11.5 million people.

The Philippines consists of 7,107 islands, of which 40 percent are inhabited. Luzon to the north and Mindanao to the south are by far the largest and comprise two thirds of the country's total area. A further nine islands have land areas in excess of 965 sq. mi. (2,500km²).Only two fifths of the islands are named, and only 350 of the islands have an area of more than 0.62 sq. mi. (1km²). The islands are volcanic in origin and are the peaks of a partly submerged mountain chain. Their terrain is rugged, with the highest point on the island of Mindanao, where Mount Apo reaches 9,689 ft. (2,954m).

## A DIVERSE LAND AND PEOPLE

The Philippines lies in the tropics and has a hot and humid year-round climate with an average annual temperature of 81°F (27°C) and average rainfall of 80 in. (203cm) per year. However, there is much variation in temperature and rainfall based on location and elevation. Around 45 percent of the country is under cultivation, and around one third remains forested, despite logging, much of it illegal, and slash-and-burn agriculture.

There are over 10,000 species of trees, shrubs, and ferns, the most common of which are palms and bamboos. There are also more than 700 species of birds and many species of amphibians and reptiles. Rice and corn are the most common staple foods, but a wide range of crops are grown for both local consumption and export. Over 100 different ethnic groups live in the country, and a large range of languages and dialects are spoken. While Pilipino is the official language, English is widely used for commercial and governmental purposes. Around 81 percent of the population are Roman Catholics, while a large Muslim minority of around five percent are found particularly on the island of Mindanao.

335

▲ Many Filipino people, especially those who live on smaller islands, survive through fishing. In 2007 more than 5.2 million tons (4.7 million metric tonnes) of fish were caught off the Philippines.

▼ The San Guillermo Parish Church lies in the settlement of Bacolor, 37 mi. (60km) northwest of Manila. Founded in 1576, the church was severely damaged by a mudflow caused by an eruption of Mount Pinatubo in 1991.

## NATURAL DISASTERS

As part of the Pacific's "Ring of Fire," the Philippines lies on some of the most geologically active parts of Earth's crust. The country regularly experiences earthquakes, including one in 1990 that struck the northern part of the island of Luzon, taking the lives of 1,600 people and leaving over 100,000 homeless. The islands also have an estimated 20 active volcanoes, including Mount Pinatubo on Luzon, which, after six centuries of lying dormant, erupted severely in 1991. The people of the Philippines also have to contend with floods, landslides, and relatively frequent typhoons (known as hurricanes in the Atlantic) that tend to occur during the wet season, particularly from September to December. In 2002 the United Nations released statistics showing that the Philippines was the most disaster-prone nation on Earth. In the first decade of the 21st century the country suffered six major disasters, floods, storms, and earthquakes.

## A HISTORIC TRADING CENTER

The Philippines came under Spanish colonial rule in 1521 when it was named Felipinas in honor of Spain's future king, Philip II. Lying in a strategic location between Asia and the "new world" of the Americas, the Philippines grew as a trading and transportation hub. Spain's colonial rule lasted until the U.S. gained possession following victories in the Spanish-American War of 1898 and the Philippine-American War (1899–1901). After occupation by Japan during World War II the Philippines became an independent republic in 1946. Ferdinand Marcos came to power in 1965, and he suppressed all political opposition. The Marcos regime was finally overturned in 1986, and despite bouts of corruption and political scandal since then, the Philippines is now an emerging democratic nation. The brutal years of the Marcos rule, as well as corruption and natural disasters since, have acted as a brake on the Philippines' economic growth. Manufacturing industries, such as textiles, electronics, chemicals, and machine parts, are growing, but there is great poverty and overcrowded slums in many cities.

# AFRICA

# AFRICA

The second-largest continent, Africa holds around one fifth of Earth's total land area. It is bordered by the Mediterranean and Red seas, as well as two oceans, the Atlantic and the Indian. Off its Indian Ocean coastline lies the world's fourth-largest island, Madagascar (see page 286). Africa's landscape is varied—from the world's largest desert, the Sahara, in the north to lush tropical jungles and rain forests in the middle of the continent. Africa is home to an amazing variety of wildlife, including the world's largest land animals such as the African elephant, the rhinoceros, and the giraffe. Africa has a rich and diverse human population consisting of more than 3,000 different ethnic groups. In the past much of Africa was ruled as colonies of major European powers such as Great Britain, France, and Belgium. They divided the land with little regard for ethnic boundaries and territories. Today Africans live in many nations, most obtaining independence in the last 50 years. Many of these countries are the least developed in the world and have been marred by ethnic conflicts, civil wars, and natural disasters, including droughts, famines, and diseases.

▲ These Nigerian women transport market goods by foot to the town of Ikere-Ekiti in southwestern Nigeria. The large majority of Africans live in rural areas and depend on farming in order to make a living.

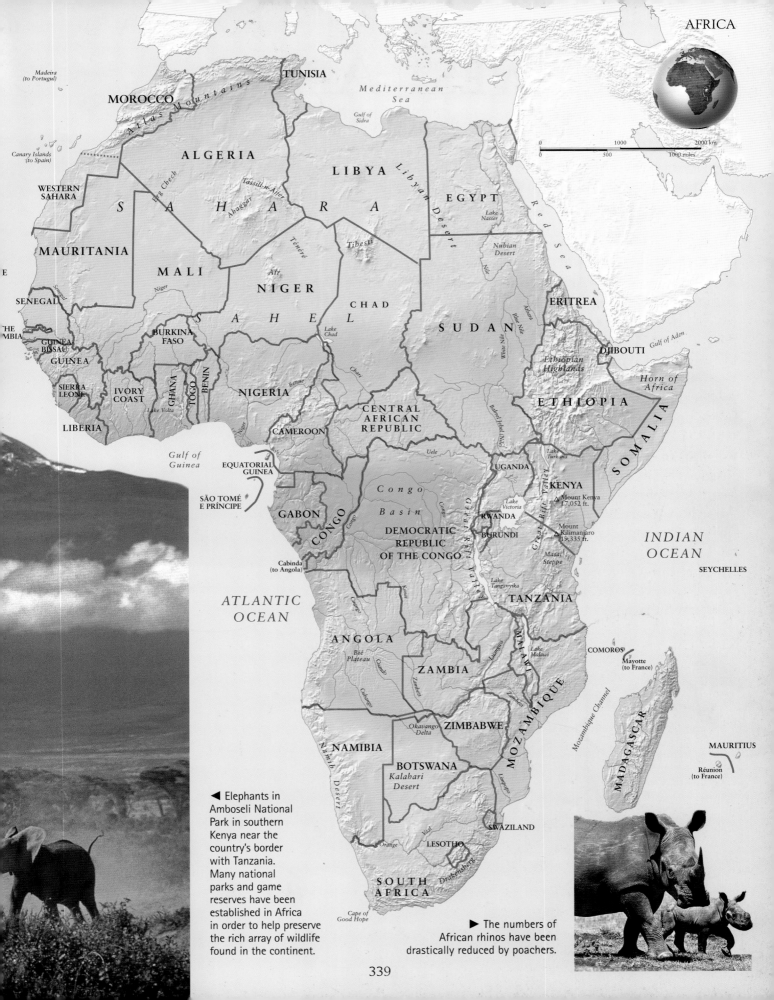

AFRICA

Madeira
(to Portugal)

MOROCCO

TUNISIA

*Mediterranean Sea*

Gulf of Sidra

Canary Islands
(to Spain)

WESTERN SAHARA

ALGERIA

*Atlas Mountains*

LIBYA

EGYPT

Lake Nasser

MAURITANIA

S A H A R A

*Eg Chech*

*Tassili-n-Ajjer*

*Ahaggar*

*Ténéré*

*Tibesti*

*Libyan Desert*

Nubian Desert

*Red Sea*

SENEGAL

MALI

NIGER

CHAD

SUDAN

ERITREA

Nile

THE GAMBIA

GUINEA BISSAU

GUINEA

S A H E L

Lake Chad

DJIBOUTI

Gulf of Aden

*Niger*

BURKINA FASO

*Benue*

Chari

Bahr el Ghazal

White Nile

Blue Nile

Atbara

Ethiopian Highlands

Horn of Africa

SIERRA LEONE

IVORY COAST

GHANA

TOGO

BENIN

NIGERIA

Lake Volta

CAMEROON

CENTRAL AFRICAN REPUBLIC

ETHIOPIA

SOMALIA

LIBERIA

*Niger*

Gulf of Guinea

EQUATORIAL GUINEA

SÃO TOMÉ E PRÍNCIPE

GABON

CONGO

Uele

*Congo Basin*

Congo

DEMOCRATIC REPUBLIC OF THE CONGO

UGANDA

Lake Turkana

KENYA

△ Mount Kenya 17,052 ft.

RWANDA

BURUNDI

Lake Victoria

Great Rift Valley

△ Mount Kilimanjaro 19,335 ft.

Masai Steppe

INDIAN OCEAN

SEYCHELLES

Cabinda (to Angola)

Congo

Kasai

ATLANTIC OCEAN

*Cuango*

Lake Tanganyika

TANZANIA

ANGOLA

Bié Plateau

*Cuanza*

*Cubango*

*Zambezi*

ZAMBIA

MALAWI

Lake Malawi

*Ruvuma*

COMOROS

Mayotte (to France)

MOZAMBIQUE

Mozambique Channel

MADAGASCAR

MAURITIUS

Réunion (to France)

Okavango Delta

ZIMBABWE

*Zambezi*

NAMIBIA

*Namib Desert*

BOTSWANA

Kalahari Desert

*Limpopo*

◄ Elephants in Amboseli National Park in southern Kenya near the country's border with Tanzania. Many national parks and game reserves have been established in Africa in order to help preserve the rich array of wildlife found in the continent.

*Orange*

*Vaal*

SWAZILAND

LESOTHO

*Drakensberg*

SOUTH AFRICA

Cape of Good Hope

► The numbers of African rhinos have been drastically reduced by poachers.

339

# NORTHWEST AFRICA

The four nations and one disputed region that comprise northwest Africa occupy a strategic location between the rest of Africa, Western Europe, and the Middle East. Much of the region borders the Mediterranean Sea to the north, while the massive desert region of the Sahara lies to the south and covers the majority of the land area of Algeria and Libya. Running through Morocco, a small part of Algeria, and into Tunisia is the region's principal mountain range, the Atlas Mountains. The majority of the population of northwest Africa are of Arab descent following invasions into the region between the A.D. 600s–1000s. More than 85 percent of the population of northwest Africa live on the narrow coastal plain that borders the Mediterranean. There the climate is hot and dry in the summer and warm and fairly wet in the winter, providing conditions in which land can be farmed. Isolated water wells and oases in the interior support the small number of people who live there. The region includes the former colony of Western Sahara, almost all of which has been occupied by Morocco since 1979. Bordering the Atlantic Ocean, a large proportion of Western Sahara's population consists of settlers from Morocco who were encouraged to move there by the country's government. Most of the native Sahrawi people of Western Sahara now live in exile in Algeria, where they have declared Western Sahara independent.

▲ The Tuareg are a native people of the Sahara desert who controlled trade across much of the Sahara for many centuries. Tuareg people today live in Algeria, Tunisia, Libya, Burkina Faso, and Mali.

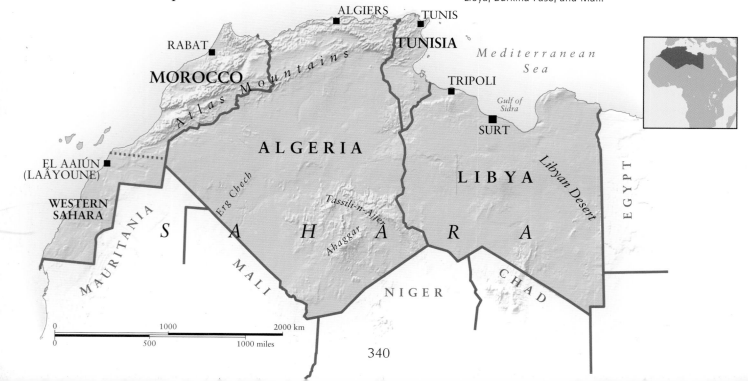

340

# MOROCCO

**The rugged and mountainous kingdom of Morocco faces Spain across the Straits of Gibraltar. It gained independence from France and Spain in 1956.**

**Area:** 177,120 sq. mi. (458,730km²) excluding the disputed Western Sahara territory, or 266,520 sq. mi. (690,275km²) including Western Sahara
**Population:** 29,892,000 (including Western Sahara, which has 417,000)
**Capital:** Rabat (1,623,000) El Aaiun, W. Sahara (184,000)
**Main languages spoken:** Arabic, Berber dialects
**Main religion:** Islam
**Currency:** dirham
**Main exports:** phosphates, food and beverages (fruit, wine, and vegetables), consumer goods, clothing
**Type of government:** constitutional monarchy

▼ The lively central square, Djemaa el Fna, of the city of Marrakech. Located on a fertile plain, the city was founded in the 1000s.

Morocco's land contains two large mountain chains. The Rif Mountains run along the Mediterranean coast, while the higher Atlas Mountains run from southwest to northeast and are heavily forested in places. A large amount of snow and rainfall falls on these mountains, and this water flows through a network of streams. To the south and southeast lies part of the Sahara Desert. Around 45 percent of the Moroccan workforce are engaged in farming and fishing. Cereals, sugarcane, sugar beets, dates, olives, and citrus fruit are key crops, while large herds of sheep and goats are raised. Fishing is important, with over 770,000 tons (700,000 metric tonnes) of fish caught every year. The country's location on both the Mediterranean and Atlantic coasts has seen a number of large ports develop, including Casablanca, the country's most populous city. Around two thirds of the people speak Arabic. Native Berber languages are also common. Almost all of the people are Muslims. Morocco controls around three fourths of the world's reserves of phosphates, substances that are an important ingredient of fertilizers, metal-cleaning agents, toothpastes, and detergents. Morocco has some deposits of coal, iron ore, lead, and other metals, while oil was discovered in the northeastern desert area in 2000. Tourism has become an increasingly important industry and is vital to Morocco's economy. The country's warm climate, beaches, scenery, and ancient cities, such as Fès, Tangier, and Marrakech, attracted 8.4 million tourists in 2009.

# ALGERIA

Algeria won independence from France in 1962 after a bitter struggle. Its land is dominated by the Sahara Desert, and its economy is overshadowed by oil and natural gas.

**Area:** 919,595 sq. mi. (2,381,741km²)
**Population:** 34,460,000
**Capital:** Algiers (2,948,000)
**Main languages spoken:** Arabic, French, Berber dialects
**Main religion:** Sunni Islam
**Currency:** Algerian dinar
**Main exports:** crude petroleum, natural gas, refined petroleum
**Type of government:** republic

▼ Located deep in the Sahara Desert, 270 mi. (430km) east of Mount Tahat, the oasis of Djanet is the main settlement in the southeast of Algeria. Recent droughts have forced many desert herders and some farmers to abandon their traditional lives and look for work in cities.

The narrow and hilly coastal plain bordering the Mediterranean Sea contains most of Algeria's best farmland and is also where most of the country's people live. Separating this area from the desert interior are the Atlas Mountains and high, barren plateaus. South of these mountains lies the Sahara Desert, which occupies more than four fifths of the country's land area. Coastal areas in Algeria have a warm temperate climate with average rainfall of around 40 in. (100cm) per year. In contrast areas deep in the Sahara may not see rainfall for years. Three fourths of Algeria's people are Arabs, and almost one fourth are of Berber descent. Today few Europeans live in Algeria. Around 99 percent of the people are Muslims. The leading crops include cereals, figs, dates, olives, and a variety of fruit and vegetables. Although farming engages around 13 percent of the workforce, the country's economy is dominated by oil and natural gas production and processing. Algeria has some of Africa's largest reserves of oil and the world's fifth-largest natural gas deposits. Despite this, Algeria's economy has struggled in recent times with high food prices, around 12 percent unemployment, and clashes between terrorists and military groups.

Map labels: Mediterranean Sea, ALGIERS, Tizi-Ouzou, Annaba, Ech Chéliff, Oran, El Boulaïda, Constantine, Sidi Bel Abbès, Sétif, Batna, Tilimsen, Atlas Mountains, MOROCCO, TUNISIA, Grand Erg Occidental, Grand Erg Oriental, ALGERIA, LIBYA, Erg Iguidi, Erg Chech, Tassili n'Ajjer, MAURITANIA, Sahara, Tahat 9,849 ft. Ahaggar, MALI, NIGER

# TUNISIA

**The smallest nation in northwest Africa, Tunisia is sandwiched between Algeria and Libya and has a historically important Mediterranean coastline.**

**Area:** 63,170 sq. mi. (163,610km²)
**Population:** 10,327,000
**Capital:** Tunis (2,140,000)
**Main languages spoken:** Arabic, French
**Main religion:** Sunni Islam
**Currency:** Tunisian dinar
**Main exports:** clothing and accessories, machinery and electrical apparatus, phosphates
**Type of government:** republic

▼ A livestock market is held each week in Douz, 70 mi. (110km) west of Gabès. Douz is the largest of Tunisia's desert oasis settlements and has a population of around 27,000. Every year the town hosts the International Festival of the Sahara, which draws performers and artists from across northern Africa.

Mountainous and very green in the north, Tunisia becomes flatter and drier toward the south. The Atlas Mountains extend into the northern section of Tunisia, forming two ranges that contain the country's highest point, the peak of Jebal Chambi, with an elevation of 5,064 ft. (1,544m). A mountainous plateau extends northeast, sloping down toward the coast. Toward the south lies a region of salt lakes, some of which are below sea level. South of these lakes the land becomes part of the Sahara Desert, with isolated watering holes and settlements. The large lake of Shatt al Jarid lies in the center of the country. In the north is the country's most fertile farming area. Compared to its neighbors, a much greater proportion of Tunisia can be farmed using irrigation. However, periodic droughts have an enormous effect on farm output. Cereals, citrus fruit, olives, and vegetables are key crops, while herds of sheep, goats, cattle, and camels are raised. Tunisia has a mixed economy in which farming, mining, manufacturing, and tourism each play a role. Much of the country's manufacturing industry has been developed since independence from France in 1956 and is based around Tunis,

its largest city. Steelmaking, food processing, chemicals, and leather products are among the leading manufacturing areas, while phosphates, lead, and oil are the most important mined products. Separated from the island of Sicily by just 100 mi. (160km) of water, Tunisia has had much contact with Europe for over three centuries. The Phoenicians established colonies in the country over 3,000 years ago. The city of Carthage, located close to Tunis, became the center of a major Mediterranean power until it was overthrown by the Romans in 146 B.C. Ancient remains from these civilizations, along with Tunisia's many sandy beaches and warm climate, attracted 6.7 million visitors in 2007.

# LIBYA

**Libya is a sparsely populated desert nation whose people have benefited from its large oil reserves.**

**Area:** 686,130 sq. mi.
(1,777,060km²)
**Population:** 5,673,000
**Capitals:** Tripoli
(1,356,000)—official and
diplomatic capital; Surt
(120,000)—legislative and
administrative capital
**Main language spoken:**
Arabic
**Main religion:** Sunni Islam
**Currency:** Libyan dinar
**Main export:** crude
petroleum
**Type of government:**
Islamic Arabic socialist
"mass state"

▼ A desert oasis in the
Sahara Desert. Large amounts
of water lie underneath the
surface of the land in south
and southeast Libya. The Great
Manmade River Project, one
of the largest engineering
programs in the world,
transports water from this
region to the cities on the
coast.

The Great Socialist People's Libyan Arab Jamahiriya borders Tunisia, Algeria, Niger, Chad, Sudan, and Egypt and has a long coastline with the Mediterranean Sea. Most of its people live in towns and cities situated on or close to the coast. Small, isolated settlements exist southward in the Sahara and in the northeastern arm of the desert. Less than one percent of the land is cultivated, with barley, tobacco, dates, figs, and grapes grown. Livestock, particularly sheep, goats, and poultry, is more important than crop growing. Until the discovery of oil in the 1950s Libya was a desperately poor nation reliant on aid and imports of food to enable its people to survive. Oil output today is around 1.9 million barrels per day, and crude oil makes up 97 percent of all of Libya's exports. Oil revenue has enabled the government to establish a welfare state in which education and health care are free, although under resourced and less common in rural areas. It has also enabled Libya to build up its military forces. Libya invaded northern Chad in the 1970s, not withdrawing until 1987. Ruled by dictator Colonel Mu'ammar Gadhafi since 1969, Libya has suffered from sanctions imposed because of its links with terrorism. It has recently regained the West's confidence, and in 2006, the United States restored full diplomatic relations with the country.

*MEDITERRANEAN SEA*

TRIPOLI
Az Zawiyah • ■ • Al Khums
TUNISIA • Misratah • *Gulf of Sidra* • Al Marj • Tubruq
Benghazi

SURT ■

ALGERIA

**L I B Y A**

*Great Sand Sea*

EGYPT

*S a h a r a*

NIGER

CHAD

△ Bikku Bitti
7,435 ft.

# NORTHEAST AFRICA

Northeast Africa is a geographically varied region through which two of Africa's most important features run—the Great Rift Valley and the Nile river. The Nile flows through Sudan and Egypt before emptying into the Mediterranean Sea and provides vital water in an otherwise dry region. The Great Rift Valley is the largest split in Earth's surface and cuts through much of Ethiopia and into the nations south of this region. The rugged terrain surrounding the Great Rift Valley makes Ethiopia the region's most mountainous country and the home of northeast Africa's highest peaks. Ethiopia is the only nation in the region that does not have a coastline with either the Red Sea or the Indian Ocean. Ships pass along these three linked stretches of water and through the Suez Canal in the north to gain access to the Mediterranean Sea and the nations of Europe. Northeast Africa's natural life varies greatly—from the plant-rich wetlands of southern Sudan to the Sahara and other large desert areas throughout the region. Northeast Africa's climate is generally characterized by low rainfall, which has led to prolonged droughts and famines in many of the nations. Millions of people have starved to death or remain undernourished, susceptible to life-threatening diseases, and reliant on foreign aid for their existence. The countries that comprise this region have been heavily influenced by their proximity to the Middle East, and many of their people are either Muslims or Christians. While Egypt has maintained prosperity and a degree of stability, the remaining nations of northeast Africa have all suffered in recent times from wars and internal conflicts.

▲ These Sudanese girls live in Camp Riang Aguer in Bahr al-Ghazal, a makeshift camp in southern Sudan for people displaced from their home areas because of conflicts.

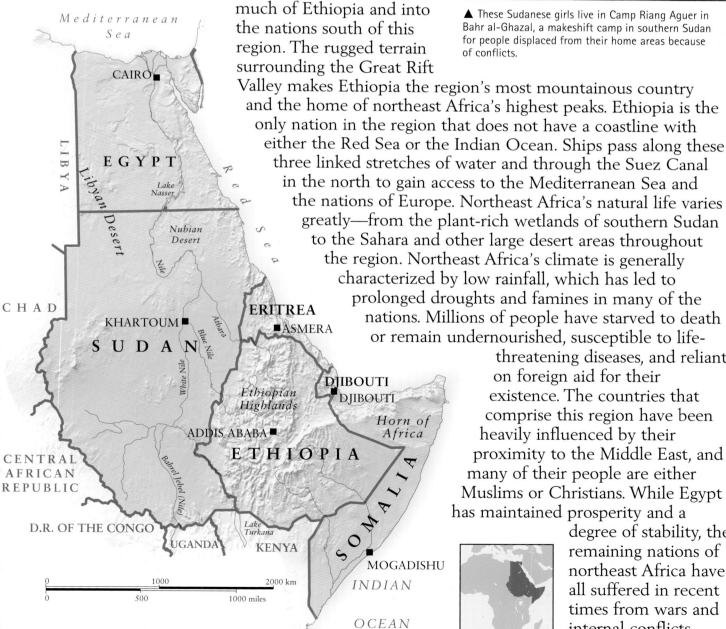

Mediterranean Sea

CAIRO

LIBYA

EGYPT

Libyan Desert

Lake Nasser

Nubian Desert

Nile

Red Sea

CHAD

KHARTOUM

S U D A N

Atbara

Blue Nile

White Nile

ERITREA

ASMERA

Ethiopian Highlands

DJIBOUTI

DJIBOUTI

Horn of Africa

ADDIS ABABA

E T H I O P I A

Bahr el Jebel (Nile)

CENTRAL AFRICAN REPUBLIC

D.R. OF THE CONGO

Lake Turkana

S O M A L I A

UGANDA

KENYA

MOGADISHU

INDIAN

OCEAN

0    1000    2000 km
0    500    1000 miles

# EGYPT

The birthplace of the great ancient Egyptian civilization, Egypt captivates and fascinates people to this day.

**Area:** 385,229 sq. mi. (997,739km²)
**Population:** 72,798,000
**Capital:** Cairo (12,200,000)
**Main language spoken:** Arabic
**Main religions:** Sunni Islam, Coptic Christian
**Currency:** Egyptian pound
**Main exports:** petroleum and petroleum products, cotton yarn and textiles, basic manufactures, clothing
**Type of government:** republic; partial democracy

E gypt is roughly square in shape with long coastlines in the north and east. The Sinai Peninsula lies between the main body of Egypt and Israel and the Gaza territory to the northeast. It is separated from the rest of Egypt by the Gulf of Suez and the Suez Canal, the artificial waterway that links the Mediterranean Sea to the Red Sea. The northern part of Sinai consists of sandy deserts, while the southern portion is mountainous and contains the country's highest point, Jabal Katrina (8,623 ft./ 2,629m). Over 90 percent of Egypt's land is very dry deserts that are split into two regions by the Nile river. The Libyan Desert is a low-lying series of gravel and sand plateaus. There are no rivers or streams, and rain that does fall gathers in depressions, forming temporary salt lakes. A smaller desert to the east is more rugged and contains mountains and plateaus that end in cliffs facing the Red Sea.

## A DESERT CLIMATE

Egypt experiences a dry climate, and even the wettest parts of the country—the coastal strip bordering the Mediterranean—receive less than 9 in. (22cm) of rainfall per year. Most of Egypt receives less than 4 in. (10cm) per year, while in some desert areas rain may not fall for years. The mountains of Sinai often receive snow in the winter, and the meltwaters are collected for use in the hot, dry summer. Egypt's deserts experience dramatic temperature changes. When the sun rises, sand and rocks begin to heat, radiating warmth into the dry air. Daytime temperatures can reach over 122°F (50°C). When the sun sets, the desert cools rapidly. Temperature changes of over 98°F (37°C) have been recorded in one 24-hour period.

▼ The ancient Egyptian pyramids near El Gîza are among the most majestic monuments to this great civilization. For nearly 3,000 years an almost unbroken line of pharoahs presided over an empire in which culture, arts, science, and technology flourished.

## THE NILE RIVER

The world's longest river, the Nile, flows more than 930 mi. (1,500km) south to north through Egypt before emptying into the Mediterranean Sea. North of the city of Cairo the Nile divides into two branches that have created the wide and fertile Nile Delta. Since ancient times the people of Egypt have been dependent on the Nile for water, transportation, and for the fertile soils from the banks on both sides of the river, known as the Nile Valley. Today the large majority of the population live on just four percent of Egypt's land, the Nile Valley or Nile Delta regions. Agriculture provides work for around one fourth of Egyptians, with the fields close to the Nile among the highest yielding in the world. Cotton, corn, wheat, sugarcane, rice, and a large range of vegetables and fruit are the leading crops.

## EGYPT'S RESOURCES AND INDUSTRY

The Nile is Egypt's greatest natural resource, yet Egypt also has a variety of mineral deposits, including gold, uranium, phosphates, and iron ore. Oil and natural gas are the most important minerals. Egypt is Africa's fifth-largest oil producer following Nigeria, Libya, Algeria, and Angola. Just over one tenth of the country's workforce are now employed in manufacturing industries, particularly processing the crops grown and minerals extracted within its borders. Egypt's cotton, textiles, and clothing industries are its largest employers behind the government, while oil refining, fertilizers, cement, and refined sugar are also major industries. Large numbers of small businesses produce pottery, perfume, and handicrafts, which are sold to around 13 million tourists who visit every year.

## THE EGYPTIAN PEOPLE

Ninety-eight percent of Egyptians are descendants of either the native ancient Egyptian population (Hamites) or of Arabs who conquered Egypt in A.D. 642 and settled in the region. Before the Arab invasion most Egyptians had been Christians, but the Arab settlers introduced the Islamic religion, and today over 90 percent of Egyptians are Muslims. Egypt's population is growing at around 1.8 percent per year, which is much faster than the world average. This is putting great pressure on both Egypt's economy and the already densely populated habitable land. Large cities—such as Alexandria, its major seaport, and, the largest of all, Cairo—are being forced to grow rapidly in size.

▲ The Nile has been a major transportation route through Egypt for over 5,000 years. The river is formed by three major tributaries: the Atbara, the White Nile, which flows from Lake Victoria in Uganda, and the Blue Nile, which begins life in the Ethiopian highlands. The Nile's waters have been harnessed near Aswân to generate large amounts of hydroelectricity. This, along with increasing demands for irrigation, has caused the river's level to drop significantly.

# SUDAN

**The largest African nation, Sudan has distinctly different northern and southern halves. The peoples of these two regions were in conflict from the 1950s to 2005.**

**Area:** 967,500 sq. mi. (2,505,815km²)
**Population:** 39,154,000
**Capital:** Khartoum (4,273,000)
**Main languages spoken:** Arabic, Nubian, Ta Bedawie
**Main religions:** Sunni Islam, indigenous beliefs, Christian
**Currency:** Sudanese dinar
**Main exports:** petroleum, cotton, sheep and lamb, sesame seeds, gum arabic, gold
**Type of government:** republic with strong military influence

▼ This Sudanese nomad tends his herd of cattle. Around two million Sudanese are nomads, making a living through herding cattle, sheep, and goats, which together numbered around 138 million in 2007.

With the exception of small areas of highlands, Sudan is mostly a land of flat plains. The northern part of the country is split by the Nile river into the Libyan Desert to the west and the Nubian Desert to the east. The clay plains in the center of the country support dry savannas that change to giant swamplands and rain forests in the south. The lands around the two key tributaries of the Nile, the Blue and White Nile, are the most fertile farming areas in the country. Sudanese people come from more than 500 different tribes, clans, and groups. Around two thirds live in rural areas and depend on agriculture, which is often hit by droughts, to survive. Cotton is the main cash crop, while a range of food crops, including wheat, millet, and sorghum, are grown. The people of northern Sudan are mainly Arab Muslims. Some non-Arab people in the north have also become Muslims. The people of southern and central Sudan are predominantly black Africans who practice traditional African religions or are Christians. In 2011 a vote will be held in the south to decide whether this region will become independent. Since 2004, a revolt by black Sudanese in the Darfur region has led to many deaths.

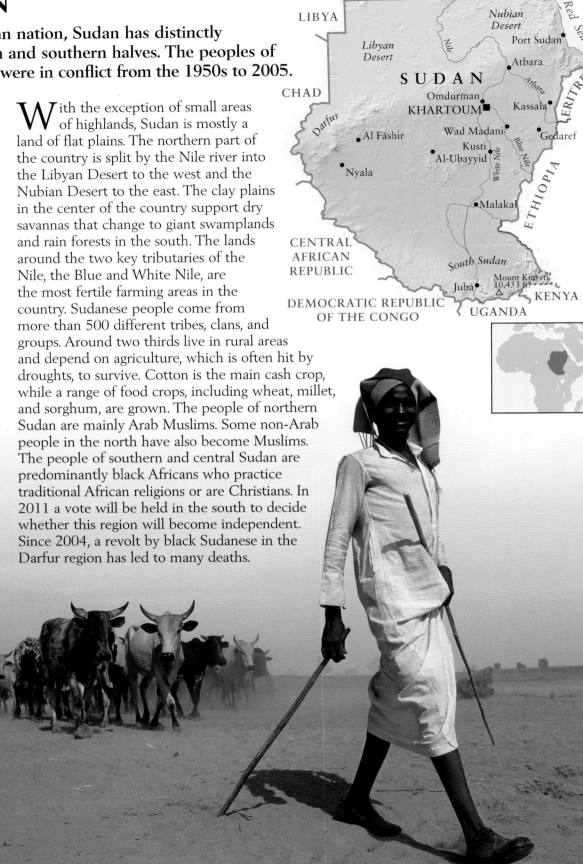

# SOMALIA

**Formed in 1960 from Italian and British Somaliland colonies, Somalia is drought- and war-ridden and is one of the poorest nations in the world.**

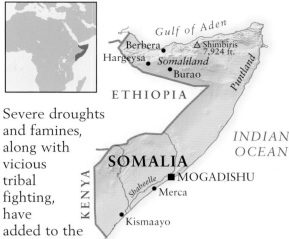

**Area:** 246,201 sq. mi. (637,657km²)
**Population:** 8,600,000
**Capital:** Mogadishu (700,000)
**Main languages spoken:** Somali, Arabic
**Main religion:** Sunni Islam
**Currency:** Somali shilling
**Main exports:** sheep and goats, bananas, camels and cattle
**Type of government:** republic; no effective national government

Somalia consists of rugged plains and plateaus. Much of the country is very dry. Fruit, corn, sugarcane, and cotton, are grown in the southwest. More than half of the population are nomadic, wandering with herds of animals. Industry, limited to processing leather and food products, largely halted in the 1990s. In 1991 a dictatorship was overthrown, and since then the country has been in political turmoil.

Severe droughts and famines, along with vicious tribal fighting, have added to the troubles of the already desperately poor people. The North, Somaliland, has effectively left Somalia, whose government only controls Mogadishu. Somali pirates regularly capture ships in the Indian Ocean.

# ETHIOPIA

**Formerly called Abyssinia, Ethiopia is one of the world's oldest nations and one of the only parts of Africa that has never been a European colony.**

**Area:** 435,186 sq. mi. (1,127,127km²)
**Population:** 73,919,000
**Capital:** Addis Ababa (2,738,000)
**Main languages spoken:** Amharic, Tigrinya, Orominga
**Main religions:** Islam, Ethiopian Orthodox, animist
**Currency:** birr
**Main exports:** coffee (accounts for almost two thirds of exports), animal hides, pulses, petroleum products
**Type of government:** federal republic

Ethiopia is dominated by highland areas and is divided by the Great Rift Valley, which runs from north to south. Three fourths of its land is above 4,590 ft. (1,400m) in elevation. Lake Tana, which lies in the north of the country, is northeast Africa's largest lake. To the east lies a semidesert plain, and north of this plain is one of the hottest places on Earth, with temperatures reaching 122°F (50°C). Rainfall varies greatly, usually with elevation, but is often not enough to prevent devastating droughts. Over 80 percent of Ethiopians are rural and rely on farming to survive, with coffee the key cash crop and livestock herding vital for domestic food. Ethiopia is one of the least developed and poorest nations in the world. Frequent droughts, famines, and wars have all damaged the economy and created great suffering among the country's people.

▼ A cascading waterfall on the Blue Nile river as it runs through Ethiopia. The Blue Nile, known as Abay to Ethiopians, is a major tributary of the Nile.

# ERITREA

**One of the youngest African nations, Eritrea became independent from Ethiopia in 1993. The country has a 620-mi.- (1,000-km-) long coastline with the Red Sea.**

**Area:** 46,760 sq. mi. (121,100km²)
**Population:** 3,622,000
**Capital:** Asmera (501,000)
**Main languages spoken:** Tigrinya, Tigre, Kunama, Afar, Amhanc, Arabic
**Main religions:** Islam, Coptic Christian, Roman Catholic, Protestant
**Currency:** nakfa
**Main exports:** raw materials (including animal hides), food products, manufactures (inc. footwear and textiles)
**Type of government:** transitional

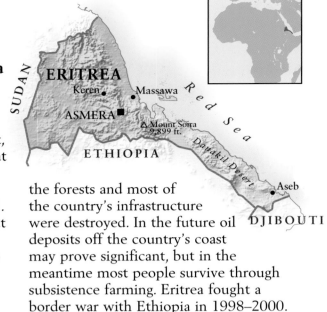

Eritrea's land consists of a hot, dry coastal plain that rises to form areas of highland plateaus with an elevation of between 4,920–8,040 ft. (1,500–2,450m). Rainfall is higher in the highland areas but is still relatively low, and at times the country suffers from droughts. Handed to Ethiopia by the United Nations in 1952, Eritreans embarked upon a 30-year-long war of independence in which many hundreds of thousands of people died, and the forests and most of the country's infrastructure were destroyed. In the future oil deposits off the country's coast may prove significant, but in the meantime most people survive through subsistence farming. Eritrea fought a border war with Ethiopia in 1998–2000. The economy of Eritrea is largely state-run.

# DJIBOUTI

... esert land that ... Its capital, ... ional port.

... to the north, with low ... center and south, most ... is hot deserts broken up ... and salt lakes. Rainfall ... ountains but even there ... (32cm), while most of ... es less than 6 in. (15cm) ... vestock is the chief ... close to two thirds of ... in or around the city of ... try's economy is highly dependent on the port's strategic location at the junction of the Red Sea and the Gulf of Aden. Much of Djibouti's income is derived from port trade since it is the main outlet for landlocked Ethiopia's

**Type of government:** republic

▶ Salt is extracted from Lake Assal in the center of Djibouti. At 515 ft. (157m) below sea level, the lake is the lowest point in Africa.

coffee crops and other produce. Djibouti became independent from France in 1977 and still relies on aid from that country. Unemployment is high, poverty is common, and tensions between the country's two main peoples, the Issa and the Afar, have resulted in occasional conflicts.

# WEST AFRICA

Most of the land that comprises west Africa lies below 4,920 ft. (1,500m) in elevation, and much of its territory consists of plains. Three large nations, Mauritania, Mali, and Niger, lie to the north—much of their land area is part of the Sahara Desert. Farther south the land and vegetation vary from semidesert to savanna, and farthest south there are large—but shrinking—tropical rain forests. South of these three desert giants are nations whose land is among the most densely populated in Africa. All, except Burkina Faso, Mali, and Niger, have coastlines with the Atlantic Ocean. The majority of the region's rivers, including its largest, the Niger, empty into this ocean. West Africa was the home of large and flourishing civilizations hundreds of years before European explorers and traders arrived on its shores. The region became subject to the rule and exploitation of its resources and people by European colonial powers. Millions were sent overseas to work as as slaves, and the region became seriously depopulated. Today west Africa comprises 16 nations and the island republic of Cape Verde. Relatively rich in mineral and natural resources, the region includes a number of countries that are developing large-scale industries.

▲ A woman grinds grain into flour using a pole, called a pestle, in the west African country of Niger. Although a number of west African nations have developed large manufacturing and service industries, agriculture still remains the biggest single employer.

# CAPE VERDE

Lying off the west coast of Africa, the island group of Cape Verde became independent from Portugal in 1975. Over half of the people live on the island of São Tiago.

**Area:** 1,557 sq. mi. (4,033km²)
**Population:** 509,000
**Capital:** Praia (125,000)
**Main languages spoken:** Portuguese, Crioulo (Portuguese Creole)
**Main religion:** Roman Catholic
**Currency:** Cape Verdean escudo
**Main exports:** shoes, clothing, and textiles, fish and fish products, salt, bananas
**Type of government:** republic

The ten islands and five islets that comprise Cape Verde are of volcanic origin and contain one active volcano, Pico do Fogo, which, at 9,279 ft. (2,829m), is also the island's highest point. Rainfall (less than 10 in./25cm per year), vegetation, and wildlife are all fairly sparse on these rugged islands, most of which are mountainous. Cape Verde suffers severe water shortages. Farming is only possible in limited areas in valleys using irrigation, and the islands have to import much of their food. The fishing industry is the country's biggest export earner. The islands are increasingly becoming a tourist destination. Aid, mainly from the European Union, has helped improve health care and education.

---

# MAURITANIA

The largely desert nation of Mauritania received its independence from France in 1960 and since that time has increased its ties with the Arab world.

**Area:** 397,955 sq. mi. (1,030,700km²)
**Population:** 3,162,000
**Capital:** Nouakchott (847,000)
**Main languages spoken:** Hasaniya, Arabic, Wolof, Pular, Soninke
**Main religion:** Islam
**Currency:** ouguiya (the world's only nondecimal currency)
**Main exports:** iron ore, fish and fish products
**Type of government:** republic; dictatorship

Like Mali, which it borders to the south and east, most of Mauritania lies within the Sahara Desert. Only its southern lands and some areas of its Atlantic coast are capable of supporting varied vegetation. Farming is mainly confined to the valley along the border area with Senegal, where millet, pulses, and dates are among the crops grown. The rich fishing grounds off its coastline make fish and fish processing one of the country's major exports behind iron ore, which accounts for 40 percent of exports. The country produces gold, copper, and petroleum and has huge, untouched gypsum deposits. Fishing and mining account for over 99 percent of its earnings from exports. The majority of Mauritania's population are either Moors, a north African people, or of mixed Arab origin. Black Africans from many different ethnic groups make up around 30 percent. Ethnic tensions and occasional conflicts exist between the Moors, who are dominant in politics, and the black minority.

► Imraguen fishermen gather a catch of golden mullet at the Banc d'Arguin National Park off the coast of Mauritania. Imraguen fishermen have fished this area for thousands of years.

# MALI

**Once the center of a great Saharan trading empire, Mali is a landlocked, underdeveloped country in which droughts and famines have created widespread poverty.**

**Area:** 482,077 sq. mi. (1,248,574km²)
**Population:** 14,517,000
**Capital:** Bamako (1,809,000)
**Main languages spoken:** Bambara, French, many African languages
**Main religions:** Islam, indigenous beliefs
**Currency:** CFA franc
**Main exports:** cotton and cotton products, live animals, gold
**Type of government:** republic

▶ Droughts and political boundaries have forced many of the Saharan nomadic Tuareg peoples to settle in towns and cities.

Almost half of Mali's land is part of the Sahara Desert, while semiarid sand areas cover much of the rest of the country. Mountains rise to the south, and hydroelectric dams on the Niger river provide 57 percent of Mali's electricity. Mali's fast-growing population is concentrated in the southern part of the country and is reliant on the Niger river for water for crop irrigation, as well as for the rich fish stocks it holds. Deforestation and desertification are rampant, and less than ten percent of the country's people have access to adequate sanitation. Most people are rural farmers and livestock herders. The key industries of the country are cotton growing and, increasingly, mining for gold and other minerals.

# NIGER

**Niger is a poor, desertlike country. The majority of its people live in a semifertile southern strip bordering Nigeria and, to the southwest, the Niger river.**

**Area:** 458,075 sq. mi. (1,186,408km²)
**Population:** 14,297,000
**Capital:** Niamey (1,033,000)
**Main languages spoken:** French, Hausa, Djerma
**Main religions:** Islam, traditional beliefs
**Currency:** CFA franc
**Main exports:** uranium, livestock, black-eyed peas
**Type of government:** republic; dictatorship

The northern two thirds of Niger are part of the Sahara Desert, which is spreading southward as desertification continues. Three fourths of the population work in agriculture, although less than four percent of the land can be cultivated. Herding livestock is a major occupation, while some people fish the Niger river. Niger is an important producer of uranium, the price of which has increased, adding value to Niger's exports. However, Niger remains one of the poorest countries in the world. Coal, phosphates, tin, and salt are also mined. Niger's population is ethnically diverse. The leading groups include the Djerma-Songhai, the Fulani, and the Hausa. Another small group are the Tuareg, many of whom live a nomadic life raising livestock in the dry north. The population of Niger is increasing rapidly, but the average life expectancy is only 53 years.

# SENEGAL

**The former French colony of Senegal lies on the bulge of western Africa, bounded by the Atlantic Ocean, Mauritania, Mali, Guinea, and Guinea-Bissau.**

**Area:** 75,951 sq. mi. (196,712km²)
**Population:** 11,343,000
**Capital:** Dakar (2,446,000)
**Main languages spoken:** French, Wolof, Pulaar, Diola, Mandingo
**Main religion:** Islam
**Currency:** CFA franc
**Main exports:** fish and crustaceans, chemicals, peanut oil, phosphates
**Type of government:** republic; democracy

▼ Senegalese women carry a harvest of millet in baskets perched on top of their heads. Millet is a staple grain used in stews and many Senegalese meals.

Senegal is a largely flat, sandy, and low-lying country with an average elevation below 656 ft. (200m). Higher land is only found in the extreme southeast, where mountains rise to elevations above 1,640 ft. (500m). Senegal has a hot, tropical climate with more rainfall toward the south. As a result of this, there are dry savannas in the north and considerably more lush areas of rain forests in the south. Four major rivers cross the country, including the large Sénégal river, which forms most of the country's border with Mauritania. The Sénégal floods every year and deposits fertile sediment over a large area on which a number of crops are grown. Around 77 percent of the workforce are employed in farming. The country is encouraging the growth of crops like sugarcane, cotton, rice, and vegetables to reduce its reliance on the single dominant crop of peanuts. The country's population consists of seven main ethnic groups, with the Wolof making up around 43 percent. Compared to many neighboring countries, Senegal is fairly wealthy. It has well-developed transportation and communications systems and a relatively large industrial sector. Senegal's capital and largest city, Dakar, is located on the Cape Verde Peninsula, which contains mainland Africa's most westerly point.

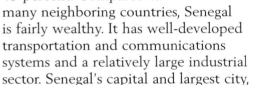

# THE GAMBIA

**Surrounded by Senegal on three sides, the Gambia is the smallest nation on the west African mainland and at no point measures more than 50 mi. (80km) wide.**

▲ Formerly a naval port, the Gambia's capital city of Banjul is located on Banjul Island. This road, Independence Drive, connects the city to the mainland.

**Area:** 4,127 sq. mi. (10,689km²)
**Population:** 1,660,000
**Capital:** Banjul (524,000)
**Main languages spoken:** English, Madinka, Wolof, Fula
**Main religion:** Islam
**Currency:** dalasi
**Main exports:** reexports (mainly to Senegal), fish and fish products, groundnuts, processed food
**Type of government:** republic

The Gambia is dominated by the Gambia river, which runs east to west through the entire country and divides it in half. Most of its land is savanna grasslands, with some forested areas and swamplands close to the river and the coast. Rice and peanuts are the two largest crops. Gambia's industry is mainly limited to processing farm products. The country has a tropical climate with a short rainy season between June and October. Gambians come from many different ethnic groups, and around 90 percent are Muslims. Many rural Gambians are migrating to towns, where incomes are often three or four times higher than in rural areas. There they work in service industries, transportation, and tourism. The country's capital city, Banjul, is located on a deep natural harbor, one of the best on the entire west coast of Africa. Revenue from tourists, most of whom come from the U.K., Germany, and other European nations, is the fastest-growing part of the country's economy.

# GUINEA-BISSAU

**Guinea-Bissau, one of the poorest nations in west Africa, has been troubled by internal strife since its independence from Portugal in 1974.**

**Area:** 13,950 sq. mi. (36,125km²)
**Population:** 1,548,000
**Capital:** Bissau (385,000)
**Main languages spoken:** Portuguese, Crioulo (Portuguese Creole), tribal languages
**Main religions:** indigenous beliefs, Islam
**Currency:** CFA franc
**Main exports:** cashews, timber, cotton, shrimp
**Type of government:** republic; democracy

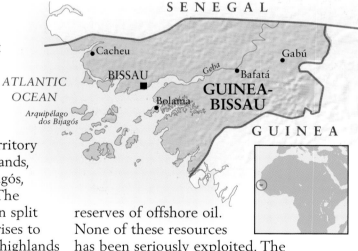

Guinea-Bissau has a heavily indented coastline, and its territory includes more than 60 offshore islands, including the Arquipélago dos Bijagós, which lies in the Atlantic Ocean. The landscape consists of a coastal plain split by many river estuaries. The land rises to a low plateau in the interior, with highlands in the northeast close to the country's border with Guinea. Guinea-Bissau has a tropical climate with heavy rainfall. Mangrove swamps and tropical jungles cover much of the land near the coast. Much of the land in the interior is savannas. Guinea-Bissau's forests contain commercially valuable hardwood trees, and the country has mineral deposits of tin, bauxite, and copper, as well as possible reserves of offshore oil. None of these resources has been seriously exploited. The population generally makes their living through subsistence farming. Fishing is also important. Guinea-Bissau has suffered instability, a civil war, and several military coups since independence. Most of the population are below the poverty line, 58 percent cannot read or write, and around ten percent of all babies die before reaching adulthood. The country is heavily reliant on foreign aid.

# GUINEA

Independent since 1958, Guinea is a poor country and is reliant on foreign aid, despite being rich in mineral reserves.

**Area:** 94,926 sq. mi. (245,857km2)
**Population:** 10,200,000
**Capital:** Conakry (1,860,000)
**Main languages spoken:** French, tribal languages
**Main religions:** Islam, Christian
**Currency:** Guinean franc
**Main exports:** bauxite, alumina, gold, coffee, diamonds, fish
**Type of government:** republic; limited democracy

Guinea consists of four regions: the wet coastal plain, the northwestern Fouta Djallon hill region, the northern dry lowlands, and the hilly, forested area of the southeast. Guinea is one of the wettest countries in west Africa, and its capital and largest city, Conakry, receives over 170 in. (430cm) of rain per year. Many crops are grown, including rice, cassava, pineapples, and peanuts. Guinea has more than 30 percent of the world's reserves of bauxite ore, from which aluminum is smelted. Bauxite makes up around two thirds of all exports. The country remains poor and underdeveloped. Corruption, instability, and a poor infrastructure hinder development.

# SIERRA LEONE

Founded in 1787 for freed African slaves, Sierra Leone became independent in 1961. Scarred by war and political instability, the country is extremely poor.

**Area:** 27,700 sq. mi. (71,740km2)
**Population:** 4,977,000
**Capital:** Freetown (791,000)
**Main languages spoken:** English, Mende, Temne, Krio (English Creole)
**Main religions:** Islam, traditional beliefs
**Currency:** leone
**Main exports:** diamonds, rutile/titanium ore, cocoa, coffee
**Type of government:** republic

Sierra Leone's land consists of a swampy coastal plain that rises to a plateau and mountains in the northeast. The capital, Freetown, is located on a rocky peninsula overlooking one of the world's largest natural harbors. Savanna grasslands are found in the northern interior, with dense rain forests in the south. Valuable tropical hardwoods, including teak and mahogany, as well as wildlife, including chimpanzees, monkeys, and numerous bird species, are under threat from heavy deforestation. Today an estimated three percent of Sierra Leone's forests are cut down each year. Seventy-six percent of the country's workforce are involved in agriculture, with rice the largest staple crop. After a devastating civil war in modern times Sierra Leone now relies heavily on foreign aid. The country remains unstable and under threat of more conflicts. Its people, comprising more than 20 ethnic groups, are among the world's poorest, with just one doctor per 15,000 people.

► A group of Sierra Leonean women tie-dye cloth to make a traditional form of brightly patterned cloth called *gara*.

# LIBERIA

**Liberia was founded in 1847 by freed African slaves from the U.S. The majority of its population are engaged in subsistence farming.**

**Area:** 43,000 sq. mi. (111,370km²)
**Population:** 3,476,000
**Capital:** Monrovia (1,015,000)
**Main languages spoken:** English, tribal languages
**Main religions:** traditional beliefs, Islam, Christian
**Currency:** Liberian dollar (the U.S. dollar is also in circulation as legal tender)
**Main exports:** iron ore, rubber, timber, diamonds, gold
**Type of government:** republic; limited democracy

Liberia's land includes a rocky coastline with lagoons and sandbars and a coastal plain on which the majority of its population live. This plain rises to a series of plateaus and low mountains. With an elevation of 4,529 ft. (1,381m), Mount Wuteve, near the border with Guinea, is Liberia's highest peak. One fifth of the country is forested. Between 1990 and 1997 a bloody civil war destroyed most of Liberia's economy. Before the war giant rubber plantations and large-scale iron ore mines accounted for most of its exports. Since the conflict the country, which had previously retained close ties with the U.S., has struggled to maintain peace. Liberia has the world's largest registered fleet of ships, but almost all of the vessels are owned by foreign companies.

▼ Digging for diamonds—Liberia is one of the world's top-20 diamond producers.

---

# TOGO

**A long, narrow country with a mixture of coastal swamps, plateaus, and low mountains, Togo stretches from the Gulf of Guinea around 320 mi. (515km) into west Africa.**

**Area:** 21,925 sq. mi. (56,785km²)
**Population:** 5,337,000
**Capital:** Lomé (1,377,000)
**Main languages spoken:** Ewe, Mina, Dagomba, Kabye
**Main religions:** indigenous beliefs, Christian, Islam
**Currency:** CFA franc
**Main exports:** cotton, reexports, phosphates, coffee
**Type of government:** republic

Around 60 percent of Togo's workforce are engaged in agriculture. Most of the country's food is grown on small farms, with staple crops such as cassava, yams, sorghum, corn, and plantains. Minerals, particularly phosphates, have become the country's leading export earner, and mining is the country's main industry. The capital city, Lomé, is also a major regional port. The people of Togo come from many ethnic groups. Tensions exist between the two largest groups—the Kabye in the north and the Ewe in the south. Isolation in international relations and lack of investment have held the economy back.

▲ This Togolese woman is at a market selling yams, which are eaten as a vegetable, ground into a flour, or boiled and eaten as a paste with soup.

357

# IVORY COAST

The Republic of Côte d'Ivoire, or the Ivory Coast, is a large, square-shaped west African nation with a tropical climate and large areas of fertile land.

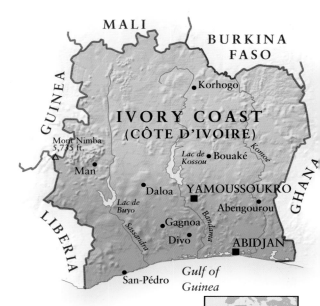

**Area:** 123,855 sq. mi. (320,783km²)
**Population:** 20,080,000
**Capitals:** Yamoussoukro (300,000)—official capital; Abidjan (4,200,000)—diplomatic and administrative capital
**Main languages spoken:** French, Dioula
**Main religions:** Islam, indigenous beliefs, Christian
**Currency:** CFA franc
**Main exports:** cocoa, coffee, wood and wood products, petroleum products, fish products
**Type of government:** republic; dictatorship

▼ Yamoussoukro's Basilica of Our Lady of Peace was modeled after St. Peter's Basilica in Rome, Italy, and is one of the largest Catholic churches in the world. It took three years to build at a cost of over $300 million.

The Ivory Coast consists of an extensive plateau rising gradually from sea level to an elevation of almost 1,640 ft. (500m). The country's coast is not easily navigable since it is fringed with lagoons, sandbars, and swamps, with some cliffs and bays to the east. A canal, completed in 1950, links the country's major city, Abidjan, to the sea so that ocean-going ships can dock. The northern part of the country is largely savanna grasslands, with mountains to the northwest, while the center is dominated by heavy rain forests that support a rich array of wildlife. Most forest clearance has occurred in the central and south-central regions of the country.

Farming is the chief occupation of the Ivory Coast's workforce. While many people grow only enough to feed their families, much of the country's farming is conducted on a larger scale. The Ivory Coast is the world's largest producer of cacao beans, used to make chocolate and cocoa. It is Africa's leading coffee producer and also grows cotton, palm oil, and rubber for export. Yamoussoukro, near the country's largest lake, Lac de Kossou, was declared the country's capital in 1983, but many government offices remain in Abidjan,

the country's major port, commercial center, and its most populous city. Compared with many of its west African neighbors, the Ivory Coast had a stable political history until almost the end of the 20th century. It became independent from France in 1960 and was ruled for 33 years by a single president, Houphouët-Boigny. During the 1960s and 1970s the country's economy flourished with financial assistance from France. Expensive projects were undertaken, including the building of some of the world's largest churches and mosques. But in the 1980s the economy took a downturn and the country faced huge foreign debts. In 1999 the country was disrupted by a military coup, followed by a civil war between the largely Muslim, rebel-held north and the mainly Christian, government-held south.

# GHANA

**Ghana is one of the most developed countries in west Africa. Its economy is based mainly on agriculture and mining.**

**Area:** 92,098 sq. mi. (238,533km²)
**Population:** 23,417,000
**Capital:** Accra (2,906,000)
**Main languages spoken:** English, Akan, Moshi-Dagomba, Ewe, Ga
**Main religions:** indigenous beliefs, Islam, Christian
**Currency:** cedi
**Main exports:** gold, cocoa, food products, timber, tuna, bauxite
**Government:** republic

▼ A traditional wooden boat, known as a pirogue, travels along the Volta river. The Volta river and lake system provide almost ten percent of the country's annual fish catch of over 485,000 tons (440,000 metric tonnes).

Ghana is a low-lying nation in west Africa. Half of its land lies below 492 ft. (150m), and its highest point, Mount Afadjato (2,886 ft./880m), is in the eastern hills near the border with Togo. Much of the country's landscape is formed by the basin of the Volta rivers. The northern region is drained by the Black Volta and White Volta rivers, which join to form the Volta. This river is crossed by the Akosombo hydroelectric dam in the southeast of the country, which forms one of the world's largest artificial lakes, Lake Volta. Almost all of Ghana's electricity is generated via hydroelectric power. Ghana has a tropical climate, with daily temperatures tending to range between 70–90°F (21–32°C). There are two rainy seasons, from March to July and from September to October. Annual rainfall varies greatly throughout the country, ranging between 40 in. (100cm) in the north to 81 in. (205cm) in the southeast. In the north large areas are savannas, while a mixture of savannas and rain forests covers the center and south of the country. Much of the original vegetation has been cleared for farming and by the country's large timber industry. Ghana is one of Africa's leading timber exporters, and cocoa is its chief export crop. Ghana was a British colony until 1957 and was known as the Gold Coast. The country lives up to its former name, being the third-largest producer of gold in Africa, producing around 145,950 lbs. (66,200kg) in 2006. It also has diamond, bauxite, and manganese mines. Despite military coups between 1966 and 1981, Ghana has been more stable than neighboring countries, and since 1992, it has been a democracy.

# NIGERIA

**The most populous country in Africa, Nigeria is home to several hundred different ethnic groups. This large nation is rich in natural resources, especially oil.**

**Area:** 356,412 sq. mi. (923,103km²)
**Population:** 140,003,000
**Capital:** Abuja (778,000)
**Main languages spoken:** English, Hausa, Yoruba, Ibo
**Main religions:** Islam, Christian
**Currency:** naira
**Main exports:** crude petroleum (over 90 percent of exports), cocoa beans, rubber, textiles
**Type of government:** republic

Nigeria's coast consists of a number of long, sandy beaches broken up by mangrove swamps where rivers meet the sea. The Niger river, which enters the country in the northwest and flows through the western region of Nigeria, is the country's major river system. As the Niger heads toward the coast it fans out to form Africa's largest river delta, around 14,000 sq. mi. (36,000km²) in area. High rainfall in the river valleys and along the coast enables a large range of crops to be grown. Along the river floodplains rice is a common crop. Along the coastal region, which extends up to 60 mi. (100km) inland, the land becomes hilly and largely covered in forests before rising to the Jos Plateau in the center of the country. North of this are savanna plains, which are the largest areas of farmland in the country. The savanna gets drier and becomes semidesert and desert in the far north.

## AN OIL-DEPENDENT ECONOMY

Nigeria is rich in natural resources, including tin, iron ore, coal, limestone, zinc, and lead. Chief among its mineral reserves, however, are oil and natural gas. Nigeria is one of the world's leading crude oil producers, extracting around 2.3 million barrels per day. Oil accounts for over 95 percent of the country's exports, but the

yams, taro, and rice. The country's fast-growing population means that Nigeria has to import a large amount of its food.

## MANY DIFFERENT PEOPLES

Nigeria has a long history, not just of settlement but also of empires and city-states—long before the region was colonized by European powers. Peoples such as the Hausa in the north, the Ibo (Igbo) in the southeast, and the Yoruba, based around the city of Ife in the southwest, had formed well-organized kingdoms centuries before European arrivals. The Hausa, Yoruba, and Ibo peoples make up over half of the country's population. The remainder belong to over 250 different ethnic groups that not only contribute to Nigeria's extremely rich culture and arts but also divide the country along both ethnic and language lines. In addition, there is a religious divide, with people in the north predominantly Muslim and those in the south mainly Christian or practicing traditional African beliefs. Keeping so many different peoples with different cultures and beliefs together in one single nation has proved difficult, especially since the divide between the Muslim north and the rest of the country is increasing. Since independence in 1960 Nigeria has had to contend with many conflicts within its borders, including a civil war (1967–1970) when the Ibo people tried to break away to form their own nation of Biafra. There have been more years of rule by military dictatorships than elected civilian governments, and the country maintains an uneasy peace to this day.

◀ Lagos is the most important city in Nigeria, with a fast-growing population rivaling Cairo, Egypt, for the title of Africa's largest city. The country's chief port, around half of the entire country's manufacturing industry is based in or around Lagos.

wealth generated has only benefited very few because corruption is rampant. In addition, the reliance on a single commodity means that the economy is severely affected by changes in oil prices. In comparison to oil, Nigeria's natural gas and other mineral deposits are underexploited. Agriculture employs 40 percent of the country's workforce, and cocoa, rubber, and textiles are the chief exports. However, the large majority of farming is performed on small family farms growing staple foods, including sorghum, millet, corn,

▼ A tugboat maneuvers a raft of logs along one of Nigeria's rivers. Logging is a major industry in Nigeria, with the majority of wood used by Nigerians as firewood.

# BURKINA FASO

**Burkina Faso is a landlocked country lying on the fringe of the Sahara. Droughts and desertification have recently increased the nation's difficulties.**

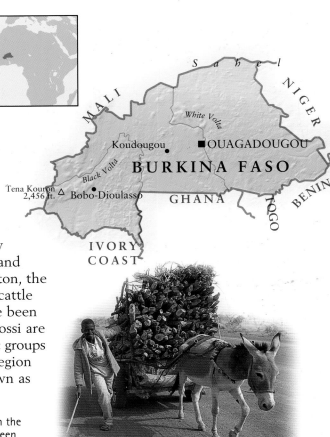

**Area:** 105,839 sq. mi.
(274,122km²)
**Population:** 15,225,000
**Capital:** Ouagadougou
(1,475,000)
**Main languages spoken:**
French, Sudanic tribal
languages
**Main religions:** Islam,
indigenous beliefs,
Roman Catholic
**Currency:** CFA franc
**Main exports:** cotton,
live animals, gold, hides
and skins
**Type of government:**
republic

Most of Burkina Faso is flat, with some rolling hills and forests in the southwest. The north of the country is dry, and frequent droughts afflict most of the country. The majority of the population are farmers who live in the south and grow either food crops, such as rice, cereals, and vegetables, or cash crops, including cotton, the leading export crop. Goats, sheep, and cattle are herded, but livestock numbers have been severely decreased by droughts. The Mossi are the largest of Burkina Faso's many ethnic groups and were the traditional rulers of the region before it became a French colony, known as Upper Volta, between 1895 and 1960.

▶ A Burkinabé man guides his cart carrying wood in the Sahel region. The Sahel is a dry transition zone between the Sahara and more lush grasslands in the south.

# BENIN

**Formerly known as Dahomey, Benin is a small west African nation that stretches north around 415 mi. (670km) from the Gulf of Guinea to the Niger river.**

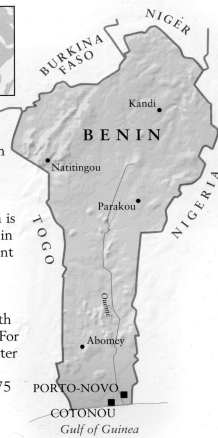

**Area:** 43,484 sq. mi.
(112,622km²)
**Population:** 7,841,000
**Capitals:** Porto-Novo
(224,000)—legislative
capital; Cotonou
(879,000)—diplomatic and
administrative capital
**Main languages spoken:**
French, Fon, Yoruba
**Main religions:** indigenous
beliefs, Islam, Christian
**Currency:** CFA franc
**Main exports:** cotton
yarn, re-exports of
manufactures, cashews
**Type of government:**
republic

Benin's sandy, 75-mi.- (121-km-) long coastal strip is indented with lagoons and mangrove swamps. North of this region is a fertile plateau that contains large marshlands. The plateau gradually rises and is crossed in the center of the country by mountains. Benin's climate is tropical but with relatively low average rainfall, which is highest in the south. Desertification is a major problem in the northern region. The people are a mixture of different ethnic groups, with the Fon, the largest group, making up just under 40 percent. The people make their living mainly through subsistence farming. Rice, corn, cassava, millet, and yams are among the crops grown. In the north goat, sheep, and cattle herding is the major occupation. For more than six centuries the city of Abomey was the center of a prosperous kingdom before coming under French control. Independence was achieved in 1960, and in 1975 the country changed its name to Benin. The early years of independence saw a number of military coups, but multiparty elections were restored in the 1990s.

# CENTRAL AND EAST AFRICA

Central and east Africa straddle the equator, and most of the 15 nations that occupy this region experience a tropical climate. The region is divided in two by a giant split in Earth's crust called the Great Rift Valley, with uplands on both sides. A chain of lakes runs along the Great Rift Valley, while Lake Victoria—Africa's largest and the world's third-largest lake, with an area of 26,830 sq. mi. (69,500km²)—lies between the two branches of the valley. West of the Great Rift Valley the Congo river, Africa's second-longest river, snakes through Congo and the Democratic Republic of the Congo, a distance of approximately 2,920 mi. (4,700km). Central and east Africa's populations have experienced varying fortunes since independence from colonial powers occurred, mainly in the 1960s. Some nations, such as the Central African Republic, are poor; others, like Rwanda, have been torn apart by war, while some nations, including Kenya, are relatively stable.

▲ Central Africa is home to the gorilla, the largest of the world's apes. The region's gorilla population is under threat from hunting and habitat destruction.

▼ Refugees from the central African nation of Rwanda in a refugee camp in Tanzania. In the mid-1990s a brutal civil war in Rwanda saw between 500,000 and one million Tutsi people killed in fighting.

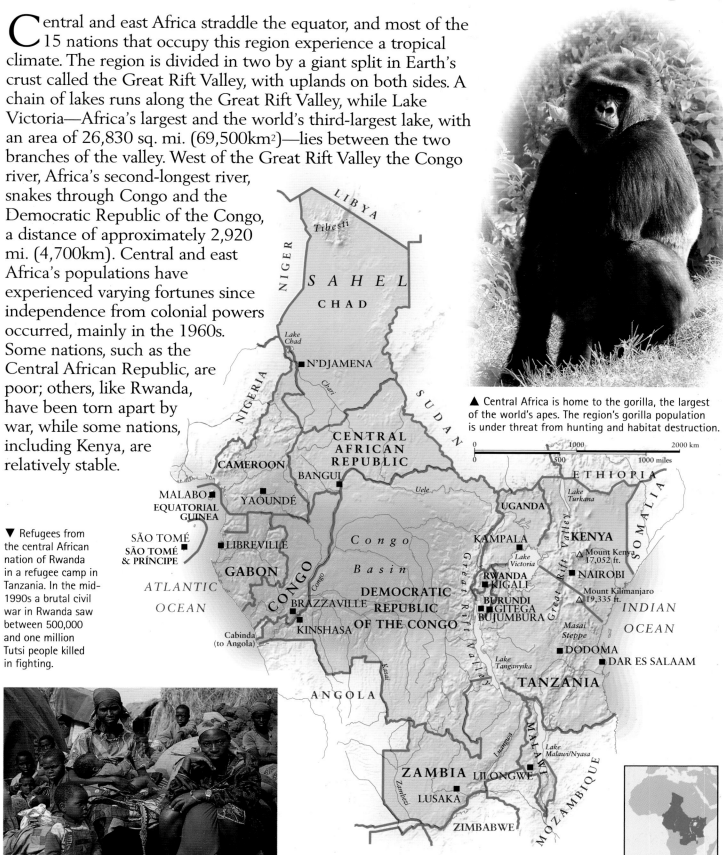

# CAMEROON

**A heavily forested country, with the majority of its people living in the south, Cameroon has developed its industry and infrastructure since independence in 1961.**

**Area:** 183,569 sq. mi. (475,442km²)
**Population:** 18,675,000
**Capital:** Yaoundé (1,248,000)
**Main languages spoken:** English, French, 24 African languages
**Main religions:** indigenous beliefs, Christian, Islam
**Currency:** CFA franc
**Main exports:** crude petroleum, timber, cocoa, coffee, aluminum, cotton
**Type of government:** republic

Cameroon is a country of varied landscapes. In the south there are coastal plains, small wetlands, and a plateau mainly covered in rain forests. In the north dry grasslands continue northward until they reach the southern shores of Lake Chad. Along the country's northern and western borders with Nigeria the land is mountainous and rises to an elevation of 13,432 ft. (4,095m)—the peak of the Cameroon mountain volcano Fako. The western slopes of this mountain are some of the wettest places in the world, with an average annual rainfall as high as 394 in. (1,000cm). Cameroon's population is very diverse, with over 210 different ethnic groups and no one dominant people. A large range of crops is grown for food and export, and for many years the country has been self-sufficient in staple foods. Over 90 percent of its electricity is generated through hydroelectric power, of which almost half is used to power a giant aluminum plant. Oil, although declining, still provides valuable export revenue, while commercial fishing is on the rise.

# CENTRAL AFRICAN REPUBLIC

**Since independence in 1960 the landlocked and poor country of the Central African Republic has been largely governed by dictators and the military.**

**Area:** 240,324 sq. mi. (622,436km²)
**Population:** 3,895,000
**Capital:** Bangui (747,000)
**Main languages spoken:** French, Sangho, Arabic, Hunsa, Swahili
**Main religions:** Protestant, Roman Catholic, indigenous beliefs, Islam
**Currency:** CFA franc
**Main exports:** diamonds, coffee, timber and timber products, cotton
**Type of government:** republic; limited democracy

Most of the Central African Republic consists of a plateau that ranges in elevation between 1,970–2,620 ft. (600–800m). The plateau is flanked by highland areas to the northeast and hill ranges to the north. Dense rain forests cover much of the south of the country, some of which are in reserves to protect wildlife, including gorillas and leopards. The remainder of the land is grasslands with some trees. Less than four percent of the country is cultivated, and subsistence agriculture dominates the lives of the people. Deposits of uranium, iron, and copper exist, but mining focuses on diamonds, which account for 40 percent of the country's exports.

▶ These Baaka pygmies in the rain forests of the Central African Republic make simple shelters from bent tree branches covered in bark and foliage.

364

# EQUATORIAL GUINEA

The small country of Equatorial Guinea consists of the mainland, called Rio Muni, and five islands, the largest of which, Bioko, is the site of the country's capital.

**Area:** 10,831 sq. mi. (28,051km²)
**Population:** 1,015,000
**Capital:** Malabo (93,000)
**Main languages spoken:** Spanish, French, Fang, Bubi
**Main religion:** Roman Catholic
**Currency:** CFA franc
**Main exports:** petroleum products, timber, cocoa
**Type of government:** republic

Surrounded by Gabon and Cameroon, the small mainland region of Equatorial Guinea is a land of few extremes in height. Inland from the coastal plain and hill ranges over half of the land is heavily forested. The country's varied wildlife includes elephants, gorillas, leopards, crocodiles, and chimpanzees. However, many creatures are endangered as a result of extensive and uncontrolled logging operations. In contrast to the landscape of the mainland, Equatorial Guinea's largest island, Bioko, has a dramatic and rugged terrain. Of volcanic origin, the island contains a number of crater lakes and extinct volcanic cones, one of which, Pico Basilé, is the country's highest point at 9,866 ft. (3,008m). Bioko is the center of the country's cacao bean production, the country's main export crop. Coffee is grown for export on the mainland, while rice, yams, and bananas are among the key staple foods. The country became independent in 1968 after a long period of Spanish rule and remained largely undeveloped until the discovery of oil in the late 1980s. Oil production today is around 360,000 barrels per day. The country is now a considerable oil exporter, but the wealth oil has brought is confined to a small group of people and the majority still live in great poverty.

# SÃO TOMÉ & PRÍNCIPE

**Lying off the coast of west Africa, the smallest country in Africa consists of one large island, São Tomé, one smaller island, Príncipe, and a small number of islets.**

**Area:** 386 sq. mi. (1,001km²)
**Population:** 170,000
**Capital:** São Tomé (52,000)
**Main language spoken:** Portuguese
**Main religion:** Roman Catholic
**Currency:** dobra
**Main exports:** cocoa (over 95 percent of exports)
**Type of government:** republic

Príncipe • Santo António

*Gulf of Guinea*

**SÃO TOMÉ & PRÍNCIPE**

*São Tomé*

Pico de São Tomé △ ■ SÃO TOMÉ
6,638 ft.

*ATLANTIC OCEAN*

Separated by 90 mi. (144km) of ocean, both islands were formed by volcanic activity and have high mountains in the south and west and lowland areas in the north. Lying on the equator, São Tomé & Príncipe has a warm, tropical climate, and dense forests cover around half of both islands. A former Portuguese colony, the people are mainly of African descent, with a minority of Portuguese origin.

The majority are Roman Catholics, although some are Protestant or practice traditional African beliefs. The country is dependent on cocoa exports to pay for food and fuel imports and is also reliant on foreign aid. However, oil exploration, tourism, and fishing offer hope for future economic development.

# CHAD

**A poor, landlocked nation in northern central Africa, Chad is more than 990 mi. (1,600km) from the ocean, and its northern region is part of the Sahara Desert.**

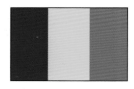

**Area:** 495,750 sq. mi. (1,284,000km²)
**Population:** 11,176,000
**Capital:** N'Djamena (993,000)
**Main languages spoken:** French, Arabic, Sara, Songo
**Main religions:** Islam, Christian, indigenous beliefs
**Currency:** CFA franc
**Main exports:** petroleum, cotton, live cattle
**Type of government:** republic; limited democracy

LIBYA

*Tibesti*

△ Emi Koussi
11,201 ft.

*Sahara*

NIGER

**CHAD**

*Sahel*

Lake Chad

Abéché •

SUDAN

■ N'DJAMENA

CAMEROON

*Chari*

Sarh •

• Moundou

CENTRAL AFRICAN REPUBLIC

Chad's landscape is dominated by the large basin that surrounds Lake Chad. This shallow lake has shrunk since the 1960s, when it covered up to 10,040 sq. mi. (26,000km²) in a season of heavy rain to around 520 sq. mi. (1,350km²) in 2007. Stretching away from the basin are plateaus that rise to mountains in the north, south, and east. Chad's climate is hot and extremely dry in the north, where the land is desert, while rainfall is relatively heavy in the south, where the majority of the country's people live. The south is mainly savanna and is the chief farming region of the country. Since independence from France Chad has been beset by internal conflicts and civil wars, which have prevented the country's development. Chad became an oil-exporting country in 2003, when a pipeline from Chadian oil fields to the Atlantic was opened.

▼ Located 490 mi. (790km) northeast of N'Djamena, Faya is one of the largest oasis towns in the Sahara desert and relies on underground water to grow dates, wheat, and figs.

# GABON

**Containing some of Africa's largest original rain forests and an array of wildlife, Gabon is a sparsely populated nation whose people are fairly prosperous.**

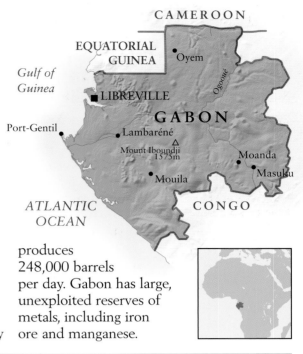

**Area:** 103,347 sq. mi.
(267,667km²)
**Population:** 1,521,000
**Capital:** Libreville
(662,000)
**Main languages spoken:**
French, Bantu dialects
**Main religion:** Christian
**Currency:** CFA franc
**Main exports:** petroleum
and petroleum products
(accounting for over 80
percent of exports), wood,
manganese ore, uranium
**Type of government:**
republic; dictatorship

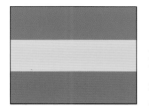

Gabon consists of a coastal plain that rises inland to form a series of mountains, valleys, and plateaus mostly covered in untouched rain forests. Unlike many African countries, Gabon has not been troubled by conflicts since independence from France in 1960. Although many Gabonese live in poverty, the country is wealthy in comparison to much of Africa, largely owing to its oil revenues—the country produces 248,000 barrels per day. Gabon has large, unexploited reserves of metals, including iron ore and manganese.

# CONGO

**The Republic of the Congo is a tropical country that was Africa's first communist state from 1970 to 1991. More than half of the land is covered in rain forests.**

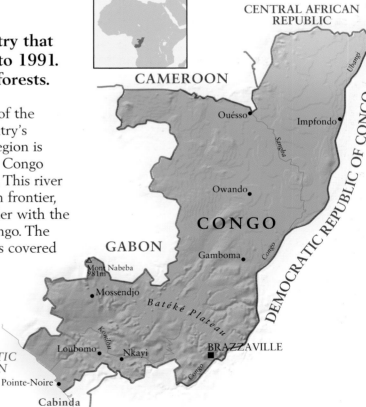

**Area:** 132,050 sq. mi.
(342,000km²)
**Population:** 4,002,000
**Capital:** Brazzaville
(1,408,000)
**Main languages spoken:**
French, Lingala, Kikongo
**Main religions:** Christian,
animist, Islam
**Currency:** CFA franc
**Main exports:** petroleum
and petroleum products,
wood and timber
products, sugar
**Type of government:**
republic; dictatorship

Much of the country's northern region is part of the Congo river basin. This river flows along the country's eastern frontier, where it forms most of the border with the Democratic Republic of the Congo. The northern region of the country is covered with swamps and dense forests, while there are grasslands to the south. Oil, first discovered in the 1970s and largely found offshore, is the country's key resource and is responsible for 75 percent of its export earnings. Other major industries are mining, timber, coffee, and cocoa. Most farmland is devoted to producing food for local consumption, with women traditionally the farmworkers.

Congo's transportation, energy, and communications are underdeveloped, and much of the country is isolated, using only dirt roads or the large river network for transportation. Most of the Congo's industry is situated in Pointe Noire, the country's main Atlantic port.

# DEMOCRATIC REP. OF THE CONGO

The Democratic Republic of the Congo, formerly Zaire, is Africa's third-largest country. Despite rich natural resources, its people are among Africa's poorest.

**Area:** 905,354 sq. mi. (2,344,856km²)
**Population:** 58,300,000
**Capital:** Kinshasa (7,274,000)
**Main language spoken:** French
**Main religions:** Roman Catholic, Protestant, Islam, Kimbanguist
**Currency:** Congolese franc
**Main exports:** diamonds, crude petroleum, coffee, copper, cobalt
**Type of government:** republic; limited democracy

▼ A small settlement in the Democratic Republic of the Congo's Ruwenzori Mountains. This rugged mountain range straddles the country's border with its neighbor, Uganda.

The Democratic Republic of the Congo is almost landlocked except for a thin strip of land on the north bank of the Congo river, which gives the country a 23-mi.- (37-km-) long Atlantic coastline. The Congo's giant river basin dominates the country's landscape, covering an area of almost 380,000 sq. mi. (1,000,000km²), and is largely covered in rain forests. The basin rises to form mountain plateaus in the west, while in the south there are grassland plains. The country's highest mountains are found in the east. Lying on the equator, the country has a tropical climate, with the hottest temperatures in the central region. The southern highlands are cooler and drier, while the eastern highlands are cooler and wetter. Over 60 percent of this large country is covered in rain forests that account for approximately half of Africa's forests. The country's poor transportation network has prevented large-scale clearance by big logging businesses. However, deforestation is occurring in order to supply local people with firewood and farmland. Most of the population farm the land, growing rice, cassava, peanuts, and fruit trees. The country is rich in natural resources and is a leading producer of copper, cobalt, and diamonds. Yet the wealth from these resources has been squandered through colonial exploitation by Belgium before 1960, civil wars, and corrupt government. Two wars, in which neighboring countries intervened, wrecked the infrastructure in 1996–1997 and 1998–2003.

CENTRAL AFRICAN REPUBLIC

SUDAN

*Ubangi*

*Uele*

*Congo*

*Aruwimi*

Lake Albert

UGANDA

Kisangani

Margherita Peak 16,760 ft.

*Tshuapa*

Mbandaka

**DEMOCRATIC REPUBLIC OF THE CONGO**

*Congo*

*Kasai*

Bukavu

RWANDA

BURUNDI

KINSHASA

*Lualaba*

Ilebo

*Lomami*

Matadi

Kikwit

Kananga

Kalémié

Lake Tanganyika

TANZANIA

Mbuji-Mayi

ANGOLA

Kamina

Likasi

Lubumbashi

ZAMBIA

# UGANDA

Uganda is a land of fertile uplands and mountains that border Africa's largest lake. It is recovering after 25 years of ethnic conflicts under dictators.

**Area:** 93,070 sq. mi. (241,040km²)
**Population:** 29,593,000
**Capital:** Kampala (1,790,000)
**Main languages spoken:** English, Luganda, Swahili
**Main religions:** Protestant, Roman Catholic, indigenous beliefs, Islam
**Currency:** Ugandan shilling
**Main exports:** coffee, cotton, tea, fish, horticultural products
**Type of government:** republic

▼ This Ugandan fisherman hauls in a freshwater fish from the waters of Lake Victoria. Uganda has one of the largest freshwater fishing catches in the world, almost all of which is consumed within the country. In 2008 the total fish catch was more than 364,000 tons (330,000 metric tonnes).

Much of Uganda consists of a plateau that rises gently from an elevation of around 2,950 ft. (900m) in the north to 4,920 ft. (1,500m) in the south. Surrounding this elevated plateau are large valleys or mountainous areas on most sides. The western mountain range is the location of the country's highest peaks. Uganda is a land of abundant freshwater sources. Many rivers flow through the country, while almost one fifth of the country's area is made up of lakes. These include Lake Kyoga in the center of the country and Lake Albert, which lies in the Great Rift Valley to the west. Uganda has a long shoreline with Africa's largest lake, Lake Victoria. This country has an essentially tropical climate, but average temperatures are cooler owing to its relatively high altitude. Rainfall varies, with the wettest areas in the south receiving around 60 in. (150cm) per year and the driest in the northeast receiving just over half that figure.

## UGANDA'S RESOURCES
Compared to some of its neighbors, Uganda is not heavily forested. The country had around 2,510 sq. mi. (6,500km²) of forests in 1960, but today this has been reduced by over one fourth. While clearing land for farming has contributed to

deforestation, the major cause has been the use of trees to burn as fuel by Uganda's mainly rural population. Almost all of Uganda's electricity is generated by hydroelectric power. Uganda is not an oil producer, nor does it have large mining or manufacturing industries. The cost of transporting goods to seaports in Kenya and Tanzania is high. The country is blessed with fertile farmland, and Uganda's largely rural population grows a range of crops for domestic use and also for export. Coffee is the leading export, followed by fish and fish products and gold. In modern times, stability and the return of Indian-Ugandan businesspeople, who were exiled in the 1970s, have helped the economy grow.

# RWANDA

Called the "land of 1,000 hills," Rwanda is heavily populated, with about 82 percent of its people living in rural areas and involved in farming.

**Area:** 10,169 sq. mi. (26,338km²)
**Population:** 9,500,000
**Capital:** Kigali (900,000)
**Main languages spoken:** French, Kinyarwanda, English
**Main religions:** Roman Catholic, indigenous beliefs
**Currency:** Rwandan franc
**Main exports:** coffee (accounts for over 70 percent of exports), tea, hides, tin
**Type of government:** republic; limited democracy

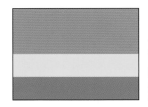

A centuries-old conflict between two major ethnic groups, the Hutu majority and the Tutsi minority, has dominated Rwanda since independence from Belgium in 1962. In 1994 violence led to the deaths of around 500,000 people, while around two million fled the country as refugees. The economy was devastated. Attempts have been made to reconcile the two peoples, but poverty and diseases are widespread, and Rwanda depends on foreign aid. It plans to develop natural gas reserves under Lake Kivu and to increase tourism in the northern forests—home to the world's largest population of mountain gorillas.

# BURUNDI

A small, landlocked, and mountainous country just south of the equator, Burundi has been troubled by ethnic conflicts between the Tutsi and Hutu peoples.

**Area:** 10,747 sq. mi. (27,834km²)
**Population:** 8,300,000
**Capital:** Bujumbura (374,000); Gitega (26,000)—capital designate
**Main languages spoken:** Kirundi, French, Swahili
**Main religions:** Roman Catholic, indigenous beliefs
**Currency:** Burundian franc
**Main exports:** coffee, tea, cotton, sugar
**Type of government:** republic; limited democracy

Lush hills and low mountains cover much of Burundi, while a large plain that borders Lake Tanganyika rises to form a plateau in the south. On the lake's northern shore is the country's capital city and chief port, Bujumbura. The fertile hill slopes are heavily farmed, with coffee the most important cash crop followed by tea and cotton. Tropical fruit are grown in the country's valleys. Burundi is one of the most densely populated countries in Africa, with 746 people per square mile. Birth rates are high, and families tend to have many children. Although the Tutsi comprise only 16 percent of the population, they retain much political and military control of the country. This has led to conflicts with the majority Hutus, resulting in over 200,000 deaths and as many as one million refugees.

# KENYA

**After independence in 1963 Kenya successfully developed its economy, but recent political and economic troubles have afflicted the country.**

**Area:** 224,961 sq. mi. (582,646km²)
**Population:** 35,112,000
**Capital:** Nairobi (2,948,000)
**Main languages spoken:** Swahili, English, indigenous languages
**Main religions:** Protestant, Roman Catholic, indigenous beliefs
**Currency:** Kenyan shilling
**Main exports:** tea, coffee, fruit and vegetables, petroleum products, cement
**Type of government:** republic

▲ A group of Masai warriors in the Masai Mara National Park, Kenya.

▼ The Samburu National Reserve is one of many large nature reserves in Kenya. Animals that roam the Samburu include elephants, lions, giraffes, zebras, and leopards.

Kenya's dramatic landscape is dominated by the Great Rift Valley, which cuts through the country from north to south. The valley, which in some places is over 1,970 ft. (600m) deep, varies in width from 9 mi. (14km) to over 50 mi. (85km). A number of lakes are found along this valley in Kenya, including Lake Rudolf, the country's largest. The Great Rift Valley divides Kenya into two areas that are unequal in area. A narrower western area consisting of plains and plateaus borders Uganda and the northeastern shore of Lake Victoria. The much larger eastern region begins with a large area of central highlands in which Kenya's loftiest peak, the 17,052-ft.- (5,199-m-) high Mount Kenya (Kirinyaga), is located. This extinct volcano is the second-highest mountain in Africa. The highlands slope down toward grassy plains before reaching the coast, which is lined with long beaches and is the home of Kenya's major port and second-largest city, Mombasa. The former British colony of Kenya has more than 50 national parks and reserves that help protect large numbers of its rich array of native wildlife. Kenya receives 1.7 million visitors a year, both those on beach vacations and those on safari. Tourism is Kenya's single largest foreign income earner.

Around two thirds of Kenyans are mostly from three ethnic groups: the Kikuyu, Luhya, and Luo. Many other minority groups exist, including Kenyan Asians and Kenyan Arabs, who, although small in number, tend to hold much commercial power. Most Kenyans are employed in agriculture, with herding livestock important in the drier regions, especially in the north. Although they tend to be on a small scale, Kenya also has some of the most developed industries in east Africa. These include the processing of foodstuffs, textiles, beer brewing, furniture, plastics, and building materials.

# TANZANIA

Tanzania is home to some of the most spectacular features on Earth, including Africa's highest mountain, Mount Kilimanjaro.

**Area:** 364,881 sq. mi. (945,037km²)
**Population:** 37,394,000
**Capitals:** Dodoma (324,000)—legislative capital and capital designate; Dar es Salaam 2,660,000)—administrative capital
**Main languages spoken:** Swahili, English
**Main religions:** Christian, Islam, traditional beliefs
**Currency:** Tanzanian shilling
**Main exports:** gold, coffee, cotton, cashews, tobacco
**Type of government:** republic

▼ Located in northeastern Tanzania, Kilimanjaro consists of three separate extinct volcanic peaks: Kibo, Mawensi, and Shira. Kibo, the youngest and highest, has a crater around 1.2 mi. (2km) in diameter. Despite lying near the equator, Kibo's 19,332-ft.- (5,895-m-) high peak has a year-round cap of snow and ice.

Tanzania's landscape varies from a low, flat coastal plain that is heavily covered in tropical vegetation to rugged, volcanic mountaintops. Much of the country, however, is located on a plateau averaging 3,940 ft. (1,200m) in elevation that is largely covered in savanna grasslands and forests but is more arid in the north. Isolated mountain groups rise in the southwest and the northeast, while both branches of the Great Rift Valley run through the country. The eastern branch divides the northeastern highlands and contains a series of small lakes. The western branch contains Lakes Malawi/Nyasa and Tanganyika and acts as a natural border separating Tanzania from nations to the west. A little over half of Africa's largest lake, Lake Victoria, lies in the north of the country. Offshore from Tanzania's Indian Ocean coastline lie a number of islands, including Pemba and Zanzibar. Zanzibar, including Pemba, merged with the mainland of Tanganyika in 1964 to form Tanzania. Around one third of the country is protected as either national parks or game reserves. These include the world-renowned Serengeti National Park, which contains over 200 species of birds and 35 species of land animals, including cheetahs, lions, elephants, and the extremely rare black rhinoceros. About 650,000 tourists per year are drawn to the country's parks, reserves, and spectacular geography. Although Tanzania has gold and diamond mines and around 44 percent of the country is forested, farming provides most of the country's exports and employs almost 80 percent of the workforce.

# MALAWI

**The landlocked country of Malawi contains most of the giant Lake Malawi/Nyasa within its territory. It is one of the least developed and poorest countries in Africa.**

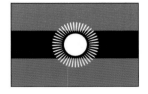

**Area:** 45,747 sq. mi. (118,484km²)
**Population:** 13,077,000
**Capital:** Lilongwe (674,000)
**Main languages spoken:** English, Chichewa
**Main religions:** Protestant, Roman Catholic, Islam
**Currency:** Malawian kwacha
**Main exports:** tobacco (which accounts for over 60 percent of exports), tea, sugar, cotton
**Type of government:** multiparty democracy

▼ Malawian fishermen bring in their boats and catch. Almost all of Malawi's 66,000 tons (60,000 metric tons) of fish caught every year are found in the waters of Lake Malawi/Nyasa.

Malawi is bordered by Zambia, Mozambique, and Tanzania. The Great Rift Valley runs along the eastern region of the country from north to south. Contained within the valley and occupying almost one third of Malawi's territory is Africa's third-largest lake, Lake Malawi/Nyasa. Much of the country consists of highland plateaus and mountains. South of Lake Malawi/Nyasa lies the Shire Highland—home to the country's highest peaks. The large majority of Malawi's people live in the countryside, where farming is the chief occupation. An almost completely agricultural nation, Malawians rely solely on their domestic food crops, and when droughts strike, they devastate the country. When adequate rainfall does occur, Malawi is Africa's second-largest producer of tobacco behind only Zimbabwe. Other major exports include tea, sugar, and peanuts, while corn, sorghum, and a wide range of fruit and vegetables are grown for local food. The country also has a growing fishing industry based on the shores of Lake Malawi/Nyasa, which catches 66,000 tons (60,000 metric tonnes) of fish per year. Malawi has few industries beyond small local companies and few mineral resources. Over 90 percent of its electricity is generated via hydroelectric power programs. Malawi was formerly known as Nyasaland when it was ruled as a British colony between 1891 and 1964. Unlike some other countries in the region, Malawi has not been beset by serious conflicts between different ethnic or religious groups. Its people come from many different tribal groups, but the Chewa people form the majority of the population, and their language, Chichewa, is an official language, alongside English. High population growth has been curbed by disease, poverty, and limited health care, and the average life expectancy is only 50 years of age. Forty-five percent of the country's population are under the age of 15.

# ZAMBIA

Zambia, formerly known as Northern Rhodesia, is one of Africa's most urbanized nations, with around 36 percent of people living in towns and cities.

**Area:** 290,586 sq. mi. (752,614km²)
**Population:** 11,570,000
**Capital:** Lusaka (2,000,000)
**Main languages spoken:** English, indigenous
**Main religions:** Christian, Hinduism, Islam
**Currency:** Zambian kwacha
**Main exports:** copper, cobalt
**Type of government:** republic

▼ The 420-ft.- (128-m-) high Kariba Dam on Zambia's border with Zimbabwe was completed in 1959. The 1,900-ft.- (579-m-) long dam is is part of a giant hydroelectric power plant.

Zambia's northern border is divided by land belonging to the Democratic Republic of the Congo. The territory extends deep into the middle of Zambia, partly dividing the country into eastern and western sections. The eastern region is more sparsely populated. Running to the west and parallel to the Luangwa river are mountains that are the home of Zambia's highest hills. The western region of Zambia is where most of the country's population and industry reside. Zambia sits on a high plateau crossed by deep river valleys and occasional lakes and swampland. The country has a tropical climate with temperatures moderated owing to its relatively high altitude. The natural vegetation is mainly savanna grasslands with areas of forests. Despite poaching, which has slashed rhinoceros and elephant herds, Zambia's land supports a large number of wild animals, many now in protected game reserves. The climate and some of the land support farming, which is the nation's biggest employer. Corn is the most frequently grown staple food, while large amounts of cassava, sugarcane, wheat, and peanuts are also harvested.

## THE ZAMBEZI, ENERGY, AND MINERALS

Winding its way from northwestern Zambia to the Indian Ocean, the Zambezi river forms much of the country's southern border. The river drops 354 ft. (108m) as it flows over one of the world's most famous waterfalls, the Mosi-oa-Tunya, or Victoria Falls, on Zambia's border with Zimbabwe. Then 300 mi. (480km) east of Victoria Falls the river flows into Lake Kariba, a giant artificial lake built to generate hydroelectric power and shared by Zambia and Zimbabwe. Zambia derives 99 percent of its electricity from hydroelectric power. Zambia has traditionally relied on just two products to generate exports: copper and cobalt. Giant reserves in the north of the country saw the formation of an urban and industrial mining region, known as the Copper Belt, in which minerals are mined and processed. Copper production fell until 2004, as copper prices fell, but, since then, rising prices and foreign investment have revived Zambia's copper industry.

# SOUTHERN AFRICA

S outhern Africa's geography is dominated by the Southern Plateau, which crosses much of the region at an elevation of between 2,950–4,920 ft. (900–1,500m). Around the edges of the plateau is a series of mountains and cliffs called the Great Escarpment, while further mountainous areas lie in places along the southern and eastern coastlines. Large stretches of the region are grasslands with both forested areas and two deserts, the Kalahari in the center and the Namib along the western coast. Southern Africa is one of the world's most mineral-rich areas. A large proportion of the world's copper, gold, uranium, and diamonds come from the area, which has had an impact on regional economies.

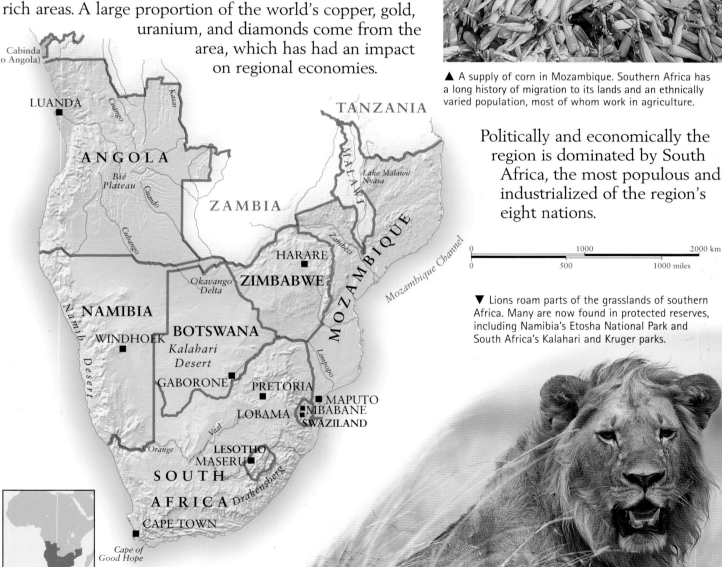

▲ A supply of corn in Mozambique. Southern Africa has a long history of migration to its lands and an ethnically varied population, most of whom work in agriculture.

Politically and economically the region is dominated by South Africa, the most populous and industrialized of the region's eight nations.

▼ Lions roam parts of the grasslands of southern Africa. Many are now found in protected reserves, including Namibia's Etosha National Park and South Africa's Kalahari and Kruger parks.

# ANGOLA

Rich in oil and diamonds, Angola suffered an almost continual civil war from its independence from Portugal in 1975 until 2002.

**Area:** 481,350 sq. mi. (1,246,700km²)
**Population:** 15,566,000
**Capital:** Luanda (2,262,000)
**Main languages spoken:** Portuguese, Bantu and tribal languages
**Main religions:** traditional beliefs, Roman Catholic, Protestant
**Currency:** readjusted kwanza
**Main exports:** petroleum, diamonds, coffee, fish
**Type of government:** republic; limited democracy

▼ The Benguela railroad is a vital transportation link connecting Angola to both the Democratic Republic of the Congo and Zimbabwe. It is currently undergoing renovation after being seriously damaged during the long civil war.

Angola's landscape is diverse. The land stretches from a coastal plain that varies in width from 16 mi. (25km) in the south to between 60–125 mi. (100–200km) in the north. Inland from the plain the land rises toward mountains and a plateau that covers almost two thirds of the country. The plateau undulates and varies in average height between 3,940–5,250 ft. (1,200–1,600m). Angola has no large lakes but does have many rivers, most of which begin in the central mountains and either flow west to the Atlantic Ocean or north. Angola's climate is essentially tropical but fairly dry. In the southwest the country is extremely dry and desertlike. Close to the coast the climate is more temperate, while the northern half of the central plateau is tropical and receives a little more rainfall. Large rain forests cover the northern part of the country, while grasslands are found in the central and south-central regions. Angola has large oil deposits, particularly offshore near the exclave of Cabinda, producing around two million barrels per day. The country also has large reserves of diamonds, iron, and many other minerals, as well as great hydroelectric potential. Along with fertile farmland, Angola has many resources and should be relatively prosperous, but a civil war between two major groups, UNITA and the MPLA, was fought for many years. The result was a shattered economy with mines, industries, and transportation links destroyed and as many as ten million unexploded land mines left across its land.

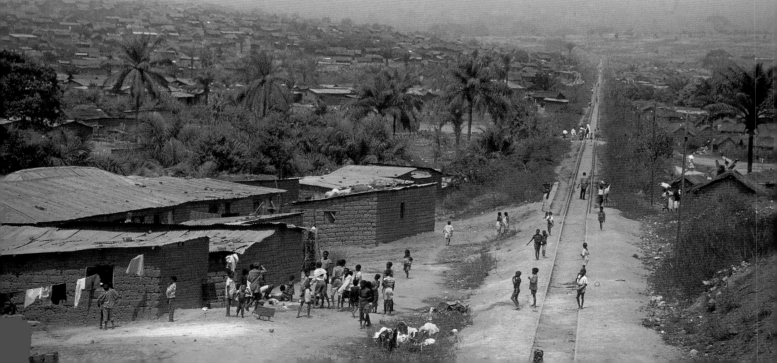

# BOTSWANA

**Landlocked and dry, much of Botswana's territory is part of the red soil, sand, and scrubland of the vast Kalahari Desert.**

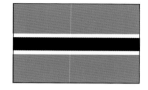

**Area:** 224,610 sq. mi. (581,730km2)
**Population:** 1,773,000
**Capital:** Gaborone (308,000)
**Main languages spoken:** English, Setswana
**Main religions:** indigenous beliefs, Christian
**Currency:** pula
**Main exports:** diamonds, copper, nickel, textiles
**Type of government:** parliamentary republic

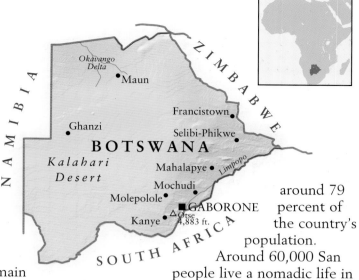

Botswana's land is largely a broad, flat plateau with some hills in the east. In the northwest the Okavango river empties inland, creating the largest inland river delta in the world. The swamplands and floodplains of the Okavango Delta are a haven for wildlife, particularly birds. Farming is the main occupation, although water is often scarce. In 1967, one year after independence from Great Britain, enormous diamond reserves were discovered. Botswana is now the world's third-largest producer of diamonds and also has huge reserves of coal, copper, and nickel. The Tswana people make up around 79 percent of the country's population.

Around 60,000 San people live a nomadic life in the Kalahari, hunting and gathering, as well as tending small herds of livestock. Despite much economic growth, the country's people are poor and beset by diseases, especially AIDS. Around 24 percent of all of Botswana's adults have HIV or AIDS, the second-highest infection rate in the world.

# NAMIBIA

**Lying on the southwestern coast of Africa, sparsely populated but mineral-rich Namibia gained independence from South Africa in 1990.**

▲ The Namib Desert is a dry, largely barren region where temperatures can reach 120°F (49°C).

**Area:** 318,252 sq. mi. (824,269km2)
**Population:** 2,215,000
**Capital:** Windhoek (250,000)
**Main languages spoken:** Afrikaans, English, German, indigenous languages
**Main religions:** Lutheran, Christian
**Currency:** Namibian dollar
**Main exports:** diamonds, fish and fish products, copper, lead
**Type of government:** republic

Namibia consists of a central plateau region that occupies around half of the country, with an elevation of between 3,810–6,560 ft. (970–2,000m). Deserts lie on both sides of this plateau—to the east the Kalahari Desert extends into the country, while the whole western coast is occupied by the Namib Desert. Namibia's climate is hot and dry, and only the central plateau supports a large amount of vegetation. Despite the hostile environment, Namibia has much wildlife, some of which is protected in reserves. Eighty-seven percent of the population are black Africans, with around ten percent white. Nambia is Africa's fourth-largest producer of nonfuel materials.

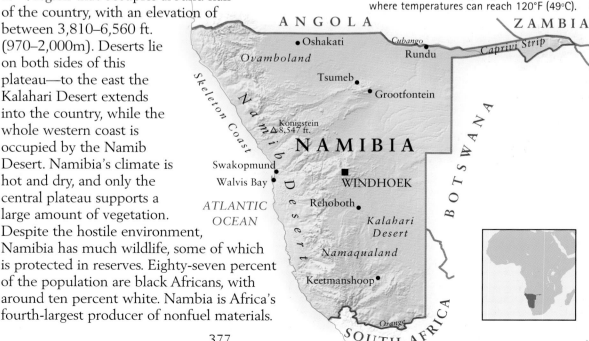

377

# ZIMBABWE

As a British colony the landlocked nation of
Zimbabwe was known as Southern Rhodesia
and, between 1965 and 1980, as Rhodesia.

**Area:** 150,872 sq. mi.
(390,757km²)
**Population:** 12,500,000
**Capital:** Harare
(1,881,000)
**Main languages spoken:**
English, Shona, Sindebele
**Main religions:** Syncretic
Christian, indigenous
beliefs
**Currency:** Zimbabwe
dollar (suspended in favour
of South African rand/US
dollar)
**Main exports:** gold, iron
alloys, nickel, cotton,
asbestos, tobacco, cut
flowers, platinum
**Type of government:**
republic

▼ Straddling the
border between Zimbabwe
and Zambia, Victoria Falls
(Mosi-oa-Tunya) is around
twice as high and twice
as wide as Niagara Falls
in North America.

Most of
Zimbabwe
lies on the Southern
Plateau of Africa
and is above 985 ft.
(300m) in elevation.
The Zambezi river
flows along Zimbabwe's
northern border and
generates almost 40 percent
of the country's electricity via
hydroelectric power. Despite large-
scale migration to the country's towns and
cities, around 63 percent of the population
still live in rural areas. Farming is practiced on
a large commercial scale, with tobacco the
leading export crop. Cotton growing and
cattle raising are also conducted on a large
scale. In contrast many Zimbabweans work
their own small farms, growing just enough
to feed their families. Huge mineral reserves
exist in Zimbabwe, including gold, nickel,
and asbestos. Zimbabwe has a wide range of
industries, from steel, chemicals, and cement
to motor vehicles, footwear, and textiles.
Ruled by an increasingly oppressive
government, Zimbabwe
has attracted international
criticism for human rights
abuses. Redistribution of
land and wealth from the
rich white minority to the
poorer black majority has occurred, sometimes
using force, but the economy has collapsed,
many live in extreme poverty, and up to three
million Zimbabweans have left the country.

# MOZAMBIQUE

**Mozambique is a large, ethnically diverse nation that is trying to rebuild after a long civil war and devastating droughts and floods.**

**Area:** 309,500 sq. mi. (801,590km²)
**Population:** 20,530,000
**Capital:** Maputo (1,775,000)
**Main languages spoken:** Portuguese, indigenous dialects
**Main religions:** indigenous beliefs, Christian, Islam
**Currency:** metical
**Main exports:** shrimp, cotton, cashews, sugar, copra
**Type of government:** republic

Two fifths of Mozambique's land is coastal lowlands that end in a 1,535-mi.- (2,470-km-) long shoreline with the Indian Ocean. Farther inland the land rises to a series of hill ranges, with mountains in the west and north. Mozambique has a tropical climate, but most of its soil is poor. Despite this, most of its people work as farmers growing corn and cassava for themselves or working on plantations growing coconuts, cashews, cotton, or sugarcane. The country's fishing industry is vital, with shrimp an important export. Mining is underdeveloped, and the country is seeking investment to tap its large reserves of copper, iron, uranium, coal, and natural gas. Following independence from Portugal in 1975 a violent civil war erupted. Mozambique has struggled to rebuild after the war ended in the early 1990s.

Apart from the legacy of destroyed towns, transportation systems, and industries, there are between two and three million unexploded land mines. Clearing land of these weapons has been a slow process. In addition, the country has suffered from floods and droughts that have killed thousands of people, while diseases, especially AIDS, are common.

▲ Zebras are one of a number of large mammals that live within Mozambique's borders. A total of 15,450 sq. mi. (40,400km²) of the country are part of the Greater Limpopo Transfrontier Park, which also extends into South Africa and Zimbabwe.

▶ A large cooking pot made from an oil drum is stirred at a Mozambique orphanage. Civil war, diseases including AIDS, and land mines have created approximately 1.2 million orphans in the country—one in six of all the country's children.

# SOUTH AFRICA

**South Africa occupies the southernmost part of Africa. A multiethnic society and a country of great mineral wealth, it has the largest economy in Africa.**

**Area:** 472,856 sq. mi. (1,224,691km²)
**Population:** 48,502,000
**Capitals:** Tshwane (Pretoria) (1,787,000)—administrative capital; Cape Town (2,872,000)—legislative capital
**Main languages spoken:** English, Afrikaans, Ndebele, Pedi, Sotho
**Main religions:** Christian, traditional beliefs
**Currency:** rand
**Main exports:** gold, base metals, diamonds, food (particularly fruit and wine)
**Type of government:** republic

South Africa borders six nations, including Lesotho, which it completely surrounds, and is the only nation with both Atlantic and Indian ocean coastlines. Fishing in the coastal waters brings in around 900,000 tons (820,000 metric tonnes) of fish every year. The lands close to the coast are low-lying, fertile plains that tend to occupy a relatively narrow strip between 18–60 mi. (30–100km) in width. The coastal plains give way to a mountainous region, known as the Great Escarpment, that separates the coast from the high inland plateau on which most of the country is situated. The Drakensberg Mountains are the highest part of the Great Escarpment and run in an arc inland from the Indian Ocean coast.

### THE VELDS AND WILDLIFE

Most of the plateau region of South Africa is called the High Veld and consists of rolling grasslands mostly above 4,920 ft. (1,500m) in elevation. The western portion of the plateau is known as the Middle Veld. Lying at an average elevation of 3,020 ft. (920m), the land there is dry and mostly used for herding

▲ A gold miner at work drilling in Savuka gold mine, around 50 mi. (80km) southwest of Johannesburg. Savuka, along with its sister mine, Mponeng, are among the deepest gold mines in the world at over 11,480 ft. (3,500m) in depth.

livestock. The Middle Veld merges with the Namib and Kalahari deserts to the west and northwest. To the northeast the High Veld descends into a large lowland area called the Bush Veld that consists mainly of savanna grasslands and scattered trees. South Africa has highly varied wildlife, with over 200 species of mammals, including elephants, hippotamuses, zebras, and lions. Hunting has slashed herd numbers, but many of these creatures are now

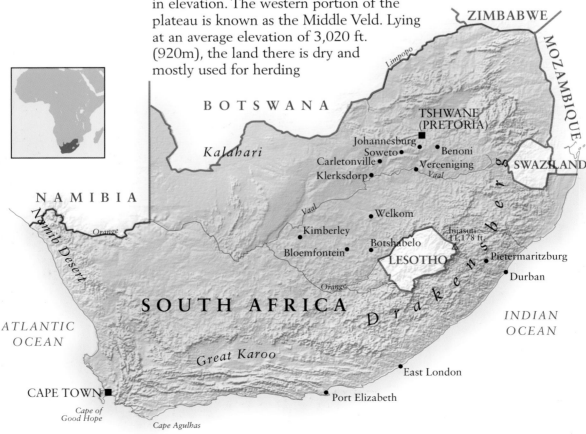

protected in the country's 30 national parks and game reserves. In addition, South Africa is incredibly rich in flowering plants, with over 20,000 different species.

## CLIMATE
South Africa lies in the temperate zone, but its climate varies greatly throughout the country. The highest temperature recorded was 125.0°F (51.7°C) in the Kalahari Desert. Sutherland, 170 mi. (270km) northeast of Cape Town, regularly sees winter temperatures drop to 5°F (-15°C). Elevation, wind, and ocean currents influence the regional differences in climate. For example, the cold Benguela Current, which flows northward along the west coast, cools temperatures and also reduces rainfall levels. South Africa is a semiarid country, and around half the land receives between 8–24 in. (20–60cm) of rainfall per year, while a further one fourth receives less than 8 in. (20cm). Rainfall levels tend to increase from west to east, with the eastern coast benefiting from the warm Mozambique Current, which raises temperature and rainfall levels.

## WATER AND AGRICULTURE
South Africa has no large lakes and only a small number of major rivers. These include the Vaal and the Limpopo, which flow in the north and form much of the country's border with Botswana and Zimbabwe. South Africa's longest river is the Orange, which travels around 1,300 mi. (2,090km) from Lesotho west through the High Veld before forming all of South Africa's border with Namibia and flowing into the Atlantic Ocean. With water at a premium, South Africa relies on large irrigation systems to water cropland. Despite only a small percentage of the land being suitable for crop growing, South Africa is usually self-sufficient in many crops, including cereals, vegetables, and sugarcane. The country is renowned for its high-quality fruit crops, including grapes, which form the basis of a large and profitable wine industry.

▲ Native bushmen in the Kgalagadi Transfrontier Park study animal tracks. This protected reserve has a huge area of 13,900 sq. mi. (36,000km²).

▼ The rugged and spectacular Drakensberg Mountains are found in the Royal Natal National Park. Peaks in this mountain chain exceed 9,840 ft. (3,000m) in places.

▲ Founded in 1886 as a gold-mining town, Johannesburg has grown into South Africa's largest urban area with a population of 6.4 million.

▼ Cape Town is the law-making capital of South Africa and one of its major ports and commercial centers. A fast-growing city, it is overlooked by the majestic Table Mountain.

## INDUSTRY

South Africa is the most industrially powerful country in the African continent. Cape Town, Johannesburg, Port Elizabeth, and Durban are large industrial centers producing a large range of goods—from chemicals, textiles, and paper to motor vehicles, electronic goods, and weapons. Much of South Africa's development has stemmed from huge reserves of valuable minerals that lie within its borders. Despite a decline in gold production, South Africa remains the world's biggest producer. It is also a world leader in platinum, manganese, chrome, and diamond production. The country has no major oil deposits but has huge reserves of coal. This is burned to generate most of the country's electricity. A huge challenge facing the country's government is how to provide electricity to the 80 percent of black South African homes that currently are not on the national electricity program.

## THE "RAINBOW NATION"

South Africa is a multiracial nation in which there are 11 officially recognized languages, with many more spoken. Approximately three fourths of the population belong to one of nine black African ethnic groups. The Zulu people are the largest group, at around 24 percent of the population. The next largest are the Xhosa (18 percent), followed by the Pedi, Tswana, Sotho,

▲ This family lives in Nyanga township close to the city of Cape Town. Township dwellers often have to contend with cramped living conditions, poor sanitation and water supplies, and high unemployment.

Tsonga, and other groups. Around ten percent of South Africa's people are white and are divided into two principal groups. Afrikaners, or Boers, are descendants of Dutch and sometimes German or French settlers. They speak Afrikaans and make up around 60 percent of the white population. Most of the remainder speak English and are of British origin. Nine percent of South Africa's people has a mixed ethnic background, and three percent are of Asian, mainly Indian, descent. Over

of different racial groups apart on public transportation, in schools, jobs, and in most walks of life. Many black people were forced to live in townships outside of major cities or in "homelands" in rural areas. In these areas the growing land, schools, and facilities were often much worse than in white-only areas. Condemnation of South Africa's racist apartheid policy occurred around the world and was followed by trade sanctions and boycotts that prevented the country from taking part in many sports and cultural events. Apartheid's grip was finally loosened in the late 1980s and early 1990s, and in 1994 elections involving all people, regardless of race or color, occurred, returning a black president, Nelson Mandela, for the first time. Since then governments have tried to create a peaceful path to a multiracial society but with great difficulties. Large inequalities in education, income, and living conditions between many blacks and whites remain, and violent crime, especially in the cities, is among the highest in the world.

▲ Workers harvest grapes in the Nuy Valley vineyards in the Western Cape. South Africa is one of the world's leading wine producers. In 2002 white wine exports reached around 57 million gallons (216 mllion liters), ten times the amount in 1992.

60 percent of South Africans live in cities, and nine in ten live in the eastern half of the country or along the southern coast. Apart from the area around Cape Town, the west is very sparsely populated.

## APARTHEID AND RECONCILIATION

South Africa's black population had been oppressed for decades before the government policy of apartheid was introduced in 1948. Meaning "apartness," apartheid was a country-wide policy, in place until the 1990s, designed to protect the interests of a white minority. Under apartheid people were classified by race. Apartheid kept people

# SWAZILAND

**Landlocked between South Africa and Mozambique, Swaziland's traditional society and customs are in contrast to its more modern industries.**

**Area:** 6,704 sq. mi. (17,363km²)
**Population:** 954,000
**Capitals:** Mbabane (58,000)—administrative capital; Lobamba (4,000)—royal and legislative capital
**Main languages spoken:** Swazi, English
**Main religions:** Christian, indigenous beliefs
**Currency:** lilangeni
**Main exports:** wood and wood products, sugar
**Type of government:** constitutional monarchy

Swaziland is divided into three regions: the mountainous high veld in the west, the grassy middle veld in the center, and the low bushveld in the east. The high veld is humid and temperate, with warm, wet summers and cold, dry winters. Originally largely treeless, there are now large plantations of pine and eucalyptus trees—part of the country's extensive forestry industry. The middle veld has a subtropical climate with the most fertile soil. The majority of the population live in this region. Many herd cattle or grow corn or work on large plantations growing sugarcane and other crops. The low veld is dry and hot in the summer. Mountains run along the border with Mozambique.

The mining of coal, gold, and diamonds, and manufacturing industries, are major sources of work for the country's people, 95 percent of whom belong to the Swazi ethnic group. Swazis retain many of their ancient traditions and are governed by an hereditary monarchy. Despite pressures for reform, political parties remain banned. The country has the highest rate of HIV infection in the world, at 26 percent.

# LESOTHO

**Lesotho is surrounded by South Africa, from which it gained independence in 1966. Its people are mainly farmers and are reliant on South Africa for trade.**

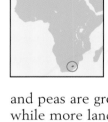

**Area:** 11,720 sq. mi. (30,355km²)
**Population:** 1,881,000
**Capital:** Maseru (198,000)
**Main languages spoken:** English, Sesotho
**Main religions:** Christian, indigenous beliefs
**Currency:** maluti
**Main exports:** clothing, furniture, footwear, food, live animals, wool
**Type of government:** modified constitutional monarchy

▶ Like most of the population, this Lesotho woman makes a living raising small herds of livestock and subsistence crop growing.

Known as the "roof of Africa," Lesotho is a mountainous land. Its lowest point is around 4,535 ft. (1,380m) in elevation, rising to almost 11,480 ft. (3,500m) in the mountains to the east. Rolling lowlands mainly in the west are the main agricultural area. Corn, wheat, root vegetables, beans, and peas are grown, while more land is used as grazing pastures for cattle, sheep, and goats. Unrestricted grazing has caused much soil erosion. Apart from some diamond mining, the country has few mineral resources. Lesotho's rugged landscape does, however, allow it to generate all the electricity it needs from hydroelectric power. Large quantities of electricity are exported to South Africa. Lesotho has few industries, and many male adults move to South Africa to find work in mines and other industries. Its people are poor; 49 percent of the population are believed to live below the poverty line.

# OCEANIA & ANTARCTICA

# OCEANIA

Oceania is a vast region of scattered islands lying across most of the Pacific Ocean. Covering approximately one third of the entire planet's surface, the Pacific occupies a total area of more than 65 million sq. mi. (169 million km²). The region called Oceania has a land area of just over 3.3 million sq. mi. (8.5 million km²) and consists of the continent of Australia, as well as larger islands including New Zealand's North and South islands, New Guinea and Tasmania, and more than 20,000 smaller islands. This latter group, often referred to as the Pacific islands, are often clustered in groups and separated by vast stretches of ocean. Most of the smaller islands have been created through coral formation or volcanic activity. Many of Oceania's islands lie on or near the edges of the Pacific tectonic plate, which is also the location of many of the world's volcanoes. The Pacific islands of Oceania are often divided into three distinct groups. Polynesia is the most easterly and consists of a huge, roughly triangular expanse of the Pacific, extending north of Hawaii, south of New Zealand, and eastward past Easter Island. Micronesia is the region west of Polynesia and closest to Southeast Asia, while Melanesia is considered the region containing New Guinea, Fiji Islands, the Solomon Islands, Vanuatu, and a small number of other island groups. While Aborigines reached Australia over 50,000 years ago and New Guinea has a long history of settlement, other parts of Oceania were the last places in the world to be settled by people.

In waves of migrations, which are estimated to have started between 6,000 and 7,000 years ago, different peoples from Southeast Asia reached the most westerly and northerly islands. Long voyages made in simple vessels saw peoples travel across much of the Pacific, reaching the most outlying islands between 2,000 and 1,000 years ago. Today Oceania's people number almost 35 million—less than one half a percent of the total world population. Over half of the continent's people are found in Australia, a giant landmass and the most developed and economically powerful nation in the continent. In contrast neighboring Papua New Guinea and many of the smaller island nations are among the least developed countries in the world. The majority of the population of these countries are reliant on fishing and forms of agriculture that have not altered much for many centuries.

▲ The scattered Pacific islands of Oceania tend to experience tropical or subtropical climates with heavy rainfall. Many of the islands are covered in lush vegetation, including palm trees.

▲ Polynesian men paddle a type of canoe with a balancing float, known as an outrigger, in the Pacific Ocean. Outrigger canoes, or double canoes, are used by many Pacific peoples, including the Melanesians and Polynesians, to complete amazingly long journeys between islands that are dwarfed by the ocean around them.

◄ These Aborigines live in Arnhem Land, a region in northeastern Australia that has been continuously settled by them for at least 40,000 years. Aboriginal Australians were among the first settlers in Oceania and are believed to have reached Australia at least 50,000—and possibly even 70,000—years ago.

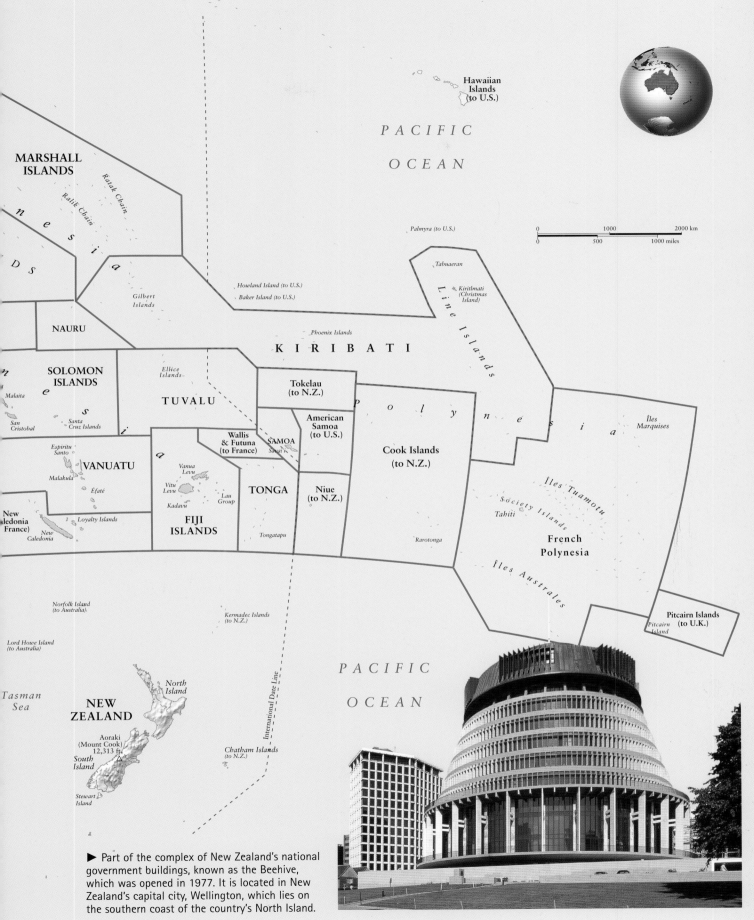

Hawaiian
Islands
(to U.S.)

*P A C I F I C*

*O C E A N*

**MARSHALL
ISLANDS**

*Ratak Chain*

*Ralik Chain*

Palmyra (to U.S.)

Tabuaeran

Howland Island (to U.S.)

Baker Island (to U.S.)

Kiritlmati
(Christmas
Island)

Gilbert
Islands

*L i n e   I s l a n d s*

**NAURU**

Phoenix Islands

**K I R I B A T I**

**SOLOMON
ISLANDS**

Ellice
Islands

*Malaita*

**TUVALU**

*San
Cristobal*

*Santa
Cruz Islands*

**Tokelau
(to N.Z.)**

*Îles
Marquises*

*P  o  l  y  n  e  s  i  a*

**American
Samoa
(to U.S.)**

Wallis
& Futuna
(to France)

**SAMOA**

*Savai'i*

**Espíritu
Santo**

**VANUATU**

*Vanua
Levu*

**Cook Islands
(to N.Z.)**

*Malakula*

*Éfaté*

*Vitu
Levu*

**TONGA**

**Niue
(to N.Z.)**

*Îles Tuamotu*

*Lau
Group*

*Kadavu*

*Society Islands*

**New
Caledonia
(France)**

*Loyalty Islands*

**FIJI
ISLANDS**

*Tahiti*

*New
Caledonia*

*Rarotonga*

**French
Polynesia**

*Tongatapu*

*Îles Australes*

Norfolk Island
(to Australia).

Kermadec Islands
(to N.Z.)

Pitcairn Islands
(to U.K.)

Lord Howe Island
(to Australia)

*Pitcairn
Island*

*Tasman
Sea*

*North
Island*

**NEW
ZEALAND**

*P A C I F I C*

*International Date Line*

Aoraki
(Mount Cook)
12,313 ft.

*South
Island*

Chatham Islands
(to N.Z.)

*O C E A N*

Stewart
Island

▶ Part of the complex of New Zealand's national
government buildings, known as the Beehive,
which was opened in 1977. It is located in New
Zealand's capital city, Wellington, which lies on
the southern coast of the country's North Island.

389

# PAPUA NEW GUINEA

**A land of rich resources and traditional cultures, Papua New Guinea occupies half of the island of New Guinea, as well as numerous other smaller islands in the Pacific.**

**Area:** 178,700 sq. mi. (462,840km²)
**Population:** 5,370,000
**Capital:** Port Moresby (255,000)
**Main languages spoken:** English, Motu, over 700 other languages
**Main religions:** indigenous beliefs, Roman Catholic, Lutheran
**Currency:** kina
**Main exports:** petroleum, gold, copper, timber, coffee, cocoa, crayfish and shrimp
**Type of government:** limited democracy

Papua New Guinea consists of over 600 islands. These include New Britain, its second-largest landmass, and the archipelago of islands located in the Bismarck Sea. Four fifths of its land area are made up of the eastern half of New Guinea. From a low-lying, often swampy coastline the land of New Guinea rises to rugged mountains. Although some of the country's smaller islands are formed from coral, many are of volcanic origin and feature mountainous interiors. Papua New Guinea's varied landscape provides habitats for large numbers of plants and animals. Recent surveys show that around five percent of the world's living species are found within its borders. Located just south of the equator, Papua New Guinea's climate is tropical, with its rainy season occurring between December and March.

▲ A Papua New Guinean tribesman paints his face in traditional decorations. Many highland tribes and groups were not discovered until the mid- to late 1900s and have lived in ways largely unchanged for thousands of years.

390

### RICH IN RESOURCES

Over 80 percent of Papua New Guinea is covered in dense tropical rain forests, although this is declining owing to large-scale logging. One third of its forests is open to timber companies, and forestry is a major industry. This is eclipsed in importance, however, by the mining sector. Papua New Guinea is rich in many minerals, including copper, gold, silver, nickel, and cobalt, while oil and natural gas reserves are also exploited. The mining sector makes the largest contribution to the country's economy. Seventy percent of the workforce are subsistence farmers, despite less than two percent of the land being suitable for crops. Larger farms grow coffee and other export crops.

### PEOPLE AND LANGUAGE

Settled for around 50,000 years, the geography of the country has acted as a barrier to movement, isolating many different groups of people who have developed their own languages and cultures. As a result, Papua New Guinea has one of the most culturally varied populations on Earth, with over 700 languages spoken. A distinction is often made between those people who live in lowland areas near the coasts and tend to have frequent contact with other groups and the more isolated highlanders. Although most of the population are Christians, traditional beliefs and customs are still widely practiced. Since independence in 1975 the people of the copper-rich island of Bougainville have pressed to break away from the country.

▲ A highland area near Goroka, close to the highest point on Papua New Guinea, Mount Wilhelm. The highland areas are cooler than on the coast, where temperatures rise to 90°F (32°C) or higher in the summer.

▼ Port Moresby, the capital of Papua New Guinea, is the manufacturing center of the country, with food processing the main industry.

# AUSTRALIA

**Australia's vast, arid interior is sparsely populated. But its rich mineral resources and highly developed agricultural base have made it a prosperous nation.**

**Area:** 2,973,880 sq. mi. (7,702,315km²)
**Population:** 21,875,000
**Capital:** Canberra (395,000)
**Main languages spoken:** English, aboriginal languages
**Main religions:** Anglican, Roman Catholic, other Christian
**Currency:** Australian dollar
**Principal exports:** food (particularly cereals and cereal preparations and meat and meat preparations), live animals, metallic ores, mineral fuels and lubricants (particularly coal and petroleum), basic manufactures
**Type of government:** democratic federal state system

▼ Sydney Harbor Bridge and Sydney Opera House are world-famous symbols of Australia's prosperity. The bridge was opened in 1932, and its total length is 3,770 ft. (1,150m), with a single arch span of 1,650 ft. (503m). It carries eight vehicle lanes, two railroad lines, a footpath, and a bicycle lane. The more modern opera house was completed in 1973, and its unique concrete roofs were designed by the Finnish architect Ove Arup.

Situated between the Indian and South Pacific oceans, Australia includes in its territory the large island of Tasmania and many other islands dotted along its 16,000-mi.- (25,760-km-) long coastline. Considered a continental landmass rather than an island, Australia has been geologically stable for over 300 million years, with few earthquakes, volcanoes, or upthrusts of land to create mountains. As a result, erosion by wind and water has created large, flat plains. Under seven percent of its huge area is above 1,970 ft. (600m) in elevation. Much of Australia is extremely dry; two thirds of the country are deserts or semideserts. Situated in the east of the country, the Great Dividing Range runs roughly north to south and separates the eastern coastline from the dry interior of Australia, known as the outback. Most of the population live in cities and towns along this eastern coast, including the country's largest and most cosmopolitan city, Sydney. Other major cities include Brisbane, Melbourne, Perth, Adelaide, and Canberra, the country's capital. Separating from other continental landmasses around 65 million years ago, Australia's isolation from the rest of the world has meant that many creatures have evolved there that are not found

▲ Also known by its aboriginal name of Uluru, Ayers Rock is the world's largest monolith. Located in the Uluru-Kata Tjuta National Park, it rises .1,141 ft. (348m) above the desert floor and has a circumference of 5 mi. (8km).

elsewhere. Most famous are creatures such as the kangaroo, koala, and duck-billed platypus. Australia's first human inhabitants arrived at least 40,000 years ago. The Aborigines settled throughout much of Australia. They lived off the land and developed a rich culture before the arrival of European settlers from the 1700s onward. Today Aborigines make up around one percent of Australia's population, most of whom are of European descent.

Cape
York

*PACIFIC
OCEAN*

*Melville
Island*

*Arafura Sea*

*Cape
York
Peninsula*

*Coral
Sea*

*Timor
Sea*

*Arnhem
Land*

*Gulf of
Carpentaria*

*Joseph
Bonaparte
Gulf*

*Kimberley
Plateau*

*INDIAN
OCEAN*

*Barkly
Tableland*

*Tanami
Desert*

*Great
Barrier
Reef*

*Great Sandy
Desert*

NORTHERN
TERRITORY

*Flinders*

*North
West Cape*

*Lake
Mackay*

*Mitchell*

QUEENSLAND

*Hamersley Range*

*Lake
Disappointment*

*Macdonnell Ranges*

*Great
Dividing
Range*

**A U S T R A L I A**

*Georgina*

WESTERN
AUSTRALIA

*Gibson
Desert*

△ Uluru
(Ayers Rock)
2,844 ft.

*Simpson
Desert*

*Buckland
Tableland*

*Lake
MacLeod*

*Lake
Carnegie*

*Diamantina*

*Thomson*

*Lake
Eyre North*

*Cooper Ck.*

*Sturt
Stony
Desert*

*Warrego*

*Lake
Barlee*

*Great Victoria
Desert*

SOUTH AUSTRALIA

*Lake
Eyre South*

*Darling*

NEW SOUTH
WALES

*Lake Torrens*

*Lake
Frome*

*Nullarbor plain*

*Lake
Gairdner*

*Flinders Ranges*

*Lachlan*

*Tasman
Sea*

*Great
Australian Bight*

*Murray*

*Great Dividing Range*

*Cape Leeuwin*

SOUTHERN
OCEAN

*Kangaroo
Island*

VICTORIA

■ CANBERRA
AUSTRALIAN
CAPITAL TERRITORY
△ Mount Kosciusko
7,314 ft.

| 0 | 300 | 600 km |
| 0 | 150 | 300 miles |

*Bass Strait*

*Furneaux
Group*

TASMANIA

*South East
Cape*

# EASTERN AUSTRALIA

**The region of Australia first settled by Europeans, eastern Australia is a land of rich mineral and natural resources and the center of industry and commerce.**

▲ The Royal Flying Doctor Service treats a patient in Queensland. Founded in 1928, its aircraft fly over 7 million mi. (11 million km) each year to isolated communities all across Australia.

Australia is divided into six states and two territories. Eastern Australia consists of the states of Queensland, Victoria, and New South Wales, as well as the Australian Capital Territory (ACT), in which the country's capital city, Canberra, is located. Australia became a federation of states on its independence in 1901, and Canberra was chosen as the seat of government shortly afterward. It is the only major Australian city that does not lie on the country's huge coastline. Australia has a 16,000-mi.-(25,760-km-) long coastline, of which eastern Australia has 30 percent. However, the country's fishing catches are relatively modest at around 330,700 tons (300,000

metric tonnes) per year. Over half of the income from fishing comes from shellfish such as lobsters, shrimp, and oysters. Inland from eastern Australia's coast lie a series of coastal plains that form much of the region's farmland. Eastern Australia's most dominant land feature is the Great Dividing Range. This broken chain of mountains runs along almost the entire length of eastern Australia from northern Queensland to the southern coast of Victoria. Averaging around 3,940 ft. (1,200km) in height, the Great Dividing Range has the highest peaks in the Snowy Mountains in New South Wales, with Australia's tallest peak, Mount Kosciuszko, rising to 7,314 ft. (2,230m). These highlands have some of the country's largest coal deposits, enabling Australia to be one of the world's largest coal exporters. West of

the Great Dividing Range the land slopes down to plains heading westward into the country's mainly flat and dry interior. A major feature of this portion of eastern Australia is the Great Artesian Basin, one of the largest regions of underground water springs, many of which are tapped for irrigation. Eastern Australia's largest river system is the Murray-Darling river system in the south of the region. It has a total length of 2,330 mi. (3,750km) and drains an area of over 386,000 sq. mi. (1,000,000km²)

## THE GREAT BARRIER REEF

One of the natural wonders of the world, the Great Barrier Reef lies off the coast of Queensland. It consists of more than 3,000 reefs, along with a number of small islands that extend around 1,240 mi. (2,000km). Covering an area close to 135,140 sq. mi. (350,000km²), it is the planet's largest coral reef system. More than 350 species of coral make up the Great Barrier Reef, and the region provides habitats for a staggering array of wildlife, including 1,500 species of fish and more than 200 species of birds. It is also a breeding ground for several species of turtles and home to dolphins, large, endangered sea mammals called dugongs (sea cows), and humpback whales. A region of great natural beauty, around two million visitors travel to the reef system every year, but such large numbers are one of the threats that the fragile reef faces. Coral is delicate and can be easily broken by divers, tourists' feet, and ships. It also suffers from pollution and rises in sea temperature. In addition, the reef faces damage from the crown-of-thorns starfish, which eat living coral.

▲ Parliament House lies in the center of Canberra and was completed in 1988. Canberra was chosen as the seat of government in 1908, seven years after Australia's independence.

▼ The tropical rain forests in Cape Tribulation National Park stretch right down to the shoreline facing Queensland's Great Barrier Reef. Most of the rain forests in the 620 sq. mi. (1,600km²) protected area have existed unchanged for around 100 million years.

### INTRODUCED ANIMALS

▲ The beautiful living coral and the breathtaking array of marine life draw millions of tourists to dive and snorkel in the waters of the Great Barrier Reef.

▼ The Canberra Deep Space Communications Complex features giant antennae, the largest 230 ft. (70m) in diameter, that are used to communicate with spacecrafts. The complex was the first to receive images of the first human on the Moon in 1969.

Many species of animals have been introduced to Australia by humans. Among the earliest was a wild Asian dog, known as a dingo, that arrived with the Aborigines at least 40,000 years ago. Some creatures have been introduced that have had a damaging effect on the environment. Creatures such as the cane toad and the rabbit, for example, have multiplied into populations of millions and have become major pests to farmers while also disrupting fragile natural ecosystems. Other introduced species have formed the backbone of Australian farming in eastern Australia and elsewhere. Australia has around 73 million sheep and around 28 million beef and dairy cattle. These graze

grasslands in almost all of the states of Australia. Grazing lands make up more than 90 percent of Australia's farmed areas. Queensland is home to over one third of all cattle, while 28 million sheep are found in New South Wales. Many of these herds are kept on vast farms called stations, with the largest over 4,600 sq. mi. (12,000km²) in area. Australia is the world's largest exporter of beef, and its large sheep herds make it the world's leading wool producer.

## THE AUSTRALIAN PEOPLE

Australia was reached by Dutch explorers in the mid-1600s and by the Englishman William Dampier in 1688 and 1699. In 1770 James Cook claimed the land for Great Britain, and in 1788 a British prison colony was established in Australia at the site of what is now the country's largest city, Sydney. From that time until 1853 the policy of transportation saw approximately 160,000 British convicts moved to Australia. Most arrived at one of eastern Australia's settlements. In 1851 gold was discovered in the state of Victoria, and a major gold rush attracted thousands of free settlers hoping to make a fortune. After World War II the Australian government promoted an extensive immigration program, and around 5.5 million people emigrated to the country. Over half of the migrants who arrived were British, with large numbers of Germans, Dutch, Italians, Greeks, and Yugoslavs. Australia adopted a whites-only immigration policy until 1973. Today around 92 percent of the population are of European descent, with growing minorities from Asia and the Middle East. The country's population of just 21.9 million represents more than 150 different nationalities. Around 68 percent of

the population are Christians, while more than 15 percent of the population are nonreligious. Australia's climate and wide, open spaces have encouraged people to live an outdoor lifestyle, and many sports, including cricket, rugby, and swimming, are avidly played and watched. The Australian people generally have a high standard of living, although downturns in the economy have led to an increase in the gap between the rich and poor. With its former major trading partner, the U.K., now part of the European Union, Australia has increased its trade links with the U.S. and many Asian nations. Although a 1999 referendum was in favor of keeping the United Kingdom monarch as the head of state, large numbers of Australians, particularly the younger generation, want their country to become a republic.

▲ Part of the Great Dividing Range, the Blue Mountains are so named owing to the blue appearance of the leaves of the large forests of eucalyptus trees that cover its slopes.

▲ Australia has an illustrious sporting heritage, and the 2000 Oympics, held in Sydney, was the largest Olympics so far, with 10,651 athletes competing in 300 events.

▼ The city of Gold Coast is a 30 mi. (50km) stretch of resorts, hotels, and apartments in Queensland, attracting over ten million tourists every year.

## EASTERN AUSTRALIAN CITIES

Australia's three largest cities are found on eastern Australia's coast: Melbourne, the capital of Victoria, Brisbane, the capital of Queensland, and Sydney, the capital of New South Wales. Built on a spectacular natural harbor, Sydney has become the country's most populous city and is also its commercial center and the Australian city that draws more of the six million foreign visitors each year than any other.

## ABORIGINAL RIGHTS AND WELFARE

As many as one million Aborigines lived in Australia before the arrival of European settlers. These immigrants brought new diseases with them against which the Aborigines had no natural protection. Thousands died from smallpox, tuberculosis, and the common cold. Many more were killed in fights over land with the settlers, many of whom treated the Aborigines as if they were savages. They were discriminated against, their lands were seized, and in many cases they were forced to change their way of life, moving to cities or housed in reservations. An estimated 100,000 aboriginal children, known as the "stolen generation," were taken from their families and placed in institutions or with white families. Until the mid-1960s adult aborigines were not even allowed to vote in elections. Since that time much progress has been made. Aboriginal culture has been increasingly embraced, welfare and education programs have been introduced, and native rights to land have started to be recognized. Despite many initiatives, Aborigines still tend to be the most disadvantaged and poverty-stricken of all Australians, with a life expectancy over 15 years lower than the rest of the population.

# TASMANIA

**Separated from mainland Australia by the Bass Strait, the island of Tasmania is Australia's smallest state. Home to 503,000 people, it has a dramatic and beautiful landscape.**

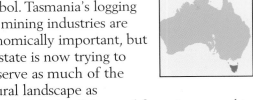

▲ A small boat nudges a salmon pen into position at the Port Esperance fish farm, 30 mi. (50km) southwest of the state capital, Hobart.

▼ The New River Lagoon lies in the Tasmanian Wilderness World Heritage Area. This 5,020 sq. mi. (13,000km²) national park is a world heritage site. More than one fifth of Tasmania is covered in national parks that are designed to protect its unique landscape and nature.

Tasmania's 26,200 sq. mi. (67,800km²) territory, including the smaller islands of Flinders, King, and Cape Barren, is less than one percent of Australia's total land area. Tasmania was linked to Australia until as little as 9,000 years ago, and geologically it is part of Australia's Great Dividing Range. Much of the main island consists of a plateau over 2,950 ft. (900m) in height and a series of mountain peaks. The land is crossed with many fast-flowing streams and rivers, a number of which have been harnessed to provide hydroelectric power. Rolling farmland and meadows and many vineyards occupy large parts of the north, east coast, and the central midlands of the island. However, to the west the landscape is less cultivated and includes large tracts of native forests with many different trees, including the blue gum eucalyptus, the state symbol. Tasmania's logging and mining industries are economically important, but the state is now trying to conserve as much of the natural landscape as possible. Much of the workforce is engaged in farming, with apples, grapes, and livestock the key products. Most of the state's limited industries are based in the southeast close to Hobart, Australia's second-oldest city and the state's chief port. Tasmania was originally settled more than 35,000 years ago by Aborigines when it was part of the Australian mainland, but after European settlement, diseases, and conflicts dramatically reduced the number of native people who now comprise only one percent of the population.

# CENTRAL AUSTRALIA

**Consisting of Northern Territory and the state of South Australia, Central Australia is a largely flat and arid land with isolated hills and mountain ranges.**

▲ Goods are often moved through central Australia by road train—a high-speed truck carrying a number of linked trailers.

▼ A bush fire rages in Kakadu National Park, around 160 mi. (250km) east of Darwin. Famous for its aboriginal art sites and its abundant wildlife, Kakadu is home to 1,200 plant, 100 reptile, 200 bird, and 50 mammal species.

Much of Central Australia is part of the hot, dry scrublands and deserts that constitute the country's Great Red Center. The Simpson, Tanami, and Great Victoria deserts occupy large areas of the region. In the center, close to the border between Northern Territory and South Australia, lie several mountain ranges— the MacDonnell Ranges, which extend over 125 mi. (200km) to the west of Alice Springs and rise to heights of over 4,920 ft. (1,500m), and the Musgrave Ranges just south of Uluru (Ayers Rock). The northernmost region of Northern Territory is known as the Top End and fetaures savanna woodlands and smaller areas of rain forests with swamps along the coast. South Australia is generally low-lying and contains the heavily forested Flinders Ranges, the largest area of highlands. Lying relatively close to the Flinders Ranges is a series of huge lakes that are salt basins most of the time and are only occasionally filled with water. The largest of these, Lake Eyre, lies

▲ Two aboriginal men wear ceremonial body paint made from crushed rocks and soil. Aboriginal gatherings, called corroborees, are held to celebrate aboriginal culture and feature music and dancing.

north of the Flinders Ranges and sometimes covers an area of over 3,440 sq. mi. (8,900km²). It drains an area of over 386,000 sq. mi. (1,000,000km²). South Australia's major river is the Murray, which flows mainly through New South Wales before entering South Australia and emptying into the ocean east of Adelaide.

## CLIMATE AND FARMING

South Australia is considered the driest state in Australia. Its coast experiences higher rainfall and a temperate climate, but inland around 80 percent of the state is arid, receiving less than 12 in. (30cm) of rain per year. The same hot, dry conditions prevail throughout most of Northern Territory. However, on and near the coast the climate is tropical and can receive more than 63 in. (160cm) of rain per year, much of it in the monsoon season from November to April. Tropical vegetable and fruit crops are grown in the Top End of Northern Territory. With poor soil and a dry climate in the center and south, farming there is largely restricted to livestock grazing, particularly cattle. Cattle and sheep herds are also found in the northern and central areas of South Australia. The southern part of the territory is more fertile, and large amounts of wheat, barley, and fruit are grown there, as well as oats, flax, and vegetables. Irrigation is also widely practiced. South Australia produces more grapes than any other state, and its wine industry has grown greatly in the past 20 years.

▲ South Australia's Lake Eyre is fed by occasional rivers, and evaporation often reduces the bed to a dry, salt-crusted area. At 52 ft. (16m) below sea level, it is the lowest point in Australia.

▼ Located 30 mi. (50km) northeast of Adelaide, the Barossa Valley is a fertile wine-growing area flanked by the Barossa Range to the east. The 30 different wine-making companies located in the Barossa Valley are responsible for around one third of Australia's total wine production, much of which is exported.

## SPARSELY POPULATED LANDS

Central Australia is a sparsely settled region, with most of the population concentrated in small areas. Vast tracts of land are largely empty. Although Northern Territory is over 517,380 sq. mi. (1,340,000km²) in area, it is only home to around 225,000 people—around one percent of the total Australian population. Small numbers of people are found in mining towns, farming communities, and aboriginal towns, but the majority of the region's population live in either Alice Springs or Darwin. Northern Territory's major port and its capital city, Darwin has had to be rebuilt on five separate occasions after tropical cyclones devastated the city. Today, fueled by the development of mining industries, defense and government jobs, and a growing tourist trade, it is a prosperous and growing city with a population of 121,000. South Australia is smaller, at around 379,925 sq. mi. (984,000km²), but its population is over seven times as large as Northern Territory's. Around 95 percent of South Australia's inhabitants live within 28 mi. (45km) of the coast. Most are concentrated in a small number of settlements, the biggest of which is the state capital of Adelaide. Australia's fifth-most-populous city, it is surrounded by parkland, while its roads are designed on a grid system. The mining of metals, the exploitation of natural gas reserves, and some manufacturing industries, particularly in and around Adelaide, supplement farming and tourism as the state's major sources of income.

▲ The low-lying, spacious town of Alice Springs lies in Northern Territory and is the headquarters of the country's flying doctor service. The town has also become a tourist base since it is the closest main settlement to the Uluru (Ayers Rock) monolith.

## ANIMALS IN ISOLATION

Australia was once part of a supercontinent known as Gondwanaland. Continental drift saw Australia break away from the rest of the continent and, over a period of between 55 and 60 million years, move gradually toward its current position. Isolation has meant that Australia's animals have evolved

animals in the central Australian deserts. In 2009 the Australian authorities estimated that there were almost one million wild camels in Australia. Australia lacks large land predators but does have some highly venomous insects, jellyfish, and reptiles, including the taipan snake, which produces the most powerful poison in the world.

## ABORIGINAL CULTURE

Aborigines live throughout Australia, but they make up a higher proportion of the population of Northern Territory than any other region in the country. The first human arrivals to Australia's shores, many different aboriginal tribal groups with their own cultures and languages developed throughout the country; there are now an estimated 250 different aboriginal languages or dialects. All lived a nomadic or seminomadic life in harmony with their environment, gathering seeds, fruit, and berries and hunting and fishing. Aboriginal culture is rich and varied, with traditional painting, stories, music, and dancing. Much of their art and storytelling concerns the origins of the land and people in a complex set of beliefs known as The Dreaming, or Dreamtime. Each tribe had its own territory granted by the Ancestors, the mythical creators of the world and people. This territory could not be sold or given away, and many sites within the land are considered sacred.

▲ South Australia is home to over three million kangaroos of several species. Kangaroos are the world's largest marsupials, with male red kangaroos growing to almost 6 ft. (2m) in height and weighing 190 lbs. (85kg).

separately from the rest of the world, generating dozens of unique species. Many of its mammals are either marsupials—creatures like kangaroos, koala bears, wombats, and wallabies that nurture their young in a pouch—or monotremes, egg-laying mammals such as the duck-billed platypus and the echidna (spiny anteater). Many marsupials and monotremes are found in central Australia, while Australia's largest bird—and the second largest in the world—the emu, is found in South Australia. Camels were introduced in the 1800s for use as pack

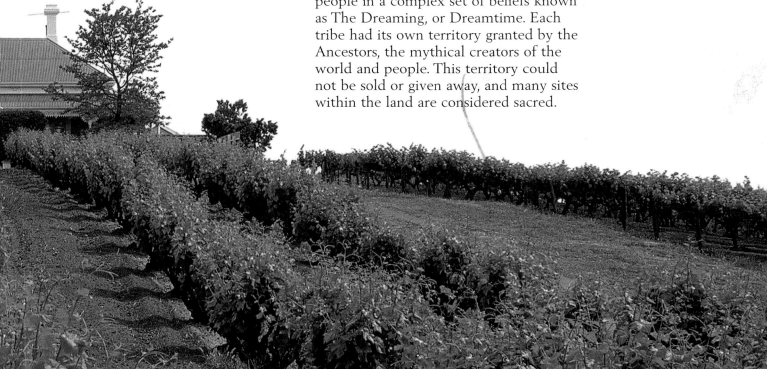

# WESTERN AUSTRALIA

**The largest state of Australia, Western Australia has a mainly dry, desertlike landscape. The state has huge mineral resources and fertile lands in the southwest.**

▲ A match between the Western Australian cricket team and a touring England team takes place at the WACA Ground in Perth.

▼ The sun sets over a beach in Broome in the Kimberley region of Western Australia. One of the few towns in northern Western Australia, Broome was once a traditional center of pearl fishing, and now people there raise oysters on pearl farms.

Western Australia is a vast, arid land area bordering the Indian Ocean to the northwest, west, and south and the Timor Sea to the north. The state has an area of around 965,260 sq. mi. (2,500,000km²). Most of it is a sandy, dry plateau with an elevation of between 980–1,970 ft. (300–600m) and little vegetation. Three large deserts cover much of its territory: the Great Sandy in the north, the Gibson in the center, and the Great Victoria in the southeast. All three contain some scrub grasslands, as well as salt marshes and lakes. However, they are arid and hostile areas, with average annual rainfall below 8 in. (20cm) and temperatures of over 86°F (30°C).

Western Australia's highland areas are isolated from each other. There are high peaks in the Hamersley Range in the northwest, while the most extensive area of uplands is the rugged Kimberley region in the northeast. Damming in the Kimberley region has created Western Australia's second-largest reservoir, Lake Argyle, in the far north of the state.

## CLIMATE AND FARMING

Western Australia is mainly hot and dry, but over such a large area there are climate variations. The extreme north has a tropical climate and is sometimes affected by tropical cyclones, while the extreme south has a Mediterranean climate. Both of these areas receive rainfall as high as 55 in. (140cm) per year. In general rainfall dwindles rapidly away from these areas and the coast. Average daily temperatures rise above 86°F (30°C) in the summer, and in the winter temperatures often fall to below 32°F (0°C).

◀ Despite being one of the most remote cities in the world, Perth's business center flourishes, with office blocks dominating the skyline. Rapid growth since the 1970s has meant that Perth has overtaken Adelaide to become Australia's fourth-most-populous city.

A series of low-lying mountains just north of Albany is the only place that receives snowfall. To the southwest there is a fertile region where most of the state's crop growing is concentrated. There are around 10,800 sq. mi. (28,000km²) of farmland in the state, on which oats, oilseeds, and wheat are grown. Western Australia is the country's biggest wheat producer. Livestock herding is also a major part of farming. Timber, largely from state-controlled forests in the southwest, and coastal fishing also make major contributions to the economy.

▼ Aboriginal children sit in the flat, dry landscape of the Gibson Desert, which lies in the center of Western Australia and occupies an approximate area of 60,040 sq. mi. (155,500km²).

### HUGE MINES AND RESERVES

Australia is very rich in mineral resources and has one of the largest and most important mining industries in the world. Large deposits of certain minerals exist in different parts of Australia, enabling major mining industries to exist in all of the country's states and territories. For example, around 70 percent of the country's copper is extracted from giant mines in Queensland, while uranium mines exist in both Northern Territory and South Australia. Western Australia, however, leads the way in mineral production, with around 38 percent of all mining and two thirds of all metals mined in the country. The state has huge reserves

▲ A huge open-cut gold mine in Western Australia. Gold makes up around 17 percent of the total mining income of the state and is its leading export ahead of iron ore, oil, natural gas, wheat, and wool.

▼ Located in the center of Nambung National Park a short distance north of Perth, the Pinnacles Desert comprises thousands of limestone pillars rising out of yellow quartz sand. It is part of over 77,220 sq. mi. (200,000km²) of parks and protected areas in Western Australia.

of minerals such as bauxite, used to make aluminum, and nickel. Around 97 percent of all of Australia's iron ore is mined in Western Australia. Over two thirds of Australia's gold output, equivalent to around eight percent of the world's production, is mined in the state. Diamond deposits were discovered in the northern Kimberley region in the 1970s, and Australia is now one of the top-five diamond producers in the world. In addition, Western Australia has major oil and natural gas deposits, particularly offshore on the northwest continental shelf.

## A FAST-DEVELOPING ECONOMY

Western Australia has had the fastest-growing economy of all Australian states since the 1960s. Its economy is based on agriculture and mining, which contribute to over one fourth of the state's income. More recently tourism has also boomed to become a major source of revenue. The manufacturing industry, mostly based around Perth, has grown rapidly in recent decades and largely involves the processing of the region's raw materials into usable materials, such as sheet steel, or finished goods such as woolen clothing. Perth has become a major business and commerce center and, situated closer to Singapore than to Sydney, has tried to strengthen trading links with Southeast Asian nations.

## MANY SMALL SETTLEMENTS AND ONE CITY

Western Australia is sparsely populated, with an average density of fewer than one person per square mile. Despite agriculture playing a large role in the region, less than 15 percent of the population live in rural areas. Western Australia's first permanent colony was established in the late 1820s. Its people struggled to prosper until larger farmlands were found, and a workforce of around 10,000 male convicts was transported to the region in the 1850s. In the late 1880s and 1890s a series of large gold discoveries generated a gold rush, and the population of the region increased dramatically. Revenue from gold wealth saw ambitious public works projects completed, including an artificial harbor in the town of Fremantle in 1899. Today Fremantle has been swallowed up by the sprawling city of Perth, Western Australia's only major settlement and the state capital. Perth's urban area is home to 1,603,000 of Western Australia's total population of 2,237,000. In contrast no other town in Western Australia has a population larger than 60,000. Perth is Australia's fourth-most-populous city.

▲ An iron ore bulk carrier approaches the docks at Port Hedland in northwest Western Australia. Australia is the third-largest iron ore producer in the world with 15 percent of total output, almost all of which comes from Western Australia.

# NEW ZEALAND

**Similar in size to Japan, New Zealand is geographically isolated from the rest of the world. Its small population lives in a varied and often spectacular landscape.**

**Area:** 104,453 sq. mi. (270,534km²)
**Population:** 4,269,000
**Capital:** Wellington (382,000)
**Main languages spoken:** English, Maori
**Main religions:** nonreligious (almost one fourth), Anglican, Presbyterian, Roman Catholic
**Currency:** New Zealand dollar
**Main exports:** meat and dairy products, wood and wood products, fish, machinery, basic manufactures, minerals
**Type of government:** parliamentary democracy

New Zealand lies around 990 mi. (1,600km) southeast of Australia. It consists of two large islands—North and South—divided by the 12-mi.- (20-km-) wide Cook Strait and a number of much smaller islands. Of these, mountainous Stewart Island off the south coast of South Island is the largest, with an area of 674 sq. mi. (1,746km²). New Zealand has strong links with a number of island territories. The Cook Islands and Niue, for example, are self-governing territories in free association with New Zealand. Tokelau is a separate territory but is dependent on New Zealand. It consists of three coral atolls more than 300 mi. (500km) north of Samoa. These islands provide homes to around 1,500 Pacific islanders who fish, farm, and export woven handicrafts.

▲ Located in New Zealand's Southern Alps in west-central South Island, Mount Cook is New Zealand's highest mountain at 12,313 ft. (3,754m) above sea level. Known to the Maoris as Aoraki, meaning "cloud piercer," the mountain is surrounded by a further 22 peaks exceeding 9,840 ft. (3,000m) in elevation.

## VOLCANIC NORTH ISLAND, MOUNTAINOUS SOUTH ISLAND

For a fairly small nation New Zealand has an incredible variety of landscapes, including fjords, glaciers, mountains, beaches, plains, swamps, and gently rolling hills. New Zealand's North Island has been greatly shaped by volcanoes. The country's largest lake, Lake Taupo, extends to over 232 sq. mi. (600km²) in area and is the crater of a huge extinct volcano. New Zealand's longest river, the Waikato, flows north and west from this lake before emptying into the Tasman Sea. Rising steeply from Lake Taupo is North Island's central plateau, on which there are four active volcanoes. The central plateau is an area of great heat and activity beneath Earth's surface, with many hot springs, geysers, and frequent small tremors and occasional larger earthquakes. Away from the plateau North Island's landscape includes rolling plains and chains of low mountains with coastal lowlands. North Island's coast is heavily indented, and both of its largest cities, Auckland and Wellington, are built around large natural harbors. The Northland region, north of Auckland, has vast, sandy beaches, subtropical vegetation, and mangrove swamps. South Island's landscape is mostly mountainous and

▼ Auckland lies on a large natural harbor. Piercing the skyline is the 1,076-ft.- (328-m-) high Sky Tower, which, on its completion in 1997, was the tallest building in New Zealand and the entire Southern Hemisphere.

## NEW ZEALAND

*North Island*

North Cape

PACIFIC
OCEAN

Whangarei

Great
Barrier
Island

Kaipara
Harbour

Hauraki
Gulf

Waitakere • North Shore

Auckland • Manukau

Coromandel
Peninsula

Manukau Harbour

Pukekohe •

Waikato

Tauranga

Bay of
Plenty

Hamilton • Cambridge

Lake
Rotorua

East
Cape

Tokoroa • Rotorua

New Plymouth •

Lake
Taupo

Taupo

Gisborne

North Taranaki
Bight

Cape
Egmont

Hawke
Bay

Mahia
Peninsula

South Taranaki
Bight

Napier •
Hastings

Wanganui •

Fielding •

Palmerston North

Levin •

Cape Farewell

D'Urville
Island

Porirua
Lower Hutt
WELLINGTON

Cook Strait

Tasman
Bay

Karamea
Bight

Nelson •

Blenheim •

Cape Palliser

Cape
Foulwind

*South
Island*

Greymouth •

Pegasus
Bay

Christchurch •

Banks
Peninsula

Aoraki
(Mount Cook)
12,313 ft.

Canterbury
Plains

Lake
Ellesmere

*Tasman
Sea*

Ashburton •

Lake
Tekapo

Timaru •

Canterbury
Bight

Lake
Wanaka

Lake
Hawea

PACIFIC
OCEAN

Fiordland

Lake
Te Anau

Lake
Wakatipu

• Oamaru

Resolution
Island

Waiau

Dunedin •
Otago
Peninsula

West
Cape

Mataura

Cape Providence

Invercargill •

Foveaux Strait

South West
Cape

Stewart Island

dominated by a large mountain chain, the Southern Alps, which runs almost the full length of the island. The large Tasman glacier is located in the Southern Alps on the slopes of the country's highest peak, Mount Cook, known to the Maoris as Aoraki. The scouring action of glaciers has created many features on South Island, including long lakes and deep valleys. Much of the island's rugged coastline is broken up by many fjords and bays.

▶ The Champagne Pool is a crater lake filled with bubbling mineral-rich waters at temperatures of over 140°F (60°C). It is found in Waiotapu Thermal Wonderland, an area of great geothermal activity around 12 mi. (20km) south of Rotorua.

409

▲ Maori men, wearing traditional dress, perform a version of the traditional war dance known as the haka.

▼ A handful of New Zealand's 39 million sheep graze pastures close to the city of Dunedin. The country also has 9.6 million cattle and more than 13 million chickens.

## A TEMPERATE CLIMATE

New Zealand experiences a temperate climate with regular rainfall all year round. No part of the country is more than 75 mi. (120km) from the ocean, which tends to moderate the climate so that extremes of temperature are rare. The summers tend to be mild to warm except in the cooler southern mountains, while the winter temperatures in lowland areas rarely fall below 32°F (0°C). Rainfall averages 30 in. (75cm) per year but varies greatly, mainly owing to the country's mountain ranges. Rainfall is highest on the mountain slopes, with the Southern Alps receiving some of the world's highest annual rainfall levels (over 315 in./800cm in some places). East of the mountains on South Island and north of the Otago Peninsula lies New Zealand's driest region, which receives an average of 13 in. (33cm) of rainfall per year.

## NATURE AND FARMING

New Zealand is geographically isolated, and as a result, many of its native plant and animal species are unique, including a number of species of flightless birds such as the kiwi and the kakapo. The country has a wide range of plant species but relatively few large native animals. Forests cover over one fourth of New Zealand, with native kauri trees, some of the tallest trees in the world, found in northern North Island. Around half of the land supports either crop growing or livestock raising, and New Zealand is the world's biggest exporter of butter and one of the leading exporters of wool, cheese, and meat products. A large range of different crops is grown, including cereals, vegetables, hops—used for brewing beer—and grapes. New Zealand is one of the world's largest exporters of fruit. The country's farming industry has been overhauled and modernized in the past 30 years and is one of the most advanced in the world.

## A MIXED ECONOMY

While agriculture is still a major part of the New Zealand economy, the country has developed other industries in the past 40 years. The cost of transporting raw materials to New Zealand has limited the development of heavy industries. Instead the country has concentrated on working with natural and mineral materials found on its own land. The processing of farm products is the country's leading industrial sector, with food-processing companies, large wool mills, and textiles, clothing, and leather businesses. Forestry and associated industries, such as timber, paper, printing, and furniture making, form an important part of the

economy. In the past much of New Zealand's dense forests were cleared, but today most of the remaining native forests are protected. Over 90 percent of the trees felled for timber and paper are tree species introduced especially for the timber industry. Nearly three fourths of the workforce is employed in service industries, including banking, insurance, and tourism. The tourist industry has grown to become the single largest earner of foreign currency in the economy. Around 3.2 million visitors arrive every year. Most are drawn to the country's beautiful scenery, the heritage of its Maori people, and its reputation as a quiet, uncrowded, friendly nation.

## ENERGY AND TRANSPORTATION

New Zealand has significant deposits of certain minerals, particularly coal, while gas and oil were discovered in the 1970s. Around four fifths of the country's electricity needs are generated by renewable methods, including geothermal power and hydroelectricity. Much of the hydroelectricity is generated in South Island but supplied to North Island, which houses around three fourths of the country's population. New Zealand has a large road network but only 107 mi. (172km) of major highways. Car ownership is high, with more than 3.8 million motor vehicles, and there are many small aircraft services and ferries linking the two islands and communities along the coast.

▲ The peaceful waters and dramatic landscape of Milford Sound, a deep fjord in New Zealand's South Island, attract many tourists. The 12-mi.- (20-km-) long fjord is an inlet of the Tasman Sea and is one of the wettest places on Earth, receiving more than 315 in. (800cm) average annual rainfall in some places.

▲ Intricate wood carvings are an important part of Maori art. The Maori are of Polynesian origin, and their wood carvings are more complex than those of any other Polynesian people.

## NEW ZEALAND'S PEOPLE

New Zealand is a country of old and new settlers. Around eight percent are the oldest arrivals—the Maori who live predominantly in North Island. The Maori are greatly outnumbered by people of European, particularly British, descent, who arrived in New Zealand mainly after 1840. European people comprise 70 percent of the population and have traditionally held most of the power and commercial positions in the country. Around four percent of the country's population originally come from other Pacific islands such as Tonga, the Cook Islands, and Samoa. They were drawn to New Zealand by the need to find work and the expansion of the New Zealand economy after World War II. Waves of more recent immigrants have come from parts of Asia, particularly Malaysia and Hong Kong. These more recent arrivals make up around six percent of the population. New Zealanders tend to enjoy a high standard of living, although the Maori suffer higher levels of unemployment and poverty. Around eight percent of New Zealanders are of mixed European and Maori descent. Despite the importance of agriculture, around 99 percent of New Zealanders live in towns and cities.

## THE MAORI CULTURE

The Maori are the indigenous people of New Zealand and are of Polynesian origin. They are believed to have reached New Zealand, possibly from the Cook Islands, from the A.D. 900s. The Maori developed a rich culture that includes intricate wood carvings and full-face tattooing, called moko, common among male warriors. Dutch explorer Abel Tasman made the first European contact with the Maori in 1642, but it was the British explorer James Cook who first landed on New Zealand soil in 1769 and claimed the country for Great Britain. The arrival of waves of European settlers from the early 1800s onward resulted in wars and diseases that reduced the Maori population to under 50,000. The Maori were forced to give up large areas of land for no more than token payments. Conflicts between the Maori and Europeans continued throughout the 1800s. Recently New Zealand has begun to focus on its past and has awarded some compensation and land to the Maori, and their children now have access to education in their own language, Maoritanga.

## POLITICS AND INTERNATIONAL RELATIONS

Although Auckland is the biggest and most populous city and the financial center of New Zealand, the seat of national government is in Wellington. New Zealand's constitution is found in several documents, and its head of state is the

▼ Located on the north coast of South Island, the beautiful 30-mi.- (49-km-) long Queen Charlotte Sound with its many bays is a popular haven for pleasure boating. The waterway was named by Captain Cook in the 1770s.

British monarch. In 1893 New Zealand was the first country in the world to give women the vote, and in 2005 Prime Minster Helen Clark was elected to a third term. Most New Zealanders are firmly in favor of staying in the Commonwealth and keeping strong ties with Great Britain, which is traditionally its most important trading partner. However, the U.K.'s entry into the European Union has forced New Zealand to strengthen its ties with other nations, particularly Australia, its largest trading partner, the U.S., Japan, and Southeast Asian nations. Around one fourth of the entire country is part of the 13 national parks and other protected areas. New Zealand strongly opposed French nuclear testing in the Pacific Ocean and has banned nuclear-powered ships and submarines from docking in its ports.

▲ The Wairakei Valley steam pipeline carries steam, heated by geothermal activity under Earth's surface, to a nearby geothermal power plant that generates electricity. Wairakei Valley lies just north of Lake Taupo, the largest lake on New Zealand's North Island.

▼ An international rugby match in progress between New Zealand, known as the All Blacks, and South Africa, held in Auckland. Rugby is the most popular sport in New Zealand, and the All Blacks have a long and illustrious history.

# GUAM & NORTHERN MARIANA ISLANDS

**Dependencies of the U.S., Guam and the Northern Mariana Islands are small island territories that have both developed successful service industries.**

### Guam

**Area:** 209 sq. mi. (541km²)
**Population:** 178,000
**Capital:** Hagatna (27,000)
**Main languages spoken:** English, Chamorro, Japanese
**Main religion:** Roman Catholic
**Currency:** U.S. dollar
**Principal exports:** reexported petroleum, construction materials, foodstuffs, fish
**Type of government:** dependency of the U.S.

### Northern Mariana Islands

**Area:** 184 sq. mi. (477km²)
**Population:** 87,000
**Capital:** Saipan (62,000)
**Main languages spoken:** English, Chamorro, Carolinian
**Main religion:** Roman Catholic
**Currency:** U.S. dollar
**Principal exports:** clothing, agricultural and fish products
**Type of government:** self-governing dependency of the U.S.

Guam was formed through the uplift of undersea volcanoes. The northern half of the island is a plateau of coral limestone. The southern half is a collection of volcanic hills and valleys. Guam's native wildlife, particularly its bird life, has been decimated by the brown tree snake, which has killed off the island's nine native bird species. A major military outpost for the U.S. in the Pacific Ocean, military bases cover one third of the island. Its palm-fringed beaches attract visitors, and tourism is the single largest industry on Guam, accounting for over half of the country's income. Along with the spending of U.S. military personnel stationed on the island, this has enabled Guam to develop its services and give its people one of the highest standards of living in the Pacific islands.

The Northern Marianas has also developed tourist resorts, particularly on the three largest islands of Saipan, Tinian, and Rota. Agriculture plays an important role in the Northern Marianas, which has a tropical climate. Cattle and pigs are raised, while sugarcane, taro, cassava, coconuts, and vegetables are grown in the fertile volcanic soil. A number of the islands' volcanoes are still active.

*Guam*
*(to U.S.)*

Asan
Agat
Hagatna
Mount Lamlan
1,332 ft.

PACIFIC OCEAN

Agrihan
Pagan
Philippine Sea
Northern Mariana Islands (to U.S.)
Tinian
Saipan
Rota
PACIFIC OCEAN

▶ More than 1.5 million tourists, especially from Japan and some from the U.S., visit Guam every year. Visitors are attracted by the island's tropical climate and duty-free shopping.

# FEDERATED STATES OF MICRONESIA

**A scattered collection of 607 small tropical islands, the Federated States of Micronesia was settled over 3,500 years ago and has a culturally diverse population.**

**Area:** 271 sq. mi. (701km²)
**Population:** 108,000
**Capital:** Palikir (6,400)
**Main languages spoken:** English, Trukese, Pohnpeian, Yapese
**Main religions:** Roman Catholic, Protestant
**Currency:** U.S. dollar
**Principal exports:** fish, clothing, bananas, black pepper
**Type of government:** republic

The Federated States of Micronesia consists of four states—Yap, Pohnpei, Kosrae, and Chuuk—that retain close ties and trade links with their former ruler, the United States. Part of the widely spread Caroline Islands archipelago, Micronesia experiences a tropical climate. The largest island, Pohnpei, is also the wettest, receiving as much as 217 in. (550cm) of rainfall per year. Although the islands stretch across a vast area of the Pacific Ocean—over 617,770 sq. mi. (1,600,000km²)—the total land area is small, no more than 271 sq. mi. (702km²).

Apart from deposits of phosphates, there are no mineral reserves and only 25 mi. (40km) of paved roads, while many homes outside of the small towns have no electricity or running water. The islanders rely on subsistence farming, growing crops, such as taro, coconuts, bananas, and yams, fishing, and raising poultry, pigs, and, sometimes, dogs for food. U.S. aid makes up more than half of the country's income. The islands have a variety of different Pacific peoples with their own distinct cultures and languages, despite Western customs being imposed by European whalers, missionaries, and traders from the early 1800s onward. Situated on Pohnpei, the giant ruins of Nan Madol are the largest ancient archaeological site found throughout the Pacific islands.

► A woman braids palm fronds into thatching for the roof of a home on Satawal Island. The most easterly of Yap's inhabited islands, with a population of around 560, Satawal had electricity installed for the first time in 2001.

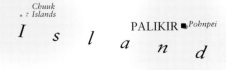

MICRONESIA

Yap

Caroline

Chuuk Islands

PALIKIR ■Pohnpei

PACIFIC OCEAN

Islands

Kosrae

# MARSHALL ISLANDS

Consisting of 1,150 coral islands, of which only 20 are inhabited, the Marshall Islands were United Nations Trust Territories under U.S. administration until 1986.

**Area:** 70 sq. mi. (181km²)
**Population:** 56,000
**Capital:** Majuro (Delap) (25,000)
**Main languages spoken:** Marshallese, English, Japanese
**Main religion:** Protestant
**Currency:** U.S. dollar
**Main exports:** copra, coconut oil, handicrafts, fish
**Type of government:** republic

The Marshall Islands consist of two chains of coral islands and islets: the Ralik, meaning "sunset," to the west and the Ratak, meaning "sunrise," to the east. The chains lie around 125 mi. (200km) apart and are around 800 mi. (1,300km) long. Many of the islands are atolls consisting of a narrow fringe of coral-based land encircling lagoons. The largest atoll, Kwajalein, is one of the largest in the world. It encircles a lagoon of around 660 sq. mi. (1,700km²) in area, yet its actual land area is only 6 sq. mi. Several of the atolls, including Bikini atoll, were used for the testing of nuclear weapons in the 1940s and 1950s, and radioactive fallout made these and neighboring islands uninhabitable for many years. Kwajalein atoll is the current home of a U.S. missile-testing range, and rent from

this base, along with U.S. aid, forms the majority of the country's income. Around one in ten of the workforce is employed in tourism, while the atoll of Majuro is the commercial center of the Marshall Islands and home to 40 percent of its population. Life away from Majuro and Kwajalein is dominated by subsistence agriculture, growing coconuts, breadfruit, taro, and fishing. Copra—dried coconut meat—is the island's major export, while many goods have to be imported.

# NAURU

A small, oval-shaped, raised coral island and the world's smallest republic, Nauru's economy is based almost solely on phosphate mining.

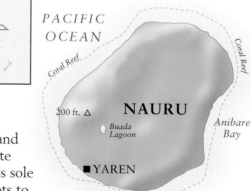

**Area:** 8 sq. mi. (21km²)
**Population:** 9,300
**Capital:** Yaren (600)
**Main languages spoken:** Nauruan, English
**Main religion:** Christian
**Currency:** Australian dollar
**Main export:** phosphates
**Type of government:** republic

A central plateau approximately 200 ft. (60m) in elevation covers the majority of the tropical island of Nauru. This plateau contains the island's phosphate reserves, with phosphate mining traditionally Nauru's sole industry. However, reserves are depleted, and attempts to diversify have led the economy into bankruptcy. Nauru has no natural harbor, docking is conducted offshore, and all drinking water, fuel, and many foodstuffs have to be imported. Most of the island's people live around the narrow but fertile coast of the island. The population includes groups of other Pacific islanders and people of Chinese and European origin. Many younger Nauruans migrate to Australia or New Zealand for work or education.

▶ Nauru has been mined for phosphates, used to make chemicals and fertilizers, for over 100 years. However, its reserves of phosphates are almost depleted.

# SOLOMON ISLANDS

**The third-largest island chain in the Pacific Ocean, the Solomon Islands consist of a mixture of rugged, mountainous islands and low-lying coral atolls.**

**Area:** 10,950 sq. mi. (28,370km²)
**Population:** 495,000
**Capital:** Honiara (59,000)
**Main languages spoken:** English, Polynesian and Melanesian languages
**Main religions:** Anglican, Roman Catholic, Baptist
**Currency:** Solomon Islands dollar
**Main exports:** timber products, fish, palm oil, copra, cocoa
**Type of government:** parliamentary democracy

▼ Many of the islands in the Solomon Islands group are fringed by coral reefs. The waters around the islands are rich in marine life, including many brightly marked species of tropical fish, sharks, and dugongs—large sea mammals also known as sea cows.

The tropical islands of the Solomons are a haven for plant life. The islands are home to over 4,500 plant species, many of which are used for building, food, medicine, and clothing. Copra, cacao, and palm oil are important cash crops, while people grow sweet potatoes, yams, taro, rice, and tropical fruit for food. The timber industry is the country's largest, and as a result, more than one tenth of the land has been cleared of trees. People have settled on around one third of the islands, with the majority living on one of the six largest islands: Malaita, Guadalcanal, New Georgia, San Cristobal (Makira), Santa Isabel, and Choiseul. The larger islands are volcanic and mountainous and have vast forests. Guadalcanal is the biggest of the islands and home of the capital, Honiara, which is also the islands' major port. First peopled approximately 3,000 years ago, the islands were settled by arrivals from many parts of the Pacific. Different peoples on different islands developed their own distinct ways of life. Most Solomon Islanders are Melanesian, and there are an estimated 115 languages spoken. Intercommunal conflict occured between 1998 and 2006, and Australian forces were invited to intervene to help restore order. They have led international forces in keeping order on the islands since 2003.

# VANUATU

Vanuatu consists of 80 islands located in a Y-shaped archipelago 1,350 mi. (2,170km) northeast of the Australian city of Sydney. The island group is renowned for its scenery.

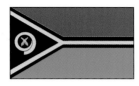

**Area:** 4,710 sq. mi. (12,190km²)
**Population:** 243,000
**Capital:** Port-Vila (46,000)
**Main languages spoken:** Bislama, English, French
**Main religions:** Presbyterian, Anglican, Roman Catholic
**Currency:** vatu
**Main exports:** copra, beef and veal, timber, cocoa, coffee
**Type of government:** republic

▼ A man from Tanna island prepares for a traditional ceremony involving the drinking of kava. The traditional drink of chiefs in many Pacific island cultures in the Melanesian part of the Pacific, kava is made from the root of a plant related to the pepper tree.

Vanuatu was formerly known as the New Hebrides and was ruled jointly by France and Great Britain until 1980. The islands experience a tropical climate, with rainfall averaging around 94 in. (240cm) per year but as high as 154 in. (390cm) in the northern islands. Tropical cyclones visit the islands from December to March. Vanuatu's islands are a mixture of coral and volcanically formed landmasses. They contain a number of active volcanoes and experience relatively frequent—but usually minor—earthquakes. Subsistence agriculture employs the majority of the workforce, but tourism and offshore banking services contribute the most money to the economy. Vanuatu's scenery, including deep ravines, heavily rain-forested mountains, clear seas, beaches, and cave systems, attracts an increasing number of tourists. Although almost all of Vanuatu's islands are inhabited, 80 percent of the population live on 11 main islands. The population is one of the most culturally diverse of all Pacific nations. The native Ni-Vanuatu people make up 98 percent, but different languages—totaling 105—and cultures have developed separately on many islands. There are also small communities of French, British, Australian, New Zealand, Vietnamese, Chinese, and other Pacific island peoples. Tourism is growing, with 200,000 visitors in 2008.

# NEW CALEDONIA

**New Caledonia is a French overseas territory. It consists of one large island, New Caledonia, on which 90 percent of the population live, as well as many smaller islands.**

**Area:** 7,172 sq. mi. (18,576km²)
**Population:** 246,000
**Capital:** Nouméa (164,000)
**Main language spoken:** French
**Main religion:** Roman Catholic
**Currency:** French Pacific franc
**Main exports:** refined ferro nickel and nickel, nickel ore, fish
**Type of government:** self-governing dependency of France

The island of New Caledonia is a little over 200 mi. (320km) long and around 30 mi. (50km) wide and has a mountainous landscape with areas of grasslands. Tourism and agriculture are the biggest employers of New Caledonians, but mining, particularly of nickel, is the most economically important industry. New Caledonia has around 25 percent of the world's reserves of nickel, and over 85 percent of the islands' income comes from nickel exports. The island came under French control in the mid-1700s. The native Kanak people form around two fifths of the population, with a large and significant minority of French origin. Tensions between the two groups have remained for many years.

▶ A traditional home on Lifou, New Caledonia's second-largest island. Lifou is part of the Loyalty Islands group, which also includes Ouvéa, Maré, and other smaller islands.

Between 2013 and 2018, the islanders will vote on whether or not they want to become independent.

# KIRIBATI

**Kiribati is a series of 33 small islands spread out over almost 2 million sq. mi. (5 million km²) of the Pacific.**

**Area:** 277 sq. mi. (717km²)
**Population:** 93,000
**Capital:** Bairiki (40,000)
**Main languages spoken:** English, Gilbertese
**Main religions:** Roman Catholic, Protestant
**Currency:** Australian dollar
**Main exports:** copra, re-exports, fish and fish products
**Type of government:** republic

Kiribati's terrain is extremely low, with its highest point just 285 ft. (87m) and almost all of its land only a few feet above sea level. Rising sea levels, caused by global warming, are a major concern to Kiribati and other low-lying island groups in the Pacific. Kiritlmati (Christmas Island) is the country's largest island, making up over half of the land area, but Tarawa is the most populous. A part of the British Gilbert and Ellice Islands colony until 1979, the people of Kiribati still refer to themselves as Gilbertese, and almost all are Christian. Most are fairly poor, relying on farming and fishing to feed their families. The majority of the islands' soils are of poor quality and support little vegetation. Islanders grow a variety of

tropical crops, including bananas, papaw, and breadfruit. The islands can also suffer from low rainfall. This occurred in 1999 when a drought emergency was declared. Phosphate mining was the principal industry until reserves of this mineral ran out in 1980. Organized resettlement from densely populated Tarawa to other less populated islands occurred during the 1990s.

# PALAU

The Republic of Palau consists of 260 islands, almost all of which lie in a large lagoon enclosed by a barrier reef that stretches a distance of over 60 mi. (100km).

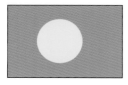

**Area:** 177 sq. mi. (458km²)
**Population:** 19,900
**Capital:** Ngerulmud-Melekeok (400)
**Main languages spoken:** English, Palauan, Sonsorolese, Angaur, Japanese, Tobi
**Main religions:** Roman Catholic, Modekngei
**Currency:** U.S. dollar
**Main exports:** shellfish, tuna, copra, clothing
**Type of government:** republic

Palau is a small nation with the fourth-smallest population in the world. Many of its people live on Babelthuap, the largest island, or Koror, the former capital on the island of Koror. The two islands are linked by a concrete bridge. Palau has one of the smallest economies in the world. Its small population, however, has a higher-than-average standard of living among the Pacific islanders. Tourism is the fastest-growing part of the economy. Palau has some of the most spectacular underwater diving sites in the world. Agreements between Palau and the U.S. have allowed U.S. military bases to be located on the islands in return for aid and trade deals. While the majority of Palauans are Christians, with about 42 percent Roman Catholic and 23 percent Protestant, and nine percent follow Modekngei.

▶ Palau's famed Rock Islands are humps of rounded, coralline limestone that are thickly covered with dense forests that have been undercut by erosion. The waters and reefs around Palau's islands are home to more than 1,400 species of fish.

# TUVALU

Lying 600 mi. (1,000km) north of Fiji, the nine coral atolls of Tuvalu were formerly known as the Ellice Islands. The islands are in danger from rising sea levels.

**Area:** 9 sq. mi. (24km²)
**Population:** 11,000
**Capital:** Fongafale (4,500)
**Main languages spoken:** Tuvaluan, English
**Main religion:** Congregational
**Currency:** Australian dollar
**Main exports:** copra, fish, clothing, fruit and vegetables
**Type of government:** dominion

Tuvalu's land is low-lying with generally poor, salty soils in which only certain plants, such as coconut palms, flourish. The tending and harvesting of coconuts and raising ducks, pigs, and chickens are key farming activities. Copra—dried coconut meat—is the only agricultural export of importance, and even this is in limited quantities. Much food has to be imported, most arriving by ships at the islands' main port on Funafuti Atoll. Tuvalu's land is very low-lying and under severe threat from rising sea levels owing to global warming. Sea water has penetrated sources of freshwater, and scientists estimate that Tuvalu may be under the waves by 2050. Plans to relocate the entire population in New Zealand or Fiji are being discussed. Opportunities for work on these tiny

islands are limited, and many younger Tuvaluans work overseas and send money back to help support their families. Tuvalu's major resources are the fish-rich seas around its islands, and the Tuvaluan government has sold licenses to foreign trawler companies. Foreign aid is also important. Sales of postage stamps also support the economy. Tuvalu's Internet country identifying code is .tv, and rights to use this for web sites were sold to a Canadian media company, bringing in many millions of dollars.

# WALLIS & FUTUNA

**Made up of two volcanic island archipelagos, Wallis & Futuna is a French overseas territory and among the least developed of all Pacific island groups.**

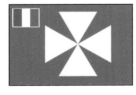

MATA'UTU■ *Wallis (Uvéa)*

*Wallis and Futuna (to France)*

*Futuna* *PACIFIC*
*Alofi* *OCEAN*

**Area:** 106 sq. mi. (274km²)
**Population:** 13,400
**Capital:** Mata'utu (1,200)
**Main languages spoken:** French, Wallisian, Futunan
**Main religion:** Roman Catholic
**Currency:** French Pacific franc
**Main exports:** copra and coconuts, construction materials
**Type of government:** dependency of France

The Wallis archipelago is made up of over 20 small islands and islets that are found on a barrier reef that encircles the main island of Wallis. It is a volcanic island but is fairly low-lying, with the highest point at 476 ft. (145m). Its terrain includes sharp sea cliffs and a number of water-filled craters. The Futuna archipelago is made up of two main islands, Futuna and Alofi, which is uninhabited. Futuna consists of a narrow coastal plain that rises sharply to heights above 1,640 ft. (500m). The islands have a tropical climate with heavy rainfall of over 118 in. (300cm) per year. The Wallis islands take their name from English navigator Samuel Wallis, who claimed possession of them for England in 1767. Both the Wallis and Futuna island groups have been under French control since 1842.

The islands are divided among three traditional kingdoms, whose rulers remain influential. The economy is limited to traditional subsistence farming, growing mostly coconut palms, breadfruit, mangoes, and vegetables. Pigs and chickens are raised, and fishing from small boats is also important. These activities engage over 80 percent of the workforce. The local government receives aid from France and sells licenses for fishing rights to Japan and South Korea. Over 15,000 Wallisians work in New Caledonia, another French territory, sending back part of their incomes to their families.

# FIJI ISLANDS

Lying 1,240 mi. (2,000km) north of New Zealand, Fiji Islands are the most populous and developed of all of the Pacific island nations.

**Area:** 7,055 sq. mi. (18,272km²)
**Population:** 837,000
**Capital:** Suva (194,000)
**Main languages spoken:** English, Fijian, Hindustani
**Main religions:** Christian, Methodist, Hinduism, Islam
**Currency:** Fijian dollar
**Main exports:** sugar, clothing, gold, fish, timber, coconuts
**Type of government:** republic; military government

▼ A casual game of rugby, one of Fiji's major sports, takes place in Albert Park in the capital city of Suva. More than 194,000 Fijians live in or around Suva, making it one of the largest settlements in the Pacific islands.

The Fiji Islands consists of around 330 islands, of which 106 are inhabited. The majority of the population live on the two largest islands: Viti Levu and Vanua Levu. These islands and a number of others are of volcanic origin and have mountainous interiors. Agriculture employs more than 70 percent of the workforce, with major crops including bananas, cocoa beans, corn, coconuts, rice, and sugarcane. Fiji exports around one-and-a-half times the amount of food it has to import. Sugar processing is the country's biggest industry and is largely government controlled. Sugar is one of the most important exports. Forestry and fishing are important industries, while tourism was the fastest-growing industry until the country's troubles in 2000. Fiji has no fossil fuels, but a large hydroelectricity plant on Viti Levu generates over three fourths of the country's electricity. Viti Levu is also the location for Fiji's largest private industry—the Vatukoula gold mine, which employs around 1,600 workers. Fiji is sometimes known as the "crossroads of the Pacific" and has seen a number of waves of settlement stretching back to the Lapita people, who are believed to have reached the islands

around 3,500 years ago. The population today includes small minorities of Chinese, Europeans, and other Pacific islanders, but they are greatly outnumbered by two large groups: native Fijians and Fijian Indians. Most Fijian Indians were brought to the islands when they were a British colony to work on the sugarcane plantations. From World War II through independence in 1970 until the 1980s Fijian Indians, most of whom are Hindus, outnumbered native Fijians—almost all of whom are Christians. Tensions between the two groups have dominated Fijian politics, with civil disorder, outbursts of violence, and a series of military coups occurring between 1987 and 2006. This has led to economic problems, and a large number of Fijian Indians have left the country.

*Vanua Levu*
*Yasawa Group*
Tavua
Lautoka
*Viti Levu* Nadi
△ Tomanivi 4,670 ft.
Savusavu *Taveuni*
*Koro*
*Koro Sea*
*Northern Lau Group*
Sigatoka
SUVA
*Gau*
*Southern Lau Group*

**FIJI ISLANDS**

*Kadavu*

*PACIFIC OCEAN*

# SAMOA

Consisting of nine islands and a number of small islets, Samoa is one of the most traditional of the Pacific island nations. It used to be known as Western Samoa.

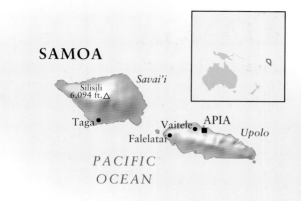

**Area:** 1,093 sq. mi. (2,831km²)
**Population:** 179,000
**Capital:** Apia (61,000)
**Main languages spoken:** Samoan, English
**Main religion:** Christian, Methodist
**Currency:** tala, local issue of New Zealand currency
**Main exports:** coconut oil, coconut cream, copra, fish, clothing, beer
**Type of government:** constitutional monarchy

▼ The interior of Samoa's major islands tends to be covered in lush plant life and cut by short, shallow, and fast-moving streams and rivers.

S amoa's land is dominated by two large islands—Savai'i and Upolo—and seven smaller islands, of which only two are inhabited. Savai'i and Upolo both have narrow coastal plains, coral reefs around their coasts, and volcanically formed, mountainous centers, much of which are densely covered in tropical forests. Samoa is a nation of farmers, with 66 percent of its people living in the countryside, mostly in the islands' 400 coastal villages. Agriculture is mainly on a small scale, although larger plantations of hardwood trees, coconut palms, and bananas provide products for export. Fishing is largely conducted using traditional outrigger canoes. Samoans tend to live in communal family groups who own 80 percent of the land— which they are not allowed to sell. Each extended family is headed by a *matai*, or elected male chief, who wields great power. Samoa faces major environmental problems, particularly deforestation and soil erosion.

More than half of its original forests have been cleared, destroying habitats of many native wildlife species. Government replanting programs and strict logging laws are helping keep the timber industry working while protecting some of the islands' land. Samoa generates over 35 percent of its electricity through hydroelectric power but has to import the remainder, along with many other goods and supplies. Despite a flourishing tourist industry, Samoa has large foreign debts and very high unemployment. Thousands of Samoans have migrated to other nations, particularly New Zealand, the U.S., and American Samoa, to seek a better living.

# TONGA

**Lying 400 mi. (640km) east of the Fiji Islands, the Kingdom of Tonga consists of 172 islands, many of which are covered in thick vegetation—but less than 40 are inhabited.**

**Area:** 289 sq. mi. (748km²)
**Population:** 102,000
**Capital:** Nuku'alofa (34,000)
**Main languages spoken:** Tongan, English
**Main religions:** Free Wesleyan, Roman Catholic, Mormon
**Currency:** pa'anga
**Principal exports:** squashes, fish, vanilla beans, root crops
**Type of government:** constitutional monarchy

▼ A sentry stands guard in front of the Royal Palace of the king of Tonga. Until 2010, political power lay with the monarch, King Siaosi Tupou V, who has reigned since 2006. In 2010, a more democratic system was introduced.

Tonga's three main island groups—Tongatapu, Ha'apai, and Vava'u—lie just west of the Tonga Trench, the second-deepest part of the Pacific Ocean floor. The eastern islands are mainly low-lying and formed of coral. Many of the western islands were formed from volcanic activity and are more rugged and mountainous, with four active volcanoes. Tonga lies over 1,365 mi. (2,200km) south of the equator and has more variation in summer and winter temperatures than many Pacific islands. Winter temperatures average between 63–72°F (17–22°C), with summer temperatures between 77–91°F (25–33°C). The islands are located within the South Pacific's cyclone belt, and tropical storms regularly strike the islands. Tonga's largest island is called Tongatapu and is home to around two thirds of the islands' people. Around 32 percent of Tongans work in agriculture, growing vanilla beans, coconuts,

and squashes for export and vegetables, such as cassava, for food. Fishing, tourism, and the sale of handicrafts contribute to the economy. Tonga has no mineral resources and mostly generates its energy needs from imported fuel.

TONGA

Niuatoputapu
Tafahi
Neiafa
Late  Vava'u Group
Tofua  Ha'apai Group
Nomuka Group
NUKU' ALOFA
Tongatapu
Eua

# AMERICAN SAMOA

**American Samoa consists of six volcanic islands and two coral atolls. The largest island is Tutuila, where the capital, Pago Pago, is located.**

**Area:** 77 sq. mi. (199km²)
**Population:** 65,000
**Capital:** Pago Pago (5,000)
**Main languages spoken:** Samoan, English
**Main religions:** Congregational, Roman Catholic
**Currency:** U.S. dollar
**Principal exports:** tuna, other fish
**Type of government:** dependency of the U.S.

American Samoa's volcanic-formed islands, which include Tutuila, Tau, and Olosega, have rugged landscapes rising to eroded mountains in their centers, with a mixture of cliffs and scooped-out bays on their coasts. The mountain interiors of these islands are heavily covered in rain forests that provide homes for many bird species, as well as flying foxes, lizards, rats, and snakes. American Samoa experiences a tropical climate with heavy rainfall. Pago Pago tends to receive an average of 197 in. (500cm) per year. The islands are susceptible to heavy storms between December and March. Unlike many Pacific island groups, American Samoa has relatively few tourists, and the economy relies on tuna canneries that process tuna caught in local waters. Textiles and handicrafts, such as woven mats, are also exported. The largest island, Tutuila, is where the majority of the territory's population live. The people of American Samoa often still live in large extended family groups, called *aiga*, but younger Samoans are becoming more Westernized and abandoning traditional ways of life.

▶ One of the finest deep-water harbors in the Pacific, Pago Pago harbor was formed from a volcanic crater that collapsed and was submerged millions of years ago.

# NIUE

**One of the largest coral islands and smallest self-governing states in the world, Niue is separately governed in free association with New Zealand.**

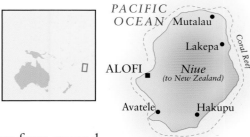

**Area:** 100 sq. mi. (259km²)
**Population:** 1,600
**Capital:** Alofi (600)
**Main languages spoken:** English, Niuean
**Main religion:** Congregational
**Currency:** New Zealand dollar
**Principal exports:** coconut cream and copra, honey, fruit
**Type of government:** self-governing dependency of New Zealand

Niue is a roughly oval-shaped island with broken and sharp cliffs facing the sea and an inland plateau rising to around 200 ft. (60m). The most fertile part of the island, where the majority of the people live, is the land near the coast, which contains wooded areas of palm and banyan trees. Almost one fourth of the island is capable of supporting some form of farming, although the soils are not of good quality. Niue lacks streams or rivers, and water tends to filter through the soil and the porous coral out into the ocean. Rainfall, which averages 79 in. (200cm) per year, has to be collected and stored. Niue's economy is tiny, with the income from around 4,000 tourists per year making a major contribution. The sale of postage stamps to foreign collectors and the exporting of copra, limes, and honey bring in further revenue. Aid, particularly from New Zealand, has enabled Niue to build a fairly extensive infrastructure, including television and telephone links. Yet opportunities for work on the island are limited, and around 20,000 Niueans have migrated to New Zealand to find work. Niue's people are mainly descended from Samoans and Tongans who settled on the island and have developed their own Pacific language, Niuean.

425

# COOK ISLANDS

**East of Tonga, the Cook Islands consist of two groups of small volcanic and coral islands scattered over around 850,000 sq. mi. (2,200,000km²) of the Pacific Ocean.**

**Area:** 92 sq. mi. (237km²)
**Population:** 19,600
**Capital:** Avarua (14,200)
**Main languages spoken:** English, Cook Islands Maori
**Main religion:** Cook Islands Church, Roman Catholic
**Currency:** New Zealand dollar
**Main exports:** copra, fresh fruit (particularly papayas), canned fruit, fish, clothing
**Type of government:** self-governing dependency of New Zealand

The Cook Islands are a self-governing dependency of new Zealand. They are made up of a northern group of six coral atolls and nine islands of volcanic origin in a southern group. The majority of the population live in the southern group, especially on the largest island, Rarotonga, where its capital, Avarua, is based. Surrounded by a coral reef, Rarotonga's land rises from a coastal plain to a volcanic peak. Cook Islanders are mostly descended from Polynesians related to the Maori people who settled in New Zealand. The Maori language, along with English, is widely spoken. While fishing and growing pineapples and other tropical crops occupy many in the small workforce, the most lucrative activities are tourism and offshore banking. Marine farms producing cultured pearls have recently been established. The expansion of New Zealand's economy has drawn many Cook Islanders to find work there. An estimated 32,000 Cook Islanders live and work in New Zealand. The islands are effectively independent, conducting their own foreign affairs, but are tied to New Zealand, which donates aid and dominates trade.

▶ Traditional dancers on the Cook Islands tell stories handed down from generation to generation. Usually accompanied by beating drums, the dancers wear traditional costumes made from palm fronds, tree bark, seashells, feathers, and flowers.

# FRENCH POLYNESIA

A collection of island archipelagos made up of over 115 islands, French Polynesia sprawls across the Pacific and is the most eastern of the Pacific island nations.

*French Polynesia* (to France) · Îles Marquises · Îles Tuamotu · Bora-Bora · Society Islands · Papeete · Tahiti · Tubuai Islands · Gambier Islands

**Area:** 1,545 sq. mi. (4,000km²)
**Population:** 260,000
**Capital:** Papeete (132,000)
**Main languages spoken:** French, Tahitian
**Main religion:** Roman Catholic
**Currency:** French Pacific franc
**Main exports:** pearls, copra and other coconut products, mother-of-pearl, vanilla
**Type of government:** dependency of France

▼ Scattered over an enormous area of the Pacific Ocean—there are over 1,240 mi. (2,000km) between the northernmost and southernmost islands—French Polynesia attracted around 200,000 tourists in 2001. Fringed by coral reefs, the tropical island paradise of Bora-Bora in the Society Islands group is a popular destination for wealthier tourists.

French Polynesia is divided into five island archipelagos: the Society Islands, the Gambier Islands, the Tubuai Islands, the Îles Marquises (Marquesa Islands), and the Tuamotu archipelago. The larger islands, which are of volcanic origin, support an array of natural life, including the large tiare flowers that are often worn by islanders. Many of the islands' plant and animal species, including wild pigs and sheep, were introduced by human settlers and have since flourished. The islands are also home to around 100 species of birds. While farming and fishing provide some employment on the outer islands, tourism is the most important industry. French Polynesia is the world leader in creating cultured pearls, particularly on the Tuamotu and Gambier islands. French Polynesia's economy, government, and transportation network are dominated by the island of Tahiti in the Society Islands. Encircled by a fertile coastal plain, Tahiti's land rises sharply to spectacular volcanic mountains. Over two thirds of the islands'

▲ Located in the Society Islands, Raiatea occupies 92 sq. mi. (238km²) and is a mountainous island surrounded by palm-fringed beaches and coral reefs.

population live on Tahiti, which is also home to the main port of Papeete. A French military presence on the islands has provided a great deal of income and employment, but French nuclear tests on Muroroa atoll in the mid-1990s provoked opposition among the islanders. Since then, France has granted increased self-rule in the islands.

# ANTARCTICA

Lying undiscovered until the early 1800s, the continent of Antarctica is a mostly icy wasteland whose interior has been barely touched by human impact or the activities of plants and animals. The continent, whose name means the opposite of Arctic, encircles the geographic South Pole. With an approximate land area of 5.5 million sq. mi. (14 million km2), it is larger than the continent of Europe. The giant Transantarctic mountain range, almost 3,100 mi. (5,000km) long and containing peaks over 13,120 ft. (4,000m) in elevation, splits the continent into two regions: a larger eastern region and the western region, which includes the Antarctic Peninsula. This peninsula extends 800 mi. (1,300km) northward toward the southernmost tip of South America and is covered in mountain ranges. Its loftiest peak, the 16,062-ft.-(4,897-m-) high Vinson Massif, is also the highest point on the continent. Around 90 percent of the world's freshwater is contained in Antarctica, locked together as ice. All except around five percent of its land surface is covered by a thick ice sheet, averaging 1.4 mi. (2.3km) in depth. It is the coldest, windiest region on Earth and also one of the driest. With a temporary human population of around 4,000 in the summer and less than 1,000 in the winter, Antarctica is the most unspoiled and hostile environment on the planet.

South Orkney
Islands
(to U.K.)

South
Shetland
Islands

James Ross Island

Antarctic
Peninsula

Anvers
Island

Palmer Land

Adelaide Island

Alexander Island

Bellingshausen
Sea

Ellsworth
Land

Thurston
Island

Amundsen
Sea

Carney Island

Siple Island

◄ An ice-breaker ship travels slowly through an open but narrow sea-lane in the ice off the continent of Antarctica.

SOUTHERN
OCEAN

Fimbul
Ice Shelf

Riiser-Larsen
Peninsula

Riiser-Larsen
Ice Shelf

Queen
Maud
Land

Enderby
Land

Weddell
Sea

Coats
Land

Kemp
Land

Berkner Island

Filchner
Ice Shelf

Cape Darnley

Amery
Ice Shelf

Ronne
Ice Shelf

Henry
Ice Rise

ANTARCTICA

Princess
Elizabeth
Land

orff
Rise

△ Vinson Massif
16,062 ft.

• South Pole

Greater
Antarctica

Willhelm II
Land

Shackleton
Ice Shelf

Lesser
Antarctica

Davis
Sea

Ross
Ice Shelf

Queen Mary
Land

Vincennes
Bay

Roosevelt Island

Cape Poinsett

Ross
Sea

Ross Island

Victoria
Land

Wilkes Land

Transantarctic Mountains

Adélie
Land

Porpoise Bay

OUTHERN
OCEAN

Oates
Land

George V
Land

• South Magnetic
Pole (1990)

Cape Adare

Dumont
d'Urville
Sea

| 0 | | 1000 | | 2000 km |
|---|---|---|---|---|

| 0 | 500 | 1000 miles |
|---|---|---|

including most of the Antarctic Peninsula, Wilkes Land, southern Victoria Land, and much of Ross Island. The peaks and some valleys in parts of the Transantarctic mountain range and the Ellsworth Mountains are also exposed rock, and because of global warming, Antarctica's ice cap appears to be receding in places. Despite the harsh climate, the continent attracts around 13,000 tourists during its summer months, who travel on organized tours to experience Antarctica. Most visit the Antarctic Peninsula or travel through the Ross Sea, which contains Ross Island, the home of one of Antarctica's two active volcanoes, the 12,444-ft.- (3,794-m-) high Mount Erebus.

**▲** The largest of all penguins, the Emperor penguin journeys up to 60 mi. (100km) inland on Antarctica to its breeding ground. Dense layers of fat and thick waterproof feathers enable these birds to survive the incredibly harsh Antarctic winter on land—the only large creature to do so.

**▼** The rugged, icebound Mount Lister has a height of 13,202 ft. (4,025m). The mountain is part of the giant Transantarctic mountain range that cuts across the continent, dividing it into two distinct halves.

Antarctica is dominated by a giant ice cap that is over 13,120 ft. (4,000m) in depth in some places, while thinning to 4,920 ft. (1,500m) near the coast. The weight of the ice cap is phenomenal, enough to push parts of the continent's rocky base down below sea level. Antarctica doubles its effective size in the winter when a huge buildup of sea ice surrounds the coastline. Some of this ice calves, or breaks off, to form icebergs. In other places the floating sea ice stays attached to the land and builds up to form an ice shelf. Ice shelves make up around ten percent of the continent's area, with the Ross Ice Shelf and the Ronne Ice Shelf the two largest examples. Not all of Antarctica is covered in ice. Around 108,100 sq. mi. (280,000km²) of land are ice free,

## COLD AND DRY

Antarctica is the location of the coldest-known temperature on Earth. In 1983 the former Soviet Union's Vostok scientific station recorded a temperature of -128.6°F (-89.2°C). The warmest temperatures recorded on the continent are in the northern part of the Antarctic Peninsula, which has seen summer temperatures of 52°F (11°C). However, temperatures for the majority of the continent most of the time remain below 32°F (0°C). Average temperatures during the winter vary from between -40 and -94°F (-40 and -70°C) in the interior to between -4 and -22°F (-20 and -30°C) on the coast. These temperatures can feel colder to creatures owing to the

owing to the wind-chill factor brought about by the powerful, sweeping winds that scour the continent. In the interior winds as high as 200 mph (320km/h) have been recorded. The interior of Antarctica is a desert in which annual rainfall averages less than 2 in. (5cm) per year. This increases at the coast to around 12 in. (30cm) per year.

## BARREN LANDS—FOOD-RICH SEAS

Antarctica's climate is so severe that few species of living things can survive there. The continent's plant life consists mainly of different types of simple algae, lichens, and mosses. These provide food for some small insects and microorganisms, as well as Antarctica's 43 different species of seabirds, including albatross and many species of penguins. In contrast to the barren land the waters around Antarctica hold large amounts of marine life. The ocean abounds with microscopic plants and animals, known as plankton, which are fed upon by a small, shrimplike creature called krill. Krill live in giant swarms and provide rich feeding grounds for fish and larger marine creatures, including squid, seals, penguins, and whales. Many species of whales migrate to Antarctica in the summer to feed off the rich krill stocks. Trawlers from many nations fish the seas surrounding the continent, but a ban on whaling in the region was agreed in 1994.

▲ This 164-ft.- (50-m-) wide, 52-ft.- (16-m-) high dome covers part of the Amundsen-Scott research station located close to the South Pole. Named after the two explorers who memorably raced to reach the South Pole in 1911, it is home to over 130 people in the summer months but only 85 people in the winter. Work on a new, enlarged South Pole research station is currently underway.

# EXPLORATION AND RESEARCH

Antarctica was first discovered in the 1820s. Gradually expeditions began to cross parts of the continent, and in 1911 the Norwegian Roald Amundsen was the first person to reach the South Pole. Antarctica has no permanent human population. Its residents are temporary and are mainly scientists and researchers from 25 nations working at over 70 research stations. Many of these research stations study aspects of the continent and its geology, ice sheets, and impact on world weather systems. With its clear skies and isolated location, Antarctica is also used as a base for radio astronomers studying distant galaxies and deep space. Geological surveys have shown that the Transantarctic mountain range may be part of the world's biggest coalfield, while reserves of a number of valuable minerals, including iron ore, gold, chromium, and uranium, have also been found. Large deposits of oil and natural gas are believed to exist in Antarctica's continental shelf. However, in 1990 the international community agreed to ban mining and mineral exploitation on Antarctica for 50 years. A greater threat to Antarctica's environment comes from pollution, particularly global warming. The depletion of the atmosphere's ozone layer over Antarctica was discovered by an Antarctic research station in 1985.

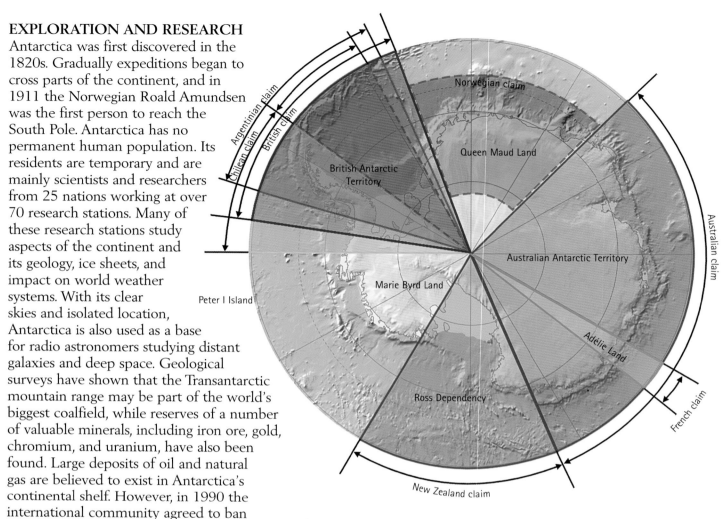

▲ This map shows the seven nations that have made territorial claims on Antarctica. Some of the claimed areas overlap, and all radiate out from the South Pole. The Antarctic Treaty of 1959 was signed by the 12 nations that then had research stations on the continent. It agreed to reserve the continent for peaceful, scientific use, to cooperate on scientific matters, and to protect the environment. Now, 47 nations have signed the treaty.

▼ Argentina's Esperanza station was founded in 1952 in Hope Bay to study Antarctica's weather and geology. Today the base is home to around 55 people, including families with children.

# READY
# REFERENCE

# WORLD BIOMES

Plants and animals rarely live in isolation. They live in their natural home, or habitat, and exist as part of an interdependent community of different living things. The world's large general habitats are called biogeographical regions, or biomes.

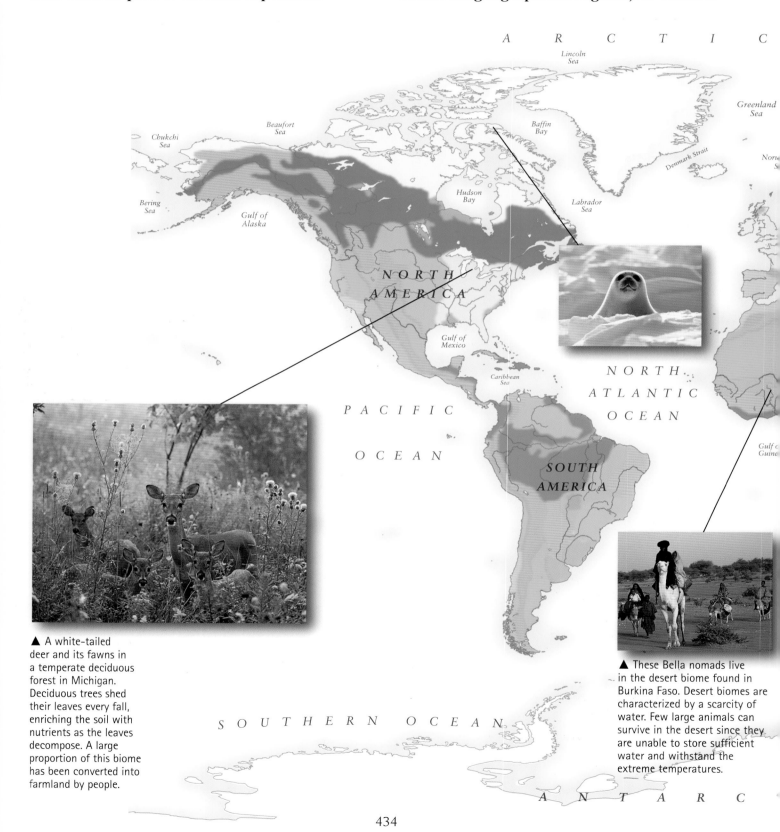

▲ A white-tailed deer and its fawns in a temperate deciduous forest in Michigan. Deciduous trees shed their leaves every fall, enriching the soil with nutrients as the leaves decompose. A large proportion of this biome has been converted into farmland by people.

▲ These Bella nomads live in the desert biome found in Burkina Faso. Desert biomes are characterized by a scarcity of water. Few large animals can survive in the desert since they are unable to store sufficient water and withstand the extreme temperatures.

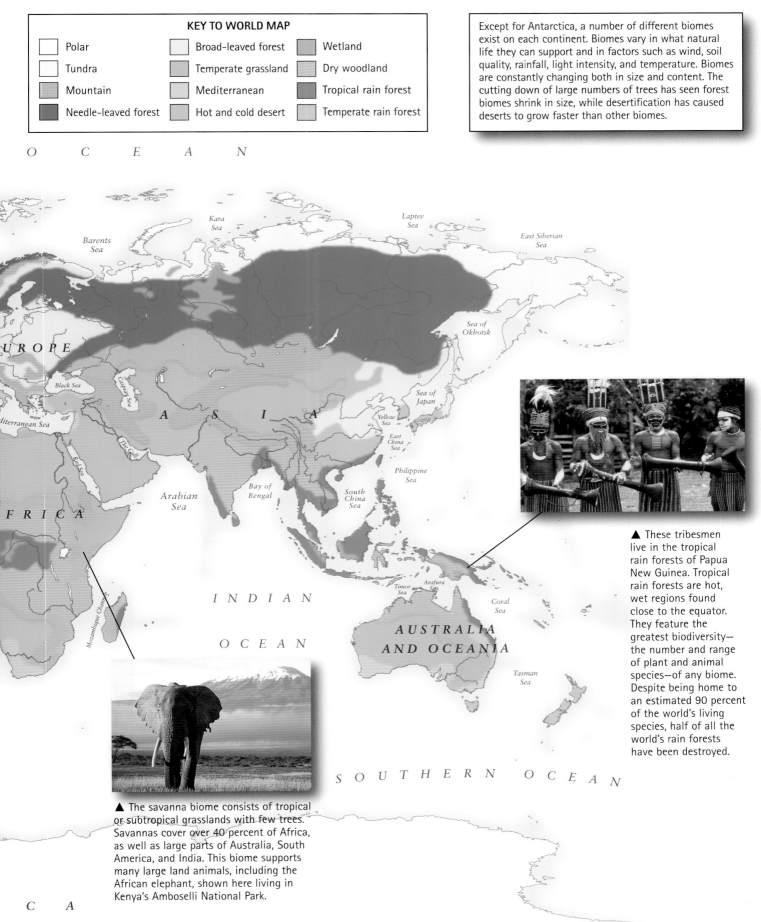

**KEY TO WORLD MAP**

- ☐ Polar
- ☐ Tundra
- ☐ Mountain
- ☐ Needle-leaved forest
- ☐ Broad-leaved forest
- ☐ Temperate grassland
- ☐ Mediterranean
- ☐ Hot and cold desert
- ☐ Wetland
- ☐ Dry woodland
- ☐ Tropical rain forest
- ☐ Temperate rain forest

Except for Antarctica, a number of different biomes exist on each continent. Biomes vary in what natural life they can support and in factors such as wind, soil quality, rainfall, light intensity, and temperature. Biomes are constantly changing both in size and content. The cutting down of large numbers of trees has seen forest biomes shrink in size, while desertification has caused deserts to grow faster than other biomes.

OCEAN

Kara Sea

Barents Sea

Laptev Sea

East Siberian Sea

EUROPE

Black Sea

Caspian Sea

Sea of Okhotsk

Mediterranean Sea

ASIA

The Gulf

Red Sea

Sea of Japan

Yellow Sea

East China Sea

AFRICA

Arabian Sea

Bay of Bengal

Philippine Sea

South China Sea

Mozambique Channel

INDIAN

OCEAN

Timor Sea

Arafura Sea

Coral Sea

AUSTRALIA AND OCEANIA

Tasman Sea

SOUTHERN OCEAN

▲ These tribesmen live in the tropical rain forests of Papua New Guinea. Tropical rain forests are hot, wet regions found close to the equator. They feature the greatest biodiversity— the number and range of plant and animal species—of any biome. Despite being home to an estimated 90 percent of the world's living species, half of all the world's rain forests have been destroyed.

▲ The savanna biome consists of tropical or subtropical grasslands with few trees. Savannas cover over 40 percent of Africa, as well as large parts of Australia, South America, and India. This biome supports many large land animals, including the African elephant, shown here living in Kenya's Amboselli National Park.

C A

# WORLD WATER

**Water is the most precious resource on Earth. Despite the existence of large quantities, water supplies are often scarce and are distributed unevenly around the planet.**

| BOTTOM 20 COUNTRIES WITH LEAST ACCESS TO SANITATION FACILITIES By percentage of population | |
|---|---|
| Senegal | 28% |
| Nepal | 27% |
| Micronesia | 25% |
| Ivory Coast | 24% |
| Mauritania | 24% |
| Sao Tomé & Príncipe | 24% |
| Rwanda | 23% |
| Somalia | 23% |
| Congo-Brazzaville | 20% |
| Guinea | 19% |
| Haiti | 19% |
| Burkina Faso | 13% |
| Togo | 12% |
| Madagascar | 12% |
| Ethiopia | 11% |
| Sierra Leone | 11% |
| Ghana | 10% |
| Chad | 9% |
| Niger | 7% |
| Eritrea | 5% |

▲ Sanitation is essential to prevent the spread of diseases and to stop water supplies from becoming contaminated. The list of nations above illustrates how many nations still struggle to offer adequate sanitation to their people.

Although people require only a small amount of drinking water each day to survive, water is also vital to ensure public health and hygiene through sanitation systems. People in more developed nations each tend to use between 40–104 gallons (150–400 liters) of water each day for cooking and cleaning. Flushing a toilet can use between 2.6–6.5 gallons (10–25 liters), a washing machine 20 gallons (75 liters), and a bath as much as 21 gallons (80 liters) of freshwater. In contrast in nations where water is not so easily available consumption is much lower. The domestic use of water is dwarfed by the amount used in agriculture; around 70 percent of all water used in human activities is consumed by farming. Without adequate water supplies, crops fail, livestock die, and food supplies shrink drastically. Cheap, plentiful supplies of water are also essential to industry, which uses almost one fourth of all water consumed. Industries use water as a coolant, a solvent, in washing and cleaning applications, and as an ingredient in many chemical, food, and drink products.

## NOT JUST FOR CONSUMPTION

Water is exploited in other ways to benefit people and nations besides being consumed directly by people or used in public health, agriculture, or industry. Water is a rich habitat for many forms of life that, in turn, provide important sources of food for millions of people. Natural inland waterways provide important transportation routes through many regions, enhanced by the construction of artificial waterways or canals. The power held in moving water is exploited in many nations to generate electricity through hydroelectric power stations.

## WATER SUPPLIES

Around three fourths of the planet is covered in water, but the large majority of this is saltwater found in the seas and oceans. Only 2.5 percent of the world's water is freshwater, and over 70 percent

▶ A sudden excess of water in the form of a flood can kill people, destroy villages, and ruin crops, crippling an area's economy. Bangladesh is considered one of the most flood-prone regions in the world. This Bangladeshi village has been flooded by the rising waters of the Jamuna river.

▲ An Omani worker examines part of a desalination plant. Desalination removes the salt from seawater in order to make it drinkable. Desalination is expensive but is used in many of the wealthier Middle Eastern nations.

of this freshwater is trapped in the polar ice caps. Rivers and lakes are an important water source, while a huge amount of freshwater is stored as groundwater beneath Earth's surface in the soil, in the pores between particles of sedimentary rocks, and in the cracks and fissures between other rocks. Approximately one tenth of the world's groundwater supplies are easy to reach, and, increasingly groundwater is being tapped by countries in order to fulfill the demand for water. Over 1.5 billion people rely on groundwater supplies for their

drinking water, but groundwater levels take a fairly long time to replenish and can become exhausted if used at a rapid rate. In the southern Indian state of Tamil Nadu, for example, the level of groundwater fell by over 65 ft. (20m) in a period of ten years, owing to so much of the water being trapped.

## THE WATER CRISIS

The water cycle, which sees water circulate between Earth and the atmosphere, is a finely balanced natural cycle that produces enough clean water to support life in many regions. Yet the increasing demands of a booming human population and, with it, pollution— from domestic sewage and dumped industrial chemicals to poisonous agricultural pesticides—reduce the levels of freshwater in many places. In large regions of Africa, the Middle East, and Asia the problem is considerably more serious. Over 880 million people currently lack access to clean water. Thousands die from hunger, frequently caused by a lack of water to sustain local crops. Even more people—more than 1.5 billion—lack safe sanitation. As a result, many people die every year from avoidable water-related diseases. While access to safe drinking water is improving, in many places, access to safe sanitation is not.

| THE 20 COUNTRIES WITH LEAST ACCESS TO IMPROVED DRINKING WATER By percentage of population | |
| --- | --- |
| Togo | 59% |
| Haiti | 58% |
| Zambia | 58% |
| Kenya | 57% |
| Guinea-Bissau | 57% |
| Tanzania | 55% |
| Sierra Leone | 53% |
| Angola | 51% |
| Chad | 48% |
| Fiji | 47% |
| Madagascar | 47% |
| Nigeria | 47% |
| Mozambique | 46% |
| Congo, D.R. | 46% |
| Equatorial Guinea | 43% |
| Ethiopia | 42% |
| Niger | 42% |
| Somalia | 29% |
| Papua New Guinea | 40% |
| Afghanistan | 22% |

▲ In many wealthy countries every person has access to clean and safe drinking water. This is not the case in many poor countries.

▼ The Cahora Bassa dam in Mozambique is the country's largest hydroelectric power dam, generating thousands of megawatts of electricity.

# WINDS AND OCEAN CURRENTS

Our climate is influenced by two systems of currents: the circulation of moving air in the atmosphere and the circulation of water in the oceans. Together these currents generate a region's climate and weather, as well as helping form the distinct features of the world's biomes.

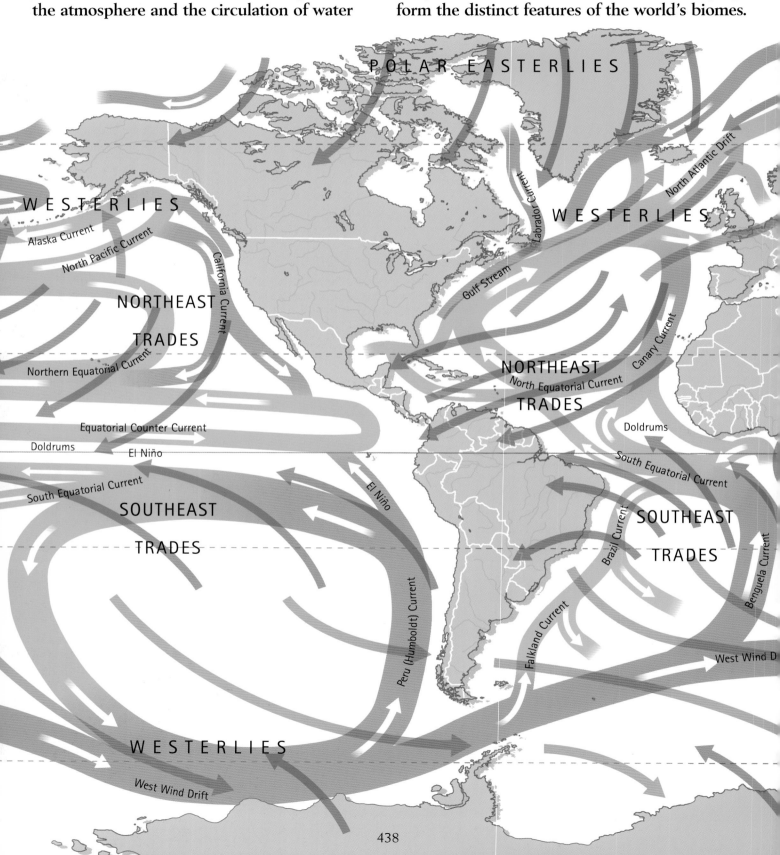

POLAR EASTERLIES

WESTERLIES

WESTERLIES

North Atlantic Drift

Alaska Current

North Pacific Current

California Current

Labrador Current

Gulf Stream

NORTHEAST

TRADES

NORTHEAST

Canary Current

Northern Equatorial Current

North Equatorial Current

TRADES

Doldrums

Equatorial Counter Current

Doldrums     El Niño

South Equatorial Current

SOUTHEAST

SOUTHEAST

El Niño

TRADES

South Equatorial Current

Brazil Current

TRADES

Benguela Current

Peru (Humboldt) Current

Falkland Current

West Wind D

WESTERLIES

West Wind Drift

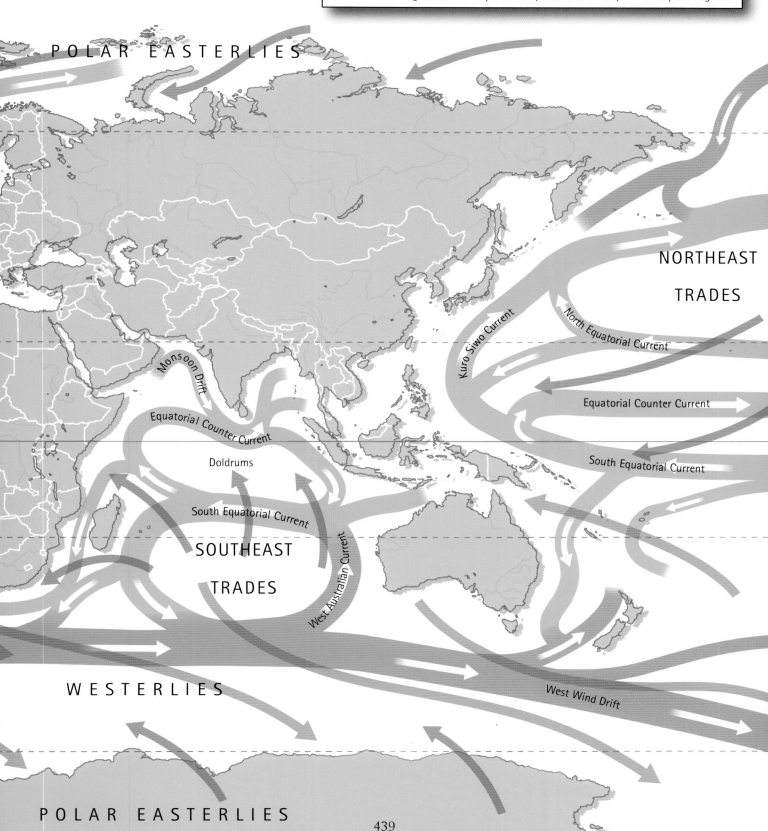

This map depicts the world's major wind and ocean current systems. Winds are named according to the direction from which they blow, and those shown are the usual, or prevailing, winds. Ocean currents circulate in paths that are called gyres. These move in a counterclockwise direction in the Southern Hemisphere. In the Northern Hemisphere they move in a clockwise direction. When these currents move toward the poles, they carry warm water away from the equatorial regions. Currents returning toward the equator carry cold water away from the polar regions.

POLAR EASTERLIES

NORTHEAST TRADES

Monsoon Drift

Kuro Siwo Current

North Equatorial Current

Equatorial Counter Current

Equatorial Counter Current

Doldrums

South Equatorial Current

South Equatorial Current

South Equatorial Current

SOUTHEAST TRADES

West Australian Current

WESTERLIES

West Wind Drift

POLAR EASTERLIES

439

# WORLD POLLUTION

Pollution is the introduction of waste energy or a substance, called a pollutant, into an environment that has a harmful effect.

Human impact on the planet has generated many different forms of pollution that affect the air, seas and oceans, and land.

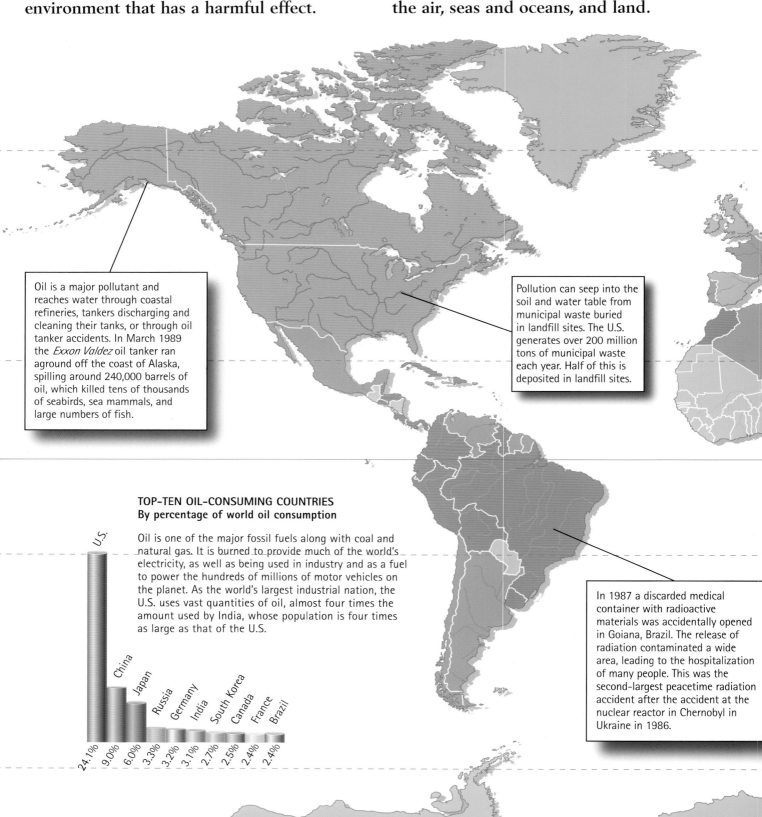

Oil is a major pollutant and reaches water through coastal refineries, tankers discharging and cleaning their tanks, or through oil tanker accidents. In March 1989 the *Exxon Valdez* oil tanker ran aground off the coast of Alaska, spilling around 240,000 barrels of oil, which killed tens of thousands of seabirds, sea mammals, and large numbers of fish.

Pollution can seep into the soil and water table from municipal waste buried in landfill sites. The U.S. generates over 200 million tons of municipal waste each year. Half of this is deposited in landfill sites.

## TOP-TEN OIL-CONSUMING COUNTRIES
### By percentage of world oil consumption

Oil is one of the major fossil fuels along with coal and natural gas. It is burned to provide much of the world's electricity, as well as being used in industry and as a fuel to power the hundreds of millions of motor vehicles on the planet. As the world's largest industrial nation, the U.S. uses vast quantities of oil, almost four times the amount used by India, whose population is four times as large as that of the U.S.

In 1987 a discarded medical container with radioactive materials was accidentally opened in Goiana, Brazil. The release of radiation contaminated a wide area, leading to the hospitalization of many people. This was the second-largest peacetime radiation accident after the accident at the nuclear reactor in Chernobyl in Ukraine in 1986.

| Country | Percentage |
|---|---|
| U.S. | 24.1% |
| China | 9.0% |
| Japan | 6.0% |
| Russia | 3.3% |
| Germany | 3.2% |
| India | 3.1% |
| South Korea | 2.7% |
| Canada | 2.5% |
| France | 2.4% |
| Brazil | 2.4% |

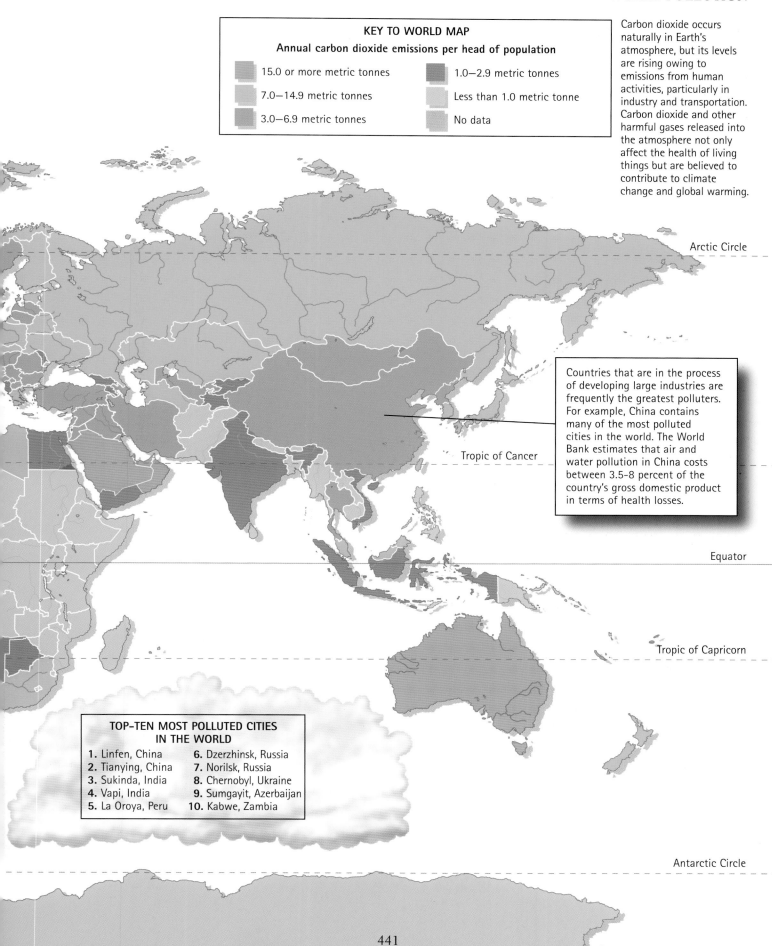

**KEY TO WORLD MAP**

**Annual carbon dioxide emissions per head of population**

- 15.0 or more metric tonnes
- 7.0—14.9 metric tonnes
- 3.0—6.9 metric tonnes
- 1.0—2.9 metric tonnes
- Less than 1.0 metric tonne
- No data

Carbon dioxide occurs naturally in Earth's atmosphere, but its levels are rising owing to emissions from human activities, particularly in industry and transportation. Carbon dioxide and other harmful gases released into the atmosphere not only affect the health of living things but are believed to contribute to climate change and global warming.

Arctic Circle

Tropic of Cancer

Countries that are in the process of developing large industries are frequently the greatest polluters. For example, China contains many of the most polluted cities in the world. The World Bank estimates that air and water pollution in China costs between 3.5-8 percent of the country's gross domestic product in terms of health losses.

Equator

Tropic of Capricorn

**TOP-TEN MOST POLLUTED CITIES IN THE WORLD**

1. Linfen, China
2. Tianying, China
3. Sukinda, India
4. Vapi, India
5. La Oroya, Peru
6. Dzerzhinsk, Russia
7. Norilsk, Russia
8. Chernobyl, Ukraine
9. Sumgayit, Azerbaijan
10. Kabwe, Zambia

Antarctic Circle

# BIODIVERSITY AND EXTINCTION

A region's biodiversity is the range and number of animal and plant species it supports. Earth is home to many millions of different species, yet thousands are under threat from extinction—their permanent disappearance from the planet.

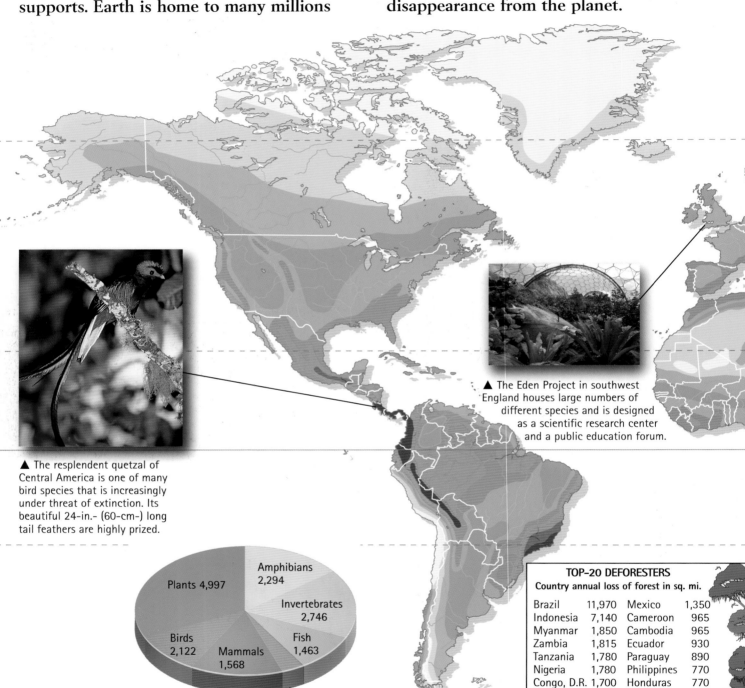

▲ The resplendent quetzal of Central America is one of many bird species that is increasingly under threat of extinction. Its beautiful 24-in.- (60-cm-) long tail feathers are highly prized.

▲ The Eden Project in southwest England houses large numbers of different species and is designed as a scientific research center and a public education forum.

Plants 4,997
Amphibians 2,294
Invertebrates 2,746
Birds 2,122
Fish 1,463
Mammals 1,568
Reptiles 503

▲ This chart outlines the number of species considered to be at risk of extinction. There are many reasons for a species being endangered. Some creatures are hunted and killed for food or to sell parts of their body, while others have been threatened by climate change or habitat loss. Some species that are critically endangered are considered unlikely to survive unless humans intervene.

### TOP-20 DEFORESTERS
**Country annual loss of forest in sq. mi.**

| Country | Loss | Country | Loss |
|---|---|---|---|
| Brazil | 11,970 | Mexico | 1,350 |
| Indonesia | 7,140 | Cameroon | 965 |
| Myanmar | 1,850 | Cambodia | 965 |
| Zambia | 1,815 | Ecuador | 930 |
| Tanzania | 1,780 | Paraguay | 890 |
| Nigeria | 1,780 | Philippines | 770 |
| Congo, D.R. | 1,700 | Honduras | 770 |
| Zimbabwe | 1,660 | Ethiopia | 730 |
| Venezuela | 1,540 | Malaysia | 700 |
| Bolivia | 1,500 | Papua N.G. | 700 |

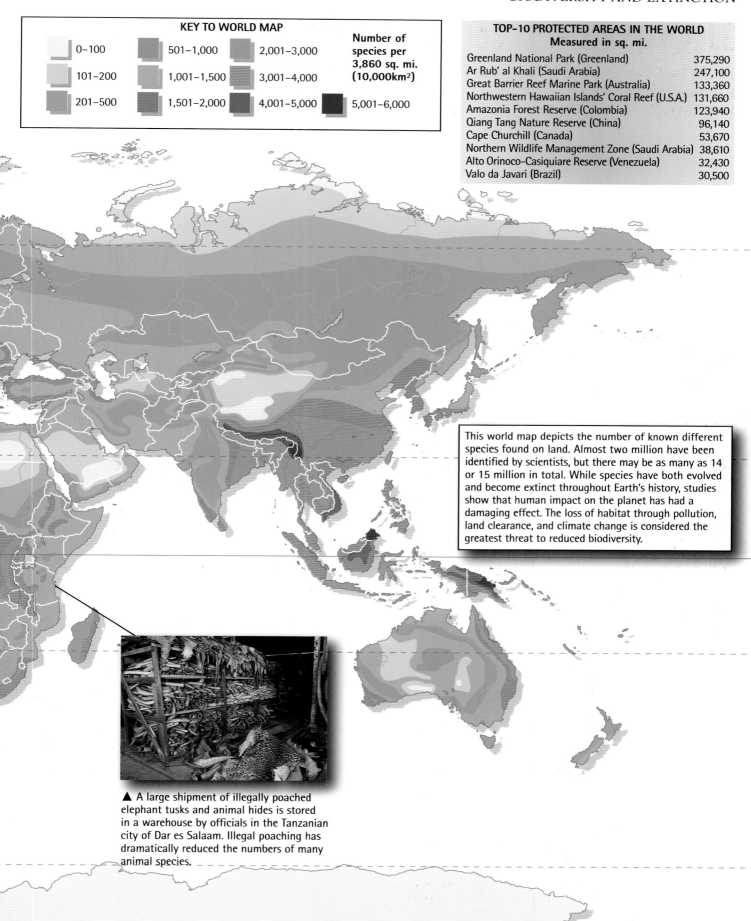

## KEY TO WORLD MAP

| | | | **Number of species per 3,860 sq. mi. (10,000km²)** |
|---|---|---|---|
| 0–100 | 501–1,000 | 2,001–3,000 | |
| 101–200 | 1,001–1,500 | 3,001–4,000 | |
| 201–500 | 1,501–2,000 | 4,001–5,000 | 5,001–6,000 |

### TOP-10 PROTECTED AREAS IN THE WORLD
Measured in sq. mi.

| | |
|---|---|
| Greenland National Park (Greenland) | 375,290 |
| Ar Rub' al Khali (Saudi Arabia) | 247,100 |
| Great Barrier Reef Marine Park (Australia) | 133,360 |
| Northwestern Hawaiian Islands' Coral Reef (U.S.A.) | 131,660 |
| Amazonia Forest Reserve (Colombia) | 123,940 |
| Qiang Tang Nature Reserve (China) | 96,140 |
| Cape Churchill (Canada) | 53,670 |
| Northern Wildlife Management Zone (Saudi Arabia) | 38,610 |
| Alto Orinoco-Casiquiare Reserve (Venezuela) | 32,430 |
| Valo da Javari (Brazil) | 30,500 |

This world map depicts the number of known different species found on land. Almost two million have been identified by scientists, but there may be as many as 14 or 15 million in total. While species have both evolved and become extinct throughout Earth's history, studies show that human impact on the planet has had a damaging effect. The loss of habitat through pollution, land clearance, and climate change is considered the greatest threat to reduced biodiversity.

▲ A large shipment of illegally poached elephant tusks and animal hides is stored in a warehouse by officials in the Tanzanian city of Dar es Salaam. Illegal poaching has dramatically reduced the numbers of many animal species.

# WORLD HEALTH

In the past century many major advances have been made in ways to improve the health of the world's human population.

However, access to ways of improving health— from a good diet to medicine and health care—varies greatly all over the world.

In the U.S. there is one doctor for around 340 people. However, in more than 20 nations, mainly in Africa, less than half of the population have access to essential drugs. The nations of Eritrea, Malawi, Tanzania, and Togo have just one doctor for every 20,000 people.

▲ A patient is surrounded by advanced monitoring and life-support systems in an intensive care unit in Hamburg, Germany.

## LIFE EXPECTANCY AT BIRTH

| TOP-20 COUNTRIES | | BOTTOM-20 COUNTRIES | |
|---|---|---|---|
| Andorra | 82.5 years | Niger | 52.6 years |
| Japan | 82.1 years | Tanzania | 52.0 years |
| Singapore | 82.0 years | Mali | 51.8 years |
| Australia | 81.6 years | Sudan | 51.4 years |
| Canada | 81.2 years | Namibia | 51.2 years |
| France | 81.0 years | Malawi | 50.0 years |
| Sweden | 80.9 years | Somalia | 49.6 years |
| Switzerland | 80.9 years | South Africa | 49.0 years |
| San Marino | 80.8 years | Guinea-Bissau | 47.9 years |
| Israel | 80.7 years | Swaziland | 47.9 years |
| Iceland | 80.7 years | Chad | 47.7 years |
| New Zealand | 80.4 years | Nigeria | 46.9 years |
| Italy | 80.2 years | Zimbabwe | 45.8 years |
| Monaco | 80.1 years | Cen. Af. Rep. | 44.5 years |
| Liechtenstein | 80.1 years | Afghanistan | 44.4 years |
| Spain | 80.1 years | Liberia | 41.8 years |
| Norway | 80.0 years | Mozambique | 41.2 years |
| Jordan | 79.9 years | Lesotho | 40.4 years |
| Greece | 79.7 years | Zambia | 38.6 years |
| Austria | 79.5 years | Angola | 38.2 years |

## TOP-20 COUNTRIES AIDS ORPHANS

| | | | |
|---|---|---|---|
| South Africa | 1,400,000 | Mozambique | 470,000 |
| Nigeria | 1,200,000 | Ivory Coast | 420,000 |
| Zimbabwe | 1,000,000 | Thailand | 300,000 |
| Tanzania | 970,000 | Burkina Faso | 260,000 |
| Uganda | 940,000 | Cameroon | 240,000 |
| Congo, D.R. | 770,000 | Burundi | 200,000 |
| Ethiopia | 650,000 | Ghana | 170,000 |
| Kenya | 650,000 | Rwanda | 160,000 |
| Zambia | 600,000 | Haiti | 155,000 |
| Malawi | 560,000 | Botswana | 120,000 |

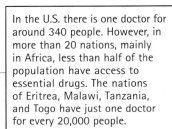

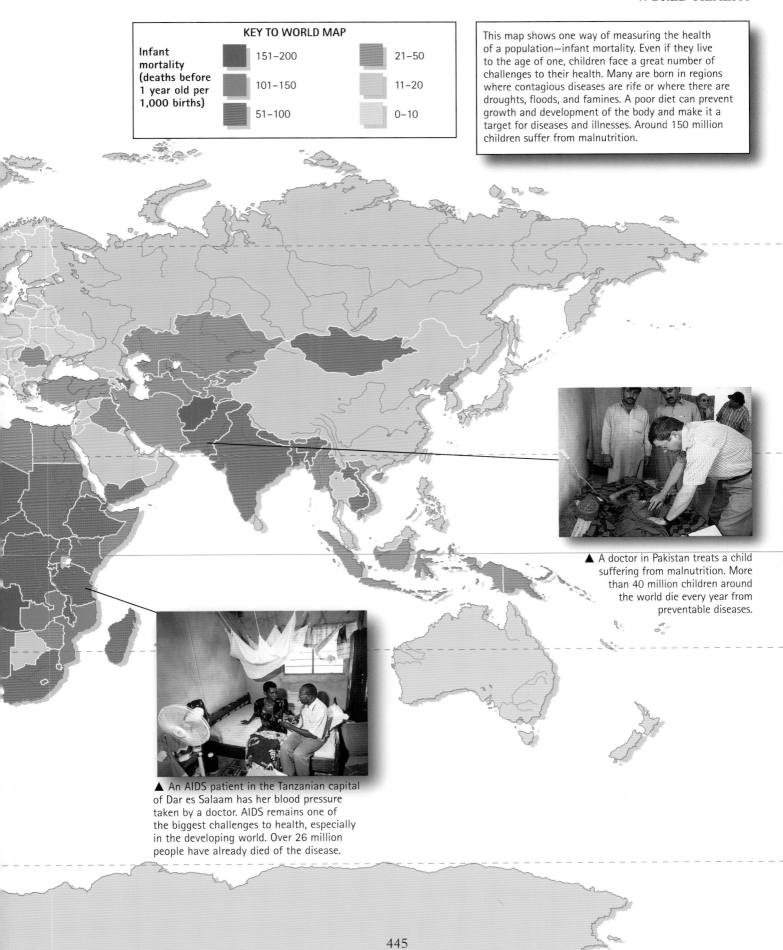

**KEY TO WORLD MAP**

Infant mortality (deaths before 1 year old per 1,000 births)

- 151–200
- 101–150
- 51–100
- 21–50
- 11–20
- 0–10

This map shows one way of measuring the health of a population—infant mortality. Even if they live to the age of one, children face a great number of challenges to their health. Many are born in regions where contagious diseases are rife or where there are droughts, floods, and famines. A poor diet can prevent growth and development of the body and make it a target for diseases and illnesses. Around 150 million children suffer from malnutrition.

▲ A doctor in Pakistan treats a child suffering from malnutrition. More than 40 million children around the world die every year from preventable diseases.

▲ An AIDS patient in the Tanzanian capital of Dar es Salaam has her blood pressure taken by a doctor. AIDS remains one of the biggest challenges to health, especially in the developing world. Over 26 million people have already died of the disease.

# WORLD EDUCATION

Education enables people to read, write, and communicate with others. It also provides people with the opportunity to work and the potential to improve their lives. The standard and quantity of education people receive vary greatly across the world.

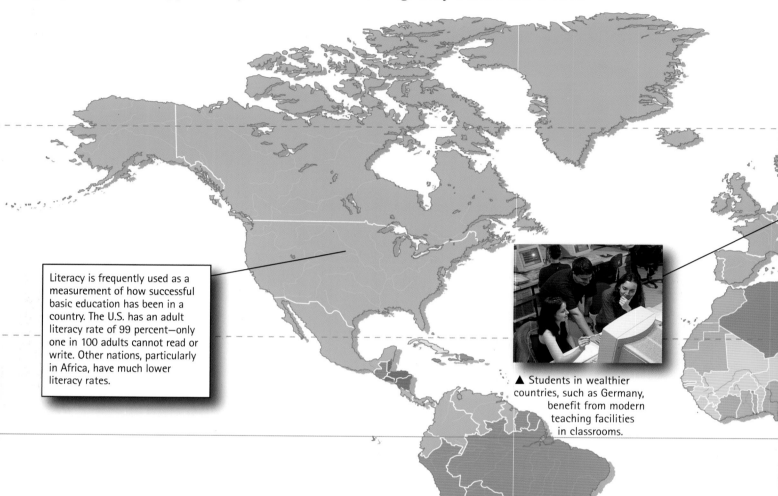

Literacy is frequently used as a measurement of how successful basic education has been in a country. The U.S. has an adult literacy rate of 99 percent—only one in 100 adults cannot read or write. Other nations, particularly in Africa, have much lower literacy rates.

▲ Students in wealthier countries, such as Germany, benefit from modern teaching facilities in classrooms.

## PERCENTAGE OF BOYS AND GIRLS IN SECONDARY EDUCATION

Not all of the world's children have the opportunity to pursue secondary education. In many societies, fewer girls than boys do.

| | | | |
|---|---|---|---|
| Chad | 22%/8% | China | 75%/76% |
| Afghanistan | 28%/9% | Australia | 100%/100% |
| Guinea | 41%/21% | France | 100%/100% |
| Yemen | 61%/30% | Germany | 100%/100% |
| Benin | 41%/23% | Italy | 100%/99% |
| Iraq | 54%/36% | Japan | 100%/100% |
| India | 59%/49% | Spain | 100%/100% |
| Nepal | 46%/41% | Bangladesh | 43%/45% |
| Papua N.G. | 30%/21% | U.K. | 100%/100% |
| Russia | 92%/91% | Namibia | 53%/60% |
| U.S.A. | 99%/98% | Sweden | 100%/100% |

▲ Bolivia has one of the lowest literacy rates in South America. This adult literacy class seeks to educate adult Bolivians who missed out on education as children.

446

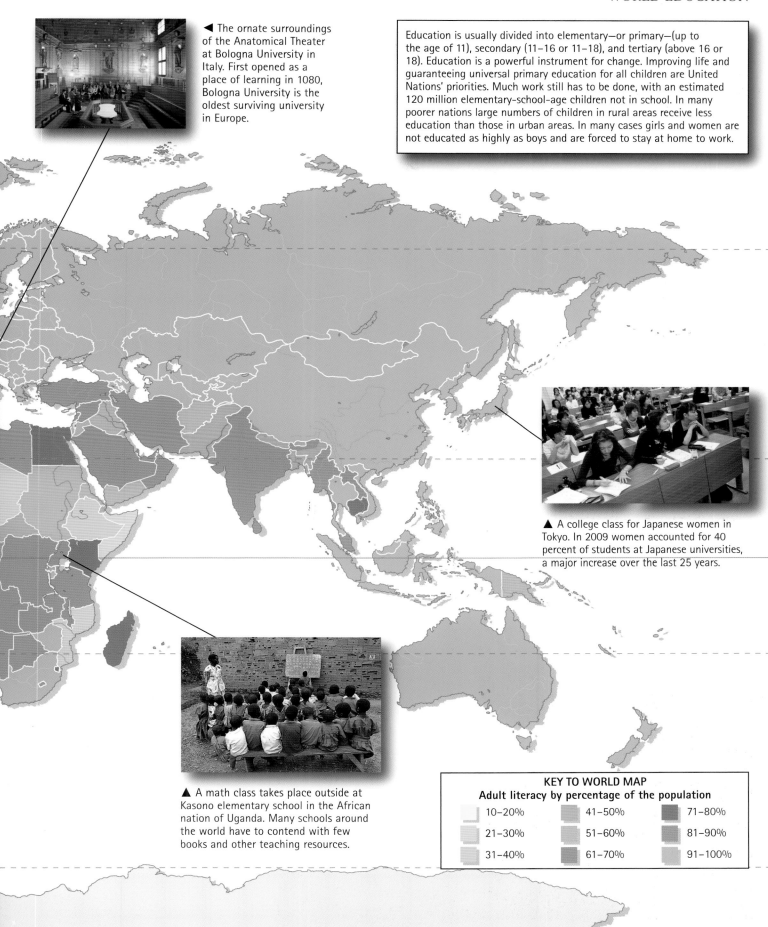

◄ The ornate surroundings of the Anatomical Theater at Bologna University in Italy. First opened as a place of learning in 1080, Bologna University is the oldest surviving university in Europe.

Education is usually divided into elementary—or primary—(up to the age of 11), secondary (11–16 or 11–18), and tertiary (above 16 or 18). Education is a powerful instrument for change. Improving life and guaranteeing universal primary education for all children are United Nations' priorities. Much work still has to be done, with an estimated 120 million elementary-school-age children not in school. In many poorer nations large numbers of children in rural areas receive less education than those in urban areas. In many cases girls and women are not educated as highly as boys and are forced to stay at home to work.

▲ A college class for Japanese women in Tokyo. In 2009 women accounted for 40 percent of students at Japanese universities, a major increase over the last 25 years.

▲ A math class takes place outside at Kasono elementary school in the African nation of Uganda. Many schools around the world have to contend with few books and other teaching resources.

**KEY TO WORLD MAP**
**Adult literacy by percentage of the population**

| | | |
|---|---|---|
| 10–20% | 41–50% | 71–80% |
| 21–30% | 51–60% | 81–90% |
| 31–40% | 61–70% | 91–100% |

# WORLD WEALTH

The world's nations vary enormously in the size and wealth of their economies—and so do the world's people. While millionaires exist in many countries, over one fifth of the total world population has a standard of living that is estimated at less than $1.50 per day.

The U.S. is the world's greatest economic power in terms of gross national product (GNP) and is the eighth highest in terms of gross national income (GNI) per capita, behind Liechtenstein, Qatar, Luxembourg, Norway, Kuwait, Singapore, and Brunei. The country has abundant natural resources producing almost one fifth of the world's oil and coal and almost half of its corn. The U.S. owes its economic position to its huge and highly developed industries.

The wealth found in a country does not necessarily reach many of its people. However, Sweden is an exception, with relatively high taxes on wealth and an extensive welfare state. It distributes its national wealth more equally than many nations around the world.

## THE DEVELOPMENT GAP

The development of industries and economies around the world has not occurred at an even speed or brought equal benefits to all people. The huge difference in conditions found in many of the more developed nations compared to many of the less developed is known as the development gap. This gap can be seen in terms of income. According to World Bank estimates, the citizens of Luxembourg enjoy the highest gross national income per person—estimated in 2009 at $78,000 per year. In contrast, the African nations of Burundi and the Democratic Republic of the Congo had per capita GNIs of $300. The gap is also apparent in the quality of diet, sanitation,

▲ French doctors treat patients in an oasis in Mauritania.

and health, which leads to large differences in life expectancy. The development gap can also be seen in the way resources are used unequally around the world. For example, around 20 percent of the world's population use 65 percent of the energy.

Exploitation by their former colonial rulers, internal conflicts and wars with neighbors, a lack of resources, famines, and droughts have blighted many sub-Saharan nations, making their people the poorest in the world. Guinea-Bissau's people have a gross national income of just $600 per year. Twelve of the 13 nations with the lowest gross national incomes are found in sub-Saharan Africa.

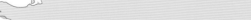

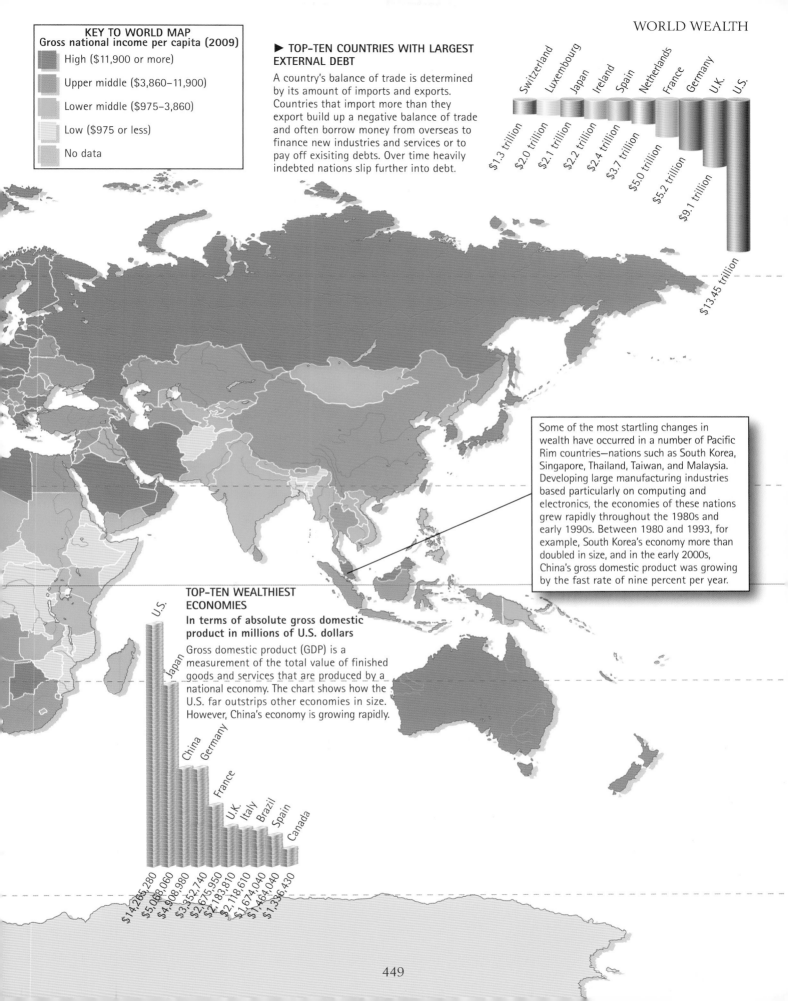

**KEY TO WORLD MAP**
Gross national income per capita (2009)

High ($11,900 or more)

Upper middle ($3,860–11,900)

Lower middle ($975–3,860)

Low ($975 or less)

No data

► **TOP-TEN COUNTRIES WITH LARGEST EXTERNAL DEBT**

A country's balance of trade is determined by its amount of imports and exports. Countries that import more than they export build up a negative balance of trade and often borrow money from overseas to finance new industries and services or to pay off exisiting debts. Over time heavily indebted nations slip further into debt.

Switzerland $1.3 trillion
Luxembourg $2.0 trillion
Japan $2.1 trillion
Ireland $2.2 trillion
Spain $2.4 trillion
Netherlands $3.7 trillion
France $5.0 trillion
Germany $5.2 trillion
U.K. $9.1 trillion
U.S. $13.45 trillion

Some of the most startling changes in wealth have occurred in a number of Pacific Rim countries—nations such as South Korea, Singapore, Thailand, Taiwan, and Malaysia. Developing large manufacturing industries based particularly on computing and electronics, the economies of these nations grew rapidly throughout the 1980s and early 1990s. Between 1980 and 1993, for example, South Korea's economy more than doubled in size, and in the early 2000s, China's gross domestic product was growing by the fast rate of nine percent per year.

**TOP-TEN WEALTHIEST ECONOMIES**

**In terms of absolute gross domestic product in millions of U.S. dollars**

Gross domestic product (GDP) is a measurement of the total value of finished goods and services that are produced by a national economy. The chart shows how the U.S. far outstrips other economies in size. However, China's economy is growing rapidly.

U.S. $14,265,280
Japan $5,068,060
China $4,908,980
Germany $3,352,740
France $2,675,950
U.K. $2,183,810
Italy $2,118,610
Brazil $1,674,040
Spain $1,464,040
Canada $1,336,430

# WORLD ENERGY

Energy exists in many forms. Converting energy into types that can be used to provide heat, light, and power is of vital importance to the world's human population. Chief among these forms are electricity and fuels that can be burned to provide power.

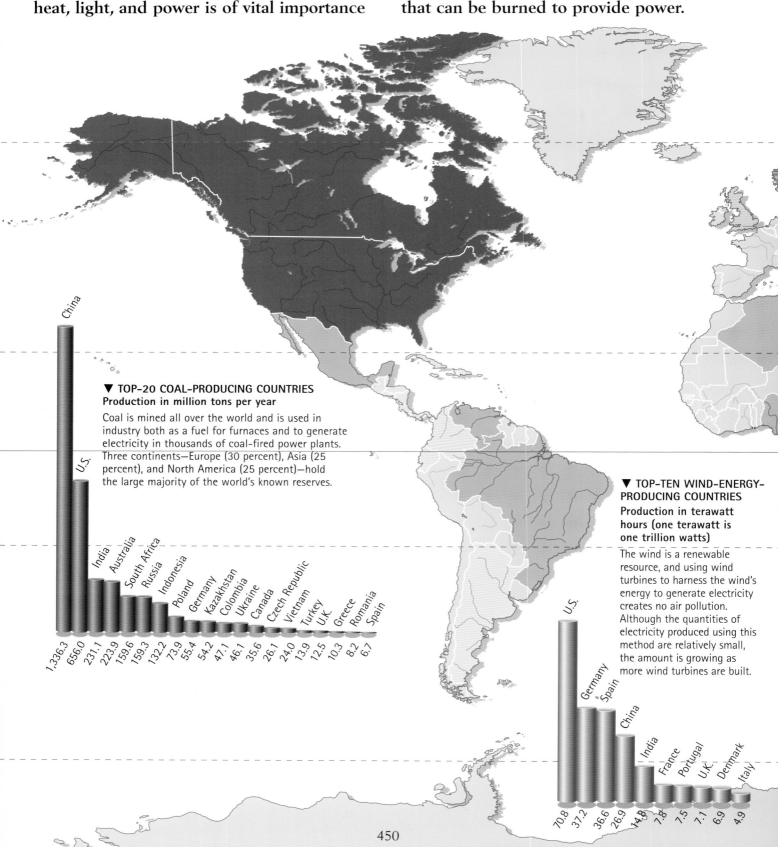

### ▼ TOP-20 COAL-PRODUCING COUNTRIES
**Production in million tons per year**

Coal is mined all over the world and is used in industry both as a fuel for furnaces and to generate electricity in thousands of coal-fired power plants. Three continents—Europe (30 percent), Asia (25 percent), and North America (25 percent)—hold the large majority of the world's known reserves.

| Country | Production |
| --- | --- |
| China | 1,336.3 |
| U.S. | 656.0 |
| India | 231.1 |
| Australia | 223.9 |
| South Africa | 159.6 |
| Russia | 159.3 |
| Indonesia | 132.2 |
| Poland | 73.9 |
| Germany | 55.4 |
| Kazakhstan | 54.2 |
| Colombia | 47.1 |
| Ukraine | 46.1 |
| Canada | 35.6 |
| Czech Republic | 26.1 |
| Vietnam | 24.0 |
| Turkey | 13.9 |
| U.K. | 12.5 |
| Greece | 10.3 |
| Romania | 8.2 |
| Spain | 6.7 |

### ▼ TOP-TEN WIND-ENERGY-PRODUCING COUNTRIES
**Production in terawatt hours (one terawatt is one trillion watts)**

The wind is a renewable resource, and using wind turbines to harness the wind's energy to generate electricity creates no air pollution. Although the quantities of electricity produced using this method are relatively small, the amount is growing as more wind turbines are built.

| Country | Production |
| --- | --- |
| U.S. | 70.8 |
| Germany | 37.2 |
| Spain | 36.6 |
| China | 26.9 |
| India | 14.8 |
| France | 7.8 |
| Portugal | 7.5 |
| U.K. | 7.1 |
| Denmark | 6.9 |
| Italy | 4.9 |

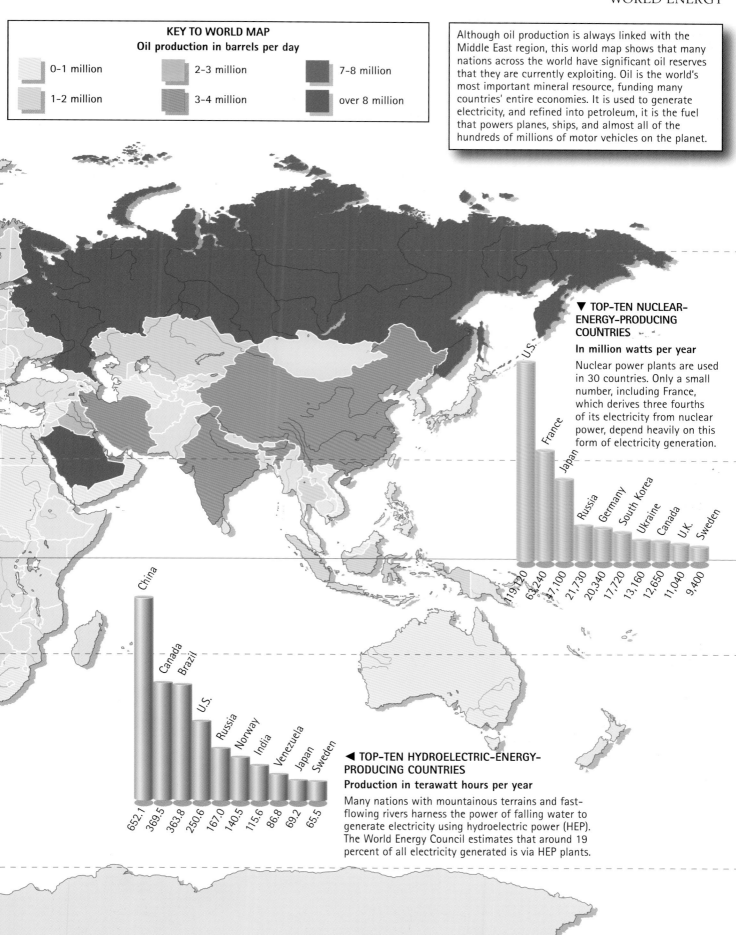

## KEY TO WORLD MAP
### Oil production in barrels per day

- 0–1 million
- 1–2 million
- 2–3 million
- 3–4 million
- 7–8 million
- over 8 million

Although oil production is always linked with the Middle East region, this world map shows that many nations across the world have significant oil reserves that they are currently exploiting. Oil is the world's most important mineral resource, funding many countries' entire economies. It is used to generate electricity, and refined into petroleum, it is the fuel that powers planes, ships, and almost all of the hundreds of millions of motor vehicles on the planet.

## ▼ TOP-TEN NUCLEAR-ENERGY-PRODUCING COUNTRIES
### In million watts per year

Nuclear power plants are used in 30 countries. Only a small number, including France, which derives three fourths of its electricity from nuclear power, depend heavily on this form of electricity generation.

| Country | Value |
|---|---|
| U.S. | 119,120 |
| France | 63,240 |
| Japan | 47,100 |
| Russia | 21,730 |
| Germany | 20,340 |
| South Korea | 17,720 |
| Ukraine | 13,160 |
| Canada | 12,650 |
| U.K. | 11,040 |
| Sweden | 9,400 |

## ◄ TOP-TEN HYDROELECTRIC-ENERGY-PRODUCING COUNTRIES
### Production in terawatt hours per year

Many nations with mountainous terrains and fast-flowing rivers harness the power of falling water to generate electricity using hydroelectric power (HEP). The World Energy Council estimates that around 19 percent of all electricity generated is via HEP plants.

| Country | Value |
|---|---|
| China | 652.1 |
| Canada | 369.5 |
| Brazil | 363.8 |
| U.S. | 250.6 |
| Russia | 167.0 |
| Norway | 140.5 |
| India | 115.6 |
| Venezuela | 86.8 |
| Japan | 69.2 |
| Sweden | 65.5 |

# WORLD COMMODITIES

**Our planet has yielded large quantities of many commodities—partly refined or raw materials—that are used to make goods or other materials.**

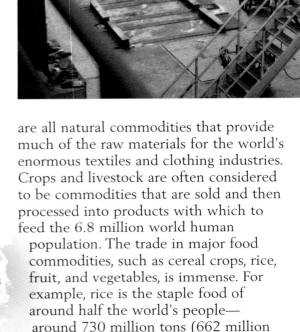

| TOP-TEN SOFTWOOD-PRODUCING COUNTRIES | |
|---|---|
| Production per annum in trillion ft.³ | |
| U.S. | 15.9 |
| India | 11.2 |
| China | 10.1 |
| Brazil | 8.4 |
| Canada | 6.9 |
| Russia | 5.9 |
| Indonesia | 4.0 |
| Ethiopia | 3.3 |
| Congo, D.R. | 3.2 |
| Nigeria | 2.5 |

▼ Timber is a valuable commodity in many forms, including paper. This giant paper-making operation is underway in Skutskar, Sweden. Sweden is the world's fourth-largest exporter of paper-based products and the second-largest exporter of sawed-softwood products.

Commodities are valued according to the cost of finding, extracting, or harvesting them, as well as their relative scarcity. Today many of the nations in the Southern Hemisphere are primarily occupied with the production of commodities that are mostly sold to nations in the Northern Hemisphere with more developed manufacturing industries. The value of commodities rises and falls, sometimes extremely sharply. This can bring additional wealth to a nation such as when oil shortages and subsequent price rises boost the economies of many Middle Eastern nations. Yet this more frequently creates major economic crises when price falls occur, especially in nations that are overreliant on one or a handful of commodities. Certain Central American nations, for example, are overdependent on the value of coffee or cocoa, creating economic difficulties when prices drop.

## NATURAL COMMODITIES

Many commodities are natural products that are potentially renewable such as timber and natural rubber. Cotton, flax, and silk are all natural commodities that provide much of the raw materials for the world's enormous textiles and clothing industries. Crops and livestock are often considered to be commodities that are sold and then processed into products with which to feed the 6.8 million world human population. The trade in major food commodities, such as cereal crops, rice, fruit, and vegetables, is immense. For example, rice is the staple food of around half the world's people— around 730 million tons (662 million metric tonnes) of rice are grown worldwide every year.

### TOP-20 STEEL-PRODUCING COUNTRIES
**Production in million tons p.a.**

|  | |
|---|---|
| China | 1,462.2 |
| Japan | 130.1 |
| U.S. | 100.8 |
| Russia | 75.5 |
| India | 60.8 |
| South Korea | 59.1 |
| Germany | 50.5 |
| Ukraine | 40.9 |
| Brazil | 37.1 |
| Italy | 33.7 |
| Turkey | 29.5 |
| Taiwan | 21.9 |
| Spain | 20.5 |
| France | 19.7 |
| Mexico | 19.0 |
| Canada | 16.3 |
| U.K. | 14.9 |
| Belgium | 11.8 |
| Iran | 11.0 |
| Poland | 10.7 |

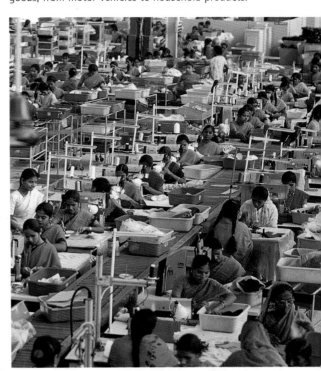

◀ Hot steel is cooled during the manufacturing process in a factory in Bochum, Germany. Steel is used in all forms of construction and the manufacture of many goods, from motor vehicles to household products.

▲ A large textiles factory in India uses cotton as a raw material to make clothing. India is the third-largest producer of cotton in the world and one of the world's foremost manufacturers of clothing. India's textiles industry is the country's second-largest employer.

## MINERAL COMMODITIES

Minerals tend to be valuable commodities because they do not occur everywhere, and they are not renewable. Manufacturing depends on mineral commodities, especially metals, to produce many of the world's finished goods. Iron ore is the basis of the world's largest metal industry, steel manufacturing. Bauxite, the ore from which aluminum is processed, is another valuable metal commodity that has generated large amounts of revenue for nations such as Australia—the world's largest bauxite exporter. The most financially important of all mineral commodities is oil, which is not only used as a vital source of energy but is also necessary for the manufacture of plastics, polymers, and many artificial materials. The 1900s saw more mineral commodities extracted from the planet than in all other centuries put together. While no mineral commodity has yet been exhausted, there are fears that some are dwindling fast.

### TOP-TEN WHEAT-PRODUCING COUNTRIES
**Production in tons p.a.**

|  | |
|---|---|
| China | 106,000,000 |
| India | 79,400,000 |
| U.S. | 62,900,000 |
| Russia | 50,200,000 |
| France | 40,700,000 |
| Canada | 26,600,000 |
| Australia | 22,800,000 |
| Germany | 26,000,000 |
| Pakistan | 23,800,000 |
| Turkey | 23,100,000 |

▶ Bags of rice are loaded onto ships at Indonesia's Sunda Kelapa port on the island of Java. Rice, along with cereal crops such as wheat, is a fundamental source of food for much of the world's human population.

### TOP-20 COTTON-PRODUCING COUNTRIES
**Production in tons p.a.**

|  | |
|---|---|
| China | 8,770,000 |
| India | 5,400,000 |
| U.S. | 3,060,000 |
| Pakistan | 2,150,000 |
| Brazil | 1,312,000 |
| Uzbekistan | 1,100,000 |
| Turkey | 463,000 |
| Australia | 364,000 |
| Turkmenistan | 309,000 |
| Syria | 243,000 |
| Greece | 220,000 |
| Burkina Faso | 198,000 |
| Iran | 176,000 |
| Argentina | 143,000 |
| Mexico | 143,000 |
| Ivory Coast | 132,000 |
| Tanzania | 132,000 |
| Egypt | 121,000 |
| Colombia | 121,000 |
| Peru | 121,000 |

# WORLD TRADE

Trading goods and services is vital in order for countries to prosper and progress economically. Many countries have joined regional trade blocs or international organizations to gain favorable treatment or to exert more influence on the world stage.

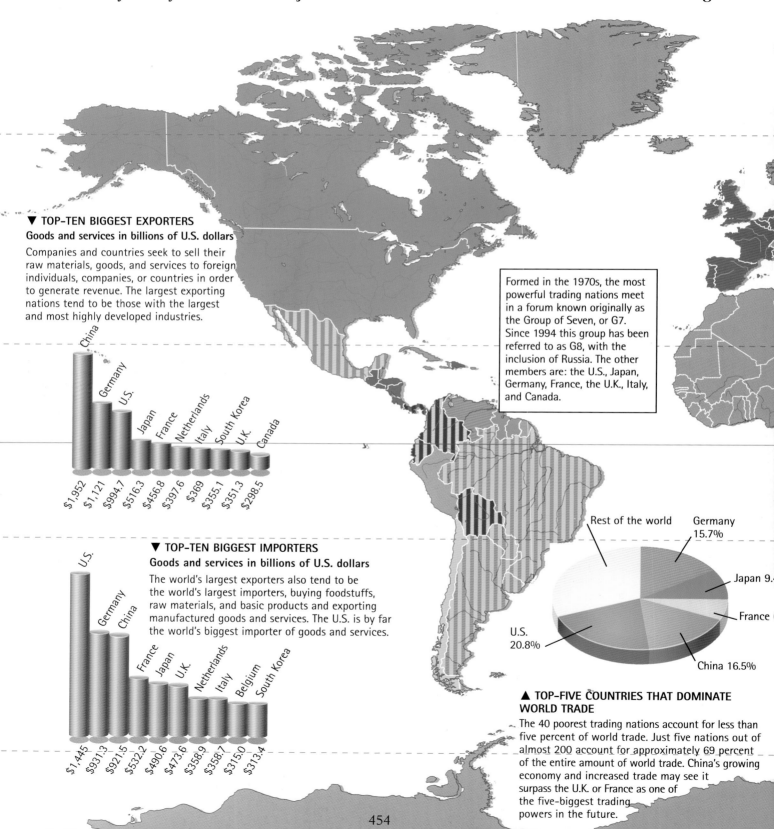

## ▼ TOP-TEN BIGGEST EXPORTERS
**Goods and services in billions of U.S. dollars**

Companies and countries seek to sell their raw materials, goods, and services to foreign individuals, companies, or countries in order to generate revenue. The largest exporting nations tend to be those with the largest and most highly developed industries.

China $1,952
Germany $1,121
U.S. $994.7
Japan $516.3
France $456.8
Netherlands $397.6
Italy $369
South Korea $355.1
U.K. $351.3
Canada $298.5

Formed in the 1970s, the most powerful trading nations meet in a forum known originally as the Group of Seven, or G7. Since 1994 this group has been referred to as G8, with the inclusion of Russia. The other members are: the U.S., Japan, Germany, France, the U.K., Italy, and Canada.

## ▼ TOP-TEN BIGGEST IMPORTERS
**Goods and services in billions of U.S. dollars**

The world's largest exporters also tend to be the world's largest importers, buying foodstuffs, raw materials, and basic products and exporting manufactured goods and services. The U.S. is by far the world's biggest importer of goods and services.

U.S. $1,445
Germany $931.3
China $921.5
France $532.2
Japan $490.6
U.K. $473.6
Netherlands $358.9
Italy $358.7
Belgium $315.0
South Korea $313.4

Rest of the world

Germany 15.7%

Japan 9.

France

China 16.5%

U.S. 20.8%

## ▲ TOP-FIVE COUNTRIES THAT DOMINATE WORLD TRADE

The 40 poorest trading nations account for less than five percent of world trade. Just five nations out of almost 200 account for approximately 69 percent of the entire amount of world trade. China's growing economy and increased trade may see it surpass the U.K. or France as one of the five-biggest trading powers in the future.

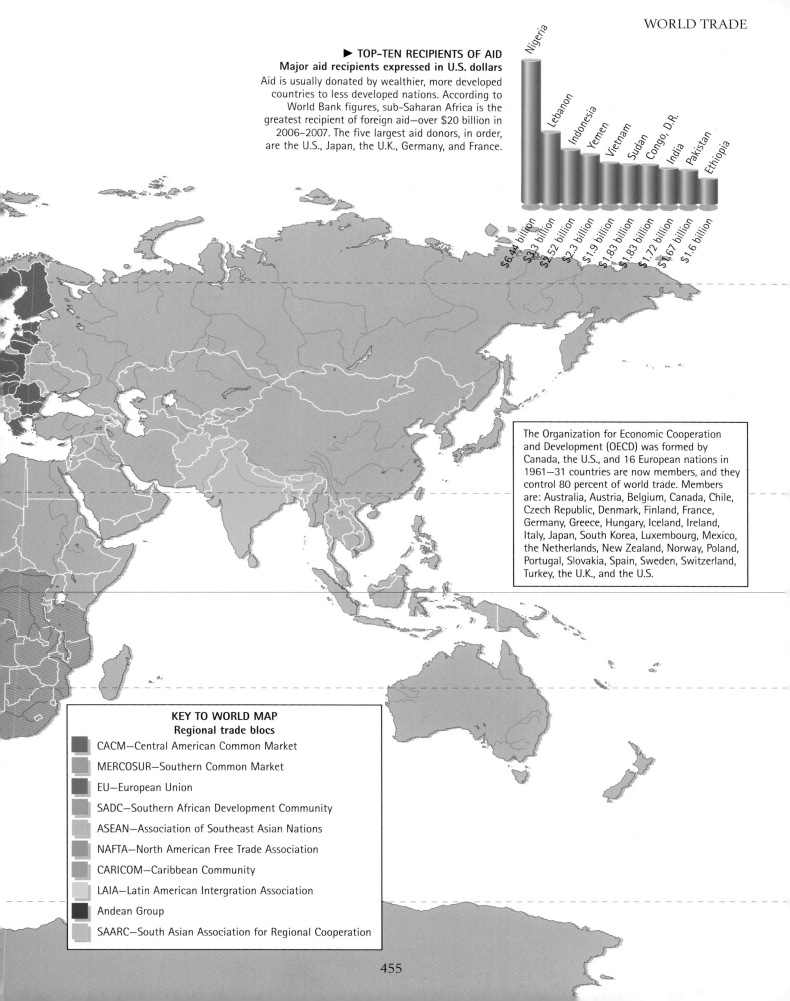

▶ TOP-TEN RECIPIENTS OF AID
**Major aid recipients expressed in U.S. dollars**
Aid is usually donated by wealthier, more developed
countries to less developed nations. According to
World Bank figures, sub-Saharan Africa is the
greatest recipient of foreign aid—over $20 billion in
2006–2007. The five largest aid donors, in order,
are the U.S., Japan, the U.K., Germany, and France.

Nigeria — $6.44 billion
Lebanon — $3.3 billion
Indonesia — $2.52 billion
Yemen — $2.3 billion
Vietnam — $1.9 billion
Sudan — $1.83 billion
Congo, D.R. — $1.83 billion
India — $1.72 billion
Pakistan — $1.67 billion
Ethiopia — $1.6 billion

The Organization for Economic Cooperation
and Development (OECD) was formed by
Canada, the U.S., and 16 European nations in
1961—31 countries are now members, and they
control 80 percent of world trade. Members
are: Australia, Austria, Belgium, Canada, Chile,
Czech Republic, Denmark, Finland, France,
Germany, Greece, Hungary, Iceland, Ireland,
Italy, Japan, South Korea, Luxembourg, Mexico,
the Netherlands, New Zealand, Norway, Poland,
Portugal, Slovakia, Spain, Sweden, Switzerland,
Turkey, the U.K., and the U.S.

**KEY TO WORLD MAP**
**Regional trade blocs**

CACM—Central American Common Market

MERCOSUR—Southern Common Market

EU—European Union

SADC—Southern African Development Community

ASEAN—Association of Southeast Asian Nations

NAFTA—North American Free Trade Association

CARICOM—Caribbean Community

LAIA—Latin American Intergration Association

Andean Group

SAARC—South Asian Association for Regional Cooperation

# TIME ZONES

Millions of people now travel around the world using modern transportation systems. Traveling long distances from east to west or west to east means crossing up to 24 time zones—measured in hours ahead of, or behind, the time found at the Greenwich Meridian at 0° longitude.

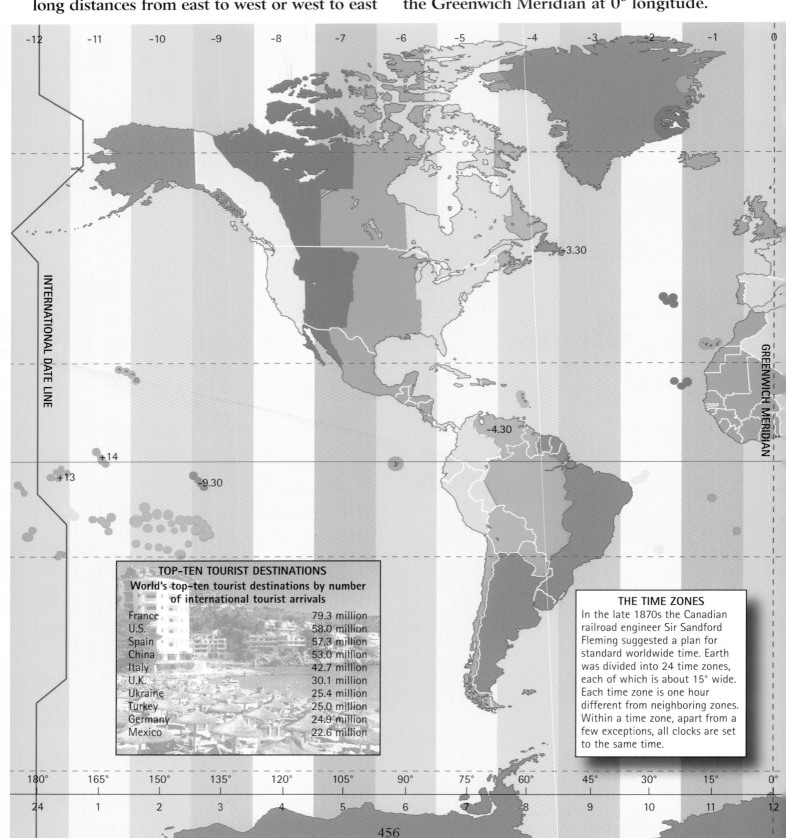

-12 -11 -10 -9 -8 -7 -6 -5 -4 -3 -2 -1 0

INTERNATIONAL DATE LINE

GREENWICH MERIDIAN

-3.30

-4.30

+14

+13

-9.30

**TOP-TEN TOURIST DESTINATIONS**

**World's top-ten tourist destinations by number of international tourist arrivals**

| | |
|---|---|
| France | 79.3 million |
| U.S. | 58.0 million |
| Spain | 57.3 million |
| China | 53.0 million |
| Italy | 42.7 million |
| U.K. | 30.1 million |
| Ukraine | 25.4 million |
| Turkey | 25.0 million |
| Germany | 24.9 million |
| Mexico | 22.6 million |

**THE TIME ZONES**

In the late 1870s the Canadian railroad engineer Sir Sandford Fleming suggested a plan for standard worldwide time. Earth was divided into 24 time zones, each of which is about 15° wide. Each time zone is one hour different from neighboring zones. Within a time zone, apart from a few exceptions, all clocks are set to the same time.

180° 165° 150° 135° 120° 105° 90° 75° 60° 45° 30° 15° 0°

24 1 2 3 4 5 6 7 8 9 10 11 12

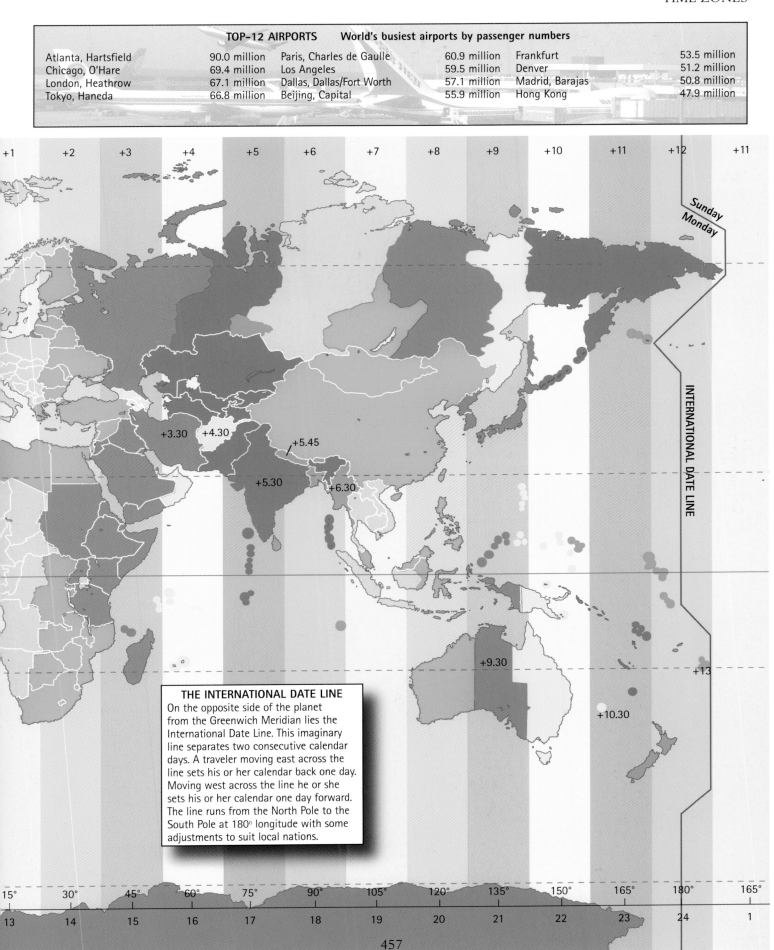

### TOP-12 AIRPORTS    World's busiest airports by passenger numbers

| | | | |
|---|---|---|---|
| Atlanta, Hartsfield | 90.0 million | Paris, Charles de Gaulle | 60.9 million |
| Chicago, O'Hare | 69.4 million | Los Angeles | 59.5 million |
| London, Heathrow | 67.1 million | Dallas, Dallas/Fort Worth | 57.1 million |
| Tokyo, Haneda | 66.8 million | Beijing, Capital | 55.9 million |

| | |
|---|---|
| Frankfurt | 53.5 million |
| Denver | 51.2 million |
| Madrid, Barajas | 50.8 million |
| Hong Kong | 47.9 million |

+1  +2  +3  +4  +5  +6  +7  +8  +9  +10  +11  +12  +11

Sunday
Monday

INTERNATIONAL DATE LINE

+3.30  +4.30

+5.45

+5.30  +6.30

+9.30

+10.30

+13

### THE INTERNATIONAL DATE LINE
On the opposite side of the planet from the Greenwich Meridian lies the International Date Line. This imaginary line separates two consecutive calendar days. A traveler moving east across the line sets his or her calendar back one day. Moving west across the line he or she sets his or her calendar one day forward. The line runs from the North Pole to the South Pole at 180° longitude with some adjustments to suit local nations.

15°  30°  45°  60°  75°  90°  105°  120°  135°  150°  165°  180°  165°

13  14  15  16  17  18  19  20  21  22  23  24  1

# WORLD ORGANIZATIONS

**As the number of independent nations has risen the need for countries to share information, conduct research, debate topics, and settle disputes has grown.**

▲ The flag of the European Union, adopted on its formation under the Treaty of Maastricht in 1993. Formerly called the European Community, it had 27 members in 2007.

▲ The distinctive five rings symbol of the Olympic Games. The International Olympic Committee (IOC) organizes the Winter and Summer Olympic Games. The Summer Games is the world's single largest sporting event.

▼ Ethiopian refugees are cared for in a camp by the International Red Cross and Red Crescent Movement. Formed in the 1800s to care for the victims of wars, it also assists victims of natural disasters in peacetime.

Historically nations aligned with each other in pacts to gain territory and for military reasons in the event of war. Security organizations, such as the North Atlantic Treaty Organization (NATO) (1949–present), were modern versions of international alliances of the past. After World War II there was a large rise in international organizations devoted to issues other than military involvement. International organizations are often split into two types. Intergovernmental organizations, such as the United Nations (UN) or NATO, involve the governments of different countries. Nongovernmental organizations (NGOs) are private organizations that work on or campaign for—or against—single issues. For example, the International Whaling Commission conducts research into and seeks to conserve whales, while the International Atomic Energy Agency (IAEA) promotes the peaceful use of nuclear energy. Many NGOs are concerned with the welfare of the world's poor. There are over 500 intergovernmental and an estimated 5,500 nongovernmental organizations in the world today.

▲ The United Nations Security Council in session in its New York City headquarters. The council consists of five permanent members: the U.S., Russia, China, France, and the U.K.—plus ten further member states that are elected for two-year terms.

## THE UNITED NATIONS

Since its formation in the aftermath of World War II the United Nations has grown into the largest of all international organizations. Almost every nation of the world is a member of the UN, although not all sign the UN's many agreements, treaties, and conventions. The United Nations has a large and complex structure, with a General Assembly in which all members are represented, a Security

▲ Armored vehicles of a UN peace-keeping force patrol and protect a convoy bringing humanitarian aid to Bosnia during the Balkans conflict in the 1990s.

Council, and more than 30 programs and specialized agencies such as the Food and Agriculture Organization (FAO), the World Health Organization (WHO), and the United Nations Children's Fund (UNICEF). One of the UN's fundamental aims is to put an end to war. UN peace-keeping forces, made up of civilian police and observers and volunteer soldiers, have been employed around the world to restore and maintain peace. UN peacekeepers have helped disarm former fighters, train and monitor civilian police, and organize and observe elections. Working with UN agencies and other organizations, they have helped refugees return home, monitored respect for human rights, cleared land mines, and started the process of reconstructing war-torn areas.

### REGIONAL ORGANIZATIONS

A number of international organizations have been formed by countries in a region to solve issues affecting their region or to promote that region's interests. For example, ASEAN (the Association of Southeast Asian Nations) promotes economic and military cooperation between ten nations in Southeast Asia. As of January 2007, the European Union (EU) is an organization of 27 member nations. Its key goal is for greater economic unity between its member states, with the free movement of people, goods, and services within its borders, and one currency—the euro—which was introduced in 1999 and adopted by 16 of the member states.

**LEAGUE OF ARAB STATES**

Algeria
Bahrain
Comoros
Djibouti
Egypt
Iraq
Jordan
Kuwait
Lebanon
Mauritania
Morocco
Oman
Palestine
Qatar
Saudi Arabia
Somalia
Sudan
Syria
Tunisia
United Arab Emirates
Yemen

▲ The League of Arab States, also known as the Arab League, was formed in 1945 to protect and promote the interests of many Arab nations in the Middle East region.

459

# WORLD RELIGIONS

**Many of the world's people live their lives according to sets of beliefs and practices that define their relationship with others, the universe, and its creation.**

▲ The head of the Roman Catholic Church is the Pope, seen here blessing a crowd of followers, who resides in the independent city-state of the Vatican.

Religious beliefs first developed many thousands of years ago. Today there are hundreds of different religions, with a few that have hundreds of millions of followers. One of the oldest surviving major religions is Judaism, the religion of the Jewish people, which developed around 4,000 years ago. The state of Israel was established in 1948 as a homeland for the Jewish people, but the largest community of Jews in a single country is found in the U.S., numbering over five million. Religions have had a major impact on world history and continue to shape the world and its people to this day.

## THE SPREAD OF RELIGIONS

In the past religious beliefs were spread by traders and missionaries and were also imposed by conquering forces. The fastest-growing religion today is believed to be Islam, whose followers are called Muslims.

The largest communities of Muslims are found in Indonesia, Pakistan, Bangladesh, and India, with many of the nations of the Middle East also Islamic states. Migrations of peoples from one nation to another have seen many countries become multifaith nations with sizable minorities of many different religious persuasions. For example, the largest community of followers of the Sikh religion outside of India is found in the United Kingdom. Christianity is the most widely followed religion and is divided into many different forms. A little over half of all

▼ LARGEST RELIGIONS By number of followers

This chart shows the estimated number of people who follow each of the world's main religions. Almost all of the major religions have different branches, or sects. In addition, there are numerous other religions with smaller numbers of followers.

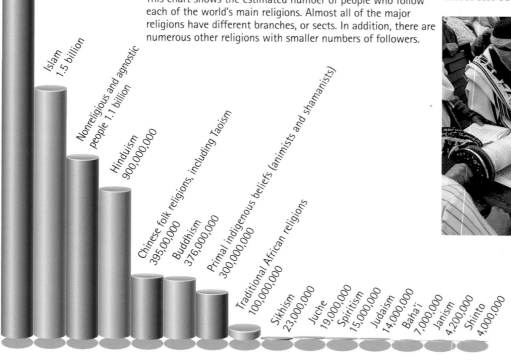

Christianity 2.1 billion

Islam 1.5 billion

Nonreligious and agnostic people 1.1 billion

Hinduism 900,000,000

Chinese folk religions, including Taoism 395,00,000

Buddhism 376,000,000

Primal indigenous beliefs (animists and shamanists) 300,000,000

Traditional African religions 100,000,000

Sikhism 23,000,000

Juche 19,000,000

Spiritism 15,000,000

Judaism 14,000,000

Baha'i 7,000,000

Janism 4,200,000

Shinto 4,000,000

▲ This 13-year-old Jewish boy is undergoing his bar mitzvah ceremony in which he will become an adult in Jewish religious life. A bat mitvah, a similar ceremony for girls, usually occurs at age 12.

◀ Two Buddhist monks stand in front of Vat Xieng Thong royal temple in Laos. Buddhism is especially followed in the nations of Southeast Asia and in China and Japan.

▶ Two Sikhs with their distinctive turbans attend the world conference Unity of Man held in Punjab, India. Punjab is the homeland of the Sikh religion and the one region on Earth where Sikhs are in the majority.

Christians are Roman Catholics. There are large numbers of Catholics in South and Central America and Europe, while the Philippines is home to the world's fourth-largest community of Catholics. The Protestant Church split from the Catholic Church around 500 years ago.

Today almost one fifth of all Christians are Protestants, particularly in northern Europe and North America. The Eastern Orthodox Churches of Russia and Eastern Europe account for a further ten percent of all Christians. Some religions are less widely spread. Most of the world's 860 million Hindus live in India, with the second- and third-largest Hindu communities found in the neighboring nations of Nepal and Bangladesh.

▼ Muslims at midday prayer in the Jami Masjid mosque in the Indian city of Delhi. Completed in 1650, it is the largest mosque in India and one of the largest in the world.

# WORLD COMMUNICATIONS

**The range of communication methods has increased dramatically, giving people the greater ability to share information and ideas with other parts of the world.**

| TOP-20 COUNTRIES FOR TV OWNERSHIP IN MILLIONS | |
| --- | --- |
| China | 493 |
| U.S. | 252.4 |
| India | 130 |
| Japan | 92.6 |
| Russia | 77 |
| Brazil | 62.9 |
| Germany | 51 |
| U.K. | 40.3 |
| France | 38.6 |
| Indonesia | 32 |
| Turkey | 31.2 |
| Italy | 30.3 |
| Mexico | 29 |
| Canada | 28 |
| Spain | 27.7 |
| Ukraine | 21.4 |
| Pakistan | 21.3 |
| South Korea | 18.5 |
| Thailand | 18.3 |
| Australia | 16.1 |

▼ Television has extended its reach into almost all parts of the world. These villagers in Tsatan Uul in northern Mongolia are among the most isolated people in Asia. Yet with a portable electricity generator they are able to watch television.

Communication comes in many forms—from hand gestures and facial expressions to sophisticated electronic communication devices such as cellular phones. Spoken language is the most common form of communication, while the development of written language has allowed people to record spoken language and ideas and to pass them on to others.

## PRINTED COMMUNICATION

Despite the rise of radio, television, and electronic media such as the Internet, the printed word, in the form of books, newspapers, and journals, remains a major form of mass communication throughout the world. The United Kingdom has one of the world's largest book publishing industries. According to the International Publishing Association, around 100,000 new titles are published in the U.K. every year, double that of France, Italy, and Russia. More newspapers are sold daily in China than in any other nation—93.5 million copies in 2008. India, with 78.8 million, and Japan, with 68.5 million copies daily, were second and third.

▲ Telecommunication and the Internet allow distance learning by children and adults in isolated areas. This young Australian student uses a CB to contact her teacher, who is hundreds of miles away.

## TELECOMMUNICATION

Much early communication was directly between people in the same place. As transportation improved and people explored greater distances a need for longer-distance communication devices arose. Telecommunication is a type of medium that enables communication over long distances. The first major telecommunication device was the telegraph, pioneered in Europe and the U.S. This was followed by the telephone, radio, and television. Television has had a profound impact on the way many people view the world; there are now over two billion TV sets in existence. Television audiences for major global events, such as wars or sports events, are measured in their millions. The past 20 years have seen the rise of cell phone services. In 2002, 72.7 percent of Germans, 64.5 percent of Australians, 64.9 percent of French, and 63.7 percent of Japanese had cell phones. In contrast, cell phone ownership in Africa is restricted: in 2009 only six percent of all Africans had a cell phone.

### ▼ MOST COMMON FIRST LANGUAGES BY NUMBER OF USERS

Around 3,000 languages and dialects (versions of a language differing in some words and pronunciations) are spoken in the world today. This chart shows the most commonly spoken first languages. The large number of Spanish speakers reflects Spain's historical impact in South and Central America. Some languages are much more widely spoken than is reflected by their number of first-language users. Although less than one tenth of the world uses English as its first language, the number of people who speak English as their second or third language is much higher. English is often the language used internationally in business and information technology.

Chinese (Guoyo) 850,000,000
Hindi 420,000,000
Spanish 360,000,000
English 340,000,000
Bengali 210,000,000
Arabic 200,000,000
Portuguese 175,000,000
Malay-Bahasa Indonesia (includes Javanese) 165,000,000
Japanese 127,000,000
Russia 120,000,000
German 100,000,000
Punjabi 90,000,000
Vietnamese 80,000,000
Korean 78,000,000
French 77,000,000
Wu 77,000,000
Marathi 72,000,000
Cantonese 71,000,000
Telugu 69,000,000
Urdu 65,000,000

▲ A Chinese newspaper stand selling some of the 60 million newspapers purchased every day in China. There are more than 2,100 daily newspapers, and in some parts of the country renting newspapers for one hour for a fraction of the cover price is practiced to save money.

▼ The Main Reading Room of the Library of Congress in Washington, D.C. The largest library in the world, it has over 32 million books in 470 different languages.

| INTERNET USAGE Top ten countries (millions of users) | |
|---|---|
| China | 298.0 |
| U.S. | 231.0 |
| Japan | 90.9 |
| India | 81.0 |
| Brazil | 64.9 |
| Germany | 62.0 |
| United Kingdom | 48.8 |
| Russia | 45.3 |
| France | 42.9 |
| South Korea | 37.5 |
| **Countries with highest numbers of people online** | |
| Iceland | 93.2% |
| Norway | 90.9% |
| Greenland | 90.3% |
| Sweden | 89.2% |
| Netherlands | 85.6% |
| Denmark | 84.2% |
| Finland | 83.5% |
| Australia | 80.1% |
| New Zealand | 79.7% |
| Luxembourg | 78.7% |

## PERSONAL COMPUTING

The past 30 years have seen a dramatic change in communication powered by personal computing and, more recently, the Internet. Computers are now found in millions of people's homes all over the world, enabling access to information stored on media such as CD-ROMs, as well as new methods of communication and information handling such as word processing, spreadsheets, and electronic books. Personal computer ownership has boomed since the mid-1980s—Israel leads the way in this, with more personal computers in the country than people. Australia, New Zealand, and the nations of Western Europe and Southeast Asia are not far behind. In contrast, less than half of one percent of the population in many African nations has access to a computer.

## INTERNET COMMUNICATION

The linking of computers together in a network started in the 1960s in academic institutions and with the network of U.S. defense computers called ARPAnet developed by the Pentagon in 1969. By 1990 around 160,000 computers around the world were linked to the Internet, but it was the arrival of the World Wide Web with web sites containing pages of linked

▲ Modern telecommunication allows businesses to span the globe. This call center for a cell phone company in the Indian city of Delhi deals with questions about its services from customers in the United Kingdom.

information that fueled the boom of the Internet. Its growth has been explosive. The amount of access to the Internet increased by 1,000 percent in 1995 and 1996 and has doubled in almost every year since. By 2009, 1.7 billion people had direct Internet access. Many more use Internet facilities in schools and at Internet cafés. According to the International Telecommunications Union, Iceland is the country with the highest level of Internet usage among its population. The Internet is revolutionizing communications for many people. E-mail, Internet chat rooms, and instant messaging allow people to make immediate contact with people on the other side of the world.

Many governments and international organizations publish important documents on the World Wide Web, allowing access to increasing amounts of information. In the Dhar district of India, for example, the Gyandoot program provides 39 computer kiosks to farmers who can check produce prices and ship to whatever markets offer the best price. For small businesses in poorer countries, isolated a long distance away from potential markets, the Internet offers a chance to sell directly to consumers. Internet access is expected to continue to rise dramatically, especially in developing countries. Some of the most powerful Pacific Rim nations are leading the way in upgrading Internet connections to allow fast business and information access. Singapore has the highest level of broadband Internet access, with 90 percent of computers linked to broadband by 2009.

▼ Global cell phone technology has evolved using geostationary satellites orbiting Earth to enable worldwide communication in even the remotest regions. This member of the Mount Vaughan expedition is using a global satellite phone to make a call from the icy wastelands of Antarctica.

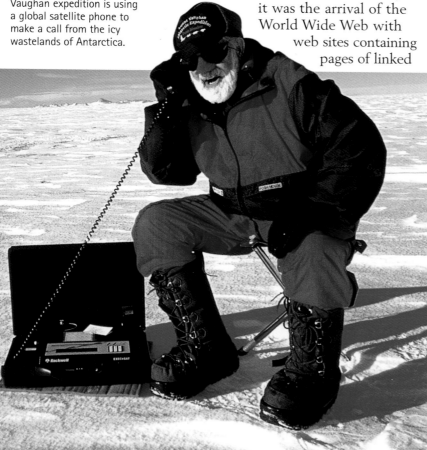

# WORLD STATISTICS

## AUSTRALIA
### STATES AND TERRITORIES

**NEW SOUTH WALES**
Area: 309,500 sq. mi.
Population: 7,100,000
Capital: Sydney

**QUEENSLAND**
Area: 666,875 sq. mi.
Population: 4,407,000
Capital: Brisbane

**SOUTH AUSTRALIA**
Area: 379,925 sq. mi.
Population: 1,623,000
Capital: Adelaide

**TASMANIA**
Area: 26,180 sq. mi.
Population: 503,000
Capital: Hobart

**VICTORIA**
Area: 87,880 sq. mi.
Population: 5,428,000
Capital: Melbourne

**WESTERN AUSTRALIA**
Area: 975,100 sq. mi.
Population: 2,237,000
Capital: Perth

**AUSTRALIAN CAPITAL TERRITORY**
Area: 900 sq. mi.
Population: 351,000
Capital: Canberra

**JERVIS BAY TERRITORY**
Area: 30 sq. mi.
Population: 390
Capital: administered from Canberra

**NORTHERN TERRITORY**
Area: 519,770 sq. mi.
Population: 225,000
Capital: Darwin

## AUSTRIA
### FEDERAL STATES

**BURGENLAND**
Area: 1,530 sq. mi.
Population: 281,000
Capital: Eisenstadt

**CARINTHIA (KÄRNTEN)**
Area: 3,681 sq. mi.
Population: 561,000
Capital: Klagenfurt

**LOWER AUSTRIA (NIEDERÖSTERREICH)**
Area: 7,403 sq. mi.
Population: 1,597,000
Capital: Sankt Pölten

**SALZBURG**
Area: 2,762 sq. mi.
Population: 531,000
Capital: Salzburg

**STYRIA (STEIERMARK)**
Area: 6,327 sq. mi.
Population: 1,206,000
Capital: Graz

**TIROL**
Area: 4,883 sq. mi.
Population: 704,000
Capital: Innsbruck

**UPPER AUSTRIA (OBERÖSTERREICH)**
Area: 4,625 sq. mi.
Population: 1,408,000
Capital: Linz

**VIENNA (WIEN)**
Area: 160 sq. mi.
Population: 1,678,000
Capital: Vienna

**VORARLBERG**
Area: 1,004 sq. mi.
Population: 366,000
Capital: Bregenz

## BELGIUM
### FEDERAL REGIONS

**BRUSSELS (BRUXELLES OR BRUSSEL)**
Area: 62 sq. mi.
Population: 1,049,000
Capital: Brussels

**FLANDERS (VLAANDEREN)**
Area: 5,220 sq. mi.
Population: 6,162,000
Capitals: Brussels

**WALLONIA (WALLONIE)**
Area: 6,504 sq. mi.
Population: 3,467,000
Capital: Namur

## BRAZIL
### STATES

**ACRE**
Area: 59,130 sq. mi.
Population: 653,000
Capital: Rio Branco

**ALAGOAS**
Area: 10,785 sq. mi.
Population: 3,015,000
Capital: Maceió

**AMAPÁ**
Area: 55,388 sq. mi.
Population: 585,000
Capital: Macapá

**AMAZONAS**
Area: 609,200 sq. mi.
Population: 3,168,000
Capital: Manaus

**BAHIA**
Area: 219,035 sq. mi.
Population: 14,080,000
Capital: Salvador

**CEARÁ**
Area: 56,505 sq. mi.
Population: 8,184,000
Capital: Fortaleza

**DISTRITO FEDERAL**
Area: 2,248 sq. mi.
Population: 2,456,000
Capital: Brasília

**ESPÍRITO SANTO**
Area: 17,831 sq. mi.
Population: 3,351,000
Capital: Vitória

**GOIÁS**
Area: 131,772 sq. mi.
Population: 5,645,000
Capital: Goiânia

**MARANHÃO**
Area: 128,713 sq. mi.
Population: 6,118,000
Capital: São Luís

**MATO GROSSO**
Area: 350,120 sq. mi.
Population: 2,854,000
Capital: Cuiabá

**MATO GROSSO DO SUL**
Area: 138,286 sq. mi.
Population: 2,265,000
Capital: Campo Grande

**MINAS GERAIS**
Area: 227,176 sq. mi.
Population: 19,262,000
Capital: Belo Horizonte

**PARÁ**
Area: 483,850 sq. mi.
Population: 7,071,000
Capital: Belém

**PARAÍBA**
Area: 21,850 sq. mi.
Population: 3,641,000
Capital: João Pessoa

**PARANÁ**
Area: 77,108 sq. mi.
Population: 10,280,000
Capital: Curitiba

**PERNAMBUCO**
Area: 37,992 sq. mi.
Population: 8,487,000
Capital: Recife

**PIAUÍ**
Area: 97,444 sq. mi.
Population: 3,030,000
Capital: Teresina

**RIO DE JANEIRO**
Area: 16,955 sq. mi.
Population: 15,406,000
Capital: Rio de Janeiro

**RIO GRANDE DO NORTE**
Area: 20,581 sq. mi.
Population: 3,014,000
Capital: Natal

**RIO GRANDE DO SUL**
Area: 108,905 sq. mi.
Population: 10,582,000
Capital: Pôrto Alegre

**RONDÔNIA**
Area: 92,090 sq. mi.
Population: 1,454,000
Capital: Pôrto Velho

**RORAIMA**
Area: 86,918 sq. mi.
Population: 394,000
Capital: Boa Vista

**SANTA CATARINA**
Area: 36,851 sq. mi.
Population: 5,868,000
Capital: Florianópolis

**SÃO PAULO**
Area: 96,066 sq. mi.
Population: 39,838,000
Capital: São Paulo

**SERGIPE**
Area: 8,515 sq. mi.
Population: 1,939,000
Capital: Aracaju

**TOCANTINS**
Area: 107,499 sq. mi.
Population: 1,248,000
Capital: Palmas

## CANADA
### PROVINCES AND TERRITORIES

**ALBERTA**
Area: 255,286 sq. mi.
Population: 3,688,000
Capital: Edmonton

**BRITISH COLUMBIA**
Area: 365,950 sq. mi.
Population: 4,455,000
Capital: Victoria

**MANITOBA**
Area: 250,950 sq. mi.
Population: 1,222,000
Capital: Winnipeg

**NEW BRUNSWICK**
Area: 28,355 sq. mi.
Population: 749,000
Capital: Fredericton

**NEWFOUNDLAND & LABRADOR**
Area: 156,650 sq. mi.
Population: 509,000
Capital: St. John's

**NOVA SCOTIA**
Area: 21,425 sq. mi.
Population: 938,000
Capital: Halifax

**ONTARIO**
Area: 412,580 sq. mi.
Population: 13,069,000
Capital: Toronto

**PRINCE EDWARD ISLAND**
Area: 2,185 sq. mi.
Population: 141,000
Capital: Charlottetown

**QUÉBEC**
Area: 594,860 sq. mi.
Population: 7,829,000
Capital: Québec

**SASKATCHEWAN**
Area: 251,870 sq. mi.
Population: 1,030,000
Capital: Regina

**NORTHWEST TERRITORIES**
Area: 503,950
Population: 43,000
Capital: Yellowknife

**NUNAVUT**
Area: 818,960 sq. mi.
Population: 32,000
Capital: Iqaluit

**YUKON TERRITORY**
Area: 186,660 sq. mi.
Population: 34,000
Capital: Whitehorse

## CHINA
### PROVINCES AND REGIONS

**ANHUI**
Area: 54,020 sq. mi.
Population: 61,180,000
Capital: Hefei

**BEIJING (PEKING)**
(municipal province)
Area: 6,490 sq. mi.
Population: 16,330,000
Capital: Beijing

**CHONGQING
(CH'UNG-CH'ING)**
(municipal province)
Area: 31,660 sq. mi.
Population: 28,160,000
Capital: Chongqing

**FUJIAN**
Area: 47,530 sq. mi.
Population: 35,810,000
Capital: Fuzhou

**GANSU**
Area: 141,500 sq. mi.
Population: 26,170,000
Capital: Lanzhou

**GUANGDONG**
Area: 76,100 sq. mi.
Population: 94,490,000
Capital: Guangzhou
(Canton)

**GUANGXI**
(autonomous region)
Area: 86,000 sq. mi.
Population: 47,680,000
Capital: Nanning

**GUIZHOU**
Area: 67,180 sq. mi.
Population: 37,620,000
Capital: Guiyang

**HAINAN**
Area: 13,240 sq. mi.
Population: 8,450,000
Capital: Haikou

**HEBEI**
Area: 78,260 sq. mi.
Population: 69,430,000
Capital: Shijiazhuang

**HEILONGJIANG**
Area: 179,000 sq. mi.
Population: 38,240,000
Capital: Harbin

**HENAN**
Area: 64,480 sq. mi.
Population: 93,600,000
Capital: Zhengzhou

**HONG KONG (OR
XIANGGANG)**
(autonomous
special administrative
region)
Area: 415 sq. mi.
Population: 7,094,000
Capital: Xianggang
(Hong Kong)

**HUBEI**
Area: 72,390 sq. mi.
Population: 56,990,000
Capital: Wuhan

**HUNAN**
Area: 81,275 sq. mi.
Population: 63,550,000
Capital: Changsha

**JIANGSU**
Area: 39,610 sq. mi.
Population: 76,250,000
Capital: Nanjing

**JIANGXI**
Area: 63,630 sq. mi.
Population: 43,680,000
Capital: Nanchang

**JILIN**
Area: 72,200 sq. mi.
Population: 27,300,000
Capital: Changchun

**LIAONING**
Area: 58,300 sq. mi.
Population: 42,980,000
Capital: Shenyang

**MACAU (AOMEN)**
(autonomous special
administrative region)
Area: 10.6 sq. mi.
Population: 502,000
Capital: Macau (Aomen)

**NEI MONGGOL
(INNER MONGOLIA)**
(autonomous region)
Area: 454,635 sq. mi.
Population: 24,050,000
Capital: Hohhot

**NINGXIA HUI**
(autonomous region)
Area: 25,640 sq. mi.
Population: 6,100,000
Capital: Yinchuan

**QINGHAI**
Area: 278,380 sq. mi.
Population: 5,520,000
Capital: Xining

**SHAANXI**
Area: 75,600 sq. mi.
Population: 37,480,000
Capital: Xi'an

**SHANDONG**
Area: 59,190 sq. mi.
Population: 93,670,000
Capital: Jinan

**SHANGHAI**
(municipal province)
Area: 2,400 sq. mi.
Population: 18,580,000
Capital: Shanghai

**SHANXI**
Area: 60,660 sq. mi.
Population: 33,930,000
Capital: Taiyuan

**SICHUAN**
Area: 188,030 sq. mi.
Population: 81,270,000
Capital: Chengdu

**TIANJIN
(TIENTSIN)**
(municipal province)
Area: 4,360 sq. mi.
Population: 11,150,000
Capital: Tianjin

**XINJIANG UYGUR
(SINKIANG)**
(autonomous region)
Area: 635,870 sq. mi.
Population: 20,250,000
Capital: Ürümqi

**XIZANG
(TIBET)**
(autonomous region)
Area: 471,660 sq. mi.
Population: 2,840,000
Capital: Lhasa

**YUNNAN**
Area: 168,420 sq. mi.
Population: 45,140,000
Capital: Kunming

**ZHEJIANG**
Area: 39,300 sq. mi.
Population: 50,600,000
Capital: Hangzhou

## FRANCE
### REGIONS

**ALSACE**
Area: 3,200 sq. mi.
Population: 1,827,000
Capital: Strasbourg

**AQUITAINE**
Area: 15,950 sq. mi.
Population: 3,151,000
Capital: Bordeaux

**AUVERGNE**
Area: 10,040 sq. mi.
Population: 1,339,000
Capital: Clermont-Ferrand

**BRITTANY (BRETAGNE)**
Area: 10,500 sq. mi.
Population: 3,120,000
Capital: Rennes

**BURGUNDY (BOURGOGNE)**
Area: 12,195 sq. mi.
Population: 1,634,000
Capital: Dijon

**CENTRE-VAL DE LOIRE**
Area: 15,120 sq. mi.
Population: 2,527,000
Capital: Orléans

**CHAMPAGNE-ARDENNE**
Area: 9,890 sq. mi.
Population: 1,339,000
Capital: Reims

**CORSICA (CORSE)**
Area: 3,351 sq. mi.
Population: 299,000
Capital: Ajaccio

**FRANCHE-COMTÉ**
Area: 6,256 sq. mi.
Population: 1,159,000
Capital: Besançon

**ÎLE-DE-FRANCE**
Area: 4,637 sq. mi.
Population: 11,599,000
Capital: Paris

**LANGUEDOC-ROUSSILLON**
Area: 10,570 sq. mi.
Population: 2,561,000
Capital: Montpellier

**LIMOUSIN**
Area: 6,541 sq. mi.
Population: 737,000
Capital: Limoges

**LORRAINE**
Area: 9,092 sq. mi.
Population: 2,340,000
Capital: Nancy

**LOWER NORMANDY
(BASSE-NORMANDIE)**
Area: 6,791 sq. mi.
Population: 1,461,000
Capital: Caen

**MIDI-PYRÉNÉES**
Area: 17,509 sq. mi.
Population: 2,811,000
Capital: Toulouse

**NORD-PAS-DE-CALAIS**
Area: 4,793 sq. mi.
Population: 4,022,000
Capital: Lille

**PAYS DE LA LOIRE**
Area: 12,387 sq. mi.
Population: 3,483,000
Capital: Nantes

**PICARDY (PICARDIE)**
Area: 7,490 sq. mi.
Population: 1,900,000
Capital: Amiens

**POITOU-CHARENTES**
Area: 9,965 sq. mi.
Population: 1,740,000
Capital: Poitiers

**PROVENCE-ALPES-CÔTE-D'AZUR**
Area: 12,120 sq. mi.
Population: 4,864,000
Capital: Marseille

**RHÔNE-ALPES**
Area: 16,872 sq. mi.
Population: 6,066,000
Capital: Lyon

**UPPER NORMANDY
(HAUTE NORMANDIE)**
Area: 4,756 sq. mi.
Population: 1,817,000
Capital: Rouen

# GERMANY
## STATES (LÄNDER)

**BADEN-WÜRTTEMBERG**
Area: 13,804 sq. mi.
Population: 10,750,000
Capital: Stuttgart

**BAVARIA (BAYERN)**
Area: 27,239 sq. mi.
Population: 12,520,000
Capital: Munich (München)

**BERLIN**
Area: 343 sq. mi.
Population: 3,432,000
Capital: Berlin

**BRANDENBURG**
Area: 11,383 sq. mi.
Population: 2,522,000
Capital: Potsdam

**BREMEN**
Area: 156 sq. mi.
Population: 662,000
Capital: Bremen

**HAMBURG**
Area: 292 sq. mi.
Population: 1,772,000
Capital: Hamburg

**HESSE (HESSEN)**
Area: 8,152 sq. mi.
Population: 6,065,000
Capital: Wiesbaden

**LOWER SAXONY
(NIEDERSACHSEN)**
Area: 18,381 sq. mi.
Population: 7,947,000
Capital: Hannover

**MECKLENBURG-WESTERN
POMERANIA (MECKLENBURG-
VORPOMMERN)**
Area: 8,946 sq. mi.
Population: 1,664,000
Capital: Schwerin

**NORTH RHINE-WESTPHALIA
(NORDRHEIN-WESTFALEN)**
Area: 13,155 sq. mi.
Population: 17,933,000
Capital: Düsseldorf

**RHINELAND-PALATINATE
(RHEINLAND-PFALZ)**
Area: 7,662 sq. mi.
Population: 4,028,000
Capital: Mainz

**SAAR**
Area: 992 sq. mi.
Population: 1,030,000
Capital: Saarbrücken

**SAXONY (SACHSEN)**
Area: 7,108 sq. mi.
Population: 4,193,000
Capital: Dresden

**SAXONY-ANHALT
(SACHSEN-ANHALT)**
Area: 7,894 sq. mi.
Population: 2,382,000
Capital: Magdeburg

**SCHLESWIG-HOLSTEIN**
Area: 6,077 sq. mi.
Population: 2,834,000
Capital: Kiel

**THURINGIA
(THÜRINGEN)**
Area: 6,245 sq. mi.
Population: 2,268,000
Capital: Erfurt

# INDIA
## STATES AND
## TERRITORIES

**ANDHRA PRADESH**
Area: 106,204 sq. mi.
Population: 82,180,000
Capital: Hyderabad

**ARUNACHAL PRADESH**
Area: 32,333 sq. mi.
Population: 1,200,000
Capital: Itanagar

**ASSAM**
Area: 30,285 sq. mi.
Population: 29,929,000
Capital: Dispur

**BIHAR**
Area: 36,357 sq. mi.
Population: 93,823,000
Capital: Patna

**CHHATTISGARH**
Area: 52,198 sq. mi.
Population: 23,636,000
Capital: Raipur

**GOA**
Area: 1,429 sq. mi.
Population: 1,628,000
Capital: Panaji

**GUJARAT**
Area: 75,685 sq. mi.
Population: 56,408,000
Capital: Gandhinagar

**HARYANA**
Area: 17,070 sq. mi.
Population: 23,772,000
Capital: Chandigarh

**HIMACHAL PRADESH**
Area: 21,495 sq. mi.
Population: 6,550,000
Capital: Shimla

**JAMMU AND KASHMIR**
Area: 85,806 sq. mi.,
of which 46,976 sq. mi.
are occupied by China
and Pakistan
Population: 12,366,000 in
Indian-administered areas
Capital: Srinagar and Jammu

**JHARKHAND**
Area: 30,778 sq. mi.
Population: 30,010,000
Capital: Ranchi

**KARNATAKA**
Area: 74,051 sq. mi.
Population: 57,399,000
Capital: Bangalore (Bengaluru)

**KERALA**
Area: 15,005 sq. mi.
Population: 34,232,000
Capital: Thiruvananthapuram
(Trivandrum)

**MADHYA PRADESH**
Area: 119,014 sq. mi.
Population: 69,279,000
Capital: Bhopal

**MAHARASHTRA**
Area: 118,800 sq. mi.
Population: 106,894,000
Capital: Mumbai (Bombay)

**MANIPUR**
Area 8,621 sq. mi.
Population: 2,627,000
Capital: Imphal

**MEGHALAYA**
Area: 8,660 sq. mi.
Population: 2,536,000
Capital: Shillong

**MIZORAM**
Area: 8,139 sq. mi.
Population: 980,000
Capital: Aizawl

**NAGALAND**
Area: 6,401 sq. mi.
Population: 2,187,000
Capital: Kohima

**ORISSA**
Area: 60,119 sq. mi.
Population: 39,899,000
Capital: Bhubaneshwar

**PUNJAB**
Area: 19,445 sq. mi.
Population: 26,591,000
Capital: Chandigarh

**RAJASTHAN**
Area: 132,139 sq. mi.
Population: 64,641,000
Capital: Jaipur

**SIKKIM**
Area: 2,740 sq. mi.
Population: 594,000
Capital: Gangtok

**TAMIL NADU**
Area: 50,216 sq. mi.
Population: 66,396,000
Capital: Madras (Chennai)

**TRIPURA**
Area: 4,049 sq. mi.
Population: 3,510,000
Capital: Agartala

**UTTARANCHAL**
Area: 20,650 sq. mi.
Population: 9,497,000
Capital: Dehra Dun

**UTTAR PRADESH**
Area: 93,023 sq. mi.
Population: 190,891,000
Capital: Lucknow

**WEST BENGAL (BANGLA)**
Area: 34,267 sq. mi.
Population: 87,869,000
Capital: Kolkata (Calcutta)

**ANDAMAN AND NICOBAR ISLANDS UNION TERRITORY**
Area: 3,185 sq. mi.
Population: 411,000
Capital: Port Blair

**CHANDIGARH UNION TERRITORY**
Area: 44 sq. mi.
Population: 1,063,000
Capital: Chandigarh

**DADRA AND NAGAR HAVELI UNION TERRITORY**
Area: 190 sq. mi.
Population: 262,000
Capital: Silvassa

**DAMAN AND DIU UNION TERRITORY**
Area: 43 sq. mi.
Population: 188,000
Capital: Daman

**DELHI UNION TERRITORY**
Area: 573 sq. mi.
Population: 17,076,000
Capital: Delhi

**LAKSHADWEEP UNION TERRITORY**
Area: 12 sq. mi.
Population: 69,000
Capital: Kavaratti

**PONDICHERRY (PUDUCHERRY) UNION TERRITORY**
Area: 190 sq. mi.
Population: 1,074,000
Capital: Pondicherry (Puducherry)

# ITALY
## REGIONS

**ABRUZZI**
Area: 4,168 sq. mi.
Population: 1,324,000
Capital: Pescara and Sulmona
(The status of L'Aquila as capital was placed in abeyance in 2009 following its devastation in an earthquake.)

**BASILICATA**
Area: 3,858 sq. mi.
Population: 591,000
Capital: Potenza

**CALABRIA**
Area: 5,822 sq. mi.
Population: 2,008,000
Capital: Catanzaro

**CAMPANIA**
Area: 5,249 sq. mi.
Population: 5,811,000
Capital: Naples (Napoli)

**EMILIA-ROMAGNA**
Area: 8,542 sq. mi.
Population: 4,276,000
Capital: Bologna

**FRIULI-VENEZIA GIULIA**
Area: 3,029 sq. mi.
Population: 1,222,000
Capital: Trieste

**LAZIO**
Area: 6,642 sq. mi.
Population: 5,561,000
Capital: Rome (Roma)

**LIGURIA**
Area: 2,092 sq. mi.
Population: 1,610,000
Capital: Genoa (Genova)

**LOMBARDY (LOMBARDIA)**
Area: 9,211 sq. mi.
Population: 9,642,000
Capital: Milan (Milano)

**MARCHE**
Area: 3,742 sq. mi.
Population: 1,553,000
Capital: Ancona

**MOLISE**
Area: 1,714 sq. mi.
Population: 321,000
Capital: Campobasso

**PIEDMONT (PIEMONTE)**
Area: 9,807 sq. mi.
Population: 4,401,000
Capital: Turin (Torino)

**PUGLIA**
Area: 7,470 sq. mi.
Population: 4,077,000
Capital: Bari

**SARDINIA (SARDEGNA)**
Area: 9,301 sq. mi.
Population: 1,666,000
Capital: Cagliari

**SICILY (SICILIA)**
Area: 9,926 sq. mi.
Population: 5,030,000
Capital: Palermo

**TUSCANY (TOSCANA)**
Area: 8,877 sq. mi.
Population: 3,677,000
Capital: Florence (Firenze)

**TRENTINO-ALTO ADIGE/ TRIENT-SÜDTIROL**
Area: 5,258 sq. mi.
Population: 1,007,000
Capitals: Bolzano-Bozen and Trento

**UMBRIA**
Area: 3,265 sq. mi.
Population: 884,000
Capital: Perugia

**VALLE D'AOSTA**
Area: 1,259 sq. mi.
Population: 126,000
Capital: Aosta

**VENETIA (VENETO)**
Area: 7,090 sq. mi.
Population: 4,832,000
Capital: Venice (Venezia)

# MALAYSIA
## STATES AND TERRITORIES

**JOHORE (JOHOR)**
Area: 7,331 sq. mi.
Population: 3,385,000
Capital: Johore Bahru (Johor Baharu)

**KEDAH**
Area: 3,639 sq. mi.
Population: 2,000,000
Capital: Alor Star (Alor Setar)

**KELANTAN**
Area: 5,770 sq. mi.
Population: 1,634,000
Capital: Kota Bahru (Kota Baharu)

**MALACCA (MELAKA)**
Area: 637 sq. mi.
Population: 769,000
Capital: Malacca (Melaka)

**NEGERI SEMBILAN**
Area: 2,565 sq. mi.
Population: 1,014,000
Capital: Seremban

**PAHANG**
Area: 13,886 sq. mi.
Population: 1,543,000
Capital: Kuantan

**PERAK**
Area: 8,110 sq. mi.
Population: 2,393,000
Capital: Ipoh

**PERLIS**
Area: 307 sq. mi.
Population: 241,000
Capital: Kangar

**PENANG (PULAU PINANG)**
Area: 398 sq. mi.
Population: 1,577,000
Capital: George Town (Penang)

**SABAH**
Area: 28,425 sq. mi.
Population: 3,201,000
Capital: Kota Kinabalu

**SARAWAK**
Area: 48,050 sq. mi.
Population: 2,504,000
Capital: Kuching

**SELANGOR**
Area: 3,056 sq. mi.
Population: 5,168,000
Capital: Shah Alam

TRENGGANU (TERENGGANU)
Area: 5,002 sq. mi.
Population: 1,121,000
Capital: Trengganu Bahru
(Terengganu Baharu)

FEDERAL CAPITAL TERRITORY
(WILAYAH PERSEKUTUAN)
Area: 94 sq. mi.
Population: 1,655,000
Capital: Kuala Lumpur

LABUAN TERRITORY
Area: 35 sq. mi.
Population: 89,000
Capital: Labuan (formerly
Victoria)

PUTRAJAYA TERRITORY
Area: 15 sq. mi.
Population: 12,000
Capital: Putrajaya

## MEXICO
### STATES AND TERRITORIES

AGUASCALIENTES
Area: 2,112 sq. mi.
Population: 1,065,000
Capital: Aguascalientes

BAJA CALIFORNIA NORTE
Area: 26,997 sq. mi.
Population: 2,844,000
Capital: Mexicali

BAJA CALIFORNIA SUR
Area: 28,369 sq. mi.
Population: 512,000
Capital: La Paz

CAMPECHE
Area: 19,619 sq. mi.
Population: 755,000
Capital: Campeche

CHIAPAS
Area: 28,653 sq. mi.
Population: 4,294,000
Capital: Tuxtla Gutiérrez

CHIHUAHUA
Area: 94,571 sq. mi.
Population: 3,241,000
Capital: Chihuahua

COAHUILA
Area: 57,908 sq. mi.
Population: 2,495,000
Capital: Saltillo

COLIMA
Area: 2,004 sq. mi.
Population: 568,000
Capital: Colima

DURANGO
Area: 47,560 sq. mi.
Population: 1,509,000
Capital: Durango

GUANAJUATO
Area: 11,773 sq. mi.
Population: 4,894,000
Capital: Guanajuato

GUERRERO
Area: 24,819 sq. mi.
Population: 3,115,000
Capital: Chilpancingo

HIDALGO
Area: 8,036 sq. mi.
Population: 2,346,000
Capital: Pachuca

JALISCO
Area: 31,211 sq. mi.
Population: 6,752,000
Capital: Guadalajara

MÉXICO
Area: 8,245 sq. mi.
Population: 14,008,000
Capital: Toluca

MICHOACÁN
Area: 23,138 sq. mi.
Population: 3,966,000
Capital: Morelia

MORELOS
Area: 1,911 sq. mi.
Population: 1,612,000
Capital: Cuernavaca

NAYARIT
Area: 10,417 sq. mi.
Population: 950,000
Capital: Tepic

NUEVO LEÓN
Area: 25,067 sq. mi.
Population: 4,199,000
Capital: Monterrey

OAXACA
Area: 36,275 sq. mi.
Population: 3,509,000
Capital: Oaxaca

PUEBLA
Area: 13,090 sq. mi.
Population: 5,383,000
Capital: Puebla

QUERÉTARO
Area: 4,420 sq. mi.
Population: 1,598,000
Capital: Querétaro

QUINTANA ROO
Area: 19,387 sq. mi.
Population: 1,135,000
Capital: Chetumal

SAN LUIS POTOSÍ
Area: 24,351 sq. mi.
Population: 2,410,000
Capital: San Luis Potosí

SINALOA
Area: 22,520 sq. mi.
Population: 2,608,000
Capital: Culiacán

SONORA
Area: 70,291 sq. mi.
Population: 2,395,000
Capital: Hermosillo

TABASCO
Area: 9,756 sq. mi.
Population: 1,990,000
Capital: Villahermosa

TAMAULIPAS
Area: 30,650 sq. mi.
Population: 3,024,000
Capital: Ciudad Victoria

TLAXCALA
Area: 1,551 sq. mi.
Population: 1,068,000
Capital: Tlaxcala

VERACRUZ
Area: 27,683 sq. mi.
Population: 7,110,000
Capital: Jalapa

YUCATÁN
Area: 14,827 sq. mi.
Population: 1,819,000
Capital: Mérida

ZACATECAS
Area: 28,283 sq. mi.
Population: 1,368,000
Capital: Zacatecas

FEDERAL DISTRICT
(DISTRITO FEDERAL)
Area: 571 sq. mi.
Population: 8,721,000
Capital: Mexico City

## RUSSIA
### REPUBLICS

ADYGEA
Area: 2,935 sq. mi.
Population: 443,000
Capital: Maykop

ALTAY
Area: 35,750 sq. mi.
Population: 209,000
Capital: Gorno-Altajsk

BASHKORTOSTAN
Area: 55,445 sq. mi.
Population: 4,057,000
Capital: Ufa

BURYATIA
Area: 135,640 sq. mi.
Population: 961,000
Capital: Ulan-Ude

CHECHNYA
Area: 4,750 sq. mi.
Population: 1,238,000
Capital: Grozny (called
Dzhokhar-Ghala by
the Chechens)

CHUVASHIA
Area: 7,070 sq. mi.
Population: 1,279,000
Capital: Cheboksary

DAGESTAN
Area: 19,420 sq. mi.
Population: 2,712,000
Capital: Makhachkala

INGUSHETIA
Area: 1,450 sq. mi.
Population: 508,000
Capital: Magas

KABARDINO-BALKARIA
Area: 4,830 sq. mi.
Population: 892,000
Capital: Nalchik

KALMYKIA (KHALMG TANGCH)
Area: 29,380 sq. mi.
Population: 284,000
Capital: Elista

KARACHAY-CHERKESSIA
Area: 5,445 sq. mi.
Population: 427,000
Capital: Cherkessk

KARELIA
Area: 66,565 sq. mi.
Population: 688,000
Capital: Petrozavodsk

KHAKASSIA
Area: 23,900 sq. mi.
Population: 538,000
Capital: Abakan

KOMI
Area: 160,580 sq. mi.
Population: 959,000
Capital: Syktyvkar

MARI-EL
Area: 8,960 sq. mi.
Population: 700,000
Capital: Yoshkar-Ola

MORDVINIA
Area: 10,115 sq. mi.
Population: 833,000
Capital: Saransk

NORTH OSSETIA-ALANIA
(SEVERO-OSSETIYA)
Area: 3,090 sq. mi.
Population: 702,000
Capital: Vladikavkaz

**RUSSIA**
Area: 4,709,790 sq. mi.
Population: 120,623,000
Capital: Moscow (Moskva)
*Unlike the republics, Russia has no government but is divided into autonomous regions, districts and cities, each with its own administration.*

**SAKHA (FORMERLY YAKUTIJA)**
Area: 1,198,150 sq. mi.
Population: 950,000
Capital: Yakutsk

**TATARSTAN**
Area: 26,255 sq. mi.
Population: 3,769,000
Capital: Kazan

**TYVA (FORMERLY TUVA)**
Area: 65,830 sq. mi.
Population: 314,000
Capital: Kyzyl-Orda

**UDMURTJA**
Area: 16,255 sq. mi.
Population: 1,528,000
Capital: Izhevsk

## SPAIN
### AUTONOMOUS COMMUNITIES (REGIONS)

**ANDALUSIA (ANDALUCÍA)**
Area: 33,822 sq. mi.
Population: 8,303,000
Capital: Seville

**ARAGÓN**
Area: 18,425 sq. mi.
Population: 1,345,000
Capital: Zaragoza

**ASTURIAS**
Area: 4,094 sq. mi.
Population: 1,085,000
Capital: Oviedo

**BALEARIC ISLANDS (BALEARES)**
Area: 1,927 sq. mi.
Population: 1,095,000
Capital: Palma de Mallorca

**BASQUE COUNTRY (PAÍS VASCO OR EUSKAL HERRIKO)**
Area: 2,793 sq. mi.
Population: 2,172,000
Capital: Vitoria (Gasteiz)

**CANARY ISLANDS (ISLAS CANARIAS)**
Area: 2,875 sq. mi.
Population: 2,172,000
Joint capitals: Santa Cruz de Tenerife and Las Palmas de Gran Canaria

**CANTABRIA**
Area: 2,054 sq. mi.
Population: 589,000
Capital: Santander

**CASTILE-LA MANCHA (CASTILLA-LA MANCHA)**
Area: 30,680 sq. mi.
Population: 2,081,000
Capital: Toledo

**CASTILE AND LEÓN (CASTILLA Y LEÓN)**
Area: 36,380 sq. mi.
Population: 2,564,000
Capital: Valladolid

**CATALONIA (CATALUÑA OR CATALUNYA)**
Area: 12,399 sq. mi.
Population: 7,475,000
Capital: Barcelona

**CEUTA**
Area: 8 sq. mi.
Population: 79,000
Capitals: Ceuta

**ESTRAMADURA**
Area: 16,075 sq. mi.
Population: 1,102,000
Capital: Mérida

**GALICIA (GALIZA)**
Area: 11,419 sq. mi.
Population: 2,796,000
Capital: Santiago de Compostela

**LA RIOJA**
Area: 1,948 sq. mi.
Population: 322,000
Capital: Logroño

**MADRID**
Area: 3,100 sq. mi.
Population: 6,387,000
Capital: Madrid

**MELILLA**
Area: 5 sq. mi.
Population: 73,000
Capital: Melilla

**MURCIA**
Area: 4,368 sq. mi.
Population: 1,447,000
Capital: Murcia (although the regional parliament meets in Cartagena)

**NAVARRE (NAVARRA)**
Area: 4,012 sq. mi.
Population: 631,000
Capital: Pamplona

**VALENCIA**
Area: 8,979 sq. mi.
Population: 5,095,000
Capital: Valencia

## SWITZERLAND
### CANTONS

**AARGAU**
Area: 542 sq. mi.
Population: 582,000
Capital: Aarau

**APPENZELL AUSSER-RHODEN (half-canton)**
Area: 94 sq. mi.
Population: 53,000
Capital: Herisau

**APPENZELL INNER-RHODEN (half-canton)**
Area: 67 sq. mi.
Population: 15,000
Capital: Appenzell

**BASEL-LANDSCHAFT (half-canton)**
Area: 200 sq. mi.
Population: 269,000
Capital: Liestal

**BASEL-STADT (half-canton)**
Area: 14 sq. mi.
Population: 185,000
Capital: Basel

**BERN (BERNE)**
Area: 2,302 sq. mi.
Population: 963,000
Capital: Bern

**FRIBOURG**
Area: 645 sq. mi.
Population: 263,000
Capital: Fribourg

**GENEVA (GENÈVE)**
Area: 109 sq. mi.
Population: 438,000
Capital: Geneva

**GLARUS**
Area: 264 sq. mi.
Population: 38,000
Capital: Glarus

**GRAUBÜNDEN (GRISONS)**
Area: 2,743 sq. mi.
Population: 189,000
Capital: Chur

**JURA**
Area: 323 sq. mi.
Population: 70,000
Capital: Delémont

**LUCERNE (LUZERN)**
Area: 576 sq. mi.
Population: 363,000
Capital: Lucerne

**NEUCHÂTEL**
Area: 310 sq. mi.
Population: 170,000
Capital: Neuchâtel

**NIDWALDEN (half-canton)**
Area: 107 sq. mi.
Population: 40,000
Capital: Stans

**OBWALDEN (half-canton)**
Area: 189 sq. mi.
Population: 34,000
Capital: Sarnen

**ST. GALLEN (SANKT GALLEN)**
Area: 782 sq. mi.
Population: 466,000
Capital: St. Gallen

**SCHAFFHAUSEN**
Area: 115 sq. mi.
Population: 75,000
Capital: Schaffhausen

**SCHWYZ**
Area: 351 sq. mi.
Population: 141,000
Capital: Schwyz

**SOLOTHURN**
Area: 305 sq. mi.
Population: 250,000
Capital: Solothurn

**THURGAU**
Area: 383 sq. mi.
Population: 238,000
Capital: Frauenfeld

**TICINO**
Area: 1,086 sq. mi.
Population: 329,000
Capital: Bellinzona

**URI**
Area: 416 sq. mi.
Population: 35,000
Capital: Altdorf

**VALAIS**
Area: 2,017 sq. mi.
Population: 299,000
Capital: Sion

**VAUD**
Area: 1,240 sq. mi.
Population: 672,000
Capital: Lausanne

**ZUG**
Area: 92 sq. mi.
Population: 109,000
Capital: Zug

**ZÜRICH**
Area: 668 sq. mi.
Population: 1,308,000
Capital: Zürich

## UNITED KINGDOM
### COUNTRIES

**ENGLAND**
Area: 50,363 sq. mi.
Population: 51,466,000
Capital: London

**NORTHERN IRELAND**
Area: 5,453 sq. mi.
Population: 1,775,000
Capital: Belfast

**SCOTLAND**
Area: 30,409 sq. mi.
Population: 5,169,000
Capital: Edinburgh

**WALES**
Area: 8,019 sq. mi.
Population: 2,993,000
Capital: Cardiff

## U.S.
### STATES

**ALABAMA**
Area: 51,705 sq. mi.
Population: 4,628,000
Capital: Montgomery

**ALASKA**
Area: 591,004 sq. mi.
Population: 683,000
Capital: Juneau

**ARIZONA**
Area: 114,000 sq. mi.
Population: 6,339,000
Capital: Phoenix

**ARKANSAS**
Area: 53,187 sq. mi.
Population: 2,835,000
Capital: Little Rock

**CALIFORNIA**
Area: 158,845 sq. mi.
Population: 36,553,000
Capital: Sacramento

**COLORADO**
Area: 104,091 sq. mi.
Population: 4,862,000
Capital: Denver

**CONNECTICUT**
Area: 5,018 sq. mi.
Population: 3,502,000
Capital: Hartford

**DELAWARE**
Area: 2,044 sq. mi.
Population: 865,000
Capital: Dover

**DISTRICT OF COLUMBIA
(WASHINGTON, D.C.)**
Federal district
Area: 69 sq. mi.
Population: 588,000

**FLORIDA**
Area: 58,664 sq. mi.
Population: 18,251,000
Capital: Tallahassee

**GEORGIA**
Area: 58,910 sq. mi.
Population: 9,545,000
Capital: Atlanta

**HAWAII**
Area: 6,470 sq. mi.
Population: 1,283,000
Capital: Honolulu

**IDAHO**
Area: 83,565 sq. mi.
Population: 1,499,000
Capital: Boise

**ILLINOIS**
Area: 57,871 sq. mi.
Population: 12,853,000
Capital: Springfield

**INDIANA**
Area: 36,413 sq. mi.
Population: 6,345,000
Capital: Indianapolis

**IOWA**
Area: 56,275 sq. mi.
Population: 2,988,000
Capital: Des Moines

**KANSAS**
Area: 82,277 sq. mi.
Population: 2,776,000
Capital: Topeka

**KENTUCKY**
Area: 40,409 sq. mi.
Population: 4,241,000
Capital: Frankfort

**LOUISIANA**
Area: 47,752 sq. mi.
Population: 4,293,000
Capital: Baton Rouge

**MAINE**
Area: 33,265 sq. mi.
Population: 1,317,000
Capital: Augusta

**MARYLAND**
Area: 10,460 sq. mi.
Population: 5,618,000
Capital: Annapolis

**MASSACHUSETTS**
Area: 8,284 sq. mi.
Population: 6,450,000
Capital: Boston

**MICHIGAN**
Area: 97,102 sq. mi.
Population: 10,072,000
Capital: Lansing

**MINNESOTA**
Area: 86,614 sq. mi.
Population: 5,198,000
Capital: St. Paul

**MISSISSIPPI**
Area: 47,689 sq. mi.
Population: 2,919,000
Capital: Jackson

**MISSOURI**
Area: 69,697 sq. mi.
Population: 5,878,000
Capital: Jefferson City

**MONTANA**
Area: 147,046 sq. mi.
Population: 958,000
Capital: Helena

**NEBRASKA**
Area: 77,355 sq. mi.
Population: 1,775,000
Capital: Lincoln

**NEVADA**
Area: 110,561 sq. mi.
Population: 2,565,000
Capital: Carson City

**NEW HAMPSHIRE**
Area: 9,279 sq. mi.
Population: 1,316,000
Capital: Concord

**NEW JERSEY**
Area: 7,787 sq. mi.
Population: 8,686,000
Capital: Trenton

**NEW MEXICO**
Area: 121,593 sq. mi.
Population: 1,970,000
Capital: Santa Fe

**NEW YORK**
Area: 52,735 sq. mi.
Population: 19,298,000
Capital: Albany

**NORTH CAROLINA**
Area: 52,669 sq. mi.
Population: 9,061,000
Capital: Raleigh

**NORTH DAKOTA**
Area: 70,702 sq. mi.
Population: 640,000
Capital: Bismarck

**OHIO**
Area: 44,787 sq. mi.
Population: 11,467,000
Capital: Columbus

**OKLAHOMA**
Area: 69,956 sq. mi.
Population: 3,617,000
Capital: Oklahoma City

**OREGON**
Area: 97,073 sq. mi.
Population: 3,747,000
Capital: Salem

**PENNSYLVANIA**
Area: 46,043 sq. mi.
Population: 12,433,000
Capital: Harrisburg

**RHODE ISLAND**
Area: 1,212 sq. mi.
Population: 1,058,000
Capital: Providence

**SOUTH CAROLINA**
Area: 31,113 sq. mi.
Population: 4,408,000
Capital: Columbia

**SOUTH DAKOTA**
Area: 77,116 sq. mi.
Population: 796,000
Capital: Pierre

**TENNESSEE**
Area: 42,144 sq. mi.
Population: 6,157,000
Capital: Nashville

**TEXAS**
Area: 266,807 sq. mi.
Population: 23,904,000
Capital: Austin

**UTAH**
Area: 84,899 sq. mi.
Population: 2,646,000
Capital: Salt Lake City

**VERMONT**
Area: 9,614 sq. mi.
Population: 621,000
Capital: Montpelier

**VIRGINIA**
Area: 40,767 sq. mi.
Population: 7,712,000
Capital: Richmond

**WASHINGTON**
Area: 68,139 sq. mi.
Population: 6,468,000
Capital: Olympia

**WEST VIRGINIA**
Area: 24,231 sq. mi.
Population: 1,812,000
Capital: Charleston

**WISCONSIN**
Area: 66,215 sq. mi.
Population: 5,601,000
Capital: Madison

**WYOMING**
Area: 97,809 sq. mi.
Population: 523,000
Capital: Cheyenne

# GLOSSARY

**abrasion** physical wearing and grinding of a surface through friction and impact by material carried in air, water, or ice.

**acid rain** rain and snow containing poisonous or harmful chemicals, such as sulfur dioxide, released by burning fossil fuels.

**aquaculture** the farming of freshwater and saltwater species, including fish, shellfish, and seaweed.

**archipelago** a chain or set of islands grouped together, often in a curving arc.

**arid** dry with little rainfall.

**atmosphere** the collection of different gases that surrounds Earth.

**atoll** a coral reef, usually circular, that encloses a shallow lagoon.

**avalanche** a downward slide of snow, ice, and debris.

**bedrock** the solid rock that underlies all soil or other loose material; the rock material that breaks down to form soil eventually.

**biodiversity** short for biological diversity, the range of different species of living things. The greater the biodiversity of an area, the greater the number of species it contains.

**biome** a large, general habitat that covers a region of Earth such as tundra or desert.

**biosphere** the name given to all parts of Earth where living things are found.

**caldera** a bowl-shaped circular depression caused by the destruction of the peak of a volcano.

**cartography** the art and science of making maps.

**census** an investigation or count of a population.

**cirque** a bowl-shaped depression on a mountain that is carved out by a glacier.

**climate** the general weather conditions of a region or the entire Earth over a long period of time.

**colonialism** the system by which one country controls and dominates another country or territory politically and economically.

**confluence** the place at which two streams join to form one larger stream.

**conifer** a plant that reproduces by making cones. Conifers are mainly evergreen trees and bushes that keep their leaves throughout the year.

**continent** one of Earth's largest landmasses. In order of size, they are: Asia, Africa, North America, South America, Antarctica, Europe, and Australia.

**continental climate** the type of climate found in the interior of major continents in temperate latitudes. This climate is characterized by a large seasonal variation in temperature and relatively low annual rainfall.

**continental shelf** the extension of the continents into the ocean.

**contour map** a map that shows points of equal elevation as a line.

**conurbation** several towns and cities that adjoin or run into one another. *See also* **metropolitan area**.

**core** the metallic center of Earth made up of a molten outer core and a solid inner core.

**crust** the outermost part of Earth.

**cyclone** *see* **hurricane**.

**deciduous** trees that lose their leaves in the fall.

**decomposer** a living thing that gains nutrients by breaking down dead bodies, releasing the minerals they contain into the environment.

**deforestation** the cutting down of large numbers of trees for fuel or timber or to clear the land for settlements or farms.

**delta** the often triangular-shaped area at the mouth of a river.

**demography** the study of population statistics and trends such as births, deaths, and diseases.

**desert** an area with little precipitation or where evaporation exceeds precipitation and thus has sparse or no vegetation.

**desertification** the way a desert expands and spreads, reducing the land's ability to support life. Desertification is brought

about by the planet's changing climate, by overfarming, overgrazing, and removing trees and plants that hold the soil in place.

**dictatorship** a form of government where the ruler, known as a dictator, has absolute power.

**earthquake** a large, sudden movement of Earth's crust.

**ecology** the branch of science that studies the relationships between different living things and living things and their environment.

**economy** the way in which natural resources are used and goods and services are produced, distributed (sold or passed on to people), and consumed (used by organizations or people).

**ecosystem** a collection of all living things and their nonliving surroundings in a defined area.

**El Niño** a periodic warming of the ocean waters in the eastern Pacific Ocean that affects global weather patterns.

**elevation** the height of a point on Earth's surface above sea level.

**emissions** harmful gases released into the air by industry, fires, and motor vehicles.

**enclave** a territory of one nation enclosed within another state or country.

**endangered species** species of living thing that is seriously threatened with extinction.

**enhanced greenhouse effect** the buildup of carbon dioxide, methane, and other gases in the atmosphere, trapping the Sun's heat and affecting the climate.

**epicenter** the point on Earth's surface directly above the hypocenter, where the energy of an earthquake is first released.

**equator** the imaginary line drawn around the center of Earth an equal distance from the North and South poles.

**equinox** the beginning of fall and spring, the two days each year when the Sun is directly overhead at the equator.

**escarpment** a long cliff or steep slope separating two comparatively level or more gently sloping surfaces and resulting from erosion or faulting.

**estuary** the wide end of a river when it meets the sea.

**evaporation** the process where a liquid changes into a gas. The warming of the air by the Sun causes water to evaporate and change into water vapor.

**extinction** the permanent disappearance of a species.

**fault** a fracture or crack in Earth's crust where blocks of rock slip past each other.

**fauna** animal life.

**federation** a form of government in which powers and functions are divided between a central government and a number of political subdivisions that have significant control over their own affairs.

**fjord** a coastal valley that was sculpted by glacial action.

**floodplain** a flat, low-lying area near a river or stream that is subject to flooding.

**flora** plant life.

**fold** a bend in the layers of rock that make up Earth's crust.

**food chain** the links between different animals that feed on plants and each other. Food chains show how energy is passed up through the chain.

**fossil fuels** materials that were formed from living things that have decayed and been buried in the ground for millions of years and that can now be burned to generate energy.

**geological time** the calendar of Earth's history since its birth. Geological time is divided into eras, epochs, and periods.

**geyser** a fountain of hot water and steam found in volcanic areas.

**glacier** a mass of ice carrying rocks and soil formed from densely packed snow that does not melt. Pressure forces the glacier to move slowly downhill.

**greenhouse gases** gases, such as carbon dioxide, methane, and nitrous oxide, in the atmosphere that trap heat from the Sun and warm Earth.

**gross domestic product (GDP)** a common measurement of a country's economic strength and wealth. GDP represents the total value of all goods and services produced by a nation during a given year.

**habitat** the surroundings that a particular species needs in order to survive. Habitats include coral reefs, grasslands, freshwater lakes, and deserts. Some creatures can live in more than one habitat.

**hemisphere** one of the halves of Earth. The equator divides Earth into the Southern Hemisphere and Northern Hemisphere.

**humidity** the amount of water vapor in the air.

**humus** partially decomposed organic soil material.

**hurricane** a tropical storm that contains winds of at least 74 mph (120km/h). Hurricanes are also known as cyclones in the northern Indian Ocean and as typhoons in the western Pacific Ocean.

**hydrography** the study of the surface waters of Earth.

**hydroponics** the growing of plants, especially vegetables, in water containing essential mineral nutrients rather than in soil.

**hypocenter** the point under Earth's surface where the energy of an earthquake is first released.

**ice sheet** a large, thick layer of ice covering a vast area of land.

**igneous rock** a rock formed from the cooling and hardening of hot, liquid magma, or lava.

**indigenous** the earliest known inhabitants of a country.

**industrialization** the process in which more and more emphasis is placed on industry and manufacturing in a country's economy.

**International Date Line** an imaginary line on or around 180° longitude that separates the two simultaneous days that exist on Earth at the same time.

**introduced species** a species that people have taken from one part of the world and released into another.

**irrigation** a human-made system of watering the land using pipes and ditches to channel water.

**jet stream** a narrow band of fast-moving winds that is found at high altitudes.

**karst** a landscape composed of limestone features, including sinkholes, caves, and underground streams.

**lagoon** a small, shallow body of water between a barrier island or a coral reef and the mainland; also a small body of water surrounded by an atoll.

**latitude** an imaginary line around Earth parallel to the equator and used to measure distances from the equator.

**lava** magma that reaches Earth's surface through a volcanic vent or fissure.

**life expectancy** the length of time people can expect to live on average from when they are born. Life expectancy is affected by factors such as disease, nutrition, poverty, and living conditions.

**literacy** the ability to read and write.

**lithosphere** the solid outer layer of Earth, including the crust and the top of the mantle.

**longitude** an imaginary line around Earth from the North Pole to the South Pole. Lines of longitude are used to measure distances from east and west.

**magma** hot, liquid rock that lies beneath the surface of Earth.

**mantle** the rocky middle layer of Earth between the core and the crust.

**manufacturing industry** industry that brings together materials or products in order to offer them for sale.

**map** a graphic representation of Earth's surface.

**map projection** a mathematical way of representing the curved surface of Earth on the flat surface of a map.

**map scale** the relationship between distance on a map and the distance on Earth's surface.

**maritime climate** a climate strongly influenced by an ocean, found on islands and the windward shores of continents. It is characterized by small daily and yearly temperature ranges and high humidity.

**meander** a curve in the course of a river.

**meridian** a line of longitude.

**mesa** a large, flat-topped but steep-sided landform.

**mestizo** a person of mixed European and native Indian descent.

**metamorphic rock** a type of rock formed when igneous or sedimentary rock is altered by great heat and pressure.

**metropolitan area** a large city and its surrounding suburbs, forming one built-up area.

**microclimate** the climate of a small, defined area such as a valley.

**migration** a move by people or animals from one location to another.

**monarchy** a country whose head of state is a king, queen, or prince who usually inherits the position rather than being elected.

**monsoon** a wind system, especially in southern Asia, that changes direction seasonally, creating rainy and dry seasons.

**moraine** the rocks and soil carried and deposited by a glacier.

**multilingual** the ability to use more than one language when speaking or writing.

**municipal waste** unwanted by-products generated by people living in an urban area.

**nomads** people who do not have a fixed home and usually keep moving, traveling to wherever food can be found.

**nutrient** any material taken in by a living thing to help it sustain life.

**oasis** a fertile area with a good water supply found in a desert.

**ocean current** the regular movement of seawater in or near the surface of a sea or ocean.

**ore** a type of mineral that contains useful metals, such as iron, copper, or zinc, that can be extracted.

**ozone layer** a thin layer of the atmosphere consisting of ozone gas that absorbs the majority of the harmful ultraviolet rays from the Sun.

**parallel** a line of latitude.

**parasite** an animal that feeds on or inside another living animal, which is called its host. Parasites are usually much smaller than—and do not necessarily harm— their hosts.

**peninsula** a narrow area of land that stretches into the sea or a lake.

**permafrost** ground that is permanently frozen below the surface.

**photosynthesis** the process by which plants make food using water and sunlight.

**physical geography** the branch of geography dealing with the natural features of Earth.

**plateau** a raised area of mostly flat ground often surrounded by steep slopes.

**pollution** waste products or heat that damage the environment in some way.

**population** density of the number of people per unit of area, often per square mile.

**porous** something through which water can pass.

**prairie** a type of mostly treeless, grassy plain found in the center of the North American continent.

**precipitation** any form of water that falls from the atmosphere to the surface of Earth such as rain, snow, or hail.

**predator** an animal that kills and feeds on another animal, which is known as its prey.

**prevailing wind** the wind that blows in an area most often.

**quarry** an open pit made by digging for rocks or minerals.

**rapids** fast-flowing parts of a river.

**recycling** recovering waste materials to make new products. Can also mean to reuse discarded products.

**reef** a line of hard rocks or coral at or near the surface of the sea.

**republic** a country that has an elected government but no monarch.

**reservoir** an artificial lake built to store water.

**resources** natural things found on Earth, such as water, rocks, wood, and coal, that can be used in some way.

**ridge** a narrow, raised stretch of land.

**rift valley** a long, deep valley formed when part of Earth's crust collapses along a fault line. The Great Rift Valley in Africa is the world's largest rift valley.

**runoff** the part of rainfall that reaches streams or rivers. The remainder either evaporates into the atmosphere or seeps below ground.

**rural** belonging to the countryside.

**salinity** a measurement of the amount of salt dissolved in water.

**savanna** a type of plain covered in grasses with occasional trees.

**scree** a collection of loose rocks around the bottoms of steep slopes in upland areas.

**sea level** the average height of the surface of the sea.

**seamount** a single volcanic mountain rising up from the seabed that does not break the surface of the sea.

**sediment** the solid that settles to the bottom of a liquid.

**sedimentary rock** a type of rock formed from sediment that is compressed to form a solid over time.

**seismic waves** waves of energy that travel through Earth following an earthquake.

**seismology** the study of seismic waves in order to learn about earthquakes and the structure of Earth.

**service industries** types of work activities that provide services for people such as banking, retailing, education, and tourism.

**sewage** liquid and solid wastes that are channeled into the ground, rivers, or ocean.

**silt** a fine-grained substance made up of tiny particles of rock.

**sinkhole** a crater formed when the roof of a cavern collapses; usually found in areas of limestone rock.

**soil erosion** the process by which loose soil is washed or blown away.

**soluble** capable of being dissolved.

**source** the place where a stream or river begins to flow.

**species** a set of organisms that can be grouped together owing to their similarity and their potential ability to breed with each other.

**spit** a long, narrow stretch of sand or gravel running into the sea.

**spring** a place where a stream or river rises out of the ground.

**stalactite** a pointed piece of limestock rock hanging down from the roof of a cave like an icicle.

**stalagmite** a spike or mound of limestock rock rising up from the floor of a cave.

**strait** a narrow strip of sea connecting two seas or oceans.

**strata** layers of sedimentary rock.

**subduction** the process by which one of Earth's plates is forced beneath another as they collide.

**subsistence farming** a form of agriculture in which farmers aim to produce enough food to feed only their families.

**subterranean** something that is below the surface of the ground such as a cave or underground river.

**summit** the highest point of a hill or mountain.

**tableland** a large area of high, flat land.

**taiga** a moist, subarctic coniferous forest that begins where the tundra ends and is dominated by spruces and firs.

**temperate** term used to describe a region or climate that is neither very hot nor very cold. Temperate zones lie between the tropics and the polar regions.

**thaw** the melting of a substance that has been previously frozen.

**thermal** a rising column of warm air.

**tide** a regular movement of seawater toward and away from the land. Tides are caused by the gravity exerted by the Sun and the Moon.

**topography** the surface features of a landscape, both natural and artificial.

**tor** an isolated mass of eroded rock such as granite.

**tornado** a small but fast-moving, violent storm caused by rotating winds.

**toxic** any substance that is poisonous or harmful to life.

**tree line** a limit in elevation on a mountain above which trees cannot grow. Also used as a limit in latitude toward the North and South poles beyond which trees cannot grow.

**trench** a long, deep valley on the ocean floor.

**tributaries** streams or small rivers that flow into larger rivers.

**tropics** the region around the equator that remains warm all year-round.

**tsunami** a huge ocean wave, often known as a tidal wave, usually generated by earthquakes or volcanic eruptions.

**tundra** a treeless plain characteristic of the Arctic and subarctic regions.

**typhoon** *see* **hurricane**.

**urban** belonging to a city or town.

**urbanization** an increase in people moving to urban areas.

**valley** a trough-shaped dip in the landscape. Many valleys contain a river.

**vegetation** the total plant cover of an area.

**veld** a type of dry, open grassland found in southern Africa.

**wadi** a dried-up river in a desert.

**water cycle** the continual flow of Earth's water. Water vapor from the ocean and land rises into the atmosphere, becoming rain, snow, or hail, and then falls back to Earth. Rivers carry it back to the ocean.

**water table** the level below the land surface that is fully saturated with water.

**weathering** the gradual breaking down of rocks and minerals into sand and soil.

**wetland** an area or region that is usually flooded such as a swamp, marsh, or bog.

# INDEX

# The publishers wish to thank the following for their contribution to this book:

**Photographs** (*t* = top; *b* = bottom; *m* = middle; *l* = left; *r* = right)

Page i *b* Corbis; ii/iii *b* Corbis; iv *tl* NASA; iv *bl* Robert Glusic/PhotoDisc; iv *m* Philip Coblentz/Brand X Pictures; iv *mr* Philip Coblentz/Brand X Pictures; v *tl* David Lorenz Winston/Brand X Pictures; v *m* Corbis; v *mr* Corbis; v *b* Corbis; vi *tl* Herbert Maeder/Still Pictures; vi *m* Steve Allen/Brand X Pictures; vi *b* Corbis; vii *b* MediaFocus International; 1 NASA; 2 *b* NASA; 3 *br* Adalberto Rios Szalay/Sexto Sol/PhotoDisc; 4 *tr* MediaFocus Internrational; 5 *tl* Emanuele Taroni/PhotoDisc; 6 *tr* Chris Madeley/Science Photo Library; 7 *tr* US Geological Surveys/Science Photo Library; 8 *b* Jeremy Horner/Panos Pictures; 11 *tl* Bernhard Edmaier/Science Photo Library; 11 *br* Rob Huibers/Panos Pictures; 12 *tl* Photo 24/Brand X Pictures; 13 *tl* Photo 24/Brand X Pictures; 13 *l* John Mead/Science Photo Library; 15 *tl* Photo 24/Brand X Pictures; 15 *b* Corbis; 16/17 MediaFocus International; 16 *tl* MediaFocus International; 16/17 *t* Lyndon Harvey; 17 *br* Bernhard Edmaier/Science Photo Library; 18/19 MediaFocus International; 19 *t* MediaFocus International; 19 *br* Photo 24/Brand X Pictures; 20 *tl* Glen Allison/PhotoDisc; 20 *b* Tom Van Saint, Geosphere Project/Planetary Visions/Science Photo Library; 22 *tl* Julian Holland; 22/23 *t* Photo 24/Brand X Pictures; 23 *br* MediaFocus International; 24/25 *t* MediaFocus International; 25 *br* MediaFocus International; 26 *tl* MediaFocus International; 26 *tr* MediaFocus International; 26 *b* MediaFocus International; 27 *tr* Charles O'Rear/Corbis; 28 *tr* NASA; 28 *b* NASA/Science Photo Library; 31 *bl* Photo 24/Brand X Pictures; 31 *br* Corbis; 32 *tl* Photo 24/Brand X Pictures; 32 *bl* MediaFocus International; 33 *bl* Amanda Clement/PhotoDisc; 33 *r* David Lorenz Winston/Brand X Pictures; 33 *mr* Alain Le Garsmeur/Panos Pictures; 33 *r* MediaFocus International; 33 *br* Photo 24/Brand X Pictures; 34 *tl* Rouxaime & Jacana/Science Photo Library; 34 *tr* Philip Coblentz/Brand X Pictures; 35 *r* Julian Holland; 35 *b* NASA; 36 *tr* Bernhard Edmaier/Science Photo Library; 36 *b* Edouard Parker/Hutchison Library; 37 *t* Michael S. Yamashita/Corbis; 40 *tl* Trygve Bolstad/Panos Pictures; 41 *t* Liba Taylor/Panos Pictures; 41 *br* John Mead/Science Photo Library; 42 *tr* Julian Holland; 43 *br* NASA; 49 PhotoDisc/Robert Glusic; 50 *b* B & C Alexander/Still Pictures; 51 *b* B & C Alexander/Still Pictures; 52/53 Photo 24/Brand X Pictures; 52 *tr* MediaFocus International; 52 *b* John Wang/PhotoDisc; 54 *b* Corbis; 54/55 *t* Corbis; 55 *r* Gerry Ellis/DigitalVision; 56 *tl* Ron Watts/Corbis; 56 *b* Steve Allen/Brand X Pictures; 57 *t* David Lorenz Winston/Brand X Pictures; 58 *tl* Alain Le Garsmeur/Panos Pictures; 58 *bl* Bob Krist/Corbis; 58/59 *b* Glen Allison/PhotoDisc; 60 *tl* Gerry Ellis/DigitalVision; 60 *b* Steve Allen/Brand X Pictures; 61 *t* Corbis; 62 *tl* Trevor Page/Hutchison Library; 62 *b* Robert Glusic/PhotoDisc; 63 *tr* Gerry Ellis/PhotoDisc; 63 *bl* Staffan Widstrand/Corbis; 64 *tr* Gerry Ellis/PhotoDisc; 64 *b* Steve Allen/Brand X Pictures; 65 *t* Corbis; 65 *br* Photo 24/Brand X Pictures; 66 *tl* Steve Allen/Brand X Pictures; 66 *tr* David Lorenz Winston/Brand X Pictures; 66 *b* Steve Allen/Brand X Pictures; 67 *b* Jim Wark/Still Pictures; 68 *tl* Steve Allen/Brand X Pictures; 68/69 *t* Photo 24/Brand X Pictures; 68/69 *b* Jeremy Woodhouse/PhotoDisc; 69 *tr* Steve Allen/Brand X Pictures; 69 *r* Joseph Sohm; ChromoSohm Inc./Corbis; 70 *tl* Sandy Felsenthal/Corbis; 70 *tr* Photo 24/Brand X Pictures; 70 *bl* Jeri Gleiter/Still Pictures; 71 *tr* Gerry Ellis/PhotoDisc; 71 *br* Jeff Greenberg/Still Pictures; 72 *tl* Glen Allison/PhotoDisc; 72 *l* Photo 24/Brand X Pictures; 72 *b* Photo 24/Brand X Pictures; 73 *t* Photo 24/Brand X Pictures; 73 *br* Ken Redding/Corbis; 74 *t* Bob Krist/Corbis; 74 *tr* Photo 24/Brand X Pictures; 74 *b* Corbis; 75 *b* Bob Rowan; Progressive Image/Corbis; 76 *tl* Photo 24/Brand X Pictures; 76 *bl* Richard Weiss/Still Pictures; 77 *tl* NASA; 77 *b* Richard Hamilton Smith/Corbis; 78 *tl* Photo 24/Brand X Pictures; 78 *b* Steve Allen/Brand X Pictures; 78/79 *t* Robert Glusic/PhotoDisc; 79 *bl* MediaFocus International; 79 *br* Rick Doyle/Corbis; 80/81 Photo 24/Brand X Pictures; 80 *l* Steve Allen/Brand X Pictures; 80 *bl* Jeff Greenberg/Still Pictures; 80/81 *t* Gunter Marx Photography/Corbis; 81 *tr* Gerry Ellis/PhotoDisc; 81 *br* Photo 24/Brand X Pictures; 82 *tl* Kevin Schafer/Still Pictures; 82 *r* Gerry Ellis/PhotoDisc; 82 *b* MediaFocus International; 83 *b* Philip Coblentz/Brand X Pictures; 84 *t* Mark Henley/Panos Pictures; 85 *t* Philip Coblentz/Brand X Pictures; 85 *bl* Philip Coblentz/Brand X Pictures; 86 *tr* Philip Coblentz/Brand X Pictures; 86 *b* Adalberto Rios Szalay/Sexto Sol/PhotoDisc; 87 *tr* MediaFocus International; 87 *br* Neil Beer/PhotoDisc; 88 *tl* IMS Communications; 88 *b* Edward Parker/Hutchison Library; 89 *tl* Phil Schermeister/Corbis; 89 *tr* Gerry Ellis/PhotoDisc; 89 *b* Adalberto Rios Lanz/Sexto Sol/PhotoDisc; 90 *b* Sean Sprague/Panos Pictures; 91 *tl* Nigel Dickinson/Still Pictures; 91 *bl* Gerry Ellis/PhotoDisc; 91 *br* Steve Allen/Brand X Pictures; 92 *ml* Philip Coblentz/Brand X Pictures; 92 *b* Mike Kolloffel/Still Pictures; 93 *r* David Reed/Panos Pictures; 93 *bl* S. Sprague/Panos Pictures; 94 *bl* Nik Wheeler/Corbis; 95 *m!* Philip Coblentz/Brand X Pictures; 95 *b* Philip Coblentz/Brand X Pictures; 95 *r* Philip Coblentz/Brand X Pictures; 96 *l* IMS Communications; 96 *b* Gerard & Margi Moss/Still Pictures; 97 Philip Coblentz/Brand X Pictures; 98 Philip Coblentz/Brand X Pictures; 99 *t* Mark Edwards/Still Pictures; 99 *b* Philip Coblentz/Brand X Pictures; 100 *tr* Klaus Andrews/Still Pictures; 100 *b* Mark Edwards/Still Pictures; 101 *tr* Rolando Pujol/South American Pictures; 102 *b* Marc French/Panos Pictures; 103 *m* Hisham F. Ibrahim/PhotoDisc; 104 *mr* Marc French/Panos Pictures; 105 *mr* Philip Wolmuth/Panos Pictures; 108 *b* Neil Cooper/Panos Pictures; 109 *mr* Philip Coblentz/Brand X Pictures; 110 *mr* Jonathan Blair/Corbis; 110 *br* Veronica Garbutt/Panos Pictures; 111 *t* Philip Wolmuth/Panos Pictures; 111 *b* Philip Coblentz/Brand X Pictures; 112 *tr* Hubert Stadler/Corbis; 112/113 *b* Graham Neden; Ecoscene/Corbis; 113 *tr* Corbis; 113 *br* David Lorenz Winston/Brand X Pictures; 114 *tr* Corbis; 114/115 *b* Philip Coblentz/Brand X Pictures; 115 *bl* Philip Coblentz/Brand X Pictures; 115 *br* Philip Coblentz/Brand X Pictures; 116/117 *b* Tony Morrison/South American Pictures; 116/117 *t* Caroline Penn/Panos Pictures; 117 *br* Kevin Schafer/Still Pictures; 118 *t* Alfredo Cedeño/Panos Pictures; 118 *bl* IMS Communications; 119 *bl* Jonathan Kaplan/Still Pictures; 119 *br* Staffan Widstrand/Corbis; 120 *b* James L. Amos/Corbis; 121 *bl* Philip Coblentz/Brand X Pictures; 121 *br* European Space Agency; 122 *bl* IMS Communications; 123 *t* Jon Spaull/Panos Pictures; 123 *bl* Clive Gifford; 124 *bl* IMS Communications; 124/125 *b* Jeremy Horner/Panos Pictures; 125 *t* Julian Holland; 125 *r* Corbis; 126/127 *t* Tony Morrison/South American Pictures; 127 *tr* David Lorenz Winston/Brand X Pictures; 127 *br* Glen Allison/PhotoDisc; 128 *bl* Ron Giling/Still Pictures; 129 *tl* Mark Edwards/Still Pictures; 129 *b* Jeremy A. Horner/Panos Pictures; 130 *tr* MediaFocus International; 130 *b* Mark Edwards/Still Pictures; 132 *bl* Ricardo Azoury/Corbis; 132/133 *b* Richard T. Nowitz/Corbis; 133 *t* Philip Coblentz/Brand X Pictures; 133 *br* MediaFocus International; 134/135 *t* Ernesto Rios Lanz/Sexto Sol/PhotoDisc; 134/135 *b* Chris Sattlberger/Panos Pictures; 136 *b* Tony Morrison/South American Pictures; 137 *b* Nick Haslam/Hutchison Library; 137 *mr* Philip Coblentz/Brand X Pictures; 138 *b* Philip Coblentz/Brand X Pictures; 138/139 *t* Jeremy Horner/Panos Pictures; 138/139 *m* Philip Coblentz/Brand X Pictures; 139 *br* Philip Coblentz/Brand X Pictures; 140 *bl* Philip Coblentz/Brand X Pictures; 141 *tl* Frank Nowikowski/South American Pictures; 141 *tr* Javier Pierini/PhotoDisc; 141 *b* MediaFocus International; 142 *tl* Kit Houghton/Corbis; 142 *b* MediaFocus International; 143 *tl* Gerry Ellis/DigitalVision; 143 *b* John Farmar; Ecoscene/Corbis; 144 *b* John Noble/Corbis; 145 Philip Coblentz/Brand X Pictures; 146 *bl* Charles & Josette Lenars/Corbis; 146 *tr* MediaFocus International; 147 *br* Ellerbrock & Schaft/Network; 148 *tr* MediaFocus International; 148 *b* Gavin Hellier/Robert Harding Picture Library; 149 *br* Steve Allen/Brand X Pictures; 150 *bl* Yann Arthus-Bertrand/Corbis; 151 *t* Galen Rowell/Corbis; 151 *b* Chris Lisle/Corbis; 152 *b* W. Herbert/Robert Harding Picture Library; 153 *t* Duncan Maxwell/Robert Harding Picture Library; 153 *mr* Pal Hermansen/Still Pictures; 153 *b* Bengt Andreasson/Robert Harding Picture Library; 154 *l* Dylan Garcia/Still Pictures; 155 *t* Wally Herbert/Robert Harding Picture Library; 155 *mr* K. Gillham/Robert Harding Picture Library; 155 *b* Robert Harding Picture Library;,156 *ml* MediaFocus International; 156 *b* MediaFocus International; 157 *tr* Adam Woolfitt/Corbis; 158 *ml* MediaFocus International; 158 *b* Dave G. Houser/Corbis; 159 *b* Steve Allen/Brand X Pictures; 160 *tl* David Toase/PhotoDisc; 160 *b* Stephanie Maze/Corbis; 161 *tl* Christopher Tordai/Hutchison Library; 161 *br* Tuck Goh/Hutchison Library; 162/163 *b* Roger Ressmeyer/Corbis; 163 *tl* Julian Holland; 163 *bl* Julian Holland; 163 *t* Pawel Libera/Corbis; 163 *mr* Julian Holland; 164 *tl* David Toase/PhotoDisc; 164/165 *t* Robert Laberge/Getty Images; 164 *b* Michael St. Maur Sheil/Corbis; 165 *tr* Philip Coblentz/Brand X Pictures; 165 *mr* Philip Coblentz/Brand X Pictures; 166 *tr* R. Rainford/Robert Harding Picture Library; 166 *ml* MediaFocus International; 166 *b* MediaFocus International; 167 *t* MediaFocus International; 168 *b* Sylvain Grandadam/Robert Harding Picture Library; 169 *t* Thomas Raupach/Still Pictures; 169 *br* MediaFocus International; 170/171 *b* Thomas Raupach/Still Pictures; 171 *t* MediaFocus International; 171 *br* MediaFocus International; 172 *tl* Emanuele Taroni/PhotoDisc; 172 *bl* John Wang/PhotoDisc; 172/173 *t* David Turnley/Corbis; 173 *tr* MediaFocus International; 173 *b* Hartmut Schwarzbach/Still Pictures; 174 *t* MediaFocus International; 174 *bl* MediaFocus International; 175 *b* Andy Williams/Robert Harding Picture Library; 176 *tl* MediaFocus International; 176/177 *b* MediaFocus International; 177 *tr* Martial Colomb/PhotoDisc; 177 *mr* Michael Busselle/Corbis; 178 *t* MediaFocus International; 178 *bl* Michael Short/Robert Harding Picture Library; 179 *tr* Philip Coblentz/Brand X Pictures; 179 *br* Martial Colomb/PhotoDisc; 180/181 *t* Tamas Revesz/Still Pictures; 180/181 *b* Ray Juno/Corbis; 182 *b* MediaFocus International; 183 *tr* Reuter Raymond/Corbis Sygma; 183 *b* Roy Rainford/Robert Harding Picture Library; 184 *b* S. Grandadam/Robert Harding Picture Library; 185 *t* Mike McQueen/Impact; 186/187 *b* Corbis; 187 *t* Barry Lewis/Corbis; 187 *br* Philip Coblentz/Brand X Pictures; 188 *b* Emma Lee/Life File/PhotoDisc; 189 *tr* Liba Taylor/Hutchison Library; 189 *b* Jan Hacad/Woodfall Wild Images; 190 *b* John Hatt/Hutchison Library; 191 *tl* Ron Giling/Still Pictures; 191 *tr* Phil Robinson/Robert Harding Picture Library; 191 *b* David Hoffman/Still Pictures; 192 *b* Liba Taylor/Hutchison Library; 193 David Lorenz Winston/Brand X Pictures; 194/195 *b* MediaFocus International; 195 *br* Edward Parker/Hutchison Library; 196 *bl* Philip Coblentz/Brand X Pictures; 197 *tr* Jose Fuste Raga/Corbis; 197 *b* Fin Costello/Robert Harding Picture Library; 198 *tl* Ryan MacVay/PhotoDisc; 198 *b* Steve Allen/Brand X Pictures; 199 *tr* Mark Henley/Impact; 200 *b* MediaFocus International; 201 *t* MediaFocus International; p.201 *r* Philip Coblentz/Brand X Pictures; 201 *br* Joerg Boethling/Still Pictures; 202/203 *b* Marco Cristofori/Still Pictures; 203 *t* Corbis; 203 *br* Explorer/Robert Harding Picture Library; 204 *tl* MediaFocus International; 204 *b* Martyn Goddard/Corbis; 205 *br* Philip Coblentz/Brand X Pictures; 206 *b* Janez Stock/Corbis; 207 *b* MediaFocus International; 208 *bl* Colin Paterson/PhotoDisc; 208 *tr* Marc French/Panos Pictures; 209 *b* MediaFocus International; 210 *b* Michael Short/Robert Harding Picture Library; 211 *b* Ed Kashi/Corbis; 212 *b* Leif Skoogfors/Corbis; 213 *b* Melanie Friend/Hutchison Library; 214/215 *b* Toma Babovic/Still Pictures; 215 *t* Mark Henley/Impact; 215 *br* Mark Henley/Impact; 216/217 *b* MediaFocus International; 216/217 *t* Christopher Bluntzer/Impact; 218 *ml* Gregory Wrona/Panos Pictures; 218 *b* Dean Conger/Corbis; 219 *bl* Steve Raymer/Corbis; 220 *b* Chris Lisle/Corbis; 221 *b* Nik Wheeler/Corbis; 222/223 *b* Peter Turnley/Corbis; 223 *tr* Gyori Antoine/Corbis Sygma; 224 *ml* Jeff Greenberg/Robert Harding Picture Library; 224 *b* Barry Lewis/Corbis; 225 *b* C. Bowman/Robert Harding Picture Library; 226 *b* Sandro Vannini/Corbis; 227 *b* David B.A. Jones/Robert Harding Picture Library; 228 *tl* Dave G. Houser/Corbis; 228/229 *b* Michael Nicholson/Corbis; 229 *br* Janet Wishnetsky/Impact; 230 *tl* David Turnley/Corbis; 230 *b* Gregor Schmid/Corbis; 231 *tl* Wolfgang Kaehler/Corbis; 232 *tl* Bojan Vreceljj/Corbis; 232/233 *b* Christina Dodwell/Hutchison Library; 233 *tr* Paul A. Souders/Corbis; 234 *tr* Rhodri Jones/Panos Pictures; 235 *b* Heidi Bradner/Panos Pictures; 236 *b* Rhodri Jones/Panos Pictures; 237 *ml* Heidi Bradner/Panos Pictures; 237 *b* Jon Spaull/Panos Pictures; 238/239 *t* MediaFocus International; 239 *tr* Adam Woolfitt/Robert Harding Picture Library; 239 *b* Joan Klatchko/Hutchison Library; 240 *b* Philip Woolmuth/Hutchison Library; 241 Corbis; 242 *tr* Jochen Tack/Still Pictures; 242 *b* Giacomo Pirozzi/Panos Pictures; 243 *bl* Lindsay Hebberd/Corbis; 244 *tr* Jean-Léo Dugast/Panos Pictures; 244 *b* Robin Constable/Hutchison Library; 245 *br* MediaFocus International; 246/247 *t* K. M. Westermann/Corbis; 246/247 *b* K. M. Westermann/Corbis; 247 *mr* Dave Bartruff/Corbis; 248 *bl* Ricki Rosen/Corbis; 248/249 *b* Ricki Rosen/Corbis; 250 *ml* Edward Parker/Hutchison Library; 250 *b* Alan Keohane/Impact; 251 *ml* Toby Adamson/Still Pictures; 251 *b* Charles & Josette Lenars/Corbis; 252 *ml* Caroline Penn/Panos Pictures; 252 *b* Michael S. Yamashita/Corbis; 253 *tr* Mohamed Ansar/Impact; 253 *b* John Isaac/Still Pictures; 254 *tr* Robin Laurance/Impact; 254/255 *b* Marcus Rose/Panos Pictures; 255 *tr* Charles & Josette Lenars/Corbis; 256 *tr* Hutchison Library; 257 *b* Hutchison Library; 256/257 *b* Bernard Gerard/Hutchison Library; 258 *tl* Alex Majoli/Magnum; 258 *b* Mohamed Amin/Robert Harding Picture Library; 259 *b* Adrian Arbib/Still Pictures; 260 *mr* Guy Mansfield/Panos Pictures; 261 *br* MediaFocus International; 262 *b* Nick Haslam/Hutchison Library; 263 *tr* John Miles/Panos Pictures; 263 *ml* John Miles/Panos Pictures; 264/265 *b* Dieter Telemans/Panos Pictures; 265 *b* John McDermott/Panos Pictures; 266 *tr* Liba Taylor/Corbis; 266 *l* ESA/Starsem; 267 *b* Jon Spaull/Panos Pictures; 267 *b* Marcus Rose/Panos Pictures; 268 *b* Brian Goddard/Panos Pictures; 270/271 *b* Dr Petocz/Still Pictures; 271 *tr* Joe Raedle/Getty Images; 272 *tr* Alain Le Garsmeur/Panos Pictures; 272/273 *b* Hartmut Schwarzbach/Still Pictures; 273 *br* Fred Hoogervorst/Panos Pictures; 274 *tr* Friedrich Stark/Still Pictures; 275 *tr* Henning Christoph/Still Pictures; 275 *br* Dermot Tatlow/Panos Pictures; 276/277 *t* Ingo Jezierski/PhotoDisc; 276 *b* Hutchison Library; 277 *tr* Jeremy Horner/Corbis; 277 *br* Gerry Ellis/DigitalVision; 278 *tl* Jeremy Horner/Panos Pictures; 278 *bl* Corbis; 278/279 Mark Henley/Panos Pictures; 278/279 *t* Bob Krist/Corbis; 278/279 *b* Wolfgang Schmidt/Still Pictures; 280 *tl* Daniel O'Leary/Panos Pictures; 280/281 *t* Piers Cavendish/Impact; 281 *b* Jochen Tack/Still Pictures; 280/281 *b* Christopher Cormack/Corbis; 282 *b* Shehzad Nooran/Still Pictures; 283 *mr* David Lorenz Winston/Brand X Pictures; 284 *b* Chris Stowers/Panos Pictures; 285 *b* MediaFocus International; 286 *b* Thierry Thomas/Still Pictures; 287 *b* MediaFocus International; 288 *b* Sarvottam Rajkoomar/Still Pictures; 289 Corbis; 290 *b* Corbis; 291 *b* B.S.P.I/Corbis; 292/293 *t* Corbis; 292 *b* Corbis; 293 *tr* Gerry Ellis/DigitalVision; 294/295 *b* Corbis; 294/295 *b* Corbis; 295 *tr* Ron Giling/Still Pictures; 296 *tl* MediaFocus International; 296/297 *b* Adam Crowley/PhotoDisc; 296/297 *t* Liu Liqun/Corbis; 297 *br* SETBOUN/Corbis; 298 *t* Adam Crowley/PhotoDisc; 298 *b* Corbis; 299 *bl* Chris Stowers/Panos Pictures; 300/301 *t* Mark Henley/Impact; 301 *tl* Toby Adamson/Still Pictures; 301 *br* PERN/Hutchison Library; 302 *b* Friedrich Stark/Still Pictures; 303 *t* Jeremy Horner/Panos Pictures; 303 *b* Friedrich Stark/Still Pictures; 304 *b* R. Ian Lloyd/Hutchison Library; 305 *t* Jim Holmes/Panos Pictures; 305 *br* Friedrich Stark/Still Pictures; 306 *b* Corbis; 306/307 *t* Dean Conger/Corbis; 307 *br* Akira Kaede/PhotoDisc; 308 *b* Corbis; 308/309 *t* Corbis; 309 *br* Akira Kaede/PhotoDisc; 310 *b* Philip Coblentz/Brand X Pictures; 311 *tl* Philip Coblentz/Brand X Pictures; 311 *br* Chris Stowers/Panos Pictures; 312 *bl* Philip Coblentz/Brand X Pictures; 313 *t* Amanda Leung/Panos Pictures; 313 *b* Ingo Jezierski/PhotoDisc; 314 *bl* Jeremy Horner/Hutchison Library; 315 *t* Philip Coblentz/Brand X Pictures; 316 *b* Jean-Léo Dugast/Panos Pictures; 316/317 *b* Sarah Murray/Hutchison Library; 317 *tr* Caroline Penn/Panos Pictures; 318/319 *b* Glen Allison/PhotoDisc; 319 *tr* Hartmut Schwarzbach/Still Pictures; 320/321 *b* J. Holmes/Still Pictures; 321 *t* Jorgen Schytte/Still Pictures; 321 *br* Jorgen Schytte/Still Pictures; 322 *bl* Jim Olive/Still Pictures; 323 *ml* R. Ian Lloyd/Hutchison Library; 323 *br* Corbis; 324 *tr* Steve Allen/Brand X Pictures; 325 *tl* Gerard & Margi Moss/Still Pictures; 325 *b* Macduff Everton/Corbis; 326 *tl* Fred Hoogervorst/Panos Pictures; 326 *b* Mark Edwards/Still Pictures; 326/327 *b* Nigel Dickinson/Still Pictures; 327 *t* Corbis; 327 *b* Robert Francis/Hutchison Library; 328/329 *t* Russell Gordon/Still Pictures; 329 *br* Chris Stowers/Panos Pictures; 330 *tl* Mark Edwards/Still Pictures; 330 *b* Philip Coblentz/Brand X Pictures; 331 *t* Dani & Jeske/Still Pictures; 331 *br* Michael Macintyre/Hutchison Library; 332 *b* Mark Edwards/Still Pictures; 333 *t* Robert Francis/Hutchison Library; 333 *br* T. Turner/Times Picayune/Still Pictures; 334 *b* Friedrich Stark/Still Pictures; 335 *bl* IMS Communications; 336 *tl* Dean Conger/Corbis; 336 *b* Yann Arthus-Bertrand/Corbis; 337 Herbert Maeder/Still Pictures; 338 *b* Betty Press/Panos Pictures; 338/339 *b* M & C Denis-Huot/Still Pictures; 339 *br* Gerry Ellis/DigitalVision; 340 *tr* Adrian Arbib/Still Pictures; 341 *b* Ron Giling/Still Pictures; 342 *b* Georges Lopez/Still Pictures; 343 *bl* Mark Henley/Impact; 344 *b* Voltchev-Unep/Still Pictures; 345 *tr* Markus Matzel/Still Pictures; 346/347 *b* MediaFocus International; 347 *tr* Tibor Bognar/Corbis; 348 *b* Paul O'Driscoll/Impact; 349 *br* Dan Charlish-Christian Aid/Still Pictures; 350 *b* Maya Kardum/Panos Pictures; 351 *b* Henning Christoph/Still Pictures; 352 *b* Mark Edwards/Still Pictures; 353 *mr* Clive Shirley/Panos Pictures; 354 *b* Ron Giling/Still Pictures; 355 *b* Friedrich Stark/Still Pictures; 356 *b* Caroline Penn/Corbis; 357 *br* Betty Press/Panos Pictures; 358 *b* Sebastian Bolesch/Still Pictures; 359 *b* Gallo Images/Corbis; 360/361 *b* Bruce Paton/Panos Pictures; 360/361 *b* Mark Edwards/Still Pictures; 362 *mr* Knut Müller/Still Pictures; 363 *tr* Julian Holland; 363 *b* Liba Taylor/Panos Pictures; 365 *b* Genevieve Renson/Still Pictures; 366 *b* Edgar Cleijne/Still Pictures; 368 *b* James Sugar/Still Pictures; 369 *b* Ron Giling/Still Pictures; 370/371 *b* Fred Hoogervorst/Panos Pictures; 371 *ml* Anthony Bannister; Gallo Images/Corbis; 372 *b* Yann Arthus-Bertrand/Corbis; 373 *b* Brian Moser/Hutchison Library; 374 *b* Michael Busselle/Corbis; 375 *tr* Trygve Bolstad/Panos Pictures; 375 *b* Gerry Ellis/DigitalVision; 376 *b* Hjalte Tin/Still Pictures; 377 *mr* Jeremy Woodhouse/PhotoDisc; 378 *b* Gerard & Margi Moss/Still Pictures; 379 *b* Gerry Ellis/DigitalVision; 379 *b* Friedrich Stark/Still Pictures; 380 *tr* Michael S. Lewis/Corbis; 380/381 *b* Roderick Johnson/Panos Pictures; 381 *tr* Roger de la Harpe/Still Pictures; 382 *tl* IMS Communications; 382/383 *b* Jeremy Woodhouse/PhotoDisc; 382/383 *t* Friedrich Stark/Still Pictures; 383 *tr* Caroline Penn/Panos Pictures; 384 *b* Billie Rafaeli/Hutchison Library; 385 Steve Allen/Brand X Pictures; 386/387 Philip Coblentz/Brand X Pictures; 388 *tl* Bob Abraham/Still Pictures; 388 *bl* Penny Tweedie/Corbis; 389 *br* Paul A. Souders/Corbis; 390/391 *t* Corbis; 391 *tr* Michael Macintyre/Hutchison Library; 391 *b* Michael Macintyre/Hutchison Library; 392 *tr* Glen Allison/Still Pictures; 392/393 *b* Steve Allen/Brand X Pictures; 394 *tl* Patrick Ward/Corbis; 394/395 *t* MediaFocus International; 394/395 *b* Corbis; 396/397 *b* Corbis; 397 *tr* Paul A. Souders/Corbis; 398 *tl* Nick Wilson/Getty Images; 398 *b* MediaFocus International; 399 *tl* Paul A. Souders/Corbis; 399 *b* Martin Hawes/Still Pictures; 400 *tl* O. Alamany & E. Vicens/Corbis; 400 *tr* Penny Tweedie/Corbis; 400/401 *b* Corbis; 402 *tl* Ted Spiegel/Corbis; 402/403 *t* L. Clarke/Corbis; 402/403 *b* Dave G. Houser/Corbis; 403 *tr* Gerry Ellis/DigitalVision; 404 *tl* Nick Wilson/Getty Images; 404/405 *t* Paul A. Souders/Corbis; 404/405 *b* Corbis; 405 *b* Robert Garvey/Corbis; 406 *t* Roger Garwood & Trish Ainslie/Corbis; 406/407 *b* Massimo Mastrorillo/Corbis; 407 *tr* Robert Garvey/Corbis; 408 *b* Steve Allen/Brand X Pictures; 408/409 *t* Pat O'Hara/Corbis; 409 *br* Steve Allen/Brand X Pictures; 410 *tl* Anders Ryman/Corbis; 410/411 *b* Corbis; 411 *t* Robert Dowling/Corbis; 412 *tl* Steve Allen/Brand X Pictures; 412 *b* Steve Allen/Brand X Pictures; 413 *t* Paul A. Souders/Corbis; 413 *br* Scott Barbour/Getty Images; 414 *b* J. G. Fuller/Hutchison Library; 415 *m* Anders Ryman/Corbis; 416 *br* Andy Crump/Still Pictures; 417 *b* Stephen Frink/Corbis; 418 *b* Roger Ressmeyer/Corbis; 419 *mr* Glen Allison/PhotoDisc; 420/421 Norbert Wu/Still Pictures; 422 *b* Jan Butchofsky-Houser/Corbis; 423 *b* Michael Macintyre/Hutchison Library; 424 *b* Patricio Goycoolea/Hutchison Library; 425 *mr* Jack Fields/Corbis; 426 *mr* Philipp Hympendahl/Still Pictures; 426/427 *b* Glen Allison/PhotoDisc; 427 *b* Philip Coblentz/Brand X Pictures; 428 *b* W. Perry Conway/Corbis; 430 *tl* Fritz Polking/Still Pictures; 430/431 *b* Galen Rowell/Corbis; 432 *b* Mark Carwardine/Still Pictures; 434 *ml* Carl R. Sams II/Still Pictures; 434 *r* Gerry Ellis/DigitalVision; 434 *br* Mark Edwards/Still Pictures; 435 *mr* Corbis; 435 *bl* Diane Blell/Still Pictures; 436/437 *b* Bojan Brecelj/Still Pictures; 436/437 *b* Gil Moti/Still Pictures; 437 *br* Rui Vieira/Panos Pictures; 442 *ml* Kevin Schafer/Still Pictures; 442 *mr* Caron Philippe/Corbis; 443 *bl* Sabine Vielmo/Still Pictures; 444 *mr* Mike Schroder/Still Pictures; 445 *mr* Shehzad Noorani/Still Pictures; 445 *bl* Jorgen Schytte/Still Pictures; 446 *mr* Wolfgang M. Weber/Still Pictures; 446 *b* Ron Giling/Still Pictures; 447 *tl* Robert Holmes/Corbis; 447 *mr* Tom Wagner/Corbis; 447 *bl* Caroline Penn/Panos Pictures; 448 *bl* Pierre Gleizes/Still Pictures; 452/453 *t* Manfred Voller/Corbis; 452 *b* Claes Lofgren/Still Pictures; 453 *tr* Ron Giling/Still Pictures; 453 *b* Chris Stowers/Panos Pictures; 458 *mr* Ron Giling/Still Pictures; 458/459 *b* Heine Pedersen/Still Pictures; 459 *t* Nigel Dickinson/Still Pictures; 460 *t* Bettmann/Corbis; 460/461 *t* Jorgen Schytte/Still Pictures; 460 *br* Robert Mulder/Still Pictures; 461 *tr* Sabine Sauer/Still Pictures; 461 *b* Hartmut Schwarzbach/Still Pictures; 462 *tr* Penny Tweedie/Panos Pictures; 462 *bl* Adrian Arbib/Still Pictures; 463 *tr* John Van Hasselt/Corbis Sygma; 463 *b* Catherine Karnow/Corbis; 464 *tr* Mark Henley/Panos Pictures; 464 *bl* Gordon Wiltsie/Still Pictures

**Additional artwork:** Julian Baker

488